OXFORD WORLD

ALFRED TE

ALFRED TENNYSON was born in rural Lincolnshire in 1809. He grew up introspective and somewhat brooding, but he was drawn to poetry from an early age, writing *The Devil and the Lady* (a polished imitation of Elizabethan tragedy) at the age of 14. From 1827 he attended Trinity College Cambridge, where he met Arthur Hallam, whose friendship was of enormous importance to him. Hallam brought him out of his shell, and encouraged his poetry; and with him Tennyson joined the Cambridge debating group 'The Apostles' in 1829. Tennyson won the Chancellor's Gold Medal for Poetry with 'Timbuctoo', and the publication of *Poems, Chiefly Lyrical* (1830) and *Poems* (1832) brought him a wider reputation. When in 1833 Hallam died unexpectedly of a brain haemorrhage, Tennyson was plunged into profound grief. He began writing lyrics in an attempt to come to terms with his bereavement. Tennyson continued writing in a variety of forms throughout the 1830s and 1840s, and *The Princess* (1847) enhanced his reputation. By the time he published a collection of the lyrics he had written after Hallam's death as *In Memoriam A. H. H.* (1850) he was acknowledged as one of the chief poetic voices of his age. He married Emily Sellwood in 1850, and later in the same year he was appointed Poet Laureate. In 1853 he settled in the Isle of Wight, and continued to produce poetic masterpieces, including *Maud* (1855) and *Enoch Arden* (1864). Queen Victoria, grieving for the death of her beloved Albert after 1861, took a particular comfort from *In Memoriam*, and Tennyson was offered a baronetcy many times before he finally accepted ennoblement in 1883. Much of his later career was taken up with finishing a long-gestated Arthurian epic, *Idylls of the King* (the first element of which was published in 1842, but which was not completed until 1874), and a late flurry of stage-plays, beginning with *Queen Mary*, which was produced in 1875. He died in 1892.

ADAM ROBERTS is Professor of Nineteenth-Century Literature at Royal Holloway, University of London. He has published widely on a variety of nineteenth-century topics, and is the editor (with Daniel Karlin) of the Oxford World's Classics *Robert Browning: The Major Works*.

OXFORD WORLD'S CLASSICS

*For over 100 years Oxford World's Classics have brought
readers closer to the world's great literature. Now with over 700
titles—from the 4,000-year-old myths of Mesopotamia to the
twentieth century's greatest novels—the series makes available
lesser-known as well as celebrated writing.*

*The pocket-sized hardbacks of the early years contained
introductions by Virginia Woolf, T. S. Eliot, Graham Greene,
and other literary figures which enriched the experience of reading.
Today the series is recognized for its fine scholarship and
reliability in texts that span world literature, drama and poetry,
religion, philosophy and politics. Each edition includes perceptive
commentary and essential background information to meet the
changing needs of readers.*

OXFORD WORLD'S CLASSICS

Alfred Tennyson
The Major Works

Edited with an Introduction and Notes by
ADAM ROBERTS

OXFORD
UNIVERSITY PRESS

OXFORD

UNIVERSITY PRESS

Great Clarendon Street, Oxford OX2 6DP

Oxford University Press is a department of the University of Oxford.
It furthers the University's objective of excellence in research, scholarship,
and education by publishing worldwide in

Oxford New York

Auckland Bangkok Buenos Aires Cape Town Chennai
Dar es Salaam Delhi Hong Kong Istanbul Karachi Kolkata
Kuala Lumpur Madrid Melbourne Mexico City Mumbai Nairobi
São Paulo Shanghai Taipei Tokyo Toronto

Oxford is a registered trade mark of Oxford University Press
in the UK and in certain other countries

Published in the United States
by Oxford University Press Inc., New York

Introduction and editorial matter © Adam Roberts 2000, 2009

The moral rights of the author have been asserted
Database right Oxford University Press (maker)

First Published 2000
First Published as an Oxford World's Classics paperback 2009

British Library Cataloguing in Publication Data

Data available

Library of Congress Cataloging in Publication Data

ISBN 978-0-19-957276-2

11

Typeset by SPI Publisher Services, Pondicherry, India
Printed in Great Britain
on acid-free paper by
Clays Ltd, Elcograf S.p.A

CONTENTS

PROSE

Letters and Journal Entries

INTRODUCTION

OF all Victorian poets, Tennyson is the one whose reputation has tied him most intimately to the age in which he lived. As poet laureate, and the first poet to be ennobled, he spent the last four decades of his life as the official poetic voice of his day. It was a duty he took very seriously. And yet, Tennyson began his career as the most private of poets; a shy, introspective individual whose writing explored the personal agonies of an oversensitive consciousness. There is something striking about this, an apparent division at the core of Tennyson's poetic talent. We can begin by drawing a crude dividing line between early and late at 1850. The later period of his career follows his appointment to the laureateship in 1850, and is largely occupied with poetry that performs in a public and therefore relatively impersonal voice. It is characterized by works such as the stately (in several senses) 'Ode on the Death of the Duke of Wellington' (1852), the famous articulation of patriotic militarism 'The Charge of the Light Brigade' (1854), and the long-gestated epic that sought to define Englishness via a retelling of Arthurian legends, *The Idylls of the King* (worked on mostly between 1855 and 1885)—all this is exactly the sort of poetry we might expect a national laureate to write. Indeed even a more individual, or perhaps idiosyncratic, production like *Maud; A Monodrama* (1854) ties the exploration of diseased consciousness to national events (in this case the Crimean War). We might draw the conclusion from this that Tennyson's genius was inherently public, that he was well suited to the role of Establishment poet. But he remained an extremely private man. He took his laureateship seriously but he was never comfortable with it. The poetry that made his reputation and which led to his appointment as laureate (which is to say, the poetry written between 1829 and 1850) is amongst the most personal and private of the period. In contrast with the laureate work, in the early period Tennyson avoids public topics with a studiousness that begins to seem rather forced. Many of these extraordinary early lyrics are precisely concerned with a withdrawal from the world, with women cloistered away ('The Lady of Shalott', 'Mariana'), with men living hermetic lives ('St Simeon Stylites'), with speakers trapped in the private hell of suicidal contemplation ('The Two Voices'). A creature such as the Kraken (1830) is as far removed from the world (the public) as it is possible to imagine, slumbering through time in the deeps of the ocean.

And the dissociated subject-matter was matched by an intense, personal style of vivid imagery and exquisite prosody that enacts a distinctive, private voice. This reaches a sort of apotheosis in Tennyson's master-piece, *In Memoriam*, which occupied him from 1833 through to its publication in 1850. One of the most personal texts produced in the nineteenth century, it marks with the acute and sometimes morbid precision which we nowadays would tend to call 'confessional' the process of Tennyson's profound grief over the death of his closest friend. That this poem went on to become the characteristic poem of its period owed something to chance; Queen Victoria's own bereavement (in 1861) was much consoled by the work, and as the cultural tenor of the nineteenth century shifted towards mourning and Christian fortitude Tennyson's lyrical exposition of emotional pain operated more and more as a model of public behaviour.

In Memoriam is the hinge, then, a work both intensely private and extremely public, sitting Janus-faced in the centre of Tennyson's career. 'It happens now and then,' T. S. Eliot commented on Tennyson's elegy, 'that a poet by some strange accident expresses the mood of his generation, at the same time that he is expressing a mood of his own which is quite remote from that of his generation.'[1] Harold Bloom makes the same point with a little more force: 'one never ceases to be puzzled that *In Memoriam*, an outrageously personal poem of Romantic apotheosis, a poem indeed of vastly eccentric mythmaking, should have been accepted as a work of consolation and moral resolution in the tradition of Christian humanism.'[2] This is the creative tension that runs through Tennyson's writing. One of the accounts of his career traces exactly this shift from personal acuteness to public occupation, the expansion into the public realm of the particular emphases of Tennyson's personal myth-making. It is precisely the tension between public and private that provides one of the continuities of this trajectory, and this in turn grows out of the early Tennyson's fascination with withdrawal from the world and anatomization of involuted consciousness.

Tennyson's early private poetry was shaped by the particulars of his upbringing. Born in Somersby amongst the Lincolnshire flats, he was the third surviving son of a gloomy and emotionally unstable Rector. Lonely and often miserable, Tennyson's retreat into subjectivity and the

---

[1] T. S. Eliot, '*In Memoriam*' (1936), in Frank Kermode (ed.), *Selected Prose of T. S. Eliot* (London: Faber, 1987), 243.

[2] Harold Bloom, *The Ringers in the Tower: Studies in Romantic Tradition* (Chicago: Univ. of Chicago Press, 1971), 153–4.

fantasy offered by literature gave his first poetic expressions an intro-
spection that bordered on the morbid. In the words of Paul Turner, 'the
need to escape into subjectivity tended to inspire poetry about sleep,
dream, vision, madness, intoxication, and other states of heightened
sensation and lowered intellectual control.'[3] His very first poetic pro-
nouncement at the age of 4 (see below, p. 527)—walking on a stormy day
and declaring 'I hear a voice that's speaking in the wind'—also records
the way this intense subjectivity found an intimate correlative in the nat-
ural world. A poem such as 'Mariana' expresses all these intensely per-
sonal sentiments in the figure of the isolated and miserable protagonist
('She said, "I am aweary, aweary, | I would that I were dead!" '); but at
every point in the poem her negative subjectivity is linked, indeed inter-
penetrated, by the close presence of the natural world.

> About a stone-cast from the wall
>   A sluice with blacken'd waters slept,
> And o'er it many, round and small,
>   The cluster'd marish-mosses crept.
> Hard by a poplar shook alway,
>   All silver-green with gnarled bark:
> For leagues no other tree did mark
>   The level waste, the rounding gray.

> ('Mariana', 37–44)

This landscape, which so precisely matches and externalizes Mariana's
mood, is the Lincolnshire wolds of Tennyson's youth. The precise evo-
cation of the natural world is one of the most distinctive features of
Tennyson's poetry.

> Willows whiten, aspens quiver,
> Little breezes dusk and shiver
> Thro' the wave that runs for ever
> By the island in the river
>   Flowing down to Camelot.

> ('Lady of Shalott', 10–14)

The willows 'whiten' because, as Tennyson had noticed, wind ruffles the
leaves of the tree and the white undersides become momentarily visible
(Tennyson was so fond of this observation that he used it again in *In
Memoriam*—'blasts that blow the poplar white'—and again in 'Merlin

---

[3] Paul Turner, *Victorian Poetry, Drama, and Miscellaneous Prose 1832–1890*
(Oxford: Clarendon Press, 1989), 19.

and the Gleam'—'Silent river | Silvery willow'). The breezes 'dusk' the surface of the water by pushing down the wavelets (which reflect the light more noticeably) and creating patterns of a darker colour. This is exquisitely observed, but married to this visual acuity is an extraordinary sense of the cadences of language, the musical patterns of sound that structure poetry: the sensuousness of the alliterative 'w's in the first two words ('willows whiten'), the way they operate the lips, those most sensuous parts of the body; the way movement is implied rather than actually stated; the word 'dusk' apparently being used as a verb, but also connecting with a pattern whereby motion is described in terms of colour; the third line is a *half*-rhyme, as if falling away, as if the rhyme-scheme is not static but is also in motion. Arthur Hallam's early essay on his friend's poetry makes this point: 'Mr Tennyson belongs decidedly to the class we have already described as Poets of Sensation. He sees all forms of nature with the "*eruditus oculus*" [erudite eye] and his ear has a fairy fineness.'[4]

Tennyson's early youth separated him from the broader currents of Britain in the 1820s, the aftermath of the Napoleonic Wars and the quickening of those processes of growth and development that characterize the Victorianism that was to follow. Close to his brothers (his first volume of verse, 1827's *Poems by Two Brothers*, was co-authored with both Tennyson's brothers), he was otherwise intensely shy. After going up to Cambridge he is said to have fled in a panic from the dining hall of Trinity crowded with people. It is not surprising that this intense and involuted personality should fixate on one particular individual rather than developing a wide circle of friends. That individual, Arthur Hallam, exercised a deeper and more lasting influence on Tennyson's poetic career than anybody else. He became the poet's best friend, gave constructive criticism of his poetry, and published positive reviews. The two went travelling together, and Hallam became engaged to Tennyson's sister. But the central relationship was between Hallam and Tennyson himself; indeed, the love these two men had for one another was so intense that some critics today suggest we can really only begin to understand it within the context of gay discourse.[5] It is extremely unlikely that Tennyson and Hallam were lovers in the modern-day sense of the term, or that Tennyson thought of himself as

4 Arthur Hallam, 'On Some of the Characteristics of Modern Poetry, and on the Lyrical Poems of Alfred Tennyson', *Englishman's Magazine* (Aug. 1831), 624.

5 See Alan Sinfield's sensitive readings in his *Alfred Tennyson* (Oxford: Blackwell, 1986).

homosexual, but there is some point in deploying this sort of critical perspective none the less: it reflects both the intensity of Tennyson's feelings and the exquisite sensuality of the way his imagination captured it in poetry. His rendering of another intensely subjective state of mind—the passive surrender of the mariners in 'The Lotos-Eaters'—infuses a representation of the natural world with an intense, drowsy sensitivity.

> There is sweet music here that softer falls
> Than petals from blown roses on the grass,
> Or night-dews on still waters between walls
> Of shadowy granite, in a gleaming pass;
> Music that gentlier on the spirit lies,
> Than tir'd eyelids upon tir'd eyes;
> Music that brings sweet sleep down from the blissful skies.
> Here are cool mosses deep,
> And thro' the moss the ivies creep,
> And in the stream the long-leaved flowers weep,
> And from the craggy ledge the poppy hangs in sleep.
>
> ('The Lotos-Eaters', 46–56)

It is not that this poem embodies a specific erotic charge, but it is so acutely aware of sensual bliss as to almost do so. It is a sort of withdrawal from the world into sensual delight and sleep. Music is the apparent correlative, but the languorous physical prosody ('tired' in particular is a deliciously slow monosyllable) makes it clear that the important music is the music of words and the melody of Tennyson's own language.

The most obvious criticism of this sort of poetry (and it is one that was made many times by critics in Tennyson's day) is that it is tantamount to mere escapism. It weakens Tennyson's aesthetic if it does indeed refuse to engage with the real world, with for instance politics or the concerns of the day. But it is not always easy to contextualize early Tennyson in historical or cultural terms. His early poem 'The Kraken' is an example:

> Below the thunders of the upper deep;
> Far, far beneath in the abysmal sea,
> His ancient, dreamless, uninvaded sleep
> The Kraken sleepeth: faintest sunlights flee
> About his shadowy sides: above him swell
> Huge sponges of millennial growth and height;
> And far away into the sickly light,
> From many a wondrous grot and secret cell

> Unnumber'd and enormous polypi
> Winnow with giant arms the slumbering green.
> There hath he lain for ages and will lie
> Battening upon huge seaworms in his sleep,
> Until the latter fire shall heat the deep;
> Then once by men and angels to be seen,
> In roaring he shall rise and on the surface die.

The awkwardness of line 8 aside, this is a beautifully constructed and sensually evocative piece of writing that, again, embodies a dissociated subjectivity: the majestic cadences of the polysyllabic words rumbling and rolling along their pentameters—'unnumber'd and enormous polypi'—'his ancient, dreamless, uninvaded sleep'—mirroring the slow, rumbling life of its subject; the evocative sense of place conjured up with light and the slow motion of the winnowing polypi. But is it more than that? Critics have been tempted to read it as a symbolic portrait, but nobody has agreed what the symbol represents. Isobel Armstrong suggests that the Kraken, like Demogorgon from Shelley's *Prometheus Unbound*, represents the slumbering political might of the working classes, the difference (in Tennyson's final line) suggesting his difference in political affiliation—that for Tennyson the eventual revolution was doomed to failure.[6] But it is difficult to assign a political reading to this poem, because it focuses so minutely on its strange, cut-off subject. As Armstrong herself points out, 'the poem insists upon the inert, unconscious life of the Kraken ... it is the living embodiment of oblivion because its actions occur without volition'. Tennyson's early poetry explores with horrified fascination the passive life, the life of inaction; his is a poetry of impotence.

Paradoxically, Hallam's full impact on Tennyson's poetry did not become apparent until 1833, with Hallam's premature death of an aneurism. There is no doubting the profundity of the grief that settled over Tennyson's life in the years immediately following this event, a grief that worked its way through a hundred and thirty lyrics into 1850's *In Memoriam*. It may seem callous to say it, but Hallam's death gave Tennyson a subject other than his own morbid subjectivity: the subject of loss. It is a facile critical exercise to contrast the rather dissociated melancholia of 'The Kraken' or 'Mariana' with the aching precision of 'Ulysses', mourning the passing of his heroic youth and striving even to

---

[6] Isobel Armstrong, *Victorian Poetry: Poetry, Poetics and Politics* (London: Routledge, 1993), 53.

death in the attempt not to give up. For 'Tithonus' even immortality is a kind of loss, a 'withering' removed from the lilting downward trajectory of mortal existence:

> The woods decay, the woods decay and fall,
> The vapours weep their burthen to the ground,
> Man comes and tills the field and lies beneath,
> And after many a summer dies the swan.
>
> ('Tithonus', 1–4)

This is still not a public Tennyson; these sentiments are still removed from what might be called 'official' or 'establishment' Victorian pieties of work, duty, and religious resignation. But by working through his grief during the long composition of *In Memoriam* Tennyson was also, it seems by chance, working towards the expression of something absolutely, classically of his age. *In Memoriam* is, in many ways, a poem that perfectly embodies Victorian pieties: it explores the consolations of religion, the proper responses to the death of a loved one, it manifests typically nineteenth-century anxieties about change, scientific erosion of divinity, and so on. When Queen Victoria lost her husband, and adopted the mourning dress and habits by which she is now most closely identified—exaggerating the nation's already keen interest in the rituals of mourning—it was *In Memoriam* she kept on her bedside table. But at the same time *In Memoriam* is a profoundly non-Establishment work. It remains a fiercely personal elaboration of the love of a man for a man, one charged with such erotic tension that at least one contemporary reviewer assumed the (anonymous) volume must have been written by a grief-stricken widow.

It is possible to miss the sensuality of *In Memoriam*, because the object of love is necessarily absent throughout the piece. Death has removed the physicality of Hallam, although that physicality lives on in the poem both directly and by virtue of the sensuous intensity with which Tennyson records his own emotional states. The tree growing in the graveyard is able to embrace the dead in a way denied to Tennyson:

> Old Yew, which graspest at the stones
>   That name the under-lying dead,
>   Thy fibres net the dreamless head,
> Thy roots are wrapt about the bones.   (II: 1–4)

There is a grisly aspect to this image (underlined by the plosive 't's of 'graspest', 'net', 'wrapt'); but a tenderness also, and an awareness of the physical reality of death. It is moments like this in Tennyson's evolving career that wrench him back from the idealized escapism of his earlier subjective misery, and do so with a bitter sense of a hard, unyielding materiality. Section VII of *In Memoriam* sees the bereaved speaker return to the dead man's house. It ends:

> He is not here; but far away
>   The noise of life begins again,
>   And ghastly thro' the drizzling rain
> On the bald street breaks the blank day.   (VII: 9–12)

The verse here teeters on the edge of egregiousness, the awkward inversion of 'On the bald street breaks' coupled with the bald/breaks/blank 'b' alliteration. But the alliteration here at the end of the lyric is only clearly marking out, underscoring in a sense, a musical pattern of word-sound that has played through the whole.

In Memoriam marked a turning point in Tennyson's life and poetic career. It was only after its publication that Emily Sellwood, the woman he had courted for nearly twenty years, finally agreed to marry him; and it was later the same year that *In Memoriam* appeared that Tennyson was appointed to the laureateship. *Maud* (1854) is centred on a portrait of a pathological consciousness, and Tennyson's original, though superseded, title ('the Madness') harks back to early monologues of insanity like 'St Simeon Stylites'. But the poem reaches a more official conclusion; the speaker recovers his sanity by deliberately and dutifully moving from the private introspection of his passion for Maud to the official patriotism of joining the army and sailing off to fight in the Crimean War.

> It is better to fight for the good than to rail at the ill;
> I have felt with my native land, I am one with my kind,
> I embrace the purpose of God, and the doom assign'd.
>   (*Maud*, III: 57–9)

This forceful statement of public connection is so completely at odds with the private, subjective isolation of earlier Tennyson (the separation of a Mariana or a Lady of Shalott *from* society) that most critics have assumed an irony here. There is no early Tennyson character who could or would assert 'I am at one with my kind', it is true, and it provides a plausible reading of the poem to see the narrator still mad at the end, if mad with a different emphasis. But we don't need to follow this path. It is the very fact that the speaker here is now operating in a public domain, performing patriotism and 'the better mind' of the people, that marks out the shift in Tennyson's own poetic role. This is not to make the naïve mistake of assuming Tennyson and speaker to be the same in this poem: clearly they are not. The point is not one of identity, but of register. We find the jingoistic sentiments of the speaker offensive today, and so they may be, but it is not the content that is especially important here. It is rather the domain of the discourse. The speaker of *Maud* has killed the 'old hysterical mock-disease' (III: 33) of his madness by abandoning the 'passionate heart and morbid eye' of his old mode of subjective perception and expression, and adopting instead a public discourse, 'mix[ing] my breath | With a loyal people' (III: 32–5).

Tennyson, in the 1850s and 1860s, worked towards this same aim. It is this fact, coupled to the archaic ideologies that constituted 'public discourse' in Tennyson's day, that make much of his later 'public' period so much less appealing to us today than the sensitive, introverted verse of his youth. In place of shyness and fantasy, Tennyson took upon himself the conventional attitudes of his day, and these can make his verse 'Victorian' in a bad way. It is hard to know how to deal with the offensive racism that occasionally manifests itself ('Ev'n the black Australian dying hopes he shall return, a white', 'Locksley Hall, Sixty Years After', 70). Reading the account of Tennyson's endorsement of the atrocities committed against black West Indians by Governor Eyre (see below, p. 513) leaves a very unpleasant taste in the mouth indeed.

The extent to which we will want merely to dismiss *this* Tennyson as offensive and not worth our attention will probably depend upon the extent to which we are interested in the cultural and historical phenomenon of 'Victorianism'—and, particularly, white, middle-class English Victorianism. Public Tennyson has his role here. If we want to find a representation of (for instance) a truly Victorian celebration of the sanctity of home and family life, then we will not find it in Browning, Barrett-Browning, Arnold, Rossetti, or Swinburne. But Enoch Arden looks through the window of his former home into exactly such a scene:

> For cups and silver on the burnish'd board
> Sparkled and shone; so genial was the hearth:
> And on the right hand of the hearth he saw
> Philip, the slighted suitor of old times,
> Stout, rosy, with his babe across his knees;
> And o'er her second father stoopt a girl,
> A later but a loftier Annie Lee,
> Fair-hair'd and tall, and from her lifted hand
> Dangled a length of ribbon and a ring
> To tempt the babe, who rear'd his creasy arms,
> Caught at and ever miss'd it, and they laugh'd;

> And on the left hand of the hearth he saw
> The mother glancing often toward her babe,
> But turning now and then to speak with him,
> Her son, who stood beside her tall and strong
> And saying that which pleased him, for he smiled.
>
> (*Enoch Arden*, 738–53)

This dull, fussily composed tableau ('And on the right hand . . . And on the left hand') might stand as an emblem of everything in 'Victorianism' that seems to us today unappealing: a restrictive, essentialist, and sexist belief in the 'hearth and the home' as the ethical centre of the universe. We do need to acknowledge that there is a certain sort of reader, less common now than then, for whom this is the *point* of Tennyson's poetry. This sort of reader might feel their heartbeat quicken reading 'The Revenge' as the plucky English ship, hopelessly outnumbered, battles heroically against the Spanish, and the Captain utters his defiant last order:

> Sink me the ship, Master Gunner—sink her, split her in twain!
> Fall into the hands of God, not into the hands of Spain!
>
> ('The Revenge', 89–90)

These notional readers might similarly have nodded in agreement to 'You ask me, why', with its fears that 'banded unions' of the working class could drive the affluent, such as Tennyson, out of the country. These readers would have identified with the England of that poem, the land that 'sober-suited Freedom chose', and such sober suits are another manifestation of this narrowly conceived Victorianism.

If this were all that remained of Tennyson after he 'went public' in 1850, then he would cut a very unappealing figure indeed. But the subjective, introverted Tennyson never absents himself from the poetry. In a way, the public persona, the public voice, only intensifies the earlier subjectivity, intensifies it because it drives it underground. Fame brought Tennyson a certain wealth and status; but it also acted as a sort of prison. An incident at Dickens's funeral in 1870 illustrates this fact neatly; the speaker here (we have lost his name) recalls Tennyson's presence at that well-attended event:

There was an immense congregation that day in the Abbey—and when the service was over—we stood up waiting a long time to pass out through the rails. But instead of dispersing by the outer door the people all turned eastward and flocked toward the altar, pressing closer and closer up to the Sacrarium. The chances of getting out became less and less, and I turned to Tennyson and said,

'I don't know what all this means, but we seem to be so hemmed in that it is use-less to move as yet.' Then a man, standing close by me whispered, 'I don't think they will go, sir, so long as your friend stands there.' Of course I saw at once what was happening—it had got to be known that Tennyson was present, and the solid throng was bent on seeing him. Such a popularity had never occurred to me or to him.[7]

The general public popularity hemmed Tennyson in as much as his morbid introspection had in his private days. It is the sense of being trapped, imprisoned, crushed by the multiplicity of the world that is one of the most striking features of Tennyson's verse, early and late. More importantly, this aesthetic of imprisonment also functions as a cri-tique of that selfsame stifling 'Victorianism' that Tennyson's public voice set out to celebrate. Many critics have noticed this: the strand in his poetic vision that runs from his earliest poems—Mariana confined in the moated grange—through to his latest—Merlin (Tennyson's own symbol of himself) trapped in the oak by Vivien in the *Idylls of the King*. On one level these actual 'prisons' correlate to states of mind, to what today we might call 'depression', but which Tennyson would have known as either 'melancholia' (when there was no specific referent for the mood) or 'sorrow' (when there was, for instance with the death of Hallam). *In Memoriam* is, amongst other things, an exploration of what it is to be trapped and locked away by grief. But the eruption of Ten-nyson into the public realm, into an official status, also takes this impris-onment away from the merely personal and into the political. 'Official' Victorian ideologies *were* prisons, amongst other things. Patriotism may be exhilarating, but in Tennyson ('The Revenge', 'The Charge of the Light Brigade') it always leads to death: it closes down possibilities, it operates as a trap. Bigotry such as racism becomes just one more way in which Tennyson cuts himself off from communion with his fellow men and women. Enoch Arden on his island is alone, just as completely as the Kraken had been in his deep-sea slumber. This isolation, this 'death', this depression, almost always underwrites Tennyson's public voice.

This is to say more than that Tennyson wrote a poetry fascinated with depression. Tennyson's Mariana endures a despairing melancholy it is true, but the more acute form of consciousness in Tennysonian poetics is that of a strange, visionary fugue-state. In a letter to Benjamin Blood (below, p. 520) he talked about 'a kind of waking trance (this for

---

[7] Quoted in Norman Page (ed.), *Tennyson: Interviews and Recollections* (London: Macmillan, 1983), 123.

lack of a better word)' that he had 'frequently had quite up from boy-
hood when I have been all alone. This has often come upon me through
repeating my own name to myself silently, till all at once as it were out of
the intensity of the consciousness of individuality the individuality
itself seemed to dissolve and fade away into boundless being.' This hal-
lucinatory state of mind crops up again and again in his poetry, early *and*
late. Tennyson actually revised *The Princess* after publication in order to
insert passages that described his hero as susceptible to exactly this sort
of 'weird seizure' ('I seem'd to move among a world of ghosts, | And
feel myself the shadow of a dream', I: 17–18). This state of mind is also
crucial to the *Idylls of the King*. Sometimes it is conceptualized as a
straightforward melancholia, as with Merlin:

> Then fell on Merlin a great melancholy;
> He walk'd with dreams and darkness, and he found
> A doom that ever poised itself to fall.
>
> (*Merlin and Vivien*, 187–9)

More centrally, it is represented as a state of mind that leaves conven-
tional emotional states behind and represents a more mystic trance.
After his knights return from the fruitless quest for the Holy Grail, King
Arthur makes a remarkable speech:

> Let visions of the night or of the day
> Come, as they will; and many a time they come,
> Until this earth he walks on seems not earth,
> This light that strikes his eyeball is not light,
> This air that smites his forehead is not air
> But vision—
>
> (*Holy Grail*, 906–11)

This mystic light, whatever it is, still does strike his eyeball; and the
vision it provides is of a weird, inexpressible sense. It may be this cleav-
age of visual with visionary that constitutes Tennyson's highest achieve-
ment; his particular variety of the visionary, one always and at all points
rooted in observation of the actual. This might seem an odd, almost con-
tradictory use of the word 'visionary', but it is in that contradiction that
Tennyson's peculiar genius most finds its expression. To put this
another way, these moments of 'weird visionary seizure' operate directly
upon the ordinary, the everyday. These two sorts of vision, the Victorian
and the extraordinary, coexist.

A little earlier I called a scene from the end of *Enoch Arden* fussy and
dull; but it would be wrong to give the impression that those two words

applied to that poem as a whole. There is nothing dull or narrow about
the emotional sweep of this Hardyesque fable about the arbitrariness of
fate and the way certain individuals find themselves tragically unable to
fit into the ordinary world. Indeed, in *Enoch Arden* the dullness of every-
day home-based banality is necessary to the poetic effectiveness of the
whole work, in order to offset the extraordinary experience that Enoch
has. To put this another way: at the core of Enoch's experience is pre-
cisely this shift from the real to the visionary, and the poem *needs* the real
(howsoever dull, conventional, or limited) in order to contextualize the
visionary. The real in this case is the home, the family life that is Enoch's
emotional core; the life to protect the sanctity of which he is prepared, at
the end of the poem, literally to lie down and die. But his interlude on
the desert island, the imprisonment that it represents, partakes of the
visionary in some of Tennyson's most lucid, luminous poetry. It is not
the 'kindly human face' or 'kindly voice' of the affective pole-star of the
poem (such as the domestic scene quoted above), but something
stranger, something more alien and beautiful:

> what he fain had seen
> He could not see, the kindly human face,
> Nor ever hear a kindly voice, but heard
> The myriad shriek of wheeling ocean-fowl,
> The league-long roller thundering on the reef,
> The moving whisper of huge trees that branch'd
> And blossom'd in the zenith, or the sweep
> Of some precipitous rivulet to the wave
>
>   .   .   .   .   .   .
>
> A shipwreck'd sailor, waiting for a sail:
> No sail from day to day, but every day
> The sunrise broken into scarlet shafts
> Among the palms and ferns and precipices;
> The blaze upon the waters to the east;
> The blaze upon his island overhead;
> The blaze upon the waters to the west;
> Then the great stars that globed themselves in Heaven,
> The hollower-bellowing ocean, and again
> The scarlet shafts of sunrise—but no sail.

                    (*Enoch Arden*, 576–83, 586–95)

It is not really proper to say that in poetry such as this landscape is stand-
ing in for states of mind; this does not correlate to the 'state of mind' of
Enoch at all. It is something altogether more unsettling, a vision of
paradise *as* hell, a collocation of Tennysonian intensity, colour, beauty,

and warmth that none the less is a prison. Beauty as monotony, time as torment, nature as a fugue-state. The last six lines quoted here, with their astonishing, almost heartbreaking apprehension of the passage of a day and a night, are unlike anything else in Victorian poetry. Once he has been touched by this strange, trance-like state of existence Enoch cannot return to the pieties of conventional Victorian living. He has, in some unspeakable sense, crossed the bar.

'Can anybody in his senses,' asked a Victorian critic, 'imagine posterity speaking of our age as the age of Tennyson?'[8] Paul Turner adds that 'we may reasonably call it just that; for all its main features are reflected in his poetry'. But there is more to Tennyson's Victorianism than a ticking off of a list of period characteristics. It is the coexistence in Tennyson's poetry of the visionary and the mundane, of subjective and objective, that points to something more penetrating, a multifariousness that we can also legitimately call Victorian, an opening up to the multiple possibilities of interpretation. Tennyson's poetry embodies both a rootedness in the specificities of nineteenth-century society and attitudes, and a deeply personal, anti-rational attempt to transcend the ordinariness of these roots. His voice is uniquely public and private.

[8] Quoted in Paul Turner, *Tennyson* (London: Routledge, 1976), 1.

CHRONOLOGY

1809   Alfred Tennyson born at Somersby, Lincolnshire, the third surviving son of George Tennyson, the Rector, and Elizabeth Tennyson. His father is an alcoholic, melancholic, and sometimes violent man.

1816   Enrols at Louth Grammar School.

1820   Leaves school. His education continues at home, directed by his father.

1824   George Tennyson's health collapses.

1827   In April Tennyson publishes *Poems by Two Brothers*, a volume that actually contains poetry by three of the Tennyson brothers (Alfred, Charles, and Frederick). The volume is little noticed. In November he goes up to Trinity College Cambridge.

1829   Meets Arthur Hallam; their friendship grows. Tennyson wins the Chancellor's Gold Medal with his poem 'Timbuctoo', the first blank-verse poem to win the prize. Later in the year, he joins the debating society 'The Apostles'.

1830   Publishes *Poems, Chiefly Lyrical*; it is unfavourably reviewed by Lockhart and John Wilson. Tennyson travels in Europe with Hallam.

1831   After the death of his father, Tennyson leaves Cambridge without taking a degree.

1832   Travels in Europe with Hallam a second time; Hallam is now engaged to Tennyson's sister, Emily. In December *Poems* is published.

1833   Some poor reviews of *Poems*. Hallam dies suddenly in September, whilst in Vienna. Tennyson overwhelmed by grief; he begins writing the lyrics that will become *In Memoriam*.

1836   Tennyson falls in love with Emily Sellwood (whom he had first met in 1830). They will not marry until 1850.

1837   Tennyson's engagement with Emily is recognized by their families.

1840   The engagement is broken off, for reasons that remain unclear but may have had to do with Tennyson's financial insecurity.

1840–3   Tennyson invests his money (about £3,000) in a scheme based on a new wood-carving machine. This has collapsed by 1843.

1842   Publishes *Poems* in two volumes, the first containing a selection of his earlier work and the second with all new poems. Some more favourable critical attention.

1845   Awarded a Civil List pension of £200 a year.

1847   Publishes *The Princess*.

1850   *In Memoriam* is published anonymously in May. In June Tennyson finally marries Emily. Following Wordsworth's death in April there is much speculation concerning who will be the next poet laureate; Tennyson is appointed to the post in November.

1851   The Tennysons' first child is stillborn.

1852   Hallam Tennyson born. *Ode on the Death of the Duke of Wellington* published in November.

1853   Settles in Farringford, on the Isle of Wight.

1854   Lionel Tennyson born.

1855   *Maud and Other Poems* published.

1859   *Idylls of the King* published (it contains four idylls: *Enid, Vivien, Elaine,* and *Guinevere*).

1861   Prince Albert, the Queen's Consort, dies in December. The following month Tennyson writes a dedication to the new edition of *Idylls of the King*: 'These to His Memory—since he held them dear'.

1862   First meeting with Queen Victoria.

1864   *Enoch Arden* published.

1869   *The Holy Grail and Other Poems* published.

1871   *Gareth and Lynette* published.

1872–3 *Collected Works* published (The Imperial Library edition), which brings together all but one of the *Idylls of the King* (the one remaining, *Balin and Balan,* will be written in 1874).

1875   Publishes his first play, *Queen Mary*. He will go on to publish another seven plays between 1875 and 1892, many of which are staged by Henry Irving.

1880   *Ballads and Other Poems* published.

1883   Is offered, and accepts, a barony (he had been offered a baronetcy in 1865, 1873, 1874, and 1880, refusing it on each occasion). Takes his seat in the House of Lords in March 1884.

1885   *Tiresias, and Other Poems* published.

1886   In April Tennyson's son Lionel dies (aged 32) on the way back from a trip to India.

1889   *Demeter and Other Poems* published.

1890   Edison makes a recording of Tennyson reading some of his poems.

1892   Tennyson dies, at Aldworth, Haslemere, 6 October. *The Death of Œnone, Akbar's Dream and Other Poems* published posthumously.

NOTE ON THE TEXT

THE copy text for this edition is the nine-volume edition of Tennyson's complete works edited by his son, Hallam Tennyson, and published by Macmillan in 1907–8, known as the 'Eversley' edition. This incorporates Tennyson's last revisions and therefore his ultimate desires as to the shape of his poetry. The 'Eversley' also includes copious notes by Hallam Tennyson, many of which quote directly from Tennyson's own statements about his poetry; many of these comments are given in the notes to this edition, identified by the provenance '[T]'. Hallam Tennyson's *Memoir*, a life of his father, also contains a great deal of interesting material that relates to how Tennyson and his contemporaries saw his poetry; such extracts from the *Memoir* as relate to the poetry are excerpted and included at the end of this edition, after a selection of some of the more interesting of Tennyson's letters and journal entries.

The degree sign (°) indicates a note at the end of the book. Annotation has been kept to a minimum; notes record first publication date and, when known, date of composition; they include relevant comments by Tennyson if these elucidate the poems. The more general headnotes to individual poems are not cued.

POEMS

JUVENILIA

Timbuctoo

Deep in that lion-haunted inland lies
A mystic city, goal of high emprise.

Chapman

I stood upon the Mountain which o'erlooks°
The narrow seas, whose rapid interval
Parts Afric from green Europe, when the Sun
Had fall'n below th' Atlantic, and above
The silent heavens were blench'd with faëry light,
Uncertain whether faëry light or cloud,
Flowing Southward, and the chasms of deep, deep blue
Slumber'd unfathomable, and the stars
Were flooded over with clear glory and pale.
I gazed upon the sheeny coast beyond,   [10]
There where the Giant of old Time infix'd°
The limits of his prowess, pillars high
Long time erased from Earth: even as the Sea
When weary of wild inroad buildeth up
Huge mounds whereby to stay his yeasty waves.°
And much I mused on legends quaint and old
Which whilom won the hearts of all on earth
Toward their brightness, ev'n as flame draws air;
But had their being in the heart of man
As air is th' life of flame: and thou wert then   [20]
A center'd glory-circled memory,
Divinest Atalantis, whom the waves
Have buried deep, and thou of later name,
Imperial Eldorado, roof'd with gold:
Shadows to which, despite all shocks of change,
All on-set of capricious Accident,
Men clung with yearning Hope which would not die.
As when in some great City where the walls
Shake, and the streets with ghastly faces throng'd,

Do utter forth a subterranean voice,   [30]
Among the inner columns far retired
At midnight, in the lone Acropolis,
Before the awful Genius of the place°
Kneels the pale Priestess in deep faith, the while
Above her head the weak lamp dips and winks
Unto the fearful summoning without:
Nathless she ever clasps the marble knees,
Bathes the cold hands with tears, and gazeth on
Those eyes which wear no light but that wherewith
Her phantasy informs them.
                                        Where are ye,   [40]
Thrones of the Western wave, fair Islands green?
Where are your moonlight halls, your cedarn glooms,
The blossoming abysses of your hills?
Your flowering Capes, and your gold-sanded bays
Blown round with happy airs of odorous winds?
Where are the infinite ways, which, Seraph-trod,
Wound thro' your great Elysian solitudes,
Whose lowest deeps were, as with visible love,
Fill'd with Divine effulgence, circumfused,
Flowing between the clear and polish'd stems,   [50]
And ever circling round their emerald cones
In coronals and glories, such as gird
The unfading foreheads of the Saints in Heaven?
For nothing visible, they say, had birth
In that blest ground, but it was play'd about
With its peculiar glory. Then I raised
My voice and cried, 'Wide Afric, doth thy Sun
Lighten, thy hills enfold a City as fair
As those which starr'd the night o' the elder world?
Or is the rumour of thy Timbuctoo   [60]
A dream as frail as those of ancient Time?'
    A curve of whitening, flashing, ebbing light!
A rustling of white wings! the bright descent
Of a young Seraph! and he stood beside me
There on the ridge, and look'd into my face
With his unutterable, shining orbs.°
So that with hasty motion I did veil
My vision with both hands, and saw before me
Such colour'd spots as dance athwart the eyes

Of those, that gaze upon the noonday Sun.   [70]
Girt with a zone of flashing gold beneath°
His breast, and compass'd round about his brow
With triple arch of everchanging bows,
And circled with the glory of living light
And alternation of all hues, he stood.
    'O child of man, why muse you here alone
Upon the Mountain, on the dreams of old
Which fill'd the earth with passing loveliness,
Which flung strange music on the howling winds,
And odours rapt from remote Paradise?   [80]
Thy sense is clogg'd with dull mortality;
Thy spirit fetter'd with the bond of clay:
Open thine eyes and see.'
                              I look'd, but not
Upon his face, for it was wonderful
With its exceeding brightness, and the light
Of the great Angel Mind which look'd from out
The starry glowing of his restless eyes.
I felt my soul grow mighty, and my spirit
With supernatural excitation bound
Within me, and my mental eye grew large   [90]
With such a vast circumference of thought,
That in my vanity I seem'd to stand
Upon the outward verge and bound alone
Of full beatitude. Each failing sense,
As with a momentary flash of light,
Grew thrillingly distinct and keen. I saw
The smallest grain that dappled the dark earth,
The indistinctest atom in deep air,
The Moon's white cities, and the opal width
Of her small glowing lakes, her silver heights   [100]
Unvisited with dew of vagrant cloud,
And the unsounded, undescended depth
Of her black hollows. The clear Galaxy
Shorn of its hoary lustre, wonderful,
Distinct and vivid with sharp points of light,
Blaze within blaze, an unimagin'd depth
And harmony of planet-girded suns
And moon-encircled planets, wheel in wheel,
Arch'd the wan sapphire. Nay—the hum of men,°

Or other things talking in unknown tongues,   [110]
And notes of busy life in distant worlds
Beat like a far wave on my anxious ear.

    A maze of piercing, trackless, thrilling thoughts,
Involving and embracing each with each,
Rapid as fire, inextricably link'd,
Expanding momently with every sight
And sound which struck the palpitating sense,
The issue of strong impulse, hurried through
The riv'n rapt brain; as when in some large lake
From pressure of descendant crags, which lapse   [120]
Disjointed, crumbling from their parent slope
At slender interval, the level calm
Is ridg'd with restless and increasing spheres
Which break upon each other, each th' effect
Of separate impulse, but more fleet and strong
Than its precursor, till the eye in vain
Amid the wild unrest of swimming shade
Dappled with hollow and alternate rise
Of interpenetrated arc, would scan
Definite round.

                I know not if I shape   [130]
These things with accurate similitude
From visible objects, for but dimly now,
Less vivid than a half-forgotten dream,
The memory of that mental excellence
Comes o'er me, and it may be I entwine
The indecision of my present mind
With its past clearness, yet it seems to me
As even then the torrent of quick thought
Absorbed me from the nature of itself
With its own fleetness. Where is he, that borne   [140]
Adown the sloping of an arrowy stream,
Could link his shallop to the fleeting edge,°
And muse midway with philosophic calm
Upon the wondrous laws which regulate
The fierceness of the bounding Element?

    My thoughts which long had grovell'd in the slime
Of this dull world, like dusky worms which house°
Beneath unshaken waters, but at once
Upon some Earth-awakening day of Spring

Do pass from gloom to glory, and aloft   [150]
Winnow the purple, bearing on both sides
Double display of star-lit wings, which burn
Fan-like and fibred with intensest bloom;
Ev'n so my thoughts, erewhile so low, now felt
Unutterable buoyancy and strength
To bear them upward through the trackless fields
Of undefin'd existence far and free.
    Then first within the South methought I saw
A wilderness of spires, and chrystal pile
Of rampart upon rampart, dome on dome,   [160]
Illimitable range of battlement
On battlement, and the Imperial height
Of Canopy o'ercanopied.
               Behind
In diamond light upsprung the dazzling peaks
Of Pyramids, as far surpassing earth's
As heaven than earth is fairer. Each aloft
Upon his narrow'd eminence bore globes
Of wheeling Suns, or Stars, or semblances
Of either, showering circular abyss
Of radiance. But the glory of the place   [170]
Stood out a pillar'd front of burnish'd gold,
Interminably high, if gold it were
Or metal more etherial, and beneath
Two doors of blinding brilliance, where no gaze
Might rest, stood open, and the eye could scan,
Through length of porch and valve and boundless hall,°
Part of a throne of fiery flame, wherefrom
The snowy skirting of a garment hung,
And glimpse of multitudes of multitudes
That minister'd around it—if I saw   [180]
These things distinctly, for my human brain
Stagger'd beneath the vision, and thick night
Came down upon my eyelids, and I fell.
    With ministering hand he rais'd me up:
Then with a mournful and ineffable smile,
Which but to look on for a moment fill'd
My eyes with irresistible sweet tears,
In accents of majestic melody,
Like a swoln river's gushings in still night

Mingled with floating music, thus he spake: [190]
    'There is no mightier Spirit than I to sway
The heart of man: and teach him to attain
By shadowing forth the Unattainable;
And step by step to scale that mighty stair
Whose landing-place is wrapt about with clouds
Of glory' of heaven. With earliest light of Spring,°
And in the glow of sallow Summertide,
And in red Autumn when the winds are wild
With gambols, and when full-voiced Winter roofs
The headland with inviolate white snow,   [200]
I play about his heart a thousand ways,
Visit his eyes with visions, and his ears
With harmonies of wind and wave and wood,
—Of winds which tell of waters, and of waters
Betraying the close kisses of the wind—
And win him unto me: and few there be
So gross of heart who have not felt and known
A higher than they see: They with dim eyes
Behold me darkling. Lo! I have given thee
To understand my presence, and to feel   [210]
My fullness; I have fill'd thy lips with power.
I have rais'd thee nigher to the spheres of Heaven
Man's first, last home: and thou with ravish'd sense
Listenest the lordly music flowing from
Th' illimitable years. I am the Spirit,
The permeating life which courseth through
All th' intricate and labyrinthine veins
Of the great vine of Fable, which, outspread°
With growth of shadowing leaf and clusters rare,
Reacheth to every corner under Heaven,   [220]
Deep-rooted in the living soil of truth;
So that men's hopes and fears take refuge in
The fragrance of its complicated glooms,
And cool impleachèd twilights. Child of Man,
See'st thou yon river, whose translucent wave,
Forth issuing from the darkness, windeth through
The argent streets o' th' City, imaging
The soft inversion of her tremulous Domes,°
Her gardens frequent with the stately Palm,

Her pagods hung with music of sweet bells,   [230]
Her obelisks of rangèd chrysolite,°
Minarets and towers? Lo! how he passeth by,
And gulphs himself in sands, as not enduring°
To carry through the world those waves, which bore
The reflex of my City in their depths.
Oh City! oh latest Throne! where I was rais'd
To be a mystery of loveliness
Unto all eyes, the time is well-nigh come
When I must render up this glorious home
To keen Discovery: soon yon brilliant towers   [240]
Shall darken with the waving of her wand;
Darken, and shrink and shiver into huts,
Black specks amid a waste of dreary sand,
Low-built, mud-wall'd, barbarian settlements.
How chang'd from this fair City!'
                                Thus far the Spirit:
Then parted Heaven-ward on the wing: and I
Was left alone on Calpe, and the Moon°
Had fallen from the night, and all was dark!

'The Idealist'

A mighty matter I rehearse,
A mighty matter undescried;
Come listen all who can.
I am the spirit of a man,
I weave the universe,
And indivisible divide,
Creating all I hear and see.
All souls are centres: I am one,
I am the earth, the stars, the sun,
I am the clouds, the sea.   [10]
I am the citadels and palaces
Of all great cities: I am Rome,
Tadmor, and Cairo: I am Place°
And Time, yet is my home

Eternity: (let no man think it odd,
 For I am these,
And every other birth of every other race;)
I am all things save souls of fellow men and
 very God!

POEMS, CHIEFLY LYRICAL
(1830)

Mariana

'Mariana in the moated grange.'
Measure for Measure

With blackest moss the flower-plots
    Were thickly crusted, one and all:
The rusted nails fell from the knots
    That held the pear to the gable-wall.
The broken sheds look'd sad and strange:
    Unlifted was the clinking latch;
    Weeded and worn the ancient thatch
Upon the lonely moated grange.
        She only said, 'My life is dreary,
           He cometh not,' she said;   [10]
        She said, 'I am aweary, aweary,
           I would that I were dead!'

Her tears fell with the dews at even;
    Her tears fell ere the dews were dried;
She could not look on the sweet heaven,
    Either at morn or eventide.
After the flitting of the bats,
    When thickest dark did trance the sky,
    She drew her casement-curtain by,
And glanced athwart the glooming flats.   [20]
        She only said, 'The night is dreary,
           He cometh not,' she said;
        She said, 'I am aweary, aweary,
           I would that I were dead!'

Upon the middle of the night,
    Waking she heard the night-fowl crow:
The cock sung out an hour ere light:

From the dark fen the oxen's low
  Came to her: without hope of change,
    In sleep she seem'd to walk forlorn,
    Till cold winds woke the gray-eyed morn   [30]
About the lonely moated grange.
      She only said, 'The day is dreary,
        He cometh not,' she said;
      She said, 'I am aweary, aweary,
        I would that I were dead!'

About a stone-cast from the wall
  A sluice with blacken'd waters slept,°
And o'er it many, round and small,
  The cluster'd marish-mosses crept.°   [40]
Hard by a poplar shook alway,
  All silver-green with gnarled bark:
  For leagues no other tree did mark
The level waste, the rounding gray.
      She only said, 'My life is dreary,
        He cometh not,' she said;
      She said, 'I am aweary, aweary,
        I would that I were dead!'

And ever when the moon was low,
  And the shrill winds were up and away,   [50]
In the white curtain, to and fro,
  She saw the gusty shadow sway.
But when the moon was very low,
  And wild winds bound within their cell,
  The shadow of the poplar fell
Upon her bed, across her brow.
      She only said, 'The night is dreary,
        He cometh not,' she said;
      She said, 'I am aweary, aweary,
        I would that I were dead!'   [60]

All day within the dreamy house,
  The doors upon their hinges creak'd;
The blue fly sung in the pane; the mouse°
  Behind the mouldering wainscot shriek'd,°
Or from the crevice peer'd about.
      Old faces glimmer'd thro' the doors,

Old footsteps trod the upper floors,
Old voices called her from without.
  She only said, 'My life is dreary,
    He cometh not,' she said;   [70]
  She said, 'I am aweary, aweary,
    I would that I were dead!'

The sparrow's chirrup on the roof,
  The slow clock ticking, and the sound
Which to the wooing wind aloof
  The poplar made, did all confound
Her sense; but most she loathed the hour
  When the thick-moted sunbeam lay
Athwart the chambers, and the day
Was sloping toward his western bower.   [80]
  Then, said she, 'I am very dreary,
    He will not come,' she said;
  She wept, 'I am aweary, aweary,
    Oh God, that I were dead!'

Supposed Confessions of a Second-Rate Sensitive Mind

O God! my God! have mercy now.
I faint, I fall. Men say that Thou
Didst die for me, for such as *me*,
Patient of ill, and death, and scorn,
And that my sin was as a thorn
Among the thorns that girt Thy brow,
Wounding Thy soul.—That even now,
In this extremst misery
Of ignorance, I should require
A sign! and if a bolt of fire   [10]
Would rive the slumbrous summer noon°
While I do pray to Thee alone,
Think my belief would stronger grow!
Is not my human pride brought low?
The boastings of my spirit still?

The joy I had in my freewill
All cold, and dead, and corpse-like grown?
And what is left to me, but Thou,
And faith in Thee? Men pass me by;
Christians with happy countenances—   [20]
And children all seem full of Thee!
And women smile with saint-like glances
Like Thine own mother's when she bow'd
Above Thee, on that happy morn
When angels spake to men aloud,
And Thou and peace to earth were born.
Goodwill to me as well as all—
I one of them: my brothers they:
Brothers in Christ—a world of peace
And confidence, day after day;   [30]
And trust and hope till things should cease,
And then one Heaven receive us all.

How sweet to have a common faith!
To hold a common scorn of death!
And at a burial to hear
The creaking cords which wound and eat
Into my human heart, whene'er
Earth goes to earth, with grief, not fear,
With hopeful grief, were passing sweet!

Thrice happy state again to be   [40]
The trustful infant on the knee!
Who lets his rosy fingers play
About his mother's neck, and knows
Nothing beyond his mother's eyes.
They comfort him by night and day;
They light his little life alway;
He hath no thought of coming woes;
He hath no care of life or death;
Scarce outward signs of joy arise,
Because the Spirit of happiness   [50]
And perfect rest so inward is;
And loveth so his innocent heart,
Her temple and her place of birth,
Where she would ever wish to dwell,
Life of the fountain there, beneath

Its salient springs, and far apart,°
Hating to wander out on earth,
Or breathe into the hollow air,
Whose chillness would make visible
Her subtil, warm, and golden breath,   [60]
Which mixing with the infant's blood,
Fulfils him with beatitude.
Oh! sure it is a special care
Of God, to fortify from doubt,
To arm in proof, and guard about
With triple-mailèd trust, and clear
Delight, the infant's dawning year.

Would that my gloomed fancy were
As thine, my mother, when with brows
Propt on thy knees, my hands upheld   [70]
In thine, I listen'd to thy vows,
For me outpour'd in holiest prayer—
For me unworthy!—and beheld
Thy mild deep eyes upraised, that knew
The beauty and repose of faith,
And the clear spirit shining thro'.
Oh! wherefore do we grow awry
From roots which strike so deep? why dare
Paths in the desert? Could not I
Bow myself down, where thou hast knelt,   [80]
To the earth—until the ice would melt
Here, and I feel as thou hast felt?
What Devil had the heart to scathe°
Flowers thou hadst rear'd—to brush the dew
From thine own lily, when thy grave
Was deep, my mother, in the clay?
Myself? Is it thus? Myself? Had I
So little love for thee? But why
Prevail'd not thy pure prayers? Why pray
To one who heeds not, who can save   [90]
But will not? Great in faith, and strong
Against the grief of circumstance
Wert thou, and yet unheard. What if
Thou pleadest still, and seest me drive
Thro' utter dark a full-sail'd skiff,

Unpiloted i' the echoing dance
Of reboant whirlwinds, stooping low°
Unto the death, not sunk! I know
At matins and at evensong,
That thou, if thou wert yet alive,   [100]
In deep and daily prayers would'st strive
To reconcile me with thy God.
Albeit, my hope is gray, and cold
At heart, thou wouldest murmur still—
'Bring this lamb back into Thy fold,
My Lord, if so it be Thy will.'
Would'st tell me I must brook the rod
And chastisement of human pride;
That pride, the sin of devils, stood
Betwixt me and the light of God!   [110]
That hitherto I had defied
And had rejected God—that grace
Would drop from his o'er-brimming love,
As manna on my wilderness,
If I would pray—that God would move
And strike the hard, hard rock, and thence,
Sweet in their utmost bitterness,
Would issue tears of penitence
Which would keep green hope's life. Alas!
I think that pride hath now no place   [120]
Nor sojourn in me. I am void,
Dark, formless, utterly destroyed.

Why not believe then? Why not yet
Anchor thy frailty there, where man
Hath moor'd and rested? Ask the sea
At midnight, when the crisp slope waves°
After a tempest, rib and fret
The broad-imbased beach, why he
Slumbers not like a mountain tarn?°
Wherefore his ridges are not curls   [130]
And ripples of an inland mere?°
Wherefore he moaneth thus, nor can
Draw down into his vexed pools
All that blue heaven which hues and paves
The other? I am too forlorn,

Too shaken: my own weakness fools
My judgment, and my spirit whirls,
Moved from beneath with doubt and fear.

'Yet,' said I, in my morn of youth,
The unsunn'd freshness of my strength,   [140]
When I went forth in quest of truth,
'It is man's privilege to doubt,
If so be that from doubt at length,
Truth may stand forth unmoved of change,
An image with profulgent brows,
And perfect limbs, as from the storm
Of running fires and fluid range
Of lawless airs, at last stood out
This excellence and solid form
Of constant beauty. For the Ox   [150]
Feeds in the herb, and sleeps, or fills
The horned valleys all about,
And hollows of the fringèd hills
In summer heats, with placid lows
Unfearing, till his own blood flows
About his hoof. And in the flocks
The lamb rejoiceth in the year,
And raceth freely with his fere,°
And answers to his mother's calls
From the flower'd furrow. In a time,   [160]
Of which he wots not, run short pains
Thro' his warm heart; and then, from whence
He knows not, on his light there falls
A shadow; and his native slope,
Where he was wont to leap and climb,
Floats from his sick and filmèd eyes,
And something in the darkness draws
His forehead earthward, and he dies.
Shall man live thus, in joy and hope
As a young lamb, who cannot dream,   [170]
Living, but that he shall live on?
Shall we not look into the laws
Of life and death, and things that seem,
And things that be, and analyse
Our double nature, and compare

All creeds till we have found the one,
If one there be?' Ay me! I fear
All may not doubt, but everywhere
Some must clasp Idols. Yet, my God,
Whom call I Idol? Let Thy dove   [180]
Shadow me over, and my sins°
Be unremember'd and Thy love
Enlighten me. Oh teach me yet
Somewhat before the heavy clod
Weighs on me, and the busy fret
Of that sharp-headed worm begins
In the gross blackness underneath.

O weary life! O weary death!
O spirit and heart made desolate!
O damned vacillating state!   [190]

Song

I

I' the glooming light
Of middle night
So cold and white,
Worn Sorrow sits by the moaning wave;
    Beside her are laid
    Her mattock and spade,
For she hath half delved her own deep grave.
    Alone she is there:
The white clouds drizzle: her hair falls loose;
    Her shoulders are bare;   [10]
Her tears are mixed with the beaded dews.

II

Death standeth by;
She will not die;
With glazèd eye
She looks at her grave: she cannot sleep;
    Ever alone

She maketh her moan:
She cannot speak; she can only weep,
   For she will not hope.
The thick snow falls on her flake by flake,
   The dull wave mourns down the slope,   [20]
The world will not change, and her heart will not break.

Song

I

A spirit haunts the year's last hours
Dwelling amid these yellowing bowers:
     To himself he talks;
For at eventide, listening earnestly,
At his work you may hear him sob and sigh
     In the walks;
     Earthward he boweth the heavy stalks
Of the mouldering flowers:
     Heavily hangs the broad sunflower
       Over its grave i' the earth so chilly;   [10]
     Heavily hangs the hollyhock,
       Heavily hangs the tiger-lily.

II

The air is damp, and hush'd, and close,
As a sick man's room when he taketh repose
     An hour before death;
My very heart faints and my whole soul grieves
At the moist rich smell of the rotting leaves,
     And the breath
     Of the fading edges of box beneath,°
And the year's last rose.   [20]
     Heavily hangs the broad sunflower
       Over its grave i' the earth so chilly;
     Heavily hangs the hollyhock,
       Heavily hangs the tiger-lily.

The Kraken

Below the thunders of the upper deep;
Far, far beneath in the abysmal sea,
His ancient, dreamless, uninvaded sleep
The Kraken sleepeth: faintest sunlights flee
About his shadowy sides: above him swell
Huge sponges of millennial growth and height;
And far away into the sickly light,
From many a wondrous grot and secret cell
Unnumber'd and enormous polypi
Winnow with giant arms the slumbering green.   [10]
There hath he lain for ages and will lie
Battening upon huge seaworms in his sleep,°
Until the latter fire shall heat the deep;°
Then once by men and angels to be seen,
In roaring he shall rise and on the surface die.

POEMS (1832)

The Lady of Shalott

Part I

On either side the river lie
Long fields of barley and of rye,
That clothe the wold and meet the sky;
And thro' the field the road runs by
    To many-tower'd Camelot;
And up and down the people go,
Gazing where the lilies blow
Round an island there below,
    The island of Shalott.

Willows whiten, aspens quiver,°   [10]
Little breezes dusk and shiver
Thro' the wave that runs for ever
By the island in the river
    Flowing down to Camelot.
Four gray walls, and four gray towers,
Overlook a space of flowers,
And the silent isle imbowers
    The Lady of Shalott.

By the margin, willow-veil'd,
Slide the heavy barges trail'd   [20]
By slow horses; and unhail'd
The shallop flitteth silken-sail'd°
    Skimming down to Camelot:
But who hath seen her wave her hand?
Or at the casement seen her stand?
Or is she known in all the land,
    The Lady of Shalott?

Only reapers, reaping early
In among the bearded barley,

Hear a song that echoes cheerly   [30]
From the river winding clearly,
        Down to tower'd Camelot:
And by the moon the reaper weary,
Piling sheaves in uplands airy,
Listening, whispers ''Tis the fairy
        Lady of Shalott.'

Part II

There she weaves by night and day
A magic web with colours gay.
She has heard a whisper say,
A curse is on her if she stay   [40]
        To look down to Camelot.
She knows not what the curse may be,
And so she weaveth steadily,
And little other care hath she,
        The Lady of Shalott.

And moving thro' a mirror clear
That hangs before her all the year,
Shadows of the world appear.
There she sees the highway near
        Winding down to Camelot: [50]
There the river eddy whirls,
And there the surly village-churls,
And the red cloaks of market girls,
        Pass onward from Shalott.

Sometimes a troop of damsels glad,
An abbot on an ambling pad,°
Sometimes a curly shepherd-lad,
Or long-hair'd page in crimson clad,
        Goes by to tower'd Camelot;
And sometimes thro' the mirror blue   [60]
The knights come riding two and two:
She hath no loyal knight and true,
        The Lady of Shalott.

But in her web she still delights
To weave the mirror's magic sights,

For often thro' the silent nights
A funeral, with plumes and lights
  And music, went to Camelot:
Or when the moon was overhead,
Came two young lovers lately wed;   [70]
'I am half sick of shadows,' said°
  The Lady of Shalott.

Part III

A bow-shot from her bower-eaves,
He rode between the barley-sheaves,
The sun came dazzling thro' the leaves,
And flamed upon the brazen greaves°
  Of bold Sir Lancelot.
A red-cross knight for ever kneel'd°
To a lady in his shield,
That sparkled on the yellow field,   [80]
  Beside remote Shalott.

The gemmy bridle glitter'd free,
Like to some branch of stars we see
Hung in the golden Galaxy.
The bridle bells rang merrily
  As he rode down to Camelot:
And from his blazon'd baldric slung°
A mighty silver bugle hung,
And as he rode his armour rung,
  Beside remote Shalott.   [90]

All in the blue unclouded weather
Thick-jewell'd shone the saddle-leather,
The helmet and the helmet-feather
Burn'd like one burning flame together,
  As he rode down to Camelot.
As often thro' the purple night,
Below the starry clusters bright,
Some bearded meteor, trailing light,
  Moves over still Shalott.

His broad clear brow in sunlight glow'd;   [100]
On burnish'd hooves his war-horse trode;

From underneath his helmet flow'd
His coal-black curls as on he rode,
    As he rode down to Camelot.
From the bank and from the river
He flash'd into the crystal mirror,
'Tirra lirra,' by the river°
    Sang Sir Lancelot.

She left the web, she left the loom,
She made three paces thro' the room,   [110]
She saw the water-lily bloom,
She saw the helmet and the plume,
    She look'd down to Camelot.
Out flew the web and floated wide;
The mirror crack'd from side to side;
'The curse is come upon me,' cried
    The Lady of Shalott.

Part IV

In the stormy east-wind straining,
The pale yellow woods were waning,
The broad stream in his banks complaining,   [120]
Heavily the low sky raining
    Over tower'd Camelot;
Down she came and found a boat
Beneath a willow left afloat,
And round about the prow she wrote
    The Lady of Shalott.

And down the river's dim expanse
Like some bold seër in a trance,
Seeing all his own mischance—
With a glassy countenance   [130]
    Did she look to Camelot.
And at the closing of the day
She loosed the chain, and down she lay;
The broad stream bore her far away,
    The Lady of Shalott.

Lying, robed in snowy white
That loosely flew to left and right—

The leaves upon her falling light—
Thro' the noises of the night
    She floated down to Camelot: [140]
And as the boat-head wound along
The willowy hills and fields among,
They heard her singing her last song,
    The Lady of Shalott.

Heard a carol, mournful, holy,
Chanted loudly, chanted lowly,
Till her blood was frozen slowly,
And her eyes were darken'd wholly,
    Turn'd to tower'd Camelot.
For ere she reach'd upon the tide   [150]
The first house by the water-side,
Singing in her song she died,
    The Lady of Shalott.

Under tower and balcony,
By garden-wall and gallery,
A gleaming shape she floated by,
Dead-pale between the houses high,
    Silent into Camelot.
Out upon the wharfs they came,
Knight and burgher, lord and dame,   [160]
And round the prow they read her name,
    The Lady of Shalott.

Who is this? and what is here?
And in the lighted palace near
Died the sound of royal cheer;
And they cross'd themselves for fear,
    All the knights at Camelot:
But Lancelot mused a little space;
He said, 'She has a lovely face;
God in his mercy lend her grace,   [170]
    The Lady of Shalott.'°

Mariana in the South

With one black shadow at its feet,
    The house thro' all the level shines,
Close-latticed to the brooding heat,
    And silent in its dusty vines:
A faint-blue ridge upon the right,
    An empty river-bed before,
    And shallows on a distant shore,
In glaring sand and inlets bright.
        But 'Ave Mary,' made she moan,
            And 'Ave Mary,' night and morn,   [10]
        And 'Ah,' she sang, 'to be all alone,
            To live forgotten, and love forlorn.'

She, as her carol sadder grew,
    From brow and bosom slowly down
Thro' rosy taper fingers drew
    Her streaming curls of deepest brown
To left and right, and made appear
    Still-lighted in a secret shrine,
    Her melancholy eyes divine,
The home of woe without a tear.   [20]
        And 'Ave Mary,' was her moan,
            'Madonna, sad is night and morn,'
        And 'Ah,' she sang, 'to be all alone,
            To live forgotten, and love forlorn.'

Till all the crimson changed, and past
    Into deep orange o'er the sea,
Low on her knees herself she cast,
    Before Our Lady murmur'd she;
Complaining, 'Mother, give me grace
    To help me of my weary load.'   [30]
    And on the liquid mirror glow'd
The clear perfection of her face.
        'Is this the form,' she made her moan,
            'That won his praises night and morn?'
        And 'Ah,' she said, 'but I wake alone,
            I sleep forgotten, I wake forlorn.'

Nor bird would sing, nor lamb would bleat,
    Nor any cloud would cross the vault,

But day increased from heat to heat,
    On stony drought and steaming salt;   [40]
Till now at noon she slept again,
    And seem'd knee-deep in mountain grass,
    And heard her native breezes pass,
And runlets babbling down the glen.
        She breathed in sleep a lower moan,
            And murmuring, as at night and morn,
        She thought, 'My spirit is here alone,
            Walks forgotten, and is forlorn.'

Dreaming, she knew it was a dream:
    She felt he was and was not there.   [50]
She woke: the babble of the stream
    Fell, and, without, the steady glare
Shrank one sick willow sere and small.
    The river-bed was dusty-white;
    And all the furnace of the light
Struck up against the blinding wall.
        She whisper'd, with a stifled moan
            More inward than at night or morn,
        'Sweet Mother, let me not here alone
            Live forgotten and die forlorn.'   [60]

And, rising, from her bosom drew
    Old letters, breathing of her worth,
For 'Love,' they said, 'must needs be true,
    To what is loveliest upon earth.'
An image seem'd to pass the door,
    To look at her with slight, and say
    'But now thy beauty flows away,
So be alone for evermore.'
        'O cruel heart,' she changed her tone,
            'And cruel love, whose end is scorn,   [70]
        Is this the end, to be left alone,
            To live forgotten, and die forlorn?'

But sometimes in the falling day
    An image seem'd to pass the door,
To look into her eyes and say,
    'But thou shalt be alone no more.'
And flaming downward over all

From heat to heat the day decreased,
    And slowly rounded to the east
The one black shadow from the wall.   [80]
        'The day to night,' she made her moan,
            'The day to night, the night to morn,
        And day and night I am left alone
            To live forgotten, and love forlorn.'

At eve a dry cicala sung,°
    There came a sound as of the sea;
Backward the lattice-blind she flung,
    And lean'd upon the balcony.
There all in spaces rosy-bright
    Large Hesper glitter'd on her tears,   [90]
        And deepening thro' the silent spheres
Heaven over Heaven rose the night.
And weeping then she made her moan,
    'The night comes on that knows not morn,
When I shall cease to be all alone,
    To live forgotten, and love forlorn.'

Œnone

There lies a vale in Ida, lovelier°
Than all the valleys of Ionian hills.°
The swimming vapour slopes athwart the glen,
Puts forth an arm, and creeps from pine to pine,
And loiters, slowly drawn. On either hand
The lawns and meadow-ledges midway down
Hang rich in flowers, and far below them roars
The long brook falling thro' the clov'n ravine
In cataract after cataract to the sea.
Behind the valley topmost Gargarus°   [10]
Stands up and takes the morning: but in front
The gorges, opening wide apart, reveal
Troas and Ilion's column'd citadel,
The crown of Troas.
                        Hither came at noon
Mournful Œnone, wandering forlorn
Of Paris, once her playmate on the hills.°

Her cheek had lost the rose, and round her neck
Floated her hair or seem'd to float in rest.
She, leaning on a fragment twined with vine,
Sang to the stillness, till the mountain-shade   [20]
Sloped downward to her seat from the upper cliff.

   'O mother Ida, many-fountain'd Ida,
Dear mother Ida, harken ere I die.
For now the noonday quiet holds the hill:
The grasshopper is silent in the grass:
The lizard, with his shadow on the stone,
Rests like a shadow, and the winds are dead.
The purple flower droops: the golden bee
Is lily-cradled: I alone awake.
My eyes are full of tears, my heart of love,   [30]
My heart is breaking, and my eyes are dim,
And I am all aweary of my life.

   'O mother Ida, many-fountain'd Ida,
Dear mother Ida, harken ere I die.
Hear me, O Earth, hear me, O Hills, O Caves
That house the cold crown'd snake! O mountain brooks,
I am the daughter of a River-God,°
Hear me, for I will speak, and build up all
My sorrow with my song, as yonder walls
Rose slowly to a music slowly breathed,   [40]
A cloud that gather'd shape: for it may be
That, while I speak of it, a little while
My heart may wander from its deeper woe.

   'O mother Ida, many-fountain'd Ida,
Dear mother Ida, harken ere I die.
I waited underneath the dawning hills,
Aloft the mountain lawn was dewy-dark,
And dewy dark aloft the mountain pine:
Beautiful Paris, evil-hearted Paris,
Leading a jet-black goat white-horn'd, white-hooved,   [50]
Came up from reedy Simois all alone.

   'O mother Ida, harken ere I die.
Far-off the torrent call'd me from the cleft:
Far up the solitary morning smote

The streaks of virgin snow. With down-dropt eyes
I sat alone: white-breasted like a star
Fronting the dawn he moved; a leopard skin
Droop'd from his shoulder, but his sunny hair
Cluster'd about his temples like a God's:
And his cheek brighten'd as the foam-bow brightens°   [60]
When the wind blows the foam, and all my heart
Went forth to embrace him coming ere he came.

    'Dear mother Ida, harken ere I die.
He smiled, and opening out his milk-white palm
Disclosed a fruit of pure Hesperian gold,°
That smelt ambrosially, and while I look'd
And listen'd, the full-flowing river of speech
Came down upon my heart.
                              ' "My own Œnone,
Beautiful-brow'd Œnone, my own soul,
Behold this fruit, whose gleaming rind ingrav'n   [70]
'For the most fair,' would seem to award it thine,
As lovelier than whatever Oread haunt°
The knolls of Ida, loveliest in all grace
Of movement, and the charm of married brows."

    'Dear mother Ida, harken ere I die.
He prest the blossom of his lips to mine,
And added "This was cast upon the board,
When all the full-faced presence of the Gods
Ranged in the halls of Peleus; whereupon°
Rose feud, with question unto whom 'twere due: [80]
But light-foot Iris brought it yester-eve,
Delivering, that to me, by common voice
Elected umpire, Herè comes to-day,
Pallas and Aphroditè, claiming each
This meed of fairest. Thou, within the cave
Behind yon whispering tuft of oldest pine,
Mayst well behold them unbeheld, unheard
Hear all, and see thy Paris judge of Gods."

    'Dear mother Ida, harken ere I die.
It was the deep midnoon: one silvery cloud   [90]
Had lost his way between the piney sides
Of this long glen. Then to the bower they came,

Naked they came to that smooth-swarded bower,
And at their feet the crocus brake like fire,
Violet, amaracus, and asphodel,
Lotos and lilies: and a wind arose,
And overhead the wandering ivy and vine,
This way and that, in many a wild festoon
Ran riot, garlanding the gnarled boughs
With bunch and berry and flower thro' and thro'.   [100]

   'O mother Ida, harken ere I die.
On the tree-tops a crested peacock lit,
And o'er him flow'd a golden cloud, and lean'd
Upon him, slowly dropping fragrant dew.
Then first I heard the voice of her, to whom°
Coming thro' Heaven, like a light that grows
Larger and clearer, with one mind the Gods
Rise up for reverence. She to Paris made
Proffer of royal power, ample rule
Unquestion'd, overflowing revenue   [110]
Wherewith to embellish state, "from many a vale
And river-sunder'd champaign clothed with corn,
Or labour'd mine undrainable of ore.
Honour," she said, "and homage, tax and toll,
From many an inland town and haven large,
Mast-throng'd beneath her shadowing citadel
In glassy bays among her tallest towers."

   'O mother Ida, harken ere I die.
Still she spake on and still she spake of power,
"Which in all action is the end of all;   [120]
Power fitted to the season; wisdom-bred
And throned of wisdom—from all neighbour crowns
Alliance and allegiance, till thy hand
Fail from the sceptre-staff. Such boon from me,
From me, Heaven's Queen, Paris, to thee king-born,
A shepherd all thy life but yet king-born,
Should come most welcome, seeing men, in power
Only, are likest gods, who have attain'd
Rest in a happy place and quiet seats
Above the thunder, with undying bliss   [130]
In knowledge of their own supremacy."

'Dear mother Ida, harken ere I die.
She ceased, and Paris held the costly fruit
Out at arm's-length, so much the thought of power
Flatter'd his spirit; but Pallas where she stood
Somewhat apart, her clear and bared limbs
O'erthwarted with the brazen-headed spear
Upon her pearly shoulder leaning cold,
The while, above, her full and earnest eye
Over her snow-cold breast and angry cheek   [140]
Kept watch, waiting decision, made reply.

  ' "Self-reverence, self-knowledge, self-control,
These three alone lead life to sovereign power.
Yet not for power (power of herself
Would come uncall'd for) but to live by law,
Acting the law we live by without fear;
And, because right is right, to follow right
Were wisdom in the scorn of consequence."

'Dear mother Ida, harken ere I die.
Again she said: "I woo thee not with gifts.   [150]
Sequel of guerdon could not alter me°
To fairer. Judge thou me by what I am,
So shalt thou find me fairest.
                     Yet, indeed,
If gazing on divinity disrobed
Thy mortal eyes are frail to judge of fair,
Unbias'd by self-profit, oh! rest thee sure
That I shall love thee well and cleave to thee,
So that my vigour, wedded to thy blood,
Shall strike within thy pulses, like a God's,
To push thee forward thro' a life of shocks,   [160]
Dangers, and deeds, until endurance grow
Sinew'd with action, and the full-grown will,
Circled thro' all experiences, pure law,
Commeasure perfect freedom."
                     'Here she ceas'd,
And Paris ponder'd, and I cried, "O Paris,
Give it to Pallas!" but he heard me not,
Or hearing would not hear me, woe is me!

'O mother Ida, many-fountain'd Ida,
Dear mother Ida, harken ere I die.
Idalian Aphroditè beautiful,   [170]
Fresh as the foam, new-bathed in Paphian wells,°
With rosy slender fingers backward drew
From her warm brows and bosom her deep hair
Ambrosial, golden round her lucid throat
And shoulder: from the violets her light foot
Shone rosy-white, and o'er her rounded form
Between the shadows of the vine-bunches
Floated the glowing sunlights, as she moved.

'Dear mother Ida, harken ere I die.
She with a subtle smile in her mild eyes,   [180]
The herald of her triumph, drawing nigh
Half-whisper'd in his ear, "I promise thee
The fairest and most loving wife in Greece,"
She spoke and laugh'd: I shut my sight for fear:
But when I look'd, Paris had raised his arm,
And I beheld great Herè's angry eyes,
As she withdrew into the golden cloud,
And I was left alone within the bower;
And from that time to this I am alone,
And I shall be alone until I die.   [190]

'Yet, mother Ida, harken ere I die.
Fairest—why fairest wife? am I not fair?
My love hath told me so a thousand times.
Methinks I must be fair, for yesterday,
When I past by, a wild and wanton pard,°
Eyed like the evening star, with playful tail
Crouch'd fawning in the weed. Most loving is she?
Ah me, my mountain shepherd, that my arms
Were wound about thee, and my hot lips prest
Close, close to thine in that quick-falling dew   [200]
Of fruitful kisses, thick as Autumn rains
Flash in the pools of whirling Simois.

'O mother, hear me yet before I die.
They came, they cut away my tallest pines,
My tall dark pines, that plumed the craggy ledge
High over the blue gorge, and all between

The snowy peak and snow-white cataract
Foster'd the callow eaglet—from beneath
Whose thick mysterious boughs in the dark morn
The panther's roar came muffled, while I sat   [210]
Low in the valley. Never, never more
Shall lone Œnone see the morning mist
Sweep thro' them; never see them overlaid
With narrow moon-lit slips of silver cloud,
Between the loud stream and the trembling stars.

   'O mother, hear me yet before I die.
I wish that somewhere in the ruin'd folds,
Among the fragments tumbled from the glens,
Or the dry thickets, I could meet with her
The Abominable, that uninvited came°   [220]
Into the fair Peleïan banquet-hall,
And cast the golden fruit upon the board,
And bred this change; that I might speak my mind,
And tell her to her face how much I hate
Her presence, hated both of Gods and men.

   'O mother, hear me yet before I die.
Hath he not sworn his love a thousand times,
In this green valley, under this green hill,
Ev'n on this hand, and sitting on this stone?
Seal'd it with kisses? water'd it with tears?   [230]
O happy tears, and how unlike to these!
O happy Heaven, how canst thou see my face?
O happy earth, how canst thou bear my weight?
O death, death, death, thou ever-floating cloud,
There are enough unhappy on this earth,
Pass by the happy souls, that love to live:
I pray thee, pass before my light of life,
And shadow all my soul, that I may die.
Thou weighest heavy on the heart within,
Weigh heavy on my eyelids: let me die.   [240]

   'O mother, hear me yet before I die.
I will not die alone, for fiery thoughts
Do shape themselves within me, more and more,
Whereof I catch the issue, as I hear
Dead sounds at night come from the inmost hills,

Like footsteps upon wool. I dimly see
My far-off doubtful purpose, as a mother
Conjectures of the features of her child
Ere it is born: her child!—a shudder comes
Across me: never child be born of me,   [250]
Unblest, to vex me with his father's eyes!

   'O mother, hear me yet before I die.
Hear me, O earth. I will not die alone,
Lest their shrill happy laughter come to me
Walking the cold and starless road of Death
Uncomforted, leaving my ancient love
With the Greek woman. I will rise and go
Down into Troy, and ere the stars come forth
Talk with the wild Cassandra, for she says°
A fire dances before her, and a sound   [260]
Rings ever in her ears of armed men.
What this may be I know not, but I know
That, wheresoe'er I am by night and day,
All earth and air seem only burning fire.'

The Palace of Art

I built my soul a lordly pleasure-house,°
    Wherein at ease for aye to dwell.
I said, 'O Soul, make merry and carouse,
    Dear soul, for all is well.'

A huge crag-platform, smooth as burnish'd brass
    I chose. The ranged ramparts bright
From level meadow-bases of deep grass
    Suddenly scaled the light.

Thereon I built it firm. Of ledge or shelf
    The rock rose clear, or winding stair.   [10]
My soul would live alone unto herself
    In her high palace there.

And 'while the world runs round and round,' I said,
    'Reign thou apart, a quiet king,
Still as, while Saturn whirls, his stedfast shade
    Sleeps on his luminous ring.'°

To which my soul made answer readily:
    'Trust me, in bliss I shall abide
In this great mansion, that is built for me,
    So royal-rich and wide.'   [20]

    .   .   .   .   .   .

   .   .   .   .

Four courts I made, East, West and South and North,
    In each a squared lawn, wherefrom
The golden gorge of dragons spouted forth
    A flood of fountain-foam.

And round the cool green courts there ran a row
    Of cloisters, branch'd like mighty woods,
Echoing all night to that sonorous flow
    Of spouted fountain-floods.

And round the roofs a gilded gallery
    That lent broad verge to distant lands,   [30]
Far as the wild swan wings, to where the sky
    Dipt down to sea and sands.

From those four jets four currents in one swell
    Across the mountain stream'd below
In misty folds, that floating as they fell
    Lit up a torrent-bow.

And high on every peak a statue seem'd
    To hang on tiptoe, tossing up
A cloud of incense of all odour steam'd
    From out a golden cup.   [40]

So that she thought, 'And who shall gaze upon°
    My palace with unblinded eyes,
While this great bow will waver in the sun,
    And that sweet incense rise?'

For that sweet incense rose and never fail'd,
    And, while day sank or mounted higher
The light aërial gallery, golden-rail'd,
    Burnt like a fringe of fire.

Likewise the deep-set windows, stain'd and traced,
    Would seem slow-flaming crimson fires   [50]
From shadow'd grots of arches interlaced,
    And tipt with frost-like spires.

.   .   .   .

.   .   .   .

Full of long-sounding corridors it was,
    That over-vaulted grateful gloom,
Thro' which the livelong day my soul did pass,
    Well-pleased, from room to room.

Full of great rooms and small the palace stood,
    All various, each a perfect whole
From living Nature, fit for every mood
    And change of my still soul.   [60]

For some were hung with arras green and blue,°
    Showing a gaudy summer-morn,
Where with puff'd cheek the belted hunter blew
    His wreathed bugle-horn.

One seem'd all dark and red—a tract of sand,
    And some one pacing there alone,
Who paced for ever in a glimmering land,
    Lit with a low large moon.

One show'd an iron coast and angry waves.
    You seem'd to hear them climb and fall   [70]
And roar rock-thwarted under bellowing caves
    Beneath the windy wall.

And one, a full-fed river winding slow
    By herds upon an endless plain,
The ragged rims of thunder brooding low,
    With shadow-streaks of rain.

And one, the reapers at their sultry toil.
    In front they bound the sheaves. Behind
Were realms of upland, prodigal in oil,
    And hoary to the wind.°   [80]

And one a foreground black with stones and slags,
    Beyond, a line of heights, and higher
All barr'd with long white cloud the scornful crags,
    And highest, snow and fire.

And one, an English home—gray twilight pour'd
    On dewy pastures, dewy trees,
Softer than sleep—all things in order stored,
    A haunt of ancient Peace.

Nor these alone, but every landscape fair,
    As fit for every mood of mind,   [90]
Or gay, or grave, or sweet, or stern, was there
    Not less than truth design'd.

   .   .   .   .   .
     .   .   .   .   .

Or the maid-mother by a crucifix,
    In tracts of pasture sunny-warm,
Beneath branch-work of costly sardonyx°
    Sat smiling, babe in arm.

Or in a clear-wall'd city on the sea,
    Near gilded organ-pipes, her hair
Wound with white roses, slept St Cecily;°
    An angel look'd at her.   [100]

Or thronging all one porch of Paradise
    A group of Houris bow'd to see°
The dying Islamite, with hands and eyes
    That said, We wait for thee.

Or mythic Uther's deeply-wounded son
    In some fair space of sloping greens
Lay, dozing in the vale of Avalon,°
    And watch'd by weeping queens.

Or hollowing one hand against his ear,
    To list a foot-fall, ere he saw   [110]
The wood-nymph, stay'd the Ausonian king to hear°
    Of wisdom and of law.

Or over hills with peaky tops engrail'd,°
    And many a tract of palm and rice,
The throne of Indian Cama slowly sail'd°
    A summer fann'd with spice.

Or sweet Europa's mantle blew unclasp'd,°
    From off her shoulder backward borne:
From one hand droop'd a crocus: one hand grasp'd
    The mild bull's golden horn.   [120]

Or else flush'd Ganymede, his rosy thigh°
    Half-buried in the Eagle's down,
Sole as a flying star shot thro' the sky
    Above the pillar'd town.

Nor these alone: but every legend fair
    Which the supreme Caucasian mind
Carved out of Nature for itself, was there,
    Not less than life, design'd.

    .   .   .   .
    .   .   .   .

Then in the towers I placed great bells that swung,
    Moved of themselves, with silver sound;   [130]
And with choice paintings of wise men I hung
    The royal dais round.

For there was Milton like a seraph strong,
    Beside him Shakespeare bland and mild;
And there the world-worn Dante grasp'd his song,
    And somewhat grimly smiled.

And there the Ionian father of the rest;°
    A million wrinkles carved his skin;
A hundred winters snow'd upon his breast,
    From cheek and throat and chin.   [140]

Above, the fair hall-ceiling stately-set
    Many an arch high up did lift,
And angels rising and descending met
    With interchange of gift.

Below was all mosaic choicely plann'd
    With cycles of the human tale
Of this wide world, the times of every land
    So wrought, they will not fail.

The people here, a beast of burden slow,
    Toil'd onward, prick'd with goads and stings;   [150]
Here play'd, a tiger, rolling to and fro
    The heads and crowns of kings;

Here rose, an athlete, strong to break or bind
    All force in bonds that might endure,
And here once more like some sick man declined,
    And trusted any cure.

But over these she trod: and those great bells
    Began to chime. She took her throne:
She sat betwixt the shining Oriels,°
    To sing her songs alone.   [160]

And thro' the topmost Oriels' coloured flame
        Two godlike faces gazed below;
Plato the wise, and large-brow'd Verulam,°
        The first of those who know.

And all those names, that in their motion were
        Full-welling fountain-heads of change,
Betwixt the slender shafts were blazon'd fair
        In diverse raiment strange:

Thro' which the lights, rose, amber, emerald, blue,
        Flush'd in her temples and her eyes,   [170]
And from her lips, as morn from Memnon, drew°
        Rivers of melodies.

No nightingale delighteth to prolong
        Her low preamble all alone,
More than my soul to hear her echo'd song
        Throb thro' the ribbed stone;

Singing and murmuring in her feastful mirth,
        Joying to feel herself alive,
Lord over Nature, Lord of the visible earth,
        Lord of the senses five;   [180]

Communing with herself: 'All these are mine,
        And let the world have peace or wars,
'Tis one to me.' She—when young night divine
        Crown'd dying day with stars,

Making sweet close of his delicious toils—
        Lit light in wreaths and anadems,
And pure quintessences of precious oils
        In hollow'd moons of gems,

To mimic heaven; and clapt her hands and cried,
        'I marvel if my still delight   [190]
In this great house so royal-rich, and wide,
        Be flatter'd to the height.

'O all things fair to sate my various eyes!
        O shapes and hues that please me well!
O silent faces of the Great and Wise,
        My Gods, with whom I dwell!

'O God-like isolation which art mine,
    I can but count thee perfect gain,
What time I watch the darkening droves of swine
       That range on yonder plain.   [200]

'In filthy sloughs they roll a prurient skin,
    They graze and wallow, breed and sleep;
And oft some brainless devil enters in,
       And drives them to the deep.'°

Then of the moral instinct would she prate
    And of the rising from the dead,
As hers by right of full-accomplish'd Fate;
       And at the last she said:

'I take possession of man's mind and deed.
    I care not what the sects may brawl.   [210]
I sit as God holding no form of creed,
       But contemplating all.'

   .   .   .   .   .   .

   .   .   .   .   .   .

Full oft the riddle of the painful earth
    Flash'd thro' her as she sat alone,
Yet not the less held she her solemn mirth,
       And intellectual throne.

And so she throve and prosper'd: so three years
    She prosper'd: on the fourth she fell,
Like Herod, when the shout was in his ears,°
       Struck thro' with pangs of hell.   [220]

Lest she should fail and perish utterly,
    God, before whom ever lie bare
The abysmal deeps of Personality,
       Plagued her with sore despair.

When she would think, where'er she turn'd her sight
    The airy hand confusion wrought,
Wrote, 'Mene, mene,' and divided quite°
       The kingdom of her thought.

Deep dread and loathing of her solitude
    Fell on her, from which mood was born   [230]
Scorn of herself; again, from out that mood
       Laughter at her self-scorn.

'What! is not this my place of strength,' she said,
    'My spacious mansion built for me,
Whereof the strong foundation-stones were laid
        Since my first memory?'

But in dark corners of her palace stood
    Uncertain shapes; and unawares
On white-eyed phantasms weeping tears of blood,
        And horrible nightmares,   [240]

And hollow shades enclosing hearts of flame,
    And, with dim fretted foreheads all,
On corpses three-months-old at noon she came,
        That stood against the wall.

A spot of dull stagnation, without light
    Or power of movement, seem'd my soul,
'Mid onward-sloping motions infinite
        Making for one sure goal.

A still salt pool, lock'd in with bars of sand,
    Left on the shore; that hears all night   [250]
The plunging seas draw backward from the land
        Their moon-led waters white.

A star that with the choral starry dance
    Join'd not, but stood, and standing saw
The hollow orb of moving Circumstance
        Roll'd round by one fix'd law.

Back on herself her serpent pride had curl'd.
    'No voice,' she shriek'd in that lone hall,
'No voice breaks thro' the stillness of this world:
        One deep, deep silence all!'   [260]

She, mouldering with the dull earth's mouldering sod,
    Inwrapt tenfold in slothful shame,
Lay there exiled from eternal God,
        Lost to her place and name;

And death and life she hated equally,
    And nothing saw, for her despair,
But dreadful time, dreadful eternity,
        No comfort anywhere;

Remaining utterly confused with fears,
    And ever worse with growing time,   [270]
And ever unrelieved by dismal tears,
    And all alone in crime:

Shut up as in a crumbling tomb, girt round
    With blackness as a solid wall,
Far off she seem'd to hear the dully sound
    Of human footsteps fall.

As in strange lands a traveller walking slow,
    In doubt and great perplexity,
A little before moon-rise hears the low
    Moan of an unknown sea;   [280]

And knows not if it be thunder, or a sound
    Of rocks thrown down, or one deep cry
Of great wild beasts; then thinketh, 'I have found
    A new land, but I die.'

She howl'd aloud, 'I am on fire within.
    There comes no murmur of reply.
What is it that will take away my sin,
    And save me lest I die?'

So when four years were wholly finished
    She threw her royal robes away.   [290]
'Make me a cottage in the vale,' she said,
    'Where I may mourn and pray.

'Yet pull not down my palace towers, that are
    So lightly, beautifully built:
Perchance I may return with others there
    When I have purged my guilt.'

The Hesperides

Hesperus and his daughters three
That sing about the golden tree.

Comus°

The North wind fall'n, in the new-starréd night
Zidonian Hanno, wandering beyond

The hoary promontory of Soloë,
Past Thymiaterion in calmèd bays°
Between the southern and the western Horn,
Heard neither warbling of the nightingale,
Nor melody of the Libyan Lotus-flute°
Blown seaward from the shore; but from a slope
That ran bloom-bright into the Atlantic blue,
Beneath a highland leaning down a weight   [10]
Of cliffs, and zoned below with cedar-shade,
Came voices like the voices in a dream
Continuous; till he reach'd the outer sea:—

Song of the Three Sisters

I

The Golden Apple, the Golden Apple, the hallow'd fruit,
Guard it well, guard it warily,
Singing airily,
Standing about the charmèd root.
Round about all is mute,
As the snowfield on the mountain-peaks,
As the sandfield at the mountain-foot.   [20]
Crocodiles in briny creeks
Sleep and stir not: all is mute.
If ye sing not, if ye make false measure,
We shall lose eternal pleasure,
Worth eternal want of rest.
Laugh not loudly: watch the treasure
Of the wisdom of the West.
In a corner wisdom whispers. Five and three°
(Let it not be preach'd abroad) make an awful mystery:
For the blossom unto threefold music bloweth;   [30]
Evermore it is born anew,
And the sap to threefold music floweth,
From the root,
Drawn in the dark,
Up to the fruit,
Creeping under the fragrant bark,

Líquid góld, hóneyswéet thró and thró.
Keen-eyed Sisters, singing airily,
Looking warily
Every way,   [40]
Guard the apple night and day,
Lest one from the East come and take it away.°

II

Father Hesper, Father Hesper, Watch, watch, ever and aye,
Looking under silver hair with a silver eye.
Father, twinkle not thy stedfast sight:
Kingdoms lapse, and climates change, and races die;
Honour comes with mystery;
Hoarded wisdom brings delight.
Number, tell them over, and number
How many the mystic fruit-tree holds,   [50]
Lest the red-comb'd dragon slumber
Roll'd together in purple folds.
Look to him, father, lest he wink, and the golden apple be
     stol'n away,
For his ancient heart is drunk with overwatchings night
     and day
Round about the hallow'd fruit-tree curl'd—
Sing awáy, sing aloúd evermóre in the wínd without   (*Anapœst*)
     stóp,
Lest his scaléd eyelid drop,
For he is older than the world.
If *hé* waken, *wé* waken,
Rapidly levelling eager eyes   [60]
If *hé* sleep, *wé* sleep,
Dropping the eyelid over the eyes.
If the golden apple be taken
The world will be overwise.
Five links, a golden chain are we,
Hesper, the Dragon, and Sisters three
Bound about the golden tree.

III

Father Hesper, Father Hesper, Watch, watch, night and day,
Lest the old wound of the world be healéd,

The glory unsealéd,   [70]
The golden apple stol'n away,
And the ancient secret revealéd.
Look from West to East along:
Father, old Himala weakens, Caucasus is bold and strong.°
Wandering waters unto wandering waters call;
Let them clash together, foam and fall.
Out of watchings, out of wiles,
Comes the bliss of secret smiles.
All things are not told to all,
Half-round the mantling night is drawn.   [80]
Purplefringéd with even and dawn
Hesper hateth Phosphor, evening hateth morn.°

IV

Every flower and every fruit the redolent breath
    Of the warm seawind ripeneth,
        Arching the billow in his sleep:
But the land-wind wandereth,
        Broken by the highland steep,
        Two streams upon the violet deep.
For the Western Sun, and the Western Star,
And the low west-wind, breathing afar,   [90]
        The end of day and beginning of night
        Make the apple Holy and Bright;
Holy and Bright, round and full, bright and blest,
            Mellow'd in a land of rest:
            Watch it warily day and night;
            All good things are in the West.
Till mid-noon the cool East light
Is shut out by the round of the tall hill brow,
        But, when the full-faced Sunset yellowly
        Stays on the flowering arch of the bough,   [100]
        The luscious fruitage clustereth mellowly,
            Golden-kernell'd, Golden-cored,
        Sunset-ripen'd above on the tree.
        The world is wasted with fire and sword,
        But the Apple of gold hangs over the Sea!
        Five links—a Golden chain are we—
        Hesper, the Dragon, and Sisters three,

Daughters three,
Round about,
All round about   [110]
The gnarléd bole of the charméd tree.
The Golden Apple, The Golden Apple, The hallow'd fruit,
Guard it well
Guard it warily,
Watch it warily,
Singing airily,
Standing about the charméd root.

The Lotos-Eaters

'Courage!' he said, and pointed toward the land,°
'This mounting wave will roll us shoreward soon.'
In the afternoon they came unto a land
In which it seemed always afternoon.
All round the coast the languid air did swoon,
Breathing like one that hath a weary dream.
Full-faced above the valley stood the moon;
And like a downward smoke, the slender stream
Along the cliff to fall and pause and fall did seem.

A land of streams! some, like a downward smoke,   [10]
Slow-dropping veils of thinnest lawn, did go;°
And some thro' wavering lights and shadows broke,
Rolling a slumbrous sheet of foam below.
They saw the gleaming river seaward flow
From the inner land: far off, three mountain-tops,
Three silent pinnacles of aged snow,
Stood sunset-flush'd: and, dew'd with showery drops,
Up-clomb the shadowy pine above the woven copse.

The charmed sunset linger'd low adown
In the red West: thro' mountain clefts the dale   [20]
Was seen far inland, and the yellow down
Border'd with palm, and many a winding vale
And meadow, set with slender galingale;°
A land where all things always seem'd the same!
And round about the keel with faces pale,

Dark faces pale against that rosy flame,
The mild-eyed melancholy Lotos-eaters came.

Branches they bore of that enchanted stem,
Laden with flower and fruit, whereof they gave
To each, but whoso did receive of them,   [30]
And taste, to him the gushing of the wave
Far far away did seem to mourn and rave
On alien shores; and if his fellow spake,
His voice was thin, as voices from the grave;
And deep-asleep he seem'd, yet all awake,
And music in his ears his beating heart did make.

They sat them down upon the yellow sand,
Between the sun and moon upon the shore;
And sweet it was to dream of Fatherland,
Of child, and wife, and slave; but evermore   [40]
Most weary seem'd the sea, weary the oar,
Weary the wandering fields of barren foam.
Then some one said, 'We will return no more;'
And all at once they sang, 'Our island home
Is far beyond the wave; we will no longer roam.'

Choric Song

I

There is sweet music here that softer falls
Than petals from blown roses on the grass,
Or night-dews on still waters between walls
Of shadowy granite, in a gleaming pass;
Music that gentlier on the spirit lies,   [50]
Than tir'd eyelids upon tir'd eyes;
Music that brings sweet sleep down from the blissful skies.
Here are cool mosses deep,
And thro' the moss the ivies creep,
And in the stream the long-leaved flowers weep,
And from the craggy ledge the poppy hangs in sleep.

II

Why are we weigh'd upon with heaviness,
And utterly consumed with sharp distress,

While all things else have rest from weariness?
All things have rest: why should we toil alone,   [60]
We only toil, who are the first of things,
And make perpetual moan,
Still from one sorrow to another thrown:
Nor ever fold our wings,
And cease from wanderings,
Nor steep our brows in slumber's holy balm;
Nor harken what the inner spirit sings,
'There is no joy but calm!'
Why should we only toil, the roof and crown of things?

III

Lo! in the middle of the wood,   [70]
The folded leaf is woo'd from out the bud
With winds upon the branch, and there
Grows green and broad, and takes no care,
Sun-steep'd at noon, and in the moon
Nightly dew-fed; and turning yellow
Falls, and floats adown the air.
Lo! sweeten'd with the summer light,
The full-juiced apple, waxing over-mellow,
Drops in a silent autumn night.
All its allotted length of days,   [80]
The flower ripens in its place,
Ripens and fades, and falls, and hath no toil,
Fast-rooted in the fruitful soil.

IV

Hateful is the dark-blue sky,
Vaulted o'er the dark-blue sea.
Death is the end of life; ah, why
Should life all labour be?
Let us alone. Time driveth onward fast,
And in a little while our lips are dumb.
Let us alone. What is it that will last?   [90]
All things are taken from us, and become
Portions and parcels of the dreadful Past.
Let us alone. What pleasure can we have
To war with evil? Is there any peace

In ever climbing up the climbing wave?
All things have rest, and ripen toward the grave
In silence; ripen, fall and cease:
Give us long rest or death, dark death, or dreamful ease.

V

How sweet it were, hearing the downward stream,
With half-shut eyes ever to seem   [100]
Falling asleep in a half-dream!
To dream and dream, like yonder amber light,
Which will not leave the myrrh-bush on the height;
To hear each other's whisper'd speech;
Eating the Lotos day by day,
To watch the crisping ripples on the beach,
And tender curving lines of creamy spray;
To lend our hearts and spirits wholly
To the influence of mild-minded melancholy;
To muse and brood and live again in memory,   [110]
With those old faces of our infancy
Heap'd over with a mound of grass,
Two handfuls of white dust, shut in an urn of brass!

VI

Dear is the memory of our wedded lives,
And dear the last embraces of our wives
And their warm tears: but all hath suffer'd change:
For surely now our household hearths are cold:
Our sons inherit us: our looks are strange:
And we should come like ghosts to trouble joy.
Or else the island princes over-bold   [120]
Have eat our substance, and the minstrel sings
Before them of the ten years' war in Troy,
And our great deeds, as half-forgotten things.
Is there confusion in the little isle?
Let what is broken so remain.
The Gods are hard to reconcile:
'Tis hard to settle order once again.
There *is* confusion worse than death,
Trouble on trouble, pain on pain,
Long labour unto aged breath,   [130]

Sore task to hearts worn out by many wars
And eyes grown dim with gazing on the pilot-stars.

VII

But, propt on beds of amaranth and moly,°
How sweet (while warm airs lull us, blowing lowly)
With half-dropt eyelid still,
Beneath a heaven dark and holy,
To watch the long bright river drawing slowly
His waters from the purple hill—
To hear the dewy echoes calling
From cave to cave thro' the thick-twined vine—   [140]
To watch the emerald-colour'd water falling
Thro' many a wov'n acanthus-wreath divine!°
Only to hear and see the far-off sparkling brine,
Only to hear were sweet, stretch'd out beneath the pine.

VIII

The Lotos blooms below the barren peak:
The Lotos blows by every winding creek:
All day the wind breathes low with mellower tone:
Thro' every hollow cave and alley lone
Round and round the spicy downs the yellow Lotos-dust is blown.
We have had enough of action, and of motion we,   [150]
Roll'd to starboard, roll'd to larboard, when the surge was
    seething free,
Where the wallowing monster spouted his foam-fountains
    in the sea.
Let us swear an oath, and keep it with an equal mind,
In the hollow Lotos-land to live and lie reclined
On the hills like Gods together, careless of mankind.
For they lie beside their nectar, and the bolts are hurl'd°
Far below them in the valleys, and the clouds are lightly
    curl'd
Round their golden houses, girdled with the gleaming world:
Where they smile in secret, looking over wasted lands,
Blight and famine, plague and earthquake, roaring deeps
    and fiery sands,   [160]
Clanging fights, and flaming towns, and sinking ships, and
    praying hands.

But they smile, they find a music centred in a doleful song
Steaming up, a lamentation and an ancient tale of wrong,
Like a tale of little meaning tho' the words are strong;
Chanted from an ill-used race of men that cleave the soil,
Sow the seed, and reap the harvest with enduring toil,
Storing yearly little dues of wheat, and wine and oil;
Till they perish and they suffer—some, 'tis whisper'd—
     down in hell
Suffer endless anguish, others in Elysian valleys dwell,
Resting weary limbs at last on beds of asphodel.°   [170]
Surely, surely, slumber is more sweet than toil, the shore
Than labour in the deep mid-ocean, wind and wave and oar;
Oh rest ye, brother mariners, we will not wander more.

A Dream of Fair Women

I read, before my eyelids dropt their shade,
     '*The Legend of Good Women*,' long ago
Sung by the morning star of song, who made
     His music heard below;

Dan Chaucer, the first warbler, whose sweet breath°
     Preluded those melodious bursts that fill
The spacious times of great Elizabeth
     With sounds that echo still.

And, for a while, the knowledge of his art
     Held me above the subject, as strong gales   [10]
Hold swollen clouds from raining, tho' my heart,
     Brimful of those wild tales,

Charged both mine eyes with tears. In every land
     I saw, wherever light illumineth,
Beauty and anguish walking hand in hand
     The downward slope to death.

Those far-renowned brides of ancient song
     Peopled the hollow dark, like burning stars,
And I heard sounds of insult, shame, and wrong,
     And trumpets blown for wars;   [20]

And clattering flints batter'd with clanging hoofs;
    And I saw crowds in column'd sanctuaries;
And forms that pass'd at windows and on roofs
    Of marble palaces;

Corpses across the threshold; heroes tall
    Dislodging pinnacle and parapet
Upon the tortoise creeping to the wall;°
    Lances in ambush set;

And high shrine-doors burst thro' with heated blasts
    That run before the fluttering tongues of fire;   [30]
White surf wind-scatter'd over sails and masts,
    And ever climbing higher;

Squadrons and squares of men in brazen plates,
    Scaffolds, still sheets of water, divers woes,
Ranges of glimmering vaults with iron grates,
    And hush'd seraglios.°

So shape chased shape as swift as, when to land
    Bluster the winds and tides the self-same way,
Crisp foam-flakes scud along the level sand,
    Torn from the fringe of spray.   [40]

I started once, or seem'd to start in pain,
    Resolved on noble things, and strove to speak,
As when a great thought strikes along the brain,
    And flushes all the cheek.

And once my arm was lifted to hew down
    A cavalier from off his saddle-bow,
That bore a lady from a leaguer'd town;
    And then, I know not how,

All those sharp fancies, by down-lapsing thought
    Stream'd onward, lost their edges, and did creep   [50]
Roll'd on each other, rounded, smooth'd, and brought
    Into the gulfs of sleep.

At last methought that I had wander'd far
    In an old wood: fresh-wash'd in coolest dew°
The maiden splendours of the morning star
    Shook in the stedfast blue.

Enormous elm-tree-boles did stoop and lean
    Upon the dusky brushwood underneath
Their broad curved branches, fledged with clearest green,
    New from its silken sheath.   [60]

The dim red morn had died, her journey done,
    And with dead lips smiled at the twilight plain,
Half-fall'n across the threshold of the sun,
    Never to rise again.

There was no motion in the dumb dead air,
    Not any song of bird or sound of rill;
Gross darkness of the inner sepulchre
    Is not so deadly still

As that wide forest. Growths of jasmine turn'd
    Their humid arms festooning tree to tree,   [70]
And at the root thro' lush green grasses burn'd
    The red anemone.

I knew the flowers, I knew the leaves, I knew
    The tearful glimmer of the languid dawn
On those long, rank, dark wood-walks drench'd in dew,
    Leading from lawn to lawn.

The smell of violets, hidden in the green,
    Pour'd back into my empty soul and frame
The times when I remember to have been
    Joyful and free from blame.   [80]

And from within me a clear under-tone
    Thrill'd thro' mine ears in that unblissful clime,
'Pass freely thro': the wood is all thine own,
    Until the end of time.'

At length I saw a lady within call,°
    Stiller than chisell'd marble, standing there;
A daughter of the gods, divinely tall,
    And most divinely fair.

Her loveliness with shame and with surprise
    Froze my swift speech: she turning on my face   [90]
The star-like sorrows of immortal eyes,
    Spoke slowly in her place.

'I had great beauty: ask thou not my name:
  No one can be more wise than destiny.
Many drew swords and died. Where'er I came
  I brought calamity.'

'No marvel, sovereign lady: in fair field
  Myself for such a face had boldly died,'
I answer'd free; and turning I appeal'd
  To one that stood beside.°   [100]

But she, with sick and scornful looks averse,
  To her full height her stately stature draws;
'My youth,' she said, 'was blasted with a curse:
  This woman was the cause.

'I was cut off from hope in that sad place,
  Which men call'd Aulis in those iron years:
My father held his hand upon his face;
  I, blinded with my tears,

'Still strove to speak: my voice was thick with sighs
  As in a dream. Dimly I could descry   [110]
The stern black-bearded kings with wolfish eyes,
  Waiting to see me die.

'The high masts flicker'd as they lay afloat;
  The crowds, the temples, waver'd, and the shore;
The bright death quiver'd at the victim's throat;
  Touch'd; and I knew no more.'

Whereto the other with a downward brow:
  'I would the white cold heavy-plunging foam,
Whirl'd by the wind, had roll'd me deep below,
  Then when I left my home.'   [120]

Her slow full words sank thro' the silence drear,
  As thunder-drops fall on a sleeping sea:
Sudden I heard a voice that cried, 'Come here,
  That I may look on thee.'

I turning saw, throned on a flowery rise,
  One sitting on a crimson scarf unroll'd;°
A queen, with swarthy cheeks and bold black eyes,°
  Brow-bound with burning gold.

She, flashing forth a haughty smile, began:
    'I govern'd men by change, and so I sway'd   [130]
All moods. 'Tis long since I have seen a man.
    Once, like the moon, I made

'The ever-shifting currents of the blood
    According to my humour ebb and flow.
I have no men to govern in this wood:
    That makes my only woe.

'Nay—yet it chafes me that I could not bend
    One will; nor tame and tutor with mine eye
That dull cold-blooded Cæsar. Prythee, friend,
    Where is Mark Antony?   [140]

'The man, my lover, with whom I rode sublime
    On Fortune's neck: we sat as God by God:
The Nilus would have risen before his time
    And flooded at our nod.

'We drank the Libyan Sun to sleep, and lit
    Lamps which out-burn'd Canopus. O my life°
In Egypt! O the dalliance and the wit,
    The flattery and the strife,

'And the wild kiss, when fresh from war's alarms,
    My Hercules, my Roman Antony,   [150]
My mailed Bacchus leapt into my arms,
    Contented there to die!

'And there he died: and when I heard my name
    Sigh'd forth with life I would not brook my fear
Of the other: with a worm I balk'd his fame.
    What else was left? look here!'

(With that she tore her robe apart, and half
    The polish'd argent of her breast to sight
Laid bare. Thereto she pointed with a laugh,
    Showing the aspick's bite.)   [160]

'I died a Queen. The Roman soldier found
    Me lying dead, my crown about my brows,
A name for ever!—lying robed and crown'd,
    Worthy a Roman spouse.'

Her warbling voice, a lyre of widest range
  Struck by all passion, did fall down and glance
From tone to tone, and glided thro' all change
  Of liveliest utterance.

When she made pause I knew not for delight;
  Because with sudden motion from the ground   [170]
She raised her piercing orbs, and fill'd with light
  The interval of sound.

Still with their fires Love tipt his keenest darts;
  As once they drew into two burning rings
All beams of Love, melting the mighty hearts
  Of captains and of kings.

Slowly my sense undazzled. Then I heard
  A noise of some one coming thro' the lawn,°
And singing clearer than the crested bird
  That claps his wings at dawn.   [180]

'The torrent brooks of hallow'd Israel
  From craggy hollows pouring, late and soon,
Sound all night long, in falling thro' the dell,
  Far-heard beneath the moon.

'The balmy moon of blessed Israel
  Floods all the deep-blue gloom with beams divine:
All night the splinter'd crags that wall the dell
  With spires of silver shine.'

As one that museth where broad sunshine laves
  The lawn by some cathedral, thro' the door   [190]
Hearing the holy organ rolling waves
  Of sound on roof and floor

Within, and anthem sung, is charm'd and tied
  To where he stands,—so stood I, when that flow
Of music left the lips of her that died
  To save her father's vow;

The daughter of the warrior Gileadite,
  A maiden pure; as when she went along
From Mizpeh's tower'd gate with welcome light,
  With timbrel and with song.   [200]

My words leapt forth: 'Heaven heads the count of crimes
　　With that wild oath.' She render'd answer high:
'Not so, nor once alone; a thousand times
　　I would be born and die.

'Single I grew, like some green plant, whose root
　　Creeps to the garden water-pipes beneath,
Feeding the flower; but ere my flower to fruit
　　Changed, I was ripe for death.

'My God, my land, my father—these did move
　　Me from my bliss of life, that Nature gave,   [210]
Lower'd softly with a threefold cord of love
　　Down to a silent grave.

'And I went mourning, "No fair Hebrew boy
　　Shall smile away my maiden blame among
The Hebrew mothers"—emptied of all joy,
　　Leaving the dance and song,

'Leaving the olive-gardens far below,
　　Leaving the promise of my bridal bower,
The valleys of grape-loaded vines that glow
　　Beneath the battled tower.   [220]

'The light white cloud swam over us. Anon
　　We heard the lion roaring from his den;
We saw the large white stars rise one by one,
　　Or, from the darken'd glen,

'Saw God divide the night with flying flame,
　　And thunder on the everlasting hills.
I heard Him, for He spake, and grief became
　　A solemn scorn of ills.

'When the next moon was roll'd into the sky,
　　Strength came to me that equall'd my desire.   [230]
How beautiful a thing it was to die
　　For God and for my sire!

'It comforts me in this one thought to dwell,
　　That I subdued me to my father's will;
Because the kiss he gave me, ere I fell,
　　Sweetens the spirit still.

'Moreover it is written that my race
    Hew'd Ammon, hip and thigh, from Aroer
On Arnon unto Minneth.' Here her face°
    Glow'd, as I look'd at her.   [240]

She lock'd her lips: she left me where I stood:
    'Glory to God,' she sang, and past afar,
Thridding the sombre boskage of the wood,°
    Toward the morning-star.

Losing her carol I stood pensively,
    As one that from a casement leans his head,
When midnight bells cease ringing suddenly,
    And the old year is dead.

'Alas! alas!' a low voice, full of care,°
    Murmur'd beside me: 'Turn and look on me: [250]
I am that Rosamond, whom men call fair,
    If what I was I be.

'Would I had been some maiden coarse and poor!
    O me, that I should ever see the light!
Those dragon eyes of anger'd Eleanor
    Do hunt me, day and night.'

She ceased in tears, fallen from hope and trust:
    To whom the Egyptian: 'O, you tamely died!°
You should have clung to Fulvia's waist, and thrust
    The dagger thro' her side.'   [260]

With that sharp sound the white dawn's creeping beams,
    Stol'n to my brain, dissolved the mystery
Of folded sleep. The captain of my dreams°
    Ruled in the eastern sky.

Morn broaden'd on the borders of the dark,
    Ere I saw her, who clasp'd in her last trance°
Her murder'd father's head, or Joan of Arc,
    A light of ancient France;

Or her who knew that Love can vanquish Death,°
    Who kneeling, with one arm about her king,   [270]
Drew forth the poison with her balmy breath,
    Sweet as new buds in Spring.

No memory labours longer from the deep
    Gold-mines of thought to lift the hidden ore
That glimpses, moving up, than I from sleep
    To gather and tell o'er

Each little sound and sight. With what dull pain
    Compass'd, how eagerly I sought to strike
Into that wondrous track of dreams again!
    But no two dreams are like.   [280]

As when a soul laments, which hath been blest,
    Desiring what is mingled with past years,
In yearnings that can never be exprest
    By signs or groans or tears;

Because all words, tho' cull'd with choicest art,
    Failing to give the bitter of the sweet,
Wither beneath the palate, and the heart
    Faints, faded by its heat.

POEMS (1842)

The Two Voices

A still small voice spake unto me,
'Thou art so full of misery,
Were it not better not to be?'

Then to the still small voice I said;
'Let me not cast in endless shade
What is so wonderfully made.'

To which the voice did urge reply;
'To-day I saw the dragon-fly°
Come from the wells where he did lie.

'An inner impulse rent the veil   [10]
Of his old husk: from head to tail
Came out clear plates of sapphire mail.

'He dried his wings: like gauze they grew;
Thro' crofts and pastures wet with dew
A living flash of light he flew.'

I said, 'When first the world began,
Young Nature thro' five cycles ran,
And in the sixth she moulded man.°

'She gave him mind, the lordliest
Proportion, and, above the rest,   [20]
Dominion in the head and breast.'

Thereto the silent voice replied;
'Self-blinded are you by your pride:
Look up thro' night: the world is wide.

'This truth within thy mind rehearse,
That in a boundless universe
Is boundless better, boundless worse.

'Think you this mould of hopes and fears
Could find no statelier than his peers
In yonder hundred million spheres?'   [30]

It spake, moreover, in my mind:
'Tho' thou wert scatter'd to the wind,
Yet is there plenty of the kind.'

Then did my response clearer fall:
'No compound of this earthly ball
Is like another, all in all.'

To which he answer'd scoffingly;
'Good soul! suppose I grant it thee,
Who'll weep for thy deficiency?

'Or will one beam be less intense,   [40]
When thy peculiar difference
Is cancell'd in the world of sense?'

I would have said, 'Thou canst not know,'
But my full heart, that work'd below,
Rain'd thro' my sight its overflow.

Again the voice spake unto me:
'Thou art so steep'd in misery,
Surely 'twere better not to be.

'Thine anguish will not let thee sleep,
Nor any train of reason keep: [50]
Thou canst not think, but thou wilt weep.'

I said, 'The years with change advance:
If I make dark my countenance,
I shut my life from happier chance.

'Some turn this sickness yet might take,
Ev'n yet.' But he: 'What drug can make
A wither'd palsy cease to shake?'

I wept, 'Tho' I should die, I know
That all about the thorn will blow
In tufts of rosy-tinted snow;   [60]

'And men, thro' novel spheres of thought
Still moving after truth long sought,
Will learn new things when I am not.'

'Yet,' said the secret voice, 'some time,
Sooner or later, will gray prime
Make thy grass hoar with early rime.

'Not less swift souls that yearn for light,
Rapt after heaven's starry flight,
Would sweep the tracts of day and night.

'Not less the bee would range her cells, [70]
The furzy prickle fire the dells,
The foxglove cluster dappled bells.'

I said that 'all the years invent;
Each month is various to present
The world with some development.

'Were this not well, to bide mine hour,
Tho' watching from a ruin'd tower
How grows the day of human power?'

'The highest-mounted mind,' he said,
'Still sees the sacred morning spread [80]
The silent summit overhead.

'Will thirty seasons render plain
Those lonely lights that still remain,
Just breaking over land and main?

'Or make that morn, from his cold crown
And crystal silence creeping down,
Flood with full daylight glebe and town?

'Forerun thy peers, thy time, and let
Thy feet, millenniums hence, be set
In midst of knowledge, dream'd not yet. [90]

'Thou hast not gain'd a real height,
Nor art thou nearer to the light,
Because the scale is infinite.

' 'Twere better not to breathe or speak,
Than cry for strength, remaining weak,
And seem to find, but still to seek.

'Moreover, but to seem to find
Asks what thou lackest, thought resign'd,
A healthy frame, a quiet mind.'

I said, 'When I am gone away, [100]
"He dared not tarry," men will say,
Doing dishonour to my clay.'

'This is more vile,' he made reply,
'To breathe and loathe, to live and sigh,
Than once from dread of pain to die.

'Sick art thou—a divided will
Still heaping on the fear of ill
The fear of men, a coward still.

'Do men love thee? Art thou so bound
To men, that how thy name may sound   [110]
Will vex thee lying underground?

'The memory of the wither'd leaf
In endless time is scarce more brief
Than of the garner'd Autumn-sheaf.

'Go, vexed Spirit, sleep in trust;
The right ear, that is fill'd with dust,
Hears little of the false or just.'

'Hard task, to pluck resolve,' I cried,
'From emptiness and the waste wide
Of that abyss, or scornful pride!   [120]

'Nay—rather yet that I could raise
One hope that warm'd me in the days
While still I yearn'd for human praise.

'When, wide in soul and bold of tongue,
Among the tents I paused and sung,
The distant battle flash'd and rung.

'I sung the joyful Pæan clear,°
And, sitting, burnish'd without fear
The brand, the buckler, and the spear—

'Waiting to strive a happy strife,   [130]
To war with falsehood to the knife,
And not to lose the good of life—

'Some hidden principle to move,
To put together, part and prove,
And mete the bounds of hate and love—

'As far as might be, to carve out
Free space for every human doubt,
That the whole mind might orb about—

'To search thro' all I felt or saw,
The springs of life, the depths of awe,   [140]
And reach the law within the law:

'At least, not rotting like a weed,
But, having sown some generous seed,
Fruitful of further thought and deed,

'To pass, when Life her light withdraws,
Not void of righteous self-applause,
Nor in a merely selfish cause—

'In some good cause, not in mine own,
To perish, wept for, honour'd, known,
And like a warrior overthrown;   [150]

'Whose eyes are dim with glorious tears,
When, soil'd with noble dust, he hears
His country's war-song thrill his ears:

'Then dying of a mortal stroke,
What time the foeman's line is broke,
And all the war is roll'd in smoke.'

'Yea!' said the voice, 'thy dream was good,
While thou abodest in the bud.
It was the stirring of the blood.

'If Nature put not forth her power   [160]
About the opening of the flower,
Who is it that could live an hour?

'Then comes the check, the change, the fall,
Pain rises up, old pleasures pall.
There is one remedy for all.

'Yet hadst thou, thro' enduring pain,
Link'd month to month with such a chain
Of knitted purport, all were vain.

'Thou hadst not between death and birth
Dissolved the riddle of the earth.   [170]
So were thy labour little-worth.

'That men with knowledge merely play'd,
I told thee—hardly nigher made,
Tho' scaling slow from grade to grade;

'Much less this dreamer, deaf and blind,
Named man, may hope some truth to find,
That bears relation to the mind.

'For every worm beneath the moon
Draws different threads, and late and soon
Spins, toiling out his own cocoon.   [180]

'Cry, faint not: either Truth is born
Beyond the polar gleam forlorn,
Or in the gateways of the morn.

'Cry, faint not, climb: the summits slope
Beyond the furthest flights of hope,
Wrapt in dense cloud from base to cope.°

'Sometimes a little corner shines,
As over rainy mist inclines
A gleaming crag with belts of pines.

'I will go forward, sayest thou,   [190]
I shall not fail to find her now.
Look up, the fold is on her brow.

'If straight thy track, or if oblique,
Thou know'st not. Shadows thou dost strike,
Embracing cloud, Ixion-like;°

'And owning but a little more
Than beasts, abidest lame and poor,
Calling thyself a little lower

'Than angels. Cease to wail and brawl!
Why inch by inch to darkness crawl?   [200]
There is one remedy for all.'

'O dull, one-sided voice,' said I,
'Wilt thou make everything a lie,
To flatter me that I may die?

'I know that age to age succeeds,
Blowing a noise of tongues and deeds,
A dust of systems and of creeds.

'I cannot hide that some have striven,
Achieving calm, to whom was given
The joy that mixes man with Heaven: [210]

'Who, rowing hard against the stream,
Saw distant gates of Eden gleam,
And did not dream it was a dream;

'But heard, by secret transport led,
Ev'n in the charnels of the dead,
The murmur of the fountain-head—

'Which did accomplish their desire,
Bore and forbore, and did not tire,
Like Stephen, an unquenched fire.°

'He heeded not reviling tones,   [220]
Nor sold his heart to idle moans,
Tho' cursed and scorn'd, and bruised with stones:

'But looking upward, full of grace,
He pray'd, and from a happy place
God's glory smote him on the face.'

The sullen answer slid betwixt:
'Not that the grounds of hope were fix'd,
The elements were kindlier mix'd.'

I said, 'I toil beneath the curse,
But, knowing not the universe,   [230]
I fear to slide from bad to worse.

'And that, in seeking to undo
One riddle, and to find the true,
I knit a hundred others new:

'Or that this anguish fleeting hence,
Unmanacled from bonds of sense,
Be fix'd and froz'n to permanence:

'For I go, weak from suffering here:
Naked I go, and void of cheer:
What is it that I may not fear?'   [240]

'Consider well,' the voice replied,
'His face, that two hours since hath died;
Wilt thou find passion, pain or pride?

'Will he obey when one commands?
Or answer should one press his hands?
He answers not, nor understands.

'His palms are folded on his breast:
There is no other thing express'd
But long disquiet merged in rest.

'His lips are very mild and meek: [250]
Tho' one should smite him on the cheek,
And on the mouth, he will not speak.

'His little daughter, whose sweet face
He kiss'd, taking his last embrace,
Becomes dishonour to her race—

'His sons grow up that bear his name,
Some grow to honour, some to shame,—
But he is chill to praise or blame.

'He will not hear the north-wind rave,
Nor, moaning, household shelter crave   [260]
From winter rains that beat his grave.

'High up the vapours fold and swim:
About him broods the twilight dim:
The place he knew forgetteth him.'

'If all be dark, vague voice,' I said,
'These things are wrapt in doubt and dread,
Nor canst thou show the dead are dead.

'The sap dries up: the plant declines.
A deeper tale my heart divines.
Know I not Death? the outward signs?   [270]

'I found him when my years were few;°
A shadow on the graves I knew,
And darkness in the village yew.

'From grave to grave the shadow crept:
In her still place the morning wept:
Touch'd by his feet the daisy slept.

'The simple senses crown'd his head:
"Omega! thou art Lord," they said,
"We find no motion in the dead."

'Why, if man rot in dreamless ease, [280]
Should that plain fact, as taught by these,
Not make him sure that he shall cease?

'Who forged that other influence,
That heat of inward evidence,
By which he doubts against the sense?

'He owns the fatal gift of eyes,
That read his spirit blindly wise,
Not simple as a thing that dies.

'Here sits he shaping wings to fly:
His heart forebodes a mystery: [290]
He names the name Eternity.

'That type of Perfect in his mind
In Nature can he nowhere find.
He sows himself on every wind.

'He seems to hear a Heavenly Friend,
And thro' thick veils to apprehend
A labour working to an end.

'The end and the beginning vex
His reason: many things perplex,
With motions, checks, and counterchecks. [300]

'He knows a baseness in his blood
At such strange war with something good,
He may not do the thing he would.

'Heaven opens inward, chasms yawn,
Vast images in glimmering dawn,
Half shown, are broken and withdrawn.

'Ah! sure within him and without,
Could his dark wisdom find it out,
There must be answer to his doubt,

'But thou canst answer not again. [310]
With thine own weapon art thou slain,
Or thou wilt answer but in vain.

'The doubt would rest, I dare not solve.
In the same circle we revolve.
Assurance only breeds resolve.'

As when a billow, blown against,
Falls back, the voice with which I fenced
A little ceased, but recommenced.

'Where wert thou when thy father play'd
In his free field, and pastime made,   [320]
A merry boy in sun and shade?

'A merry boy they call'd him then,
He sat upon the knees of men
In days that never come again.

'Before the little ducts began°
To feed thy bones with lime, and ran
Their course, till thou wert also man:

'Who took a wife, who rear'd his race,
Whose wrinkles gather'd on his face,
Whose troubles number with his days: [330]

'A life of nothings, nothing-worth,
From that first nothing ere his birth
To that last nothing under earth!'

'These words,' I said, 'are like the rest;
No certain clearness, but at best
A vague suspicion of the breast:

'But if I grant, thou mightst defend
The thesis which thy words intend—
That to begin implies to end;

'Yet how should I for certain hold,   [340]
Because my memory is so cold,
That I first was in human mould?

'I cannot make this matter plain,
But I would shoot, howe'er in vain,
A random arrow from the brain.

'It may be that no life is found,
Which only to one engine bound
Falls off, but cycles always round.

'As old mythologies relate,
Some draught of Lethe might await°   [350]
The slipping thro' from state to state.

'As here we find in trances, men
Forget the dream that happens then,
Until they fall in trance again.

'So might we, if our state were such
As one before, remember much,
For those two likes might meet and touch.

'But, if I lapsed from nobler place,
Some legend of a fallen race
Alone might hint of my disgrace;   [360]

'Some vague emotion of delight
In gazing up an Alpine height,
Some yearning toward the lamps of night;

'Or if thro' lower lives I came—
Tho' all experience past became
Consolidate in mind and frame—

'I might forget my weaker lot;
For is not our first year forgot?
The haunts of memory echo not.

'And men, whose reason long was blind,   [370]
From cells of madness unconfined,
Oft lose whole years of darker mind.

'Much more, if first I floated free,
As naked essence, must I be
Incompetent of memory:

'For memory dealing but with time,
And he with matter, could she climb
Beyond her own material prime?

'Moreover, something is or seems,
That touches me with mystic gleams,   [380]
Like glimpses of forgotten dreams—

'Of something felt, like something here;
Of something done, I know not where;
Such as no language may declare.'

The still voice laugh'd. 'I talk,' said he,
'Not with thy dreams. Suffice it thee
Thy pain is a reality.'

'But thou,' said I, 'hast missed thy mark,
Who sought'st to wreck my mortal ark,
By making all the horizon dark. [390]

'Why not set forth, if I should do
This rashness, that which might ensue
With this old soul in organs new?

'Whatever crazy sorrow saith,
No life that breathes with human breath
Has ever truly long'd for death.

' 'Tis life, whereof our nerves are scant,
Oh life, not death, for which we pant;
More life, and fuller, that I want.'

I ceased, and sat as one forlorn. [400]
Then said the voice, in quiet scorn,
'Behold, it is the Sabbath morn.'

And I arose, and I released
The casement, and the light increased
With freshness in the dawning east.

Like soften'd airs that blowing steal,
When meres begin to uncongeal,
The sweet church bells began to peal.

On to God's house the people prest:
Passing the place where each must rest, [410]
Each enter'd like a welcome guest.

One walk'd between his wife and child,
With measured footfall firm and mild,
And now and then he gravely smiled.

The prudent partner of his blood
Lean'd on him, faithful, gentle, good,
Wearing the rose of womanhood.

And in their double love secure,
The little maiden walk'd demure,
Pacing with downward eyelids pure. [420]

These three made unity so sweet,
My frozen heart began to beat,
Remembering its ancient heat.

I blest them, and they wander'd on:
I spoke, but answer came there none:
The dull and bitter voice was gone.

A second voice was at mine ear,
A little whisper silver-clear,
A murmur, 'Be of better cheer.'

As from some blissful neighbourhood,   [430]
A notice faintly understood,
'I see the end, and know the good.'

A little hint to solace woe,
A hint, a whisper breathing low,
'I may not speak of what I know.'

Like an Æolian harp that wakes°
No certain air, but overtakes
Far thought with music that it makes:

Such seem'd the whisper at my side:
'What is it thou knowest, sweet voice?' I cried.   [440]
'A hidden hope,' the voice replied:

So heavenly-toned, that in that hour
From out my sullen heart a power
Broke, like the rainbow from the shower,

To feel, altho' no tongue can prove,
That every cloud, that spreads above
And veileth love, itself is love.

And forth into the fields I went,
And Nature's living motion lent
The pulse of hope to discontent.   [450]

I wonder'd at the bounteous hours,
The slow result of winter showers:
You scarce could see the grass for flowers.

I wonder'd, while I paced along:
The woods were fill'd so full with song,
There seem'd no room for sense of wrong;

And all so variously wrought,
I marvell'd how the mind was brought
To anchor by one gloomy thought;

And wherefore rather I made choice   [460]
To commune with that barren voice,
Than him that said, 'Rejoice! Rejoice!'

St Simeon Stylites

Altho' I be the basest of mankind,
From scalp to sole one slough and crust of sin,
Unfit for earth, unfit for heaven, scarce meet
For troops of devils, mad with blasphemy,
I will not cease to grasp the hope I hold
Of saintdom, and to clamour, mourn and sob,
Battering the gates of heaven with storms of prayer,
Have mercy, Lord, and take away my sin.

Let this avail, just, dreadful, mighty God,
This not be all in vain, that thrice ten years,   [10]
Thrice multiplied by superhuman pangs,
In hungers and in thirsts, fevers and cold,
In coughs, aches, stitches, ulcerous throes and cramps,
A sign betwixt the meadow and the cloud,
Patient on this tall pillar I have borne
Rain, wind, frost, heat, hail, damp, and sleet, and snow;
And I had hoped that ere this period closed
Thou wouldst have caught me up into thy rest,
Denying not these weather-beaten limbs
The meed of saints, the white robe and the palm.   [20]

O take the meaning, Lord: I do not breathe,
Not whisper, any murmur of complaint.
Pain heap'd ten-hundred-fold to this, were still
Less burthen, by ten-hundred-fold, to bear,
Than were those lead-like tons of sin, that crush'd
My spirit flat before thee.

                                   O Lord, Lord,
Thou knowest I bore this better at the first,
For I was strong and hale of body then;
And tho' my teeth, which now are dropt away,

Would chatter with the cold, and all my beard [30]
Was tagg'd with icy fringes in the moon,
I drown'd the whoopings of the owl with sound
Of pious hymns and psalms, and sometimes saw
An angel stand and watch me, as I sang.
Now am I feeble grown; my end draws nigh;
I hope my end draws nigh: half deaf I am,
So that I scarce can hear the people hum
About the column's base, and almost blind,
And scarce can recognise the fields I know;
And both my thighs are rotted with the dew; [40]
Yet cease I not to clamour and to cry,
While my stiff spine can hold my weary head,
Till all my limbs drop piecemeal from the stone,
Have mercy, mercy: take away my sin.

O Jesus, if thou wilt not save my soul,
Who may be saved? who is it may be saved?
Who may be made a saint, if I fail here?
Show me the many hath suffer'd more than I.
For did not all thy martyrs die one death?
For either they were stoned, or crucified, [50]
Or burn'd in fire, or boil'd in oil, or sawn
In twain beneath the ribs; but I die here
To-day, and whole years long, a life of death.
Bear witness, if I could have found a way
(And heedfully I sifted all my thought)
More slowly-painful to subdue this home
Of sin, my flesh, which I despise and hate,
I had not stinted practice, O my God.

For not alone this pillar-punishment, [60]
Not this alone I bore: but while I lived
In the white convent down the valley there,
For many weeks about my loins I wore
The rope that haled the buckets from the well,
Twisted as tight as I could knot the noose;
And spake not of it to a single soul,
Until the ulcer, eating thro' my skin,
Betray'd my secret penance, so that all
My brethren marvell'd greatly. More than this
I bore, whereof, O God, thou knowest all.

Three winters, that my soul might grow to thee,   [70]
I lived up there on yonder mountain side.
My right leg chain'd into the crag, I lay
Pent in a roofless close of ragged stones;
Inswathed sometimes in wandering mist, and twice
Black'd with thy branding thunder, and sometimes
Sucking the damps for drink, and eating not,
Except the spare chance-gift of those that came
To touch my body and be heal'd, and live:
And they say then that I work'd miracles,
Whereof my fame is loud amongst mankind,   [80]
Cured lameness, palsies, cancers. Thou, O God,
Knowest alone whether this was or no.
Have mercy, mercy! cover all my sin.

Then, that I might be more alone with thee,
Three years I lived upon a pillar, high
Six cubits, and three years on one of twelve;
And twice three years I crouch'd on one that rose
Twenty by measure; last of all, I grew
Twice ten long weary weary years to this,
That numbers forty cubits from the soil.   [90]

I think that I have borne as much as this—
Or else I dream—and for so long a time,
If I may measure time by yon slow light,
And this high dial, which my sorrow crowns—°
So much—even so.
                              And yet I know not well,
For that the evil ones come here, and say,
'Fall down, O Simeon: thou hast suffer'd long
For ages and for ages!' then they prate
Of penances I cannot have gone thro',
Perplexing me with lies; and oft I fall,   [100]
Maybe for months, in such blind lethargies
That Heaven, and Earth, and Time are choked.
                                                But yet
Bethink thee, Lord, while thou and all the saints
Enjoy themselves in heaven, and men on earth
House in the shade of comfortable roofs,
Sit with their wives by fires, eat wholesome food,
And wear warm clothes, and even beasts have stalls,

I, 'tween the spring and downfall of the light,
Bow down one thousand and two hundred times,
To Christ, the Virgin Mother, and the saints; [110]
Or in the night, after a little sleep,
I wake: the chill stars sparkle; I am wet
With drenching dews, or stiff with crackling frost.
I wear an undress'd goatskin on my back;
A grazing iron collar grinds my neck;
And in my weak, lean arms I lift the cross,
And strive and wrestle with thee till I die:
O mercy, mercy! wash away my sin.

O Lord, thou knowest what a man I am;
A sinful man, conceived and born in sin: [120]
'Tis their own doing; this is none of mine;
Lay it not to me. Am I to blame for this,
That here come those that worship me? Ha! ha!
They think that I am somewhat. What am I?
The silly people take me for a saint,
And bring me offerings of fruit and flowers:
And I, in truth (thou wilt bear witness here)
Have all in all endured as much, and more
Than many just and holy men, whose names
Are register'd and calendar'd for saints. [130]

Good people, you do ill to kneel to me.
What is it I can have done to merit this?
I am a sinner viler than you all.
It may be I have wrought some miracles,
And cured some halt and maim'd; but what of that?
It may be, no one, even among the saints,
May match his pains with mine; but what of that?
Yet do not rise; for you may look on me,
And in your looking you may kneel to God.
Speak! is there any of you halt or maim'd? [140]
I think you know I have some power with Heaven
From my long penance: let him speak his wish.

Yes, I can heal him. Power goes forth from me.
They say that they are heal'd. Ah, hark! they shout
'St Simeon Stylites.' Why, if so,
God reaps a harvest in me. O my soul,

God reaps a harvest in thee. If this be,
Can I work miracles and not be saved?
This is not told of any. They were saints.
It cannot be but that I shall be saved;   [150]
Yea, crown'd a saint. They shout, 'Behold a saint!'
And lower voices saint me from above.
Courage, St Simeon! This dull chrysalis°
Cracks into shining wings, and hope ere death
Spreads more and more and more, that God hath now
Sponged and made blank of crimeful record all
My mortal archives.
             O my sons, my sons,
I, Simeon of the pillar, by surname
Stylites, among men; I, Simeon,
The watcher on the column till the end;   [160]
I, Simeon, whose brain the sunshine bakes;
I, whose bald brows in silent hours become
Unnaturally hoar with rime, do now
From my high nest of penance here proclaim
That Pontius and Iscariot by my side
Show'd like fair seraphs. On the coals I lay,°
A vessel full of sin: all hell beneath
Made me boil over. Devils pluck'd my sleeve,
Abaddon and Asmodeus caught at me.°
I smote them with the cross; they swarm'd again.   [170]
In bed like monstrous apes they crush'd my chest:
They flapp'd my light out as I read: I saw
Their faces grow between me and my book;
With colt-like whinny and with hoggish whine
They burst my prayer. Yet this way was left,
And by this way I 'scaped them. Mortify
Your flesh, like me, with scourges and with thorns;
Smite, shrink not, spare not. If it may be, fast
Whole Lents, and pray. I hardly, with slow steps,
With slow, faint steps, and much exceeding pain,   [180]
Have scrambled past those pits of fire, that still
Sing in mine ears. But yield not me the praise:
God only thro' his bounty hath thought fit,
Among the powers and princes of this world,
To make me an example to mankind,
Which few can reach to. Yet I do not say

But that a time may come—yea, even now,
Now, now, his footsteps smite the threshold stairs
Of life—I say, that time is at the doors
When you may worship me without reproach;   [190]
For I will leave my relics in your land,
And you may carve a shrine about my dust,
And burn a fragrant lamp before my bones,
When I am gather'd to the glorious saints.

While I spake then, a sting of shrewdest pain
Ran shrivelling thro' me, and a cloudlike change,
In passing, with a grosser film made thick
These heavy, horny eyes. The end! the end!
Surely the end! What's here? a shape, a shade,
A flash of light. Is that the angel there   [200]
That holds a crown? Come, blessed brother, come.
I know thy glittering face. I waited long;
My brows are ready. What! deny it now?
Nay, draw, draw, draw nigh. So I clutch it. Christ!
'Tis gone: 'tis here again; the crown! the crown!°
So now 'tis fitted on and grows to me,
And from it melt the dews of Paradise,
Sweet! sweet! spikenard, and balm, and frankincense.
Ah! let me not be fool'd, sweet saints: I trust
That I am whole, and clean, and meet for Heaven.   [210]

Speak, if there be a priest, a man of God,
Among you there, and let him presently
Approach, and lean a ladder on the shaft,
And climbing up into my airy home,
Deliver me the blessed sacrament;
For by the warning of the Holy Ghost,
I prophesy that I shall die to-night,
A quarter before twelve.
                        But thou, O lord,
Aid all this foolish people; let them take
Example, pattern: lead them to thy light.   [220]

Ulysses

It little profits that an idle king,
By this still hearth, among these barren crags,
Match'd with an aged wife, I mete and dole°
Unequal laws unto a savage race,
That hoard, and sleep, and feed, and know not me.

I cannot rest from travel: I will drink
Life to the lees: all times I have enjoy'd
Greatly, have suffer'd greatly, both with those
That loved me, and alone; on shore, and when
Thro' scudding drifts the rainy Hyades°   [10]
Vext the dim sea: I am become a name;
For always roaming with a hungry heart
Much have I seen and known; cities of men
And manners, climates, councils, governments,
Myself not least, but honour'd of them all;
And drunk delight of battle with my peers,
Far on the ringing plains of windy Troy.
I am a part of all that I have met;
Yet all experience is an arch wherethro'
Gleams that untravell'd world, whose margin fades   [20]
For ever and for ever when I move.
How dull it is to pause, to make an end,
To rust unburnish'd, not to shine in use!
As tho' to breathe were life. Life piled on life
Were all too little, and of one to me
Little remains: but every hour is saved
From that eternal silence, something more,
A bringer of new things; and vile it were
For some three suns to store and hoard myself,
And this gray spirit yearning in desire   [30]
To follow knowledge like a sinking star,
Beyond the utmost bound of human thought.

    This is my son, mine own Telemachus,
To whom I leave the sceptre and the isle—
Well-loved of me, discerning to fulfil
This labour, by slow prudence to make mild
A rugged people, and thro' soft degrees

Subdue them to the useful and the good.
Most blameless is he, centred in the sphere
Of common duties, decent not to fail [40]
In offices of tenderness, and pay
Meet adoration to my household gods,
When I am gone. He works his work, I mine.

There lies the port; the vessel puffs her sail:
There gloom the dark broad seas. My mariners,
Souls that have toil'd, and wrought, and thought with me—
That ever with a frolic welcome took
The thunder and the sunshine, and opposed
Free hearts, free foreheads—you and I are old;
Old age hath yet his honour and his toil; [50]
Death closes all: but something ere the end,
Some work of noble note, may yet be done,
Not unbecoming men that strove with Gods.
The lights begin to twinkle from the rocks:
The long day wanes: the slow moon climbs: the deep
Moans round with many voices. Come, my friends,
'Tis not too late to seek a newer world.
Push off, and sitting well in order smite
The sounding furrows; for my purpose holds
To sail beyond the sunset, and the baths [60]
Of all the western stars, until I die.
It may be that the gulfs will wash us down:
It may be we shall touch the Happy Isles,
And see the great Achilles, whom we knew.°
Tho' much is taken, much abides; and tho'
We are not now that strength which in old days
Moved earth and heaven; that which we are, we are;
One equal temper of heroic hearts,
Made weak by time and fate, but strong in will
To strive, to seek, to find, and not to yield. [70]

Tithon (First Version)

Ay me! ay me! the woods decay and fall,
The vapours weep their substance to the ground,
Man comes and tills the earth and lies beneath,

And after many summers dies the rose.
Me only fatal immortality
Consumes: I wither slowly in thine arms,
Here at the quiet limit of the world,
A white-haired shadow roaming like a dream
The ever-silent spaces of the East,
Far-folded mists, and gleaming halls of morn.   [10]

    Ay me! ay me! what everlasting pain,
Being immortal with a mortal heart,
To live confronted with eternal youth:
To look on what is beautiful nor know
Enjoyment save through memory. Can thy love,
Thy beauty, make amends, though even now,
Close over us, the silver star, thy guide,
Shines in those tremulous eyes that fill with tears?
Release me: let me go: take back thy gift:
Why should a man desire in any shape   [20]
To vary from his kind, or beat the roads
Of life, beyond the goal of ordinance°
Where all should pause, as is most meet for all?
Or let me call thy ministers, the hours,
To take me up, to wind me in their arms,
To shoot the sunny interval of day,
And lap me deep within the lonely west.

    A soft air fans the cloud apart; there comes
A glimpse of that dark world where I was born.
Once more the old mysterious glimmer steals   [30]
From thy pure brows, and from thy shoulders pure,
And bosom throbbing with a fresher heart.
Thy cheek begins to bloom a fuller red,
Thy sweet eyes brighten slowly close to mine,
Ere yet they blind the stars, and thy wild team,
Spreading a rapid glow with loosened manes,
Fly, trampling twilight into flakes of fire.

    'Tis ever thus: thou growest more beautiful,
Thou partest: when a little warmth returns
Thou partest, and thy tears are on my cheek.   [40]

    Ay me! ay me! with what another heart,
By thy divine embraces circumfused,
Thy black curls burning into sunny rings,
With thy change changed, I felt this wondrous glow

That, gradually blooming, flushes all
Thy pale fair limbs: what time my mortal frame
Molten in thine immortal, I lay wooed,
Lips, forehead, eyelids, growing dewy-warm
With kisses balmier than opening buds;
Anon the lips that dealt them moved themselves   [50]
In wild and airy whisperings more sweet
Than that strange song I heard Apollo sing,
While Ilion like a mist rose into towers.°

    Ah! keep me not for ever in the East:
How can my nature longer mix with thine?
Coldly thy rosy shadows bathe me, cold
Are all thy lights, and cold my wrinkled feet
Upon these glimmering thresholds, when the steam
Floats up from those still fields that dream below.
Release me! so restore me to the ground;   [60]
Thou seest all things, thou wilt see my grave:
Thou wilt renew thy beauty with the morn;
I earth in earth forget these empty courts,
And thee returning on thy silver wheels.

The Epic / Morte d'Arthur

The Epic

At Francis Allen's on the Christmas-eve,—
The game of forfeits done—the girls all kiss'd
Beneath the sacred bush and past away—°
The parson Holmes, the poet Everard Hall,
The host, and I sat round the wassail-bowl,
Then half-way ebb'd: and there we held a talk,
How all the old honour had from Christmas gone,
Or gone, or dwindled down to some odd games
In some odd nooks like this; till I, tired out
With cutting eights that day upon the pond,°   [10]
Where, three times slipping from the outer edge,
I bump'd the ice into three several stars,

Fell in a doze; and half-awake I heard
The parson taking wide and wider sweeps,
Now harping on the church-commissioners,
Now hawking at Geology and schism;°
Until I woke, and found him settled down
Upon the general decay of faith
Right thro' the world, 'at home was little left,
And none abroad: there was no anchor, none,   [20]
To hold by.' Francis, laughing, clapt his hand
On Everard's shoulder, with 'I hold by him.'
'And I,' quoth Everard, 'by the wassail-bowl.'
'Why yes,' I said, 'we knew your gift that way
At college: but another which you had,
I mean of verse (for so we held it then),
What came of that?' 'You know,' said Frank, 'he burnt
His epic, his King Arthur, some twelve books'—
And then to me demanding why? 'Oh, sir,
He thought that nothing new was said, or else   [30]
Something so said 'twas nothing—that a truth
Looks freshest in the fashion of the day:
God knows: he has a mint of reasons: ask.
It pleased *me* well enough.' 'Nay, nay,' said Hall,
'Why take the style of those heroic times?
For nature brings not back the Mastodon,°
Nor we those times; and why should any man
Remodel models? these twelve books of mine
Were faint Homeric echoes, nothing-worth,
Mere chaff and draff, much better burnt.' 'But I,'   [40]
Said Francis, 'pick'd the eleventh from this hearth
And have it: keep a thing, its use will come.
I hoard it as a sugar-plum for Holmes.'
He laugh'd, and I, tho' sleepy, like a horse
That hears the corn-bin open, prick'd my ears;
For I remember'd Everard's college fame
When we were Freshmen: then at my request
He brought it; and the poet little urged,
But with some prelude of disparagement,
Read, mouthing out his hollow oes and aes,   [50]
Deep-chested music, and to this result.

Morte d'Arthur

So all day long the noise of battle roll'd
Among the mountains by the winter sea;
Until King Arthur's table, man by man,
Had fallen in Lyonnesse about their Lord,°
King Arthur: then, because his wound was deep,
The bold Sir Bedivere uplifted him,
Sir Bedivere, the last of all his knights,
And bore him to a chapel nigh the field,
A broken chancel with a broken cross,
That stood on a dark strait of barren land.   [10]
On one side lay the Ocean, and on one
Lay a great water, and the moon was full.

    Then spake King Arthur to Sir Bedivere:
'The sequel of to-day unsolders all
The goodliest fellowship of famous knights
Whereof this world holds record. Such a sleep
They sleep—the men I loved. I think that we
Shall never more, at any future time,
Delight our souls with talk of knightly deeds,
Walking about the gardens and the halls   [20]
Of Camelot, as in the days that were.
I perish by this people which I made,—
Tho' Merlin sware that I should come again
To rule once more—but let what will be, be,
I am so deeply smitten thro' the helm
That without help I cannot last till morn.
Thou therefore take my brand Excalibur,
Which was my pride: for thou rememberest how
In those old days, one summer noon, an arm
Rose up from out the bosom of the lake,   [30]
Clothed in white samite, mystic, wonderful,
Holding the sword—and how I row'd across
And took it, and have worn it, like a king:
And, wheresoever I am sung or told
In aftertime, this also shall be known:
But now delay not: take Excalibur,
And fling him far into the middle mere:
Watch what thou seëst, and lightly bring me word.'°

To him replied the bold Sir Bedivere:
'It is not meet, Sir King, to leave thee thus,   [40]
Aidless, alone, and smitten thro' the helm.
A little thing may harm a wounded man.
Yet I thy hest will all perform at full,
Watch what I see, and lightly bring thee word.'

So saying, from the ruin'd shrine he stept
And in the moon athwart the place of tombs,
Where lay the mighty bones of ancient men,
Old knights, and over them the sea-wind sang
Shrill, chill, with flakes of foam. He, stepping down
By zig-zag paths, and juts of pointed rock,   [50]
Came on the shining levels of the lake.

There drew he forth the brand Excalibur,
And o'er him, drawing it, the winter moon,
Brightening the skirts of a long cloud, ran forth
And sparkled keen with frost against the hilt:
For all the haft twinkled with diamond sparks,°
Myriads of topaz-lights, and jacinth-work°
Of subtlest jewellery. He gazed so long
That both his eyes were dazzled, as he stood,
This way and that dividing the swift mind,   [60]
In act to throw: but at the last it seem'd
Better to leave Excalibur conceal'd
There in the many-knotted waterflags,
That whistled stiff and dry about the marge.
So strode he back slow to the wounded King.

Then spake King Arthur to Sir Bedivere:
'Hast thou perform'd my mission which I gave?
What is it thou hast seen? or what hast heard?'

And answer made the bold Sir Bedivere:
'I heard the ripple washing in the reeds,   [70]
And the wild water lapping on the crag.'

To whom replied King Arthur, faint and pale:
'Thou hast betray'd thy nature and thy name,
Not rendering true answer, as beseem'd
Thy fëalty, nor like a noble knight:
For surer sign had follow'd, either hand,

Or voice, or else a motion of the mere.
This is a shameful thing for men to lie.
Yet now, I charge thee, quickly go again
As thou art lief and dear, and do the thing°   [80]
I bad thee, watch, and lightly bring me word.'

    Then went Sir Bedivere the second time
Across the ridge, and paced beside the mere,
Counting the dewy pebbles, fix'd in thought;
But when he saw the wonder of the hilt,
How curiously and strangely chased, he smote
His palms together, and he cried aloud,

    'And if indeed I cast the brand away,
Surely a precious thing, one worthy note,
Should thus be lost for ever from the earth,   [90]
Which might have pleased the eyes of many men.
What good should follow this, if this were done?
What harm, undone? deep harm to disobey,
Seeing obedience is the bond of rule.
Were it well to obey then, if a king demand
An act unprofitable, against himself?
The King is sick, and knows not what he does.
What record, or what relic of my lord
Should be to aftertime, but empty breath
And rumours of a doubt? but were this kept,   [100]
Stored in some treasure-house of mighty kings,
Some one might show it at a joust of arms,
Saying, "King Arthur's sword, Excalibur,
Wrought by the lonely maiden of the Lake.
Nine years she wrought it, sitting in the deeps
Upon the hidden bases of the hills."
So might some old man speak in the aftertime
To all the people, winning reverence.
But now much honour and much fame were lost.'

    So spake he, clouded with his own conceit,   [110]
And hid Excalibur the second time,
And so strode back slow to the wounded King.

    Then spoke King Arthur, breathing heavily:
'What is it thou hast seen? or what hast heard?'

And answer made the bold Sir Bedivere:
'I heard the water lapping on the crag,
And the long ripple washing in the reeds.'

To whom replied King Arthur, much in wrath:
'Ah, miserable and unkind, untrue,
Unknightly, traitor-hearted! Woe is me!   [120]
Authority forgets a dying king,
Laid widow'd of the power in his eye
That bow'd the will. I see thee what thou art,
For thou, the latest-left of all my knights,
In whom should meet the offices of all,
Thou wouldst betray me for the precious hilt;
Either from lust of gold, or like a girl
Valuing the giddy pleasure of the eyes.
Yet, for a man may fail in duty twice,
And the third time may prosper, get thee hence: [130]
But, if thou spare to fling Excalibur,
I will arise and slay thee with my hands.'

Then quickly rose Sir Bedivere, and ran,
And, leaping down the ridges lightly, plunged
Among the bulrush-beds, and clutch'd the sword,
And strongly wheel'd and threw it. The great brand
Made lightnings in the splendour of the moon,
And flashing round and round, and whirl'd in an arch,
Shot like a streamer of the northern morn,°
Seen where the moving isles of winter shock°   [140]
By night, with noises of the northern sea.
So flash'd and fell the brand Excalibur:
But ere he dipt the surface, rose an arm
Clothed in white samite, mystic, wonderful,
And caught him by the hilt, and brandish'd him
Three times, and drew him under in the mere.
And lightly went the other to the King.

Then spoke King Arthur, drawing thicker breath:
'Now see I by thine eyes that this is done.
Speak out: what is it thou hast heard, or seen?'   [150]

And answer made the bold Sir Bedivere:
'Sir King, I closed mine eyelids, lest the gems
Should blind my purpose, for I never saw,

Nor shall see, here or elsewhere, till I die,
Not tho' I live three lives of mortal men,
So great a miracle as yonder hilt.
Then with both hands I flung him, wheeling him;
But when I look'd again, behold an arm,
Clothed in white samite, mystic, wonderful,
That caught him by the hilt, and brandish'd him   [160]
Three times, and drew him under in the mere.'

And answer made King Arthur, breathing hard:
'My end draws nigh; 'tis time that I were gone.
Make broad thy shoulders to receive my weight,
And bear me to the margin; yet I fear
My wound hath taken cold, and I shall die.'

So saying, from the pavement he half rose,
Slowly, with pain, reclining on his arm,
And looking wistfully with wide blue eyes
As in a picture. Him Sir Bedivere   [170]
Remorsefully regarded thro' his tears,
And would have spoken, but he found not words,
Then took with care, and kneeling on one knee,
O'er both his shoulders drew the languid hands,
And rising bore him thro' the place of tombs.

But, as he walk'd, King Arthur panted hard,
Like one that feels a nightmare on his bed
When all the house is mute. So sigh'd the King,
Muttering and murmuring at his ear, 'Quick, quick!
I fear it is too late, and I shall die.'   [180]
But the other swiftly strode from ridge to ridge,
Clothed with his breath, and looking, as he walk'd,
Larger than human on the frozen hills.
He heard the deep behind him, and a cry
Before. His own thought drove him, like a goad.
Dry clash'd his harness in the icy caves
And barren chasms, and all to left and right
The bare black cliff clang'd round him, as he based
His feet on juts of slippery crag that rang
Sharp-smitten with the dint of armed heels—   [190]
And on a sudden, lo! the level lake,
And the long glories of the winter moon.

Then saw they how there hove a dusky barge,
Dark as a funeral scarf from stem to stern,
Beneath them; and descending they were ware
That all the decks were dense with stately forms
Black-stoled, black-hooded, like a dream—by these
Three Queens with crowns of gold—and from them rose°
A cry that shiver'd to the tingling stars,
And, as it were one voice, an agony   [200]
Of lamentation, like a wind, that shrills
All night in a waste land, where no one comes,
Or hath come, since the making of the world.

Then murmur'd Arthur, 'Place me in the barge,'
And to the barge they came. There those three Queens
Put forth their hands, and took the King, and wept.
But she, that rose the tallest of them all
And fairest, laid his head upon her lap,
And loosed the shatter'd casque, and chafed his hands,°
And call'd him by his name, complaining loud,   [210]
And dropping bitter tears against his brow
Striped with dark blood: for all his face was white
And colourless, and like the wither'd moon
Smote by the fresh beam of the springing east;
And all his greaves and cuisses dash'd with drops
Of onset; and the light and lustrous curls—°
That made his forehead like a rising sun
High from the daïs-throne—were parch'd with dust;
Or, clotted into points and hanging loose,
Mix'd with the knightly growth that fringed his lips.   [220]
So like a shatter'd column lay the King;
Not like that Arthur who, with lance in rest,
From spur to plume a star of tournament,
Shot thro' the lists at Camelot, and charged
Before the eyes of ladies and of kings.

Then loudly cried the bold Sir Bedivere,
'Ah! my Lord Arthur, whither shall I go?
Where shall I hide my forehead and my eyes?
For now I see the true old times are dead,
When every morning brought a noble chance,   [230]
And every chance brought out a noble knight.
Such times have been not since the light that led

The holy Elders with the gift of myrrh.
But now the whole ROUND TABLE is dissolved
Which was an image of the mighty world;
And I, the last, go forth companionless,
And the days darken round me, and the years,
Among new men, strange faces, other minds.'

    And slowly answered Arthur from the barge:
'The old order changeth, yielding place to new,   [240]
And God fulfils Himself in many ways,
Lest one good custom should corrupt the world.
Comfort thyself: what comfort is in me?
I have lived my life, and that which I have done
May He within Himself make pure! but thou,
If thou shouldst never see my face again,
Pray for my soul. More things are wrought by prayer
Than this world dreams of. Wherefore, let thy voice
Rise like a fountain for me night and day.
For what are men better than sheep or goats   [250]
That nourish a blind life within the brain,
If, knowing God, they lift not hands of prayer
Both for themselves and those who call them friend?
For so the whole round earth is every way
Bound by gold chains about the feet of God.
But now farewell. I am going a long way
With these thou seëst—if indeed I go—
(For all my mind is clouded with a doubt)
To the island-valley of Avilion;°
Where falls not hail, or rain, or any snow,   [260]
Nor ever wind blows loudly; but it lies
Deep-meadow'd, happy, fair with orchard-lawns
And bowery hollows crown'd with summer sea,
Where I will heal me of my grievous wound.'

    So said he, and the barge with oar and sail
Moved from the brink, like some full-breasted swan
That, fluting a wild carol ere her death,
Ruffles her pure cold plume, and takes the flood
With swarthy webs. Long stood Sir Bedivere
Revolving many memories, till the hull   [270]
Look'd one black dot against the verge of dawn,
And on the mere the wailing died away.

[*The Epic*]

Here ended Hall, and our last light, that long
Had wink'd and threaten'd darkness, flared and fell:
At which the Parson, sent to sleep with sound,
And waked with silence, grunted 'Good!' but we
Sat rapt: it was the tone with which he read—
Perhaps some modern touches here and there
Redeem'd it from the charge of nothingness—
Or else we loved the man, and prized his work;   [280]
I know not: but we sitting, as I said,
The cock crew loud; as at that time of year
The lusty bird takes every hour for dawn:
Then Francis, muttering, like a man ill-used,
'There now—that's nothing!' drew a little back,
And drove his heel into the smoulder'd log,
That sent a blast of sparkles up the flue:
And so to bed; where yet in sleep I seem'd
To sail with Arthur under looming shores,
Point after point; till on to dawn, when dreams   [290]
Begin to feel the truth and stir of day,
To me, methought, who waited with a crowd,
There came a bark that, blowing forward, bore
King Arthur, like a modern gentleman
Of stateliest port; and all the people cried,
'Arthur is come again: he cannot die.'
Then those that stood upon the hills behind
Repeated—'Come again, and thrice as fair;'
And, further inland, voices echo'd—'Come
With all good things, and war shall be no more.'   [300]
At this a hundred bells began to peal,
That with the sound I woke, and heard indeed
The clear church-bells ring in the Christmas-morn.

'*You ask me, why, tho' ill at ease*'

You ask me, why, tho' ill at ease,
    Within this region I subsist,
    Whose spirits falter in the mist,
And languish for the purple seas.

It is the land that freemen till,
 That sober-suited Freedom chose,
 The land, where girt with friends or foes
A man may speak the thing he will;

A land of settled government,
 A land of just and old renown,   [10]
 Where Freedom slowly broadens down
From precedent to precedent:

Where faction seldom gathers head,
 But by degrees to fulness wrought,
 The strength of some diffusive thought
Hath time and space to work and spread.

Should banded unions persecute°
 Opinion, and induce a time
 When single thought is civil crime,
And individual freedom mute;   [20]

Tho' Power should make from land to land
 The name of Britain trebly great—
 Tho' every channel of the State
Should fill and choke with golden sand—

Yet waft me from the harbour-mouth,
 Wild wind! I seek a warmer sky,
 And I will see before I die
The palms and temples of the South.

Audley Court

'The Bull, the Fleece are cramm'd, and not a room
For love or money. Let us picnic there
At Audley Court.'
                    I spoke, while Audley feast
Humm'd like a hive all round the narrow quay,
To Francis, with a basket on his arm,
To Francis just alighted from the boat,
And breathing of the sea. 'With all my heart,'
Said Francis. Then we shoulder'd thro' the swarm,

And rounded by the stillness of the beach
To where the bay runs up its latest horn.   [10]

    We left the dying ebb that faintly lipp'd
The flat red granite; so by many a sweep
Of meadow smooth from aftermath we reach'd
The griffin-guarded gates, and pass'd thro' all
The pillar'd dusk of sounding sycamores,
And cross'd the garden to the gardener's lodge,
With all its casements bedded, and its walls
And chimneys muffled in the leafy vine.

    There, on a slope of orchard, Francis laid
A damask napkin wrought with horse and hound,   [20]
Brought out a dusky loaf that smelt of home,
And, half-cut-down, a pasty costly-made,
Where quail and pigeon, lark and leveret lay,°
Like fossils of the rock, with golden yolks
Imbedded and injellied; last, with these,
A flask of cider from his father's vats,
Prime, which I knew; and so we sat and eat
And talk'd old matters over; who was dead,
Who married, who was like to be, and how
The races went, and who would rent the hall: [30]
Then touch'd upon the game, how scarce it was
This season; glancing thence, discuss'd the farm,
The four-field system, and the price of grain;
And struck upon the corn-laws, where we split,°
And came again together on the king
With heated faces; till he laugh'd aloud;
And, while the blackbird on the pippin hung°
To hear him, clapt his hand in mine and sang—

    'Oh! who would fight and march and countermarch,
Be shot for sixpence in a battle-field,   [40]
And shovell'd up into some bloody trench
Where no one knows? but let me live my life.
    'Oh! who would cast and balance at a desk,
Perch'd like a crow upon a three-legg'd stool,
Till all his juice is dried, and all his joints
Are full of chalk? but let me live my life.
    'Who'd serve the state? for if I carved my name

Upon the cliffs that guard my native land,
I might as well have traced it in the sands;
The sea wastes all: but let me live my life.   [50]
    'Oh! who would love? I woo'd a woman once,
But she was sharper than an eastern wind,
And all my heart turn'd from her, as a thorn
Turns from the sea; but let me live my life.'

He sang his song, and I replied with mine:
I found it in a volume, all of songs,
Knock'd down to me, when old Sir Robert's pride,
His books—the more the pity, so I said—
Came to the hammer here in March—and this—
I set the words, and added names I knew.   [60]

    'Sleep, Ellen Aubrey, sleep, and dream of me:
Sleep, Ellen, folded in thy sister's arm,
And sleeping, haply dream her arm is mine.
    'Sleep, Ellen, folded in Emilia's arm;
Emilia, fairer than all else but thou,
For thou art fairer than all else that is.
    'Sleep, breathing health and peace upon her breast:
Sleep, breathing love and trust against her lip:
I go to-night: I come to-morrow morn.
    'I go, but I return: I would I were   [70]
The pilot of the darkness and the dream.
Sleep, Ellen Aubrey, love, and dream of me.'

    So sang we each to either, Francis Hale,
The farmer's son, who lived across the bay,
My friend; and I, that having wherewithal,
And in the fallow leisure of my life
A rolling stone of here and everywhere,
Did what I would; but ere the night we rose
And saunter'd home beneath a moon, that, just
In crescent, dimly rain'd about the leaf   [80]
Twilights of airy silver, till we reach'd
The limit of the hills; and as we sank
From rock to rock upon the glooming quay,
The town was hush'd beneath us: lower down
The bay was oily calm; the harbour-buoy,
Sole star of phosphorescence in the calm,°

With one green sparkle ever and anon
Dipt by itself, and we were glad at heart.

'Break, break, break'

Break, break, break,
　　On thy cold gray stones, O Sea!
And I would that my tongue could utter
　　The thoughts that arise in me.

O well for the fisherman's boy,
　　That he shouts with his sister at play!
O well for the sailor lad,
　　That he sings in his boat on the bay!

And the stately ships go on
　　To their haven under the hill;　　　　　　　[10]
But O for the touch of a vanish'd hand,
　　And the sound of a voice that is still!

Break, break, break,
　　At the foot of thy crags, O Sea!
But the tender grace of a day that is dead
　　Will never come back to me.

Sir Galahad

My good blade carves the casques of men,°
　　My tough lance thrusteth sure,
My strength is as the strength of ten,
　　Because my heart is pure.
The shattering trumpet shrilleth high,
　　The hard brands shiver on the steel,
The splinter'd spear-shafts crack and fly,
　　The horse and rider reel:
They reel, they roll in clanging lists,
　　And when the tide of combat stands,　　　　[10]
Perfume and flowers fall in showers,
　　That lightly rain from ladies' hands.

How sweet are looks that ladies bend
    On whom their favours fall!
For them I battle till the end,
    To save from shame and thrall:
But all my heart is drawn above,
    My knees are bow'd in crypt and shrine:
I never felt the kiss of love,
    Nor maiden's hand in mine.   [20]
More bounteous aspects on me beam,
    Me mightier transports move and thrill;
So keep I fair thro' faith and prayer
    A virgin heart in work and will.

When down the stormy crescent goes,°
    A light before me swims,
Between dark stems the forest glows,
    I hear a noise of hymns:
Then by some secret shrine I ride;
    I hear a voice but none are there;   [30]
The stalls are void, the doors are wide,
    The tapers burning fair.
Fair gleams the snowy altar-cloth,
    The silver vessels sparkle clean,
The shrill bell rings, the censer swings,
    And solemn chaunts resound between.

Sometimes on lonely mountain-meres
    I find a magic bark;
I leap on board: no helmsman steers:
    I float till all is dark.   [40]
A gentle sound, an awful light!
    Three angels bear the holy Grail:°
With folded feet, in stoles of white,
    On sleeping wings they sail.
Ah, blessed vision! blood of God!
    My spirit beats her mortal bars,
As down dark tides the glory slides,
    And star-like mingles with the stars.

When on my goodly charger borne
    Thro' dreaming towns I go,   [50]

The cock crows ere the Christmas morn,
    The streets are dumb with snow.
The tempest crackles on the leads,
    And, ringing, springs from brand and mail;
But o'er the dark a glory spreads,
    And gilds the driving hail.
I leave the plain, I climb the height;
    No branchy thicket shelter yields;
But blessed forms in whistling storms
    Fly o'er waste fens and windy fields.   [60]

A maiden knight—to me is given
    Such hope, I know not fear;
I yearn to breathe the airs of heaven
    That often meet me here.
I muse on joy that will not cease,
    Pure spaces clothed in living beams,
Pure lilies of eternal peace,
    Whose odours haunt my dreams;
And, stricken by an angel's hand,
    This mortal armour that I wear,   [70]
This weight and size, this heart and eyes,
Are touch'd, are turn'd to finest air.

The clouds are broken in the sky,
    And thro' the mountain-walls
A rolling organ-harmony
    Swells up, and shakes and falls.
Then move the trees, the copses nod,
    Wings flutter, voices hover clear:
'O just and faithful knight of God!
    Ride on! the prize is near.'   [80]
So pass I hostel, hall, and grange;
    By bridge and ford, by park and pale,°
All-arm'd I ride, whate'er betide,
    Until I find the holy Grail.

A Farewell

Flow down, cold rivulet, to the sea,
  Thy tribute wave deliver:
No more by thee my steps shall be,
  For ever and for ever.

Flow, softly flow, by lawn and lea,
  A rivulet then a river:
No where by thee my steps shall be,
  For ever and for ever.

But here will sigh thine alder tree,
  And here thine aspen shiver;   [10]
And here by thee will hum the bee,
  For ever and for ever.

A thousand suns will stream on thee,
  A thousand moons will quiver;
But not by thee my steps shall be,
  For ever and for ever.

'Oh! that 'twere possible'

Oh! that 'twere possible,
  After long grief and pain,
To find the arms of my true-love
  Round me once again!

When I was wont to meet her
  In the silent woody places
    Of the land that gave me birth,
  We stood tranced in long embraces,
Mixt with kisses sweeter, sweeter,
    Than any thing on earth.   [10]

A shadow flits before me—
    Not thou, but like to thee.
Ah God! that it were possible
    For one short hour to see
The souls we loved, that they might tell us
    What and where they be.

It leads me forth at Evening,
    It lightly winds and steals
In a cold white robe before me,
    When all my spirit reels   [20]
At the shouts, the leagues of lights,
    And the roaring of the wheels.

Half the night I waste in sighs,
    In a wakeful doze I sorrow
For the hand, the lips, the eyes—
    For the meeting of tomorrow,
      The delight of happy laughter,
The delight of low replies.

Do I hear the pleasant ditty,
    That I heard her chant of old?   [30]
      But I wake—my dream is fled.
Without knowledge, without pity—
    In the shuddering dawn behold,
    By the curtains of my bed,
That abiding phantom cold.

Then I rise: the eave-drops fall
    And the yellow-vapours choke
      The great city sounding wide;
The day comes—a dull red ball,
    Wrapt in drifts of lurid smoke,   [40]
      On the misty river-tide.

Through the hubbub of the market
    I steal, a wasted frame;
It crosseth here, it crosseth there—
Through all that crowd, confused and loud,
    The shadow still the same;
And on my heavy eyelids
    My anguish hangs like shame.

Alas for her that met me,
    That heard me softly call—   [50]
Came glimmering through the laurels
    At the quiet even-fall,
In the garden by the turrets
    Of the old Manorial Hall.

Then the broad light glares and beats,
    And the sunk eye flits and fleets,
And will not let me be.
    I loathe the squares and streets,
And the faces that one meets,
    Hearts with no love for me;   [60]
Always I long to creep
To some still cavern deep,
And to weep, and weep and weep
    My whole soul out to thee.

Get thee hence, nor come again,
    Pass and cease to move about—
Pass, thou death-like type of pain,
    Mix not memory with doubt.
'Tis the blot upon the brain
    That *will* show itself without.   [70]

Would the happy Spirit descend
    In the chamber or the street
        As she looks among the blest;
Should I fear to greet my friend,
    Or to ask her, 'Take me, sweet,
        To the region of thy rest.'

But she tarries in her place,
And I paint the beauteous face
    Of the maiden, that I lost,
        In my inner eyes again,   [80]
Lest my heart be overborne
By the thing I hold in scorn,
    By a dull mechanic ghost
        And a juggle of the brain.

I can shadow forth my bride
    As I knew her fair and kind,
        As I wooed her for my wife;
She is lovely by my side
        In the silence of my life—
'Tis a phantom of the mind.   [90]
'Tis a phantom fair and good;
    I can call it to my side,

So to guard my life from ill,
Though its ghastly sister glide
    And be moved around me still
With the moving of the blood,
    That is moved not of the will.

Let it pass, the dreary brow,
Let the dismal face go by.
Will it lead me to the grave?   [100]
    Then I lose it: it will fly:
Can it overlast the nerves?
    Can it overlive the eye?
But the other, like a star,
Through the channel windeth far
    Till it fade and fail and die,
To its Archetype that waits,
Clad in light by golden gates—
Clad in light the Spirit waits
    To embrace me in the sky.   [110]

Locksley Hall

Comrades, leave me here a little, while as yet 'tis early morn:°
Leave me here, and when you want me, sound upon the
    bugle-horn.

'Tis the place, and all around it, as of old, the curlews call,
Dreary gleams about the moorland flying over Locksley Hall;

Locksley Hall, that in the distance overlooks the sandy tracts,
And the hollow ocean-ridges roaring into cataracts.

Many a night from yonder ivied casement, ere I went to rest,
Did I look on great Orion sloping slowly to the West.

Many a night I saw the Pleiads, rising thro' the mellow shade,°
Glitter like a swarm of fire-flies tangled in a silver braid.   [10]

Here about the beach I wander'd, nourishing a youth sublime
With the fairy tales of science, and the long result of Time;

When the centuries behind me like a fruitful land reposed;
When I clung to all the present for the promise that it closed:

When I dipt into the future far as human eye could see;
Saw the Vision of the world, and all the wonder that would
be.——

In the Spring a fuller crimson comes upon the robin's breast;
In the Spring the wanton lapwing gets himself another crest;

In the Spring a livelier iris changes on the burnish'd dove;
In the Spring a young man's fancy lightly turns to thoughts
of love. [20]

Then her cheek was pale and thinner than should be for one so
young,
And her eyes on all my motions with a mute observance hung.

And I said, 'My cousin Amy, speak, and speak the truth to me,
Trust me, cousin, all the current of my being sets to thee.'

On her pallid cheek and forehead came a colour and a light,
As I have seen the rosy red flushing in the northern night.

And she turn'd—her bosom shaken with a sudden storm of
sighs—
All the spirit deeply dawning in the dark of hazel eyes—

Saying, 'I have hid my feelings, fearing they should do me
wrong;'
Saying, 'Dost thou love me, cousin?' weeping, 'I have loved
thee long.' [30]

Love took up the glass of Time, and turn'd it in his glowing
hands;
Every moment, lightly shaken, ran itself in golden sands.

Love took up the harp of Life, and smote on all the chords with
might;
Smote the chord of Self, that, trembling, pass'd in music out of
sight.

Many a morning on the moorland did we hear the copses ring,
And her whisper throng'd my pulses with the fulness of the
Spring.

Many an evening by the waters did we watch the stately ships,
And our spirits rush'd together at the touching of the lips.

O my cousin, shallow-hearted! O my Amy, mine no more!
O the dreary, dreary moorland! O the barren, barren shore!   [40]

Falser than all fancy fathoms, falser than all songs have sung,°
Puppet to a father's threat, and servile to a shrewish tongue!

Is it well to wish thee happy?—having known me—to decline
On a range of lower feelings and a narrower heart than mine!

Yet it shall be: thou shalt lower to his level day by day,
What is fine within thee growing coarse to sympathise with clay.

As the husband is, the wife is: thou art mated with a clown,°
And the grossness of his nature will have weight to drag thee down.

He will hold thee, when his passion shall have spent its novel
    force,
Something better than his dog, a little dearer than his horse.   [50]

What is this? his eyes are heavy: think not they are glazed with
    wine.
Go to him: it is thy duty: kiss him: take his hand in thine.

It may be my lord is weary, that his brain is overwrought:
Soothe him with thy finer fancies, touch him with thy lighter
    thought.

He will answer to the purpose, easy things to understand—
Better thou wert dead before me, tho' I slew thee with my hand!

Better thou and I were lying, hidden from the heart's disgrace,
Roll'd in one another's arms, and silent in a last embrace.

Cursed be the social wants that sin against the strength of youth!
Cursed be the social lies that warp us from the living truth!   [60]

Cursed be the sickly forms that err from honest Nature's rule!
Cursed be the gold that gilds the straiten'd forehead of the fool!°

Well—'tis well that I should bluster!—Hadst thou less unworthy
    proved—
Would to God—for I had loved thee more than ever wife was loved.

Am I mad, that I should cherish that which bears but bitter fruit?
I will pluck it from my bosom, tho' my heart be at the root.

Never, tho' my mortal summers to such length of years should
    come
As the many-winter'd crow that leads the clanging rookery home.

Where is comfort? in division of the records of the mind?
Can I part her from herself, and love her, as I knew her, kind?   [70]

I remember one that perish'd: sweetly did she speak and move:
Such a one do I remember, whom to look at was to love.

Can I think of her as dead, and love her for the love she bore?
No—she never loved me truly: love is love for evermore.

Comfort? comfort scorn'd of devils! this is truth the poet sings,°
That a sorrow's crown of sorrow is remembering happier things.

Drug thy memories, lest thou learn it, lest thy heart be put to
    proof,
In the dead unhappy night, and when the rain is on the roof.

Like a dog, he hunts in dreams, and thou art staring at the wall,
Where the dying night-lamp flickers, and the shadows rise
    and fall.   [80]

Then a hand shall pass before thee, pointing to his drunken
    sleep,
To thy widow'd marriage-pillows, to the tears that thou wilt
    weep.°

Thou shalt hear the 'Never, never,' whisper'd by the phantom
    years,
And a song from out the distance in the ringing of thine ears;

And an eye shall vex thee, looking ancient kindness on thy pain.
Turn thee, turn thee on thy pillow: get thee to thy rest again.

Nay, but Nature brings thee solace; for a tender voice will cry.
'Tis a purer life than thine; a lip to drain thy trouble dry.

Baby lips will laugh me down: my latest rival brings thee rest.
Baby fingers, waxen touches, press me from the mother's breast.   [90]

O, the child too clothes the father with a dearness not his due.
Half is thine and half is his: it will be worthy of the two.

O, I see thee old and formal, fitted to thy petty part,
With a little hoard of maxims preaching down a daughter's heart.

'They were dangerous guides the feelings—she herself was not
    exempt—
Truly, she herself had suffer'd'—Perish in thy self-contempt!

Overlive it—lower yet—be happy! wherefore should I care?
I myself must mix with action, lest I wither by despair.

What is that which I should turn to, lighting upon days like
    these?
Every door is barr'd with gold, and opens but to golden keys.°   [100]

Every gate is throng'd with suitors, all the markets overflow.
I have but an angry fancy: what is that which I should do?

I had been content to perish, falling on the foeman's ground,
When the ranks are roll'd in vapour, and the winds are laid with
    sound.

But the jingling of the guinea helps the hurt that Honour feels,
And the nations do but murmur, snarling at each other's heels.

Can I but relive in sadness? I will turn that earlier page.
Hide me from my deep emotion, O thou wondrous Mother-Age!

Make me feel the wild pulsation that I felt before the strife,
When I heard my days before me, and the tumult of my life;   [110]

Yearning for the large excitement that the coming years would
    yield,
Eager-hearted as a boy when first he leaves his father's field,

And at night along the dusky highway near and nearer drawn,
Sees in heaven the light of London flaring like a dreary dawn;

And his spirit leaps within him to be gone before him then,
Underneath the light he looks at, in among the throngs of men:

Men, my brothers, men the workers, ever reaping something new:
That which they have done but earnest of the things that they
    shall do:°

For I dipt into the future, far as human eye could see,
Saw the Vision of the world, and all the wonder that would be;   [120]

Saw the heavens fill with commerce, argosies of magic sails,°
Pilots of the purple twilight, dropping down with costly bales;

Heard the heavens fill with shouting, and there rain'd a ghastly
    dew
From the nations' airy navies grappling in the central blue;

Far along the world-wide whisper of the south-wind rushing
    warm,
With the standards of the peoples plunging thro' the thunder-
    storm;

Till the war-drum throbb'd no longer, and the battle-flags were
    furl'd
In the Parliament of man, the Federation of the world.

There the common sense of most shall hold a fretful realm
    in awe,
And the kindly earth shall slumber, lapt in universal law. [130]

So I triumph'd ere my passion sweeping thro' me left me dry,
Left me with the palsied heart, and left me with the jaundiced
    eye;

Eye, to which all order festers, all things here are out of joint:
Science moves, but slowly slowly, creeping on from point to
    point:

Slowly comes a hungry people, as a lion creeping nigher,
Glares at one that nods and winks behind a slowly-dying fire.

Yet I doubt not thro' the ages one increasing purpose runs,
And the thoughts of men are widen'd with the process of the
    suns.

What is that to him that reaps not harvest of his youthful joys,
Tho' the deep heart of existence beat for ever like a boy's? [140]

Knowledge comes, but wisdom lingers, and I linger on the shore,
And the individual withers, and the world is more and more.

Knowledge comes, but wisdom lingers, and he bears a laden
    breast,
Full of sad experience, moving toward the stillness of his rest.

Hark, my merry comrades call me, sounding on the bugle-horn,
They to whom my foolish passion were a target for their scorn:

Shall it not be scorn to me to harp on such a moulder'd string?
I am shamed thro' all my nature to have loved so slight a thing.

Weakness to be wroth with weakness! woman's pleasure, woman's pain°—

Nature made them blinder motions bounded in a shallower brain: [150]

Woman is the lesser man, and all thy passions, match'd with mine,
Are as moonlight unto sunlight, and as water unto wine—

Here at least, where nature sickens, nothing. Ah, for some retreat
Deep in yonder shining Orient, where my life began to beat;

Where in wild Mahratta-battle fell my father evil-starr'd;—°
I was left a trampled orphan, and a selfish uncle's ward.

Or to burst all links of habit—there to wander far away,
On from island unto island at the gateways of the day.

Larger constellations burning, mellow moons and happy skies,
Breadths of tropic shade and palms in cluster, knots of Paradise.   [160]

Never comes the trader, never floats an European flag,
Slides the bird o'er lustrous woodland, swings the trailer from the crag;°

Droops the heavy-blossom'd bower, hangs the heavy-fruited tree—
Summer isles of Eden lying in dark-purple spheres of sea.

There methinks would be enjoyment more than in this march of mind,
In the steamship, in the railway, in the thoughts that shake mankind.

There the passions cramp'd no longer shall have scope and breathing space;
I will take some savage woman, she shall rear my dusky race.

Iron-jointed, supple-sinew'd, they shall dive, and they shall run,
Catch the wild goat by the hair, and hurl their lances in the sun;   [170]

Whistle back the parrot's call, and leap the rainbows of the brooks,
Not with blinded eyesight poring over miserable books—

Fool, again the dream, the fancy! but I *know* my words are wild,
But I count the gray barbarian lower than the Christian child.

I, to herd with narrow foreheads, vacant of our glorious gains,
Like a beast with lower pleasures, like a beast with lower pains!

Mated with a squalid savage—what to me were sun or clime?
I the heir of all the ages, in the foremost files of time—

I that rather held it better men should perish one by one,
Than that earth should stand at gaze like Joshua's moon
    in Ajalon!°   [180]

Not in vain the distance beacons. Forward, forward let us range,
Let the great world spin for ever down the ringing grooves of
    change.°

Thro' the shadow of the globe we sweep into the younger day:
Better fifty years of Europe than a cycle of Cathay.°

Mother-Age (for mine I knew not) help me as when life begun:
Rift the hills, and roll the waters, flash the lightnings, weigh
    the Sun.

O, I see the crescent promise of my spirit hath not set.
Ancient founts of inspiration well thro' all my fancy yet.

Howsoever these things be, a long farewell to Locksley Hall!
Now for me the woods may wither, now for me the roof-tree fall.   [190]

Comes a vapour from the margin, blackening over heath and holt,
Cramming all the blast before it, in its breast a thunderbolt.

Let it fall on Locksley Hall, with rain or hail, or fire or snow;
For the mighty wind arises, roaring seaward, and I go.

The Vision of Sin

I

I had a vision when the night was late:
A youth came riding toward a palace-gate.
He rode a horse with wings, that would have flown,°
But that his heavy rider kept him down.
And from the palace came a child of sin,

And took him by the curls, and led him in,
Where sat a company with heated eyes,
Expecting when a fountain should arise:
A sleepy light upon their brows and lips—
As when the sun, a crescent of eclipse,   [10]
Dreams over lake and lawn, and isles and capes—
Suffused them, sitting, lying, languid shapes,
By heaps of gourds, and skins of wine, and piles of grapes.

II

Then methought I heard a mellow sound,
Gathering up from all the lower ground;
Narrowing in to where they sat assembled
Low voluptuous music winding trembled,
Wov'n in circles: they that heard it sigh'd,
Panted hand-in-hand with faces pale,
Swung themselves, and in low tones replied;   [20]
Till the fountain spouted, showering wide
Sleet of diamond-drift and pearly hail;
Then the music touch'd the gates and died;
Rose again from where it seem'd to fail,
Storm'd in orbs of song, a growing gale;
Till thronging in and in, to where they waited,
As 'twere a hundred-throated nightingale,
The strong tempestuous treble throbb'd and palpitated;
Ran into its giddiest whirl of sound,
Caught the sparkles, and in circles,   [30]
Purple gauzes, golden hazes, liquid mazes,
Flung the torrent rainbow round:
Then they started from their places,
Moved with violence, changed in hue,
Caught each other with wild grimaces,
Half-invisible to the view,
Wheeling with precipitate paces
To the melody, till they flew,
Hair, and eyes, and limbs, and faces,
Twisted hard in fierce embraces,   [40]
Like to Furies, like to Graces,°
Dash'd together in blinding dew:
Till, kill'd with some luxurious agony,

The nerve–dissolving melody
Flutter'd headlong from the sky.

III

And then I look'd up toward a mountain-tract,
That girt the region with high cliff and lawn:
I saw that every morning, far withdrawn
Beyond the darkness and the cataract,
God made Himself an awful rose of dawn,   [50]
Unheeded: and detaching, fold by fold,
From those still heights, and, slowly drawing near,
A vapour heavy, hueless, formless, cold,
Came floating on for many a month and year,
Unheeded: and I thought I would have spoken,
And warn'd that madman ere it grew too late:
But, as in dreams, I could not. Mine was broken,
When that cold vapour touch'd the palace gate,
And link'd again. I saw within my head
A gray and gap-tooth'd man as lean as death,   [60]
Who slowly rode across a wither'd heath,
And lighted at a ruin'd inn, and said:

IV

'Wrinkled ostler, grim and thin!°
    Here is custom come your way;
Take my brute, and lead him in,
    Stuff his ribs with mouldy hay.

'Bitter barmaid, waning fast!
    See that sheets are on my bed;
What! the flower of life is past:
    It is long before you wed.   [70]

'Slip-shod waiter, lank and sour,
    At the Dragon on the heath!
Let us have a quiet hour,
    Let us hob-and-nob with Death.

'I am old, but let me drink;
    Bring me spices, bring me wine;
I remember, when I think,
    That my youth was half divine.

'Wine is good for shrivell'd lips,
  When a blanket wraps the day,   [80]
When the rotten woodland drips,
  And the leaf is stamp'd in clay.

'Sit thee down, and have no shame,
  Cheek by jowl, and knee by knee:
What care I for any name?
  What for order or degree?

'Let me screw thee up a peg:
  Let me loose thy tongue with wine:
Callest thou that thing a leg?
  Which is thinnest? thine or mine?   [90]

'Thou shalt not be saved by works:°
  Thou hast been a sinner too:
Ruin'd trunks on wither'd forks,°
  Empty scarecrows, I and you!

'Fill the cup, and fill the can:
  Have a rouse before the morn:
Every moment dies a man,
  Every moment one is born.

'We are men of ruin'd blood;
  Therefore comes it we are wise.   [100]
Fish are we that love the mud,
  Rising to no fancy-flies.

'Name and fame! to fly sublime
  Thro' the courts, the camps, the schools,
Is to be the ball of Time,
  Bandied by the hands of fools.

'Friendship!—to be two in one—
  Let the canting liar pack!
Well I know, when I am gone,
  How she mouths behind my back.   [110]

'Virtue!—to be good and just—
  Every heart, when sifted well,
Is a clot of warmer dust,
  Mix'd with cunning sparks of hell.

'O! we two as well can look
   Whited thought and cleanly life
As the priest, above his book
   Leering at his neighbour's wife.

'Fill the cup, and fill the can:
   Have a rouse before the morn: [120]
Every moment dies a man,
   Every moment one is born.

'Drink, and let the parties rave:
   They are fill'd with idle spleen;
Rising, falling, like a wave,
   For they know not what they mean.

'He that roars for liberty
   Faster binds a tyrant's power;
And the tyrant's cruel glee
   Forces on the freer hour.   [130]

'Fill the can, and fill the cup:
   All the windy ways of men
Are but dust that rises up,
   And is lightly laid again.

'Greet her with applausive breath,
   Freedom, gaily doth she tread;°
In her right a civic wreath,
   In her left a human head.

'No, I love not what is new;
   She is of an ancient house: [140]
And I think we know the hue
   Of that cap upon her brows.

'Let her go! her thirst she slakes
   Where the bloody conduit runs,
Then her sweetest meal she makes
   On the first-born of her sons.

'Drink to lofty hopes that cool—
   Visions of a perfect State:
Drink we, last, the public fool,
   Frantic love and frantic hate.   [150]

'Chant me now some wicked stave,
    Till thy drooping courage rise,
And the glow-worm of the grave
    Glimmer in thy rheumy eyes.

'Fear not thou to loose thy tongue;
    Set thy hoary fancies free;
What is loathsome to the young
    Savours well to thee and me.

'Change, reverting to the years,
    When thy nerves could understand   [160]
What there is in loving tears,
    And the warmth of hand in hand.

'Tell me tales of thy first love—
    April hopes, the fools of chance;
Till the graves begin to move,
    And the dead begin to dance.

'Fill the can, and fill the cup:
    All the windy ways of men
Are but dust that rises up,
    And is lightly laid again.   [170]

'Trooping from their mouldy dens
    The chap-fallen circle spreads:
Welcome, fellow-citizens,
    Hollow hearts and empty heads!

'You are bones, and what of that?
    Every face, however full,
Padded round with flesh and fat,
    Is but modell'd on a skull.

'Death is king, and Vivat Rex!°
    Tread a measure on the stones,   [180]
Madam—if I know your sex,
    From the fashion of your bones.

'No, I cannot praise the fire
    In your eye—nor yet your lip:
All the more do I admire
    Joints of cunning workmanship.

'Lo! God's likeness—the ground-plan—
    Neither modell'd, glazed, nor framed:
Buss me, thou rough sketch of man,°
    Far too naked to be shamed!   [190]

'Drink to Fortune, drink to Chance,
    While we keep a little breath!
Drink to heavy Ignorance!
    Hob-and-nob with brother Death!

'Thou art mazed, the night is long,
    And the longer night is near:
What! I am not all as wrong
    As a bitter jest is dear.

'Youthful hopes, by scores, to all,
    When the locks are crisp and curl'd;   [200]
Unto me my maudlin gall
    And my mockeries of the world.

'Fill the cup, and fill the can:
    Mingle madness, mingle scorn!
Dregs of life, and lees of man:
    Yet we will not die forlorn.'

V

The voice grew faint: there came a further change:
Once more uprose the mystic mountain-range:
Below were men and horses pierced with worms,
And slowly quickening into lower forms;   [210]
By shards and scurf of salt, and scum of dross,°
Old plash of rains, and refuse patch'd with moss.
Then some one spake: 'Behold! it was a crime
Of sense avenged by sense that wore with time.'
Another said: 'The crime of sense became
The crime of malice, and is equal blame.'
And one: 'He had not wholly quench'd his power;
A little grain of conscience made him sour.'
At last I heard a voice upon the slope
Cry to the summit, 'Is there any hope?'   [220]
To which an answer peal'd from that high land,

But in a tongue no man could understand;
And on the glimmering limit far withdrawn
God made Himself an awful rose of dawn.

The Eagle

Fragment

He clasps the crag with crooked hands;
Close to the sun in lonely lands,
Ring'd with the azure world, he stands.

The wrinkled sea beneath him crawls;
He watches from his mountain walls,
And like a thunderbolt he falls.

THE PRINCESS (1847)

A Medley

Sir Walter Vivian all a summer's day
Gave his broad lawns until the set of sun
Up to the people: thither flock'd at noon
His tenants, wife and child, and thither half
The neighbouring borough with their Institute°
Of which he was the patron. I was there
From college, visiting the son,—the son
A Walter too,—with others of our set,
Five others: we were seven at Vivian-place.

And me that morning Walter show'd the house,   [10]
Greek, set with busts: from vases in the hall
Flowers of all heavens, and lovelier than their names,
Grew side by side; and on the pavement lay
Carved stones of the Abbey-ruin in the park,
Huge Ammonites, and the first bones of Time;°
And on the tables every clime and age
Jumbled together; celts and calumets,
Claymore and snowshoe, toys in lava, fans°
Of sandal, amber, ancient rosaries,°
Laborious orient ivory sphere in sphere,   [20]
The cursed Malayan crease, and battle-clubs°
From the isles of palm: and higher on the walls,
Betwixt the monstrous horns of elk and deer,
His own forefathers' arms and armour hung.

And 'this' he said 'was Hugh's at Agincourt;
And that was old Sir Ralph's at Ascalon:°
A good knight he! we keep a chronicle
With all about him'—which he brought, and I

Dived in a hoard of tales that dealt with knights,
Half–legend, half–historic, counts and kings   [30]
Who laid about them at their wills and died;
And mixt with these, a lady, one that arm'd°
Her own fair head, and sallying thro' the gate,
Had beat her foes with slaughter from her walls.

'O miracle of women,' said the book,
'O noble heart who, being strait–besieged
By this wild king to force her to his wish,
Nor bent, nor broke, nor shunn'd a soldier's death,
But now when all was lost or seem'd as lost—
Her stature more than mortal in the burst   [40]
Of sunrise, her arm lifted, eyes on fire—
Brake with a blast of trumpets from the gate,
And, falling on them like a thunderbolt,
She trampled some beneath her horses' heels,
And some were whelm'd with missiles of the wall,
And some were push'd with lances from the rock,
And part were drown'd within the whirling brook:
O miracle of noble womanhood!'

So sang the gallant glorious chronicle;
And, I all rapt in this, 'Come out,' he said,   [50]
'To the Abbey: there is Aunt Elizabeth
And sister Lilia with the rest.' We went
(I kept the book and had my finger in it)
Down thro' the park: strange was the sight to me;
For all the sloping pasture murmur'd, sown
With happy faces and with holiday.
There moved the multitude, a thousand heads:
The patient leaders of their Institute
Taught them with facts. One rear'd a font of stone
And drew, from butts of water on the slope,   [60]
The fountain of the moment, playing, now
A twisted snake, and now a rain of pearls,
Or steep–up spout whereon the gilded ball
Danced like a wisp: and somewhat lower down
A man with knobs and wires and vials fired
A cannon: Echo answer'd in her sleep
From hollow fields: and here were telescopes
For azure views; and there a group of girls

In circle waited, whom the electric shock
Dislink'd with shrieks and laughter: round the lake   [70]
A little clock-work steamer paddling plied
And shook the lilies: perch'd about the knolls
A dozen angry models jetted steam:
A petty railway ran: a fire-balloon
Rose gem-like up before the dusky groves
And dropt a fairy parachute and past:
And there thro' twenty posts of telegraph
They flash'd a saucy message to and fro
Between the mimic stations; so that sport°
Went hand in hand with Science; otherwhere   [80]
Pure sport: a herd of boys with clamour bowl'd
And stump'd the wicket; babies roll'd about°
Like tumbled fruit in grass; and men and maids
Arranged a country dance, and flew thro' light
And shadow, while the twangling violin
Struck up with Soldier-laddie, and overhead°
The broad ambrosial aisles of lofty lime
Made noise with bees and breeze from end to end.

Strange was the sight and smacking of the time;
And long we gazed, but satiated at length   [90]
Came to the ruins. High-arch'd and ivy-claspt,
Of finest Gothic lighter than a fire,
Thro' one wide chasm of time and frost they gave
The park, the crowd, the house; but all within
The sward was trim as any garden lawn:
And here we lit on Aunt Elizabeth,
And Lilia with the rest, and lady friends
From neighbour seats: and there was Ralph himself,
A broken statue propt against the wall,
As gay as any. Lilia, wild with sport,   [100]
Half child half woman as she was, had wound
A scarf of orange round the stony helm,
And robed the shoulders in a rosy silk,
That made the old warrior from his ivied nook
Glow like a sunbeam: near his tomb a feast
Shone, silver-set; about it lay the guests,
And there we join'd them: then the maiden Aunt
Took this fair day for text, and from it preach'd

An universal culture for the crowd,
And all things great; but we, unworthier, told   [110]
Of college: he had climb'd across the spikes,
And he had squeezed himself betwixt the bars,
And he had breathed the Proctor's dogs; and one°
Discuss'd his tutor, rough to common men,
But honeying at the whisper of a lord;
And one the Master, as a rogue in grain°
Veneer'd with sanctimonious theory.

But while they talk'd, above their heads I saw
The feudal warrior lady-clad; which brought
My book to mind: and opening this I read   [120]
Of old Sir Ralph a page or two that rang
With tilt and tourney; then the tale of her
That drove her foes with slaughter from her walls,
And much I praised her nobleness, and 'Where,'
Ask'd Walter, patting Lilia's head (she lay
Beside him) 'lives there such a woman now?'

Quick answer'd Lilia 'There are thousands now
Such women, but convention beats them down:
It is but bringing up; no more than that:
You men have done it: how I hate you all!   [130]
Ah, were I something great! I wish I were
Some mighty poetess, I would shame you then,
That love to keep us children! O I wish
That I were some great princess, I would build
Far off from men a college like a man's,
And I would teach them all that men are taught;
We are twice as quick!' And here she shook aside
The hand that play'd the patron with her curls.

And one said smiling 'Pretty were the sight
If our old halls could change their sex, and flaunt   [140]
With prudes for proctors, dowagers for deans,
And sweet girl-graduates in their golden hair.
I think they should not wear our rusty gowns,
But move as rich as Emperor-moths, or Ralph
Who shines so in the corner; yet I fear,
If there were many Lilias in the brood,
However deep you might embower the nest,
Some boy would spy it.'

At this upon the sward°
She tapt her tiny silken-sandal'd foot:
'That's your light way; but I would make it death   [150]
For any male thing but to peep at us.'

Petulant she spoke, and at herself she laugh'd;
A rosebud set with little wilful thorns,
And sweet as English air could make her, she:
But Walter hail'd a score of names upon her,
And 'petty Ogress,' and 'ungrateful Puss,'
And swore he long'd at college, only long'd,
All else was well, for she-society.
They boated and they cricketed; they talk'd
At wine, in clubs, of art, of politics;   [160]
They lost their weeks; they vext the souls of deans;
They rode; they betted; made a hundred friends,
And caught the blossom of the flying terms,
But miss'd the mignonette of Vivian-place,
The little hearth-flower Lilia. Thus he spoke,
Part banter, part affection.

'True,' she said,
'We doubt not that. O yes, you miss'd us much.
I'll stake my ruby ring upon it you did.'

She held it out; and as a parrot turns
Up thro' gilt wires a crafty loving eye,   [170]
And takes a lady's finger with all care,
And bites it for true heart and not for harm,
So he with Lilia's. Daintily she shriek'd
And wrung it. 'Doubt my word again!' he said.
'Come, listen! here is proof that you were miss'd:
We seven stay'd at Christmas up to read;
And there we took one tutor as to read:
The hard-grain'd Muses of the cube and square°
Were out of season: never man, I think,
So moulder'd in a sinecure as he: [180]
For while our cloisters echo'd frosty feet,
And our long walks were stript as bare as brooms,
We did but talk you over, pledge you all
In wassail; often, like as many girls—°
Sick for the hollies and the yews of home—
As many little trifling Lilias—play'd

Charades and riddles as at Christmas here,
And *what's my thought* and *when* and *where* and *how*,
And often told a tale from mouth to mouth
As here at Christmas.'
                  She remember'd that: [190]
A pleasant game, she thought: she liked it more
Than magic music, forfeits, all the rest.
But these—what kind of tales did men tell men,
She wonder'd, by themselves?
                  A half-disdain
Perch'd on the pouted blossom of her lips:
And Walter nodded at me; '*He* began,
The rest would follow, each in turn; and so
We forged a sevenfold story. Kind? what kind?
Chimeras, crotchets, Christmas solecisms,°
Seven-headed monsters only made to kill   [200]
Time by the fire in winter.'
                  'Kill him now,
The tyrant! kill him in the summer too,'
Said Lilia; 'Why not now?' the maiden Aunt.
'Why not a summer's as a winter's tale?°
A tale for summer as befits the time,
And something it should be to suit the place,
Heroic, for a hero lies beneath,
Grave, solemn!'
           Walter warp'd his mouth at this
To something so mock-solemn, that I laugh'd
And Lilia woke with sudden-shrilling mirth   [210]
An echo like a ghostly woodpecker,
Hid in the ruins; till the maiden Aunt
(A little sense of wrong had touch'd her face
With colour) turn'd to me with 'As you will;
Heroic if you will, or what you will,
Or be yourself your hero if you will.'

   'Take Lilia, then, for heroine' clamour'd he,
'And make her some great Princess, six feet high,
Grand, epic, homicidal; and be you
The Prince to win her!'
             'Then follow me, the Prince,'   [220]
I answer'd, 'each be hero in his turn!

Seven and yet one, like shadows in a dream.—
Heroic seems our Princess as required—
But something made to suit with Time and place,
A Gothic ruin and a Grecian house,
A talk of college and of ladies' rights,
A feudal knight in silken masquerade,
And, yonder, shrieks and strange experiments
For which the good Sir Ralph had burnt them all—
This *were* a medley! we should have him back   [230]
Who told the "Winter's tale" to do it for us.
No matter: we will say whatever comes.
And let the ladies sing us, if they will,
From time to time, some ballad or a song
To give us breathing-space.'
                                        So I began,
And the rest follow'd: and the women sang
Between the rougher voices of the men,
Like linnets in the pauses of the wind:
And here I give the story and the songs.

                                        I

A prince I was, blue-eyed, and fair in face,
Of temper amorous, as the first of May,
With lengths of yellow ringlet, like a girl,
For on my cradle shone the Northern star.

    There lived an ancient legend in our house.
Some sorcerer, whom a far-off grandsire burnt
Because he cast no shadow, had foretold,
Dying, that none of all our blood should know
The shadow from the substance, and that one
Should come to fight with shadows and to fall.   [10]
For so, my mother said, the story ran.
And, truly, waking dreams were, more or less,
An old and strange affection of the house.
Myself too had weird seizures, Heaven knows what:°
On a sudden in the midst of men and day,
And while I walk'd and talk'd as heretofore,
I seem'd to move among a world of ghosts,
And feel myself the shadow of a dream.

Our great court-Galen poised his gilt-head cane,°
And paw'd his beard, and mutter'd 'catalepsy.'   [20]
My mother pitying made a thousand prayers;
My mother was as mild as any saint,
Half-canonized by all that look'd on her,
So gracious was her tact and tenderness:
But my good father thought a king a king;
He cared not for the affection of the house;
He held his sceptre like a pedant's wand
To lash offence, and with long arms and hands
Reach'd out, and pick'd offenders from the mass
For judgment.
                         Now it chanced that I had been,   [30]
While life was yet in bud and blade, betroth'd
To one, a neighbouring Princess: she to me
Was proxy-wedded with a bootless calf°
At eight years old; and still from time to time
Came murmurs of her beauty from the South,
And of her brethren, youths of puissance;°
And still I wore her picture by my heart,
And one dark tress; and all around them both
Sweet thoughts would swarm as bees about their queen.

   But when the days drew nigh that I should wed,   [40]
My father sent ambassadors with furs
And jewels, gifts, to fetch her: these brought back
A present, a great labour of the loom;
And therewithal an answer vague as wind:
Besides, they saw the king; he took the gifts;
He said there was a compact; that was true:
But then she had a will; was he to blame?
And maiden fancies; loved to live alone
Among her women; certain, would not wed.

   That morning in the presence room I stood   [50]
With Cyril and with Florian, my two friends:
The first, a gentleman of broken means
(His father's fault) but given to starts and bursts
Of revel; and the last, my other heart,
And almost my half-self, for still we moved
Together, twinn'd as horse's ear and eye.

Now, while they spake, I saw my father's face
Grow long and troubled like a rising moon,
Inflamed with wrath: he started on his feet,
Tore the king's letter, snow'd it down, and rent   [60]
The wonder of the loom thro' warp and woof
From skirt to skirt; and at the last he sware
That he would send a hundred thousand men,
And bring her in a whirlwind: then he chew'd
The thrice-turn'd cud of wrath, and cook'd his spleen,°
Communing with his captains of the war.

At last I spoke. 'My father, let me go.
It cannot be but some gross error lies
In this report, this answer of a king,
Whom all men rate as kind and hospitable: [70]
Or, maybe, I myself, my bride once seen,
Whate'er my grief to find her less than fame,
May rue the bargain made.' And Florian said:
'I have a sister at the foreign court,
Who moves about the Princess; she, you know,
Who wedded with a nobleman from thence:
He, dying lately, left her, as I hear,
The lady of three castles in that land:
Thro' her this matter might be sifted clean.'
And Cyril whisper'd: 'Take me with you too.'   [80]
Then laughing 'what, if these weird seizures come
Upon you in those lands, and no one near
To point you out the shadow from the truth!
Take me: I'll serve you better in a strait;
I grate on rusty hinges here:' but 'No!'
Roar'd the rough king, 'you shall not; we ourself
Will crush her pretty maiden fancies dead
In iron gauntlets: break the council up.'

But when the council broke, I rose and past
Thro' the wild woods that hung about the town;   [90]
Found a still place, and pluck'd her likeness out;
Laid it on flowers, and watch'd it lying bathed
In the green gleam of dewy-tassell'd trees:
What were those fancies? wherefore break her troth?
Proud look'd the lips: but while I meditated
A wind arose and rush'd upon the South,

And shook the songs, the whispers, and the shrieks
Of the wild woods together; and a Voice
Went with it, 'Follow, follow, thou shalt win.'

Then, ere the silver sickle of that month°   [100]
Became her golden shield, I stole from court
With Cyril and with Florian, unperceived,
Cat-footed thro' the town and half in dread
To hear my father's clamour at our backs
With Ho! from some bay-window shake the night;
But all was quiet: from the bastion'd walls
Like threaded spiders, one by one, we dropt,
And flying reach'd the frontier: then we crost
To a livelier land; and so by tilth and grange,
And vines, and blowing bosks of wilderness,°   [110]
We gain'd the mother-city thick with towers,
And in the imperial palace found the king.

His name was Gama; crack'd and small his voice,
But bland the smile that like a wrinkling wind
On glassy water drove his cheek in lines;
A little dry old man, without a star,
Not like a king: three days he feasted us,
And on the fourth I spake of why we came,
And my betroth'd. 'You do us, Prince,' he said,
Airing a snowy hand and signet gem,   [120]
'All honour. We remember love ourselves
In our sweet youth: there did a compact pass
Long summers back, a kind of ceremony—
I think the year in which our olives fail'd.
I would you had her, Prince, with all my heart,
With my full heart: but there were widows here,
Two widows, Lady Psyche, Lady Blanche;
They fed her theories, in and out of place
Maintaining that with equal husbandry
The woman were an equal to the man.   [130]
They harp'd on this; with this our banquets rang;
Our dances broke and buzz'd in knots of talk;
Nothing but this; my very ears were hot
To hear them: knowledge, so my daughter held,
Was all in all: they had but been, she thought,
As children; they must lose the child, assume

The woman: then, Sir, awful odes she wrote,
Too awful, sure, for what they treated of,
But all she is and does is awful; odes
About this losing of the child; and rhymes   [140]
And dismal lyrics, prophesying change
Beyond all reason: these the women sang;
And they that know such things—I sought but peace;
No critic I—would call them masterpieces:
They master'd *me*. At last she begg'd a boon,
A certain summer-palace which I have
Hard by your father's frontier: I said no,
Yet being an easy man, gave it: and there,
All wild to found an University
For maidens, on the spur she fled; and more   [150]
We know not,—only this: they see no men,
Not ev'n her brother Arac, nor the twins
Her brethren, tho' they love her, look upon her
As on a kind of paragon; and I
(Pardon me saying it) were much loth to breed
Dispute betwixt myself and mine: but since
(And I confess with right) you think me bound
In some sort, I can give you letters to her;
And yet, to speak the truth, I rate your chance
Almost at naked nothing.'
                                  Thus the king;   [160]
And I, tho' nettled that he seem'd to slur
With garrulous ease and oily courtesies
Our formal compact, yet, not less (all frets
But chafing me on fire to find my bride)
Went forth again with both my friends. We rode
Many a long league back to the North. At last
From hills, that look'd across a land of hope,
We dropt with evening on a rustic town
Set in a gleaming river's crescent-curve,
Close at the boundary of the liberties;   [170]
There, enter'd an old hostel, call'd mine host
To council, plied him with his richest wines,
And show'd the late-writ letters of the king.

He with a long low sibilation, stared
As blank as death in marble; then exclaim'd

Averring it was clear against all rules
For any man to go: but as his brain
Began to mellow, 'If the king,' he said,
'Had given us letters, was he bound to speak?
The king would bear him out;' and at the last—   [180]
The summer of the vine in all his veins—
'No doubt that we might make it worth his while.
She once had past that way; he heard her speak;
She scared him; life! he never saw the like;
She look'd as grand as doomsday and as grave:
And he, he reverenced his liege-lady there;
He always made a point to post with mares;
His daughter and his housemaid were the boys:
The land, he understood, for miles about
Was till'd by women; all the swine were sows,   [190]
And all the dogs'—
                        But while he jested thus,
A thought flash'd thro' me which I clothed in act,
Remembering how we three presented Maid
Or Nymph, or Goddess, at high tide of feast,
In masque or pageant at my father's court.
We sent mine host to purchase female gear;
He brought it, and himself, a sight to shake
The midriff of despair with laughter, holp°
To lace us up, till, each, in maiden plumes
We rustled: him we gave a costly bribe   [200]
To guerdon silence, mounted our good steeds,°
And boldly ventured on the liberties.

We follow'd up the river as we rode,
And rode till midnight when the college lights
Began to glitter firefly-like in copse
And linden alley: then we past an arch,
Whereon a woman-statue rose with wings
From four wing'd horses dark against the stars;
And some inscription ran along the front,
But deep in shadow: further on we gain'd   [210]
A little street half garden and half house;
But scarce could hear each other speak for noise
Of clocks and chimes, like silver hammers falling
On silver anvils, and the splash and stir

Of fountains spouted up and showering down
In meshes of the jasmine and the rose:
And all about us peal'd the nightingale,
Rapt in her song, and careless of the snare.

There stood a bust of Pallas for a sign,°
By two sphere lamps blazon'd like Heaven and
        Earth   [220]
With constellation and with continent,
Above an entry: riding in, we call'd;
A plump–arm'd Ostleress and a stable wench°
Came running at the call, and help'd us down.
Then stept a buxom hostess forth, and sail'd,
Full-blown, before us into rooms which gave
Upon a pillar'd porch, the bases lost
In laurel: her we ask'd of that and this,
And who were tutors. 'Lady Blanche' she said,
'And Lady Psyche.' 'Which was prettiest,   [230]
Best-natured?' 'Lady Psyche.' 'Hers are we,'
One voice, we cried; and I sat down and wrote,
In such a hand as when a field of corn
Bows all its ears before the roaring East;

'Three ladies of the Northern empire pray
Your Highness would enroll them with your own,
As Lady Psyche's pupils.'

                                This I seal'd:
The seal was Cupid bent above a scroll,
And o'er his head Uranian Venus hung,°
And raised the blinding bandage from his eyes: [240]
I gave the letter to be sent with dawn;
And then to bed, where half in doze I seem'd
To float about a glimmering night, and watch
A full sea glazed with muffled moonlight, swell
On some dark shore just seen that it was rich.

        As thro' the land at eve we went,
            And pluck'd the ripen'd ears,
        We fell out, my wife and I,
        O we fell out I know not why,

And kiss'd again with tears.
And blessings on the falling out
    That all the more endears,
When we fall out with those we love
    And kiss again with tears!
For when we came where lies the child   [10]
    We lost in other years,
There above the little grave,
O there above the little grave,
    We kiss'd again with tears.

II

At break of day the College Portress came:
She brought us Academic silks, in hue
The lilac, with a silken hood to each,
And zoned with gold; and now when these were on,°
And we as rich as moths from dusk cocoons,
She, curtseying her obeisance, let us know
The Princess Ida waited: out we paced,
I first, and following thro' the porch that sang
All round with laurel, issued in a court
Compact of lucid marbles, boss'd with lengths   [10]
Of classic frieze, with ample awnings gay
Betwixt the pillars, and with great urns of flowers.
The Muses and the Graces, group'd in threes,
Enring'd a billowing fountain in the midst;
And here and there on lattice edges lay
Or book or lute; but hastily we past,
And up a flight of stairs into the hall.

    There at a board by tome and paper sat,
With two tame leopards couch'd beside her throne,
All beauty compass'd in a female form,   [20]
The Princess; liker to the inhabitant
Of some clear planet close upon the Sun,
Than our man's earth; such eyes were in her head,
And so much grace and power, breathing down
From over her arch'd brows, with every turn

Lived thro' her to the tips of her long hands,
And to her feet. She rose her height, and said:

'We give you welcome: not without redound
Of use and glory to yourselves ye come,
The first-fruits of the stranger: aftertime,   [30]
And that full voice which circles round the grave,
Will rank you nobly, mingled up with me.
What! are the ladies of your land so tall?'
'We of the court' said Cyril. 'From the court'
She answer'd, 'then ye know the Prince?' and he:
'The climax of his age! as tho' there were
One rose in all the world, your Highness that,
He worships your ideal:' she replied:
'We scarcely thought in our own hall to hear
This barren verbiage, current among men,   [40]
Light coin, the tinsel clink of compliment.
Your flight from out your bookless wilds would seem
As arguing love of knowledge and of power;
Your language proves you still the child. Indeed,
We dream not of him: when we set our hand
To this great work, we purposed with ourself
Never to wed. You likewise will do well,
Ladies, in entering here, to cast and fling
The tricks, which make us toys of men, that so,
Some future time, if so indeed you will,   [50]
You may with those self-styled our lords ally
Your fortunes, justlier balanced, scale with scale.'

At those high words, we conscious of ourselves,
Perused the matting; then an officer
Rose up, and read the statutes, such as these:
Not for three years to correspond with home;
Not for three years to cross the liberties;
Not for three years to speak with any men;
And many more, which hastily subscribed,
We enter'd on the boards: and 'Now,' she cried,   [60]
'Ye are green wood, see ye warp not. Look, our hall!
Our statues!—not of those that men desire,
Sleek Odalisques, or oracles of mode,°
Nor stunted squaws of West or East; but she

That taught the Sabine how to rule, and she°
The foundress of the Babylonian wall,
The Carian Artemisia strong in war,
The Rhodope, that built the pyramid,°
Clelia, Cornelia, with the Palmyrene
That fought Aurelian, and the Roman brows   [70]
Of Agrippina. Dwell with these, and lose°
Convention, since to look on noble forms
Makes noble thro' the sensuous organism
That which is higher. O lift your natures up:
Embrace our aims: work out your freedom. Girls,
Knowledge is now no more a fountain seal'd:
Drink deep, until the habits of the slave,
The sins of emptiness, gossip and spite
And slander, die. Better not be at all
Than not be noble. Leave us: you may go: [80]
To-day the Lady Psyche will harangue
The fresh arrivals of the week before;
For they press in from all the provinces,
And fill the hive.'
                      She spoke, and bowing waved
Dismissal: back again we crost the court
To Lady Psyche's: as we enter'd in,
There sat along the forms, like morning doves
That sun their milky bosoms on the thatch,
A patient range of pupils; she herself
Erect behind a desk of satin-wood,   [90]
A quick brunette, well-moulded, falcon-eyed,
And on the hither side, or so she look'd,
Of twenty summers. At her left, a child,
In shining draperies, headed like a star,°
Her maiden babe, a double April old,
Aglaïa slept. We sat: the Lady glanced:
Then Florian, but no livelier than the dame°
That whisper'd 'Asses' ears,' among the sedge,
'My sister.' 'Comely, too, by all that's fair,'
Said Cyril. 'O hush, hush!' and she began.   [100]

    'This world was once a fluid haze of light,
Till toward the centre set the starry tides,
And eddied into suns, that wheeling cast

The planets: then the monster, then the man;
Tattoo'd or woaded, winter-clad in skins,°
Raw from the prime, and crushing down his mate;
As yet we find in barbarous isles, and here
Among the lowest.'
                              Thereupon she took
A bird's-eye-view of all the ungracious past;
Glanced at the legendary Amazon°   [110]
As emblematic of a nobler age;
Appraised the Lycian custom, spoke of those
That lay at wine with Lar and Lucumo;°
Ran down the Persian, Grecian, Roman lines
Of empire, and the woman's state in each,
How far from just; till warming with her theme
She fulmined out her scorn of laws Salique
And little-footed China, touch'd on Mahomet°
With much contempt, and came to chivalry:
When some respect, however slight, was paid   [120]
To woman, superstition all awry:
However then commenced the dawn: a beam
Had slanted forward, falling in a land
Of promise; fruit would follow. Deep, indeed,
Their debt of thanks to her who first had dared
To leap the rotten pales of prejudice,
Disyoke their necks from custom, and assert
None lordlier than themselves but that which made
Woman and man. She had founded; they must build.
Here might they learn whatever men were taught: [130]
Let them not fear: some said their heads were less:
Some men's were small; not they the least of men;
For often fineness compensated size:
Besides the brain was like the hand, and grew
With using; thence the man's, if more was more;
He took advantage of his strength to be
First in the field: some ages had been lost;
But woman ripen'd earlier, and her life
Was longer; and albeit their glorious names
Were fewer, scatter'd stars, yet since in truth   [140]
The highest is the measure of the man,
And not the Kaffir, Hottentot, Malay,°
Nor those horn-handed breakers of the glebe,°

But Homer, Plato, Verulam; even so°
With woman: and in arts of government
Elizabeth and others; arts of war
The peasant Joan and others; arts of grace
Sappho and others vied with any man:°
And, last not least, she who had left her place,
And bow'd her state to them, that they might grow   [150]
To use and power on this Oasis, lapt
In the arms of leisure, sacred from the blight
Of ancient influence and scorn.
                          At last
She rose upon a wind of prophecy
Dilating on the future; 'everywhere
Two heads in council, two beside the hearth,
Two in the tangled business of the world,
Two in the liberal offices of life,
Two plummets dropt for one to sound the abyss
Of science, and the secrets of the mind: [160]
Musician, painter, sculptor, critic, more:
And everywhere the broad and bounteous Earth
Should bear a double growth of those rare souls,
Poets, whose thoughts enrich the blood of the world.'

    She ended here, and beckon'd us: the rest
Parted; and, glowing full-faced welcome, she
Began to address us, and was moving on
In gratulation, till as when a boat
Tacks, and the slacken'd sail flaps, all her voice°
Faltering and fluttering in her throat, she cried   [170]
'My brother!' 'Well, my sister.' 'O,' she said,
'What do you here? and in this dress? and these?
Why who are these? a wolf within the fold!
A pack of wolves! the Lord be gracious to me!
A plot, a plot, a plot, to ruin all!'
'No plot, no plot,' he answer'd. 'Wretched boy,
How saw you not the inscription on the gate,
LET NO MAN ENTER IN ON PAIN OF DEATH?'
'And if I had,' he answer'd, 'who could think
The softer Adams of your Academe,°   [180]
O sister, Sirens tho' they be, were such°
As chanted on the blanching bones of men?'

'But you will find it otherwise' she said.
'You jest: ill jesting with edge-tools! my vow
Binds me to speak, and O that iron will,
That axelike edge unturnable, our Head,
The Princess.' 'Well then, Psyche, take my life,
And nail me like a weasel on a grange
For warning: bury me beside the gate,
And cut this epitaph above my bones;   [190]
Here lies a brother by a sister slain,
All for the common good of womankind.'
'Let me die too,' said Cyril, 'having seen
And heard the Lady Psyche.'
                              I struck in:
'Albeit so mask'd, Madam, I love the truth;
Receive it; and in me behold the Prince
Your countryman, affianced years ago
To the Lady Ida: here, for here she was,
And thus (what other way was left) I came.'
'O Sir, O Prince, I have no country; none;   [200]
If any, this; but none. Whate'er I was
Disrooted, what I am is grafted here.
Affianced, Sir? love-whispers may not breathe
Within this vestal limit, and how should I,
Who am not mine, say, live: the thunderbolt
Hangs silent; but prepare: I speak; it falls.'
'Yet pause,' I said: 'for that inscription there,
I think no more of deadly lurks therein,
Than in a clapper clapping in a garth,°
To scare the fowl from fruit: if more there be,   [210]
If more and acted on, what follows? war;
Your own work marr'd: for this your Academe,
Whichever side be Victor, in the halloo
Will topple to the trumpet down, and pass
With all fair theories only made to gild
A stormless summer.' 'Let the Princess judge
Of that' she said: 'farewell, Sir—and to you.
I shudder at the sequel, but I go.'

   'Are you that Lady Psyche,' I rejoin'd,
'The fifth in line from that old Florian,   [220]
Yet hangs his portrait in my father's hall

(The gaunt old Baron with his beetle brow
Sun-shaded in the heat of dusty fights)
As he bestrode my Grandsire, when he fell,
And all else fled? we point to it, and we say,
The loyal warmth of Florian is not cold,
But branches current yet in kindred veins.'
'Are you that Psyche,' Florian added; 'she
With whom I sang about the morning hills,
Flung ball, flew kite, and raced the purple fly,   [230]
And snared the squirrel of the glen? are you
That Psyche, wont to bind my throbbing brow,
To smoothe my pillow, mix the foaming draught
Of fever, tell me pleasant tales, and read
My sickness down to happy dreams? are you
That brother-sister Psyche, both in one?
You were that Psyche, but what are you now?'
'You are that Psyche,' Cyril said, 'for whom
I would be that for ever which I seem,
Woman, if I might sit beside your feet,   [240]
And glean your scatter'd sapience.'
                                    Then once more,
'Are you that Lady Psyche,' I began,
'That on her bridal morn before she past
From all her old companions, when the king
Kiss'd her pale cheek, declared that ancient ties
Would still be dear beyond the southern hills;
That were there any of our people there
In want or peril, there was one to hear
And help them? look! for such are these and I.'
'Are you that Psyche,' Florian ask'd, 'to whom,   [250]
In gentler days, your arrow-wounded fawn
Came flying while you sat beside the well?
The creature laid his muzzle on your lap,
And sobb'd, and you sobb'd with it, and the blood
Was sprinkled on your kirtle, and you wept.
That was fawn's blood, not brother's, yet you wept.
O by the bright head of my little niece,
You were that Psyche, and what are you now?'
'You are that Psyche,' Cyril said again,
'The mother of the sweetest little maid,   [260]
That ever crow'd for kisses.'

'Out upon it!'
She answer'd, 'peace! and why should I not play
The Spartan Mother with emotion, be
The Lucius Junius Brutus of my kind?°
Him you call great: he for the common weal,
The fading politics of mortal Rome,
As I might slay this child, if good need were,
Slew both his sons: and I, shall I, on whom
The secular emancipation turns°
Of half this world, be swerved from right to save   [270]
A prince, a brother? a little will I yield.
Best so, perchance, for us, and well for you.
O hard, when love and duty clash! I fear
My conscience will not count me fleckless; yet—
Hear my conditions: promise (otherwise
You perish) as you came, to slip away
To–day, to–morrow, soon: it shall be said,
These women were too barbarous, would not learn;
They fled, who might have shamed us: promise, all.'

         What could we else, we promised each; and she,   [280]
Like some wild creature newly–caged, commenced
A to–and–fro, so pacing till she paused
By Florian; holding out her lily arms
Took both his hands, and smiling faintly said:
'I knew you at the first: tho' you have grown
You scarce have alter'd: I am sad and glad
To see you, Florian. *I* give thee to death
My brother! it was duty spoke, not I.
My needful seeming harshness, pardon it.
Our mother, is she well?'
                    With that she kiss'd   [290]
His forehead, then, a moment after, clung
About him, and betwixt them blossom'd up
From out a common vein of memory
Sweet household talk, and phrases of the hearth,
And far allusion, till the gracious dews
Began to glisten and to fall: and while
They stood, so rapt, we gazing, came a voice,
'I brought a message here from Lady Blanche.'
Back started she, and turning round we saw

The Lady Blanche's daughter where she stood,   [300]
Melissa, with her hand upon the lock,
A rosy blonde, and in a college gown,
That clad her like an April daffodilly
(Her mother's colour) with her lips apart,
And all her thoughts as fair within her eyes,
As bottom agates seen to wave and float°
In crystal currents of clear morning seas.

So stood that same fair creature at the door.
Then Lady Psyche, 'Ah—Melissa—you!
You heard us?' and Melissa, 'O pardon me   [310]
I heard, I could not help it, did not wish:
But, dearest Lady, pray you fear me not,
Nor think I bear that heart within my breast,
To give three gallant gentlemen to death.'
'I trust you,' said the other, 'for we two
Were always friends, none closer, elm and vine:
But yet your mother's jealous temperament—
Let not your prudence, dearest, drowse, or prove
The Danaïd of a leaky vase, for fear°
This whole foundation ruin, and I lose   [320]
My honour, these their lives.' 'Ah, fear me not'
Replied Melissa; 'no—I would not tell,
No, not for all Aspasia's cleverness,°
No, not to answer, Madam, all those hard things
That Sheba came to ask of Solomon.'°
'Be it so' the other, 'that we still may lead
The new light up, and culminate in peace,
For Solomon may come to Sheba yet.'
Said Cyril, 'Madam, he the wisest man
Feasted the woman wisest then, in halls   [330]
Of Lebanonian cedar: nor should you
(Tho', Madam, *you* should answer, *we* would ask)
Less welcome find among us, if you came
Among us, debtors for our lives to you,
Myself for something more.' He said not what,
But 'Thanks,' she answer'd 'Go: we have been too long
Together: keep your hoods about the face;

They do so that affect abstraction here.
Speak little; mix not with the rest; and hold
Your promise: all, I trust, may yet be well.'   [340]

We turn'd to go, but Cyril took the child,
And held her round the knees against his waist,
And blew the swoll'n cheek of a trumpeter,
While Psyche watch'd them, smiling, and the child
Push'd her flat hand against his face and laugh'd;
And thus our conference closed.
                                        And then we stroll'd
For half the day thro' stately theatres
Bench'd crescent-wise. In each we sat, we heard
The grave Professor. On the lecture slate
The circle rounded under female hands   [350]
With flawless demonstration: follow'd then
A classic lecture, rich in sentiment,
With scraps of thundrous Epic lilted out
By violet-hooded Doctors, elegies
And quoted odes, and jewels five-words-long
That on the stretch'd forefinger of all Time
Sparkle for ever: then we dipt in all
That treats of whatsoever is, the state,
The total chronicles of man, the mind,
The morals, something of the frame, the rock,   [360]
The star, the bird, the fish, the shell, the flower,
Electric, chemic laws, and all the rest,
And whatsoever can be taught and known;
Till like three horses that have broken fence,
And glutted all night long breast-deep in corn,
We issued gorged with knowledge, and I spoke:
'Why, Sirs, they do all this as well as we.'
'They hunt old trails' said Cyril 'very well;
But when did woman ever yet invent?'
'Ungracious!' answer'd Florian; 'have you learnt   [370]
No more from Psyche's lecture, you that talk'd
The trash that made me sick, and almost sad?'
'O trash' he said, 'but with a kernel in it.
Should I not call her wise, who made me wise?
And learnt? I learnt more from her in a flash,

Than if my brainpan were an empty hull,
And every Muse tumbled a science in.
A thousand hearts lie fallow in these halls,
And round these halls a thousand baby loves
Fly twanging headless arrows at the hearts,　　　　　[380]
Whence follows many a vacant pang; but O
With me, Sir, enter'd in the bigger boy,°
The Head of all the golden-shafted firm,
The long-limb'd lad that had a Psyche too;
He cleft me thro' the stomacher; and now
What think you of it, Florian? do I chase
The substance or the shadow? will it hold?
I have no sorcerer's malison on me,
No ghostly hauntings like his Highness. I
Flatter myself that always everywhere　　　　　　　[390]
I know the substance when I see it. Well,
Are castles shadows? Three of them? Is she
The sweet proprietress a shadow? If not,
Shall those three castles patch my tatter'd coat?
For dear are those three castles to my wants,
And dear is sister Psyche to my heart,
And two dear things are one of double worth,
And much I might have said, but that my zone
Unmann'd me: then the Doctors! O to hear
The Doctors! O to watch the thirsty plants　　　　　[400]
Imbibing! once or twice I thought to roar,
To break my chain, to shake my mane: but thou,
Modulate me, Soul of mincing mimicry!
Make liquid treble of that bassoon, my throat;
Abase those eyes that ever loved to meet
Star-sisters answering under crescent brows;
Abate the stride, which speaks of man, and loose
A flying charm of blushes o'er this cheek,
Where they like swallows coming out of time
Will wonder why they came: but hark the bell　　　　[410]
For dinner, let us go!'
　　　　　　　　　And in we stream'd
Among the columns, pacing staid and still
By twos and threes, till all from end to end
With beauties every shade of brown and fair
In colours gayer than the morning mist,

The long hall glitter'd like a bed of flowers.
How might a man not wander from his wits
Pierced thro' with eyes, but that I kept mine own
Intent on her, who rapt in glorious dreams,
The second-sight of some Astræan age,°   [420]
Sat compass'd with professors: they, the while,
Discuss'd a doubt and tost it to and fro:
A clamour thicken'd, mixt with inmost terms
Of art and science: Lady Blanche alone
Of faded form and haughtiest lineaments,
With all her autumn tresses falsely brown,
Shot sidelong daggers at us, a tiger-cat
In act to spring.

                    At last a solemn grace
Concluded, and we sought the gardens: there
One walk'd reciting by herself, and one   [430]
In this hand held a volume as to read,
And smoothed a petted peacock down with that:
Some to a low song oar'd a shallop by,°
Or under arches of the marble bridge
Hung, shadow'd from the heat: some hid and sought
In the orange thickets: others tost a ball
Above the fountain-jets, and back again
With laughter: others lay about the lawns,
Of the older sort, and murmur'd that their May
Was passing: what was learning unto them?   [440]
They wish'd to marry; they could rule a house;
Men hated learned women: but we three
Sat muffled like the Fates; and often came
Melissa hitting all we saw with shafts
Of gentle satire, kin to charity,
That harm'd not: then day droopt; the chapel bells
Call'd us: we left the walks; we mixt with those
Six hundred maidens clad in purest white,
Before two streams of light from wall to wall,
While the great organ almost burst his pipes,   [450]
Groaning for power, and rolling thro' the court
A long melodious thunder to the sound
Of solemn psalms, and silver litanies,
The work of Ida, to call down from Heaven
A blessing on her labours for the world.

Sweet and low, sweet and low,
     Wind of the western sea,
Low, low, breathe and blow,
     Wind of the western sea!
Over the rolling waters go,
Come from the dying moon, and blow,
     Blow him again to me;
While my little one, while my pretty one, sleeps.

Sleep and rest, sleep and rest,
     Father will come to thee soon;   [10]
Rest, rest, on mother's breast,
     Father will come to thee soon;
Father will come to his babe in the nest,
Silver sails all out of the west
     Under the silver moon:
Sleep, my little one, sleep, my pretty one, sleep.

III

Morn in the white wake of the morning star
Came furrowing all the orient into gold.
We rose, and each by other drest with care
Descended to the court that lay three parts
In shadow, but the Muses' heads were touch'd
Above the darkness from their native East.

     There while we stood beside the fount, and watch'd
Or seem'd to watch the dancing bubble, approach'd
Melissa, tinged with wan from lack of sleep,
Or grief, and glowing round her dewy eyes   [10]
The circled Iris of a night of tears;
'And fly,' she cried, 'O fly, while yet you may!
My mother knows:' and when I ask'd her 'how,'
'My fault' she wept 'my fault! and yet not mine;
Yet mine in part. O hear me, pardon me.
My mother, 'tis her wont from night to night
To rail at Lady Psyche and her side.
She says the Princess should have been the Head,
Herself and Lady Psyche the two arms;

And so it was agreed when first they came;   [20]
But Lady Psyche was the right hand now,
And she the left, or not, or seldom used;
Hers more than half the students, all the love.
And so last night she fell to canvass you:
Her countrywomen! she did not envy her.
"Who ever saw such wild barbarians?
Girls?—more like men!" and at these words the snake,
My secret, seem'd to stir within my breast;
And oh, Sirs, could I help it, but my cheek
Began to burn and burn, and her lynx eye   [30]
To fix and make me hotter, till she laugh'd:
"O marvellously modest maiden, you!
Men! girls, like men! why, if they had been men
You need not set your thoughts in rubric thus
For wholesale comment." Pardon, I am shamed
That I must needs repeat for my excuse
What looks so little graceful: "men" (for still
My mother went revolving on the word)
"And so they are,—very like men indeed—
And with that woman closeted for hours!"   [40]
Then came these dreadful words out one by one,
"Why—these—*are*—men:" I shudder'd: "and you
       know it."
"O ask me nothing," I said: "And she knows too,
And she conceals it." So my mother clutch'd
The truth at once, but with no word from me;
And now thus early risen she goes to inform
The Princess: Lady Psyche will be crush'd;
But you may yet be saved, and therefore fly:
But heal me with your pardon ere you go.'

'What pardon, sweet Melissa, for a blush?'   [50]
Said Cyril: 'Pale one, blush again: than wear
Those lilies, better blush our lives away.
Yet let us breathe for one hour more in Heaven'
He added, 'lest some classic Angel speak
In scorn of us, "They mounted, Ganymedes,
To tumble, Vulcans, on the second morn."°
But I will melt this marble into wax
To yield us farther furlough:' and he went.

    Melissa shook her doubtful curls, and thought
He scarce would prosper. 'Tell us,' Florian ask'd,   [60]
'How grew this feud betwixt the right and left.'
'O long ago,' she said, 'betwixt these two
Division smoulders hidden; 'tis my mother,
Too jealous, often fretful as the wind
Pent in a crevice: much I bear with her:
I never knew my father, but she says
(God help her) she was wedded to a fool;
And still she rail'd against the state of things.
She had the care of Lady Ida's youth,
And from the Queen's decease she brought her up.   [70]
But when your sister came she won the heart
Of Ida: they were still together, grew
(For so they said themselves) inosculated;°
Consonant chords that shiver to one note;
One mind in all things: yet my mother still
Affirms your Psyche thieved her theories,
And angled with them for her pupil's love:
She calls her plagiarist; I know not what:
But I must go: I dare not tarry,' and light,
As flies the shadow of a bird, she fled.   [80]

    Then murmur'd Florian gazing after her,
'An open-hearted maiden, true and pure.
If I could love, why this were she: how pretty
Her blushing was, and how she blush'd again,
As if to close with Cyril's random wish:
Not like your Princess cramm'd with erring pride,
Nor like poor Psyche whom she drags in tow.'

    'The crane,' I said, 'may chatter of the crane,
The dove may murmur of the dove, but I
An eagle clang an eagle to the sphere.   [90]
My princess, O my princess! true she errs,
But in her own grand way: being herself
Three times more noble than three score of men,
She sees herself in every woman else,
And so she wears her error like a crown
To blind the truth and me: for her, and her,
Hebes are they to hand ambrosia, mix°
The nectar; but—ah she—whene'er she moves

The Samian Herè rises and she speaks°
A Memnon smitten with the morning Sun.'°   [100]

    So saying from the court we paced, and gain'd
The terrace ranged along the Northern front,
And leaning there on those balusters, high
Above the empurpled champaign, drank the gale°
That blown about the foliage underneath,
And sated with the innumerable rose,
Beat balm upon our eyelids. Hither came
Cyril, and yawning 'O hard task,' he cried;
'No fighting shadows here! I forced a way
Thro' solid opposition crabb'd and gnarl'd.   [110]
Better to clear prime forests, heave and thump
A league of street in summer solstice down,
Than hammer at this reverend gentlewoman.
I knock'd and, bidden, enter'd; found her there
At point to move, and settled in her eyes
The green malignant light of coming storm.
Sir, I was courteous, every phrase well-oil'd,
As man's could be; yet maiden-meek I pray'd
Concealment: she demanded who we were,
And why we came? I fabled nothing fair,   [120]
But, your example pilot, told her all.
Up went the hush'd amaze of hand and eye.
But when I dwelt upon your old affiance,
She answer'd sharply that I talk'd astray.
I urged the fierce inscription on the gate,
And our three lives. True—we had limed ourselves°
With open eyes, and we must take the chance.
But such extremes, I told her, well might harm
The woman's cause. "Not more than now," she said,
"So puddled as it is with favouritism."   [130]
I tried the mother's heart. Shame might befall
Melissa, knowing, saying not she knew:
Her answer was "Leave me to deal with that."
I spoke of war to come and many deaths,
And she replied, her duty was to speak,
And duty duty, clear of consequences.
I grew discouraged, Sir; but since I knew
No rock so hard but that a little wave

May beat admission in a thousand years,
I recommenced; "Decide not ere you pause.   [140]
I find you here but in the second place,
Some say the third—the authentic foundress you.
I offer boldly: we will seat you highest:
Wink at our advent: help my prince to gain
His rightful bride, and here I promise you
Some palace in our land, where you shall reign
The head and heart of all our fair she-world,
And your great name flow on with broadening time
For ever." Well, she balanced this a little,
And told me she would answer us to-day,   [150]
Meantime be mute: thus much, nor more I gain'd.'

    He ceasing, came a message from the Head.
'That afternoon the Princess rode to take
The dip of certain strata to the North.°
Would we go with her? we should find the land
Worth seeing; and the river made a fall
Out yonder:' then she pointed on to where
A double hill ran up his furrowy forks
Beyond the thick-leaved platans of the vale.°

    Agreed to, this, the day fled on thro' all   [160]
Its range of duties to the appointed hour.
Then summon'd to the porch we went. She stood
Among her maidens, higher by the head,
Her back against a pillar, her foot on one
Of those tame leopards. Kittenlike he roll'd
And paw'd about her sandal. I drew near;
I gazed. On a sudden my strange seizure came
Upon me, the weird vision of our house:
The Princess Ida seem'd a hollow show,
Her gay-furr'd cats a painted fantasy,   [170]
Her college and her maidens, empty masks,
And I myself the shadow of a dream,
For all things were and were not. Yet I felt
My heart beat thick with passion and with awe;
Then from my breast the involuntary sigh
Brake, as she smote me with the light of eyes
That lent my knee desire to kneel, and shook
My pulses, till to horse we got, and so

Went forth in long retinue following up
The river as it narrow'd to the hills.   [180]

    I rode beside her and to me she said:
'O friend, we trust that you esteem'd us not
Too harsh to your companion yestermorn;
Unwillingly we spake.' 'No—not to her,'
I answer'd, 'but to one of whom we spake
Your Highness might have seem'd the thing you say.'
'Again?' she cried, 'are you ambassadresses
From him to me? we give you, being strange,
A license: speak, and let the topic die.'

    I stammer'd that I knew him—could have wish'd—   [190]
'Our king expects—was there no precontract?
There is no truer-hearted—ah, you seem
All he prefigured, and he could not see
The bird of passage flying south but long'd
To follow: surely, if your Highness keep
Your purport, you will shock him ev'n to death,
Or baser courses, children of despair.'

    'Poor boy,' she said, 'can he not read—no books?
Quoit, tennis, ball—no games? nor deals in that°
Which men delight in, martial exercise?   [200]
To nurse a blind ideal like a girl,
Methinks he seems no better than a girl;
As girls were once, as we ourself have been:
We had our dreams; perhaps he mixt with them:
We touch on our dead self, nor shun to do it,
Being other—since we learnt our meaning here,
To lift the woman's fall'n divinity
Upon an even pedestal with man.'

    She paused, and added with a haughtier smile
'And as to precontracts, we move, my friend,   [210]
At no man's beck, but know ourself and thee,
O Vashti, noble Vashti! Summon'd out°
She kept her state, and left the drunken king
To brawl at Shushan underneath the palms.'

    'Alas your Highness breathes full East,' I said,°
'On that which leans to you. I know the Prince,
I prize his truth: and then how vast a work

To assail this gray preëminence of man!
You grant me license; might I use it? think;
Ere half be done perchance your life may fail;   [220]
Then comes the feebler heiress of your plan,
And takes and ruins all; and thus your pains
May only make that footprint upon sand
Which old-recurring waves of prejudice
Resmooth to nothing: might I dread that you,
With only Fame for spouse and your great deeds
For issue, yet may live in vain, and miss,
Meanwhile, what every woman counts her due,
Love, children, happiness?'
                                        And she exclaim'd,
'Peace, you young savage of the Northern wild!   [230]
What! tho' your Prince's love were like a God's,
Have we not made ourself the sacrifice?
You are bold indeed: we are not talk'd to thus:
Yet will we say for children, would they grew
Like field-flowers everywhere! we like them well:
But children die; and let me tell you, girl,
Howe'er you babble, great deeds cannot die;
They with the sun and moon renew their light
For ever, blessing those that look on them.
Children—that men may pluck them from our hearts,   [240]
Kill us with pity, break us with ourselves—
O—children—there is nothing upon earth
More miserable than she that has a son
And sees him err: nor would we work for fame;
Tho' she perhaps might reap the applause of Great,
Who learns the one POU STO whence after-hands°
May move the world, tho' she herself effect
But little: wherefore up and act, nor shrink
For fear our solid aim be dissipated
By frail successors. Would, indeed, we had been,   [250]
In lieu of many mortal flies, a race
Of giants living, each, a thousand years,
That we might see our own work out, and watch
The sandy footprint harden into stone.'

    I answer'd nothing, doubtful in myself
If that strange Poet-princess with her grand

Imaginations might at all be won.
And she broke out interpreting my thoughts:

'No doubt we seem a kind of monster to you;
We are used to that: for women, up till this   [260]
Cramp'd under worse than South-sea-isle taboo,
Dwarfs of the gynæceum, fail so far°
In high desire, they know not, cannot guess
How much their welfare is a passion to us.
If we could give them surer, quicker proof—
Oh if our end were less achievable
By slow approaches, than by single act
Of immolation, any phase of death,
We were as prompt to spring against the pikes,
Or down the fiery gulf as talk of it,   [270]
To compass our dear sisters' liberties.'

She bow'd as if to veil a noble tear;
And up we came to where the river sloped
To plunge in cataract, shattering on black blocks
A breadth of thunder. O'er it shook the woods,
And danced the colour, and, below, stuck out
The bones of some vast bulk that lived and roar'd
Before man was. She gazed awhile and said,
'As these rude bones to us, are we to her
That will be.' 'Dare we dream of that,' I ask'd,   [280]
'Which wrought us, as the workman and his work,
That practice betters?' 'How,' she cried, 'you love
The metaphysics! read and earn our prize,
A golden brooch: beneath an emerald plane
Sits Diotima, teaching him that died°
Of hemlock; our device; wrought to the life;
She rapt upon her subject, he on her:
For there are schools for all.' 'And yet' I said
'Methinks I have not found among them all
One anatomic.' 'Nay, we thought of that,'°   [290]
She answer'd, 'but it pleased us not: in truth
We shudder but to dream our maids should ape
Those monstrous males that carve the living hound,
And cram him with the fragments of the grave,
Or in the dark dissolving human heart,
And holy secrets of this microcosm,

Dabbling a shameless hand with shameful jest,
Encarnalize their spirits: yet we know
Knowledge is knowledge, and this matter hangs:
Howbeit ourself, foreseeing casualty,   [300]
Nor willing men should come among us, learnt,
For many weary moons before we came,
This craft of healing. Were you sick, ourself
Would tend upon you. To your question now,
Which touches on the workman and his work.
Let there be light and there was light: 'tis so:
For was, and is, and will be, are but is;
And all creation is one act at once,
The birth of light: but we that are not all,
As parts, can see but parts, now this, now that,   [310]
And live, perforce, from thought to thought, and make
One act a phantom of succession: thus
Our weakness somehow shapes the shadow, Time;
But in the shadow will we work, and mould
The woman to the fuller day.'
                              She spake
With kindled eyes: we rode a league beyond,
And, o'er a bridge of pinewood crossing, came
On flowery levels underneath the crag,
Full of all beauty. 'O how sweet' I said
(For I was half-oblivious of my mask)   [320]
'To linger here with one that loved us.' 'Yea,'
She answer'd, 'or with fair philosophies
That lift the fancy; for indeed these fields
Are lovely, lovelier not the Elysian lawns,°
Where paced the Demigods of old, and saw
The soft white vapour streak the crowned towers
Built to the Sun:' then, turning to her maids,
'Pitch our pavilion here upon the sward;
Lay out the viands.' At the word, they raised
A tent of satin, elaborately wrought   [330]
With fair Corinna's triumph; here she stood,°
Engirt with many a florid maiden-cheek,
The woman-conqueror; woman-conquer'd there
The bearded Victor of ten-thousand hymns,
And all the men mourn'd at his side: but we
Set forth to climb; then, climbing, Cyril kept

With Psyche, with Melissa Florian, I
With mine affianced. Many a little hand
Glanced like a touch of sunshine on the rocks,
Many a light foot shone like a jewel set   [340]
In the dark crag: and then we turn'd, we wound
About the cliffs, the copses, out and in,
Hammering and clinking, chattering stony names
Of shale and hornblende, rag and trap and tuff,
Amygdaloid and trachyte, till the Sun°
Grew broader toward his death and fell, and all
The rosy heights came out above the lawns.

     The splendour falls on castle walls
          And snowy summits old in story:
     The long light shakes across the lakes,
          And the wild cataract leaps in glory.
     Blow, bugle, blow, set the wild echoes flying,
     Blow, bugle; answer, echoes, dying, dying, dying.

     O hark, O hear! how thin and clear,
          And thinner, clearer, farther going!
     O sweet and far from cliff and scar
          The horns of Elfland faintly blowing!   [10]
     Blow, let us hear the purple glens replying:
     Blow, bugle; answer, echoes, dying, dying, dying.

     O love, they die in yon rich sky,
          They faint on hill or field or river:
     Our echoes roll from soul to soul,
          And grow for ever and for ever.
     Blow, bugle, blow, set the wild echoes flying,
     And answer, echoes, answer, dying, dying, dying.

                    IV

'There sinks the nebulous star we call the Sun,
If that hypothesis of theirs be sound'°
Said Ida; 'let us down and rest;' and we

Down from the lean and wrinkled precipices,
By every coppice-feather'd chasm and cleft,
Dropt thro' the ambrosial gloom to where below
No bigger than a glow-worm shone the tent
Lamp-lit from the inner. Once she lean'd on me,
Descending; once or twice she lent her hand,
And blissful palpitations in the blood,   [10]
Stirring a sudden transport rose and fell.

But when we planted level feet, and dipt
Beneath the satin dome and enter'd in,°
There leaning deep in broider'd down we sank
Our elbows: on a tripod in the midst
A fragrant flame rose, and before us glow'd
Fruit, blossom, viand, amber wine, and gold.

Then she, 'Let some one sing to us: lightlier move
The minutes fledged with music:' and a maid,
Of those beside her, smote her harp, and sang.   [20]

'Tears, idle tears, I know not what they mean,
Tears from the depth of some divine despair
Rise in the heart, and gather to the eyes,
In looking on the happy Autumn-fields,
And thinking of the days that are no more.

'Fresh as the first beam glittering on a sail,
That brings our friends up from the underworld,
Sad as the last which reddens over one
That sinks with all we love below the verge;
So sad, so fresh, the days that are no more.   [30]

'Ah, sad and strange as in dark summer dawns
The earliest pipe of half-awaken'd birds
To dying ears, when unto dying eyes
The casement slowly grows a glimmering square;
So sad, so strange, the days that are no more.

'Dear as remember'd kisses after death,
And sweet as those by hopeless fancy feign'd
On lips that are for others; deep as love,
Deep as first love, and wild with all regret;
O Death in Life, the days that are no more.'   [40]

She ended with such passion that the tear,
She sang of, shook and fell, an erring pearl
Lost in her bosom: but with some disdain
Answer'd the Princess, 'If indeed there haunt
About the moulder'd lodges of the Past
So sweet a voice and vague, fatal to men,
Well needs it we should cram our ears with wool
And so pace by: but thine are fancies hatch'd
In silken-folded idleness; nor is it
Wiser to weep a true occasion lost,   [50]
But trim our sails, and let old bygones be,
While down the streams that float us each and all
To the issue, goes, like glittering bergs of ice,
Throne after throne, and molten on the waste
Becomes a cloud: for all things serve their time
Toward that great year of equal mights and rights,
Nor would I fight with iron laws, in the end
Found golden: let the past be past; let be
Their cancell'd Babels: tho' the rough kex break°
The starr'd mosaic, and the beard-blown goat   [60]
Hang on the shaft, and the wild figtree split
Their monstrous idols, care not while we hear
A trumpet in the distance pealing news
Of better, and Hope, a poising eagle, burns
Above the unrisen morrow:' then to me;
'Know you no song of your own land,' she said,
'Not such as moans about the retrospect,
But deals with the other distance and the hues
Of promise; not a death's-head at the wine.'

Then I remember'd one myself had made,   [70]
What time I watch'd the swallow winging south
From mine own land, part made long since, and part
Now while I sang, and maidenlike as far
As I could ape their treble, did I sing.

　　'O Swallow, Swallow, flying, flying South,
　　Fly to her, and fall upon her gilded eaves,
　　And tell her, tell her, what I tell to thee.

　　'O tell her, Swallow, thou that knowest each,
　　That bright and fierce and fickle is the South,
　　And dark and true and tender is the North.   [80]

    'O Swallow, Swallow, if I could follow, and light
Upon her lattice, I would pipe and trill,
And cheep and twitter twenty million loves.

    'O were I thou that she might take me in,
And lay me on her bosom, and her heart
Would rock the snowy cradle till I died.

    'Why lingereth she to clothe her heart with love,
Delaying as the tender ash delays
To clothe herself, when all the woods are green?

    'O tell her, Swallow, that thy brood is flown: [90]
Say to her, I do but wanton in the South,
But in the North long since my nest is made.

    'O tell her, brief is life but love is long,
And brief the sun of summer in the North,
And brief the moon of beauty in the South.

    'O Swallow, flying from the golden woods,
Fly to her, and pipe and woo her, and make her mine,
And tell her, tell her, that I follow thee.'

I ceased, and all the ladies, each at each,
Like the Ithacensian suitors in old time,°   [100]
Stared with great eyes, and laugh'd with alien lips,°
And knew not what they meant; for still my voice
Rang false: but smiling 'Not for thee,' she said,
'O Bulbul, any rose of Gulistan°
Shall burst her veil: marsh-divers, rather, maid,
Shall croak thee sister, or the meadow-crake°
Grate her harsh kindred in the grass: and this
A mere love-poem! O for such, my friend,
We hold them slight: they mind us of the time
When we made bricks in Egypt. Knaves are men,°   [110]
That lute and flute fantastic tenderness,
And dress the victim to the offering up,
And paint the gates of Hell with Paradise,
And play the slave to gain the tyranny.
Poor soul! I had a maid of honour once;
She wept her true eyes blind for such a one,
A rogue of canzonets and serenades.°
I loved her. Peace be with her. She is dead.
So they blaspheme the muse! But great is song

Used to great ends: ourself have often tried   [120]
Valkyrian hymns, or into rhythm have dash'd°
The passion of the prophetess; for song
Is duer unto freedom, force and growth
Of spirit than to junketing and love.
Love is it? Would this same mock-love, and this
Mock-Hymen were laid up like winter bats,°
Till all men grew to rate us at our worth,
Not vassals to be beat, nor pretty babes
To be dandled, no, but living wills, and sphered
Whole in ourselves and owed to none. Enough!   [130]
But now to leaven play with profit, you,
Know you no song, the true growth of your soil,
That gives the manners of your country-women?'

     She spoke and turn'd her sumptuous head with eyes
Of shining expectation fixt on mine.
Then while I dragg'd my brains for such a song,
Cyril, with whom the bell-mouth'd glass had wrought,
Or master'd by the sense of sport, began°
To troll a careless, careless tavern-catch
Of Moll and Meg, and strange experiences   [140]
Unmeet for ladies. Florian nodded at him,
I frowning; Psyche flush'd and wann'd and shook;
The lilylike Melissa droop'd her brows;
'Forbear,' the Princess cried; 'Forbear, Sir' I;
And heated thro' and thro' with wrath and love,
I smote him on the breast; he started up;
There rose a shriek as of a city sack'd;
Melissa clamour'd 'Flee the death;' 'To horse'
Said Ida; 'home! to horse!' and fled, as flies
A troop of snowy doves athwart the dusk,   [150]
When some one batters at the dovecote-doors,
Disorderly the women. Alone I stood
With Florian, cursing Cyril, vext at heart,
In the pavilion: there like parting hopes
I heard them passing from me: hoof by hoof,
And every hoof a knell to my desires,
Clang'd on the bridge; and then another shriek,
'The Head, the Head, the Princess, O the Head!'
For blind with rage she miss'd the plank, and roll'd

In the river. Out I sprang from glow to gloom: [160]
There whirl'd her white robe like a blossom'd branch
Rapt to the horrible fall: a glance I gave,
No more; but woman-vested as I was
Plunged; and the flood drew; yet I caught her; then
Oaring one arm, and bearing in my left
The weight of all the hopes of half the world,
Strove to buffet to land in vain. A tree
Was half-disrooted from his place and stoop'd
To drench his dark locks in the gurgling wave
Mid-channel. Right on this we drove and caught,   [170]
And grasping down the boughs I gain'd the shore.

    There stood her maidens glimmeringly group'd
In the hollow bank. One reaching forward drew
My burthen from mine arms; they cried 'she lives:'
They bore her back into the tent: but I,
So much a kind of shame within me wrought,
Not yet endured to meet her opening eyes,
Nor found my friends; but push'd alone on foot
(For since her horse was lost I left her mine)
Across the woods, and less from Indian craft   [180]
Than beelike instinct hiveward, found at length
The garden portals. Two great statues, Art
And Science, Caryatids, lifted up°
A weight of emblem, and betwixt were valves°
Of open-work in which the hunter rued
His rash intrusion, manlike, but his brows
Had sprouted, and the branches thereupon
Spread out at top, and grimly spiked the gates.

    A little space was left between the horns,
Thro' which I clamber'd o'er at top with pain,   [190]
Dropt on the sward, and up the linden walks,
And, tost on thoughts that changed from hue to hue,
Now poring on the glowworm, now the star,
I paced the terrace, till the Bear had wheel'd°
Thro' a great arc his seven slow suns.
                             A step
Of lightest echo, then a loftier form
Than female, moving thro' the uncertain gloom,
Disturb'd me with the doubt 'if this were she,'

But it was Florian. 'Hist O Hist,' he said,
'They seek us: out so late is out of rules.   [200]
Moreover "seize the strangers" is the cry.
How came you here?' I told him: 'I' said he,
'Last of the train, a moral leper, I,
To whom none spake, half-sick at heart, return'd.
Arriving all confused among the rest
With hooded brows I crept into the hall,
And, couch'd behind a Judith, underneath°
The head of Holofernes peep'd and saw.
Girl after girl was call'd to trial: each
Disclaim'd all knowledge of us: last of all,   [210]
Melissa: trust me, Sir, I pitied her.
She, question'd if she knew us men, at first
Was silent; closer prest, denied it not:
And then, demanded if her mother knew,
Or Psyche, she affirm'd not, or denied:
From whence the Royal mind, familiar with her,
Easily gather'd either guilt. She sent
For Psyche, but she was not there; she call'd
For Psyche's child to cast it from the doors;
She sent for Blanche to accuse her face to face;   [220]
And I slipt out: but whither will you now?
And where are Psyche, Cyril? both are fled:
What, if together? that were not so well.
Would rather we had never come! I dread
His wildness, and the chances of the dark.'

'And yet,' I said, 'you wrong him more than I
That struck him: this is proper to the clown,
Tho' smock'd, or furr'd and purpled, still the clown,
To harm the thing that trusts him, and to shame
That which he says he loves: for Cyril, howe'er   [230]
He deal in frolic, as to-night—the song
Might have been worse and sinn'd in grosser lips
Beyond all pardon—as it is, I hold
These flashes on the surface are not he.
He has a solid base of temperament:
But as the waterlily starts and slides
Upon the level in little puffs of wind,
Tho' anchor'd to the bottom, such is he.'

Scarce had I ceased when from a tamarisk near
Two Proctors leapt upon us, crying, 'Names:'   [240]
He, standing still, was clutch'd; but I began
To thrid the musky-circled mazes, wind
And double in and out the boles, and race°
By all the fountains: fleet I was of foot:
Before me shower'd the rose in flakes; behind
I heard the puff'd pursuer; at mine ear
Bubbled the nightingale and heeded not,
And secret laughter tickled all my soul.
At last I hook'd my ankle in a vine,
That claspt the feet of a Mnemosyne,   [250]
And falling on my face was caught and known.

They haled us to the Princess where she sat
High in the hall: above her droop'd a lamp,
And made the single jewel on her brow
Burn like the mystic fire on a mast-head,°
Prophet of storm: a handmaid on each side
Bow'd toward her, combing out her long black hair
Damp from the river; and close behind her stood
Eight daughters of the plough, stronger than men,
Huge women blowzed with health, and wind, and
          rain,°   [260]
And labour. Each was like a Druid rock;°
Or like a spire of land that stands apart
Cleft from the main, and wail'd about with mews.

Then, as we came, the crowd dividing clove
An advent to the throne: and there beside,
Half-naked as if caught at once from bed
And tumbled on the purple footcloth, lay
The lily-shining child; and on the left,
Bow'd on her palms and folded up from wrong,
Her round white shoulder shaken with her sobs,   [270]
Melissa knelt; but Lady Blanche erect
Stood up and spake, an affluent orator.

'It was not thus, O Princess, in old days:
You prized my counsel, lived upon my lips:
I led you then to all the Castalies;°
I fed you with the milk of every Muse;

I loved you like this kneeler, and you me
Your second mother: those were gracious times.
Then came your new friend: you began to change—
I saw it and grieved—to slacken and to cool;   [280]
Till taken with her seeming openness
You turn'd your warmer currents all to her,
To me you froze: this was my meed for all.
Yet I bore up in part from ancient love,
And partly that I hoped to win you back,
And partly conscious of my own deserts,
And partly that you were my civil head,
And chiefly you were born for something great,
In which I might your fellow-worker be,
When time should serve; and thus a noble scheme   [290]
Grew up from seed we two long since had sown;
In us true growth, in her a Jonah's gourd,°
Up in one night and due to sudden sun:
We took this palace; but even from the first
You stood in your own light and darken'd mine.
What student came but that you planed her path
To Lady Psyche, younger, not so wise,
A foreigner, and I your countrywoman,
I your old friend and tried, she new in all?
But still her lists were swell'd and mine were lean;   [300]
Yet I bore up in hope she would be known:
Then came these wolves: *they* knew her: *they* endured,
Long-closeted with her the yestermorn,
To tell her what they were, and she to hear:
And me none told: not less to an eye like mine
A lidless watcher of the public weal,°
Last night, their mask was patent, and my foot
Was to you: but I thought again: I fear'd
To meet a cold "We thank you, we shall hear of it
From Lady Psyche:" you had gone to her,   [310]
She told, perforce; and winning easy grace,
No doubt, for slight delay, remain'd among us
In our young nursery still unknown, the stem
Less grain than touchwood, while my honest heat°
Were all miscounted as malignant haste
To push my rival out of place and power.
But public use required she should be known;

And since my oath was ta'en for public use,
I broke the letter of it to keep the sense.
I spoke not then at first, but watch'd them well,   [320]
Saw that they kept apart, no mischief done;
And yet this day (tho' you should hate me for it)
I came to tell you; found that you had gone,
Ridd'n to the hills, she likewise: now, I thought,
That surely she will speak; if not, then I:
Did she? These monsters blazon'd what they were,
According to the coarseness of their kind,
For thus I hear; and known at last (my work)
And full of cowardice and guilty shame,
I grant in her some sense of shame, she flies;   [330]
And I remain on whom to wreak your rage,
I, that have lent my life to build up yours,
I that have wasted here health, wealth, and time,
And talent, I—you know it—I will not boast:
Dismiss me, and I prophesy your plan,
Divorced from my experience, will be chaff
For every gust of chance, and men will say
We did not know the real light, but chased
The wisp that flickers where no foot can tread.'

    She ceased: the Princess answer'd coldly, 'Good: [340]
Your oath is broken: we dismiss you: go.
For this lost lamb (she pointed to the child)
Our mind is changed: we take it to ourself.'

    Thereat the Lady stretch'd a vulture throat,
And shot from crooked lips a haggard smile.
'The plan was mine. I built the nest' she said
'To hatch the cuckoo. Rise!' and stoop'd to updrag
Melissa: she, half on her mother propt,
Half-drooping from her, turn'd her face, and cast
A liquid look on Ida, full of prayer,   [350]
Which melted Florian's fancy as she hung,
A Niobëan daughter, one arm out,°
Appealing to the bolts of Heaven; and while
We gazed upon her came a little stir
About the doors, and on a sudden rush'd
Among us, out of breath, as one pursued,
A woman-post in flying raiment. Fear

Stared in her eyes, and chalk'd her face, and wing'd
Her transit to the throne, whereby she fell
Delivering seal'd dispatches which the Head   [360]
Took half-amazed, and in her lion's mood
Tore open, silent we with blind surmise
Regarding, while she read, till over brow
And cheek and bosom brake the wrathful bloom
As of some fire against a stormy cloud,
When the wild peasant rights himself, the rick
Flames, and his anger reddens in the heavens;
For anger most it seem'd, while now her breast,
Beaten with some great passion at her heart,
Palpitated, her hand shook, and we heard   [370]
In the dead hush the papers that she held
Rustle: at once the lost lamb at her feet
Sent out a bitter bleating for its dam;
The plaintive cry jarr'd on her ire; she crush'd
The scrolls together, made a sudden turn
As if to speak, but, utterance failing her,
She whirl'd them on to me, as who should say
'Read,' and I read—two letters—one her sire's.

'Fair daughter, when we sent the Prince your way
We knew not your ungracious laws, which learnt,   [380]
We, conscious of what temper you are built,
Came all in haste to hinder wrong, but fell
Into his father's hands, who has this night,
You lying close upon his territory,
Slipt round and in the dark invested you,
And here he keeps me hostage for his son.'

The second was my father's running thus:
'You have our son: touch not a hair of his head:
Render him up unscathed: give him your hand:
Cleave to your contract: tho' indeed we hear   [390]
You hold the woman is the better man;
A rampant heresy, such as if it spread
Would make all women kick against their Lords
Thro' all the world, and which might well deserve
That we this night should pluck your palace down;
And we will do it, unless you send us back
Our son, on the instant, whole.'

                                    So far I read;
And then stood up and spoke impetuously.

'O not to pry and peer on your reserve,
But led by golden wishes, and a hope   [400]
The child of regal compact, did I break
Your precinct; not a scorner of your sex
But venerator, zealous it should be
All that it might be: hear me, for I bear,
Tho' man, yet human, whatsoe'er your wrongs,
From the flaxen curl to the gray lock a life
Less mine than yours: my nurse would tell me of you;
I babbled for you, as babies for the moon,
Vague brightness; when a boy, you stoop'd to me
From all high places, lived in all fair lights,   [410]
Came in long breezes rapt from inmost south
And blown to inmost north; at eve and dawn
With Ida, Ida, Ida, rang the woods;
The leader wildswan in among the stars
Would clang it, and lapt in wreaths of glowworm light
The mellow breaker murmur'd Ida. Now,
Because I would have reach'd you, had you been
Sphered up with Cassiopëia, or the enthroned
Persephonè in Hades, now at length,°
Those winters of abeyance all worn out,   [420]
A man I came to see you: but, indeed,
Not in this frequence can I lend full tongue,
O noble Ida, to those thoughts that wait
On you, their centre: let me say but this,
That many a famous man and woman, town
And landskip, have I heard of, after seen
The dwarfs of presage: tho' when known, there grew°
Another kind of beauty in detail
Made them worth knowing; but in you I found
My boyish dream involved and dazzled down   [430]
And master'd, while that after-beauty makes
Such head from act to act, from hour to hour,
Within me, that except you slay me here,
According to your bitter statute-book,
I cannot cease to follow you, as they say
The seal does music; who desire you more

Than growing boys their manhood; dying lips,
With many thousand matters left to do,
The breath of life; O more than poor men wealth,
Than sick men health—yours, yours, not
      mine—but half   [440]
Without you; with you, whole; and of those halves
You worthiest; and howe'er you block and bar
Your heart with system out from mine, I hold
That it becomes no man to nurse despair,
But in the teeth of clench'd antagonisms
To follow up the worthiest till he die:
Yet that I came not all unauthorized
Behold your father's letter.'
                On one knee
Kneeling, I gave it, which she caught, and dash'd
Unopen'd at her feet: a tide of fierce   [450]
Invective seem'd to wait behind her lips,
As waits a river level with the dam
Ready to burst and flood the world with foam:
And so she would have spoken, but there rose
A hubbub in the court of half the maids
Gather'd together: from the illumined hall
Long lanes of splendour slanted o'er a press
Of snowy shoulders, thick as herded ewes,
And rainbow robes, and gems and gemlike eyes,
And gold and golden heads; they to and fro   [460]
Fluctuated, as flowers in storm, some red, some pale,
All open-mouth'd, all gazing to the light,
Some crying there was an army in the land,
And some that men were in the very walls,
And some they cared not; till a clamour grew
As of a new-world Babel, woman-built,
And worse-confounded: high above them stood
The placid marble Muses, looking peace.

    Not peace she look'd, the Head: but rising up
Robed in the long night of her deep hair, so   [470]
To the open window moved, remaining there
Fixt like a beacon-tower above the waves
Of tempest, when the crimson-rolling eye
Glares ruin, and the wild birds on the light

Dash themselves dead. She stretch'd her arms and
    call'd
Across the tumult and the tumult fell.

   'What fear ye, brawlers? am not I your head?
On me, me, me, the storm first breaks: *I* dare
All these male thunderbolts: what is it ye fear?
Peace! there are those to avenge us and they come: [480]
If not,—myself were like enough, O girls,
To unfurl the maiden banner of our rights,
And clad in iron burst the ranks of war,
Or, falling, protomartyr of our cause,°
Die: yet I blame you not so much for fear;
Six thousand years of fear have made you that
From which I would redeem you: but for those
That stir this hubbub—you and you—I know
Your faces there in the crowd—to-morrow morn
We hold a great convention: then shall they   [490]
That love their voices more than duty, learn
With whom they deal, dismiss'd in shame to live
No wiser than their mothers, household stuff,
Live chattels, mincers of each other's fame,
Full of weak poison, turnspits for the clown,
The drunkard's football, laughing-stocks of Time,
Whose brains are in their hands and in their heels,
But fit to flaunt, to dress, to dance, to thrum,
To tramp, to scream, to burnish, and to scour,
For ever slaves at home and fools abroad.'   [500]

   She, ending, waved her hands: thereat the crowd
Muttering, dissolved: then with a smile, that look'd
A stroke of cruel sunshine on the cliff,
When all the glens are drown'd in azure gloom
Of thunder-shower, she floated to us and said:

   'You have done well and like a gentleman,
And like a prince: you have our thanks for all:
And you look well too in your woman's dress:
Well have you done and like a gentleman.
You saved our life: we owe you bitter thanks: [510]
Better have died and spilt our bones in the flood—

Then men had said—but now—What hinders me
To take such bloody vengeance on you both?—
Yet since our father—Wasps in our good hive,
You would-be quenchers of the light to be,
Barbarians, grosser than your native bears—
O would I had his sceptre for one hour!
You that have dared to break our bound, and gull'd
Our servants, wrong'd and lied and thwarted us—
I wed with thee! *I* bound by precontract   [520]
Your bride, your bondslave! not tho' all the gold
That veins the world were pack'd to make your crown,
And every spoken tongue should lord you. Sir,
Your falsehood and yourself are hateful to us:
I trample on your offers and on you:
Begone: we will not look upon you more.
Here, push them out at gates.'

                    In wrath she spake.
Then those eight mighty daughters of the plough
Bent their broad faces toward us and address'd
Their motion: twice I sought to plead my cause,   [530]
But on my shoulder hung their heavy hands,
The weight of destiny: so from her face
They push'd us, down the steps, and thro' the court,
And with grim laughter thrust us out at gates.

    We cross'd the street and gain'd a petty mound
Beyond it, whence we saw the lights and heard
The voices murmuring. While I listen'd, came
On a sudden the weird seizure and the doubt:
I seem'd to move among a world of ghosts;
The Princess with her monstrous woman-guard,   [540]
The jest and earnest working side by side,
The cataract and the tumult and the kings
Were shadows; and the long fantastic night
With all its doings had and had not been,
And all things were and were not.

                   This went by
As strangely as it came, and on my spirits
Settled a gentle cloud of melancholy;
Not long; I shook it off; for spite of doubts
And sudden ghostly shadowings I was one

To whom the touch of all mischance but came   [550]
As night to him that sitting on a hill
Sees the midsummer, midnight, Norway sun
Set into sunrise; then we moved away.

  Thy voice is heard thro' rolling drums,
   That beat to battle where he stands;
  Thy face across his fancy comes,
   And gives the battle to his hands:
  A moment, while the trumpets blow,
   He sees his brood about thy knee;
  The next, like fire he meets the foe,
   And strikes him dead for thine and thee.

So Lilia sang: we thought her half-possess'd,
She struck such warbling fury thro' the words;   [10]
And, after, feigning pique at what she call'd
The raillery, or grotesque, or false sublime—
Like one that wishes at a dance to change
The music—clapt her hands and cried for war,
Or some grand fight to kill and make an end:
And he that next inherited the tale
Half turning to the broken statue, said,
'Sir Ralph has got your colours: if I prove
Your knight, and fight your battle, what for me?'
It chanced, her empty glove upon the tomb   [20]
Lay by her like a model of her hand.
She took it and she flung it. 'Fight' she said,
'And make us all we would be, great and good.'
He knightlike in his cap instead of casque,
A cap of Tyrol borrow'd from the hall,
Arranged the favour, and assumed the Prince.

        V

Now, scarce three paces measured from the mound,
We stumbled on a stationary voice,
And 'Stand, who goes?' 'Two from the palace' I.

'The second two: they wait,' he said, 'pass on;
His Highness wakes:' and one, that clash'd in arms,
By glimmering lanes and walls of canvas led
Threading the soldier-city, till we heard
The drowsy folds of our great ensign shake
From blazon'd lions o'er the imperial tent
Whispers of war.
             Entering, the sudden light   [10]
Dazed me half-blind: I stood and seem'd to hear,
As in a poplar grove when a light wind wakes
A lisping of the innumerous leaf and dies,
Each hissing in his neighbour's ear; and then
A strangled titter, out of which there brake
On all sides, clamouring etiquette to death,
Unmeasured mirth; while now the two old kings
Began to wag their baldness up and down,
The fresh young captains flash'd their glittering teeth,
The huge bush-bearded Barons heaved and blew,   [20]
And slain with laughter roll'd the gilded Squire.

   At length my Sire, his rough cheek wet with tears,
Panted from weary sides 'King, you are free!
We did but keep you surety for our son,
If this be he,—or a draggled mawkin, thou,°
That tends her bristled grunters in the sludge:'
For I was drench'd with ooze, and torn with briers,
More crumpled than a poppy from the sheath,
And all one rag, disprinced from head to heel.
Then some one sent beneath his vaulted palm   [30]
A whisper'd jest to some one near him, 'Look,
He has been among his shadows.' 'Satan take
The old women and their shadows! (thus the King
Roar'd) make yourself a man to fight with men.
Go: Cyril told us all.'
              As boys that slink
From ferule and the trespass-chiding eye,°
Away we stole, and transient in a trice°
From what was left of faded woman-slough
To sheathing splendours and the golden scale
Of harness, issued in the sun, that now   [40]
Leapt from the dewy shoulders of the Earth,

And hit the Northern hills. Here Cyril met us.
A little shy at first, but by and by
We twain, with mutual pardon ask'd and given
For stroke and song, resolder'd peace, whereon
Follow'd his tale. Amazed he fled away
Thro' the dark land, and later in the night
Had come on Psyche weeping: 'then we fell
Into your father's hand, and there she lies,
But will not speak, nor stir.'
                        He show'd a tent   [50]
A stone-shot off: we enter'd in, and there
Among piled arms and rough accoutrements,
Pitiful sight, wrapp'd in a soldier's cloak,
Like some sweet sculpture draped from head to foot,
And push'd by rude hands from its pedestal,
All her fair length upon the ground she lay:
And at her head a follower of the camp,
A charr'd and wrinkled piece of womanhood,
Sat watching like a watcher by the dead.

    Then Florian knelt, and 'Come' he whisper'd to her,   [60]
'Lift up your head, sweet sister: lie not thus.
What have you done but right? you could not slay
Me, nor your prince: look up: be comforted:
Sweet is it to have done the thing one ought,
When fall'n in darker ways.' And likewise I:
'Be comforted: have I not lost her too,
In whose least act abides the nameless charm
That none has else for me?' She heard, she moved,
She moan'd, a folded voice; and up she sat,
And raised the cloak from brows as pale and smooth   [70]
As those that mourn half-shrouded over death
In deathless marble. 'Her,' she said, 'my friend—
Parted from her—betray'd her cause and mine—
Where shall I breathe? why kept ye not your faith?
O base and bad! what comfort? none for me!'
To whom remorseful Cyril, 'Yet I pray
Take comfort: live, dear lady, for your child!'
At which she lifted up her voice and cried.

    'Ah me, my babe, my blossom, ah, my child,
My one sweet child, whom I shall see no more!   [80]

For now will cruel Ida keep her back;
And either she will die from want of care,
Or sicken with ill-usage, when they say
The child is hers—for every little fault,
The child is hers; and they will beat my girl
Remembering her mother: O my flower!
Or they will take her, they will make her hard,
And she will pass me by in after-life
With some cold reverence worse than were she dead.
Ill mother that I was to leave her there,   [90]
To lag behind, scared by the cry they made,
The horror of the shame among them all:
But I will go and sit beside the doors,
And make a wild petition night and day,
Until they hate to hear me like a wind
Wailing for ever, till they open to me,
And lay my little blossom at my feet,
My babe, my sweet Aglaïa, my one child:
And I will take her up and go my way,
And satisfy my soul with kissing her: [100]
Ah! what might that man not deserve of me
Who gave me back my child?' 'Be comforted,'
Said Cyril, 'you shall have it:' but again
She veil'd her brows, and prone she sank, and so
Like tender things that being caught feign death,
Spoke not, nor stirr'd.

           By this a murmur ran
Thro' all the camp and inward raced the scouts
With rumour of Prince Arac hard at hand.
We left her by the woman, and without
Found the gray kings at parle: and 'Look you' cried   [110]
My father 'that our compact be fulfill'd:
You have spoilt this child; she laughs at you and man:
She wrongs herself, her sex, and me, and him:
But red-faced war has rods of steel and fire;
She yields, or war.'

           Then Gama turn'd to me:
'We fear, indeed, you spent a stormy time
With our strange girl: and yet they say that still
You love her. Give us, then, your mind at large:
How say you, war or not?'

                           'Not war, if possible,
O king,' I said, 'lest from the abuse of war,   [120]
The desecrated shrine, the trampled year,°
The smouldering homestead, and the household flower
Torn from the lintel—all the common wrong—
A smoke go up thro' which I loom to her
Three times a monster: now she lightens scorn
At him that mars her plan, but then would hate
(And every voice she talk'd with ratify it,
And every face she look'd on justify it)
The general foe. More soluble is this knot,
By gentleness than war. I want her love.   [130]
What were I nigher this altho' we dash'd
Your cities into shards with catapults,
She would not love;—or brought her chain'd, a slave,
The lifting of whose eyelash is my lord,
Not ever would she love; but brooding turn
The book of scorn, till all my flitting chance
Were caught within the record of her wrongs,
And crush'd to death: and rather, Sire, than this
I would the old God of war himself were dead,
Forgotten, rusting on his iron hills,   [140]
Rotting on some wild shore with ribs of wreck,
Or like an old-world mammoth bulk'd in ice, °
Not to be molten out.'
                         And roughly spake
My father, 'Tut, you know them not, the girls.
Boy, when I hear you prate I almost think
That idiot legend credible. Look you, Sir!
Man is the hunter; woman is his game:
The sleek and shining creatures of the chase,
We hunt them for the beauty of their skins;
They love us for it, and we ride them down.   [150]
Wheedling and siding with them! Out! for shame!
Boy, there's no rose that's half so dear to them
As he that does the thing they dare not do,
Breathing and sounding beauteous battle, comes
With the air of the trumpet round him, and leaps in
Among the women, snares them by the score
Flatter'd and fluster'd, wins, tho' dash'd with death
He reddens what he kisses: thus I won

Your mother, a good mother, a good wife,
Worth winning; but this firebrand—gentleness   [160]
To such as her! if Cyril spake her true,
To catch a dragon in a cherry net,
To trip a tigress with a gossamer,
Were wisdom to it.'
                             'Yea but Sire,' I cried,
'Wild natures need wise curbs. The soldier? No:
What dares not Ida do that she should prize
The soldier? I beheld her, when she rose
The yesternight, and storming in extremes,
Stood for her cause, and flung defiance down
Gagelike to man, and had not shunn'd the death,   [170]
No, not the soldier's: yet I hold her, king,
True woman: but you clash them all in one,
That have as many differences as we.
The violet varies from the lily as far
As oak from elm: one loves the soldier, one
The silken priest of peace, one this, one that,
And some unworthily; their sinless faith,
A maiden moon that sparkles on a sty,
Glorifying clown and satyr; whence they need
More breadth of culture: is not Ida right?   [180]
They worth it? truer to the law within?
Severer in the logic of a life?
Twice as magnetic to sweet influences
Of earth and heaven? and she of whom you speak,
My mother, looks as whole as some serene
Creation minted in the golden moods
Of sovereign artists; not a thought, a touch,
But pure as lines of green that streak the white
Of the first snowdrop's inner leaves; I say,
Not like the piebald miscellany, man,   [190]
Bursts of great heart and slips in sensual mire,
But whole and one: and take them all-in-all,
Were we ourselves but half as good, as kind,
As truthful, much that Ida claims as right
Had ne'er been mooted, but as frankly theirs
As dues of Nature. To our point: not war:
Lest I lose all.'
                        'Nay, nay, you spake but sense'

Said Gama. 'We remember love ourself
In our sweet youth; we did not rate him then
This red-hot iron to be shaped with blows.   [200]
You talk almost like Ida: *she* can talk;
And there is something in it as you say:
But you talk kindlier: we esteem you for it.—
He seems a gracious and a gallant Prince,
I would he had our daughter: for the rest,
Our own detention, why, the causes weigh'd,
Fatherly fears—you used us courteously—
We would do much to gratify your Prince—
We pardon it; and for your ingress here
Upon the skirt and fringe of our fair land,   [210]
You did but come as goblins in the night,
Nor in the furrow broke the ploughman's head,
Nor burnt the grange, nor buss'd the milking-maid,°
Nor robb'd the farmer of his bowl of cream:
But let your Prince (our royal word upon it,
He comes back safe) ride with us to our lines,
And speak with Arac: Arac's word is thrice
As ours with Ida: something may be done—
I know not what—and ours shall see us friends.
You, likewise, our late guests, if so you will,   [220]
Follow us: who knows? we four may build some plan
Foursquare to opposition.'
                              Here he reach'd
White hands of farewell to my sire, who growl'd
An answer which, half-muffled in his beard,
Let so much out as gave us leave to go.

Then rode we with the old king across the lawns
Beneath huge trees, a thousand rings of Spring
In every bole, a song on every spray
Of birds that piped their Valentines, and woke
Desire in me to infuse my tale of love   [230]
In the old king's ears, who promised help, and oozed
All o'er with honey'd answer as we rode
And blossom-fragrant slipt the heavy dews
Gather'd by night and peace, with each light air
On our mail'd heads: but other thoughts than Peace
Burnt in us, when we saw the embattled squares,

And squadrons of the Prince, trampling the flowers
With clamour: for among them rose a cry
As if to greet the king; they made a halt;
The horses yell'd; they clash'd their arms; the drum   [240]
Beat; merrily-blowing shrill'd the martial fife;
And in the blast and bray of the long horn
And serpent-throated bugle, undulated
The banner: anon to meet us lightly pranced
Three captains out; nor ever had I seen
Such thews of men: the midmost and the highest
Was Arac: all about his motion clung
The shadow of his sister, as the beam
Of the East, that play'd upon them, made them
    glance
Like those three stars of the airy Giant's zone,°   [250]
That glitter burnish'd by the frosty dark;
And as the fiery Sirius alters hue,
And bickers into red and emerald, shone
Their morions, wash'd with morning, as they came.°

    And I that prated peace, when first I heard
War-music, felt the blind wildbeast of force,
Whose home is in the sinews of a man,
Stir in me as to strike: then took the king
His three broad sons; with now a wandering hand
And now a pointed finger, told them all: [260]
A common light of smiles at our disguise
Broke from their lips, and, ere the windy jest
Had labour'd down within his ample lungs,
The genial giant, Arac, roll'd himself
Thrice in the saddle, then burst out in words.

    'Our land invaded, 'sdeath! and he himself°
Your captive, yet my father wills not war:
And, 'sdeath! myself, what care I, war or no?
But then this question of your troth remains:
And there's a downright honest meaning in her;   [270]
She flies too high, she flies too high! and yet
She ask'd but space and fairplay for her scheme;
She prest and prest it on me—I myself,
What know I of these things? but, life and soul!
I thought her half-right talking of her wrongs;

I say she flies too high, 'sdeath! what of that?
I take her for the flower of womankind,
And so I often told her, right or wrong,
And, Prince, she can be sweet to those she loves,
And, right or wrong, I care not: this is all,   [280]
I stand upon her side: she made me swear it—
'Sdeath—and with solemn rites by candle-light—
Swear by St something—I forget her name—
Her that talk'd down the fifty wisest men;°
She was a princess too; and so I swore.
Come, this is all; she will not: waive your claim:
If not, the foughten field, what else, at once
Decides it, 'sdeath! against my father's will.'

    I lagg'd in answer loth to render up
My precontract, and loth by brainless war   [290]
To cleave the rift of difference deeper yet;
Till one of those two brothers, half aside
And fingering at the hair about his lip,
To prick us on to combat 'Like to like!
The woman's garment hid the woman's heart.'
A taunt that clench'd his purpose like a blow!
For fiery-short was Cyril's counter-scoff,
And sharp I answer'd, touch'd upon the point
Where idle boys are cowards to their shame,
'Decide it here: why not? we are three to three.'   [300]

    Then spake the third 'But three to three? no more?
No more, and in our noble sister's cause?
More, more, for honour: every captain waits
Hungry for honour, angry for his king.
More, more, some fifty on a side, that each
May breathe himself, and quick! by overthrow
Of these or those, the question settled die.'

    'Yea,' answer'd I, 'for this wild wreath of air,
This flake of rainbow flying on the highest
Foam of men's deeds—this honour, if ye will.   [310]
It needs must be for honour if at all:
Since, what decision? if we fail, we fail,
And if we win, we fail: she would not keep
Her compact.' ''Sdeath! but we will send to her,'

Said Arac, 'worthy reasons why she should
Bide by this issue: let our missive thro',
And you shall have her answer by the word.'

   'Boys!' shriek'd the old king, but vainlier than a hen
To her false daughters in the pool; for none
Regarded; neither seem'd there more to say: [320]
Back rode we to my father's camp, and found
He thrice had sent a herald to the gates,
To learn if Ida yet would cede our claim,
Or by denial flush her babbling wells
With her own people's life: three times he went:
The first, he blew and blew, but none appear'd:
He batter'd at the doors; none came: the next,
An awful voice within had warn'd him thence:
The third, and those eight daughters of the plough
Came sallying thro' the gates, and caught his hair,   [330]
And so belabour'd him on rib and cheek
They made him wild: not less one glance he caught
Thro' open doors of Ida station'd there
Unshaken, clinging to her purpose, firm
Tho' compass'd by two armies and the noise
Of arms; and standing like a stately Pine
Set in a cataract on an island–crag,
When storm is on the heights, and right and left
Suck'd from the dark heart of the long hills roll
The torrents, dash'd to the vale: and yet her will   [340]
Bred will in me to overcome it or fall.

   But when I told the king that I was pledged
To fight in tourney for my bride, he clash'd
His iron palms together with a cry;
Himself would tilt it out among the lads:
But overborne by all his bearded lords
With reasons drawn from age and state, perforce
He yielded, wroth and red, with fierce demur:
And many a bold knight started up in heat,
And sware to combat for my claim till death.   [350]

   All on this side the palace ran the field
Flat to the garden-wall: and likewise here,
Above the garden's glowing blossom-belts,

A column'd entry shone and marble stairs,
And great bronze valves, emboss'd with Tomyris°
And what she did to Cyrus after fight,
But now fast barr'd: so here upon the flat
All that long morn the lists were hammer'd up,
And all that morn the heralds to and fro,
With message and defiance, went and came;   [360]
Last, Ida's answer, in a royal hand,
But shaken here and there, and rolling words
Oration-like. I kiss'd it and I read.

   'O brother, you have known the pangs we felt,
What heats of indignation when we heard
Of those that iron-cramp'd their women's feet;
Of lands in which at the altar the poor bride
Gives her harsh groom for bridal-gift a scourge;
Of living hearts that crack within the fire°
Where smoulder their dead despots; and of those,—   [370]
Mothers,—that, all prophetic pity, fling
Their pretty maids in the running flood, and swoops°
The vulture, beak and talon, at the heart
Made for all noble motion: and I saw
That equal baseness lived in sleeker times
With smoother men: the old leaven leaven'd all:°
Millions of throats would bawl for civil rights,
No woman named: therefore I set my face
Against all men, and lived but for mine own.
Far off from men I built a fold for them: [380]
I stored it full of rich memorial:
I fenced it round with gallant institutes,°
And biting laws to scare the beasts of prey
And prosper'd; till a rout of saucy boys
Brake on us at our books, and marr'd our peace,
Mask'd like our maids, blustering I know not what
Of insolence and love, some pretext held
Of baby troth, invalid, since my will
Seal'd not the bond—the striplings!—for their
     sport!—
I tamed my leopards: shall I not tame these?   [390]
Or you? or I? for since you think me touch'd
In honour—what, I would not aught of false—

Is not our cause pure? and whereas I know
Your prowess, Arac, and what mother's blood
You draw from, fight: you failing, I abide
What end soever: fail you will not. Still
Take not his life: he risk'd it for my own;
His mother lives: yet whatsoe'er you do,
Fight and fight well; strike and strike home. O dear
Brothers, the woman's Angel guards you, you   [400]
The sole men to be mingled with our cause,
The sole men we shall prize in the after-time,
Your very armour hallow'd, and your statues
Rear'd, sung to, when, this gad-fly brush'd aside,
We plant a solid foot into the Time,
And mould a generation strong to move
With claim on claim from right to right, till she
Whose name is yoked with children's, know herself;
And Knowledge in our own land make her free,
And, ever following those two crowned twins,   [410]
Commerce and conquest, shower the fiery grain
Of freedom broadcast over all that orbs
Between the Northern and the Southern morn.'

      Then came a postscript dash'd across the rest.
'See that there be no traitors in your camp:
We seem a nest of traitors—none to trust
Since our arms fail'd—this Egypt-plague of men!°
Almost our maids were better at their homes,
Than thus man-girdled here: indeed I think
Our chiefest comfort is the little child   [420]
Of one unworthy mother; which she left:
She shall not have it back: the child shall grow
To prize the authentic mother of her mind.
I took it for an hour in mine own bed
This morning: there the tender orphan hands
Felt at my heart, and seem'd to charm from thence
The wrath I nursed against the world: farewell.'

      I ceased; he said, 'Stubborn, but she may sit
Upon a king's right hand in thunder-storms,
And breed up warriors! See now, tho' yourself   [430]
Be dazzled by the wildfire Love to sloughs
That swallow common sense, the spindling king,

This Gama swamp'd in lazy tolerance.
When the man wants weight, the woman takes it up,
And topples down the scales; but this is fixt
As are the roots of earth and base of all;
Man for the field and woman for the hearth:
Man for the sword and for the needle she:
Man with the head and woman with the heart:
Man to command and woman to obey;   [440]
All else confusion. Look you! the gray mare
Is ill to live with, when her whinny shrills
From tile to scullery, and her small goodman
Shrinks in his arm-chair while the fires of Hell
Mix with his hearth: but you—she's yet a colt—
Take, break her: strongly groom'd and straitly curb'd
She might not rank with those detestable
That let the bantling scald at home, and brawl
Their rights or wrongs like potherbs in the street.°
They say she's comely; there's the fairer chance: [450]
I like her none the less for rating at her!
Besides, the woman wed is not as we,
But suffers change of frame. A lusty brace
Of twins may weed her of her folly. Boy,
The bearing and the training of a child
Is woman's wisdom.'

                    Thus the hard old king:
I took my leave, for it was nearly noon:
I pored upon her letter which I held,
And on the little clause 'take not his life:'
I mused on that wild morning in the woods,   [460]
And on the 'Follow, follow, thou shalt win:'
I thought on all the wrathful king had said,
And how the strange betrothment was to end:
Then I remember'd that burnt sorcerer's curse
That one should fight with shadows and should fall;
And like a flash the weird affection came:
King, camp and college turn'd to hollow shows;
I seem'd to move in old memorial tilts,
And doing battle with forgotten ghosts,
To dream myself the shadow of a dream: [470]
And ere I woke it was the point of noon,

The lists were ready. Empanoplied and plumed
We enter'd in, and waited, fifty there
Opposed to fifty, till the trumpet blared
At the barrier like a wild horn in a land
Of echoes, and a moment, and once more
The trumpet, and again: at which the storm
Of galloping hoofs bare on the ridge of spears
And riders front to front, until they closed
In conflict with the crash of shivering points, [480]
And thunder. Yet it seem'd a dream, I dream'd
Of fighting. On his haunches rose the steed,
And into fiery splinters leapt the lance,
And out of stricken helmets sprang the fire.
Part sat like rocks: part reel'd but kept their seats:
Part roll'd on the earth and rose again and drew:
Part stumbled mixt with floundering horses. Down
From those two bulks at Arac's side, and down
From Arac's arm, as from a giant's flail,
The large blows rain'd, as here and everywhere [490]
He rode the mellay, lord of the ringing lists,
And all the plain,—brand, mace, and shaft, and shield—
Shock'd, like an iron-clanging anvil bang'd
With hammers; till I thought, can this be he
From Gama's dwarfish loins? if this be so,
The mother makes us most—and in my dream
I glanced aside, and saw the palace-front
Alive with fluttering scarfs and ladies' eyes,
And highest, among the statues, statuelike,
Between a cymbal'd Miriam and a Jael,° [500]
With Psyche's babe, was Ida watching us,
A single band of gold about her hair,
Like a Saint's glory up in heaven: but she
No saint—inexorable—no tenderness—
Too hard, too cruel: yet she sees me fight,
Yea, let her see me fall! with that I drave
Among the thickest and bore down a Prince,
And Cyril, one. Yea, let me make my dream
All that I would. But that large-moulded man,
His visage all agrin as at a wake, [510]
Made at me thro' the press, and, staggering back
With stroke on stroke the horse and horseman, came

As comes a pillar of electric cloud,
Flaying the roofs and sucking up the drains,
And shadowing down the champaign till it strikes
On a wood, and takes, and breaks, and cracks, and splits,
And twists the grain with such a roar that Earth
Reels, and the herdsmen cry; for everything
Gave way before him: only Florian, he
That loved me closer than his own right eye,   [520]
Thrust in between; but Arac rode him down:
And Cyril seeing it, push'd against the Prince,
With Psyche's colour round his helmet, tough,
Strong, supple, sinew-corded, apt at arms;
But tougher, heavier, stronger, he that smote
And threw him: last I spurr'd; I felt my veins
Stretch with fierce heat; a moment hand to hand,
And sword to sword, and horse to horse we hung,
Till I struck out and shouted; the blade glanced,
I did but shear a feather, and dream and truth   [530]
Flow'd from me; darkness closed me; and I fell.

Home they brought her warrior dead:
    She nor swoon'd, nor utter'd cry:
All her maidens, watching, said,
    'She must weep or she will die.'

Then they praised him, soft and low,
    Call'd him worthy to be loved,
Truest friend and noblest foe;
    Yet she neither spoke nor moved.

Stole a maiden from her place,
    Lightly to the warrior stept,   [10]
Took the face-cloth from the face;
    Yet she neither moved nor wept.

Rose a nurse of ninety years,
    Set his child upon her knee—
Like summer tempest came her tears—
    'Sweet my child, I live for thee.'

My dream had never died or lived again.
As in some mystic middle state I lay;
Seeing I saw not, hearing not I heard:
Tho', if I saw not, yet they told me all
So often that I speak as having seen.

    For so it seem'd, or so they said to me,
That all things grew more tragic and more strange;
That when our side was vanquish'd and my cause
For ever lost, there went up a great cry,
The Prince is slain. My father heard and ran   [10]
In on the lists, and there unlaced my casque
And grovell'd on my body, and after him
Came Psyche, sorrowing for Aglaïa.

    But high upon the palace Ida stood
With Psyche's babe in arm: there on the roofs
Like that great dame of Lapidoth she sang.°

      'Our enemies have fall'n, have fall'n: the seed,
The little seed they laugh'd at in the dark,
Has risen and cleft the soil, and grown a bulk
Of spanless girth, that lays on every side   [20]
A thousand arms and rushes to the Sun.

      'Our enemies have fall'n, have fall'n: they came;
The leaves were wet with women's tears: they heard
A noise of songs they would not understand:
They mark'd it with the red cross to the fall,
And would have strown it, and are fall'n themselves.

      'Our enemies have fall'n, have fall'n: they came,
The woodmen with their axes: lo the tree!
But we will make it faggots for the hearth,
And shape it plank and beam for roof and floor,   [30]
And boats and bridges for the use of men.

      'Our enemies have fall'n, have fall'n: they struck;
With their own blows they hurt themselves, nor knew
There dwelt an iron nature in the grain:
The glittering axe was broken in their arms,
Their arms were shatter'd to the shoulder blade.

'Our enemies have fall'n, but this shall grow
A night of Summer from the heat, a breadth
Of Autumn, dropping fruits of power: and roll'd
With music in the growing breeze of Time,   [40]
The tops shall strike from star to star, the fangs
Shall move the stony bases of the world.

'And now, O maids, behold our sanctuary
Is violate, our laws broken: fear we not
To break them more in their behoof, whose arms
Champion'd our cause and won it with a day
Blanch'd in our annals, and perpetual feast,
When dames and heroines of the golden year
Shall strip a hundred hollows bare of Spring,
To rain an April of ovation round   [50]
Their statues, borne aloft, the three: but come,
We will be liberal, since our rights are won.
Let them not lie in the tents with coarse mankind,
Ill nurses; but descend, and proffer these
The brethren of our blood and cause, that there
Lie bruised and maim'd, the tender ministries
Of female hands and hospitality.'

She spoke, and with the babe yet in her arms,
Descending, burst the great bronze valves, and led°
A hundred maids in train across the Park.   [60]
Some cowl'd, and some bare-headed, on they came,
Their feet in flowers, her loveliest: by them went
The enamour'd air sighing, and on their curls
From the high tree the blossom wavering fell,
And over them the tremulous isles of light
Slided, they moving under shade: but Blanche
At distance follow'd: so they came: anon
Thro' open field into the lists they wound
Timorously; and as the leader of the herd
That holds a stately fretwork to the Sun,   [70]
And follow'd up by a hundred airy does,
Steps with a tender foot, light as on air,
The lovely, lordly creature floated on
To where her wounded brethren lay; there stay'd;
Knelt on one knee,—the child on one,—and prest
Their hands, and call'd them dear deliverers,

And happy warriors, and immortal names,
And said 'You shall not lie in the tents but here,
And nursed by those for whom you fought, and served
With female hands and hospitality.'   [80]

    Then, whether moved by this, or was it chance,
She past my way. Up started from my side
The old lion, glaring with his whelpless eye,
Silent; but when she saw me lying stark,
Dishelm'd and mute, and motionlessly pale,
Cold ev'n to her, she sigh'd; and when she saw
The haggard father's face and reverend beard
Of grisly twine, all dabbled with the blood
Of his own son, shudder'd, a twitch of pain
Tortured her mouth, and o'er her forehead past   [90]
A shadow, and her hue changed, and she said:
'He saved my life: my brother slew him for it.'
No more: at which the king in bitter scorn
Drew from my neck the painting and the tress,
And held them up: she saw them, and a day
Rose from the distance on her memory,
When the good Queen, her mother, shore the tress
With kisses, ere the days of Lady Blanche:
And then once more she look'd at my pale face:
Till understanding all the foolish work   [100]
Of Fancy, and the bitter close of all,
Her iron will was broken in her mind;
Her noble heart was molten in her breast;
She bow'd, she set the child on the earth; she laid
A feeling finger on my brows, and presently
'O Sire,' she said, 'he lives: he is not dead:
O let me have him with my brethren here
In our own palace: we will tend on him
Like one of these; if so, by any means,
To lighten this great clog of thanks, that make   [110]
Our progress falter to the woman's goal.'

    She said: but at the happy word 'he lives'
My father stoop'd, re-father'd o'er my wounds.
So those two foes above my fallen life,
With brow to brow like night and evening mixt
Their dark and gray, while Psyche ever stole

A little nearer, till the babe that by us,
Half-lapt in glowing gauze and golden brede,°
Lay like a new-fall'n meteor on the grass,
Uncared for, spied its mother and began   [120]
A blind and babbling laughter, and to dance
Its body, and reach its fatling innocent arms
And lazy lingering fingers. She the appeal
Brook'd not, but clamouring out 'Mine—mine—
          not yours,
It is not yours, but mine: give me the child'
Ceased all on tremble: piteous was the cry:
So stood the unhappy mother open-mouth'd,
And turn'd each face her way: wan was her cheek
With hollow watch, her blooming mantle torn,
Red grief and mother's hunger in her eye,   [130]
And down dead-heavy sank her curls, and half
The sacred mother's bosom, panting, burst
The laces toward her babe; but she nor cared
Nor knew it, clamouring on, till Ida heard,
Look'd up, and rising slowly from me, stood
Erect and silent, striking with her glance
The mother, me, the child; but he that lay
Beside us, Cyril, batter'd as he was,
Trail'd himself up on one knee: then he drew
Her robe to meet his lips, and down she look'd   [140]
At the arm'd man sideways, pitying as it seem'd,
Or self-involved; but when she learnt his face,
Remembering his ill-omen'd song, arose
Once more thro' all her height, and o'er him grew
Tall as a figure lengthen'd on the sand
When the tide ebbs in sunshine, and he said:

      'O fair and strong and terrible! Lioness
That with your long locks play the Lion's mane!
But Love and Nature, these are two more terrible
And stronger. See, your foot is on our necks,   [150]
We vanquish'd, you the Victor of your will.
What would you more? give her the child! remain
Orb'd in your isolation: he is dead,
Or all as dead: henceforth we let you be:
Win you the hearts of women; and beware

Lest, where you seek the common love of these,
The common hate with the revolving wheel
Should drag you down, and some great Nemesis
Break from a darken'd future, crown'd with fire,
And tread you out for ever: but howsoe'er　　　　[160]
Fix'd in yourself, never in your own arms
To hold your own, deny not hers to her,
Give her the child! O if, I say, you keep
One pulse that beats true woman, if you loved
The breast that fed or arm that dandled you,
Or own one port of sense not flint to prayer,°
Give her the child! or if you scorn to lay it,
Yourself, in hands so lately claspt with yours,
Or speak to her, your dearest, her one fault
The tenderness, not yours, that could not kill,　　　　[170]
Give *me* it: *I* will give it her.'

　　　　　　　　　　　He said:
At first her eye with slow dilation roll'd
Dry flame, she listening; after sank and sank
And, into mournful twilight mellowing, dwelt
Full on the child; she took it: 'Pretty bud!
Lily of the vale! half open'd bell of the woods!
Sole comfort of my dark hour, when a world
Of traitorous friend and broken system made
No purple in the distance, mystery,
Pledge of a love not to be mine, farewell;　　　　[180]
These men are hard upon us as of old,
We two must part: and yet how fain was I
To dream thy cause embraced in mine, to think
I might be something to thee, when I felt
Thy helpless warmth about my barren breast
In the dead prime: but may thy mother prove°
As true to thee as false, false, false to me!
And, if thou needs must bear the yoke, I wish it
Gentle as freedom'—here she kiss'd it: then—
'All good go with thee! take it Sir,' and so　　　　[190]
Laid the soft babe in his hard-mailed hands,
Who turn'd half-round to Psyche as she sprang
To meet it, with an eye that swum in thanks;
Then felt it sound and whole from head to foot,
And hugg'd and never hugg'd it close enough,

And in her hunger mouth'd and mumbled it,
And hid her bosom with it; after that
Put on more calm and added suppliantly:

'We two were friends: I go to mine own land
For ever: find some other: as for me   [200]
I scarce am fit for your great plans: yet speak to me,
Say one soft word and let me part forgiven.'

But Ida spoke not, rapt upon the child.
Then Arac. 'Ida—'sdeath! you blame the man;
You wrong yourselves—the woman is so hard
Upon the woman. Come, a grace to me!
I am your warrior: I and mine have fought
Your battle: kiss her; take her hand, she weeps:
'Sdeath! I would sooner fight thrice o'er than see it.'

But Ida spoke not, gazing on the ground,   [210]
And reddening in the furrows of his chin,
And moved beyond his custom, Gama said:

'I've heard that there is iron in the blood,
And I believe it. Not one word? not one?
Whence drew you this steel temper? not from me,
Not from your mother, now a saint with saints.
She said you had a heart—I heard her say it—
"Our Ida has a heart"—just ere she died—
"But see that some one with authority
Be near her still" and I—I sought for one—   [220]
All people said she had authority—
The Lady Blanche: much profit! Not one word;
No! tho' your father sues: see how you stand
Stiff as Lot's wife, and all the good knights maim'd,°
I trust that there is no one hurt to death,
For your wild whim: and was it then for this,
Was it for this we gave our palace up,
Where we withdrew from summer heats and state,
And had our wine and chess beneath the planes,
And many a pleasant hour with her that's gone,   [230]
Ere you were born to vex us? Is it kind?
Speak to her I say: is this not she of whom,
When first she came, all flush'd you said to me
Now had you got a friend of your own age,

Now could you share your thought; now should men see
Two women faster welded in one love
Than pairs of wedlock; she you walk'd with, she
You talk'd with, whole nights long, up in the tower,
Of sine and arc, spheroïd and azimuth,°
And right ascension, Heaven knows what; and now   [240]
A word, but one, one little kindly word,
Not one to spare her: out upon you, flint!
You love nor her, nor me, nor any; nay,
You shame your mother's judgment too. Not one?
You will not? well—no heart have you, or such
As fancies like the vermin in a nut
Have fretted all to dust and bitterness.'
So said the small king moved beyond his wont.

But Ida stood nor spoke, drain'd of her force
By many a varying influence and so long.   [250]
Down thro' her limbs a drooping langour wept:
Her head a little bent; and on her mouth
A doubtful smile dwelt like a clouded moon
In a still water: then brake out my sire,
Lifting his grim head from my wounds. 'O you,
Woman, whom we thought woman even now,
And were half fool'd to let you tend our son,
Because he might have wish'd it—but we see
The accomplice of your madness unforgiven,
And think that you might mix his draught with death,   [260]
When your skies change again: the rougher hand
Is safer: on to the tents: take up the Prince.'

He rose, and while each ear was prick'd to attend
A tempest, thro' the cloud that dimm'd her broke
A genial warmth and light once more, and shone
Thro' glittering drops on her sad friend.
                                   'Come hither.
O Psyche,' she cried out, 'embrace me, come,
Quick while I melt; make reconcilement sure
With one that cannot keep her mind an hour:
Come to the hollow heart they slander so!   [270]
Kiss and be friends, like children being chid!
I seem no more: *I* want forgiveness too:
I should have had to do with none but maids,

That have no links with men. Ah false but dear,
Dear traitor, too much loved, why?—why?—Yet see,
Before these kings we embrace you yet once more
With all forgiveness, all oblivion,
And trust, not love, you less.

            And now, O sire,
Grant me your son, to nurse, to wait upon him,
Like mine own brother. For my debt to him,   [280]
This nightmare weight of gratitude, I know it;
Taunt me no more: yourself and yours shall have
Free adit; we will scatter all our maids°
Till happier times each to her proper hearth:
What use to keep them here—now? grant my prayer.
Help, father, brother, help; speak to the king:
Thaw this male nature to some touch of that
Which kills me with myself, and drags me down
From my fixt height to mob me up with all
The soft and milky rabble of womankind,   [290]
Poor weakling ev'n as they are.'

              Passionate tears
Follow'd: the king replied not: Cyril said:
'Your brother, Lady,—Florian,—ask for him
Of your great head—for he is wounded too—
That you may tend upon him with the prince.'
'Ay so,' said Ida with a bitter smile,
'Our laws are broken: let him enter too.'
Then Violet, she that sang the mournful song,
And had a cousin tumbled on the plain,
Petition'd too for him. 'Ay so,' she said,   [300]
'I stagger in the stream: I cannot keep
My heart an eddy from the brawling hour:
We break our laws with ease, but let it be.'
'Ay so?' said Blanche: 'Amazed am I to hear
Your Highness: but your Highness breaks with ease
The law your Highness did not make: 'twas I.
I had been wedded wife, I knew mankind,
And block'd them out; but these men came to woo
Your Highness—verily I think to win.'

    So she, and turn'd askance a wintry eye: [310]
But Ida with a voice, that like a bell

Toll'd by an earthquake in a trembling tower,
Rang ruin, answer'd full of grief and scorn.

'Fling our doors wide! all, all, not one, but all,
Not only he, but by my mother's soul,
Whatever man lies wounded, friend or foe,
Shall enter, if he will. Let our girls flit,
Till the storm die! but had you stood by us,
The roar that breaks the Pharos from his base°
Had left us rock. She fain would sting us too,   [320]
But shall not. Pass, and mingle with your likes.
We brook no further insult but are gone.'

She turn'd; the very nape of her white neck
Was rosed with indignation: but the Prince
Her brother came; the king her father charm'd
Her wounded soul with words: nor did mine own
Refuse her proffer, lastly gave his hand.

Then us they lifted up, dead weights, and bare
Straight to the doors: to them the doors gave way
Groaning, and in the Vestal entry shriek'd   [330]
The virgin marble under iron heels:
And on they moved and gain'd the hall, and there
Rested: but great the crush was, and each base,
To left and right, of those tall columns drown'd
In silken fluctuation and the swarm
Of female whisperers: at the further end
Was Ida by the throne, the two great cats
Close by her, like supporters on a shield,
Bow-back'd with fear: but in the centre stood
The common men with rolling eyes; amazed   [340]
They glared upon the women, and aghast
The women stared at these, all silent, save
When armour clash'd or jingled, while the day,
Descending, struck athwart the hall, and shot
A flying splendour out of brass and steel
That o'er the statues leapt from head to head,
Now fired an angry Pallas on the helm,
Now set a wrathful Dian's moon on flame,
And now and then an echo started up,

And shuddering fled from room to room, and died   [350]
Of fright in far apartments.
                              Then the voice
Of Ida sounded, issuing ordinance:
And me they bore up the broad stairs, and thro'
The long-laid galleries past a hundred doors
To one deep chamber shut from sound, and due
To languid limbs and sickness; left me in it;
And others otherwhere they laid; and all
That afternoon a sound arose of hoof
And chariot, many a maiden passing home
Till happier times; but some were left of those   [360]
Held sagest, and the great lords out and in,
From those two hosts that lay beside the walls,
Walk'd at their will, and everything was changed.

Ask me no more: the moon may draw the sea;
    The cloud may stoop from heaven and take the shape
    With fold to fold, of mountain or of cape;
But O too fond, when have I answered thee?
                    Ask me no more.

Ask me no more: what answer should I give?
    I love not hollow cheek or faded eye:
    Yet, O my friend, I will not have thee die!
Ask me no more, lest I should bid thee live;
                    Ask me no more.   [10]

Ask me no more: thy fate and mine are seal'd:
    I strove against the stream and all in vain:
    Let the great river take me to the main:
No more, dear love, for at a touch I yield;
                    Ask me no more.

VII

So was their sanctuary violated,
So their fair college turn'd to hospital;
At first with all confusion: by and by

Sweet order lived again with other laws:
A kindlier influence reign'd; and everywhere
Low voices with the ministering hand
Hung round the sick: the maidens came, they talk'd,
They sang, they read: till she not fair began
To gather light, and she that was, became
Her former beauty treble; and to and fro   [10]
With books, with flowers, with Angel offices,
Like creatures native unto gracious act,
And in their own clear element, they moved.

But sadness on the soul of Ida fell,
And hatred of her weakness, blent with shame.
Old studies fail'd; seldom she spoke: but oft
Clomb to the roofs, and gazed alone for hours
On that disastrous leaguer, swarms of men
Darkening her female field: void was her use,°
And she as one that climbs a peak to gaze   [20]
O'er land and main, and sees a great black cloud
Drag inward from the deeps, a wall of night,
Blot out the slope of sea from verge to shore,
And suck the blinding splendour from the sand,
And quenching lake by lake and tarn by tarn
Expunge the world: so fared she gazing there;
So blacken'd all her world in secret, blank
And waste it seem'd and vain; till down she came,
And found fair peace once more among the sick.

And twilight dawn'd; and morn by morn the lark   [30]
Shot up and shrill'd in flickering gyres, but I°
Lay silent in the muffled cage of life:
And twilight gloom'd; and broader-grown the bowers
Drew the great night into themselves, and Heaven,
Star after star, arose and fell; but I,
Deeper than those weird doubts could reach me, lay
Quite sunder'd from the moving Universe,
Nor knew what eye was on me, nor the hand
That nursed me, more than infants in their sleep.

But Psyche tended Florian: with her oft,   [40]
Melissa came; for Blanche had gone, but left
Her child among us, willing she should keep

Court-favour: here and there the small bright head,
A light of healing, glanced about the couch,
Or thro' the parted silks the tender face
Peep'd, shining in upon the wounded man
With blush and smile, a medicine in themselves
To wile the length from languorous hours, and draw
The sting from pain; nor seem'd it strange that soon
He rose up whole, and those fair charities   [50]
Join'd at her side; nor stranger seem'd that hearts
So gentle, so employ'd, should close in love,
Than when two dewdrops on the petal shake
To the same sweet air, and tremble deeper down,
And slip at once all-fragrant into one.

    Less prosperously the second suit obtain'd°
At first with Psyche. Not tho' Blanche had sworn
That after that dark night among the fields
She needs must wed him for her own good name;
Not tho' he built upon the babe restored;   [60]
Nor tho' she liked him, yielded she, but fear'd
To incense the Head once more; till on a day
When Cyril pleaded, Ida came behind
Seen but of Psyche: on her foot she hung
A moment, and she heard, at which her face
A little flush'd, and she past on; but each
Assumed from thence a half-consent involved
In stillness, plighted troth, and were at peace.

    Nor only these: Love in the sacred halls
Held carnival at will, and flying struck   [70]
With showers of random sweet on maid and man.
Nor did her father cease to press my claim,
Nor did mine own, now reconciled; nor yet
Did those twin-brothers, risen again and whole;
Nor Arac, satiate with his victory.

    But I lay still, and with me oft she sat:
Then came a change; for sometimes I would catch
Her hand in wild delirium, gripe it hard,
And fling it like a viper off, and shriek
'You are not Ida;' clasp it once again,   [80]
And call her Ida, tho' I knew her not,

And call her sweet, as if in irony,
And call her hard and cold which seem'd a truth:
And still she fear'd that I should lose my mind,
And often she believed that I should die:
Till out of long frustration of her care,
And pensive tendance in the all-weary noons,
And watches in the dead, the dark, when clocks
Throbb'd thunder thro' the palace floors, or call'd
On flying Time from all their silver tongues—   [90]
And out of memories of her kindlier days,
And sidelong glances at my father's grief,
And at the happy lovers heart in heart—
And out of hauntings of my spoken love,
And lonely listenings to my mutter'd dream,
And often feeling of the helpless hands,
And wordless broodings on the wasted cheek—
From all a closer interest flourish'd up,
Tenderness touch by touch, and last, to these,
Love, like an Alpine harebell hung with tears   [100]
By some cold morning glacier; frail at first
And feeble, all unconscious of itself,
But such as gather'd colour day by day.

Last I woke sane, but well-nigh close to death
For weakness: it was evening: silent light
Slept on the painted walls, wherein were wrought
Two grand designs; for on one side arose
The women up in wild revolt, and storm'd
At the Oppian law. Titanic shapes, they cramm'd°
The forum, and half-crush'd among the rest   [110]
A dwarf-like Cato cower'd. On the other side
Hortensia spoke against the tax; behind,°
A train of dames: by axe and eagle sat,
With all their foreheads drawn in Roman scowls,
And half the wolf's-milk curdled in their veins,
The fierce triumvirs; and before them paused
Hortensia pleading: angry was her face.

I saw the forms: I knew not where I was:
They did but look like hollow shows; nor more
Sweet Ida: palm to palm she sat: the dew   [120]
Dwelt in her eyes, and softer all her shape

And rounder seem'd: I moved: I sigh'd: a touch
Came round my wrist, and tears upon my hand:
Then all for languor and self-pity ran
Mine down my face, and with what life I had,
And like a flower that cannot all unfold,
So drench'd it is with tempest, to the sun,
Yet, as it may, turns toward him, I on her
Fixt my faint eyes, and utter'd whisperingly:

'If you be, what I think you, some sweet dream,   [130]
I would but ask you to fulfil yourself:
But if you be that Ida whom I knew,
I ask you nothing: only, if a dream,
Sweet dream, be perfect. I shall die to-night.
Stoop down and seem to kiss me ere I die.'

I could no more, but lay like one in trance,
That hears his burial talk'd of by his friends,
And cannot speak, nor move, nor make one sign,
But lies and dreads his doom. She turn'd; she paused;
She stoop'd; and out of languor leapt a cry;   [140]
Leapt fiery Passion from the brinks of death;
And I believed that in the living world
My spirit closed with Ida's at the lips;
Till back I fell, and from mine arms she rose
Glowing all over noble shame; and all
Her falser self slipt from her like a robe,
And left her woman, lovelier in her mood
Than in her mould that other, when she came
From barren deeps to conquer all with love;
And down the streaming crystal dropt; and she   [150]
Far-fleeted by the purple island-sides,
Naked, a double light in air and wave,
To meet her Graces, where they deck'd her out
For worship without end; nor end of mine,
Stateliest, for thee! but mute she glided forth,
Nor glanced behind her, and I sank and slept,
Fill'd thro' and thro' with Love, a happy sleep.

Deep in the night I woke: she, near me, held
A volume of the Poets of her land:°
There to herself, all in low tones, she read.   [160]

'Now sleeps the crimson petal, now the white;
Nor waves the cypress in the palace walk;
Nor winks the gold fin in the porphyry font:
The fire-fly wakens: waken thou with me.

Now droops the milkwhite peacock like a ghost,
And like a ghost she glimmers on to me.

Now lies the Earth all Danaë to the stars,°
And all thy heart lies open unto me.

Now slides the silent meteor on, and leaves
A shining furrow, as thy thoughts in me.   [170]

Now folds the lily all her sweetness up,
And slips into the bosom of the lake:
So fold thyself, my dearest, thou, and slip
Into my bosom and be lost in me.'

I heard her turn the page; she found a small
Sweet Idyl, and once more, as low, she read:°

'Come down, O maid, from yonder mountain height:
What pleasure lives in height (the shepherd sang)
In height and cold, the splendour of the hills?
But cease to move so near the Heavens, and cease   [180]
To glide a sunbeam by the blasted Pine,
To sit a star upon the sparkling spire;
And come, for Love is of the valley, come,
For Love is of the valley, come thou down
And find him; by the happy threshold, he,
Or hand in hand with Plenty in the maize,
Or red with spirted purple of the vats,
Or foxlike in the vine; nor cares to walk
With Death and Morning on the silver horns,
Nor wilt thou snare him in the white ravine,   [190]
Nor find him dropt upon the firths of ice,
That huddling slant in furrow-cloven falls
To roll the torrent out of dusky doors:
But follow; let the torrent dance thee down
To find him in the valley; let the wild
Lean-headed Eagles yelp alone, and leave
The monstrous ledges there to slope, and spill

Their thousand wreaths of dangling water-smoke,
That like a broken purpose waste in air:
So waste not thou: but come; for all the vales   [200]
Await thee; azure pillars of the hearth
Arise to thee; the children call, and I
Thy shepherd pipe, and sweet is every sound,
Sweeter thy voice, but every sound is sweet;
Myriads of rivulets hurrying thro' the lawn,
The moan of doves in immemorial elms,
And murmuring of innumerable bees.

    So she low-toned; while with shut eyes I lay
Listening; then look'd. Pale was the perfect face;
The bosom with long sighs labour'd; and meek   [210]
Seem'd the full lips, and mild the luminous eyes,
And the voice trembled and the hand. She said
Brokenly, that she knew it, she had fail'd
In sweet humility; had failed in all;
That all her labour was but as a block
Left in the quarry; but she still were loth,
She still were loth to yield herself to one
That wholly scorn'd to help their equal rights
Against the sons of men, and barbarous laws.
She pray'd me not to judge their cause from her   [220]
That wrong'd it, sought far less for truth than power
In knowledge: something wild within her breast,
A greater than all knowledge, beat her down.
And she had nursed me there from week to week:
Much had she learnt in little time. In part
It was ill counsel had misled the girl
To vex true hearts: yet was she but a girl—
'Ah fool, and made myself a Queen of farce!
When comes another such? never, I think,
Till the Sun drop, dead, from the signs.'
                                  Her voice   [230]
Choked, and her forehead sank upon her hands,
And her great heart thro' all the faultful Past
Went sorrowing in a pause I dared not break;
Till notice of a change in the dark world
Was lispt about the acacias, and a bird,
That early woke to feed her little ones,

Sent from a dewy breast a cry for light:
She moved, and at her feet the volume fell.

    'Blame not thyself too much,' I said, 'nor blame
Too much the sons of men and barbarous laws; [240]
These were the rough ways of the world till now.
Henceforth thou hast a helper, me, that know
The woman's cause is man's: they rise or sink
Together, dwarf'd or godlike, bond or free:
For she that out of Lethe scales with man
The shining steps of Nature, shares with man
His nights, his days, moves with him to one goal,
Stays all the fair young planet in her hands—
If she be small, slight-natured, miserable,
How shall men grow? but work no more alone! [250]
Our place is much: as far as in us lies
We two will serve them both in aiding her—
Will clear away the parasitic forms
That seem to keep her up but drag her down—
Will leave her space to burgeon out of all°
Within her—let her make herself her own
To give or keep, to live and learn and be
All that not harms distinctive womanhood.
For woman is not undevelopt man,
But diverse: could we make her as the man, [260]
Sweet Love were slain: his dearest bond is this,
Not like to like, but like in difference.
Yet in the long years liker must they grow;
The man be more of woman, she of man;
He gain in sweetness and in moral height,
Nor lose the wrestling thews that throw the world;
She mental breadth, nor fail in childward care,
Nor lose the childlike in the larger mind;
Till at the last she set herself to man,
Like perfect music unto noble words; [270]
And so these twain, upon the skirts of Time,
Sit side by side, full-summ'd in all their powers,
Dispensing harvest, sowing the To-be,
Self-reverent each and reverencing each,
Distinct in individualities,
But like each other ev'n as those who love.

Then comes the statelier Eden back to men:
Then reign the world's great bridals, chaste and calm:
Then springs the crowning race of humankind.
May these things be!'

Sighing she spoke 'I fear   [280]

They will not.'

'Dear, but let us type them now

In our own lives, and this proud watchword rest
Of equal; seeing either sex alone
Is half itself, and in true marriage lies
Nor equal, nor unequal: each fulfils
Defect in each, and always thought in thought,
Purpose in purpose, will in will, they grow,
The single pure and perfect animal,
The two-cell'd heart beating, with one full stroke,
Life.'

And again sighing she spoke: 'A dream   [290]

That once was mine! what woman taught you this?'

'Alone,' I said, 'from earlier than I know,
Immersed in rich foreshadowings of the world,
I loved the woman: he, that doth not, lives
A drowning life, besotted in sweet self,
Or pines in sad experience worse than death,
Or keeps his wing'd affections clipt with crime:
Yet was there one thro' whom I loved her, one
Not learned, save in gracious household ways,
Not perfect, nay, but full of tender wants,   [300]
No Angel, but a dearer being, all dipt
In Angel instincts, breathing Paradise,
Interpreter between the Gods and men,
Who look'd all native to her place, and yet
On tiptoe seem'd to touch upon a sphere
Too gross to tread, and all male minds perforce
Sway'd to her from their orbits as they moved,
And girdled her with music. Happy he
With such a mother! faith in womankind
Beats with his blood, and trust in all things high   [310]
Comes easy to him, and tho' he trip and fall
He shall not blind his soul with clay.'

'But I,'

Said Ida, tremulously, 'so all unlike—
It seems you love to cheat yourself with words:
This mother is your model. I have heard
Of your strange doubts: they well might be: I seem
A mockery to my own self. Never, Prince;
You cannot love me.'
                              'Nay but thee' I said
'From yearlong poring on thy pictured eyes,
Ere seen I loved, and loved thee seen, and saw   [320]
Thee woman thro' the crust of iron moods
That mask'd thee from men's reverence up, and forced
Sweet love on pranks of saucy boyhood: now,
Giv'n back to life, to life indeed, thro' thee,
Indeed I love: the new day comes, the light
Dearer for night, as dearer thou for faults
Lived over: lift thine eyes; my doubts are dead,
My haunting sense of hollow shows: the change,
This truthful change in thee has kill'd it. Dear,
Look up, and let thy nature strike on mine,   [330]
Like yonder morning on the blind half-world;
Approach and fear not; breathe upon my brows;
In that fine air I tremble, all the past
Melts mist-like into this bright hour, and this
Is morn to more, and all the rich to-come
Reels, as the golden Autumn woodland reels
Athwart the smoke of burning weeds. Forgive me,
I waste my heart in signs: let be. My bride,
My wife, my life. O we will walk this world,
Yoked in all exercise of noble end,   [340]
And so thro' those dark gates across the wild
That no man knows. Indeed I love thee: come,
Yield thyself up: my hopes and thine are one:
Accomplish thou my manhood and thyself;
Lay thy sweet hands in mine and trust to me.'

CONCLUSION

So closed our tale, of which I give you all
The random scheme as wildly as it rose:
The words are mostly mine; for when we ceased
There came a minute's pause, and Walter said,

'I wish she had not yielded!' then to me,
'What, if you drest it up poetically!'
So pray'd the men, the women: I gave assent:
Yet how to bind the scatter'd scheme of seven
Together in one sheaf? What style could suit?
The men required that I should give throughout   [10]
The sort of mock-heroic gigantesque,
With which we banter'd little Lilia first:
The women—and perhaps they felt their power,
For something in the ballads which they sang,
Or in their silent influence as they sat,
Had ever seem'd to wrestle with burlesque,
And drove us, last, to quite a solemn close—
They hated banter, wish'd for something real,
A gallant fight, a noble princess—why
Not make her true-heroic—true-sublime?   [20]
Or all, they said, as earnest as the close?
Which yet with such a framework scarce could be.
Then rose a little feud betwixt the two,
Betwixt the mockers and the realists:
And I, betwixt them both, to please them both,
And yet to give the story as it rose,
I moved as in a strange diagonal,
And maybe neither pleased myself nor them.

But Lilia pleased me, for she took no part
In our dispute: the sequel of the tale   [30]
Had touch'd her; and she sat, she pluck'd the grass,
She flung it from her, thinking: last, she fixt
A showery glance upon her aunt, and said,
'You—tell us what we are' who might have told,
For she was cramm'd with theories out of books,
But that there rose a shout: the gates were closed
At sunset, and the crowd were swarming now,
To take their leave, about the garden rails.

So I and some went out to these: we climb'd
The slope to Vivian-place, and turning saw   [40]
The happy valleys, half in light, and half
Far-shadowing from the west, a land of peace;
Gray halls alone among their massive groves;
Trim hamlets; here and there a rustic tower

Half-lost in belts of hop and breadths of wheat;
The shimmering glimpses of a stream; the seas;
A red sail, or a white; and far beyond,
Imagined more than seen, the skirts of France.

'Look there, a garden!' said my college friend,
The Tory member's elder son, 'and there!   [50]
God bless the narrow sea which keeps her off,
And keeps our Britain, whole within herself,
A nation yet, the rulers and the ruled—
Some sense of duty, something of a faith,
Some reverence for the laws ourselves have made,
Some patient force to change them when we will,
Some civic manhood firm against the crowd—
But yonder, whiff! there comes a sudden heat,
The gravest citizen seems to lose his head,
The king is scared, the soldier will not fight,   [60]
The little boys begin to shoot and stab,
A kingdom topples over with a shriek
Like an old woman, and down rolls the world
In mock heroics stranger than our own;
Revolts, republics, revolutions, most
No graver than a schoolboys' barring out;
Too comic for the solemn things they are,
Too solemn for the comic touches in them,
Like our wild Princess with as wise a dream
As some of theirs—God bless the narrow seas!   [70]
I wish they were a whole Atlantic broad.'

'Have patience,' I replied, 'ourselves are full
Of social wrong; and maybe wildest dreams
Are but the needful preludes of the truth:
For me, the genial day, the happy crowd,
The sport half-science, fill me with a faith.
This fine old world of ours is but a child
Yet in the go-cart. Patience! Give it time
To learn its limbs: there is a hand that guides.'

In such discourse we gain'd the garden rails,   [80]
And there we saw Sir Walter where he stood,
Before a tower of crimson holly-hoaks,
Among six boys, head under head, and look'd

No little lily-handed Baronet he,
A great broad-shoulder'd genial Englishman,
A lord of fat prize-oxen and of sheep,
A raiser of huge melons and of pine,°
A patron of some thirty charities,
A pamphleteer on guano and on grain,°
A quarter-sessions chairman, abler none;   [90]
Fair-hair'd and redder than a windy morn;
Now shaking hands with him, now him, of those
That stood the nearest—now address'd to speech—
Who spoke few words and pithy, such as closed
Welcome, farewell, and welcome for the year
To follow: a shout rose again, and made
The long line of the approaching rookery swerve
From the elms, and shook the branches of the deer
From slope to slope thro' distant ferns, and rang
Beyond the bourn of sunset; O, a shout   [100]
More joyful than the city-roar that hails
Premier or king! Why should not these great Sirs
Give up their parks some dozen times a year
To let the people breathe? So thrice they cried,
I likewise, and in groups they stream'd away.

But we went back to the Abbey, and sat on,
So much the gathering darkness charm'd: we sat
But spoke not, rapt in nameless reverie,
Perchance upon the future man: the walls
Blacken'd about us, bats wheel'd, and owls whoop'd,   [110]
And gradually the powers of the night,
That range above the region of the wind,
Deepening the courts of twilight broke them up
Thro' all the silent spaces of the worlds,
Beyond all thought into the Heaven of Heavens.

Last little Lilia, rising quietly,
Disrobed the glimmering statue of Sir Ralph
From those rich silks, and home well-pleased we went.

IN MEMORIAM A.H.H. (1850)

OBIIT MDCCCXXXIII

PROLOGUE

Strong Son of God, immortal Love,
　　Whom we, that have not seen thy face,
　　By faith, and faith alone, embrace,
Believing where we cannot prove;

Thine are these orbs of light and shade;°
　　Thou madest Life in man and brute;
　　Thou madest Death; and lo, thy foot
Is on the skull which thou hast made.

Thou wilt not leave us in the dust:
　　Thou madest man, he knows not why,　　　　[10]
　　He thinks he was not made to die;
And thou hast made him: thou art just.

Thou seemest human and divine,
　　The highest, holiest manhood, thou:
　　Our wills are ours, we know not how,
Our wills are ours, to make them thine.

Our little systems have their day;
　　They have their day and cease to be:
　　They are but broken lights of thee,
And thou, O Lord, art more than they.　　　　[20]

We have but faith: we cannot know;
　　For knowledge is of things we see;
　　And yet we trust it comes from thee,
A beam in darkness: let it grow.

Let knowledge grow from more to more,
　　But more of reverence in us dwell;
　　That mind and soul, according well,
May make one music as before,°

But vaster. We are fools and slight;
      We mock thee when we do not fear: [30]
      But help thy foolish ones to bear;
Help thy vain worlds to bear thy light.

Forgive what seem'd my sin in me;
      What seem'd my worth since I began;
      For merit lives from man to man,
And not from man, O Lord, to thee.

Forgive my grief for one removed,
      Thy creature, whom I found so fair.
      I trust he lives in thee, and there
I find him worthier to be loved.   [40]

Forgive these wild and wandering cries,
      Confusions of a wasted youth;
      Forgive them where they fail in truth,
And in thy wisdom make me wise.

                  1849

I

I held it truth, with him who sings°
      To one clear harp in divers tones,
      That men may rise on stepping-stones
Of their dead selves to higher things.

But who shall so forecast the years
      And find in loss a gain to match?
      Or reach a hand thro' time to catch
The far-off interest of tears?

Let Love clasp Grief lest both be drown'd,
      Let darkness keep her raven gloss: [10]
      Ah, sweeter to be drunk with loss,
To dance with death, to beat the ground,

Than that the victor Hours should scorn°
      The long result of love, and boast,
      'Behold the man that loved and lost,
But all he was is overworn.'

II

Old Yew, which graspest at the stones
    That name the under-lying dead,
    Thy fibres net the dreamless head,
Thy roots are wrapt about the bones.

The seasons bring the flower again,
    And bring the firstling to the flock;
    And in the dusk of thee, the clock°
Beats out the little lives of men.

O not for thee the glow, the bloom,
    Who changest not in any gale,   [10]
    Nor branding summer suns avail
To touch thy thousand years of gloom:

And gazing on thee, sullen tree,
    Sick for thy stubborn hardihood,°
    I seem to fail from out my blood
And grow incorporate into thee.

III

O Sorrow, cruel fellowship,
    O Priestess in the vaults of Death,
    O sweet and bitter in a breath,
What whispers from thy lying lip?

'The stars,' she whispers, 'blindly run;
    A web is woven across the sky;
    From out waste places comes a cry,
And murmurs from the dying sun:

'And all the phantom, Nature, stands—
    With all the music in her tone,   [10]
    A hollow echo of my own,—
A hollow form with empty hands.'

And shall I take a thing so blind,
    Embrace her as my natural good;
    Or crush her, like a vice of blood,°
Upon the threshold of the mind?

IV

To Sleep I give my powers away;
          My will is bondsman to the dark;
          I sit within a helmless bark,
And with my heart I muse and say:

O heart, how fares it with thee now,
          That thou should'st fail from thy desire,°
          Who scarcely darest to inquire,
'What is it makes me beat so low?'

Something it is which thou hast lost,
          Some pleasure from thine early years.   [10]
          Break, thou deep vase of chilling tears,
That grief hath shaken into frost!

Such clouds of nameless trouble cross
          All night below the darken'd eyes;
          With morning wakes the will, and cries,
'Thou shalt not be the fool of loss.'

V

I sometimes hold it half a sin
          To put in words the grief I feel;
          For words, like Nature, half reveal
And half conceal the Soul within.

But, for the unquiet heart and brain,
          A use in measured language lies;
          The sad mechanic exercise,
Like dull narcotics, numbing pain.

In words, like weeds, I'll wrap me o'er,°
          Like coarsest clothes against the cold: [10]
          But that large grief which these enfold
Is given in outline and no more.

VI

One writes, that 'Other friends remain,'
          That 'Loss is common to the race'—
          And common is the commonplace,
And vacant chaff well meant for grain.

That loss is common would not make
  My own less bitter, rather more:
  Too common! Never morning wore
To evening, but some heart did break.

O father, wheresoe'er thou be,
  Who pledgest now thy gallant son;   [10]
  A shot, ere half thy draught be done,
Hath still'd the life that beat from thee.

O mother, praying God will save
  Thy sailor,—while thy head is bow'd,
  His heavy-shotted hammock-shroud
Drops in his vast and wandering grave.

Ye know no more than I who wrought
  At that last hour to please him well;
  Who mused on all I had to tell,
And something written, something thought; [20]

Expecting still his advent home;
  And ever met him on his way
  With wishes, thinking, 'here to-day,'
Or 'here to-morrow will he come.'

O somewhere, meek, unconscious dove,°
  That sittest ranging golden hair;
  And glad to find thyself so fair,
Poor child, that waitest for thy love!

For now her father's chimney glows
  In expectation of a guest;   [30]
  And thinking 'this will please him best,'
She takes a riband or a rose;

For he will see them on to-night;
  And with the thought her colour burns;
  And, having left the glass, she turns
Once more to set a ringlet right;

And, even when she turn'd, the curse
  Had fallen, and her future Lord
  Was drown'd in passing thro' the ford,
Or kill'd in falling from his horse.   [40]

O what to her shall be the end?
>> And what to me remains of good?
>> To her, perpetual maidenhood,
And unto me no second friend.

VII

Dark house, by which once more I stand°
>> Here in the long unlovely street,
>> Doors, where my heart was used to beat
So quickly, waiting for a hand,

A hand that can be clasp'd no more—
>> Behold me, for I cannot sleep,
>> And like a guilty thing I creep
At earliest morning to the door.

He is not here; but far away
>> The noise of life begins again,   [10]
>> And ghastly thro' the drizzling rain
On the bald street breaks the blank day.

VIII

A happy lover who has come
>> To look on her that loves him well,
>> Who 'lights and rings the gateway bell,
And learns her gone and far from home;

He saddens, all the magic light
>> Dies off at once from bower and hall,
>> And all the place is dark, and all
The chambers emptied of delight:

So find I every pleasant spot
>> In which we two were wont to meet,   [10]
>> The field, the chamber and the street,
For all is dark where thou art not.

Yet as that other, wandering there
>> In those deserted walks, may find
>> A flower beat with rain and wind,
Which once she foster'd up with care;

So seems it in my deep regret,
        O my forsaken heart, with thee
        And this poor flower of poesy
Which little cared for fades not yet.   [20]

But since it pleased a vanish'd eye,
        I go to plant it on his tomb,
        That if it can it there may bloom,
Or dying, there at least may die.

IX

Fair ship, that from the Italian shore°
        Sailest the placid ocean-plains
        With my lost Arthur's loved remains,
Spread thy full wings, and waft him o'er.

So draw him home to those that mourn
        In vain; a favourable speed
        Ruffle thy mirror'd mast, and lead
Thro' prosperous floods his holy urn.

All night no ruder air perplex
        Thy sliding keel, till Phosphor, bright°   [10]
        As our pure love, thro' early light
Shall glimmer on the dewy decks.

Sphere all your lights around, above;
        Sleep, gentle heavens, before the prow;
        Sleep, gentle winds, as he sleeps now,
My friend, the brother of my love;

My Arthur, whom I shall not see
        Till all my widow'd race be run;
        Dear as the mother to the son,
More than my brothers are to me.   [20]

X

I hear the noise about thy keel;
        I hear the bell struck in the night:
        I see the cabin-window bright;
I see the sailor at the wheel.

Thou bring'st the sailor to his wife,
　　　And travell'd men from foreign lands;
　　　And letters unto trembling hands;
And, thy dark freight, a vanish'd life.

So bring him: we have idle dreams:
　　　This look of quiet flatters thus   [10]
　　　Our home-bred fancies: O to us,
The fools of habit, sweeter seems

To rest beneath the clover sod,
　　　That takes the sunshine and the rains,
　　　Or where the kneeling hamlet drains
The chalice of the grapes of God;°

Than if with thee the roaring wells
　　　Should gulf him fathom–deep in brine;
　　　And hands so often clasp'd in mine,
Should toss with tangle and with shells.°   [20]

XI

Calm is the morn without a sound,
　　　Calm as to suit a calmer grief,
　　　And only thro' the faded leaf
The chestnut pattering to the ground:

Calm and deep peace on this high wold,°
　　　And on these dews that drench the furze,
　　　And all the silvery gossamers
That twinkle into green and gold:

Calm and still light on yon great plain
　　　That sweeps with all its autumn bowers,   [10]
　　　And crowded farms and lessening towers,
To mingle with the bounding main:

Calm and deep peace in this wide air,
　　　These leaves that redden to the fall;
　　　And in my heart, if calm at all,
If any calm, a calm despair:

Calm on the seas, and silver sleep,
　　　And waves that sway themselves in rest,
　　　And dead calm in that noble breast
Which heaves but with the heaving deep.   [20]

XII

Lo, as a dove when up she springs
    To bear thro' Heaven a tale of woe,
    Some dolorous message knit below
The wild pulsation of her wings;

Like her I go; I cannot stay;
    I leave this mortal ark behind,
    A weight of nerves without a mind,
And leave the cliffs, and haste away

O'er ocean-mirrors rounded large,
    And reach the glow of southern skies,   [10]
    And see the sails at distance rise,
And linger weeping on the marge,

And saying; 'Comes he thus, my friend?
    Is this the end of all my care?'
    And circle moaning in the air:
'Is this the end? Is this the end?'

And forward dart again, and play
    About the prow, and back return
    To where the body sits, and learn
That I have been an hour away.   [20]

XIII

Tears of the widower, when he sees
    A late-lost form that sleep reveals,
    And moves his doubtful arms, and feels
Her place is empty, fall like these;

Which weep a loss for ever new,
    A void where heart on heart reposed;
    And, where warm hands have prest and closed,
Silence, till I be silent too.

Which weep the comrade of my choice,
    An awful thought, a life removed,   [10]
    The human-hearted man I loved,
A Spirit, not a breathing voice.

Come Time, and teach me, many years,°
    I do not suffer in a dream;
    For now so strange do these things seem,
Mine eyes have leisure for their tears;

My fancies time to rise on wing,
    And glance about the approaching sails,
    As tho' they brought but merchants' bales,
And not the burthen that they bring.   [20]

XIV

If one should bring me this report,
    That thou hadst touch'd the land to-day,°
    And I went down unto the quay,
And found thee lying in the port;

And standing, muffled round with woe,
    Should see thy passengers in rank
    Come stepping lightly down the plank,
And beckoning unto those they know;

And if along with these should come
    The man I held as half-divine;   [10]
    Should strike a sudden hand in mind,
And ask a thousand things of home;

And I should tell him all my pain,
    And how my life had droop'd of late,
    And he should sorrow o'er my state
And marvel what possess'd my brain;

And I perceived no touch of change,
    No hint of death in all his frame,
    But found him all in all the same,
I should not feel it to be strange.   [20]

XV

To-night the winds begin to rise
    And roar from yonder dropping day:
    The last red leaf is whirl'd away,
The rooks are blown about the skies;

The forest crack'd, the waters curl'd,
    The cattle huddled on the lea;
    And wildly dash'd on tower and tree
The sunbeam strikes along the world:

And but for fancies, which aver
    That all thy motions gently pass   [10]
    Athwart a plane of molten glass,
I scarce could brook the strain and stir

That makes the barren branches loud;
    And but for fear it is not so,
    The wild unrest that lives in woe
Would dote and pore on yonder cloud

That rises upward always higher,
    And onward drags a labouring breast,
    And topples round the dreary west,
A looming bastion fringed with fire.   [20]

XVI

What words are these have fall'n from me?
    Can calm despair and wild unrest
    Be tenants of a single breast,
Or sorrow such a changeling be?

Or doth she only seem to take
    The touch of change in calm or storm;
    But knows no more of transient form
In her deep self, than some dead lake

That holds the shadow of a lark
    Hung in the shadow of a heaven?   [10]
    Or has the shock, so harshly given,
Confused me like the unhappy bark

That strikes by night a craggy shelf,
    And staggers blindly ere she sink?
    And stunn'd me from my power to think
And all my knowledge of myself;

And made me that delirious man
    Whose fancy fuses old and new,
    And flashes into false and true,
And mingles all without a plan?   [20]

XVII

Thou comest, much wept for: such a breeze
    Compell'd thy canvas, and my prayer
    Was as the whisper of an air
To breathe thee over lonely seas.

For I in spirit saw thee move
    Thro' circles of the bounding sky,
    Week after week: the days go by:
Come quick, thou bringest all I love.

Henceforth, wherever thou may'st roam,
    My blessing, like a line of light,   [10]
    Is on the waters day and night,
And like a beacon guards thee home.

So may whatever tempest mars
    Mid-ocean, spare thee, sacred bark;
    And balmy drops in summer dark
Slide from the bosom of the stars.

So kind an office hath been done,
    Such precious relics brought by thee;
    The dust of him I shall not see
Till all my widow'd race be run.   [20]

XVIII

'Tis well; 'tis something; we may stand
    Where he in English earth is laid,
    And from his ashes may be made
The violet of his native land.

'Tis little; but it looks in truth
    As if the quiet bones were blest
    Among familiar names to rest
And in the places of his youth.

Come then, pure hands, and bear the head
    That sleeps or wears the mask of sleep,   [10]
    And come, whatever loves to weep,
And hear the ritual of the dead.

Ah yet, ev'n yet, if this might be,
    I, falling on his faithful heart,
    Would breathing thro' his lips impart
The life that almost dies in me;

That dies not, but endures with pain,
    And slowly forms the firmer mind,
    Treasuring the look it cannot find,
The words that are not heard again.   [20]

XIX

The Danube to the Severn gave°
    The darken'd heart that beat no more;
    They laid him by the pleasant shore,
And in the hearing of the wave.

There twice a day the Severn fills;
    The salt sea-water passes by,
    And hushes half the babbling Wye,
And makes a silence in the hills.

The Wye is hush'd nor moved along,
    And hush'd my deepest grief of all,   [10]
    When fill'd with tears that cannot fall,
I brim with sorrow drowning song.

The tide flows down, the wave again
    Is vocal in its wooded walls;
    My deeper anguish also falls,
And I can speak a little then.

XX

The lesser griefs that may be said,
    That breathe a thousand tender vows,
    Are but as servants in a house
Where lies the master newly dead;

Who speak their feeling as it is,
        And weep the fulness from the mind:
        'It will be hard,' they say, 'to find
Another service such as this.'

My lighter moods are like to these,
        That out of words a comfort win;   [10]
        But there are other griefs within,
And tears that at their fountain freeze;

For by the hearth the children sit
        Cold in that atmosphere of Death,
        And scarce endure to draw the breath,
Or like to noiseless phantoms flit:

But open converse is there none,
        So much the vital spirits sink
        To see the vacant chair, and think,
'How good! how kind ! and he is gone.'   [20]

XXI

I sing to him that rests below,
        And, since the grasses round me wave,
        I take the grasses of the grave,
And make them pipes whereon to blow.°

The traveller hears me now and then,
        And sometimes harshly will he speak:
        'This fellow would make weakness weak,
And melt the waxen hearts of men.'

Another answers, 'Let him be,
        He loves to make parade of pain,   [10]
        That with his piping he may gain
The praise that comes to constancy.'

A third is wroth: 'Is this an hour
        For private sorrow's barren song,
        When more and more the people throng
The chairs and thrones of civil power?°

'A time to sicken and to swoon,
  When Science reaches forth her arms
  To feel from world to world, and charms
Her secret from the latest moon?'   [20]

Behold, ye speak an idle thing:
  Ye never knew the sacred dust:
  I do but sing because I must,
And pipe but as the linnets sing:

And one is glad; her note is gay,
  For now her little ones have ranged;
  And one is sad; her note is changed,
Because her brood is stol'n away.

XXII

The path by which we twain did go,
  Which led by tracts that pleased us well,
  Thro' four sweet years arose and fell,°
From flower to flower, from snow to snow:

And we with singing cheer'd the way,
  And, crown'd with all the season lent,
  From April on to April went,
And glad at heart from May to May:

But where the path we walk'd began
  To slant the fifth autumnal slope,   [10]
  As we descended following Hope,
There sat the Shadow fear'd of man;°

Who broke our fair companionship,
  And spread his mantle dark and cold,
  And wrapt thee formless in the fold,
And dull'd the murmur on thy lip,

And bore thee where I could not see
  Nor follow, tho' I walk in haste,
  And think, that somewhere in the waste
The Shadow sits and waits for me.   [20]

XXIII

Now, sometimes in my sorrow shut,
    Or breaking into song by fits,
    Alone, alone, to where he sits,
The Shadow cloak'd from head to foot,

Who keeps the keys of all the creeds,°
    I wander, often falling lame,
    And looking back to whence I came,
Or on to where the pathway leads;

And crying, How changed from where it ran
    Thro' lands where not a leaf was dumb;   [10]
    But all the lavish hills would hum
The murmur of a happy Pan:°

When each by turns was guide to each,
    And Fancy light from Fancy caught,
    And Thought leapt out to wed with Thought
Ere Thought could wed itself with Speech;

And all we met was fair and good,
    And all was good that Time could bring,
    And all the secret of the Spring
Moved in the chambers of the blood;   [20]

And many an old philosophy
    On Argive heights divinely sang,°
    And round us all the thicket rang
To many a flute of Arcady.°

XXIV

And was the day of my delight
    As pure and perfect as I say?
    The very source and fount of Day°
Is dash'd with wandering isles of night.

If all was good and fair we met,
    This earth had been the Paradise
    It never look'd to human eyes
Since our first Sun arose and set.

And is it that the haze of grief
    Makes former gladness loom so great?   [10]
    The lowness of the present state,
That sets the past in this relief?

Or that the past will always win
    A glory from its being far;
    And orb into the perfect star°
We saw not, when we moved therein?

XXV

I know that this was Life,—the track
    Whereon with equal feet we fared;
    And then, as now, the day prepared
The daily burden for the back.

But this it was that made me move
    As light as carrier-birds in air;
    I loved the weight I had to bear,
Because it needed help of Love:

Nor could I weary, heart or limb,
    When mighty Love would cleave in twain   [10]
    The lading of a single pain,°
And part it, giving half to him.

XXVI

Still onward winds the dreary way;
    I with it; for I long to prove
    No lapse of moons can canker Love,
Whatever fickle tongues may say.

And if that eye which watches guilt
    And goodness, and hath power to see
    Within the green the moulder'd tree,
And towers fall'n as soon as built—

Oh, if indeed that eye foresee
    Or see (in Him is no before)   [10]
    In more of life true life no more
And Love the indifference to be,

Then might I find, ere yet the morn
    Breaks hither over Indian seas,
    That Shadow waiting with the keys,
To shroud me from my proper scorn.°

XXVII

I envy not in any moods
    The captive void of noble rage,
    The linnet born within the cage,
That never knew the summer woods:

I envy not the beast that takes
    His license in the field of time,
    Unfetter'd by the sense of crime,
To whom a conscience never wakes;

Nor, what may count itself as blest,
    The heart that never plighted troth   [10]
    But stagnates in the weeds of sloth;
Nor any want-begotten rest.°

I hold it true, whate'er befall;
    I feel it, when I sorrow most;
    'Tis better to have loved and lost
Than never to have loved at all.°

XXVIII

The time draws near the birth of Christ:°
    The moon is hid; the night is still;
    The Christmas bells from hill to hill
Answer each other in the mist.

Four voices of four hamlets round,
    From far and near, on mead and moor,
    Swell out and fail, as if a door
Were shut between me and the sound:

Each voice four changes on the wind,°
    That now dilate, and now decrease,   [10]
    Peace and goodwill, goodwill and peace,
Peace and goodwill, to all mankind.

This year I slept and woke with pain,
    I almost wish'd no more to wake,
    And that my hold on life would break
Before I heard those bells again:

But they my troubled spirit rule,
    For they controll'd me when a boy;
    They bring me sorrow touch'd with joy,
The merry merry bells of Yule.   [20]

XXIX

With such compelling cause to grieve
    As daily vexes household peace,
    And chains regret to his decease,
How dare we keep our Christmas-eve;

Which brings no more a welcome guest
    To enrich the threshold of the night
    With shower'd largess of delight
In dance and song and game and jest?

Yet go, and while the holly boughs
    Entwine the cold baptismal font,   [10]
    Make one wreath more for Use and Wont,°
That guard the portals of the house;

Old sisters of a day gone by,°
    Gray nurses, loving nothing new;
    Why should they miss their yearly due
Before their time? They too will die.

XXX

With trembling fingers did we weave
    The holly round the Christmas hearth;
    A rainy cloud possess'd the earth,
And sadly fell our Christmas-eve.

At our old pastimes in the hall
    We gambol'd, making vain pretence
    Of gladness, with an awful sense
Of one mute Shadow watching all.°

We paused: the winds were in the beech:
    We heard them sweep the winter land;   [10]
    And in a circle hand-in-hand
Sat silent, looking each at each.

Then echo-like our voices rang;
    We sung, tho' every eye was dim,
    A merry song we sang with him
Last year: impetuously we sang:

We ceased: a gentler feeling crept
    Upon us: surely rest is meet:°
    'They rest,' we said, 'their sleep is sweet,'
And silence follow'd, and we wept.   [20]

Our voices took a higher range;
    Once more we sang: 'They do not die
    Nor lose their mortal sympathy,
Nor change to us, although they change;

'Rapt from the fickle and the frail
    With gather'd power, yet the same,
    Pierces the keen seraphic flame°
From orb to orb, from veil to veil.'

Rise, happy morn, rise, holy morn,
    Draw forth the cheerful day from night: [30]
    O Father, touch the east, and light
The light that shone when Hope was born.

XXXI

When Lazarus left his charnel-cave,°
    And home to Mary's house return'd,
    Was this demanded—if he yearn'd
To hear her weeping by his grave?

'Where wert thou, brother, those four days?'
    There lives no record of reply,
    Which telling what it is to die
Had surely added praise to praise.

From every house the neighbours met,
    The streets were fill'd with joyful sound,   [10]
    A solemn gladness even crown'd
The purple brows of Olivet.°

Behold a man raised up by Christ!
    The rest remaineth unreveal'd;
    He told it not; or something seal'd°
The lips of that Evangelist.°

XXXII

Her eyes are homes of silent prayer,°
    Nor other thought her mind admits
    But, he was dead, and there he sits,
And he that brought him back is there.

Then one deep love doth supersede
    All other, when her ardent gaze
    Roves from the living brother's face,
And rests upon the Life indeed.°

All subtle thought, all curious fears,
    Borne down by gladness so complete,   [10]
    She bows, she bathes the Saviour's feet
With costly spikenard and with tears.°

Thrice blest whose lives are faithful prayers,
    Whose loves in higher love endure;
    What souls possess themselves so pure,
Or is there blessedness like theirs?

XXXIII

O thou that after toil and storm°
    Mayst seem to have reach'd a purer air,
    Whose faith has centre everywhere,
Nor cares to fix itself to form,

Leave thou thy sister when she prays,
    Her early Heaven, her happy views;
    Nor thou with shadow'd hint confuse
A life that leads melodious days.

Her faith thro' form is pure as thine,
    Her hands are quicker unto good: [10]
    Oh, sacred be the flesh and blood
To which she links a truth divine!

See thou, that countest reason ripe
    In holding by the law within,
    Thou fail not in a world of sin,
And ev'n for want of such a type.

XXXIV

My own dim life should teach me this,
    That life shall live for evermore,
    Else earth is darkness at the core,
And dust and ashes all that is;

This round of green, this orb of flame,°
    Fantastic beauty; such as lurks
    In some wild Poet, when he works
Without a conscience or an aim.

What then were God to such as I?
    'Twere hardly worth my while to choose   [10]
    Of things all mortal, or to use
A little patience ere I die;

'Twere best at once to sink to peace,
    Like birds the charming serpent draws,
    To drop head-foremost in the jaws
Of vacant darkness and to cease.

XXXV

Yet if some voice that man could trust
    Should murmur from the narrow house,
    'The cheeks drop in; the body bows;
Man dies: nor is there hope in dust:'

Might I not say? 'Yet even here,
    But for one hour, O Love, I strive
    To keep so sweet a thing alive:'
But I should turn mine ears and hear

The moanings of the homeless sea,
    The sound of streams that swift or slow   [10]
    Draw down Æonian hills, and sow°
The dust of continents to be;

And Love would answer with a sigh,
    'The sound of that forgetful shore°
    Will change my sweetness more and more,
Half-dead to know that I shall die.'

O me, what profits it to put
    An idle case? If Death were seen
    At first as Death, Love had not been,°
Or been in narrowest working shut,   [20]

Mere fellowship of sluggish moods,
    Or in his coarsest Satyr-shape°
    Had bruised the herb and crush'd the grape,
And bask'd and batten'd in the woods.

XXXVI

Tho' truths in manhood darkly join,
    Deep-seated in our mystic frame,
    We yield all blessing to the name
Of Him that made them current coin;

For Wisdom dealt with mortal powers,
    Where truth in closest words shall fail,
    When truth embodied in a tale°
Shall enter in at lowly doors.

And so the Word had breath, and wrought°
    With human hands the creed of creeds   [10]
    In loveliness of perfect deeds,
More strong than all poetic thought;

Which he may read that binds the sheaf,
    Or builds the house, or digs the grave,
    And those wild eyes that watch the wave°
In roarings round the coral reef.

XXXVII

Urania speaks with darken'd brow:°
     'Thou pratest here where thou art least;
     This faith has many a purer priest,
And many an abler voice than thou.

'Go down beside thy native rill,
     On thy Parnassus set thy feet,°
     And hear thy laurel whisper sweet
About the ledges of the hill.'

And my Melpomene replies,°
     A touch of shame upon her cheek: [10]
     'I am not worthy even to speak
Of thy prevailing mysteries;

'For I am but an earthly Muse,
     And owning but a little art
     To lull with song an aching heart,
And render human love his dues;

'But brooding on the dear one dead,
     And all he said of things divine,
     (And dear to me as sacred wine
To dying lips is all he said),   [20]

'I murmur'd, as I came along,
     Of comfort clasp'd in truth reveal'd;
     And loiter'd in the master's field,
And darken'd sanctities with song.'

XXXVIII

With weary steps I loiter on,
     Tho' always under alter'd skies
     The purple from the distance dies,
My prospect and horizon gone.

No joy the blowing season gives,
     The herald melodies of spring,
     But in the songs I love to sing
A doubtful gleam of solace lives.

If any care for what is here
    Survive in spirits render'd free,   [10]
    Then are these songs I sing of thee
Not all ungrateful to thine ear.

XXXIX

Old warder of these buried bones,°
    And answering now my random stroke
    With fruitful cloud and living smoke,
Dark yew, that graspest at the stones

And dippest toward the dreamless head,
    To thee too comes the golden hour
    When flower is feeling after flower;
But Sorrow—fixt upon the dead,

And darkening the dark graves of men,—
    What whisper'd from her lying lips?   [10]
    Thy gloom is kindled at the tips,
And passes into gloom again.°

XL

Could we forget the widow'd hour
    And look on Spirits breathed away,
    As on a maiden in the day
When first she wears her orange-flower!

When crown'd with blessing she doth rise
    To take her latest leave of home,
    And hopes and light regrets that come
Make April of her tender eyes;

And doubtful joys the father move,
    And tears are on the mother's face,   [10]
    As parting with a long embrace
She enters other realms of love;

Her office there to rear, to teach,
    Becoming as is meet and fit
    A link among the days, to knit
The generations each with each;

And, doubtless, unto thee is given°
    A life that bears immortal fruit
    In those great offices that suit
The full-grown energies of heaven.   [20]

Ay me, the difference I discern!
    How often shall her old fireside
    Be cheer'd with tidings of the bride,
How often she herself return,

And tell them all they would have told,
    And bring her babe, and make her boast,
    Till even those that miss'd her most
Shall count new things as dear as old:

But thou and I have shaken hands,
    Till growing winters lay me low;   [30]
    My paths are in the fields I know,
And thine in undiscover'd lands.°

XLI

Thy spirit ere our fatal loss
    Did ever rise from high to higher;
    As mounts the heavenward altar-fire,
As flies the lighter thro' the gross.

But thou art turn'd to something strange,
    And I have lost the links that bound
    Thy changes; here upon the ground,
No more partaker of thy change.

Deep folly! yet that this could be—
    That I could wing my will with might   [10]
    To leap the grades of life and light,
And flash at once, my friend, to thee.

For tho' my nature rarely yields
    To that vague fear implied in death;
    Nor shudders at the gulfs beneath,
The howlings from forgotten fields;°

Yet oft when sundown skirts the moor
  An inner trouble I behold,
  A spectral doubt which makes me cold,
That I shall be thy mate no more,   [20]

Tho' following with an upward mind
  The wonders that have come to thee,
  Thro' all the secular to-be,
But evermore a life behind.°

XLII

I vex my heart with fancies dim:
  He still outstript me in the race;
  It was but unity of place
That made me dream I rank'd with him.

And so may Place retain us still,
  And he the much-beloved again,
  A lord of large experience, train
To riper growth the mind and will:

And what delights can equal those
  That stir the spirit's inner deeps,   [10]
  When one that loves but knows not, reaps
A truth from one that loves and knows?

XLIII

If Sleep and Death be truly one,
  And every spirit's folded bloom
  Thro' all its intervital gloom°
In some long trance should slumber on;

Unconscious of the sliding hour,
  Bare of the body, might it last,
  And silent traces of the past
Be all the colour of the flower:

So then were nothing lost to man;
  So that still garden of the souls   [10]
  In many a figured leaf enrolls
The total world since life began;

And love will last as pure and whole
    As when he loved me here in Time,
    And at the spiritual prime
Rewaken with the dawning soul.

XLIV

How fares it with the happy dead?
    For here the man is more and more;
    But he forgets the days before
God shut the doorways of his head.°

The days have vanish'd, tone and tint,
    And yet perhaps the hoarding sense
    Gives out at times (he knows not whence)
A little flash, a mystic hint;

And in the long harmonious years
    (If Death so taste Lethean springs),   [10]
    May some dim touch of earthly things
Surprise thee ranging with thy peers.

If such a dreamy touch should fall,
    O turn thee round, resolve the doubt;
    My guardian angel will speak out
In that high place, and tell thee all.

XLV

The baby new to earth and sky,
    What time his tender palm is prest
    Against the circle of the breast,
Has never thought that 'this is I:'

But as he grows he gathers much,
    And learns the use of 'I', and 'me,'
    And finds 'I am not what I see,
And other than the things I touch.'

So rounds he to a separate mind
    From whence clear memory may begin,   [10]
    As thro' the frame that binds him in
His isolation grows defined.

This use may lie in blood and breath,
 Which else were fruitless of their due,
 Had man to learn himself anew
Beyond the second birth of Death.

XLVI

We ranging down this lower track,
 The path we came by, thorn and flower,
 Is shadow'd by the growing hour,
Lest life should fail in looking back.

So be it: there no shade can last°
 In that deep dawn behind the tomb,
 But clear from marge to marge shall bloom°
The eternal landscape of the past;

A lifelong tract of time reveal'd;
 The fruitful hours of still increase;   [10]
 Days order'd in a wealthy peace,
And those five years its richest field.

O Love, thy province were not large,
 A bounded field, nor stretching far;
 Look also, Love, a brooding star,
A rosy warmth from marge to marge.

XLVII

That each, who seems a separate whole,
 Should move his rounds, and fusing all
 The skirts of self again, should fall
Remerging in the general Soul,°

Is faith as vague as all unsweet:
 Eternal form shall still divide
 The eternal soul from all beside;
And I shall know him when we meet:

And we shall sit at endless feast,
 Enjoying each the other's good: [10]
 What vaster dream can hit the mood
Of Love on earth? He seeks at least

Upon the last and sharpest height,
    Before the spirits fade away,
    Some landing-place, to clasp and say,
'Farewell! We lose ourselves in light.'

XLVIII

If these brief lays, of Sorrow born,
    Were taken to be such as closed
    Grave doubts and answers here proposed,
Then these were such as men might scorn:

Her care is not to part and prove;°
    She takes, when harsher moods remit,
    What slender shade of doubt may flit,
And makes it vassal unto love:

And hence, indeed, she sports with words,
    But better serves a wholesome law,   [10]
    And holds it sin and shame to draw
The deepest measure from the chords:

Nor dare she trust a larger lay,
    But rather loosens from the lip
    Short swallow-flights of song, that dip
Their wings in tears, and skim away.

XLIX

From art, from nature, from the schools,
    Let random influences glance,
    Like light in many a shiver'd lance
That breaks about the dappled pools:

The lighest wave of thought shall lisp,
    The fancy's tenderest eddy wreathe,
    The slightest air of song shall breathe
To make the sullen surface crisp.°

And look thy look, and go thy way,
    But blame not thou the winds that make   [10]
    The seeming-wanton ripple break,
The tender-pencil'd shadow play.

Beneath all fancied hopes and fears
    Ay me, the sorrow deepens down,
    Whose muffled motions blindly drown
The bases of my life in tears.

L°

Be near me when my light is low,
    When the blood creeps, and the nerves prick
    And tingle; and the heart is sick,
And all the wheels of Being slow.

Be near me when the sensuous frame
    Is rack'd with pangs that conquer trust;
    And Time, a maniac scattering dust,
And Life, a Fury slinging flame.

Be near me when my faith is dry,
    And men the flies of latter spring,   [10]
    That lay their eggs, and sting and sing
And weave their petty cells and die.

Be near me when I fade away,
    To point the term of human strife,
    And on the low dark verge of life
The twilight of eternal day.

LI

Do we indeed desire the dead
    Should still be near us at our side?
    Is there no baseness we would hide?
No inner vileness that we dread?

Shall he for whose applause I strove,
    I had such reverence for his blame,
    See with clear eye some hidden shame
And I be lessen'd in his love?

I wrong the grave with fears untrue:
    Shall love be blamed for want of faith?   [10]
    There must be wisdom with great Death:
The dead shall look me thro' and thro'.

Be near us when we climb or fall:
    Ye watch, like God, the rolling hours
    With larger other eyes than ours,
To make allowance for us all.

LII

I cannot love thee as I ought,
    For love reflects the thing beloved;
    My words are only words, and moved
Upon the topmost froth of thought.

'Yet blame not thou thy plaintive song,'
    The Spirit of true love replied;
    'Thou canst not move me from thy side,
Nor human frailty do me wrong.

'What keeps a spirit wholly true
    To that ideal which he bears?
    What record? not the sinless years°   [10]
That breathed beneath the Syrian blue:

'So fret not, like an idle girl,
    That life is dash'd with flecks of sin.
    Abide: thy wealth is gather'd in,
When Time hath sunder'd shell from pearl.'

LIII

How many a father have I seen,
    A sober man, among his boys,
    Whose youth was full of foolish noise,
Who wears his manhood hale and green:

And dare we to this fancy give,°
    That had the wild oat not been sown,
    The soil, left barren, scarce had grown
The grain by which a man may live?

Or, if we held the doctrine sound
    For life outliving heats of youth,   [10]
    Yet who would preach it as a truth
To those that eddy round and round?

Hold thou the good: define it well:
> For fear divine Philosophy
> Should push beyond her mark, and be
Procuress to the Lords of Hell.

LIV

Oh yet we trust that somehow good
> Will be the final goal of ill,
> To pangs of nature, sins of will,
Defects of doubt, and taints of blood;

That nothing walks with aimless feet;
> That not one life shall be destroy'd,
> Or cast as rubbish to the void,
When God hath made the pile complete;

That not a worm is cloven in vain;
> That not a moth with vain desire   [10]
> Is shrivell'd in a fruitless fire,
Or but subserves another's gain.

Behold, we know not anything;
> I can but trust that good shall fall
> At last—far off—at last, to all,
And every winter change to spring.

So runs my dream: but what am I?
> An infant crying in the night:
> An infant crying for the light:
And with no language but a cry.   [20]

LV

The wish, that of the living whole
> No life may fail beyond the grave,
> Derives it not from what we have
The likest God within the soul?

Are God and Nature then at strife,
> That Nature lends such evil dreams?
> So careful of the type she seems,°
So careless of the single life;

That I, considering everywhere
    Her secret meaning in her deeds,   [10]
    And finding that of fifty seeds
She often brings but one to bear,

I falter where I firmly trod,
    And falling with my weight of cares
    Upon the great world's altar-stairs
That slope thro' darkness up to God,

I stretch lame hands of faith, and grope,
    And gather dust and chaff, and call
    To what I feel is Lord of all,
And faintly trust the larger hope.   [20]

LVI°

'So careful of the type?' but no.
    From scarped cliff and quarried stone°
    She cries, 'A thousand types are gone:°
I care for nothing, all shall go.

'Thou makest thine appeal to me:
    I bring to life, I bring to death:
    The spirit does but mean the breath:
I know no more.' And he, shall he,

Man, her last work, who seem'd so fair,
    Such splendid purpose in his eyes,   [10]
    Who roll'd the psalm to wintry skies,
Who built him fanes of fruitless prayer,°

Who trusted God was love indeed
    And love Creation's final law—
    Tho' Nature, red in tooth and claw
With ravine, shriek'd against his creed—

Who loved, who suffer'd countless ills,
    Who battled for the True, the Just,
    Be blown about the desert dust,
Or seal'd within the iron hills?°   [20]

No more? A monster then, a dream,
    A discord. Dragons of the prime,°
    That tare each other in their slime,
Were mellow music match'd with him.

O life as futile, then, as frail!
    O for thy voice to soothe and bless!°
    What hope of answer, or redress?
Behind the veil, behind the veil.

LVII

Peace; come away: the song of woe
    Is after all an earthly song:
    Peace; come away: we do him wrong
To sing so wildly: let us go.

Come; let us go: your cheeks are pale;
    But half my life I leave behind:
    Methinks my friend is richly shrined;
But I shall pass; my work will fail.

Yet in these ears, till hearing dies,
    One set slow bell will seem to toll   [10]
    The passing of the sweetest soul
That ever look'd with human eyes.

I hear it now, and o'er and o'er,
    Eternal greetings to the dead;
    And 'Ave, Ave, Ave,' said,°
'Adieu, adieu' for evermore.

LVIII

In those sad words I took farewell:
    Like echoes in sepulchral halls,
    As drop by drop the water falls
In vaults and catacombs, they fell;

And, falling, idly broke the peace
    Of hearts that beat from day to day,
    Half-conscious of their dying clay,
And those cold crypts where they shall cease.

The high Muse answer'd: 'Wherefore grieve
  Thy brethren with a fruitless tear?   [10]
  Abide a little longer here,
And thou shalt take a nobler leave.'

LIX°

O Sorrow, wilt thou live with me
  No casual mistress, but a wife,
  My bosom-friend and half of life;
As I confess it needs must be;

O Sorrow, wilt thou rule my blood,
  Be sometimes lovely like a bride,
  And put thy harsher moods aside,
If thou wilt have me wise and good.

My centred passion cannot move,
  Nor will it lessen from to-day;   [10]
  But I'll have leave at times to play
As with the creature of my love;

And set thee forth, for thou art mine,
  With so much hope for years to come,
  That, howsoe'er I know thee, some
Could hardly tell what name were thine.

LX

He past; a soul of nobler tone:
  My spirit loved and loves him yet,
  Like some poor girl whose heart is set
On one whose rank exceeds her own.

He mixing with his proper sphere,
  She finds the baseness of her lot,
  Half jealous of she knows not what,
And envying all that meet him there.

The little village looks forlorn;
  She sighs amid her narrow days,   [10]
  Moving about the household ways,
In that dark house where she was born.

The foolish neighbours come and go,
    And tease her till the day draws by:
    At night she weeps, 'How vain am I!
How should he love a thing so low?'

LXI

If, in thy second state sublime,
    Thy ransom'd reason change replies
    With all the circle of the wise,
The perfect flower of human time;

And if thou cast thine eyes below,
    How dimly character'd and slight,
    How dwarf'd a growth of cold and night,
How blanch'd with darkness must I grow!

Yet turn thee to the doubtful shore,
    Where thy first form was made a man;   [10]
    I loved thee, Spirit, and love, nor can
The soul of Shakspeare love thee more.°

LXII

Tho' if an eye that's downward cast
    Could make thee somewhat blench or fail,°
    Then be my love an idle tale,
And fading legend of the past;

And thou, as one that once declined,°
    When he was little more than boy,
    On some unworthy heart with joy,
But lives to wed an equal mind;

And breathes a novel world, the while
    His other passion wholly dies,   [10]
    Or in the light of deeper eyes
Is matter for a flying smile.

LXIII

Yet pity for a horse o'er-driven,
    And love in which my hound has part,
    Can hang no weight upon my heart
In its assumptions up to heaven;

And I am so much more than these,
　　　As thou, perchance, art more than I,
　　　And yet I spare them sympathy,
And I would set their pains at ease.

So mayst thou watch me where I weep,
　　　As, unto vaster motions bound,   [10]
　　　The circuits of thine orbit round
A higher height, a deeper deep.

LXIV

Dost thou look back on what hath been,
　　　As some divinely gifted man,
　　　Whose life in low estate began
And on a simple village green;

Who breaks his birth's invidious bar,
　　　And grasps the skirts of happy chance,
　　　And breasts the blows of circumstance,
And grapples with his evil star;

Who makes by force his merit known
　　　And lives to clutch the golden keys,   [10]
　　　To mould a mighty state's decrees,
And shape the whisper of the throne;

And moving up from high to higher,
　　　Becomes on Fortune's crowning slope
　　　The pillar of a people's hope,
The centre of a world's desire;

Yet feels, as in a pensive dream,
　　　When all his active powers are still,
　　　A distant dearness in the hill,
A secret sweetness in the stream,   [20]

The limit of his narrower fate,
　　　While yet beside its vocal springs
　　　He play'd at counsellors and kings,
With one that was his earliest mate;

Who ploughs with pain his native lea
    And reaps the labour of his hands,
    Or in the furrow musing stands;
'Does my old friend remember me?'

LXV

Sweet soul, do with me as thou wilt;
    I lull a fancy trouble-tost
    With 'Love's too precious to be lost,
A little grain shall not be spilt.'

And in that solace can I sing,
    Till out of painful phases wrought
    There flutters up a happy thought,
Self-balanced on a lightsome wing:

Since we deserved the name of friends,
    And thine effect so lives in me,   [10]
    A part of mine may live in thee
And move thee on to noble ends.

LXVI

You thought my heart too far diseased;
    You wonder when my fancies play
    To find me gay among the gay,
Like one with any trifle pleased.

The shade by which my life was crost,
    Which makes a desert in the mind,
    Has made me kindly with my kind,
And like to him whose sight is lost;

Whose feet are guided thro' the land,
    Whose jest among his friends is free,   [10]
    Who takes the children on his knee,
And winds their curls about his hand:

He plays with threads, he beats his chair
    For pastime, dreaming of the sky;
    His inner day can never die,
His night of loss is always there.

LXVII

When on my bed the moonlight falls,
    I know that in thy place of rest°
    By that broad water of the west,
There comes a glory on the walls;

Thy marble bright in dark appears,
    As slowly steals a silver flame
    Along the letters of thy name,
And o'er the number of thy years.

The mystic glory swims away;
    From off my bed the moonlight dies;   [10]
    And closing eaves of wearied eyes
I sleep till dusk is dipt in gray:

And then I know the mist is drawn
    A lucid veil from coast to coast,
    And in the dark church like a ghost
Thy tablet glimmers to the dawn.

LXVIII

When in the down I sink my head,
    Sleep, Death's twin-brother, times my breath;
    Sleep, Death's twin-brother, knows not Death,
Nor can I dream of thee as dead:

I walk as ere I walk'd forlorn,
    When all our path was fresh with dew,
    And all the bugle breezes blew
Reveillée to the breaking morn.

But what is this? I turn about,
    I find a trouble in thine eye,   [10]
    Which makes me sad I know not why,
Nor can my dream resolve the doubt:

But ere the lark hath left the lea
    I wake, and I discern the truth;
    It is the trouble of my youth
That foolish sleep transfers to thee.

LXIX

I dream'd there would be Spring no more,
    That Nature's ancient power was lost:
    The streets were black with smoke and frost,
They chatter'd trifles at the door:

I wander'd from the noisy town,
    I found a wood with thorny boughs:
    I took the thorns to bind my brows,
I wore them like a civic crown:

I met with scoffs, I met with scorns
    From youth and babe and hoary hairs: [10]
    They call'd me in the public squares
The fool that wears a crown of thorns:

They call'd me fool, they call'd me child:
    I found an angel of the night;°
    The voice was low, the look was bright;
He look'd upon my crown and smiled:

He reach'd the glory of a hand,
    That seem'd to touch it into leaf:
    The voice was not the voice of grief,
The words were hard to understand.   [20]

LXX

I cannot see the features right,
    When on the gloom I strive to paint
    The face I know; the hues are faint
And mix with hollow masks of night;

Cloud-towers by ghostly masons wrought,
    A gulf that ever shuts and gapes,
    A hand that points, and palled shapes°
In shadowy thoroughfares of thought;

And crowds that stream from yawning doors,
    And shoals of pucker'd faces drive;   [10]
    Dark bulks that tumble half alive,
And lazy lengths on boundless shores;

Till all at once beyond the will
　　　　I hear a wizard music roll,
　　　　And thro' a lattice on the soul
Looks thy fair face and makes it still.

LXXI

Sleep, kinsman thou to death and trance
　　　　And madness, thou hast forged at last
　　　　A night-long Present of the Past
In which we went thro' summer France.°

Hadst thou such credit with the soul?
　　　　Then bring an opiate trebly strong,
　　　　Drug down the blindfold sense of wrong
That so my pleasure may be whole;

While now we talk as once we talk'd
　　　　Of men and minds, the dust of change,　　　　　[10]
　　　　The days that grow to something strange,
In walking as of old we walk'd

Beside the river's wooded reach,
　　　　The fortress, and the mountain ridge,
　　　　The cataract flashing from the bridge,
The breaker breaking on the beach.

LXXII

Risest thou thus, dim dawn, again,°
　　　　And howlest, issuing out of night,
　　　　With blasts that blow the poplar white,
And lash with storm the streaming pane?

Day, when my crown'd estate begun°
　　　　To pine in that reverse of doom,
　　　　Which sicken'd every living bloom,
And blurr'd the splendour of the sun;

Who usherest in the dolorous hour
　　　　With thy quick tears that make the rose　　　　[10]
　　　　Pull sideways, and the daisy close
Her crimson fringes to the shower;

Who might'st have heaved a windless flame
    Up the deep East, or, whispering, play'd
    A chequer-work of beam and shade
Along the hills, yet look'd the same,

As wan, as chill, as wild as now;
    Day, mark'd as with some hideous crime,
    When the dark hand struck down thro' time,
And cancell'd nature's best: but thou,   [20]

Lift as thou may'st thy burthen'd brows
    Thro' clouds that drench the morning star,
    And whirl the ungarner'd sheaf afar,
And sow the sky with flying boughs,

And up thy vault with roaring sound°
    Climb thy thick noon, disastrous day;
    Touch thy dull goal of joyless gray,°
And hide thy shame beneath the ground.

LXXIII

So many worlds, so much to do,
    So little done, such things to be,
    How know I what had need of thee,°
For thou wert strong as thou wert true?

The fame is quench'd that I foresaw,
    The head hath miss'd an earthly wreath:
    I curse not nature, no, nor death;
For nothing is that errs from law.

We pass; the path that each man trod
    Is dim, or will be dim, with weeds: [10]
    What fame is left for human deeds
In endless age? It rests with God.

O hollow wraith of dying fame,
    Fade wholly, while the soul exults,
    And self-infolds the large results
Of force that would have forged a name.

LXXIV

As sometimes in a dead man's face,
　　　To those that watch it more and more,
　　　A likeness, hardly seen before,
Comes out—to some one of his race:

So, dearest, now thy brows are cold,
　　　I see thee what thou art, and know
　　　Thy likeness to the wise below,
Thy kindred with the great of old.

But there is more than I can see,
　　　And what I see I leave unsaid,　　　　　　　　[10]
　　　Nor speak it, knowing Death has made
His darkness beautiful with thee.

LXXV

I leave thy praises unexpress'd
　　　In verse that brings myself relief,
　　　And by the measure of my grief
I leave thy greatness to be guess'd;

What practice howsoe'er expert
　　　In fitting aptest words to things,
　　　Or voice the richest-toned that sings,
Hath power to give thee as thou wert?

I care not in these fading days
　　　To raise a cry that lasts not long,　　　　　　[10]
　　　And round thee with the breeze of song
To stir a little dust of praise.

Thy leaf has perish'd in the green,
　　　And, while we breathe beneath the sun,
　　　The world which credits what is done
Is cold to all that might have been.

So here shall silence guard thy fame;
　　　But somewhere, out of human view,
　　　Whate'er thy hands are set to do
Is wrought with tumult of acclaim.　　　　　　　　[20]

LXXVI

Take wings of fancy, and ascend,
    And in a moment set thy face
    Where all the starry heavens of space
Are sharpen'd to a needle's end;

Take wings of foresight; lighten thro'
    The secular abyss to come,
    And lo, thy deepest lays are dumb
Before the mouldering of a yew;

And if the matin songs, that woke°
    The darkness of our planet, last,   [10]
    Thine own shall wither in the vast,
Ere half the lifetime of an oak.°

Ere these have clothed their branchy bowers
    With fifty Mays, thy songs are vain;
    And what are they when these remain
The ruin'd shells of hollow towers?

LXXVII

What hope is here for modern rhyme
    To him, who turns a musing eye
    On songs, and deeds, and lives, that lie
Foreshorten'd in the tract of time?

These mortal lullabies of pain
    May bind a book, may line a box,
    May serve to curl a maiden's locks;°
Or when a thousand moons shall wane

A man upon a stall may find,
    And, passing, turn the page that tells   [10]
    A grief, then changed to something else,
Sung by a long-forgotten mind.

But what of that? My darken'd ways
    Shall ring with music all the same;
    To breathe my loss is more than fame,
To utter love more sweet than praise.

LXXVIII

Again at Christmas did we weave°
    The holly round the Christmas hearth;
    The silent snow possess'd the earth,
And calmly fell our Christmas-eve:

The yule-clog sparkled keen with frost,°
    No wing of wind the region swept,
    But over all things brooding slept
The quiet sense of something lost.

As in the winters left behind,
    Again our ancient games had place,   [10]
    The mimic picture's breathing grace,
And dance and song and hoodman-blind.°

Who show'd a token of distress?
    No single tear, no mark of pain:
    O sorrow, then can sorrow wane?
O grief, can grief be changed to less?

O last regret, regret can die!
    No—mixt with all this mystic frame,
    Her deep relations are the same,
But with long use her tears are dry.   [20]

LXXIX

'More than my brothers are to me,'—
    Let this not vex thee, noble heart!°
    I know thee of what force thou art
To hold the costliest love in fee.

But thou and I are one in kind,
    As moulded like in Nature's mint;
    And hill and wood and field did print
The same sweet forms in either mind.

For us the same cold streamlet curl'd
    Thro' all his eddying coves; the same   [10]
    All winds that roam the twilight came
In whispers of the beauteous world.

At one dear knee we proffer'd vows,
  One lesson from one book we learn'd,
  Ere childhood's flaxen ringlet turn'd
To black and brown on kindred brows.

And so my wealth resembles thine,
  But he was rich where I was poor,
  And he supplied my want the more
As his unlikeness fitted mine.   [20]

LXXX

If any vague desire should rise,
  That holy Death ere Arthur died
  Had moved me kindly from his side,
And dropt the dust on tearless eyes;

Then fancy shapes, as fancy can,
  The grief my loss in him had wrought,
  A grief as deep as life or thought,
But stay'd in peace with God and man.°

I make a picture in the brain;
  I hear the sentence that he speaks;   [10]
  He bears the burthen of the weeks
But turns his burthen into gain.

His credit thus shall set me free;
  And, influence-rich to soothe and save,
  Unused example from the grave
Reach out dead hands to comfort me.

LXXXI

Could I have said while he was here,
  'My love shall now no further range;
  There cannot come a mellower change,
For now is love mature in ear.'°

Love, then, had hope of richer store:
  What end is here to my complaint?
  This haunting whisper makes me faint,
'More years had made me love thee more.'

But Death returns an answer sweet:
      'My sudden frost was sudden gain,   [10]
      And gave all ripeness to the grain,
It might have drawn from after-heat.'

LXXXII

I wage not any feud with Death
      For changes wrought on form and face;
      No lower life that earth's embrace
May breed with him, can fright my faith.

Eternal process moving on,
      From state to state the spirit walks;
      And these are but the shatter'd stalks,
Or ruin'd chrysalis of one.

Nor blame I Death, because he bare
      The use of virtue out of earth: [10]
      I know transplanted human worth
Will bloom to profit, otherwhere.

For this alone on Death I wreak
      The wrath that garners in my heart;
      He put our lives so far apart
We cannot hear each other speak.

LXXXIII

Dip down upon the northern shore,
      O sweet new-year delaying long;
      Thou doest expectant nature wrong;
Delaying long, delay no more.

What stays thee from the clouded noons,
      Thy sweetness from its proper place?
      Can trouble live with April days,
Or sadness in the summer moons?

Bring orchis, bring the foxglove spire,
      The little speedwell's darling blue,   [10]
      Deep tulips dash'd with fiery dew,
Laburnums, dropping-wells of fire.°

O thou, new-year, delaying long,
    Delayest the sorrow in my blood,
    That longs to burst a frozen bud
And flood a fresher throat with song.

LXXXIV

When I contemplate all alone
    The life that had been thine below,
    And fix my thoughts on all the glow
To which thy crescent would have grown;

I see thee sitting crown'd with good,
    A central warmth diffusing bliss
    In glance and smile, and clasp and kiss,
On all the branches of thy blood;

Thy blood, my friend, and partly mine;
    For now the day was drawing on,   [10]
    When thou should'st link thy life with one°
Of mine own house, and boys of thine

Had babbled 'Uncle' on my knee;
    But that remorseless iron hour
    Made cypress of her orange flower,°
Despair of Hope, and earth of thee.

I seem to meet their least desire,
    To clap their cheeks, to call them mine.
    I see their unborn faces shine
Beside the never-lighted fire.   [20]

I see myself an honour'd guest,
    Thy partner in the flowery walk
    Of letters, genial table-talk,
Or deep dispute, and graceful jest:

While now thy prosperous labour fills
    The lips of men with honest praise,
    And sun by sun the happy days
Descend below the golden hills

With promise of a morn as fair;
  And all the train of bounteous hours   [30]
  Conduct by paths of growing powers,
To reverence and the silver hair;

Till slowly worn her earthly robe,
  Her lavish mission richly wrought,
  Leaving great legacies of thought,
Thy spirit should fail from off the globe;

What time mine own might also flee,
  As link'd with thine in love and fate,
  And, hovering o'er the dolorous strait
To the other shore, involved in thee,   [40]

Arrive at last the blessed goal,
  And He that died in Holy Land
  Would reach us out the shining hand,
And take us as a single soul.

What reed was that on which I leant?
  Ah, backward fancy, wherefore wake
  The old bitterness again, and break
The low beginnings of content.

LXXXV

This truth came borne with bier and pall,
  I felt it, when I sorrow'd most,
  'Tis better to have loved and lost,
Than never to have loved at all—

O true in word, and tried in deed,
  Demanding, so to bring relief
  To this which is our common grief,
What kind of life is that I lead;

And whether trust in things above
  Be dimm'd of sorrow, or sustain'd;   [10]
  And whether love for him have drain'd
My capabilities of love;

Your words have virtue such as draws
    A faithful answer from the breast,
    Thro' light reproaches, half exprest,
And loyal unto kindly laws.

My blood an even tenor kept,
    Till on mine ear this message falls,
    That in Vienna's fatal walls
God's finger touch'd him, and he slept.   [20]

The great Intelligences fair°
    That range above our mortal state,
    In circle round the blessed gate,
Received and gave him welcome there;

And led him thro' the blissful climes,
    And show'd him in the fountain fresh
    All knowledge that the sons of flesh
Shall gather in the cycled times.

But I remain'd, whose hopes were dim,
    Whose life, whose thoughts were little worth,   [30]
    To wander on a darken'd earth,
Where all things round me breathed of him.

O friendship, equal-poised control,
    O heart, with kindliest motion warm,
    O sacred essence, other form,
O solemn ghost, O crowned soul!

Yet none could better know than I,
    How much of act at human hands
    The sense of human will demands
By which we dare to live or die.   [40]

Whatever way my days decline,
    I felt and feel, tho' left alone,
    His being working in mine own,
The footsteps of his life in mine;

A life that all the Muses deck'd
    With gifts of grace, that might express
    All-comprehensive tenderness,
All-subtilising intellect:

And so my passion hath not swerved
  To works of weakness, but I find   [50]
  An image comforting the mind,
And in my grief a strength reserved.

Likewise the imaginative woe,
  That loved to handle spiritual strife
  Diffused the shock thro' all my life,
But in the present broke the blow.

My pulses therefore beat again
  For other friends that once I met;
  Nor can it suit me to forget
The mighty hopes that make us men.   [60]

I woo your love: I count it crime
  To mourn for any overmuch;
  I, the divided half of such
A friendship as had master'd Time;

Which masters Time indeed, and is
  Eternal, separate from fears:
  The all-assuming months and years
Can take no part away from this:

But Summer on the steaming floods,
  And Spring that swells the narrow brooks, [70]
  And Autumn, with a noise of rooks,
That gather in the waning woods,

And every pulse of wind and wave
  Recalls, in change of light or gloom,
  My old affection of the tomb,
And my prime passion in the grave:

My old affection of the tomb,
  A part of stillness, yearns to speak:
  'Arise, and get thee forth and seek
A friendship for the years to come.   [80]

'I watch thee from the quiet shore;
  Thy spirit up to mine can reach;
  But in dear words of human speech
We two communicate no more.'

And I, 'Can clouds of nature stain
        The starry clearness of the free?
        How is it? Canst thou feel for me
Some painless sympathy with pain?'

And lightly does the whisper fall;
        ''Tis hard for thee to fathom this;   [90]
        I triumph in conclusive bliss,
And that serene result of all.'

So hold I commerce with the dead;
        Or so methinks the dead would say;
        Or so shall grief with symbols play
And pining life be fancy-fed.

Now looking to some settled end,
        That these things pass, and I shall prove
        A meeting somewhere, love with love,
I crave your pardon, O my friend;°   [100]

If not so fresh, with love as true,
        I, clasping brother-hands, aver
        I could not, if I would, transfer
The whole I felt for him to you.

For which be they that hold apart
        The promise of the golden hours?
        First love, first friendship, equal powers,
That marry with the virgin heart.

Still mine, that cannot but deplore,
        That beats within a lonely place,   [110]
        That yet remembers his embrace,
But at his footstep leaps no more,

My heart, tho' widow'd, may not rest
        Quite in the love of what is gone,
        But seeks to beat in time with one
That warms another living breast.

Ah, take the imperfect gift I bring,
        Knowing the primrose yet is dear,
        The primrose of the later year,
As not unlike to that of Spring.   [120]

LXXXVI

Sweet after showers, ambrosial air,
    That rollest from the gorgeous gloom
    Of evening over brake and bloom
And meadow, slowly breathing bare

The round of space, and rapt below°
    Thro' all the dewy-tassell'd wood,
    And shadowing down the horned flood
In ripples, fan my brows and blow

The fever from my cheek, and sigh
    The full new life that feeds thy breath   [10]
    Throughout my frame, till Doubt and Death,
Ill brethren, let the fancy fly

From belt to belt of crimson seas
    On leagues of odour streaming far,
    To where in yonder orient star
A hundred spirits whisper 'Peace.'

LXXXVII

I past beside the reverend walls°
    In which of old I wore the gown;
    I roved at random thro' the town,
And saw the tumult of the halls;

And heard once more in college fanes°
    The storm their high-built organs make,
    And thunder-music, rolling, shake
The prophet blazon'd on the panes;

And caught once more the distant shout,
    The measured pulse of racing oars   [10]
    Among the willows; paced the shores
And many a bridge, and all about

The same gray flats again, and felt
    The same, but not the same; and last
    Up that long walk of limes I past
To see the rooms in which he dwelt.

Another name was on the door:
  I linger'd; all within was noise
  Of songs, and clapping hands, and boys
That crash'd the glass and beat the floor;   [20]

Where once we held debate, a band°
  Of youthful friends, on mind and art,
  And labour, and the changing mart,
And all the framework of the land;

When one would aim an arrow fair,
  But send it slackly from the string;
  And one would pierce an outer ring,
And one an inner, here and there;

And last the master-bowman, he,
  Would cleave the mark. A willing ear [30]
  We lent him. Who, but hung to hear°
The rapt oration flowing free

From point to point, with power and grace
  And music in the bounds of law,
  To those conclusions when we saw
The God within him light his face,

And seem to lift the form, and glow
  In azure orbits heavenly-wise;
  And over those ethereal eyes
The bar of Michael Angelo.°   [40]

LXXXVIII

Wild bird, whose warble, liquid sweet,°
  Rings Eden thro' the budded quicks,°
  O tell me where the senses mix,
O tell me where the passions meet,

Whence radiate: fierce extremes employ
  Thy spirits in the darkening leaf,
  And in the midmost heart of grief
Thy passion clasps a secret joy:

And I—my harp would prelude woe—
    I cannot all command the strings;   [10]
    The glory of the sum of things
Will flash along the chords and go.

LXXXIX

Witch-elms that counterchange the floor°
    Of this flat lawn with dusk and bright;
    And thou, with all thy breadth and height
Of foliage, towering sycamore;

How often, hither wandering down,
    My Arthur found your shadows fair,
    And shook to all the liberal air
The dust and din and steam of town:

He brought an eye for all he saw;
    He mixt in all our simple sports;   [10]
    They pleased him, fresh from brawling courts
And dusty purlieus of the law.°

O joy to him in this retreat,
    Immantled in ambrosial dark,
    To drink the cooler air, and mark
The landscape winking thro' the heat:

O sound to rout the brood of cares,
    The sweep of scythe in morning dew,
    The gust that round the garden flew,
And tumbled half the mellowing pears!   [20]

O bliss, when all in circle drawn
    About him, heart and ear were fed
    To hear him, as he lay and read
The Tuscan poets on the lawn:°

Or in the all-golden afternoon
    A guest, or happy sister, sung,
    Or here she brought the harp and flung
A ballad to the brightening moon:

Nor less it pleased in livelier moods,
    Beyond the bounding hill to stray,   [30]
    And break the livelong summer day
With banquet in the distant woods;

Whereat we glanced from theme to theme,
    Discuss'd the books to love or hate,
    Or touch'd the changes of the state,
Or threaded some Socratic dream;°

But if I praised the busy town,
    He loved to rail against it still,
    For 'ground in yonder social mill
We rub each other's angles down,   [40]

'And merge' he said 'in form and gloss
    The picturesque of man and man.'
    We talk'd: the stream beneath us ran,
The wine-flask lying couch'd in moss,

Or cool'd within the glooming wave;
    And last, returning from afar,
    Before the crimson-circled star
Had fall'n into her father's grave,°

And brushing ankle-deep in flowers,
    We heard behind the woodbine veil   [50]
    The milk that bubbled in the pail,
And buzzings of the honied hours.

XC

He tasted love with half his mind,
    Nor ever drank the inviolate spring
    Where nighest heaven, who first could fling
This bitter seed among mankind;

That could the dead, whose dying eyes
    Were closed with wail, resume their life,°
    They would but find in child and wife
An iron welcome when they rise:

'Twas well, indeed, when warm with wine,
    To pledge them with a kindly tear,   [10]
    To talk them o'er, to wish them here,
To count their memories half divine;

But if they came who past away,
    Behold their brides in other hands;
    The hard heir strides about their lands,
And will not yield them for a day.

Yea, tho' their sons were none of these,
    Not less the yet-loved sire would make
    Confusion worse than death, and shake
The pillars of domestic peace.   [20]

Ah dear, but come thou back to me:°
    Whatever change the years have wrought,
    I find not yet one lonely thought
That cries against my wish for thee.

XCI

When rosy plumelets tuft the larch,
    And rarely pipes the mounted thrush;°
    Or underneath the barren bush
Flits by the sea-blue bird of March;°

Come, wear the form by which I know
    Thy spirit in time among thy peers;
    The hope of unaccomplish'd years
Be large and lucid round thy brow.

When summer's hourly-mellowing change
    May breathe, with many roses sweet,   [10]
    Upon the thousand waves of wheat,
That ripple round the lonely grange;

Come: not in watches of the night,
    But where the sunbeam broodeth warm,
    Come, beauteous in thine after form,
And like a finer light in light.

XCII

If any vision should reveal
    Thy likeness, I might count it vain
    As but the canker of the brain;
Yea, tho' it spake and made appeal

To chances where our lots were cast
    Together in the days behind
    I might but say, I hear a wind
Of memory murmuring the past.

Yea, tho' it spake and bared to view
    A fact within the coming year;   [10]
    And tho' the months, revolving near,
Should prove the phantom-warning true,

They might not seem thy prophecies,
    But spiritual presentiments,°
    And such refraction of events
As often rises ere they rise.

XCIII

I shall not see thee. Dare I say
    No spirit ever brake the band
    That stays him from the native land
Where first he walk'd when claspt in clay?

No visual shade of some one lost,
    But he, the Spirit himself, may come
    Where all the nerve of sense is numb;
Spirit to Spirit, Ghost to Ghost.

O, therefore from thy sightless range°
    With gods in unconjectured bliss,   [10]
    O, from the distance of the abyss
Of tenfold-complicated change,

Descend, and touch, and enter; hear
    The wish too strong for words to name;
    That in this blindness of the frame
My Ghost may feel that thine is near.

XCIV

How pure at heart and sound in head,
  With what divine affections bold
  Should be the man whose thought would hold
An hour's communion with the dead.

In vain shalt thou, or any, call
  The spirits from their golden day,
  Except, like them, thou too canst say,
My spirit is at peace with all.

They haunt the silence of the breast,
  Imaginations calm and fair,   [10]
  The memory like a cloudless air,
The conscience as a sea at rest:

But when the heart is full of din,
  And doubt beside the portal waits,
  They can but listen at the gates,
And hear the household jar within.°

XCV

By night we linger'd on the lawn,
  For underfoot the herb was dry;°
  And genial warmth; and o'er the sky
The silvery haze of summer drawn;

And calm that let the tapers burn
  Unwavering: not a cricket chirr'd:
  The brook alone far-off was heard,
And on the board the fluttering urn:°

And bats went round in fragrant skies,
  And wheel'd or lit the filmy shapes   [10]
  That haunt the dusk, with ermine capes
And woolly breasts and beaded eyes;

While now we sang old songs that peal'd
  From knoll to knoll, where, couch'd at ease,
  The white kine glimmer'd, and the trees°
Laid their dark arms about the field.

But when those others, one by one,
    Withdrew themselves from me and night,
    And in the house light after light
Went out, and I was all alone, [20]

A hunger seized my heart; I read
    Of that glad year which once had been,°
    In those fall'n leaves which kept their green,
The noble letters of the dead:

And strangely on the silence broke
    The silent-speaking words, and strange
    Was love's dumb cry defying change
To test his worth; and strangely spoke

The faith, the vigour, bold to dwell
    On doubts that drive the coward back, [30]
    And keen thro' wordy snares to track
Suggestion to her inmost cell.

So word by word, and line by line,
    The dead man touch'd me from the past,
    And all at once it seem'd at last
The living soul was flash'd on mine,

And mine in this was wound, and whirl'd
    About empyreal heights of thought,°
    And came on that which is, and caught
The deep pulsations of the world, [40]

Æonian music measuring out°
    The steps of Time—the shocks of Chance—
    The blows of Death. At length my trance
Was cancell'd, stricken thro' with doubt.

Vague words! but ah, how hard to frame
    In matter-moulded forms of speech,
    Or ev'n for intellect to reach
Thro' memory that which I became:

Till now the doubtful dusk reveal'd
    The knolls once more where, couch'd at ease, [50]
    The white kine glimmer'd, and the trees
Laid their dark arms about the field:

And suck'd from out the distant gloom
    A breeze began to tremble o'er
    The large leaves of the sycamore,
And fluctuate all the still perfume,

And gathering freshlier overhead,
    Rock'd the full-foliaged elms, and swung
    The heavy-folded rose, and flung
The lilies to and fro, and said   [60]

'The dawn, the dawn,' and died away;
    And East and West, without a breath,
    Mixt their dim lights, like life and death,
To broaden into boundless day.

XCVI

You say, but with no touch of scorn,°
    Sweet-hearted, you, whose light-blue eyes
    Are tender over drowning flies,
You tell me, doubt is Devil-born.

I know not: one indeed I knew°
    In many a subtle question versed,
    Who touch'd a jarring lyre at first,
But ever strove to make it true:

Perplext in faith, but pure in deeds,
    At last he beat his music out.   [10]
    There lives more faith in honest doubt,
Believe me, than in half the creeds.

He fought his doubts and gather'd strength,
    He would not make his judgment blind,
    He faced the spectres of the mind
And laid them: thus he came at length

To find a stronger faith his own;
    And Power was with him in the night,
    Which makes the darkness and the light,
And dwells not in the light alone,   [20]

But in the darkness and the cloud,
    As over Sinaï's peaks of old,
    While Israel made their gods of gold,
Altho' the trumpet blew so loud.°

XCVII

My love has talk'd with rocks and trees;
    He finds on misty mountain-ground
    His own vast shadow glory-crown'd;
He sees himself in all he sees.

Two partners of a married life—°
    I look'd on these and thought of thee
    In vastness and in mystery,
And of my spirit as of a wife.

These two—they dwelt with eye on eye,
    Their hearts of old have beat in tune,   [10]
    Their meetings made December June,
Their every parting was to die.

Their love has never past away;
    The days she never can forget
    Are earnest that he loves her yet,°
Whate'er the faithless people say.

Her life is lone, he sits apart,
    He loves her yet, she will not weep,
    Tho' rapt in matters dark and deep
He seems to slight her simple heart.   [20]

He thrids the labyrinth of the mind,
    He reads the secret of the star,
    He seems so near and yet so far,
He looks so cold: she thinks him kind.

She keeps the gift of years before,
    A wither'd violet is her bliss:
    She knows not what his greatness is,
For that, for all, she loves him more.

For him she plays, to him she sings
    Of early faith and plighted vows;   [30]
    She knows but matters of the house,
And he, he knows a thousand things.

Her faith is fixt and cannot move,
    She darkly feels him great and wise,
    She dwells on him with faithful eyes,
'I cannot understand: I love.'

XCVIII

You leave us: you will see the Rhine,°
    And those fair hills I sail'd below,
    When I was there with him; and go
By summer belts of wheat and vine

To where he breathed his latest breath,
    That City. All her splendour seems
    No livelier than the wisp that gleams
On Lethe in the eyes of Death.

Let her great Danube rolling fair
    Enwind her isles, unmark'd of me: [10]
    I have not seen, I will not see°
Vienna; rather dream that there,

A treble darkness, Evil haunts
    The birth, the bridal; friend from friend
    Is oftener parted, fathers bend
Above more graves, a thousand wants

Gnarr at the heels of men, and prey°
    By each cold hearth, and sadness flings
    Her shadow on the blaze of kings:
And yet myself have heard him say,   [20]

That not in any mother town°
    With statelier progress to and fro
    The double tides of chariots flow
By park and suburb under brown

Of lustier leaves; nor more content,
        He told me, lives in any crowd,
        When all is gay with lamps, and loud
With sport and song, in booth and tent,

Imperial halls, or open plain;
        And wheels the circled dance, and breaks   [30]
        The rocket molten into flakes
Of crimson or in emerald rain.

XCIX

Risest thou thus, dim dawn, again,°
        So loud with voices of the birds,
        So thick with lowings of the herds,
Day, when I lost the flower of men;

Who tremblest thro' thy darkling red
        On yon swoll'n brook that bubbles fast
        By meadows breathing of the past,
And woodlands holy to the dead;

Who murmurest in the foliaged eaves
        A song that slights the coming care,   [10]
        And Autumn laying here and there
A fiery finger on the leaves;

Who wakenest with thy balmy breath
        To myriads on the genial earth,
        Memories of bridal, or of birth,
And unto myriads more, of death.

O wheresoever those may be,
        Betwixt the slumber of the poles,°
        To-day they count as kindred souls;
They know me not, but mourn with me.   [20]

C

I climb the hill: from end to end
        Of all the landscape underneath,
        I find no place that does not breathe
Some gracious memory of my friend;

No gray old grange, or lonely fold,
  Or low morass and whispering reed,
  Or simple stile from mead to mead,
Or sheepwalk up the windy wold;

Nor hoary knoll of ash and haw
  That hears the latest linnet trill,   [10]
  Nor quarry trench'd along the hill
And haunted by the wrangling daw;

Nor runlet tinkling from the rock;
  Nor pastoral rivulet that swerves
  To left and right thro' meadowy curves,
That feed the mothers of the flock;

But each has pleased a kindred eye,
  And each reflects a kindlier day;
  And, leaving these, to pass away,
I think once more he seems to die.   [20]

CI

Unwatch'd, the garden bough shall sway,°
  The tender blossom flutter down,
  Unloved, that beech will gather brown,
This maple burn itself away;

Unloved, the sun-flower, shining fair,
  Ray round with flames her disk of seed,
  And many a rose-carnation feed
With summer spice the humming air;

Unloved, by many a sandy bar,
  The brook shall babble down the plain,   [10]
  At noon or when the lesser wain°
Is twisting round the polar star;

Uncared for, gird the windy grove,
  And flood the haunts of hern and crake;°
  Or into silver arrows break
The sailing moon in creek and cove;

Till from the garden and the wild
    A fresh association blow,
    And year by year the landscape grow
Familiar to the stranger's child;   [20]

As year by year the labourer tills
    His wonted glebe, or lops the glades;
    And year by year our memory fades
From all the circle of the hills.

CII

We leave the well-beloved place
    Where first we gazed upon the sky;
    The roofs, that heard our earliest cry,
Will shelter one of stranger race.

We go, but ere we go from home,
    As down the garden-walks I move,
    Two spirits of a diverse love°
Contend for loving masterdom.

One whispers, 'Here thy boyhood sung
    Long since its matin song, and heard°   [10]
    The low love-language of the bird
In native hazels tassel-hung.'

The other answers, 'Yea, but here
    Thy feet have stray'd in after hours
    With thy lost friend among the bowers,
And this hath made them trebly dear.'

These two have striven half the day,
    And each prefers his separate claim,
    Poor rivals in a losing game,
That will not yield each other way.   [20]

I turn to go: my feet are set
    To leave the pleasant fields and farms;
    They mix in one another's arms
To one pure image of regret.

CIII

On that last night before we went
    From out the doors where I was bred,
    I dream'd a vision of the dead,
Which left my after-morn content.

Methought I dwelt within a hall,
    And maidens with me: distant hills°
    From hidden summits fed with rills°
A river sliding by the wall.°

The hall with harp and carol rang.
    They sang of what is wise and good   [10]
    And graceful. In the centre stood
A statue veil'd, to which they sang;

And which, tho' veil'd, was known to me,
    The shape of him I loved, and love
    For ever: then flew in a dove
And brought a summons from the sea:°

And when they learnt that I must go
    They wept and wail'd, but led the way
    To where a little shallop lay
At anchor in the flood below;   [20]

And on by many a level mead,
    And shadowing bluff that made the banks,
    We glided winding under ranks
Of iris, and the golden reed;

And still as vaster grew the shore
    And roll'd the floods in grander space,
    The maidens gather'd strength and grace
And presence, lordlier than before;°

And I myself, who sat apart
    And watch'd them, wax'd in every limb;   [30]
    I felt the thews of Anakim,
The pulses of a Titan's heart;°

As one would sing the death of war,
    And one would chant the history
    Of that great race, which is to be,
And one the shaping of a star;°

Until the forward-creeping tides
    Began to foam, and we to draw
    From deep to deep, to where we saw
A great ship lift her shining sides.   [40]

The man we loved was there on deck,
    But thrice as large as man he bent
    To greet us. Up the side I went,
And fell in silence on his neck:

Whereat those maidens with one mind
    Bewail'd their lot; I did them wrong:
    'We served thee here,' they said, 'so long,
And wilt thou leave us now behind?'

So rapt I was, they could not win
    An answer from my lips, but he   [50]
    Replying, 'Enter likewise ye
And go with us:' they enter'd in.

And while the wind began to sweep
    A music out of sheet and shroud,
    We steer'd her toward a crimson cloud
That landlike slept along the deep.

CIV

The time draws near the birth of Christ;°
    The moon is hid, the night is still;
    A single church below the hill
Is pealing, folded in the mist.

A single peal of bells below,
    That wakens at this hour of rest
    A single murmur in the breast,
That these are not the bells I know.

Like strangers' voices here they sound,
    In lands where not a memory strays,   [10]
    Nor landmark breathes of other days,
But all is new unhallow'd ground.

CV

To-night ungather'd let us leave
    This laurel, let this holly stand:
    We live within the stranger's land,
And strangely falls our Christmas-eve.°

Our father's dust is left alone°
    And silent under other snows:
    There in due time the woodbine blows,
The violet comes, but we are gone.

No more shall wayward grief abuse
    The genial hour with mask and mime;   [10]
    For change of place, like growth of time,
Has broke the bond of dying use.

Let cares that petty shadows cast,
    By which our lives are chiefly proved,
    A little spare the night I loved,
And hold it solemn to the past.

But let no footstep beat the floor,
    Nor bowl of wassail mantle warm;°
    For who would keep an ancient form
Thro' which the spirit breathes no more?   [20]

Be neither song, nor game, nor feast;
    Nor harp be touch'd, nor flute be blown;
    No dance, no motion, save alone
What lightens in the lucid east

Of rising worlds by yonder wood.
    Long sleeps the summer in the seed;
    Run out your measured arcs, and lead
The closing cycle rich in good.

CVI

Ring out, wild bells, to the wild sky,
    The flying cloud, the frosty light:
    The year is dying in the night;
Ring out, wild bells, and let him die.°

Ring out the old, ring in the new,
　　Ring, happy bells, across the snow:
　　The year is going, let him go;
Ring out the false, ring in the true.

Ring out the grief that saps the mind,
　　For those that here we see no more;   [10]
　　Ring out the feud of rich and poor,
Ring in redress to all mankind.

Ring out a slowly dying cause,
　　And ancient forms of party strife;
　　Ring in the nobler modes of life,
With sweeter manners, purer laws.

Ring out the want, the care, the sin,
　　The faithless coldness of the times;
　　Ring out, ring out my mournful rhymes,
But ring the fuller minstrel in.   [20]

Ring out false pride in place and blood,
　　The civic slander and the spite;
　　Ring in the love of truth and right,
Ring in the common love of good.

Ring out old shapes of foul disease;
　　Ring out the narrowing lust of gold;
　　Ring out the thousand wars of old,
Ring in the thousand years of peace.

Ring in the valiant man and free,
　　The larger heart, the kindlier hand;   [30]
　　Ring out the darkness of the land,
Ring in the Christ that is to be.

CVII

It is the day when he was born,°
　　A bitter day that early sank
　　Behind a purple-frosty bank
Of vapour, leaving night forlorn.

The time admits not flowers or leaves
    To deck the banquet. Fiercely flies
    The blast of North and East, and ice
Makes daggers at the sharpen'd eaves,

And bristles all the brakes and thorns
    To yon hard crescent, as she hangs   [10]
    Above the wood which grides and clangs°
Its leafless ribs and iron horns

Together, in the drifts that pass
    To darken on the rolling brine
    That breaks the coast. But fetch the wine,
Arrange the board and brim the glass;

Bring in great logs and let them lie,
    To make a solid core of heat;
    Be cheerful-minded, talk and treat
Of all things ev'n as he were by;   [20]

We keep the day. With festal cheer,
    With books and music, surely we
    Will drink to him, whate'er he be,
And sing the songs he loved to hear.

CVIII

I will not shut me from my kind,
    And, lest I stiffen into stone,
    I will not eat my heart alone,
Nor feed with sighs a passing wind:

What profit lies in barren faith,
    And vacant yearning, tho' with might
    To scale the heaven's highest height,
Or dive below the wells of Death?

What find I in the highest place,
    But mine own phantom chanting hymns?   [10]
    And on the depths of death there swims
The reflex of a human face.

I'll rather take what fruit may be
    Of sorrow under human skies:
    'Tis held that sorrow makes us wise,
Whatever wisdom sleep with thee.

CIX°

Heart-affluence in discursive talk
    From household fountains never dry;
    The critic clearness of an eye,
That saw thro' all the Muses' walk;

Seraphic intellect and force
    To seize and throw the doubts of man;
    Impassion'd logic, which outran
The hearer in its fiery course;

High nature amorous of the good,
    But touch'd with no ascetic gloom;   [10]
    And passion pure in snowy bloom
Thro' all the years of April blood;

A love of freedom rarely felt,
    Of freedom in her regal seat
    Of England; not the schoolboy heat,
The blind hysterics of the Celt;

And manhood fused with female grace
    In such a sort, the child would twine
    A trustful hand, unask'd, in thine,
And find his comfort in thy face;   [20]

All these have been, and thee mine eyes
    Have look'd on: if they look'd in vain,
    My shame is greater who remain,
Nor let thy wisdom make me wise.

CX

Thy converse drew us with delight,°
    The men of rathe and riper years:°
    The feeble soul, a haunt of fears,
Forgot his weakness in thy sight.

On thee the loyal-hearted hung,
    The proud was half disarm'd of pride,
    Nor cared the serpent at thy side
To flicker with his double tongue.

The stern were mild when thou wert by,
    The flippant put himself to school   [10]
    And heard thee, and the brazen fool
Was soften'd, and he knew not why;

While I, thy nearest, sat apart,
    And felt thy triumph was as mine;
    And loved them more, that they were thine,
The graceful tact, the Christian art;

Nor mine the sweetness or the skill,
    But mine the love that will not tire,
    And, born of love, the vague desire
That spurs an imitative will.   [20]

CXI

The churl in spirit, up or down
    Along the scale of ranks, thro' all,
    To him who grasps a golden ball,°
By blood a king, at heart a clown;

The churl in spirit, howe'er he veil
    His want in forms for fashion's sake,
    Will let his coltish nature break
At seasons thro' the gilded pale:

For who can always act? but he,
    To whom a thousand memories call,   [10]
    Not being less but more than all
The gentleness he seem'd to be,

Best seem'd the thing he was, and join'd
    Each office of the social hour
    To noble manners, as the flower
And native growth of noble mind;

Nor ever narrowness or spite,
    Or villain fancy fleeting by,°
    Drew in the expression of an eye,
Where God and Nature met in light;   [20]

And thus he bore without abuse
    The grand old name of gentleman,
    Defamed by every charlatan,
And soil'd with all ignoble use.

CXII

High wisdom holds my wisdom less,
    That I, who gaze with temperate eyes
    On glorious insufficiencies,°
Set light by narrower perfectness.

But thou, that fillest all the room°
    Of all my love, art reason why
    I seem to cast a careless eye
On souls, the lesser lords of doom.

For what wert thou? some novel power
    Sprang up for ever at a touch,   [10]
    And hope could never hope too much,
In watching thee from hour to hour,

Large elements in order brought,
    And tracts of calm from tempest made,
    And world-wide fluctuation sway'd
In vassal tides that follow'd thought.

CXIII

'Tis held that sorrow makes us wise;
    Yet how much wisdom sleeps with thee
    Which not alone had guided me,
But served the seasons that may rise;

For can I doubt, who knew thee keen
    In intellect, with force and skill
    To strive, to fashion, to fulfil—
I doubt not what thou wouldst have been:

A life in civic action warm,
  A soul on highest mission sent,   [10]
  A potent voice of Parliament,
A pillar steadfast in the storm,

Should licensed boldness gather force,
  Becoming, when the time has birth,
  A lever to uplift the earth
And roll it in another course,

With thousand shocks that come and go,
  With agonies, with energies,
  With overthrowings, and with cries,
And undulations to and fro.   [20]

CXIV

Who loves not Knowledge? Who shall rail
  Against her beauty? May she mix
  With men and prosper! Who shall mix
Her pillars? Let her work prevail.°

But on her forehead sits a fire:
  She sets her forward countenance
  And leaps into the future chance,
Submitting all things to desire.

Half-grown as yet, a child, and vain—
  She cannot fight the fear of death.   [10]
  What is she, cut from love and faith,
But some wild Pallas from the brain°

Of Demons? fiery-hot to burst
  All barriers in her onward race
  For power. Let her know her place;
She is the second, not the first.

A higher hand must make her mild,°
  If all be not in vain; and guide
  Her footsteps, moving side by side
With wisdom, like the younger child: [20]

For she is earthly of the mind,
    But Wisdom heavenly of the soul.
    O, friend, who camest to thy goal
So early, leaving me behind,

I would the great world grew like thee,
    Who grewest not alone in power
    And knowledge, but by year and hour
In reverence and in charity.

CXV

Now fades the last long streak of snow,
    Now burgeons every maze of quick°
    About the flowering squares, and thick°
By ashen roots the violets blow.

Now rings the woodland loud and long,
    The distance takes a lovelier hue,
    And drown'd in yonder living blue
The lark becomes a sightless song.°

Now dance the lights on lawn and lea,
    The flocks are whiter down the vale,   [10]
    And milkier every milky sail
On winding stream or distant sea;

Where now the seamew pipes, or dives
    In yonder greening gleam, and fly°
    The happy birds, that change their sky
To build and brood; that live their lives

From land to land; and in my breast
    Spring wakens too; and my regret
    Becomes an April violet,
And buds and blossoms like the rest.   [20]

CXVI

Is it, then, regret for buried time
    That keenlier in sweet April wakes,
    And meets the year, and gives and takes
The colours of the crescent prime?

Not all: the songs, the stirring air,
    The life re-orient out of dust,
    Cry thro' the sense to hearten trust
In that which made the world so fair.

Not all regret: the face will shine
    Upon me, while I muse alone;   [10]
    And that dear voice, I once have known,
Still speak to me of me and mine:

Yet less of sorrow lives in me
    For days of happy commune dead;
    Less yearning for the friendship fled,
Than some strong bond which is to be.

CXVII

O days and hours, your work is this
    To hold me from my proper place,
    A little while from his embrace,
For fuller gain of after bliss:

That out of distance might ensue
    Desire of nearness doubly sweet;
    And unto meeting when we meet,
Delight a hundredfold accrue,

For every grain of sand that runs,
    And every span of shade that steals,   [10]
    And every kiss of toothed wheels,°
And all the courses of the suns.

CXVIII

Contemplate all this work of Time,
    The giant labouring in his youth;
    Nor dream of human love and truth,
As dying Nature's earth and lime;

But trust that those we call the dead
    Are breathers of an ampler day
    For ever nobler ends. They say,°
The solid earth whereon we tread

In tracts of fluent heat began,
  And grew to seeming-random forms,   [10]
  The seeming prey of cyclic storms,
Till at the last arose the man;

Who throve and branch'd from clime to clime,
  The herald of a higher race,
  And of himself in higher place,
If so he type this work of time°

Within himself, from more to more;
  Or, crown'd with attributes of woe
  Like glories, move his course, and show
That life is not as idle ore,   [20]

But iron dug from central gloom,
  And heated hot with burning fears,
  And dipt in baths of hissing tears,
And batter'd with the shocks of doom

To shape and use. Arise and fly
  The reeling Faun, the sensual feast;
  Move upward, working out the beast,
And let the ape and tiger die.

CXIX

Doors, where my heart was used to beat°
  So quickly, not as one that weeps
  I come once more; the city sleeps;
I smell the meadow in the street;

I hear a chirp of birds; I see
  Betwixt the black fronts long-withdrawn
  A light-blue lane of early dawn,
And think of early days and thee,

And bless thee, for thy lips are bland,
  And bright the friendship of thine eye;   [10]
  And in my thoughts with scarce a sigh
I take the pressure of thine hand.

CXX

I trust I have not wasted breath:
    I think we are not wholly brain,
    Magnetic mockeries; not in vain,
Like Paul with beasts, I fought with Death;°

Not only cunning casts in clay:
    Let Science prove we are, and then
    What matters Science unto men,
At least to me? I would not stay.

Let him, the wiser man who springs
    Hereafter, up from childhood shape   [10]
    His action like the greater ape,°
But I was *born* to other things.

CXXI

Sad Hesper o'er the buried sun°
    And ready, thou, to die with him,
    Thou watchest all things ever dim
And dimmer, and a glory done:

The team is loosen'd from the wain,°
    The boat is drawn upon the shore;
    Thou listenest to the closing door,
And life is darken'd in the brain.

Bright Phosphor, fresher for the night,
    By thee the world's great work is heard   [10]
    Beginning, and the wakeful bird;
Behind thee comes the greater light:

The market boat is on the stream,
    And voices hail it from the brink;
    Thou hear'st the village hammer clink,
And see'st the moving of the team.

Sweet Hesper–Phosphor, double name
    For what is one, the first, the last,
    Thou, like my present and my past,
Thy place is changed; thou art the same.   [20]

CXXII

Oh, wast thou with me, dearest, then,
    While I rose up against my doom,°
    And yearn'd to burst the folded gloom,
To bare the eternal Heavens again,

To feel once more, in placid awe,
    The strong imagination roll
    A sphere of stars about my soul,
In all her motion one with law;

If thou wert with me, and the grave
    Divide us not, be with me now,   [10]
    And enter in at breast and brow,
Till all my blood, a fuller wave,

Be quicken'd with a livelier breath,
    And like an inconsiderate boy,
    As in the former flash of joy,
I slip the thoughts of life and death;°

And all the breeze of Fancy blows,
    And every dew–drop paints a bow,°
    The wizard lightnings deeply glow,°
And every thought breaks out a rose.   [20]

CXXIII

There rolls the deep where grew the tree.
    O earth, what changes hast thou seen!
    There where the long street roars, hath been
The stillness of the central sea.

The hills are shadows, and they flow
    From form to form, and nothing stands;
    They melt like mist, the solid lands,
Like clouds they shape themselves and go.

But in my spirit will I dwell,
    And dream my dream, and hold it true;   [10]
    For tho' my lips may breathe adieu,
I cannot think the thing farewell.

CXXIV

That which we dare invoke to bless;
    Our dearest faith; our ghastliest doubt;
    He, They, One, All; within, without;
The Power in darkness whom we guess;

I found Him not in world or sun,
    Or eagle's wing, or insect's eye;
    Nor thro' the questions men may try,
The petty cobwebs we have spun:

If e'er when faith had fall'n asleep,
    I heard a voice 'believe no more'   [10]
    And heard an ever-breaking shore
That tumbled in the Godless deep;

A warmth within the breast would melt
    The freezing reason's colder part,
    And like a man in wrath the heart
Stood up and answer'd 'I have felt.'

No, like a child in doubt and fear:
    But that blind clamour made me wise;
    Then was I as a child that cries,
But, crying, knows his father near;   [20]

And what I am beheld again
    What is, and no man understands;
    And out of darkness came the hands
That reach thro' nature, moulding men.

CXXV

Whatever I have said or sung,
    Some bitter notes my harp would give,
    Yea, tho' there often seem'd to live
A contradiction on the tongue,

Yet Hope had never lost her youth;
    She did but look through dimmer eyes;
    Or Love but play'd with gracious lies,
Because he felt so fix'd in truth:

And if the song were full of care,
  He breathed the spirit of the song;   [10]
  And if the words were sweet and strong
He set his royal signet there;

Abiding with me till I sail
  To seek thee on the mystic deeps,
  And this electric force, that keeps
A thousand pulses dancing, fail.

CXXVI

Love is and was my Lord and King,
  And in his presence I attend
  To hear the tidings of my friend,
Which every hour his couriers bring.

Love is and was my King and Lord,
  And will be, tho' as yet I keep
  Within his court on earth, and sleep
Encompass'd by his faithful guard,

And hear at times a sentinel
  Who moves about from place to place,   [10]
  And whispers to the worlds of space,
In the deep night, that all is well.

CXXVII

And all is well, tho' faith and form
  Be sunder'd in the night of fear;°
  Well roars the storm to those that hear
A deeper voice across the storm,

Proclaiming social truth shall spread,
  And justice, ev'n tho' thrice again
  The red fool-fury of the Seine
Should pile her barricades with dead.

But ill for him that wears a crown,
  And him, the lazar, in his rags:°   [10]
  They tremble, the sustaining crags;
The spires of ice are toppled down,

And molten up, and roar in flood;
    The fortress crashes from on high,
    The brute earth lightens to the sky,
And the great Æon sinks in blood,°

And compass'd by the fires of Hell;
    While thou, dear spirit, happy star,
    O'erlook'st the tumult from afar,
And smilest, knowing all is well.					[20]

CXXVIII

The love that rose on stronger wings,
    Unpalsied when he met with Death,
    Is comrade of the lesser faith
That sees the course of human things.

No doubt vast eddies in the flood
    Of onward time shall yet be made,
    And throned races may degrade;
Yet O ye mysteries of good,

Wild Hours that fly with Hope and Fear,
    If all your office had to do					[10]
    With old results that look like new;
If this were all your mission here,

To draw, to sheathe a useless sword,
    To fool the crowd with glorious lies,
    To cleave a creed in sects and cries,
To change the bearing of a word,

To shift an arbitrary power,
    To cramp the student at his desk,
    To make old bareness picturesque
And tuft with grass a feudal tower;					[20]

Why then my scorn might well descend
    On you and yours. I see in part
    That all, as in some piece of art,
Is toil cöoperant to an end.

CXXIX

Dear friend, far off, my lost desire,
        So far, so near in woe and weal;
        O loved the most, when most I feel
There is a lower and a higher;

Known and unknown; human, divine;
        Sweet human hand and lips and eye;
        Dear heavenly friend that canst not die,
Mine, mine, for ever, ever mine;

Strange friend, past, present, and to be;
        Loved deeplier, darklier understood;   [10]
        Behold, I dream a dream of good,
And mingle all the world with thee.

CXXX

Thy voice is on the rolling air;
        I hear thee where the waters run;
        Thou standest in the rising sun,
And in the setting thou art fair.

What art thou then? I cannot guess;
        But tho' I seem in star and flower
        To feel thee some diffusive power,
I do not therefore love thee less:

My love involves the love before;
        My love is vaster passion now;   [10]
        Tho' mix'd with God and Nature thou,
I seem to love thee more and more.

Far off thou art, but ever nigh;
        I have thee still, and I rejoice;
        I prosper, circled with thy voice;
I shall not lose thee tho' I die.

CXXXI

O living will that shalt endure°
    When all that seems shall suffer shock,
    Rise in the spiritual rock,
Flow thro' our deeds and make them pure,

That we may lift from out of dust
    A voice as unto him that hears,
    A cry above the conquer'd years
To one that with us works, and trust,

With faith that comes of self-control,
    The truths that never can be proved   [10]
    Until we close with all we loved,
And all we flow from, soul in soul.

[EPILOGUE]°

O true and tried, so well and long,
    Demand not thou a marriage lay;
    In that it is thy marriage day
Is music more than any song.

Nor have I felt so much of bliss
    Since first he told me that he loved°
    A daughter of our house; nor proved
Since that dark day a day like this;

Tho' I since then have number'd o'er
    Some thrice three years: they went and came,°   [10]
    Remade the blood and changed the frame,
And yet is love not less, but more;

No longer caring to embalm
    In dying songs a dead regret,
    But like a statue solid-set,
And moulded in colossal calm.

Regret is dead, but love is more
    Than in the summers that are flown,
    For I myself with these have grown
To something greater than before;   [20]

Which makes appear the songs I made
     As echoes out of weaker times,
     As half but idle brawling rhymes,
The sport of random sun and shade.

But where is she, the bridal flower,
     That must be made a wife ere noon?
     She enters, glowing like the moon
Of Eden on its bridal bower:

On me she bends her blissful eyes
     And then on thee; they meet thy look   [30]
     And brighten like the star that shook
Betwixt the palms of paradise.

O when her life was yet in bud,
     He too foretold the perfect rose.
     For thee she grew, for thee she grows
For ever, and as fair as good.

And thou art worthy; full of power;
     As gentle; liberal-minded, great,
     Consistent; wearing all that weight
Of learning lightly like a flower.°   [40]

But now set out: the noon is near,
     And I must give away the bride;
     She fears not, or with thee beside
And me behind her, will not fear.

For I that danced her on my knee,
     That watch'd her on her nurse's arm,
     That shielded all her life from harm
At last must part with her to thee;

Now waiting to be made a wife,
     Her feet, my darling, on the dead   [50]
     Their pensive tablets round her head,°
And the most living words of life

Breathed in her ear. The ring is on,
     The 'wilt thou' answer'd, and again
     The 'wilt thou' ask'd, till out of twain
Her sweet 'I will' has made you one.

Now sign your names, which shall be read,°
  Mute symbols of a joyful morn,
  By village eyes as yet unborn;
The names are sign'd, and overhead   [60]

Begins the clash and clang that tells
  The joy to every wandering breeze;
  The blind wall rocks, and on the trees
The dead leaf trembles to the bells.

O happy hour, and happier hours
  Await them. Many a merry face
  Salutes them—maidens of the place,
That pelt us in the porch with flowers.

O happy hour, behold the bride
  With him to whom her hand I gave.   [70]
  They leave the porch, they pass the grave
That has to-day its sunny side.

To-day the grave is bright for me,
  For them the light of life increased,
  Who stay to share the morning feast,
Who rest to-night beside the sea.

Let all my genial spirits advance
  To meet and greet a whiter sun;
  My drooping memory will not shun
The foaming grape of eastern France.   [80]

It circles round, and fancy plays,
  And hearts are warm'd and faces bloom,
  As drinking health to bride and groom
We wish them store of happy days.

Nor count me all to blame if I
  Conjecture of a stiller guest,°
  Perchance, perchance, among the rest,
And, tho' in silence, wishing joy.

But they must go, the time draws on,
  And those white-favour'd horses wait;   [90]
  They rise, but linger; it is late;
Farewell, we kiss, and they are gone.

A shade falls on us like the dark
    From little cloudlets on the grass,
    But sweeps away as out we pass
To range the woods, to roam the park,

Discussing how their courtship grew,
    And talk of others that are wed,
    And how she look'd, and what he said,
And back we come at fall of dew.   [100]

Again the feast, the speech, the glee,
    The shade of passing thought, the wealth
    Of words and wit, the double health,
The crowning cup, the three-times-three,°

And last the dance;—till I retire:
    Dumb is that tower which spake so loud,
    And high in heaven the streaming cloud,
And on the downs a rising fire:

And rise, O moon, from yonder down,
    Till over down and over dale   [110]
    All night the shining vapour sail
And pass the silent-lighted town,

The white-faced halls, the glancing rills,
    And catch at every mountain head,
    And o'er the friths that branch and spread
Their sleeping silver thro' the hills;

And touch with shade the bridal doors,
    With tender gloom the roof, the wall;
    And breaking let the splendour fall
To spangle all the happy shores   [120]

By which they rest, and ocean sounds,
    And, star and system rolling past,
    A soul shall draw from out the vast
And strike his being into bounds,

And, moved thro' life of lower phase,
    Result in man, be born and think,
    And act and love, a closer link
Betwixt us and the crowning race

Of those that, eye to eye, shall look
    On knowledge; under whose command   [130]
    Is Earth and Earth's, and in their hand
Is Nature like an open book;

No longer half-akin to brute,
    For all we thought and loved and did,
    And hoped, and suffer'd, is but seed
Of what in them is flower and fruit;

Whereof the man, that with me trod
    This planet, was a noble type
    Appearing ere the times were ripe,
That friend of mine who lives in God,   [140]

That God, which ever lives and loves,
    One God, one law, one element,
    And one far-off divine event,
To which the whole creation moves.

LAUREATE POEMS

To the Queen

Revered, beloved—O you that hold
    A nobler office upon earth
    Than arms, or power of brain, or birth
Could give the warrior kings of old,

Victoria,—since your Royal grace
    To one of less desert allows
    This laurel greener from the brows
Of him that utter'd nothing base;

And should your greatness, and the care
    That yokes with empire, yield you time   [10]
    To make demand of modern rhyme
If aught of ancient worth be there;

Then—while a sweeter music wakes,
    And thro' wild March the throstle calls, °
    Where all about your palace-walls
The sun-lit almond-blossom shakes—

Take, Madam, this poor book of song;
    For tho' the faults were thick as dust
    In vacant chambers, I could trust
Your kindness. May you rule us long,   [20]

And leave us rulers of your blood
    As noble till the latest day!
    May children of our children say,
'She wrought her people lasting good;

'Her court was pure; her life serene;
    God gave her peace; her land reposed;
    A thousand claims to reverence closed
In her as Mother, Wife, and Queen;

'And statesmen at her council met
    Who knew the seasons when to take   [30]
    Occasion by the hand, and make
The bounds of freedom wider yet

'*By shaping some august decree,*
    Which kept her throne unshaken still,
    Broad-based upon her people's will,
And compass'd by the inviolate sea.'

                        March 1851

Ode on the Death of the Duke of Wellington

I

Bury the Great Duke
   With an empire's lamentation,
Let us bury the Great Duke
   To the noise of the mourning of a mighty nation,
Mourning when their leaders fall,
Warriors carry the warrior's pall,
And sorrow darkens hamlet and hall.

II

Where shall we lay the man whom we deplore?
Here, in streaming London's central roar.
Let the sound of those he wrought for,   [10]
And the feet of those he fought for,
Echo round his bones for evermore.

III

Lead out the pageant: sad and slow,
As fits an universal woe,
Let the long long procession go,
And let the sorrowing crowd about it grow,
And let the mournful martial music blow;
The last great Englishman is low.

IV

Mourn, for to us he seems the last,
Remembering all his greatness in the Past.   [20]
No more in soldier fashion will he greet
With lifted hand the gazer in the street.
O friends, our chief state-oracle is mute:
Mourn for the man of long-enduring blood,
The statesman-warrior, moderate, resolute,
Whole in himself, a common good.
Mourn for the man of amplest influence,
Yet clearest of ambitious crime,
Our greatest yet with least pretence,
Great in council and great in war,   [30]
Foremost captain of his time,
Rich in saving common-sense,
And, as the greatest only are,
In his simplicity sublime.
O good gray head which all men knew,
O voice from which their omens all men drew,
O iron nerve to true occasion true,
O fall'n at length that tower of strength
Which stood four-square to all the winds that blew!
Such was he whom we deplore.   [40]
The long self-sacrifice of life is o'er.
The great World-victor's victor will be seen no more.°

V

All is over and done:
Render thanks to the Giver,
England, for thy son.
Let the bell be toll'd.
Render thanks to the Giver,
And render him to the mould.
Under the cross of gold°
That shines over city and river,   [50]
There he shall rest for ever
Among the wise and the bold.
Let the bell be toll'd:
And a reverent people behold
The towering car, the sable steeds:

Bright let it be with its blazon'd deeds,
Dark in its funeral fold.
Let the bell be toll'd:
And a deeper knell in the heart be knoll'd;
And the sound of the sorrowing anthem roll'd   [60]
Thro' the dome of the golden cross;
And the volleying cannon thunder his loss;
He knew their voices of old.
For many a time in many a clime
His captain's-ear has heard them boom
Bellowing victory, bellowing doom:
When he with those deep voices wrought,
Guarding realms and kings from shame;
With those deep voices our dead captain taught
The tyrant, and asserts his claim   [70]
In that dread sound to the great name,
Which he has worn so pure of blame,
In praise and in dispraise the same,
A man of well-attemper'd frame.
O civic muse, to such a name,
To such a name for ages long,
To such a name,
Preserve a broad approach of fame,
And ever-echoing avenues of song.

VI

Who is he that cometh, like an honour'd guest,   [80]
With banner and with music, with soldier and with priest,
With a nation weeping, and breaking on my rest?
Mighty Seaman, this is he°
Was great by land as thou by sea.
Thine island loves thee well, thou famous man,
The greatest sailor since our world began.
Now, to the roll of muffled drums,
To thee the greatest soldier comes;
For this is he
Was great by land as thou by sea;   [90]
His foes were thine; he kept us free;
O give him welcome, this is he
Worthy of our gorgeous rites,

And worthy to be laid by thee;
For this is England's greatest son,
He that gain'd a hundred fights,
Nor ever lost an English gun;
This is he that far away
Against the myriads of Assaye°
Clash'd with his fiery few and won;   [100]
And underneath another sun,
Warring on a later day,
Round affrighted Lisbon drew°
The treble works, the vast designs
Of his labour'd rampart-lines,
Where he greatly stood at bay,
Whence he issued forth anew,
And ever great and greater grew,
Beating from the wasted vines
Back to France her banded swarms,   [110]
Back to France with countless blows,
Till o'er the hills her eagles flew
Beyond the Pyrenean pines,
Follow'd up in valley and glen
With blare of bugle, clamour of men,
Roll of cannon and clash of arms,
And England pouring on her foes.
Such a war had such a close.
Again their ravening eagle rose°
In anger, wheel'd on Europe-shadowing wings,   [120]
And barking for the thrones of kings;
Till one that sought but Duty's iron crown
On that loud sabbath shook the spoiler down;°
A day of onsets of despair!
Dash'd on every rocky square
Their surging charges foam'd themselves away;
Last, the Prussian trumpet blew;°
Thro' the long-tormented air
Heaven flash'd a sudden jubilant ray,
And down we swept and charged and overthrew.   [130]
So great a soldier taught us there,
What long-enduring hearts could do
In that world-earthquake, Waterloo!
Mighty Seaman, tender and true,

And pure as he from taint of craven guile,
O saviour of the silver-coasted isle,
O shaker of the Baltic and the Nile,°
If aught of things that here befall
Touch a spirit among things divine,
If love of country move thee there at all,   [140]
Be glad, because his bones are laid by thine!
And thro' the centuries let a people's voice
In full acclaim,
A people's voice,
The proof and echo of all human fame,
A people's voice, when they rejoice
At civic revel and pomp and game,
Attest their great commander's claim
With honour, honour, honour, honour to him,
Eternal honour to his name.   [150]

VII

A people's voice! we are a people yet.
Tho' all men else their nobler dreams forget,
Confused by brainless mobs and lawless Powers;
Thank Him who isled us here, and roughly set
His Briton in blown seas and storming showers,
We have a voice, with which to pay the debt,
Of boundless love and reverence and regret
To those great men who fought, and kept it ours.
And keep it ours, O God, from brute control;
O Statesmen, guard us, guard the eye, the soul   [160]
Of Europe, keep our noble England whole,
And save the one true seed of freedom sown
Betwixt a people and their ancient throne,
That sober freedom out of which there springs
Our loyal passion for our temperate kings;
For, saving that, ye help to save mankind
Till public wrong be crumbled into dust,
And drill the raw world for the march of mind,
Till crowds at length be sane and crowns be just.
But wink no more in slothful overtrust.   [170]
Remember him who led your hosts;
He bad you guard the sacred coasts.

Your cannons moulder on the seaward wall;
His voice is silent in your council-hall
For ever; and whatever tempests lour
For ever silent; even if they broke
In thunder, silent; yet remember all
He spoke among you, and the Man who spoke;
Who never sold the truth to serve the hour,
Nor palter'd with Eternal God for power;   [180]
Who let the turbid streams of rumour flow
Thro' either babbling world of high and low;
Whose life was work, whose language rife
With rugged maxims hewn from life;
Who never spoke against a foe;
Whose eighty winters freeze with one rebuke
All great self-seekers trampling on the right:
Truth-teller was our England's Alfred named;°
Truth-lover was our English Duke;
Whatever record leap to light   [190]
He never shall be shamed.

VIII

Lo, the leader in these glorious wars
Now to glorious burial slowly borne,
Follow'd by the brave of other lands,
He, on whom from both her open hands
Lavish Honour shower'd all her stars,
And affluent Fortune emptied all her horn.
Yea, let all good things await
Him who cares not to be great,
But as he saves or serves the state.   [200]
Not once or twice in our rough island-story
The path of duty was the way to glory:
He that walks it, only thirsting
For the right, and learns to deaden
Love of self, before his journey closes,
He shall find the stubborn thistle bursting
Into glossy purples, which outredden
All voluptuous garden-roses.
Not once or twice in our fair island-story,
The path of duty was the way to glory: [210]

He, that ever following her commands,
On with toil of heart and knees and hands,
Thro' the long gorge to the far light has won
His path upward, and prevail'd,
Shall find the toppling crags of Duty scaled
Are close upon the shining table-lands
To which our God Himself is moon and sun.
Such was he: his work is done.
But while the races of mankind endure,
Let his great example stand   [220]
Colossal, seen of every land,
And keep the soldier firm, the statesman pure:
Till in all lands and thro' all human story
The path of duty be the way to glory:
And let the land whose hearths he saved from shame
For many and many an age proclaim
At civic revel and pomp and game,
And when the long-illumined cities flame,
Their ever-loyal iron leader's fame,
With honour, honour, honour, honour to him,   [230]
Eternal honour to his name.

IX

Peace, his triumph will be sung
By some yet unmoulded tongue
Far on in summers that we shall not see:
Peace, it is a day of pain
For one about whose patriarchal knee
Late the little children clung:
O peace, it is a day of pain
For one, upon whose hand and heart and brain
Once the weight and fate of Europe hung.   [240]
Ours the pain, be his the gain!
More than is of man's degree
Must be with us, watching here
At this, our great solemnity.
Whom we see not we revere;
We revere, and we refrain
From talk of battles loud and vain,
And brawling memories all too free

For such a wise humility
As befits a solemn fane: [250]
We revere, and while we hear
The tides of Music's golden sea
Setting toward eternity,
Uplifted high in heart and hope are we,
Until we doubt not that for one so true
There must be other nobler work to do
Than when he fought at Waterloo,
And Victor he must ever be.
For tho' the Giant Ages heave the hill
And break the shore, and evermore
Make and break, and work their will; [260]
Tho' world on world in myriad myriads roll
Round us, each with different powers,
And other forms of life than ours,
What know we greater than the soul?
On God and Godlike men we build our trust.
Hush, the Dead March wails in the people's ears:
The dark crowd moves, and there are sobs and tears:
The black earth yawns: the mortal disappears;
Ashes to ashes, dust to dust; [270]
He is gone who seem'd so great.—
Gone; but nothing can bereave him
Of the force he made his own
Being here, and we believe him
Something far advanced in State,
And that he wears a truer crown
Than any wreath that man can weave him.
Speak no more of his renown,
Lay your earthly fancies down,
And in the vast cathedral leave him. [280]
God accept him, Christ receive him.

1852

The Charge of the Light Brigade

I

Half a league, half a league,
  Half a league onward,
All in the valley of Death
  Rode the six hundred.
'Forward, the Light Brigade!
Charge for the guns!' he said:
Into the valley of Death
  Rode the six hundred.

II

'Forward, the Light Brigade!'
Was there a man dismay'd?   [10]
Not tho' the soldier knew
  Some one had blunder'd:
Their's not to make reply,
Their's not to reason why,
Their's but to do and die:
Into the valley of Death
  Rode the six hundred.

III

Cannon to right of them,
Cannon to left of them,
Cannon in front of them   [20]
  Volley'd and thunder'd;
Storm'd at with shot and shell,
Boldly they rode and well,
Into the jaws of Death,
Into the mouth of Hell
  Rode the six hundred.

IV

Flash'd all their sabres bare,
Flash'd as they turn'd in air
Sabring the gunners there,
Charging an army, while   [30]

All the world wonder'd:
Plunged in the battery-smoke
Right thro' the line they broke;
Cossack and Russian
Reel'd from the sabre-stroke
   Shatter'd and sunder'd.
Then they rode back, but not
   Not the six hundred.

V

Cannon to right of them,
Cannon to left of them,   [40]
Cannon behind them
   Volley'd and thunder'd;
Storm'd at with shot and shell,
While horse and hero fell,
They that had fought so well
Came thro' the jaws of Death,
Back from the mouth of Hell,
All that was left of them,
   Left of six hundred.

VI

When can their glory fade?   [50]
O the wild charge they made!
   All the world wonder'd.
Honour the charge they made!
Honour the Light Brigade,
   Noble six hundred!

MAUD; A MONODRAMA (1855)

PART I

I

I

I hate the dreadful hollow behind the little wood,
Its lips in the field above are dabbled with blood-red heath,°
The red-ribb'd ledges drip with a silent horror of blood,
And Echo there, whatever is ask'd her, answers 'Death.'

II

For there in the ghastly pit long since a body was found,
His who had given me life—O father! O God! was it well?—
Mangled, and flatten'd, and crush'd, and dinted into the ground:
There yet lies the rock that fell with him when he fell.

III

Did he fling himself down? who knows? for a vast speculation had
    fail'd,°
And ever he mutter'd and madden'd, and ever wann'd with
    despair,   [10]
And out he walk'd when the wind like a broken worldling wail'd,
And the flying gold of the ruin'd woodlands drove thro' the air.

IV

I remember the time, for the roots of my hair were stirr'd
By a shuffled step, by a dead weight trail'd, by a whisper'd fright,
And my pulses closed their gates with a shock on my heart as I heard
The shrill-edged shriek of a mother divide the shuddering night.

V

Villainy somewhere! whose? One says, we are villains all.
Not he: his honest fame should at least by me be maintained:
But that old man, now lord of the broad estate and the Hall,
Dropt off gorged from a scheme that had left us flaccid and drain'd.   [20]

VI

Why do they prate of the blessings of Peace? we have made them
   a curse,
Pickpockets, each hand lusting for all that is not its own;
And lust of gain, in the spirit of Cain, is it better or worse
Than the heart of the citizen hissing in war on his own
   hearthstone?

VII

But these are the days of advance, the works of the men of mind,
When who but a fool would have faith in a tradesman's ware or his
   word?
Is it peace or war? Civil war, as I think, and that of a kind
The viler, as underhand, not openly bearing the sword.

VIII

Sooner or later I too may passively take the print
Of the golden age—why not? I have neither hope nor trust;   [30]
May make my heart as a millstone, set my face as a flint,
Cheat and be cheated, and die: who knows? we are ashes and dust.

IX

Peace sitting under her olive, and slurring the days gone by,
When the poor are hovell'd and hustled together, each sex, like swine,
When only the ledger lives, and when only not all men lie;
Peace in her vineyard—yes!—but a company forges the wine.

X

And the vitriol madness flushes up in the ruffian's head,°
Till the filthy by-lane rings to the yell of the trampled wife,
And chalk and alum and plaster are sold to the poor for bread,
And the spirit of murder works in the very means of life,   [40]

XI

And Sleep must lie down arm'd, for the villainous centre-bits°
Grind on the wakeful ear in the hush of the moonless nights,
While another is cheating the sick of a few last gasps, as he sits
To pestle a poison'd poison behind his crimson lights.

XII

When a Mammonite mother kills her babe for a burial fee,°
And Timour-Mammon grins on a pile of children's bones,°
Is it peace or war? better, war! loud war by land and by sea,
War with a thousand battles, and shaking a hundred thrones.

XIII

For I trust if an enemy's fleet came yonder round by the hill,
And the rushing battle-bolt sang from the three-decker out
　　of the foam,　　　　　　　　　　　　　　　　　　　　　[50]
That the smooth-faced snubnosed rogue would leap from his
　　counter and till,
And strike, if he could, were it but with his cheating yardwand,
　　home.—°

XIV

What! am I raging alone as my father raged in his mood?
Must *I* too creep to the hollow and dash myself down and die
Rather than hold by the law that I made, nevermore to brood
On a horror of shatter'd limbs and a wretched swindler's lie?

XV

Would there be sorrow for *me*? there was *love* in the passionate
　　shriek,
Love for the silent thing that had made false haste to the grave—
Wrapt in a cloak, as I saw him, and thought he would rise and speak
And rave at the lie and the liar, ah God, as he used to rave.　　[60]

XVI

I am sick of the Hall and the hill, I am sick of the moor and the main.
Why should I stay? can a sweeter chance ever come to me here?
O, having the nerves of motion as well as the nerves of pain,
Were it not wise if I fled from the place and the pit and the fear?

XVII

Workmen up at the Hall!—they are coming back from abroad;
The dark old place will be gilt by the touch of a millionaire:
I have heard, I know not whence, of the singular beauty of Maud;
I play'd with the girl when a child; she promised then to be fair.

XVIII

Maud with her venturous climbings and tumbles and childish
    escapes,
Maud the delight of the village, the ringing joy of the Hall,   [70]
Maud with her sweet purse-mouth when my father dangled
    the grapes,
Maud the beloved of my mother, the moon-faced darling of all,—

XIX

What is she now? My dreams are bad. She may bring me a curse.
No, there is fatter game on the moor; she will let me alone.
Thanks, for the fiend best knows whether woman or man be
    the worse.
I will bury myself in myself, and the Devil may pipe to his own.

II

Long have I sigh'd for a calm: God grant I may find it at last!
It will never be broken by Maud, she has neither savour nor
    salt,°
But a cold and clear-cut face, as I found when her carriage past,
Perfectly beautiful: let it be granted her: where is the fault?   [80]
All that I saw (for her eyes were downcast, not to be seen)
Faultily faultless, icily regular, splendidly null,
Dead perfection, no more; nothing more, if it had not been
For a chance of travel, a paleness, an hour's defect of the rose,
Or an underlip, you may call it a little too ripe, too full,
Or the least little delicate aquiline curve in a sensitive nose,
From which I escaped heart-free, with the least little touch of
    spleen.

III

Cold and clear-cut face, why come you so cruelly meek,
Breaking a slumber in which all spleenful folly was drown'd,
Pale with the golden beam of an eyelash dead on the cheek,   [90]
Passionless, pale, cold face, star-sweet on a gloom profound;
Womanlike, taking revenge too deep for a transient wrong
Done but in thought to your beauty, and ever as pale as before
Growing and fading and growing upon me without a sound,

Luminous, gemlike, ghostlike, deathlike, half the night long
Growing and fading and growing, till I could bear it no more,
But arose, and all by myself in my own dark garden ground,
Listening now to the tide in its broad-flung shipwrecking roar,
Now to the scream of a madden'd beach dragg'd down by the wave,
Walk'd in a wintry wind by a ghastly glimmer, and found   [100]
The shining daffodil dead, and Orion low in his grave.°

IV

I

A million emeralds break from the ruby-budded lime
In the little grove where I sit—ah, wherefore cannot I be
Like things of the season gay, like the bountiful season bland,
When the far-off sail is blown by the breeze of a softer clime,
Half-lost in the liquid azure bloom of a crescent of sea,
The silent sapphire-spangled marriage ring of the land?

II

Below me, there, is the village, and looks how quiet and small!
And yet bubbles o'er like a city, with gossip, scandal, and spite;
And Jack on his ale-house bench has as many lies as a Czar;°   [110]
And here on the landward side, by a red rock, glimmers the Hall;
And up in the high Hall-garden I see her pass like a light;
But sorrow seize me if ever that light be my leading star!

III

When have I bow'd to her father, the wrinkled head of the race?
I met her to-day with her brother, but not to her brother I bow'd:
I bow'd to his lady-sister as she rode by on the moor;
But the fire of a foolish pride flash'd over her beautiful face.
O child, you wrong your beauty, believe it, in being so proud;
Your father has wealth well-gotten, and I am nameless and poor.

IV

I keep but a man and a maid, ever ready to slander and steal;   [120]
I know it, and smile a hard-set smile, like a stoic, or like
A wiser epicurean, and let the world have its way:
For nature is one with rapine, a harm no preacher can heal;

The Mayfly is torn by the swallow, the sparrow spear'd by
    the shrike,
And the whole little wood where I sit is a world of plunder
    and prey.

V

We are puppets, Man in his pride, and Beauty fair in her flower;
Do we move ourselves, or are moved by an unseen hand at a
    game
That pushes us off from the board, and others ever succeed?
Ah yet, we cannot be kind to each other here for an hour;
We whisper, and hint, and chuckle, and grin at a brother's
    shame;   [130]
However we brave it out, we men are a little breed.

VI

A monstrous eft was of old the Lord and Master of Earth,°
For him did his high sun flame, and his river billowing ran,
And he felt himself in his force to be Nature's crowning race.
As nine months go to the shaping an infant ripe for his birth,
So many a million of ages have gone to the making of man:
He now is first, but is he the last? is he not too base?

VII

The man of science himself is fonder of glory, and vain,
An eye well-practised in nature, a spirit bounded and poor;
The passionate heart of the poet is whirl'd into folly and vice.   [140]
I would not marvel at either, but keep a temperate brain;
For not to desire or admire, if a man could learn it, were more
Than to walk all day like the sultan of old in a garden of spice.

VIII

For the drift of the Maker is dark, an Isis hid by the veil.°
Who knows the ways of the world, how God will bring them
    about?
Our planet is one, the suns are many, the world is wide.
Shall I weep if a Poland fall? shall I shriek if a Hungary fail?°
Or an infant civilisation be ruled with rod or with knout?°
I have not made the world, and He that made it will guide.

IX

Be mine a philosopher's life in the quiet woodland ways,   [150]
Where if I cannot be gay let a passionless peace be my lot,
Far-off from the clamour of liars belied in the hubbub of lies;
From the long-neck'd geese of the world that are ever hissing
        dispraise
Because their natures are little, and, whether he heed it or not,
Where each man walks with his head in a cloud of poisonous flies.

X

And most of all would I flee from the cruel madness of love,
The honey of poison-flowers and all the measureless ill.
Ah Maud, you milkwhite fawn, you are all unmeet for a wife.
Your mother is mute in her grave as her image in marble above;
Your father is ever in London, you wander about at your will;   [160]
You have but fed on the roses and lain in the lilies of life.

V

I

A voice by the cedar tree
In the meadow under the Hall!
She is singing an air that is known to me,
A passionate ballad gallant and gay,
A martial song like a trumpet's call!
Singing alone in the morning of life,
In the happy morning of life and of May,
Singing of men that in battle array,
Ready in heart and ready in hand,   [170]
March with banner and bugle and fife
To the death, for their native land.

II

Maud with her exquisite face,
And wild voice pealing up to the sunny sky,
And feet like sunny gems on an English green,
Maud in the light of her youth and her grace,
Singing of Death, and of Honour that cannot die,
Till I well could weep for a time so sordid and mean,
And myself so languid and base.

III

Silence, beautiful voice!   [180]
Be still, for you only trouble the mind
With a joy in which I cannot rejoice,
A glory I shall not find.
Still! I will hear you no more,
For your sweetness hardly leaves me a choice
But to move to the meadow and fall before
Her feet on the meadow grass, and adore,
Not her, who is neither courtly nor kind,
Not her, not her, but a voice.

VI

I

Morning arises stormy and pale,   [190]
No sun, but a wannish glare
In fold upon fold of hueless cloud,
And the budded peaks of the wood are bow'd
Caught and cuff'd by the gale:
I had fancied it would be fair.

II

Whom but Maud should I meet
Last night, when the sunset burn'd
On the blossom'd gable-ends
At the head of the village street,
Whom but Maud should I meet?   [200]
And she touch'd my hand with a smile so sweet,
She made me divine amends
For a courtesy not return'd.

III

And thus a delicate spark
Of glowing and growing light
Thro' the livelong hours of the dark
Kept itself warm in the heart of my dreams,
Ready to burst in a colour'd flame;
Till at last when the morning came
In a cloud, it faded, and seems   [210]
But an ashen-gray delight.

IV

What if with her sunny hair,
And smile as sunny as cold,
She meant to weave me a snare
Of some coquettish deceit,
Cleopatra-like as of old
To entangle me when we met,
To have her lion roll in a silken net
And fawn at a victor's feet.

V

Ah, what shall I be at fifty   [220]
Should Nature keep me alive,
If I find the world so bitter
When I am but twenty-five?
Yet, if she were not a cheat,
If Maud were all that she seem'd,
And her smile were all that I dream'd,
Then the world were not so bitter
But a smile could make it sweet.

VI

What if tho' her eye seem'd full
Of a kind intent to me,   [230]
What if that dandy-despot, he,
That jewell'd mass of millinery,
That oil'd and curl'd Assyrian Bull°
Smelling of musk and of insolence,
Her brother, from whom I keep aloof,
Who wants the finer politic sense
To mask, tho' but in his own behoof,
With a glassy smile his brutal scorn—
What if he had told her yestermorn
How prettily for his own sweet sake   [240]
A face of tenderness might be feign'd,
And a moist mirage in desert eyes,
That so, when the rotten hustings shake°
In another month to his brazen lies,
A wretched vote may be gain'd.

VII

For a raven ever croaks, at my side,
Keep watch and ward, keep watch and ward,
Or thou wilt prove their tool.
Yea, too, myself from myself I guard,
For often a man's own angry pride   [250]
Is cap and bells for a fool.

VIII

Perhaps the smile and tender tone
Came out of her pitying womanhood,
For am I not, am I not, here alone
So many a summer since she died,
My mother, who was so gentle and good?
Living alone in an empty house,
Here half-hid in the gleaming wood,
Where I hear the dead at midday moan,
And the shrieking rush of the wainscot mouse,   [260]
And my own sad name in corners cried,
When the shiver of dancing leaves is thrown
About its echoing chambers wide,
Till a morbid hate and horror have grown
Of a world in which I have hardly mixt,
And a morbid eating lichen fixt
On a heart half-turn'd to stone.

IX

O heart of stone, are you flesh, and caught
By that you swore to withstand?
For what was it else within me wrought   [270]
But, I fear, the new strong wine of love,
That made my tongue so stammer and trip
When I saw the treasured splendour, her hand,
Come sliding out of her sacred glove,
And the sunlight broke from her lip?

X

I have play'd with her when a child;
She remembers it now we meet.

Ah well, well, well, I *may* be beguiled
By some coquettish deceit.
Yet, if she were not a cheat,   [280]
If Maud were all that she seem'd,
And her smile had all that I dream'd,
Then the world were not so bitter
But a smile could make it sweet.

VII

I

Did I hear it half in a doze
    Long since, I know not where?
Did I dream it an hour ago,
    When asleep in this arm-chair?

II

Men were drinking together,°
    Drinking and talking of me;   [290]
'Well, if it prove a girl, the boy
    Will have plenty: so let it be.'

III

Is it an echo of something
    Read with a boy's delight,
Viziers nodding together°
    In some Arabian night?

IV

Strange, that I hear two men,
    Somewhere, talking of me;
'Well, if it prove a girl, my boy
    Will have plenty: so let it be.'   [300]

VIII

She came to the village church,
And sat by a pillar alone;
An angel watching an urn

Wept over her, carved in stone;
And once, but once, she lifted her eyes,
And suddenly, sweetly, strangely blush'd
To find they were met by my own;
And suddenly, sweetly, my heart beat stronger
And thicker, until I heard no longer
The snowy-banded, dilettante,   [310]
Delicate-handed priest intone;
And thought, is it pride, and mused and sigh'd
'No surely, now it cannot be pride.'

IX

I was walking a mile,
More than a mile from the shore,
The sun look'd out with a smile
Betwixt the cloud and the moor,
And riding at set of day
Over the dark moor land,
Rapidly riding far away,   [320]
She waved to me with her hand.
There were two at her side,
Something flash'd in the sun,
Down by the hill I saw them ride,
In a moment they were gone:
Like a sudden spark
Struck vainly in the night,
Then returns the dark
With no more hope of light.

X

I

Sick, am I sick of a jealous dread?   [330]
Was not one of the two at her side
This new-made lord, whose splendour plucks
The slavish hat from the villager's head?
Whose old grandfather has lately died,
Gone to a blacker pit, for whom
Grimy nakedness dragging his trucks

And laying his trams in a poison'd gloom
Wrought, till he crept from a gutted mine
Master of half a servile shire,
And left his coal all turn'd into gold   [340]
To a grandson, first of his noble line,
Rich in the grace all women desire,
Strong in the power that all men adore,
And simper and set their voices lower,
And soften as if to a girl, and hold
Awe-stricken breaths at a work divine,
Seeing his gewgaw castle shine,°
New as his title, built last year,
There amid perky larches and pine,
And over the sullen-purple moor   [350]
(Look at it) pricking a cockney ear.

II

What, has he found my jewel out?
For one of the two that rode at her side
Bound for the Hall, I am sure was he:
Bound for the Hall, and I think for a bride.
Blithe would her brother's acceptance be.
Maud could be gracious too, no doubt
To a lord, a captain, a padded shape,
A bought commission, a waxen face,°
A rabbit mouth that is ever agape—   [360]
Bought? what is it he cannot buy?
And therefore splenetic, personal, base,
A wounded thing with a rancorous cry,
At war with myself and a wretched race,
Sick, sick to the heart of life, am I.

III

Last week came one to the county town,°
To preach our poor little army down,
And play the game of the despot kings,
Tho' the state has done it and thrice as well:
This broad-brimm'd hawker of holy things,   [370]
Whose ear is cramm'd with his cotton, and rings
Even in dreams to the chink of his pence,

This huckster put down war! can he tell
Whether war be a cause or a consequence?
Put down the passions that make earth Hell!
Down with ambition, avarice, pride,
Jealousy, down! cut off from the mind
The bitter springs of anger and fear;
Down too, down at your own fireside,
With the evil tongue and the evil ear,   [380]
For each is at war with mankind.

IV

I wish I could hear again
The chivalrous battle-song
That she warbled alone in her joy!
I might persuade myself then
She would not do herself this great wrong,
To take a wanton dissolute boy
For a man and leader of men.

V

Ah God, for a man with heart, head, hand,
Like some of the simple great ones gone   [390]
For ever and ever by,
One still strong man in a blatant land,
Whatever they call him, what care I,
Aristocrat, democrat, autocrat—one
Who can rule and dare not lie.

VI

And ah for a man to arise in me,
That the man I am may cease to be!

XI

I

O let the solid ground
    Not fail beneath my feet
Before my life has found   [400]
    What some have found so sweet;

Then let come what come may,
What matter if I go mad,
I shall have had my day.

II

Let the sweet heavens endure,
    Not close and darken above me
Before I am quite quite sure
    That there is one to love me;
Then let come what come may
To a life that has been so sad,   [410]
I shall have had my day.

XII

I

Birds in the high Hall-garden
    When twilight was falling,
Maud, Maud, Maud, Maud,
    They were crying and calling

II

Where was Maud? in our wood;
    And I, who else, was with her,
Gathering woodland lilies,
    Myriads blow together.

III

Birds in our wood sang   [420]
    Ringing thro' the valleys,
Maud is here, here, here
    In among the lilies.

IV

I kiss'd her slender hand,
    She took the kiss sedately;
Maud is not seventeen,
    But she is tall and stately.

V

I to cry out on pride
    Who have won her favour!
O Maud were sure of Heaven   [430]
    If lowliness could save her.

VI

I know the way she went
    Home with her maiden posy,
For her feet have touch'd the meadows
    And left the daisies rosy.°

VII

Birds in the high Hall-garden
    Were crying and calling to her,
Where is Maud, Maud, Maud?
    One is come to woo her.

VIII

Look, a horse at the door,   [440]
    And little King Charley snarling,°
Go back, my lord, across the moor,
    You are not her darling.

XIII

I

Scorn'd, to be scorn'd by one that I scorn,
Is that a matter to make me fret?
That a calamity hard to be borne?
Well, he may live to hate me yet.
Fool that I am to be vext with his pride!
I past him, I was crossing his lands;
He stood on the path a little aside;   [450]
His face, as I grant, in spite of spite,
Has a broad-blown comeliness, red and white,
And six feet two, as I think, he stands;
But his essences turn'd the live air sick,
And barbarous opulence jewel-thick
Sunn'd itself on his breast and his hands.

II

Who shall call me ungentle, unfair,
I long'd so heartily then and there
To give him the grasp of fellowship;
But while I past he was humming an air,   [460]
Stopt, and then with a riding-whip
Leisurely tapping a glossy boot,
And curving a contumelious lip,
Gorgonised me from head to foot°
With a stony British stare.

III

Why sits he here in his father's chair?
That old man never comes to his place:
Shall I believe him ashamed to be seen?
For only once, in the village street,
Last year, I caught a glimpse of his face,   [470]
A gray old wolf and a lean.
Scarcely, now, would I call him a cheat;
For then, perhaps, as a child of deceit,
She might by a true descent be untrue;
And Maud is as true as Maud is sweet:
Tho' I fancy her sweetness only due
To the sweeter blood by the other side;
Her mother has been a thing complete,
However she came to be so allied.
And fair without, faithful within,   [480]
Maud to him is nothing akin:
Some peculiar mystic grace
Made her only the child of her mother,
And heap'd the whole inherited sin
On that huge scapegoat of the race,
All, all upon the brother.

IV

Peace, angry spirit, and let him be!
Has not his sister smiled on me?

XIV

I

Maud has a garden of roses
And lilies fair on a lawn;   [490]
There she walks in her state
And tends upon bed and bower,
And thither I climb'd at dawn
And stood by her garden-gate;
A lion ramps at the top,
He is claspt by a passion-flower.

II

Maud's own little oak-room
(Which Maud, like a precious stone
Set in the heart of the carven gloom,
Lights with herself, when alone   [500]
She sits by her music and books
And her brother lingers late
With a roystering company) looks
Upon Maud's own garden-gate:
And I thought as I stood, if a hand, as white
As ocean-foam in the moon, were laid
On the hasp of the window, and my Delight
Had a sudden desire, like a glorious ghost, to glide,
Like a beam of the seventh Heaven, down to my side,
There were but a step to be made.   [510]

III

The fancy flatter'd my mind,
And again seem'd overbold;
Now I thought that she cared for me,
Now I thought she was kind
Only because she was cold.

IV

I heard no sound where I stood
But the rivulet on from the lawn
Running down to my own dark wood;

Or the voice of the long sea-wave as it swell'd
Now and then in the dim-gray dawn; [520]
But I look'd, and round, all round the house I beheld
The death-white curtain drawn;
Felt a horror over me creep,
Prickle my skin and catch my breath,
Knew that the death-white curtain meant but sleep,
Yet I shudder'd and thought like a fool of the sleep of death.

XV

So dark a mind within me dwells,
　　And I make myself such evil cheer,
That if *I* be dear to some one else, [530]
　　　　Then some one else may have much to fear
But if *I* be dear to some one else,
　　　　Then I should be to myself more dear.
Shall I not take care of all that I think,
Yea ev'n of wretched meat and drink,
If I be dear,
If I be dear to some one else.

XVI

I

This lump of earth has left his estate°
The lighter by the loss of his weight;
And so that he find what he went to seek,
And fulsome Pleasure clog him, and drown [540]
His heart in the gross mud-honey of town,
He may stay for a year who has gone for a week:
But this is the day when I must speak,
And I see my Oread coming down,°
O this is the day!
O beautiful creature, what am I
That I dare to look her way;
Think I may hold dominion sweet,
Lord of the pulse that is lord of her breast,
And dream of her beauty with tender dread, [550]
From the delicate Arab arch of her feet

To the grace that, bright and light as the crest
Of a peacock, sits on her shining head,
And she knows it not: O, if she knew it,
To know her beauty might half undo it.
I know it the one bright thing to save
My yet young life in the wilds of Time,
Perhaps from madness, perhaps from crime,
Perhaps from a selfish grave.

II

What, if she be fasten'd to this fool lord,°   [560]
Dare I bid her abide by her word?
Should I love her so well if she
Had given her word to a thing so low?
Shall I love her as well if she
Can break her word were it even for me?
I trust that it is not so.

III

Catch not my breath, O clamorous heart,
Let not my tongue be a thrall to my eye,
For I must tell her before we part,
I must tell her, or die.   [570]

XVII

Go not, happy day,
   From the shining fields,
Go not, happy day,
   Till the maiden yields.
Rosy is the West,
   Rosy is the South,
Roses are her cheeks,
   And a rose her mouth
When the happy Yes
   Falters from her lips,   [580]
Pass and blush the news
   Over glowing ships;
Over blowing seas,
   Over seas at rest,

Pass the happy news,
   Blush it thro' the West;
Till the red man dance
   By his red cedar-tree,
And the red man's babe
   Leap, beyond the sea.   [590]
Blush from West to East,
   Blush from East to West,
Till the West is East,
   Blush it thro' the West.
Rosy is the West,
   Rosy is the South,
Roses are her cheeks,
   And a rose her mouth.

XVIII

I

I have led her home, my love, my only friend.
There is none like her, none.   [600]
And never yet so warmly ran my blood
And sweetly, on and on
Calming itself to the long-wish'd-for end,
Full to the banks, close on the promised good.

II

None like her, none.
Just now the dry-tongued laurels' pattering talk
Seem'd her light foot along the garden walk,
And shook my heart to think she comes once more;
But even then I heard her close the door,
The gates of Heaven are closed, and she is gone.   [610]

III

There is none like her, none.
Nor will be when our summers have deceased.
O, art thou sighing for Lebanon°
In the long breeze that streams to thy delicious East,
Sighing for Lebanon,
Dark cedar, tho' thy limbs have here increased,

Upon a pastoral slope as fair,
And looking to the South, and fed
With honey'd rain and delicate air,
And haunted by the starry head   [620]
Of her whose gentle will has changed my fate,
And made my life a perfumed altar-flame;
And over whom thy darkness must have spread
With such delight as theirs of old, thy great
Forefathers of the thornless garden, there
Shadowing the snow-limb'd Eve from whom she came.

IV

Here will I lie, while these long branches sway,
And you fair stars that crown a happy day
Go in and out as if at merry play,
Who am no more so all forlorn,   [630]
As when it seem'd far better to be born
To labour and the mattock-harden'd hand,
Than nursed at ease and brought to understand
A sad astrology, the boundless plan°
That makes you tyrants in your iron skies,
Innumerable, pitiless, passionless eyes,
Cold fires, yet with power to burn and brand
His nothingness into man.

V

But now shine on, and what care I,
Who in this stormy gulf have found a pearl   [640]
The countercharm of space and hollow sky,
And do accept my madness, and would die
To save from some slight shame one simple girl.

VI

Would die; for sullen-seeming Death may give
More life to Love than is or ever was
In our low world, where yet 'tis sweet to live.
Let no one ask me how it came to pass;
It seems that I am happy, that to me
A livelier emerald twinkles in the grass,
A purer sapphire melts into the sea.   [650]

VII

Not die; but live a life of truest breath,
And teach true life to fight with mortal wrongs.
O, why should Love, like men in drinking-songs,
Spice his fair banquet with the dust of death?
Make answer, Maud my bliss,
Maud made my Maud by that long loving kiss,
Life of my life, wilt thou not answer this?
'The dusky strand of Death inwoven here
With dear Love's tie, makes Love himself more dear.'

VIII

Is that enchanted moan only the swell   [660]
Of the long waves that roll in yonder bay?
And hark the clock within, the silver knell
Of twelve sweet hours that past in bridal white,
And died to live, long as my pulses play;
But now by this my love has closed her sight
And given false death her hand, and stol'n away°
To dreamful wastes where footless fancies dwell
Among the fragments of the golden day.
May nothing there her maiden grace affright!
Dear heart, I feel with thee the drowsy spell.   [670]
My bride to be, my evermore delight,
My own heart's heart, my ownest own, farewell;
It is but for a little space I go:
And ye meanwhile far over moor and fell°
Beat to the noiseless music of the night!
Has our whole earth gone nearer to the glow
Of your soft splendours that you look so bright?
I have climb'd nearer out of lonely Hell.
Beat, happy stars, timing with things below,
Beat with my heart more blest than heart can tell,   [680]
Blest, but for some dark undercurrent woe
That seems to draw—but it shall not be so:
Let all be well, be well.

XIX

I

Her brother is coming back to-night,
Breaking up my dream of delight.

II

My dream? do I dream of bliss?
I have walk'd awake with Truth.
O when did a morning shine
So rich in atonement as this
For my dark-dawning youth,   [690]
Darken'd watching a mother decline
And that dead man at her heart and mine:
For who was left to watch her but I?
Yet so did I let my freshness die.

III

I trust that I did not talk
To gentle Maud in our walk
(For often in lonely wanderings
I have cursed him even to lifeless things)
But I trust that I did not talk,
Not touch on her father's sin: [700]
I am sure I did but speak
Of my mother's faded cheek
When it slowly grew so thin,
That I felt she was slowly dying
Vext with lawyers and harass'd with debt:
For how often I caught her with eyes all wet,
Shaking her head at her son and sighing
A world of trouble within!

IV

And Maud too, Maud was moved
To speak of the mother she loved   [710]
As once scarce less forlorn,
Dying abroad and it seems apart
From him who had ceased to share her heart,

And ever mourning over the feud,
The household Fury sprinkled with blood
By which our houses are torn:
How strange was what she said,
When only Maud and the brother
Hung over her dying bed—
That Maud's dark father and mine   [720]
Had bound us one to the other,
Betrothed us over their wine,
On the day when Maud was born;
Seal'd her mine from her first sweet breath.
Mine, mine by a right, from birth till death.
Mine, mine—our fathers have sworn.

V

But the true blood spilt had in it a heat
To dissolve the precious seal on a bond,
That, if left uncancell'd, had been so sweet:
And none of us thought of a something beyond,   [730]
A desire that awoke in the heart of the child,
As it were a duty done to the tomb,
To be friends for her sake, to be reconciled;
And I was cursing them and my doom,
And letting a dangerous thought run wild
While often abroad in the fragrant gloom
Of foreign churches—I see her there,
Bright English lily, breathing a prayer
To be friends, to be reconciled!

VI

But then what a flint is he!   [740]
Abroad, at Florence, at Rome,
I find whenever she touch'd on me
This brother had laugh'd her down,
And at last, when each came home,
He had darken'd into a frown,
Chid her, and forbid her to speak
To me, her friend of the years before;
And this was what had redden'd her cheek
When I bow'd to her on the moor.

VII

Yet Maud, altho' not blind   [750]
To the faults of his heart and mind,
I see she cannot but love him,
And says he is rough but kind,
And wishes me to approve him,
And tells me, when she lay
Sick once, with a fear of worse,
That he left his wine and horses and play,
Sat with her, read to her, night and day,
And tended her like a nurse.

VIII

Kind? but the deathbed desire   [760]
Spurn'd by this heir of the liar—
Rough but kind? yet I know
He has plotted against me in this,
That he plots against me still.
Kind to Maud? that were not amiss.
Well, rough but kind; why let it be so:
For shall not Maud have her will?

IX

For, Maud, so tender and true,
As long as my life endures
I feel I shall owe you a debt,   [770]
That I never can hope to pay;
And if ever I should forget
That I owe this debt to you
And for your sweet sake to yours;
O then, what then shall I say?—
If ever I *should* forget,
May god make me more wretched
Than ever I have been yet!

X

So now I have sworn to bury
All this dead body of hate,   [780]
I feel so free and so clear

By the loss of that dead weight,
That I should grow light-headed, I fear,
Fantastically merry;
But that her brother comes, like a blight
On my fresh hope, to the Hall to-night.

XX

I

Strange, that I felt so gay,
Strange, that *I* tried to-day
To beguile her melancholy;
The Sultan, as we name him,—°   [790]
She did not wish to blame him—
But he vext her and perplext her
With his worldly talk and folly:
Was it gentle to reprove her
For stealing out of view
From a little lazy lover
Who but claims her as his due?
Or for chilling his caresses
By the coldness of her manners,
Nay, the plainness of her dresses?   [800]
Now I know her but in two,
Nor can pronounce upon it
If one should ask me whether
The habit, hat, and feather,
Or the frock and gipsy bonnet
Be the neater and completer;
For nothing can be sweeter
Than maiden Maud in either.

II

But to-morrow, if we live,
Our ponderous squire will give   [810]
A grand political dinner
To half the squirelings near;
And Maud will wear her jewels,
And the bird of prey will hover,
And the titmouse hope to win her
With his chirrup at her ear.

III

A grand political dinner
To the men of many acres,
A gathering of the Tory,°
A dinner and then a dance   [820]
For the maids and marriage-makers,
And every eye but mine will glance
At Maud in all her glory.

IV

For I am not invited,
But, with the Sultan's pardon,
I am all as well delighted,
For I know her own rose-garden,
And mean to linger in it
Till the dancing will be over;
And then, oh then, come out to me   [830]
For a minute, but for a minute,
Come out to your own true lover,
That your true lover may see
Your glory also, and render
All homage to his own darling,
Queen Maud in all her splendour.

XXI

Rivulet crossing my ground,
And bringing me down from the Hall
This garden-rose that I found,
Forgetful of Maud and me,   [840]
And lost in trouble and moving round
Here at the head of a tinkling fall,
And trying to pass to the sea;
O Rivulet, born at the Hall,
My Maud has sent it by thee
(If I read her sweet will right)
On a blushing mission to me,
Saying in odour and colour, 'Ah, be
Among the roses to-night.'

XXII

I

Come into the garden, Maud,° [850]
    For the black bat, night, has flown,
Come into the garden, Maud,
    I am here at the gate alone;
And the woodbine spices are wafted abroad,
    And the musk of the rose is blown.

II

For a breeze of morning moves,
    And the planet of Love is on high,
Beginning to faint in the light that she loves
    On a bed of daffodil sky,
To faint in the light of the sun she loves, [860]
    To faint in his light, and to die.

III

All night have the roses heard
    The flute, violin, bassoon;
All night has the casement jessamine stirr'd
    To the dancers dancing in tune;
Till a silence fell with the waking bird,
    And a hush with the setting moon.

IV

I said to the lily, 'There is but one
    With whom she has heart to be gay.
When will the dancers leave her alone? [870]
    She is weary of dance and play.'
Now half to the setting moon are gone,
    And half to the rising day;
Low on the sand and loud on the stone
    The last wheel echoes away.

V

I said to the rose, 'The brief night goes
    In babble and revel and wine.
O young lord-lover, what sighs are those,
    For one that will never be thine?
But mine, but mine,' so I sware to the rose,   [880]
    'For ever and ever, mine.'

VI

And the soul of the rose went into my blood,
    As the music clash'd in the hall;
And long by the garden lake I stood,
    For I heard your rivulet fall
From the lake to the meadow and on to the wood,
    Our wood, that is dearer than all;

VII

From the meadow your walks have left so sweet
    That whenever a March-wind sighs
He sets the jewel-print of your feet   [890]
    In violets blue as your eyes,
To the woody hollows in which we meet
    And the valleys of Paradise.

VIII

The slender acacia would not shake
    One long milk-bloom on the tree;
The white lake-blossom fell into the lake
    As the pimpernel dozed on the lea;
But the rose was awake all night for your sake,
    Knowing your promise to me;
The lilies and roses were all awake,   [900]
    They sigh'd for the dawn and thee.

IX

Queen rose of the rosebud garden of girls,
      Come hither, the dances are done,
In gloss of satin and glimmer of pearls,
      Queen lily and rose in one;
Shine out, little head, sunning over with curls,
      To the flowers, and be their sun.

X

There has fallen a splendid tear
      From the passion-flower at the gate.
She is coming, my dove, my dear;   [910]
      She is coming, my life, my fate;
The red rose cries, 'She is near, she is near;'
      And the white rose weeps, 'She is late;'
The larkspur listens, 'I hear, I hear;'
      And the lily whispers, 'I wait.'

XI

She is coming, my own, my sweet;
      Were it ever so airy a tread,
My heart would hear her and beat,
      Were it earth in an earthy bed;
My dust would hear her and beat,   [920]
      Had I lain for a century dead;
Would start and tremble under her feet,
      And blossom in purple and red.

PART II

I

I

'The fault was mine, the fault was mine'—
Why am I sitting here so stunn'd and still,
Plucking the harmless wild-flower on the hill?—
It is this guilty hand!—
And there rises ever a passionate cry
From underneath in the darkening land—
What is it, that has been done?

O dawn of Eden bright over earth and sky,
The fires of Hell brake out of thy rising sun,
The fires of Hell and of Hate;   [10]
For she, sweet soul, had hardly spoken a word.
When her brother ran in his rage to the gate,
He came with the babe-faced lord;
Heap'd on her terms of disgrace,
And while she wept, and I strove to be cool,
He fiercely gave me the lie,
Till I with as fierce an anger spoke,
And he struck me, madman, over the face,
Struck me before the languid fool,
Who was gaping and grinning by: [20]
Struck for himself an evil stroke;
Wrought for his house an irredeemable woe;
For front to front in an hour we stood,
And a million horrible bellowing echoes broke
From the red-ribb'd hollow behind the wood,
And thunder'd up into Heaven the Christless code,
That must have life for a blow.
Ever and ever afresh they seem'd to grow.
Was it he lay there with a fading eye?°
'The fault was mine,' he whisper'd, 'fly!'   [30]
Then glided out of the joyous wood
The ghastly Wraith of one that I know;°
And there rang on a sudden a passionate cry,
A cry for a brother's blood:
It will ring in my heart and my ears, till I die, till I die.

                              II

Is it gone? my pulses beat—
What was it? a lying trick of the brain?
Yet I thought I saw her stand
A shadow there at my feet,
High over the shadowy land.   [40]
It is gone; and the heavens fall in a gentle rain,
When they should burst and drown with deluging storms
The feeble vassals of wine and anger and lust,
The little hearts that know not how to forgive:
Arise, my God, and strike, for we hold Thee just,

Strike dead the whole weak race of venomous worms,
That sting each other here in the dust;
We are not worthy to live.

II

I

See what a lovely shell,
Small and pure as a pearl,   [50]
Lying close to my foot,
Frail, but a work divine,
Made so fairly well
With delicate spire and whorl,
How exquisitely minute,
A miracle of design!

II

What is it? a learned man
Could give it a clumsy name.
Let him name it who can,
The beauty would be the same.   [60]

III

The tiny cell is forlorn,
Void of the little living will
That made it stir on the shore.
Did he stand at the diamond door
Of his house in a rainbow frill?
Did he push, when he was uncurl'd,
A golden foot or a fairy horn
Thro' his dim water-world?

IV

Slight, to be crush'd with a tap
Of my finger-nail on the sand,   [70]
Small, but a work divine,
Frail, but of force to withstand,
Year upon year, the shock

Of cataract seas that snap
The three decker's oaken spine
Athwart the ledges of rock,
Here on the Breton strand!

v

Breton, not Briton; here
Like a shipwreck'd man on a coast
Of ancient fable and fear—   [80]
Plagued with a flitting to and fro,
A disease, a hard mechanic ghost
That never came from on high
Nor ever arose from below,
But only moves with the moving eye,
Flying along the land and the main—
Why should it look like Maud?
Am I to be overawed
By what I cannot but know
Is a juggle born of the brain?   [90]

VI

Back from the Breton coast,
Sick of a nameless fear,
Back to the dark sea-line
Looking, thinking of all I have lost;
An old song vexes my ear;
But that of Lamech is mine.°

VII

For years, a measureless ill,
For years, for ever, to part—
But she, she would love me still;
And as long, O God, as she   [100]
Have a grain of love for me,
So long, no doubt, no doubt,
Shall I nurse in my dark heart,
However weary, a spark of will
Not to be trampled out.

VIII

Strange, that the mind, when fraught
With a passion so intense
One would think that it well
Might drown all life in the eye,—
That it should, by being so overwrought,   [110]
Suddenly strike on a sharper sense
For a shell, or a flower, little things
Which else would have been past by!
And now I remember, I,
When he lay dying there,
I noticed one of his many rings
(For he had many, poor worm) and thought
It is his mother's hair.

IX

Who knows if he be dead?
Whether I need have fled?   [120]
Am I guilty of blood?
However this may be,
Comfort her, comfort her, all things good,
While I am over the sea!
Let me and my passionate love go by,
But speak to her all things holy and high,
Whatever happen to me!
Me and my harmful love go by;
But come to her waking, find her asleep,
Powers of the height, Powers of the deep,   [130]
And comfort her tho' I die.

III

Courage, poor heart of stone!
I will not ask thee why
Thou canst not understand
That thou art left for ever alone:°
Courage, poor stupid heart of stone.—
Or if I ask thee why,
Care not thou to reply:
She is but dead, and the time is at hand
When thou shalt more than die.   [140]

IV

I

O that 'twere possible
After long grief and pain
To find the arms of my true love
Round me once again!

II

When I was wont to meet her
In the silent woody places
By the home that gave me birth,
We stood tranced in long embraces
Mixt with kisses sweeter sweeter
Than anything on earth.   [150]

III

A shadow flits before me,
Not thou, but like to thee:
Ah Christ, that it were possible
For one short hour to see
The souls we loved, that they might tell us
What and where they be.

IV

It leads me forth at evening,
It lightly winds and steals
In a cold white robe before me,
When all my spirit reels   [160]
At the shouts, the leagues of lights,
And the roaring of the wheels.

V

Half the night I waste in sighs,
Half in dreams I sorrow after
The delight of early skies;
In a wakeful doze I sorrow
For the hand, the lips, the eyes,
For the meeting of the morrow,
The delight of happy laughter,
The delight of low replies.   [170]

VI

'Tis a morning pure and sweet,
And a dewy splendour falls
On the little flower that clings
To the turrets and the walls;
'Tis a morning pure and sweet,
And the light and shadow fleet;
She is walking in the meadow,
And the woodland echo rings;
In a moment we shall meet;
She is singing in the meadow   [180]
And the rivulet at her feet
Ripples on in light and shadow
To the ballad that she sings.

VII

Do I hear her sing as of old,
My bird with the shining head,
My own dove with the tender eye?
But there rings on a sudden a passionate cry,
There is some one dying or dead,
And a sullen thunder is roll'd;
For a tumult shakes the city,   [190]
And I wake, my dream is fled;
In the shuddering dawn, behold,
Without knowledge, without pity,
By the curtains of my bed
That abiding phantom cold.

VIII

Get thee hence, nor come again,
Mix not memory with doubt,
Pass, thou deathlike type of pain,
Pass and cease to move about!
'Tis the blot upon the brain   [200]
That *will* show itself without.

IX

Then I rise, the eavedrops fall,
And the yellow vapours choke
The great city sounding wide;

The day comes, a dull red ball
Wrapt in drifts of lurid smoke
On the misty river-tide.

X

Thro' the hubbub of the market
I steal, a wasted frame,
It crosses here, it crosses there,   [210]
Thro' all that crowd confused and loud,
The shadow still the same;
And on my heavy eyelids
My anguish hangs like shame.

XI

Alas for her that met me,
That heard me softly call,
Came glimmering thro' the laurels
At the quiet evenfall,
In the garden by the turrets
Of the old manorial hall.   [220]

XII

Would the happy spirit descend,
From the realms of light and song,
In the chamber or the street,
As she looks among the blest,
Should I fear to greet my friend
Or to say 'Forgive the wrong,'
Or to ask her, 'Take me, sweet,
To the regions of thy rest'?

XIII

But the broad light glares and beats,
And the shadow flits and fleets   [230]
And will not let me be;
And I loathe the squares and streets,
And the faces that one meets,
Hearts with no love for me:

Always I long to creep
Into some still cavern deep,
There to weep, and weep, and weep
My whole soul out to thee.

V°

I

Dead, long dead,
Long dead!   [240]
And my heart is a handful of dust,
And the wheels go over my head,
And my bones are shaken with pain,
For into a shallow grave they are thrust,
Only a yard beneath the street,
And the hoofs of the horses beat, beat,
The hoofs of the horses beat,
Beat into my scalp and my brain,
With never an end to the stream of passing feet,
Driving, hurrying, marrying, burying,   [250]
Clamour and rumble, and ringing and clatter,
And here beneath it is all as bad,
For I thought the dead had peace, but it is not so;
To have no peace in the grave, is that not sad?
But up and down and to and fro,
Ever about me the dead men go;
And then to hear a dead man chatter
Is enough to drive one mad.

II

Wretchedest age, since Time began,
They cannot even bury a man;   [260]
And tho' we paid our tithes in the days that are gone,
Not a bell was rung, not a prayer was read;
It is that which makes us loud in the world of the dead;
There is none that does his work, not one;
A touch of their office might have sufficed,
But the churchmen fain would kill their church,
As the churches have kill'd their Christ.

III

See, there is one of us sobbing,
No limit to his distress;
And another, a lord of all things, praying   [270]
To his own great self, as I guess;
And another, a statesman there, betraying
His party-secret, fool, to the press;
And yonder a vile physician, blabbing
The case of his patient—all for what?
To tickle the maggot born in an empty head,
And wheedle a world that loves him not,
For it is but a world of the dead.

IV

Nothing but idiot gabble!
For the prophecy given of old°   [280]
And then not understood,
Has come to pass as foretold;
Not let any man think for the public good,
But babble, merely for babble.
For I never whisper'd a private affair
Within the hearing of cat or mouse,
No, not to myself in the closet alone,
But I heard it shouted at once from the top of the house;
Everything came to be known.
Who told *him* we were there?°   [290]

V

Not that gray old wolf, for he came not back°
From the wilderness, full of wolves, where he used to lie;
He has gather'd the bones for his o'ergrown whelp to crack;
Crack them now for yourself, and howl, and die.

VI

Prophet, curse me the blabbing lip,
And curse me the British vermin, the rat;°
I know not whether he came in the Hanover ship,
But I know that he lies and listens mute
In an ancient mansion's crannies and holes:

Arsenic, arsenic, sure, would do it,   [300]
Except that now we poison our babes, poor souls!
It is all used up for that.

VII

Tell him now: she is standing here at my head;
Not beautiful now, not even kind;
He may take her now; for she never speaks her mind,
But is ever the one thing silent here.
She is not *of* us, as I divine;
She comes from another stiller world of the dead,
Stiller, not fairer than mine.

VIII

But I know where a garden grows,   [310]
Fairer than aught in the world beside,
All made up of the lily and rose
That blow by night, when the season is good,
To the sound of dancing music and flutes:
It is only flowers, they had no fruits,
And I almost fear they are not roses, but blood;
For the keeper was one, so full of pride,°
He linkt a dead man there to a spectral bride;°
For he, if he had not been a Sultan of brutes,
Would he have that hole in his side?   [320]

IX

But what will the old man say?
He laid a cruel snare in a pit
To catch a friend of mine one stormy day;
Yet now I could even weep to think of it;
For what will the old man say
When he comes to the second corpse in the pit?

X

Friend, to be struck by the public foe,
Then to strike him and lay him low,
That were a public merit, far,
Whatever the Quaker holds, from sin;   [330]

But the red life spilt for a private blow—
I swear to you, lawful and lawless war
Are scarcely even akin.

XI

O me, why have they not buried me deep enough?
Is it kind to have made me a grave so rough,
Me, that was never a quiet sleeper?
Maybe still I am but half-dead;
Then I cannot be wholly dumb;
I will cry to the steps above my head
And somebody, surely, some kind heart will come   [340]
To bury me, bury me
Deeper, ever so little deeper.

PART III

VI

I

My life has crept so long on a broken wing
Thro' cells of madness, haunts of horror and fear,
That I come to be grateful at last for a little thing:
My mood is changed, for it fell at a time of year°
When the face of night is fair on the dewy downs,
And the shining daffodil dies, and the Charioteer
And starry Gemini hang like glorious crowns°
Over Orion's grave low down in the west,
That like a silent lightning under the stars
She seem'd to divide in a dream from a band of the blest,°   [10]
And spoke of a hope for the world in the coming wars—
'And in that hope, dear soul, let trouble have rest,
Knowing I tarry for thee,' and pointed to Mars
As he glow'd like a ruddy shield on the Lion's breast.°

II

And it was but a dream, yet it yielded a dear delight
To have look'd, tho' but in a dream, upon eyes so fair,
That had been in a weary world my one thing bright;
And it was but a dream, yet it lighten'd my despair

When I thought that a war would arise in defence of the right,
That an iron tyranny now should bend or cease, [20]
The glory of manhood stand on his ancient height,
Nor Britain's one sole God be the millionaire:
No more shall commerce be all in all, and Peace
Pipe on her pastoral hillock a languid note,
And watch her harvest ripen, her herd increase,
Nor the cannon-bullet rust on a slothful shore,
And the cobweb woven across the cannon's throat
Shall shake its threaded tears in the wind no more.

III

And as months ran on and rumour of battle grew,
'It is time, it is time, O passionate heart,' said I [30]
(For I cleaved to a cause that I felt to be pure and true),
'It is time, O passionate heart and morbid eye,
That old hysterical mock-disease should die.'
And I stood on a giant deck and mix'd my breath°
With a loyal people shouting a battle cry,
Till I saw the dreary phantom arise and fly°
Far into the North, and battle, and seas of death.

IV

Let it go or stay, so I wake to the higher aims
Of a land that has lost for a little her lust of gold,
And love of a peace that was full of wrongs and shames [40]
Horrible, hateful, monstrous, not to be told;
And hail once more to the banner of battle unroll'd!
Tho' many a light shall darken, and many shall weep
For those that are crush'd in the clash of jarring claims,
Yet God's just wrath shall be wreak'd on a giant liar;°
And many a darkness into the light shall leap,
And shine in the sudden making of splendid names,
And noble thought be freer under the sun,
And the heart of a people beat with one desire;
For the peace, that I deem'd no peace, is over and done,° [50]
And now by the side of the Black and the Baltic deep,°
And deathful-grinning mouths of the fortress, flames
The blood-red blossom of war with a heart of fire.

V

Let it flame or fade, and the war roll down like a wind,
We have proved we have hearts in a cause, we are noble still,
And myself have awaked, as it seems, to the better mind;
It is better to fight for the good than to rail at the ill;
I have felt with my native land, I am one with my kind,
I embrace the purpose of God, and the doom assign'd.

TITHONUS (*Final Version*)

The woods decay, the woods decay and fall,
The vapours weep their burthen to the ground,
Man comes and tills the field and lies beneath,
And after many a summer dies the swan.
Me only cruel immortality
Consumes: I wither slowly in thine arms,
Here at the quiet limit of the world,
A white-hair'd shadow roaming like a dream
The ever-silent spaces of the East,
Far-folded mists, and gleaming halls of morn.   [10]

    Alas! for this gray shadow, once a man—
So glorious in his beauty and thy choice,
Who madest him thy chosen, that he seem'd
To his great heart none other than a God!
I ask'd thee, 'Give me immortality.'
Then didst thou grant mine asking with a smile,
Like wealthy men who care not how they give.
But thy strong Hours indignant work'd their wills,
And beat me down and marr'd and wasted me,
And tho' they could not end me, left me maim'd   [20]
To dwell in presence of immortal youth,
Immortal age beside immortal youth,
And all I was, in ashes. Can thy love,
Thy beauty, make amends, tho' even now,
Close over us, the silver star, thy guide,
Shines in those tremulous eyes that fill with tears
To hear me? Let me go: take back thy gift:
Why should a man desire in any way
To vary from the kindly race of men,
Or pass beyond the goal of ordinance°   [30]
Where all should pause, as is most meet for all?

    A soft air fans the cloud apart; there comes
A glimpse of that dark world where I was born.

Once more the old mysterious glimmer steals
From thy pure brows, and from thy shoulders pure,
And bosom beating with a heart renew'd.
Thy cheek begins to redden thro' the gloom,
Thy sweet eyes brighten slowly close to mine,
Ere yet they blind the stars, and the wild team
Which love thee, yearning for thy yoke, arise,   [40]
And shake the darkness from their loosen'd manes,
And beat the twilight into flakes of fire.

    Lo! ever thus thou growest beautiful
In silence, then before thine answer given
Departest, and thy tears are on my cheek.

    Why wilt thou ever scare me with thy tears,
And make me tremble lest a saying learnt,
In days far-off, on that dark earth, be true?
'The Gods themselves cannot recall their gifts.'

    Aye me! ay me! with what another heart   [50]
In days far-off, and with what other eyes
I used to watch—if I be he that watch'd—
The lucid outline forming round thee; saw
The dim curls kindle into sunny rings;
Changed with thy mystic change, and felt my blood
Glow with the glow that slowly crimson'd all
Thy presence and thy portals, while I lay,
Mouth, forehead, eyelids, growing dewy-warm
With kisses balmier than half-opening buds
Of April, and could hear the lips that kiss'd   [60]
Whispering I knew not what of wild and sweet,
Like that strange song I heard Apollo sing,
While Ilion like a mist rose into towers.°

    Yet hold me not for ever in thine East:
How can my nature longer mix with thine?
Coldly thy rosy shadows bathe me, cold
Are all thy lights, and cold my wrinkled feet
Upon thy glimmering thresholds, when the steam
Floats up from those dim fields about the homes
Of happy men that have the power to die,   [70]
And grassy barrows of the happier dead.

Release me, and restore me to the ground;
Thou seëst all things, thou wilt see my grave:
Thou wilt renew thy beauty morn by morn;
I earth in earth forget these empty courts,
And thee returning on thy silver wheels.

ENOCH ARDEN (1864)

Long lines of cliff breaking have left a chasm;
And in the chasm are foam and yellow sands;
Beyond, red roofs about a narrow wharf
In cluster; then a moulder'd church; and higher
A long street climbs to one tall-tower'd mill;
And high in heaven behind it a gray down
With Danish barrows; and a hazelwood,°
By autumn nutters haunted, flourishes
Green in a cuplike hollow of the down.

    Here on this beach a hundred years ago,   [10]
Three children of three houses, Annie Lee,
The prettiest little damsel in the port,
And Philip Ray the miller's only son,
And Enoch Arden, a rough sailor's lad
Made orphan by a winter shipwreck, play'd
Among the waste and lumber of the shore,
Hard coils of cordage, swarthy fishing-nets,
Anchors of rusty fluke, and boats updrawn;
And built their castles of dissolving sand
To watch them overflow'd, or following up   [20]
And flying the white breaker, daily left
The little footprint daily wash'd away.

    A narrow cave ran in beneath the cliff:
In this the children play'd at keeping house.
Enoch was host one day, Philip the next,
While Annie still was mistress; but at times
Enoch would hold possession for a week:
'This is my house and this my little wife.'
'Mine too' said Philip 'turn and turn about:'
When, if they quarrell'd, Enoch stronger-made   [30]
Was master: then would Philip, his blue eyes
All flooded with the helpless wrath of tears,
Shriek out 'I hate you, Enoch,' and at this

The little wife would weep for company,
And pray them not to quarrel for her sake,
And say she would be little wife to both.

But when the dawn of rosy childhood past,
And the new warmth of life's ascending sun
Was felt by either, either fixt his heart
On that one girl; and Enoch spoke his love,   [40]
But Philip loved in silence; and the girl
Seem'd kinder unto Philip than to him;
But she loved Enoch; tho' she knew it not,
And would if ask'd deny it. Enoch set
A purpose evermore before his eyes,
To hoard all savings to the uttermost,
To purchase his own boat, and make a home
For Annie: and so prosper'd that at last
A luckier or a bolder fisherman,
A carefuller in peril, did not breathe   [50]
For leagues along that breaker-beaten coast
Than Enoch. Likewise had he served a year
On board a merchantman, and made himself
Full sailor; and he thrice had pluck'd a life
From the dread sweep of the down-streaming seas:
And all men look'd upon him favourably:
And ere he touch'd his one-and-twentieth May
He purchased his own boat, and made a home
For Annie, neat and nestlike, halfway up
The narrow street that clamber'd toward the mill.   [60]

Then, on a golden autumn eventide,
The younger people making holiday,
With bag and sack and basket, great and small,
Went nutting to the hazels. Philip stay'd
(His father lying sick and needing him)
An hour behind; but as he climb'd the hill,
Just where the prone edge of the wood began
To feather toward the hollow, saw the pair,
Enoch and Annie, sitting hand-in-hand,
His large gray eyes and weather-beaten face   [70]
All-kindled by a still and sacred fire,
That burn'd as on an altar. Philip look'd,
And in their eyes and faces read his doom;

Then, as their faces drew together, groan'd,
And slipt aside, and like a wounded life
Crept down into the hollows of the wood;
There, while the rest were loud in merrymaking,
Had his dark hour unseen, and rose and past
Bearing a lifelong hunger in his heart.

So these were wed, and merrily rang the bells,   [80]
And merrily ran the years, seven happy years,
Seven happy years of health and competence,
And mutual love and honourable toil;
With children; first a daughter. In him woke,
With his first babe's first cry, the noble wish
To save all earnings to the uttermost,
And give his child a better bringing-up
Than his had been, or hers; a wish renew'd,
When two years after came a boy to be
The rosy idol of her solitudes,   [90]
While Enoch was abroad on wrathful seas,
Or often journeying landward; for in truth
Enoch's white horse, and Enoch's ocean-spoil
In ocean-smelling osier, and his face,
Rough-redden'd with a thousand winter gales,
Not only to the market-cross were known,
But in the leafy lanes behind the down,
Far as the portal-warding lion-whelp,
And peacock-yewtree of the lonely Hall,
Whose Friday fare was Enoch's ministering.°   [100]

Then came a change, as all things human change.
Ten miles to northward of the narrow port
Open'd a larger haven: thither used
Enoch at times to go by land or sea;
And once when there, and clambering on a mast
In harbour, by mischance he slipt and fell:
A limb was broken when they lifted him;
And while he lay recovering there, his wife
Bore him another son, a sickly one:
Another hand crept too across his trade   [110]
Taking her bread and theirs: and on him fell,
Altho' a grave and staid God-fearing man,
Yet lying thus inactive, doubt and gloom.

He seem'd, as in a nightmare of the night,
To see his children leading evermore
Low miserable lives of hand-to-mouth,
And her, he loved, a beggar: then he pray'd
'Save them from this, whatever comes to me.'
And while he pray'd, the master of that ship
Enoch had served in, hearing his mischance,   [120]
Came, for he knew the man and valued him,
Reporting of his vessel China-bound,
And wanting yet a boatswain. Would he go?
There yet were many weeks before she sail'd,
Sail'd from this port. Would Enoch have the place?
And Enoch all at once assented to it,
Rejoicing at that answer to his prayer.

So now that shadow of mischance appear'd
No graver than as when some little cloud
Cuts off the fiery highway of the sun,   [130]
And isles a light in the offing: yet the wife—°
When he was gone—the children—what to do?
Then Enoch lay long-pondering on his plans;
To sell the boat—and yet he loved her well—
How many a rough sea had he weather'd in her!
He knew her, as a horseman knows his horse—
And yet to sell her—then with what she brought
Buy goods and stores—set Annie forth in trade
With all that seamen needed or their wives—
So might she keep the house while he was gone.   [140]
Should he not trade himself out yonder? go
This voyage more than once? yea twice or thrice—
As oft as needed—last, returning rich,
Become the master of a larger craft,
With fuller profits lead an easier life,
Have all his pretty young ones educated,
And pass his days in peace among his own.

Thus Enoch in his heart determined all:
Then moving homeward came on Annie pale,
Nursing the sickly babe, her latest-born.   [150]
Forward she started with a happy cry,
And laid the feeble infant in his arms;
Whom Enoch took, and handled all his limbs,

Appraised his weight and fondled fatherlike,
But had no heart to break his purposes
To Annie, till the morrow, when he spoke.

Then first since Enoch's golden ring had girt
Her finger, Annie fought against his will:
Yet not with brawling opposition she,
But manifold entreaties, many a tear,   [160]
Many a sad kiss by day by night renew'd
(Sure that all evil would come out of it)
Besought him, supplicating, if he cared
For her or his dear children, not to go.
He not for his own self caring but her,
Her and her children, let her plead in vain;
So grieving held his will, and bore it thro'.

For Enoch parted with his old sea-friend,
Bought Annie goods and stores, and set his hand
To fit their little streetward sitting-room   [170]
With shelf and corner for the goods and stores.
So all day long till Enoch's last at home,
Shaking their pretty cabin, hammer and axe,
Auger and saw, while Annie seem'd to hear
Her own death-scaffold raising, shrill'd and rang,
Till this was ended, and his careful hand,—
The space was narrow,—having order'd all
Almost as neat and close as Nature packs
Her blossom or her seedling, paused; and he,
Who needs would work for Annie to the last,   [180]
Ascending tired, heavily slept till morn.

And Enoch faced this morning of farewell
Brightly and boldly. All his Annie's fears,
Save, as his Annie's, were a laughter to him.
Yet Enoch as a brave God-fearing man
Bow'd himself down, and in that mystery
Where God-in-man is one with man-in-God,
Pray'd for a blessing on his wife and babes
Whatever came to him: and then he said
'Annie, this voyage by the grace of God   [190]
Will bring fair weather yet to all of us.
Keep a clean hearth and a clear fire for me,

For I'll be back, my girl, before you know it.'
Then lightly rocking baby's cradle 'and he,
This pretty, puny, weakly little one,—
Nay—for I love him all the better for it—
God bless him, he shall sit upon my knees
And I will tell him tales of foreign parts,
And make him merry, when I come home again.
Come, Annie, come, cheer up before I go.'   [200]

Him running on thus hopefully she heard,
And almost hoped herself; but when he turn'd
The current of his talk to graver things
In sailor fashion roughly sermonizing
On providence and trust in Heaven, she heard,
Heard and not heard him; as the village girl,
Who sets her pitcher underneath the spring,
Musing on him that used to fill it for her,
Hears and not hears, and lets it overflow.

At length she spoke 'O Enoch, you are wise;   [210]
And yet for all your wisdom well know I
That I shall look upon your face no more.'

'Well then,' said Enoch, 'I shall look on yours.
Annie, the ship I sail in passes here
(He named the day) get you a seaman's glass,
Spy out my face, and laugh at all your fears.'

But when the last of those last moments came,
'Annie, my girl, cheer up, be comforted,
Look to the babes, and till I come again
Keep everything shipshape, for I must go.   [220]
And fear no more for me; or if you fear
Cast all your cares on God; that anchor holds.
Is He not yonder in those uttermost
Parts of the morning? if I flee to these
Can I go from Him? and the sea is His,
The sea is His: He made it.'
                              Enoch rose,
Cast his strong arms about his drooping wife,
And kiss'd his wonder-stricken little ones;
But for the third, the sickly one, who slept
After a night of feverous wakefulness,   [230]

When Annie would have raised him Enoch said
'Wake him not; let him sleep; how should the child
Remember this?' and kiss'd him in his cot.
But Annie from her baby's forehead clipt
A tiny curl, and gave it: this he kept
Thro' all his future; but now hastily caught
His bundle, waved his hand, and went his way.

    She when the day, that Enoch mention'd, came,
Borrow'd a glass, but all in vain: perhaps°
She could not fix the glass to suit her eye;   [240]
Perhaps her eye was dim, hand tremulous;
She saw him not: and while he stood on deck
Waving, the moment and the vessel past.

    Ev'n to the last dip of the vanishing sail
She watch'd it, and departed weeping for him;
Then, tho' she mourn'd his absence as his grave,
Set her sad will no less to chime with his,
But throve not in her trade, not being bred
To barter, nor compensating the want
By shrewdness, neither capable of lies,   [250]
Nor asking overmuch and taking less,
And still foreboding 'what would Enoch say?'
For more than once, in days of difficulty
And pressure, had she sold her wares for less
Than what she gave in buying what she sold:
She fail'd and sadden'd knowing it; and thus,
Expectant of that news which never came,
Gain'd for her own a scanty sustenance,
And lived a life of silent melancholy.

    Now the third child was sickly-born and grew   [260]
Yet sicklier, tho' the mother cared for it
With all a mother's care: nevertheless,
Whether her business often call'd her from it,
Or thro' the want of what it needed most,
Or means to pay the voice who best could tell
What most it needed—howsoe'er it was,
After a lingering,—ere she was aware,—
Like the caged bird escaping suddenly,
The little innocent soul flitted away.

In that same week when Annie buried it,
Philip's true heart, which hunger'd for her peace
(Since Enoch left he had not look'd upon her),
Smote him, as having kept aloof so long.
'Surely,' said Philip, 'I may see her now,
May be some little comfort;' therefore went,
Past thro' the solitary room in front,
Paused for a moment at an inner door,
Then struck it thrice, and, no one opening,
Enter'd; but Annie, seated with her grief,
Fresh from the burial of her little one,   [280]
Cared not to look on any human face,
But turn'd her own toward the wall and wept.
Then Philip standing up said falteringly
'Annie, I came to ask a favour of you.'

He spoke; the passion in her moan'd reply
'Favour from one so sad and so forlorn
As I am!' half abash'd him; yet unask'd,
His bashfulness and tenderness at war,
He set himself beside her, saying to her:

'I came to speak to you of what he wish'd,   [290]
Enoch, your husband: I have ever said
You chose the best among us—a strong man:
For where he fixt his heart he set his hand
To do the thing he will'd, and bore it thro'.
And wherefore did he go this weary way,
And leave you lonely? not to see the world—
For pleasure?—nay, but for the wherewithal
To give his babes a better bringing-up
Than his had been, or yours: that was his wish.
And if he come again, vext will he be   [300]
To find the precious morning hours were lost.
And it would vex him even in his grave,
If he could know his babes were running wild
Like colts about the waste. So, Annie, now—
Have we not known each other all our lives?
I do beseech you by the love you bear
Him and his children not to say me nay—
For, if you will, when Enoch comes again
Why then he shall repay me—if you will,

Annie—for I am rich and well-to-do.   [310]
Now let me put the boy and girl to school:
This is the favour that I came to ask.'

Then Annie with her brows against the wall
Answer'd 'I cannot look you in the face;
I seem so foolish and so broken down.
When you came in my sorrow broke me down;
And now I think your kindness breaks me down;
But Enoch lives; that is borne in on me:
He will repay you: money can be repaid;
Not kindness such as yours.'
                                        And Philip ask'd   [320]
'Then you will let me, Annie?'
                                        There she turn'd,
She rose, and fixt her swimming eyes upon him,
And dwelt a moment on his kindly face,
Then calling down a blessing on his head
Caught at his hand, and wrung it passionately,
And past into the little garth beyond.°
So lifted up in spirit he moved away.

Then Philip put the boy and girl to school,
And bought them needful books, and everyway,
Like one who does his duty by his own,   [330]
Made himself theirs; and tho' for Annie's sake,
Fearing the lazy gossip of the port,
He oft denied his heart his dearest wish,
And seldom crost her threshold, yet he sent
Gifts by the children, garden-herbs and fruit,
The late and early roses from his wall,
Or conies from the down, and now and then,
With some pretext of fineness in the meal
To save the offence of charitable, flour
From his tall mill that whistled on the waste.   [340]

But Philip did not fathom Annie's mind:
Scarce could the woman when he came upon her,
Out of full heart and boundless gratitude
Light on a broken word to thank him with.
But Philip was her children's all-in-all;
From distant corners of the street they ran

To greet his hearty welcome heartily;
Lords of his house and of his mill were they;
Worried his passive ear with petty wrongs
Or pleasures, hung upon him, play'd with him   [350]
And call'd him Father Philip. Philip gain'd
As Enoch lost; for Enoch seem'd to them
Uncertain as a vision or a dream,
Faint as a figure seen in early dawn
Down at the far end of an avenue,
Going we know not where: and so ten years,
Since Enoch left his hearth and native land,
Fled forward, and no news of Enoch came.

    It chanced one evening Annie's children long'd
To go with others, nutting to the wood,   [360]
And Annie would go with them; then they begg'd
For Father Philip (as they call'd him) too:
Him, like the working bee in blossom-dust,
Blanch'd with his mill, they found; and saying to him
'Come with us Father Philip' he denied;
But when the children pluck'd at him to go,
He laugh'd, and yielded readily to their wish,
For was not Annie with them? and they went.

    But after scaling half the weary down,
Just where the prone edge of the wood began   [370]
To feather toward the hollow, all her force
Fail'd her; and sighing, 'Let me rest' she said:
So Philip rested with her well-content;
While all the younger ones with jubilant cries
Broke from their elders, and tumultuously
Down thro' the whitening hazels made a plunge
To the bottom, and dispersed, and bent or broke
The lithe reluctant boughs to tear away
Their tawny clusters, crying to each other
And calling, here and there, about the wood.   [380]

    But Philip sitting at her side forgot
Her presence, and remember'd one dark hour
Here in this wood, when like a wounded life
He crept into the shadow: at last he said,
Lifting his honest forehead, 'Listen, Annie,

How merry they are down yonder in the wood.
Tired, Annie?' for she did not speak a word.
'Tired?' but her face had fall'n upon her hands;
At which, as with a kind of anger in him,
'The ship was lost,' he said, 'the ship was lost!   [390]
No more of that! why should you kill yourself
And make them orphans quite?' And Annie said
'I thought not of it: but—I know not why—
Their voices make me feel so solitary.'

   Then Philip coming somewhat closer spoke.
'Annie, there is a thing upon my mind,
And it has been upon my mind so long,
That tho' I know not when it first came there,
I know that it will out at last. O Annie,
It is beyond all hope, against all chance,   [400]
That he who left you ten long years ago
Should still be living; well then—let me speak:
I grieve to see you poor and wanting help:
I cannot help you as I wish to do
Unless—they say that women are so quick—
Perhaps you know what I would have you know—
I wish you for my wife. I fain would prove
A father to your children: I do think
They love me as a father: I am sure
That I love them as if they were mine own;   [410]
And I believe, if you were fast my wife,
That after all these sad uncertain years,
We might be still as happy as God grants
To any of his creatures. Think upon it:
For I am well-to-do—no kin, no care,
No burthen, save my care for you and yours:
And we have known each other all our lives,
And I have loved you longer than you know.'

   Then answer'd Annie; tenderly she spoke:
'You have been as God's good angel in our house.   [420]
God bless you for it, God reward you for it,
Philip, with something happier than myself.
Can one love twice? can you be ever loved
As Enoch was? what is it that you ask?'
'I am content' he answer'd 'to be loved

A little after Enoch.' 'O' she cried,
Scared as it were, 'dear Philip, wait a while:
If Enoch comes—but Enoch will not come—
Yet wait a year, a year is not so long:
Surely I shall be wiser in a year: [430]
O wait a little!' Philip sadly said
'Annie, as I have waited all my life
I well may wait a little.' 'Nay' she cried
'I am bound: you have my promise—in a year:
Will you not bide your year as I bide mine?'
And Philip answer'd 'I will bide my year.'

     Here both were mute, till Philip glancing up
Beheld the dead flame of the fallen day
Pass from the Danish barrow overhead;
Then fearing night and chill for Annie, rose   [440]
And sent his voice beneath him thro' the wood.
Up came the children laden with their spoil;
Then all descended to the port, and there
At Annie's door he paused and gave his hand,
Saying gently 'Annie, when I spoke to you,
That was your hour of weakness. I was wrong,
I am always bound to you, but you are free.'
Then Annie weeping answer'd 'I am bound.'

     She spoke; and in one moment as it were,
While yet she went about her household ways,   [450]
Ev'n as she dwelt upon his latest words,
That he had loved her longer than she knew,
That autumn into autumn flash'd again,
And there he stood once more before her face,
Claiming her promise. 'Is it a year?' she ask'd.
'Yes, if the nuts' he said 'be ripe again:
Come out and see.' But she—she put him off—
So much to look to—such a change—a month—
Give her a month—she knew that she was bound—
A month—no more. Then Philip with his eyes   [460]
Full of that lifelong hunger, and his voice
Shaking a little like a drunkard's hand,
'Take your own time, Annie, take your own time.'
And Annie could have wept for pity of him;

And yet she held him on delayingly
With many a scarce-believable excuse,
Trying his truth and his long-sufferance,
Till half-another year had slipt away.

By this the lazy gossips of the port,
Abhorrent of a calculation crost,   [470]
Began to chafe as at a personal wrong.
Some thought that Philip did but trifle with her;
Some that she but held off to draw him on;
And others laugh'd at her and Philip too,
As simple folk that knew not their own minds,
And one, in whom all evil fancies clung
Like serpent eggs together, laughingly
Would hint at worse in either. Her own son
Was silent, tho' he often look'd his wish;
But evermore the daughter prest upon her   [480]
To wed the man so dear to all of them
And lift the household out of poverty;
And Philip's rosy face contracting grew
Careworn and wan; and all these things fell on her
Sharp as reproach.
                          At last one night it chanced
That Annie could not sleep, but earnestly
Pray'd for a sign 'my Enoch is he gone?'
Then compass'd round by the blind wall of night
Brook'd not the expectant terror of her heart,
Started from bed, and struck herself a light,   [490]
Then desperately seized the holy Book,
Suddenly set it wide to find a sign,
Suddenly put her finger on the text,
'Under the palm-tree.' That was nothing to her:°
No meaning there: she closed the Book and slept:
When lo! her Enoch sitting on a height,
Under a palm-tree, over him the Sun:
'He is gone,' she thought, 'he is happy, he is singing
Hosanna in the highest: yonder shines
The Sun of Righteousness, and these be palms   [500]
Whereof the happy people strowing cried
"Hosanna in the highest!" ' Here she woke,
Resolved, sent for him and said wildly to him

'There is no reason why we should not wed.'
'Then for God's sake,' he answer'd, 'both our sakes,
So you will wed me, let it be at once.'

So these were wed and merrily rang the bells,
Merrily rang the bells and they were wed.
But never merrily beat Annie's heart.
A footstep seem'd to fall beside her path,   [510]
She knew not whence; a whisper on her ear,
She knew not what; nor loved she to be left
Alone at home, nor ventured out alone.
What ail'd her then, that ere she enter'd, often
Her hand dwelt lingeringly on the latch,
Fearing to enter: Philip thought he knew:
Such doubts and fears were common to her state,
Being with child: but when her child was born,
Then her new child was as herself renew'd,
Then the new mother came about her heart,   [520]
Then her good Philip was her all-in-all,
And that mysterious instinct wholly died.

And where was Enoch? prosperously sail'd
The ship 'Good Fortune,' tho' at setting forth
The Biscay, roughly ridging eastward, shook
And almost overwhelm'd her, yet unvext
She slipt across the summer of the world,°
Then after a long tumble about the Cape
And frequent interchange of foul and fair,
She passing thro' the summer world again,   [530]
The breath of heaven came continually
And sent her sweetly by the golden isles,
Till silent in her oriental haven.

There Enoch traded for himself, and bought
Quaint monsters for the market of those times,
A gilded dragon, also, for the babes.

Less lucky her home-voyage: at first indeed
Thro' many a fair sea-circle, day by day,
Scarce-rocking, her full-busted figure-head
Stared o'er the ripple feathering from her bows: [540]
Then follow'd calms, and then winds variable,

Then baffling, a long course of them; and last
Storm, such as drove her under moonless heavens
Till hard upon the cry of 'breakers' came
The crash of ruin, and the loss of all
But Enoch and two others. Half the night,
Buoy'd upon floating tackle and broken spars,
These drifted, stranding on an isle at morn
Rich, but the loneliest in a lonely sea.

No want was there of human sustenance,   [550]
Soft fruitage, mighty nuts, and nourishing roots;
Nor save for pity was it hard to take
The helpless life so wild that it was tame.
There in a seaward-gazing mountain-gorge
They built, and thatch'd with leaves of palm, a hut,
Half hut, half native cavern. So the three,
Set in this Eden of all plenteousness,
Dwelt with eternal summer, ill-content.

For one, the youngest, hardly more than boy,
Hurt in that night of sudden ruin and wreck,   [560]
Lay lingering out a five-years' death-in-life.
They could not leave him. After he was gone,
The two remaining found a fallen stem;
And Enoch's comrade, careless of himself,
Fire-hollowing this in Indian fashion, fell
Sun-stricken, and that other lived alone.
In those two deaths he read God's warning 'wait.'

The mountain wooded to the peak, the lawns
And winding glades high up like ways to Heaven,
The slender coco's drooping crown of plumes,   [570]
The lightning flash of insect and of bird,
The lustre of the long convolvuluses
That coil'd around the stately stems, and ran
Ev'n to the limit of the land, the glows
And glories of the broad belt of the world,
All these he saw; but what he fain had seen
He could not see, the kindly human face,
Nor ever hear a kindly voice, but heard
The myriad shriek of wheeling ocean-fowl,
The league-long roller thundering on the reef,   [580]

The moving whisper of huge trees that branch'd
And blossom'd in the zenith, or the sweep
Of some precipitous rivulet to the wave,
As down the shore he ranged, or all day long
Sat often in the seaward-gazing gorge,
A shipwreck'd sailor, waiting for a sail:
No sail from day to day, but every day
The sunrise broken into scarlet shafts
Among the palms and ferns and precipices;
The blaze upon the waters to the east;   [590]
The blaze upon his island overhead;
The blaze upon the waters to the west;
Then the great stars that globed themselves in Heaven,
The hollower-bellowing ocean, and again
The scarlet shafts of sunrise—but no sail.

    There often as he watch'd or seem'd to watch,
So still, the golden lizard on him paused,
A phantom made of many phantoms moved
Before him haunting him, or he himself
Moved haunting people, things and places, known   [600]
Far in a darker isle beyond the line;
The babes, their babble, Annie, the small house,
The climbing street, the mill, the leafy lanes,
The peacock-yewtree and the lonely Hall,
The horse he drove, the boat he sold, the chill
November dawns and dewy-glooming downs,
The gentle shower, the smell of dying leaves,
And the low moan of leaden-colour'd seas.

    Once likewise, in the ringing of his ears,
Tho' faintly, merrily—far and far away—   [610]
He heard the pealing of his parish bells;
Then, tho' he knew not wherefore, started up
Shuddering, and when the beauteous hateful isle
Return'd upon him, had not his poor heart
Spoken with That, which being everywhere
Lets none, who speaks with Him, seem all alone,
Surely the man had died of solitude.

    Thus over Enoch's early-silvering head
The sunny and rainy seasons came and went

Year after year. His hopes to see his own,   [620]
And pace the sacred old familiar fields,
Not yet had perish'd, when his lonely doom
Came suddenly to an end. Another ship
(She wanted water) blown by baffling winds,
Like the Good Fortune, from her destined course,
Stay'd by this isle, not knowing where she lay:
For since the mate had seen at early dawn
Across a break on the mist-wreathen isle
The silent water slipping from the hills,
They sent a crew that landing burst away   [630]
In search of stream or fount, and fill'd the shores
With clamour. Downward from his mountain gorge
Stept the long-hair'd long-bearded solitary,
Brown, looking hardly human, strangely clad,
Muttering and mumbling, idiotlike it seem'd,
With inarticulate rage, and making signs
They knew not what: and yet he led the way
To where the rivulets of sweet water ran;
And ever as he mingled with the crew,
And heard them talking, his long-bounden tongue   [640]
Was loosen'd, till he made them understand;
Whom, when their casks were fill'd they took aboard:
And there the tale he utter'd brokenly,
Scarce-credited at first but more and more,
Amazed and melted all who listen'd to it:
And clothes they gave him and free passage home;
But oft he work'd among the rest and shook
His isolation from him. None of these
Came from his country, or could answer him,
If question'd, aught of what he cared to know.   [650]
And dull the voyage was with long delays,
The vessel scarce sea-worthy; but evermore
His fancy fled before the lazy wind
Returning, till beneath a clouded moon
He like a lover down thro' all his blood
Drew in the dewy meadowy morning-breath
Of England, blown across her ghostly wall:°
And that same morning officers and men
Levied a kindly tax upon themselves,
Pitying the lonely man, and gave him it: [660]

Then moving up the coast they landed him,
Ev'n in that harbour whence he sail'd before.

There Enoch spoke no word to any one,
But homeward—home—what home? had he a home?
His home, he walk'd. Bright was that afternoon,
Sunny but chill; till drawn thro' either chasm,
Where either haven open'd on the deeps,
Roll'd a sea-haze and whelm'd the world in gray;
Cut off the length of highway on before,
And left but narrow breadth to left and right   [670]
Of wither'd holt or tilth or pasturage.
On the nigh-naked tree the robin piped
Disconsolate, and thro' the dripping haze
The dead weight of the dead leaf bore it down:
Thicker the drizzle grew, deeper the gloom;
Last, as it seem'd, a great mist-blotted light
Flared on him, and he came upon the place.

Then down the long street having slowly stolen,
His heart foreshadowing all calamity,
His eyes upon the stones, he reach'd the home   [680]
Where Annie lived and loved him, and his babes
In those far-off seven happy years were born;
But finding neither light nor murmur there
(A bill of sale gleam'd thro' the drizzle) crept
Still downward thinking 'dead or dead to me!'

Down to the pool and narrow wharf he went,
Seeking a tavern which of old he knew,
A front of timber-crost antiquity,
So propt, worm-eaten, ruinously old,
He thought it must have gone; but he was gone   [690]
Who kept it; and his widow Miriam Lane,
With daily-dwindling profits held the house;
A haunt of brawling seamen once, but now
Stiller, with yet a bed for wandering men.
There Enoch rested silent many days.

But Miriam Lane was good and garrulous,
Nor let him be, but often breaking in,
Told him, with other annals of the port,

Not knowing—Enoch was so brown, so bow'd,
So broken—all the story of his house. [700]
His baby's death, her growing poverty,
How Philip put her little ones to school,
And kept them in it, his long wooing her,
Her slow consent, and marriage, and the birth
Of Philip's child: and o'er his countenance
No shadow past, nor motion: any one,
Regarding, well had deem'd he felt the tale
Less than the teller: only when she closed
'Enoch, poor man, was cast away and lost'
He, shaking his gray head pathetically, [710]
Repeated muttering 'cast away and lost;'
Again in deeper inward whispers 'lost!'

But Enoch yearn'd to see her face again;
'If I might look on her sweet face again
And know that she is happy.' So the thought
Haunted and harass'd him, and drove him forth,
At evening when the dull November day
Was growing duller twilight, to the hill.
There he sat down gazing on all below;
There did a thousand memories roll upon him, [720]
Unspeakable for sadness. By and by
The ruddy square of comfortable light,
Far-blazing from the rear of Philip's house,
Allured him, as the beacon-blaze allures
The bird of passage, till he madly strikes
Against it, and beats out his weary life.

For Philip's dwelling fronted on the street,
The latest house to landward; but behind,
With one small gate that open'd on the waste,
Flourish'd a little garden square and wall'd: [730]
And in it throve an ancient evergreen,
A yewtree, and all round it ran a walk
Of shingle, and a walk divided it:
But Enoch shunn'd the middle walk and stole
Up by the wall, behind the yew; and thence
That which he better might have shunn'd, if griefs
Like his have worse or better, Enoch saw.

For cups and silver on the burnish'd board
Sparkled and shone; so genial was the hearth:
And on the right hand of the hearth he saw　　　　　　　[740]
Philip, the slighted suitor of old times,
Stout, rosy, with his babe across his knees;
And o'er her second father stoopt a girl,
A later but a loftier Annie Lee,
Fair-hair'd and tall, and from her lifted hand
Dangled a length of ribbon and a ring
To tempt the babe, who rear'd his creasy arms,
Caught at and ever miss'd it, and they laugh'd;
And on the left hand of the hearth he saw
The mother glancing often toward her babe,　　　　　　　[750]
But turning now and then to speak with him,
Her son, who stood beside her tall and strong,
And saying that which pleased him, for he smiled.

Now when the dead man come to life beheld
His wife his wife no more, and saw the babe
Hers, yet not his, upon the father's knee,
And all the warmth, the peace, the happiness,
And his own children tall and beautiful,
And him, that other, reigning in his place,
Lord of his rights and of his children's love,—　　　　　　[760]
Then he, tho' Miriam Lane had told him all,
Because things seen are mightier than things heard,
Stagger'd and shook, holding the branch, and fear'd
To send abroad a shrill and terrible cry,
Which in one moment, like the blast of doom,
Would shatter all the happiness of the hearth.

He therefore turning softly like a thief,
Lest the harsh shingle should grate underfoot,
And feeling all along the garden-wall,
Lest he should swoon and tumble and be found,　　　　　　[770]
Crept to the gate, and open'd it, and closed,
As lightly as a sick man's chamber-door,
Behind him, and came out upon the waste.

And there he would have knelt, but that his knees
Were feeble, so that falling prone he dug
His fingers into the wet earth, and pray'd.

'Too hard to bear! why did they take me thence?
O God Almighty, blessed Saviour, Thou
That didst uphold me on my lonely isle,
Uphold me, Father, in my loneliness   [780]
A little longer! aid me, give me strength
Not to tell her, never to let her know.
Help me not to break in upon her peace.
My children too! must I not speak to these?
They know me not. I should betray myself.
Never: No father's kiss for me—the girl
So like her mother, and the boy, my son.'

There speech and thought and nature fail'd a little,
And he lay tranced; but when he rose and paced
Back toward his solitary home again,   [790]
All down the long and narrow street he went
Beating it in upon his weary brain,
As tho' it were the burthen of a song,
'Not to tell her, never to let her know.'

He was not all unhappy. His resolve
Upbore him, and firm faith, and evermore
Prayer from a living source within the will,
And beating up thro' all the bitter world,
Like fountains of sweet water in the sea,
Kept him a living soul. 'This miller's wife'   [800]
He said to Miriam 'that you spoke about,
Has she no fear that her first husband lives?'
'Ay, ay, poor soul' said Miriam, 'fear enow!
If you could tell her you had seen him dead,
Why, that would be her comfort;' and he thought
'After the Lord has call'd me she shall know,
I wait His time,' and Enoch set himself,
Scorning an alms, to work whereby to live.
Almost to all things could he turn his hand.
Cooper he was and carpenter, and wrought   [810]
To make the boatmen fishing-nets, or help'd
At lading and unlading the tall barks,
That brought the stinted commerce of those days;
Thus earn'd a scanty living for himself:
Yet since he did but labour for himself,
Work without hope, there was not life in it

Whereby the man could live; and as the year
Roll'd itself round again to meet the day
When Enoch had return'd, a langour came
Upon him, gentle sickness, gradually   [820]
Weakening the man, till he could do no more,
But kept the house, his chair, and last his bed.
And Enoch bore his weakness cheerfully.
For sure no gladlier does the stranded wreck
See thro' the gray skirts of a lifting squall
The boat that bears the hope of life approach
To save the life despair'd of, than he saw
Death dawning on him, and the close of all.

    For thro' that dawning gleam'd a kindlier hope
On Enoch thinking 'after I am gone,   [830]
Then may she learn I lov'd her to the last.'
He call'd aloud for Miriam Lane and said
'Woman, I have a secret—only swear,
Before I tell you—swear upon the book
Not to reveal it, till you see me dead.'
'Dead,' clamour'd the good woman, 'hear him talk!
I warrant, man, that we shall bring you round.'
'Swear,' added Enoch sternly 'on the book.'
And on the book, half-frighted, Miriam swore.
Then Enoch rolling his gray eyes upon her,   [840]
'Did you know Enoch Arden of this town?'
'Know him?' she said 'I knew him far away.
Ay, ay, I mind him coming down the street;
Held his head high, and cared for no man, he.'
Slowly and sadly Enoch answer'd her;
'His head is low, and no man cares for him.
I think I have not three days more to live;
I am the man.' At which the woman gave
A half-incredulous, half-hysterical cry.
'You Arden, you! nay,—sure he was a foot   [850]
Higher than you be.' Enoch said again
'My God has bow'd me down to what I am;
My grief and solitude have broken me;
Nevertheless, know you that I am he
Who married—but that name has twice been changed—
I married her who married Philip Ray.

Sit, listen.' Then he told her of his voyage,
His wreck, his lonely life, his coming back,
His gazing in on Annie, his resolve,
And how he kept it. As the woman heard, [860]
Fast flow'd the current of her easy tears,
While in her heart she yearn'd incessantly
To rush abroad all round the little haven,
Proclaiming Enoch Arden and his woes;
But awed and promise-bounden she forbore,
Saying only 'See your bairns before you go!°
Eh, let me fetch 'em, Arden,' and arose
Eager to bring them down, for Enoch hung
A moment on her words, but then replied:

'Woman, disturb me not now at the last, [870]
But let me hold my purpose till I die.
Sit down again; mark me and understand,
While I have power to speak. I charge you now,
When you shall see her, tell her that I died
Blessing her, praying for her, loving her;
Save for the bar between us, loving her
As when she laid her head beside my own.
And tell my daughter Annie, whom I saw
So like her mother, that my latest breath
Was spent in blessing her and praying for her. [880]
And tell my son that I died blessing him.
And say to Philip that I blest him too;
He never meant us any thing but good.
But if my children care to see me dead,
Who hardly knew me living, let them come,
I am their father; but she must not come,
For my dead face would vex her after-life.
And now there is but one of all my blood
Who will embrace me in the world-to-be:
This hair is his: she cut it off and gave it, [890]
And I have borne it with me all these years,
And thought to bear it with me to my grave;
But now my mind is changed, for I shall see him,
My babe in bliss: wherefore when I am gone,
Take, give her this, for it may comfort her:
It will moreover be a token to her,

That I am he.'
           He ceased; and Miriam Lane
Made such a voluble answer promising all,
That once again he roll'd his eyes upon her
Repeating all he wish'd, and once again   [900]
She promised.
           Then the third night after this,
While Enoch slumber'd motionless and pale,
And Miriam watch'd and dozed at intervals,
There came so loud a calling of the sea,
That all the houses in the haven rang.
He woke, he rose, he spread his arms abroad
Crying with a loud voice 'A sail! a sail!
I am saved;' and so fell back and spoke no more.

So past the strong heroic soul away.
And when they buried him the little port   [910]
Had seldom seen a costlier funeral.

POEMS FROM THE 1860s

Milton

ALCAICS

O mighty-mouth'd inventor of harmonies,
O skill'd to sing of Time or Eternity,
    God-gifted organ-voice of England,
        Milton, a name to resound for ages;
Whose Titan angels, Gabriel, Abdiel,°
Starr'd from Jehovah's gorgeous armouries,
    Tower, as the deep-domed empyrëan
        Rings to the roar of an angel onset—
Me rather all that bowery loneliness,
The brooks of Eden mazily murmuring,   [10]
    And bloom profuse and cedar arches
        Charm, as a wanderer out in ocean,
Where some refulgent sunset of India
Streams o'er a rich ambrosial ocean isle,
    And crimson-hued the stately palm-woods
        Whisper in odorous heights of even.

HENDECASYLLABICS

O you chorus of indolent reviewers,
Irresponsible, indolent reviewers,
Look, I come to the test, a tiny poem
All composed in a metre of Catullus,
All in quantity, careful of my motion,
Like the skater on ice that hardly bears him,
Lest I fall unawares before the people,
Waking laughter in indolent reviewers.
Should I flounder awhile without a tumble

Thro' this metrification of Catullus,   [10]
They should speak to me not without a welcome,
All that chorus of indolent reviewers.
Hard, hard, hard is it, only not to tumble,
So fantastical is the dainty metre.
Wherefore slight me not wholly, nor believe me
Too presumptuous, indolent reviewers.
O blatant Magazines, regard me rather—
Since I blush to belaud myself a moment—
As some rare little rose, a piece of inmost
Horticultural art, or half coquette-like   [20]
Maiden, not to be greeted unbenignly.

Helen's Tower

Helen's Tower, here I stand,
Dominant over sea and land.
Son's love built me, and I hold
Mother's love in letter'd gold.°
Love is in and out of time,
I am mortal stone and lime.
Would my granite girth were strong
As either love, to last as long!
I should wear my crown entire
To and thro' the Doomsday fire,   [10]
And be found of angel eyes
In earth's recurring Paradise.

Northern Farmer

New Style

I

Dosn't thou 'ear my 'erse's legs, as they canters awaäy?
Proputty, proputty, proputty—that's what I 'ears 'em saäy.°
Proputty, proputty, proputty—Sam, thou's an ass for thy paaïns:
Theer's moor sense i' one o' 'is legs nor in all thy braaïns.

II

Woä—theer's a craw to pluck wi' tha, Sam: yon's parson's 'ouse—°
Dosn't thou knaw that a man mun be eäther a man or a mouse?
Time to think on it then; for thou'll be twenty to weeäk.°
Proputty, proputty—woä then woä—let ma 'ear mysén speäk.

III

Me an' thy muther, Sammy, 'as beän a-talkin o' thee;
Thou's beän talkin' to muther, an' she beän a tellin' it me.   [10]
Thou'll not marry for munny—thou's sweet upo' parson's lass—
Noä—thou'll marry for luvv—an' we boäth on us thinks tha an ass.

IV

Seeä'd her todaäy goä by—Saäint's-daäy—they was ringing the bells.
She's a beauty thou thinks—an' soä is scoors o' gells,°
Them as 'as munny an' all—wot's a beauty?—the flower as blaws.
But proputty, proputty sticks, an' proputty, proputty graws.

V

Do'ant be stunt: taäke time: I knaws what maäkes tha sa mad.°
Warn't I craäzed fur the lasses mysén when I wur a lad?
But I knaw'd a Quaäker feller as often 'as towd ma this:
'Doänt thou marry for munny, but goä wheer munny is!'   [20]

VI

An' I went wheer munny war: an' thy muther coom to 'and,
Wi' lots o' munny laaïd by, an' a nicetish bit o' land.
Maäybe she warn't a beauty:—I niver giv it a thowt—
But warn't she as good to cuddle an' kiss as a lass as 'ant nowt?°

VII

Parson's lass 'ant nowt, an' she weänt 'a nowt when 'e's deäd,
Mun be a guvness, lad, or summut, and addle her breäd:°
Why? fur 'e's nobbut a curate, an' weänt niver git hissen clear,°
An' 'e maäde the bed as 'e ligs on afoor 'e coom'd to the shere.°

VIII

An' thin 'e coom'd to the parish wi' lots o' Varsity debt,°
Stook to his taaïl they did, an' 'e 'ant got shut on 'em yet.°   [30]
An' 'e ligs on 'is back i' the grip, wi' noän to lend 'im a shuvv,°
Woorse nor a far-welter'd yowe: fur, Sammy, 'e married fur luvv.°

IX

Luvv? what's luvv? thou can luvv thy lass an' 'er munny too,
Maakin' 'em goä togither as they've good right to do.
Could'n I luvv thy muther by cause o' 'er munny laaïd by?
Naäy—fur I luvv'd 'er a vast sight moor fur it: reäson why.

X

Ay an' thy muther says thou wants to marry the lass,
Cooms of a gentleman burn: an' we boäth on us thinks tha
    an ass.°
Woä then, proputty, wiltha?—an ass as near as mays nowt—°
Woä then, wiltha? dangtha!—the bees is as fell as owt.°   [40]

XI

Breäk me a bit o' the esh for his 'eäd lad, out o' the fence!°
Gentleman burn! what's gentleman burn? is it shillins an' pence?
Proputty, proputty's ivrything 'ere, an', Sammy, I'm blest
If it isn't the saäme oop yonder, fur them as 'as it's the best.

XII

Tis'n them as 'as munny as breäks into 'ouses an' steäls,
Them as 'as coats to their backs an' taäkes their regular meäls.
Noä, but it's them as niver knaws wheer a meäl's to be 'ad.
Taäke my word for it, Sammy, the poor in a loomp is bad.

XIII

Them or thir feythers, tha sees, mun 'a beän a laäzy lot,
Fur work mun 'a gone to the gittin' whiniver munny was got.   [50]
Feyther 'ad ammost nowt; leästways 'is munny was 'id.
But 'e tued an' moil'd 'issén deäd, an' 'e died a good un, 'e did.°

XIV

Loook thou theer wheer Wrigglesby beck cooms out by the 'ill!°
Feyther run oop to the farm, an' I runs oop to the mill;
An' I'll run oop to the brig, an' that thou'll live to see;°
And if thou marries a good un I'll leäve the land to thee.

XV

Thim's my noätions, Sammy, wheerby I means to stick;
But if thou marries a bad un, I'll leäve the land to Dick.—
Coom oop, proputty, proputty—that's what I 'ears 'im saäy—
Proputty, proputty, proputty—canter an' canter awaäy.   [60]

'Flower in the crannied wall'

Flower in the crannied wall,
I pluck you out of the crannies,
I hold you here, root and all, in my hand,
Little flower—but *if* I could understand
What you are, root and all, and all in all,
I should know what God and man is.

The Higher Pantheism

The sun, the moon, the stars, the seas, the hills and the plains—
Are not these, O Soul, the Vision of Him who reigns?

Is not the Vision He? tho' He be not that which He seems?
Dreams are true while they last, and do we not live in dreams?

Earth, these solid stars, this weight of body and limb,
Are they not sign and symbol of thy division from Him?

Dark is the world to thee: thyself art the reason why;
For is He not all but that which has power to feel 'I am I'?

Glory about thee, without thee; and thou fulfillest thy doom
Making Him broken gleams, and a stifled splendour and gloom.   [10]

Speak to Him thou for He hears, and Spirit with Spirit can meet—
Closer is He than breathing, and nearer than hands and feet.

God is law, say the wise; O Soul, and let us rejoice,
For if He thunder by law the thunder is yet His voice.

Law is God, say some: no God at all, says the fool;
For all we have power to see is a straight staff bent in a pool;

And the ear of man cannot hear, and the eye of man cannot see;
But if we could see and hear, this Vision—were it not He?

Lucretius

Lucilia, wedded to Lucretius, found
Her master cold; for when the morning flush
Of passion and the first embrace had died
Between them, tho' he lov'd her none the less,
Yet often when the woman heard his foot
Return from pacings in the field, and ran
To greet him with a kiss, the master took
Small notice, or austerely, for—his mind
Half buried in some weightier argument,
Or fancy-borne perhaps upon the rise   [10]
And long roll of the Hexameter—he past°
To turn and ponder those three hundred scrolls
Left by the Teacher, whom he held divine.°
She brook'd it not; but wrathful, petulant,
Dreaming some rival, sought and found a witch
Who brew'd the philtre which had power, they said,
To lead an errant passion home again.
And this, at times, she mingled with his drink,
And this destroy'd him; for the wicked broth
Confused the chemic labour of the blood.   [20]
And tickling the brute brain within the man's
Made havock among those tender cells, and check'd

His power to shape: he loathed himself; and once
After a tempest woke upon a morn
That mock'd him with returning calm, and cried:

'Storm in the night! for thrice I heard the rain
Rushing; and once the flash of a thunderbolt—
Methought I never saw so fierce a fork—
Struck out the streaming mountain-side, and show'd
A riotous confluence of watercourses   [30]
Blanching and billowing in a hollow of it,
Where all but yester-eve was dusty-dry.

'Storm, and what dreams, ye holy Gods, what dreams!
For thrice I waken'd after dreams. Perchance
We do but recollect the dreams that come
Just ere the waking: terrible! for it seem'd
A void was made in Nature; all her bonds
Crack'd; and I saw the flaring atom-streams°
And torrents of her myriad universe,
Ruining along the illimitable inane,   [40]
Fly on to clash together again, and make
Another and another frame of things
For ever: that was mine, my dream, I knew it—
Of and belonging to me, as the dog
With inward yelp and restless forefoot plies
His function of the woodland: but the next!
I thought that all the blood by Sylla shed°
Came driving rainlike down again on earth,
And where it dash'd the reddening meadow, sprang
No dragon warriors from Cadmean teeth,°   [50]
For these I thought my dream would show to me,
But girls, Hetairai, curious in their art,°
Hired animalisms, vile as those that made
The mulberry-faced Dictator's orgies worse
Than aught they fable of the quiet Gods.
And hands they mixt, and yell'd and round me drove
In narrowing circles till I yell'd again
Half-suffocated, and sprang up, and saw—
Was it the first beam of my latest day?

'Then, then, from utter gloom stood out the breasts,   [60]
The breasts of Helen, and hoveringly a sword°

Now over and now under, now direct,
Pointed itself to pierce, but sank down shamed
At all that beauty; and as I stared, a fire,
The fire that left a roofless Ilion,
Shot out of them, and scorch'd me that I woke.

'Is this thy vengeance, holy Venus, thine,
Because I would not one of thine own doves,
Not ev'n a rose, were offer'd to thee? thine,
Forgetful how my rich procemion makes°   [70]
Thy glory fly along the Italian field,
In lays that will outlast thy Deity?

'Deity? nay, thy worshippers. My tongue
Trips, or I speak profanely. Which of these
Angers thee most, or angers thee at all?
Not if thou be'st of those who, far aloof
From envy, hate and pity, and spite and scorn,
Live the great life which all our greatest fain
Would follow, center'd in eternal calm.

'Nay, if thou canst, O Goddess, like ourselves   [80]
Touch, and be touch'd, then would I cry to thee
To kiss thy Mavors, roll thy tender arms°
Round him, and keep him from the lust of blood
That makes a steaming slaughter-house of Rome.

'Ay, but I meant not thee; I meant not her,
Whom all the pines of Ida shook to see
Slide from that quiet heaven of hers, and tempt
The Trojan, while his neat-herds were abroad;
Nor her that o'er her wounded hunter wept
Her Deity false in human-amorous tears;   [90]
Nor whom her beardless apple-arbiter°
Decided fairest. Rather, O ye Gods,
Poet-like, as the great Sicilian called
Calliope to grace his golden verse°—
Ay, and this Kypris also—did I take°
That popular name of thine to shadow forth
The all-generating powers and genial heat
Of Nature, when she strikes thro' the thick blood
Of cattle, and light is large, and lambs are glad
Nosing the mother's udder, and the bird   [100]

Makes his heart voice amid the blaze of flowers:
Which things appear the work of mighty Gods.

'The Gods! and if I go *my* work is left
Unfinish'd—*if* I go. The Gods, who haunt
The lucid interspace of world and world,
Where never creeps a cloud, or moves a wind,
Nor ever falls the least white star of snow,
Nor ever lowest roll of thunder moans,
Nor sound of human sorrow mounts to mar
Their sacred everlasting calm! and such,   [110]
Not all so fine, nor so divine a calm,
Not such, nor all unlike it, man may gain
Letting his own life go. The Gods, the Gods!
If all be atoms, how then should the Gods
Being atomic not be dissoluble,
Not follow the great law? My master held
That Gods there are, for all men so believe.
I prest my footsteps into his, and meant
Surely to lead my Memmius in a train°
Of flowery clauses onward to the proof   [120]
That Gods there are, and deathless. Meant? I meant?
I have forgotten what I meant: my mind
Stumbles, and all my faculties are lamed.

'Look where another of our Gods, the Sun,
Apollo, Delius, or of older use
All-seeing Hyperion—what you will—
Has mounted yonder; since he never sware,
Except his wrath were wreak'd on wretched man,
That he would only shine among the dead
Hereafter; tales! for never yet on earth   [130]
Could dead flesh creep, or bits of roasting ox
Moan round the spit—nor knows he what he sees;
King of the East altho' he seem, and girt
With song and flame and fragrance, slowly lifts
His golden feet on those empurpled stairs
That climb into the windy halls of heaven:
And here he glances on an eye new-born,
And gets for greeting but a wail of pain;
And here he stays upon a freezing orb
That fain would gaze upon him to the last;   [140]

And here upon a yellow eyelid fall'n
And closed by those who mourn a friend in vain,
Not thankful that his troubles are no more.
And me, altho' his fire is on my face
Blinding, he sees not, nor at all can tell
Whether I mean this day to end myself,
Or lend an ear to Plato where he says,°
That men like soldiers may not quit the post
Allotted by the Gods: but he that holds
The Gods are careless, wherefore need he care   [150]
Greatly for them, nor rather plunge at once,
Being troubled, wholly out of sight, and sink
Past earthquake—ay, and gout and stone, that break
Body toward death, and palsy, death-in-life,
And wretched age—and worst disease of all,
These prodigies of myriad nakednesses,
And twisted shapes of lust, unspeakable,
Abominable, strangers at my hearth
Not welcome, harpies miring every dish,
The phantom husks of something foully done,   [160]
And fleeting thro' the boundless universe,
And blasting the long quiet of my breast
With animal heat and dire insanity?

   'How should the mind, except it loved them, clasp
These idols to herself? or do they fly
Now thinner, and now thicker, like the flakes
In a fall of snow, and so press in, perforce
Of multitude, as crowds that in an hour
Of civic tumult jam the doors, and bear
The keepers down, and throng, their rags and they   [170]
The basest, far into that council-hall
Where sit the best and stateliest of the land?

   'Can I not fling this horror off me again,
Seeing with how great ease Nature can smile,
Balmier and nobler from her bath of storm,
At random ravage? and how easily
The mountain there has cast his cloudy slough,
Now towering o'er him in serenest air,
A mountain o'er a mountain,—ay, and within
All hollow as the hopes and fears of men?   [180]

'But who was he, that in the garden snared°
Picus and Faunus, rustic Gods? a tale
To laugh at—more to laugh at in myself—
For look! what is it? there? yon arbutus
Totters; a noiseless riot underneath
Strikes through the wood, sets all the tops quivering—
The mountain quickens into Nymph and Faun;
And here an Oread—how the sun delights°
To glance and shift about her slippery sides,
And rosy knees and supple roundedness,   [190]
And budded bosom-peaks—who this way runs
Before the rest—A satyr, a satyr, see,
Follows; but him I proved impossible;°
Twy-natured is no nature: yet he draws
Nearer and nearer, and I scan him now
Beastlier than any phantom of his kind
That ever butted his rough brother-brute
For lust or lusty blood or provender:
I hate, abhor, spit, sicken at him; and she
Loathes him as well; such a precipitate heel,   [200]
Fledged as it were with Mercury's ankle-wing,
Whirls her to me: but will she fling herself,
Shameless upon me? Catch her, goat-foot: nay,
Hide, hide them, million-myrtled wilderness,
And cavern-shadowing laurels, hide! do I wish—
What?—that the bush were leafless? or to whelm
All of them in one massacre? O ye Gods,
I know you careless, yet, behold, to you
From childly wont and ancient use I call—
I thought I lived securely as yourselves—   [210]
No lewdness, narrowing envy, monkey-spite,
No madness of ambition, avarice, none:
No larger feast than under plane or pine
With neighbours laid along the grass, to take
Only such cups as left us friendly-warm,
Affirming each his own philosophy—
Nothing to mar the sober majesties
Of settled, sweet, Epicurean life.
But now it seems some unseen monster lays
His vast and filthy hands upon my will,   [220]
Wrenching it backward into his; and spoils

My bliss in being; and it was not great;
For save when shutting reasons up in rhythm,
Or Heliconian honey in living words,°
To make a truth less harsh, I often grew
Tired of so much within our little life,
Or of so little in our little life—
Poor little life that toddles half an hour
Crown'd with a flower or two, and there an end—
And since the nobler pleasure seems to fade,　　　　[230]
Why should I, beastlike as I find myself,
Not manlike end myself?—our privilege—
What beast has heart to do it? And what man,
What Roman would be dragg'd in triumph thus?
Not I; not he, who bears one name with her°
Whose death-blow struck the dateless doom of kings,
When, brooking not the Tarquin in her veins,
She made her blood in sight of Collatine°
And all his peers, flushing the guiltless air,
Spout from the maiden fountain in her heart.　　　　[240]
And from it sprang the Commonwealth, which breaks
As I am breaking now!
　　　　　　　　　　'And therefore now
Let her, that is the womb and tomb of all,
Great Nature, take, and forcing far apart
Those blind beginnings that have made me man,
Dash them anew together at her will
Thro' all her cycles—into man once more,
Or beast or bird or fish, or opulent flower:
But till this cosmic order everywhere
Shatter'd into one earthquake in one day　　　　[250]
Cracks all to pieces,—and that hour perhaps
Is not so far when momentary man
Shall seem no more a something to himself,
But he, his hopes and hates, his homes and fanes,°
And even his bones long laid within the grave,
The very sides of the grave itself shall pass,
Vanishing, atom and void, atom and void,
Into the unseen for ever,—till that hour,
My golden work in which I told a truth
That stays the rolling Ixionian wheel,°　　　　[260]
That numbs the Fury's ringlet-snake, and plucks°

The mortal soul from out immortal hell,
Shall stand: ay, surely: then it fails at last
And perishes as I must; for O Thou,
Passionless bride, divine Tranquillity,
Yearn'd after by the wisest of the wise,
Who fail to find thee, being as thou art
Without one pleasure and without one pain,
Howbeit I know thou surely must be mine
Or soon or late, yet out of season, thus   [270]
I woo thee roughly, for thou carest not
How roughly men may woo thee so they win—
Thus—thus: the soul flies out and dies in the air.'

    With that he drove the knife into his side:
She heard him raging, heard him fall; ran in,°
Beat breast, tore hair, cried out upon herself
As having fail'd in duty to him, shriek'd
That she but meant to win him back, fell on him,
Clasp'd, kiss'd him, wail'd: he answer'd, 'Care not thou!
Thy duty? What is duty? Fare thee well!'   [280]

from THE IDYLLS OF THE KING
(1869)

Merlin and Vivien

A storm was coming, but the winds were still,
And in the wild woods of Broceliande,°
Before an oak, so hollow, huge and old
It look'd a tower of ivied masonwork,
At Merlin's feet the wily Vivien lay.

    For he that always bare in bitter grudge
The slights of Arthur and his Table, Mark
The Cornish King, had heard a wandering voice,
A minstrel of Caerleon by strong storm
Blown into shelter at Tintagil, say°   [10]
That out of naked knightlike purity
Sir Lancelot worshipt no unmarried girl°
But the great Queen herself, fought in her name,
Sware by her—vows like theirs, that high in heaven
Love most, but neither marry, nor are given
In marriage, angels of our Lord's report.

    He ceased, and then—for Vivien sweetly said
(She sat beside the banquet nearest Mark),
'And is the fair example follow'd, Sir,
In Arthur's household?'—answer'd innocently: [20]

    'Ay, by some few—ay, truly—youths that hold
It more beseems the perfect virgin knight
To worship woman as true wife beyond
All hopes of gaining, than as maiden girl.
They place their pride in Lancelot and the Queen.
So passionate for an utter purity
Beyond the limit of their bond, are these,
For Arthur bound them not to singleness.
Brave hearts and clean! and yet—God guide them—young.'

Then Mark was half in heart to hurl his cup   [30]
Straight at the speaker, but forbore: he rose
To leave the hall, and, Vivien following him,
Turn'd to her: 'Here are snakes within the grass;
And you methinks, O Vivien, save ye fear
The monkish manhood, and the mask of pure
Worn by this court, can stir them till they sting.'

And Vivien answer'd, smiling scornfully,
'Why fear? because that foster'd at *thy* court
I savour of thy—virtues? fear them? no.
As Love, if Love be perfect, casts out fear,   [40]
So Hate, if Hate be perfect, casts out fear.
My father died in battle against the King,
My mother on his corpse in open field;
She bore me there, for born from death was I
Among the dead and sown upon the wind—
And then on thee! and shown the truth betimes,
That old true filth, and bottom of the well,
Where Truth is hidden. Gracious lessons thine
And maxims of the mud! "This Arthur pure!
Great Nature thro' the flesh herself hath made   [50]
Gives him the lie! There is no being pure,
My cherub; saith not Holy Writ the same?"—°
If I were Arthur, I would have thy blood.
Thy blessing, stainless King! I bring thee back,
When I have ferreted out their burrowings,
The hearts of all this Order in mine hand—
Ay—so that fate and craft and folly close,
Perchance, one curl of Arthur's golden beard.
To me this narrow grizzled fork of thine
Is cleaner-fashion'd—Well, I loved thee first,   [60]
That warps the wit.'
                         Loud laugh'd the graceless Mark
But Vivien, into Camelot stealing, lodged°
Low in the city, and on a festal day
When Guinevere was crossing the great hall
Cast herself down, knelt to the Queen, and wail'd.
'Why kneel ye there? What evil have ye wrought?
Rise!' and the damsel bidden rise arose
And stood with folded hands and downward eyes

Of glancing corner, and all meekly said,
'None wrought, but suffer'd much, an orphan maid!   [70]
My father died in battle for thy King,
My mother on his corpse—in open field,
The sad sea-sounding wastes of Lyonnesse—
Poor wretch—no friend!—and now by Mark the King
For that small charm of feature mine, pursued—
If any such be mine—I fly to thee.
Save, save me thou—Woman of women—thine
The wreath of beauty, thine the crown of power,
Be thine the balm of pity, O Heaven's own white
Earth-angel, stainless bride of stainless King—   [80]
Help, for he follows! take me to thyself!
O yield me shelter for mine innocency
Among thy maidens!'
                    Here her slow sweet eyes
Fear-tremulous, but humbly hopeful, rose
Fixt on her hearer's, while the Queen who stood
All glittering like May sunshine on May leaves
In green and gold, and plumed with green replied,
'Peace, child! of overpraise and overblame
We choose the last. Our noble Arthur, him
Ye scarce can overpraise, will hear and know.   [90]
Nay—we believe all evil of thy Mark—
Well, we shall test thee farther; but this hour
We ride a-hawking with Sir Lancelot.
He hath given us a fair falcon which he train'd;
We go to prove it. Bide ye here the while.'

    She past; and Vivien murmur'd after 'Go!
I bide the while.' Then thro' the portal-arch
Peering askance, and muttering broken-wise,
As one that labours with an evil dream,
Beheld the Queen and Lancelot get to horse.

    'Is that the Lancelot! goodly—ay, but gaunt: [100]
Courteous—amends for gauntness—takes her hand—
That glance of theirs, but for the street, had been
A clinging kiss—how hand lingers in hand!
Let go at last!—they ride away—to hawk
For waterfowl. Royaller game is mine.
For such a supersensual sensual bond

As that gray cricket chirpt of at our hearth—°
Touch flax with flame—a glance will serve—the liars!
Ah little rat that borest in the dyke
Thy hole by night to let the boundless deep   [110]
Down upon far-off cities while they dance—
Or dream—of thee they dream'd not—nor of me
These—ay, but each of either: ride, and dream
The mortal dream that never yet was mine—
Ride, ride and dream until ye wake—to me!
Then, narrow court and lubber King, farewell!
For Lancelot will be gracious to the rat,
And our wise Queen, if knowing that I know,
Will hate, loathe, fear—but honour me the more.'

    Yet while they rode together down the plain,   [120]
Their talk was all of training, terms of art,
Diet and seeling, jesses, leash and lure.°
'She is too noble' he said 'to check at pies,
Nor will she rake: there is no baseness in her.'°
Here when the Queen demanded as by chance
'Know ye the stranger woman?' 'Let her be,'
Said Lancelot and unhooded casting off
The goodly falcon free; she tower'd; her bells,°
Tone under tone, shrill'd; and they lifted up
Their eager faces, wondering at the strength,   [130]
Boldness and royal knighthood of the bird
Who pounced her quarry and slew it. Many a time
As once—of old—among the flowers—they rode.

    But Vivien half-forgotten of the Queen
Among her damsels broidering sat, heard, watch'd
And whisper'd: thro' the peaceful court she crept
And whisper'd: then as Arthur in the highest
Leaven'd the world, so Vivien in the lowest,
Arriving at a time of golden rest,
And sowing one ill hint from ear to ear,   [140]
While all the heathen lay at Arthur's feet,
And no quest came, but all was joust and play,
Leaven'd his hall. They heard and let her be.

    Thereafter as an enemy that has left
Death in the living waters, and withdrawn,°
The wily Vivien stole from Arthur's court.

She hated all the knights, and heard in thought
Their lavish comment when her name was named.
For once, when Arthur walking all alone,
Vext at a rumour issued from herself   [150]
Of some corruption crept among his knights,
Had met her, Vivien, being greeted fair,
Would fain have wrought upon his cloudy mood
With reverent eyes mock-loyal, shaken voice,
And flutter'd adoration, and at last
With dark sweet hints of some who prized him more
Than who should prize him most; at which the King
Had gazed upon her blankly and gone by:
But one had watch'd, and had not held his peace:
It made the laughter of an afternoon   [160]
That Vivien should attempt the blameless King
And after that, she set herself to gain
Him, the most famous man of all those times,
Merlin, who knew the range of all their arts,
Had built the King his havens, ships, and halls,
Was also Bard, and knew the starry heavens;
The people call'd him Wizard; whom at first
She play'd about with slight and sprightly talk,
And vivid smiles, and faintly-venom'd points
Of slander, glancing here and grazing there;   [170]
And yielding to his kindlier moods, the Seer
Would watch her at her petulance, and play,
Ev'n when they seem'd unloveable, and laugh
As those that watch a kitten; thus he grew
Tolerant of what he half disdain'd, and she,
Perceiving that she was but half disdain'd,
Began to break her sports with graver fits,
Turn red or pale, would often when they met
Sigh fully, or all-silent gaze upon him
With such a fixt devotion, that the old man,   [180]
Tho' doubtful, felt the flattery, and at times
Would flatter his own wish in age for love,
And half believe her true: for thus at times
He waver'd; but that other clung to him,
Fixt in her will, and so the seasons went.

Then fell on Merlin a great melancholy;
He walk'd with dreams and darkness, and he found
A doom that ever poised itself to fall,
An ever-moaning battle in the mist,
World-war of dying flesh against the life,   [190]
Death in all life and lying in all love,
The meanest having power upon the highest,
And the high purpose broken by the worm.

So leaving Arthur's court he gain'd the beach;
There found a little boat, and stept into it;
And Vivien follow'd, but he mark'd her not.
She took the helm and he the sail; the boat
Drave with a sudden wind across the deeps,
And touching Breton sands, they disembark'd.
And then she follow'd Merlin all the way,   [200]
Ev'n to the wild woods of Broceliande.
For Merlin once had told her of a charm,
The which if any wrought on anyone
With woven paces and with waving arms,
The man so wrought on ever seem'd to lie
Closed in the four walls of a hollow tower,
From which was no escape for evermore;
And none could find that man for evermore,
Nor could he see but him who wrought the charm
Coming and going, and he lay as dead   [210]
And lost to life and use and name and fame.
And Vivien ever sought to work the charm
Upon the great Enchanter of the Time,
As fancying that her glory would be great
According to his greatness whom she quench'd.

There lay she all her length and kiss'd his feet,
As if in deepest reverence and in love.
A twist of gold was round her hair; a robe
Of samite without price, that more exprest
Than hid her, clung about her lissome limbs,   [220]
In colour like the satin-shining palm
On sallows in the windy gleams of March:
And while she kiss'd them, crying, 'Trample me,

Dear feet, that I have follow'd thro' the world,
And I will pay you worship; tread me down
And I will kiss you for it;' he was mute:
So dark a forethought roll'd about his brain,
As on a dull day in an Ocean cave
The blind wave feeling round his long sea-hall
In silence: wherefore, when she lifted up   [230]
A face of sad appeal, and spake and said,
'O Merlin, do ye love me?' and again,
'O Merlin, do ye love me?' and once more,
'Great Master, do ye love me?' he was mute.
And lissome Vivien, holding by his heel,
Writhed toward him, slided up his knee and sat,
Behind his ankle twined her hollow feet
Together, curved an arm about his neck,
Clung like a snake; and letting her left hand
Droop from his mighty shoulder, as a leaf,   [240]
Made with her right a comb of pearl to part
The lists of such a beard as youth gone out
Had left in ashes: then he spoke and said,
Not looking at her, 'Who are wise in love
Love most, say least,' and Vivien answer'd quick,
'I saw the little elf-god eyeless once
In Arthur's arras hall at Camelot:
But neither eyes nor tongue—O stupid child!
Yet you are wise who say it; let me think
Silence is wisdom: I am silent then,   [250]
And ask no kiss;' then adding all at once,
'And lo, I clothe myself with wisdom,' drew
The vast and shaggy mantle of his beard
Across her neck and bosom to her knee,
And call'd herself a gilded summer fly
Caught in a great old tyrant spider's web,
Who meant to eat her up in that wild wood
Without one word. So Vivien call'd herself,
But rather seem'd a lovely baleful star
Veil'd in gray vapour; till he sadly smiled: [260]
'To what request for what strange boon,' he said,
'Are these your pretty tricks and fooleries,
O Vivien, the preamble? yet my thanks,
For these have broken up my melancholy.'

   And Vivien answer'd smiling saucily,
'What, O my Master, have ye found your voice?
I bid the stranger welcome. Thanks at last!
But yesterday you never open'd lip,
Except indeed to drink: no cup had we:
In mine own lady palms I cull'd the spring   [270]
That gather'd trickling dropwise from the cleft,
And made a pretty cup of both my hands
And offer'd you it kneeling: then you drank
And knew no more, nor gave me one poor word;
O no more thanks than might a goat have given
With no more sign of reverence than a beard.
And when we halted at that other well,
And I was faint to swooning, and you lay
Foot-gilt with all the blossom-dust of those
Deep meadows we had traversed, did you know   [280]
That Vivien bathed your feet before her own?
And yet no thanks: and all thro' this wild wood
And all this morning when I fondled you:
Boon, ay, there was a boon, one not so strange—
How had I wrong'd you? Surely ye are wise,
But such a silence is more wise than kind.'

   And Merlin lock'd his hand in hers and said:
'O did ye never lie upon the shore,
And watch the curl'd white of the coming wave
Glass'd in the slippery sand before it breaks?   [290]
Ev'n such a wave, but not so pleasurable,
Dark in the glass of some presageful mood,
Had I for three days seen, ready to fall.
And then I rose and fled from Arthur's court
To break the mood. You follow'd me unask'd;
And when I look'd, and saw you following still,
My mind involved yourself the nearest thing
In that mind-mist: for shall I tell you truth?
You seem'd that wave about to break upon me
And sweep me from my hold upon the world,   [300]
My use and name and fame. Your pardon, child.
Your pretty sports have brighten'd all again.
And ask your boon, for boon I owe you thrice,

Once for wrong done you by confusion, next
For thanks it seems till now neglected, last
For these your dainty gambols: wherefore ask;
And take this boon so strange and not so strange.'

And Vivien answer'd smiling mournfully:
'O not so strange as my long asking it,
Not yet so strange as you yourself are strange,   [310]
Nor half so strange as that dark mood of yours.
I ever fear'd ye were not wholly mine;
And see, yourself have own'd ye did me wrong.
The people call you prophet: let it be:
But not of those that can expound themselves.
Take Vivien for expounder; she will call
That three-days-long presageful gloom of yours
No presage, but the same mistrustful mood
That makes you seem less noble than yourself,
Whenever I have ask'd this very boon,   [320]
Now ask'd again: for see you not, dear love,
That such a mood as that, which lately gloom'd
Your fancy when ye saw me following you,
Must make me fear still more you are not mine,
Must make me yearn still more to prove you mine,
And make me wish still more to learn this charm
Of woven paces and of waving hands,
As proof of trust. O Merlin, teach it me.
The charm so taught will charm us both to rest.
For, grant me some slight power upon your fate,   [330]
I, feeling that you felt me worthy trust,
Should rest and let you rest, knowing you mine.
And therefore be as great as ye are named,
Not muffled round with selfish reticence.
How hard you look and how denyingly!
O, if you think this wickedness in me,
That I should prove it on you unawares,
That makes me passing wrathful; then our bond
Had best be loosed for ever: but think or not,
By Heaven that hears I tell you the clean truth,   [340]
As clean as blood of babes, as white as milk:
O Merlin, may this earth, if ever I,
If these unwitty wandering wits of mine,

Ev'n in the jumbled rubbish of a dream,
Have tript on such conjectural treachery—
May this hard earth cleave to the Nadir hell
Down, down, and close again, and nip me flat,
If I be such a traitress. Yield my boon,
Till which I scarce can yield you all I am;
And grant my re-reiterated wish,   [350]
The great proof of your love: because I think,
However wise, ye hardly know me yet.'

    And Merlin loosed his hand from hers and said,
'I never was less wise, however wise,
Too curious Vivien, tho' you talk of trust,
Than when I told you first of such a charm.
Yea, if ye talk of trust I tell you this,
Too much I trusted when I told you that,
And stirr'd this vice in you which ruin'd man
Thro' woman the first hour; for howsoe'er   [360]
In children a great curiousness be well,
Who have to learn themselves and all the world,
In you, that are no child, for still I find
Your face is practised when I spell the lines,
I call it,—well, I will not call it vice:
But since you name yourself the summer fly,
I well could wish a cobweb for the gnat,
That settles, beaten back, and beaten back
Settles, till one could yield for weariness:
But since I will not yield to give you power   [370]
Upon my life and use and name and fame,
Why will ye never ask some other boon?
Yea, by God's rood, I trusted you too much.'

    And Vivien, like the tenderest-hearted maid
That ever bided tryst at village stile,
Made answer, either eyelid wet with tears:
'Nay, Master, be not wrathful with your maid;
Caress her: let her feel herself forgiven
Who feels no heart to ask another boon.
I think ye hardly know the tender rhyme   [380]
Of "trust me not at all or all in all."
I heard the great Sir Lancelot sing it once,
And it shall answer for me. Listen to it.

"In Love, if Love be Love, if Love be ours,
Faith and unfaith can ne'er be equal powers:
Unfaith in aught is want of faith in all.

"It is the little rift within the lute,
That by and by will make the music mute,
And ever widening slowly silence all.

"The little rift within the lover's lute   [390]
Or little pitted speck in garner'd fruit,
That rotting inward slowly moulders all.

"It is not worth the keeping: let it go:
But shall it? answer, darling, answer, no.
And trust me not at all or all in all."

O Master, do ye love my tender rhyme?'

And Merlin look'd and half believed her true,
So tender was her voice, so fair her face,
So sweetly gleam'd her eyes behind her tears
Like sunlight on the plain behind a shower: [400]
And yet he answer'd half indignantly:

'Far other was the song that once I heard
By this huge oak, sung nearly where we sit:
For here we met, some ten or twelve of us,
To chase a creature that was current then
In these wild woods, the hart with golden horns.
It was the time when first the question rose
About the founding of a Table Round,
That was to be, for love of God and men
And noble deeds, the flower of all the world.   [410]
And each incited each to noble deeds.
And while we waited, one, the youngest of us,
We could not keep him silent, out he flash'd,
And into such a song, such fire for fame,
Such trumpet-blowings in it, coming down
To such a stern and iron-clashing close,
That when he stopt we long'd to hurl together,
And should have done it; but the beauteous beast
Scared by the noise upstarted at our feet,
And like a silver shadow slipt away   [420]
Thro' the dim land; and all day long we rode

Thro' the dim land against a rushing wind,
That glorious roundel echoing in our ears,
And chased the flashes of his golden horns
Until they vanish'd by the fairy well
That laughs at iron—as our warriors did—
Where children cast their pins and nails, and cry,
"Laugh, little well!" but touch it with a sword,
It buzzes fiercely round the point; and there
We lost him: such a noble song was that.   [430]
But, Vivien, when you sang me that sweet rhyme,
I felt as tho' you knew this cursèd charm,
Were proving it on me, and that I lay
And felt them slowly ebbing, name and fame.'

     And Vivien answer'd smiling mournfully:
'O mine have ebb'd away for evermore,
And all thro' following you to this wild wood,
Because I saw you sad, to comfort you.
Lo now, what hearts have men! they never mount
As high as woman in her selfless mood.   [440]
And touching fame, howe'er ye scorn my song,
Take one verse more—the lady speaks it—this:

' "My name, once mine, now thine, is closelier mine,
For fame, could fame be mine, that fame were thine,
And shame, could shame be thine, that shame were mine.
So trust me not at all or all in all."

     'Says she not well? and there is more—this rhyme
Is like the fair pearl-necklace of the Queen,
That burst in dancing, and the pearls were spilt;
Some lost, some stolen, some as relics kept.   [450]
But nevermore the same two sister pearls
Ran down the silken thread to kiss each other
On her white neck—so is it with this rhyme:
It lives dispersedly in many hands,
And every minstrel sings it differently;
Yet is there one true line, the pearl of pearls:
"Man dreams of Fame while woman wakes to love."
Yea! Love, tho' Love were of the grossest, carves
A portion from the solid present, eats
And uses, careless of the rest; but Fame,   [460]
The Fame that follows death is nothing to us;

And what is Fame in life but half-disfame,
And counterchanged with darkness? ye yourself
Know well that Envy calls you Devil's son,
And since ye seem the Master of all Art,
They fain would make you Master of all vice.'

    And Merlin lock'd his hand in hers and said,
'I once was looking for a magic weed,
And found a fair young squire who sat alone,
Had carved himself a knightly shield of wood,   [470]
And then was painting on it fancied arms,
Azure, an Eagle rising or, the Sun
In dexter chief; the scroll "I follow fame."°
And speaking not, but leaning over him,
I took his brush and blotted out the bird,
And made a Gardener putting in a graff,
With this for motto, "Rather use than fame."
You should have seen him blush; but afterwards
He made a stalwart knight. O Vivien,
For you, methinks you think you love me well;   [480]
For me, I love you somewhat; rest: and Love
Should have some rest and pleasure in himself,
Not ever be too curious for a boon,
Too prurient for a proof against the grain
Of him ye say ye love: but Fame with men,
Being but ampler means to serve mankind,
Should have small rest or pleasure in herself,
But work as vassal to the larger love,
That dwarfs the petty love of one to one.
Use gave me Fame at first, and Fame again   [490]
Increasing gave me use. Lo, there my boon!
What other? for men sought to prove me vile,
Because I fain had given them greater wits:
And then did Envy call me Devil's son:
The sick weak beast seeking to help herself
By striking at her better, miss'd, and brought
Her own claw back, and wounded her own heart.
Sweet were the days when I was all unknown,
But when my name was lifted up, the storm
Brake on the mountain and I cared not for it.   [500]
Right well know I that Fame is half-disfame,

Yet needs must work my work. That other fame,
To one at least, who hath not children, vague,
The cackle of the unborn about the grave,
I cared not for it: a single misty star,°
Which is the second in a line of stars
That seem a sword beneath a belt of three,
I never gazed upon it but I dreamt
Of some vast charm concluded in that star
To make fame nothing. Wherefore, if I fear,   [510]
Giving you power upon me thro' this charm,
That you might play me falsely, having power,
However well ye think ye love me now
(As sons of kings loving in pupilage
Have turn'd to tyrants when they came to power)
I rather dread the loss of use than fame;
If you—and not so much from wickedness,
As some wild turn of anger, or a mood
Of overstrain'd affection, it may be,
To keep me all to your own self,—or else   [520]
A sudden spurt of woman's jealousy,—
Should try this charm on whom ye say ye love.'

        And Vivien answer'd smiling as in wrath:
'Have I not sworn? I am not trusted. Good!
Well, hide it, hide it; I shall find it out;
And being found take heed of Vivien.
A woman and not trusted, doubtless I
Might feel some sudden turn of anger born
Of your misfaith; and your fine epithet
Is accurate too, for this full love of mine   [530]
Without the full heart back may merit well
Your term of overstrain'd. So used as I,
My daily wonder is, I love at all.
And as to woman's jealousy, O why not?
O to what end, except a jealous one,
And one to make me jealous if I love,
Was this fair charm invented by yourself?
I well believe that all about this world
Ye cage a buxom captive here and there,
Closed in the four walls of a hollow tower   [540]
From which is no escape for evermore.'

Then the great Master merrily answer'd her:
'Full many a love in loving youth was mine;
I needed then no charm to keep them mine
But youth and love; and that full heart of yours
Whereof ye prattle, may now assure you mine;
So live uncharm'd. For those who wrought it first,
The wrist is parted from the hand that waved,
The feet unmortised from their ankle-bones
Who paced it, ages back: but will ye hear   [550]
The legend as in guerdon for your rhyme?

'There lived a king in the most Eastern East,°
Less old than I, yet older, for my blood
Hath earnest in it of far springs to be.
A tawny pirate anchor'd in his port,
Whose bark had plunder'd twenty nameless isles;
And passing one, at the high peep of dawn,
He saw two cities in a thousand boats
All fighting for a woman on the sea.
And pushing his black craft among them all,   [560]
He lightly scatter'd theirs and brought her off,
With loss of half his people arrow-slain;
A maid so smooth, so white, so wonderful,
They said a light came from her when she moved:
And since the pirate would not yield her up,
The King impaled him for his piracy;
Then made her Queen: but those isle-nurtured eyes
Waged such unwilling tho' successful war
On all the youth, they sicken'd; councils thinn'd,
And armies waned, for magnet-like she drew   [570]
The rustiest iron of old fighters' hearts;
And beasts themselves would worship; camels knelt
Unbidden, and the brutes of mountain back
That carry kings in castles, bow'd black knees
Of homage, ringing with their serpent hands,
To make her smile, her golden ankle-bells.
What wonder, being jealous, that he sent
His horns of proclamation out thro' all
The hundred under-kingdoms that he sway'd
To find a wizard who might teach the King   [580]
Some charm, which being wrought upon the Queen

Might keep her all his own: to such a one
He promised more than ever king has given,
A league of mountain full of golden mines,
A province with a hundred miles of coast,
A palace and a princess, all for him:
But on all those who tried and fail'd, the King
Pronounced a dismal sentence, meaning by it
To keep the list low and pretenders back,
Or like a king, not to be trifled with—   [590]
Their heads should moulder on the city gates.
And many tried and fail'd, because the charm
Of nature in her overbore their own:
And many a wizard brow bleach'd on the walls:
And many weeks a troop of carrion crows
Hung like a cloud above the gateway towers.'

      And Vivien breaking in upon him, said:
'I sit and gather honey; yet, methinks,
Thy tongue has tript a little: ask thyself.
The lady never made *unwilling* war   [600]
With those fine eyes: she had her pleasure in it,
And made her good man jealous with good cause.
And lived there neither dame nor damsel then
Wroth at a lover's loss? were all as tame,
I mean, as noble, as their Queen was fair?
Not one to flirt a venom at her eyes,
Or pinch a murderous dust into her drink,
Or make her paler with a poison'd rose?
Well, those were not our days: but did they find
A wizard? Tell me, was he like to thee?'   [610]

      She ceased, and made her lithe arm round his neck
Tighten, and then drew back, and let her eyes
Speak for her, glowing on him, like a bride's
On her new lord, her own, the first of men.

      He answer'd laughing, 'Nay, not like to me.
At last they found—his foragers for charms—
A little glassy-headed hairless man,
Who lived alone in a great wild on grass;
Read but one book, and ever reading grew
So grated down and filed away with thought,   [620]

So lean his eyes were monstrous; while the skin
Clung but to crate and basket, ribs and spine.
And since he kept his mind on one sole aim,
Nor ever touch'd fierce wine, nor tasted flesh,
Nor own'd a sensual wish, to him the wall
That sunders ghosts and shadow-casting men
Became a crystal, and he saw them thro' it,
And heard their voices talk behind the wall,
And learnt their elemental secrets, powers
And forces; often o'er the sun's bright eye   [630]
Drew the vast eyelid of an inky cloud,
And lash'd it at the base with slanting storm;
Or in the noon of mist and driving rain,
When the lake whiten'd and the pinewood roar'd,
And the cairn'd mountain was a shadow, sunn'd
The world to peace again: here was the man.
And so by force they dragg'd him to the King.
And then he taught the King to charm the Queen
In such-wise, that no man could see her more,
Nor saw she save the King, who wrought the charm,   [640]
Coming and going, and she lay as dead,
And lost all use of life: but when the King
Made proffer of the league of golden mines,
The province with a hundred miles of coast,
The palace and the princess, that old man
Went back to his old wild, and lived on grass,
And vanish'd, and his book came down to me.'

    And Vivien answer'd smiling saucily:
'Ye have the book: the charm is written in it:
Good: take my counsel: let me know it at once: [650]
For keep it like a puzzle chest in chest,
With each chest lock'd and padlock'd thirty-fold,
And whelm all this beneath as vast a mound
As after furious battle turfs the slain
On some wild down above the windy deep,
I yet should strike upon a sudden means
To dig, pick, open, find and read the charm:
Then, if I tried it, who should blame me then?'

    And smiling as a master smiles at one
That is not of his school, nor any school   [660]

But that where blind and naked Ignorance
Delivers brawling judgments, unashamed,
On all things all day long, he answer'd her:

'Thou read the book, my pretty Vivien!
O ay, it is but twenty pages long,
But every page having an ample marge,
And every marge enclosing in the midst
A square of text that looks a little blot,
The text no larger than the limbs of fleas;
And every square of text an awful charm, [670]
Writ in a language that has long gone by.
So long, that mountains have arisen since
With cities on their flanks—thou read the book!
And every margin scribbled, crost, and cramm'd
With comment, densest condensation, hard
To mind and eye; but the long sleepless nights
Of my long life have made it easy to me.
And none can read the text, not even I;
And none can read the comment but myself;
And in the comment did I find the charm. [680]
O, the results are simple; a mere child
Might use it to the harm of anyone,
And never could undo it: ask no more:
For tho' you should not prove it upon me,
But keep that oath ye sware, ye might, perchance,
Assay it on some one of the Table Round,
And all because ye dream they babble of you.'

And Vivien, frowning in true anger, said:
'What dare the full-fed liars say of me?
They ride abroad redressing human wrongs! [690]
They sit with knife in meat and wine in horn!
They bound to holy vows of chastity!
Were I not woman, I could tell a tale.
But you are man, you well can understand
The shame that cannot be explain'd for shame.
Not one of all the drove should touch me: swine!'

Then answer'd Merlin careless of her words:
'You breathe but accusation vast and vague,
Spleen-born, I think, and proofless. If ye know,
Set up the charge ye know, to stand or fall!' [700]

And Vivien answer'd frowning wrathfully:
'O ay, what say ye to Sir Valence, him
Whose kinsman left him watcher o'er his wife
And two fair babes, and went to distant lands;
Was one year gone, and on returning found
Not two but three? there lay the reckling, one°
But one hour old! What said the happy sire?
A seven-month's babe had been a truer gift.
Those twelve sweet moons confused his fatherhood.'

Then answer'd Merlin, 'Nay, I know the tale.   [710]
Sir Valence wedded with an outland dame:
Some cause had kept him sunder'd from his wife:
One child they had: it lived with her: she died:
His kinsman travelling on his own affair
Was charged by Valence to bring home the child.
He brought, not found it therefore: take the truth.'

'O ay,' said Vivien, 'overtrue a tale.
What say ye then to sweet Sir Sagramore,
That ardent man? "to pluck the flower in season,"
So says the song, "I trow it is no treason."   [720]
O Master, shall we call him overquick
To crop his own sweet rose before the hour?'

And Merlin answer'd, 'Overquick art thou
To catch a loathly plume fall'n from the wing
Of that foul bird of rapine whose whole prey
Is man's good name: he never wrong'd his bride.
I know the tale. An angry gust of wind
Puff'd out his torch among the myriad-room'd
And many-corridor'd complexities
Of Arthur's palace; then he found a door,   [730]
And darkling felt the sculptured ornament
That wreathen round it made it seem his own;
And wearied out made for the couch and slept,
A stainless man beside a stainless maid;
And either slept, nor knew of other there;
Till the high dawn piercing the royal rose
In Arthur's casement glimmer'd chastely down,
Blushing upon them blushing, and at once
He rose without a word and parted from her:

But when the thing was blazed about the court,   [740]
The brute world howling forced them into bonds,
And as it chanced they are happy, being pure.'

'O ay,' said Vivien, 'that were likely too.
What say ye then to fair Sir Percivale
And of the horrid foulness that he wrought,
The saintly youth, the spotless lamb of Christ,
Or some black wether of St Satan's fold.
What, in the precincts of the chapel-yard,
Among the knightly brasses of the graves,
And by the cold Hic Jacets of the dead!'°   [750]

And Merlin answer'd careless of her charge,
'A sober man is Percivale and pure;
But once in life was fluster'd with new wine,
Then paced for coolness in the chapel-yard;
Where one of Satan's shepherdesses caught
And meant to stamp him with her master's mark;
And that he sinn'd is not believable;
For, look upon his face!—but if he sinn'd,
The sin that practice burns into the blood,
And not the one dark hour which brings remorse,   [760]
Will brand us, after, of whose fold we be:
Or else were he, the holy king, whose hymns°
Are chanted in the minster, worse than all.
But is your spleen froth'd out, or have ye more?'

And Vivien answer'd frowning yet in wrath:
'O ay; what say ye to Sir Lancelot, friend
Traitor or true? that commerce with the Queen,
I ask you, is it clamour'd by the child,
Or whisper'd in the corner? Do ye know it?'

To which he answer'd sadly, 'Yea, I know it.   [770]
Sir Lancelot went ambassador, at first,
To fetch her, and she watch'd him from her walls.
A rumour runs, she took him for the King,
So fixt her fancy on him: let them be.
But have ye no one word of loyal praise
For Arthur, blameless King and stainless man?'

She answer'd with a low and chuckling laugh:
'Man! is he man at all, who knows and winks?

Sees what his fair bride is and does, and winks?
By which the good King means to blind himself,   [780]
And blinds himself and all the Table Round
To all the foulness that they work. Myself
Could call him (were it not for womanhood)
The pretty, popular name such manhood earns,
Could call him the main cause of all their crime;
Yea, were he not crown'd King, coward, and fool.'

Then Merlin to his own heart, loathing, said:
'O true and tender! O my liege and King!
O selfless man and stainless gentleman,
Who wouldst against thine own eye-witness fain   [790]
Have all men true and leal, all women pure;°
How, in the mouths of base interpreters,
From over-fineness not intelligible
To things with every sense as false and foul
As the poach'd filth that floods the middle street,
Is thy white blamelessness accounted blame!'

But Vivien, deeming Merlin overborne
By instance, recommenced, and let her tongue
Rage like a fire among the noblest names,
Polluting, and imputing her whole self,   [800]
Defaming and defacing, till she left
Not even Lancelot brave, nor Galahad clean.

Her words had issue other than she will'd.
He dragg'd his eyebrow bushes down, and made
A snowy penthouse for his hollow eyes,
And mutter'd in himself, 'Tell *her* the charm!
So, if she had it, would she rail on me
To snare the next, and if she have it not
So will she rail. What did the wanton say?
"Not mount as high;" we scarce can sink as low: [810]
For men at most differ as Heaven and earth,
But women, worst and best, as Heaven and Hell.
I know the Table Round, my friends of old;
All brave, and many generous, and some chaste.
She cloaks the scar of some repulse with lies;
I well believe she tempted them and fail'd,
Being so bitter: for fine plots may fail,

Tho' harlots paint their talk as well as face
With colours of the heart that are not theirs.
I will not let her know: nine tithes of times [820]
Face-flatterer and backbiter are the same.
And they, sweet soul, that most impute a crime
Are pronest to it, and impute themselves,
Wanting the mental range; or low desire
Not to feel lowest makes them level all;
Yea, they would pare the mountain to the plain,
To leave an equal baseness; and in this
Are harlots like the crowd, that if they find
Some stain or blemish in a name of note,
Not grieving that their greatest are so small, [830]
Inflate themselves with some insane delight,
And judge all nature from her feet of clay,
Without the will to lift their eyes, and see
Her godlike head crown'd with spiritual fire,
And touching other worlds. I am weary of her.'

He spoke in words part heard, in whispers part,
Half-suffocated in the hoary fell
And many-winter'd fleece of throat and chin.
But Vivien, gathering somewhat of his mood,
And hearing 'harlot' mutter'd twice or thrice, [840]
Leapt from her session on his lap, and stood
Stiff as a viper frozen; loathsome sight,
How from the rosy lips of life and love,
Flash'd the bare-grinning skeleton of death!
White was her cheek; sharp breaths of anger puff'd
Her fairy nostril out; her hand half-clench'd
Went faltering sideways downward to her belt,
And feeling; had she found a dagger there
(For in a wink the false love turns to hate)
She would have stabb'd him; but she found it not: [850]
His eye was calm, and suddenly she took
To bitter weeping like a beaten child,
A long, long weeping, not consolable.
Then her false voice made way, broken with sobs:

'O crueller than was ever told in tale,
Or sung in song! O vainly lavish'd love!
O cruel, there was nothing wild or strange,

Or seeming shameful—for what shame in love,
So love be true, and not as yours is—nothing
Poor Vivien had not done to win his trust   [860]
Who call'd her what he call'd her—all her crime,
All—all—the wish to prove him wholly hers.'

She mused a little, and then clapt her hands
Together with a wailing shriek, and said:
'Stabb'd through the heart's affections to the heart!
Seethed like the kid in its own mother's milk!°
Kill'd with a word worse than a life of blows!
I thought that he was gentle, being great:
O God, that I had loved a smaller man!
I should have found in him a greater heart.   [870]
O, I, that flattering my true passion, saw
The knights, the court, the King, dark in your light,
Who loved to make men darker than they are,
Because of that high pleasure which I had
To seat you sole upon my pedestal
Of worship—I am answer'd, and henceforth
The course of life that seem'd so flowery to me
With you for guide and master, only you,
Becomes the sea-cliff pathway broken short,
And ending in a ruin—nothing left,   [880]
But into some low cave to crawl, and there,
If the wolf spare me, weep my life away,
Kill'd with inutterable unkindliness.'

She paused, she turn'd away, she hung her head,
The snake of gold slid from her hair, the braid
Slipt and uncoil'd itself, she wept afresh,
And the dark wood grew darker toward the storm
In silence, while his anger slowly died
Within him, till he let his wisdom go
For ease of heart, and half believed her true: [890]
Call'd her to shelter in the hollow oak,
'Come from the storm,' and having no reply,
Gazed at the heaving shoulder, and the face
Hand-hidden, as for utmost grief or shame;
Then thrice essay'd, by tenderest-touching terms,
To sleek her ruffled peace of mind, in vain.
At last she let herself be conquer'd by him,

And as the cageling newly flown returns,
The seeming-injured simple-hearted thing
Came to her old perch back, and settled there. [900]
There while she sat, half-falling from his knees,
Half-nestled at his heart, and since he saw
The slow tear creep from her closed eyelid yet,
About her, more in kindness than in love,
The gentle wizard cast a shielding arm.
But she dislink'd herself at once and rose,
Her arms upon her breast across, and stood,
A virtuous gentlewoman deeply wrong'd,
Upright and flush'd before him: then she said:

'There must be now no passages of love [910]
Betwixt us twain henceforward evermore;
Since, if I be what I am grossly call'd,
What should be granted which your own gross heart
Would reckon worth the taking? I will go.
In truth, but one thing now—better have died
Thrice than have ask'd it once—could make me stay—
That proof of trust—so often ask'd in vain!
How justly, after that vile term of yours,
I find with grief! I might believe you then,
Who knows? once more. Lo! what was once to me [920]
Mere matter of the fancy, now hath grown
The vast necessity of heart and life.
Farewell; think gently of me, for I fear
My fate or folly, passing gayer youth
For one so old, must be to love thee still.
But ere I leave thee let me swear once more
That if I schemed against thy peace in this,
May yon just heaven, that darkens o'er me, send
One flash, that, missing all things else, may make
My scheming brain a cinder, if I lie.' [930]

Scarce had she ceased, when out of heaven a bolt
(For now the storm was close above them) struck,
Furrowing a giant oak, and javelining
With darted spikes and splinters of the wood
The dark earth round. He raised his eyes and saw
The tree that shone white-listed thro' the gloom.°
But Vivien, fearing heaven had heard her oath,

And dazzled by the livid-flickering fork,
And deafen'd with the stammering cracks and claps
That follow'd, flying back and crying out,   [940]
'O Merlin, tho' you do not love me, save,
Yet save me!' clung to him and hugg'd him close;
And call'd him dear protector in her fright,
Nor yet forgot her practice in her fright,
But wrought upon his mood and hugg'd him close.
The pale blood of the wizard at her touch
Took gayer colours, like an opal warm'd.
She blamed herself for telling hearsay tales:
She shook from fear, and for her fault she wept
Of petulancy; she call'd him lord and liege,   [950]
Her seer, her bard, her silver star of eve,
Her God, her Merlin, the one passionate love
Of her whole life; and ever overhead
Bellow'd the tempest, and the rotten branch
Snapt in the rushing of the river-rain
Above them; and in change of glare and gloom
Her eyes and neck glittering went and came;
Till now the storm, its burst of passion spent,
Moaning and calling out of other lands,
Had left the ravaged woodland yet once more   [960]
To peace; and what should not have been had been,
For Merlin, overtalk'd and overworn,
Had yielded, told her all the charm, and slept.

    Then, in one moment, she put forth the charm
Of woven paces and of waving hands,
And in the hollow oak he lay as dead,
And lost to life and use and name and fame.

    Then crying 'I have made his glory mine,'
And shrieking out 'O fool!' the harlot leapt
Adown the forest, and the thicket closed   [970]
Behind her, and the forest echo'd 'fool.'

The Holy Grail

From noiseful arms, and acts of prowess done
In tournament or tilt, Sir Percivale,
Whom Arthur and his knighthood call'd The Pure,
Had pass'd into the silent life of prayer,
Praise, fast, and alms; and leaving for the cowl
The helmet in an abbey far away
From Camelot, there, and not long after, died.

And one, a fellow-monk among the rest,
Ambrosius, loved him much beyond the rest,
And honour'd him, and wrought into his heart   [10]
A way by love that waken'd love within,
To answer that which came: and as they sat
Beneath a world-old yew-tree, darkening half
The cloisters, on a gustful April morn
That puff'd the swaying branches into smoke
Above them, ere the summer when he died,
The monk Ambrosius question'd Percivale:

'O brother, I have seen this yew-tree smoke,°
Spring after spring, for half a hundred years:
For never have I known the world without,   [20]
Nor ever stray'd beyond the pale: but thee,
When first thou camest—such a courtesy
Spake thro' the limbs and in the voice—I knew
For one of those who eat in Arthur's hall;
For good ye are and bad, and like to coins,
Some true, some light, but every one of you
Stamp'd with the image of the King; and now
Tell me, what drove thee from the Table Round,
My brother? was it earthly passion crost?'

'Nay,' said the knight; 'for no such passion mine.   [30]
But the sweet vision of the Holy Grail
Drove me from all vainglories, rivalries,
And earthly heats that spring and sparkle out
Among us in the jousts, while women watch
Who wins, who falls; and waste the spiritual strength
Within us, better offer'd up to Heaven.'

To whom the monk: 'The Holy Grail!—I trust
We are green in Heaven's eyes; but here too much
We moulder—as to things without I mean—
Yet one of your own knights, a guest of ours,   [40]
Told us of this in our refectory,
But spake with such a sadness and so low
We heard not half of what he said. What is it?
The phantom of a cup that comes and goes?'

'Nay, monk! what phantom?' answer'd Percivale.
'The cup, the cup itself, from which our Lord
Drank at the last sad supper with his own.
This, from the blessèd land of Aromat—°
After the day of darkness, when the dead
Went wandering o'er Moriah—the good saint°   [50]
Arimathæan Joseph, journeying brought
To Glastonbury, where the winter thorn°
Blossoms at Christmas, mindful of our Lord.
And there awhile it bode; and if a man
Could touch or see it, he was heal'd at once,
By faith, of all his ills. But then the times
Grew to such evil that the holy cup
Was caught away to Heaven, and disappear'd.'

To whom the monk: 'From our old books I know
That Joseph came of old to Glastonbury,   [60]
And there the heathen Prince, Arviragus,°
Gave him an isle of marsh whereon to build;
And there he built with wattles from the marsh
A little lonely church in days of yore,
For so they say, these books of ours, but seem
Mute of this miracle, far as I have read.
But who first saw the holy thing to-day?'

'A woman,' answer'd Percivale, 'a nun,
And one no further off in blood from me
Than sister; and if ever holy maid   [70]
With knees of adoration wore the stone,
A holy maid; tho' never maiden glow'd,
But that was in her earlier maidenhood,
With such a fervent flame of human love,
Which being rudely blunted, glanced and shot

Only to holy things; to prayer and praise
She gave herself, to fast and alms. And yet
Nun as she was, the scandal of the Court,
Sin against Arthur and the Table Round,
And the strange sound of an adulterous race,   [80]
Across the iron grating of her cell
Beat, and she pray'd and fasted all the more.

    'And he to whom she told her sins, or what
Her all but utter whiteness held for sin,
A man wellnigh a hundred winters old,
Spake often with her of the Holy Grail,
A legend handed down thro' five or six,
And each of these a hundred winters old,
From our Lord's time. And when King Arthur made
His Table Round, and all men's hearts became   [90]
Clean for a season, surely he had thought
That now the Holy Grail would come again;
But sin broke out. Ah, Christ, that it would come,
And heal the world of all their wickedness!
"O Father!" ask'd the maiden, "might it come
To me by prayer and fasting?" "Nay," said he,
"I know not, for thy heart is pure as snow."
And so she pray'd and fasted, till the sun
Shone, and the wind blew, thro' her, and I thought
She might have risen and floated when I saw her.   [100]

    'For on a day she sent to speak with me.
And when she came to speak, behold her eyes
Beyond my knowing of them, beautiful,
Beyond all knowing of them, wonderful,
Beautiful in the light of holiness.
And "O my brother Percivale," she said,
"Sweet brother, I have seen the Holy Grail:
For, waked at dead of night, I heard a sound
As of a silver horn from o'er the hills
Blown, and I thought, 'It is not Arthur's use   [110]
To hunt by moonlight;' and the slender sound
As from a distance beyond distance grew
Coming upon me—O never harp nor horn,
Nor aught we blow with breath, or touch with hand,
Was like that music as it came; and then

Stream'd thro' my cell a cold and silver beam,
And down the long beam stole the Holy Grail,
Rose-red with beatings in it, as if alive,
Till all the white walls of my cell were dyed
With rosy colours leaping on the wall;   [120]
And then the music faded, and the Grail
Past, and the beam decay'd, and from the walls
The rosy quiverings died into the night.
So now the Holy Thing is here again
Among us, brother, fast thou too and pray,
And tell thy brother knights to fast and pray,
That so perchance the vision may be seen
By thee and those, and all the world be heal'd."

'Then leaving the pale nun, I spake of this
To all men; and myself fasted and pray'd   [130]
Always, and many among us many a week
Fasted and pray'd even to the uttermost,
Expectant of the wonder that would be.

'And one there was among us, ever moved
Among us in white armour, Galahad.
"God make thee good as thou art beautiful,"
Said Arthur, when he dubb'd him knight; and none,
In so young youth, was ever made a knight
Till Galahad; and this Galahad, when he heard
My sister's vision, fill'd me with amaze;   [140]
His eyes became so like her own, they seem'd
Hers, and himself her brother more than I.

'Sister or brother none had he; but some
Call'd him a son of Lancelot, and some said
Begotten by enchantment—chatterers they,
Like birds of passage piping up and down,
That gape for flies—we know not whence they come;
For when was Lancelot wanderingly lewd?

'But she, the wan sweet maiden, shore away
Clean from her forehead all that wealth of hair   [150]
Which made a silken mat-work for her feet;
And out of this she plaited broad and long
A strong sword-belt, and wove with silver thread

And crimson in the belt a strange device,
A crimson grail within a silver beam;
And saw the bright boy-knight, and bound it on him,
Saying, "My knight, my love, my knight of heaven,
O thou, my love, whose love is one with mine,
I, maiden, round thee, maiden, bind my belt.
Go forth, for thou shalt see what I have seen,   [160]
And break thro' all, till one will crown thee king
Far in the spiritual city:" and as she spake
She sent the deathless passion in her eyes
Thro' him, and made him hers, and laid her mind
On him, and he believed in her belief.

'Then came a year of miracle: O brother,
In our great hall there stood a vacant chair,
Fashion'd by Merlin ere he past away,
And carven with strange figures; and in and out
The figures, like a serpent, ran a scroll   [170]
Of letters in a tongue no man could read.
And Merlin call'd it "The Siege perilous,"°
Perilous for good and ill; "for there," he said,
"No man could sit but he should lose himself:"
And once by misadvertence Merlin sat
In his own chair, and so was lost; but he,
Galahad, when he heard of Merlin's doom,
Cried, "If I lose myself, I save myself!"

'Then on a summer night it came to pass,
While the great banquet lay along the hall,   [180]
That Galahad would sit down in Merlin's chair.

'And all at once, as there we sat, we heard
A cracking and a riving of the roofs,
And rending, and a blast, and overhead
Thunder, and in the thunder was a cry.
And in the blast there smote along the hall
A beam of light seven times more clear than day:
And down the long beam stole the Holy Grail
All over cover'd with a luminous cloud,
And none might see who bare it, and it past.   [190]
But every knight beheld his fellow's face
As in a glory, and all the knights arose,

And staring each at other like dumb men
Stood, till I found a voice and sware a vow.

'I sware a vow before them all, that I,
Because I had not seen the Grail, would ride
A twelvemonth and a day in quest of it,
Until I found and saw it, as the nun
My sister saw it; and Galahad sware the vow,
And good Sir Bors, our Lancelot's cousin, sware,   [200]
And Lancelot sware, and many among the knights,
And Gawain sware, and louder than the rest.'

Then spake the monk Ambrosius, asking him,
'What said the King? Did Arthur take the vow?'

'Nay, for my lord,' said Percivale, 'the King,
Was not in hall: for early that same day,
Scaped thro' a cavern from a bandit hold,
An outraged maiden sprang into the hall
Crying on help: for all her shining hair
Was smear'd with earth, and either milky arm   [210]
Red-rent with hooks of bramble, and all she wore
Torn as a sail that leaves the rope is torn
In tempest: so the King arose and went
To smoke the scandalous hive of those wild bees
That made such honey in his realm. Howbeit
Some little of this marvel he too saw,
Returning o'er the plain that then began
To darken under Camelot; whence the King
Look'd up, calling aloud, "Lo, there! the roofs
Of our great hall are roll'd in thunder-smoke!   [220]
Pray Heaven, they be not smitten by the bolt."
For dear to Arthur was that hall of ours,
As having there so oft with all his knights
Feasted, and as the stateliest under heaven.

'O brother, had you known our mighty hall,
Which Merlin built for Arthur long ago!
For all the sacred mount of Camelot,°
And all the dim rich city, roof by roof,
Tower after tower, spire beyond spire,
By grove, and garden-lawn, and rushing brook,   [230]
Climbs to the mighty hall that Merlin built.

And four great zones of sculpture, set betwixt°
With many a mystic symbol, gird the hall:
And in the lowest beasts are slaying men,
And in the second men are slaying beasts,
And on the third are warriors, perfect men,
And on the fourth are men with growing wings,
And over all one statue in the mould
Of Arthur, made by Merlin, with a crown,
And peak'd wings pointed to the Northern Star.   [240]
And eastward fronts the statue, and the crown
And both the wings are made of gold, and flame
At sunrise till the people in far fields,
Wasted so often by the heathen hordes,
Behold it, crying, "We have still a King."

    'And, brother, had you known our hall within,
Broader and higher than any in all the lands!
Where twelve great windows blazon Arthur's wars,
And all the light that falls upon the board
Streams thro' the twelve great battles of our King.   [250]
Nay, one there is, and at the eastern end,
Wealthy with wandering lines of mount and mere,
Where Arthur finds the brand Excalibur.
And also one to the west, and counter to it,
And blank: and who shall blazon it? when and how?—
O there, perchance, when all our wars are done,
The brand Excalibur will be cast away.

    'So to this hall full quickly rode the King,
In horror lest the work by Merlin wrought,
Dreamlike, should on the sudden vanish, wrapt   [260]
In unremorseful folds of rolling fire.
And in he rode, and up I glanced, and saw
The golden dragon sparkling over all:
And many of those who burnt the hold, their arms
Hack'd, and their foreheads grimed with smoke, and sear'd,
Follow'd, and in among bright faces, ours,
Full of the vision, prest: and then the King
Spake to me, being nearest, "Percivale."
(Because the hall was all in tumult—some
Vowing, and some protesting), "what is this?"   [270]

'O brother, when I told him what had chanced,
My sister's vision, and the rest, his face
Darken'd, as I have seen it more than once,
When some brave deed seem'd to be done in vain,
Darken; and "Woe is me, my knights," he cried,
"Had I been here, ye had not sworn the vow."
Bold was mine answer, "Had thyself been here,
My King, thou wouldst have sworn." "Yea, yea," said he,
"Art thou so bold and hast not seen the Grail?"

' "Nay, lord, I heard the sound, I saw the light,   [280]
But since I did not see the Holy Thing,
I sware a vow to follow it till I saw."

'Then when he ask'd us, knight by knight, if any
Had seen it, all their answers were as one:
"Nay, lord, and therefore have we sworn our vows."

' "Lo now," said Arthur, "have ye seen a cloud?
What go ye into the wilderness to see?"

'Then Galahad on the sudden, and in a voice
Shrilling along the hall to Arthur, call'd,
"But I, Sir Arthur, saw the Holy Grail,   [290]
I saw the Holy Grail and heard a cry—
'O Galahad, and O Galahad, follow me.' "

' "Ah, Galahad, Galahad," said the King, "for such
As thou art is the vision, not for these.
Thy holy nun and thou have seen a sign—
Holier is none, my Percivale, than she—
A sign to maim this Order which I made.
But ye, that follow but the leader's bell"
(Brother, the King was hard upon his knights)
"Taliessin is our fullest throat of song,°   [300]
And one hath sung and all the dumb will sing.
Lancelot is Lancelot, and hath overborne
Five knights at once, and every younger knight,
Unproven, holds himself as Lancelot,
Till overborne by one, he learns—and ye,
What are ye? Galahads?—no, nor Perçivales"
(For thus it pleased the King to range me close
After Sir Galahad); "nay," said he, "but men

With strength and will to right the wrong'd, of power
To lay the sudden heads of violence flat, [310]
Knights that in twelve great battles splash'd and dyed
The strong White Horse in his own heathen blood—°
But one hath seen, and all the blind will see.
Go, since your vows are sacred, being made:
Yet—for ye know the cries of all my realm
Pass thro' this hall—how often, O my knights,
Your places being vacant at my side,
This chance of noble deeds will come and go
Unchallenged, while ye follow wandering fires
Lost in the quagmire! Many of you, yea most, [320]
Return no more: ye think I show myself
Too dark a prophet: come now, let us meet
The morrow morn once more in one full field
Of gracious pastime, that once more the King,
Before ye leave him for this Quest, may count
The yet-unbroken strength of all his knights,
Rejoicing in that Order which he made."

'So when the sun broke next from under ground,
All the great table of our Arthur closed
And clash'd in such a tourney and so full, [330]
So many lances broken—never yet
Had Camelot seen the like, since Arthur came;
And I myself and Galahad, for a strength
Was in us from the vision, overthrew
So many knights that all the people cried,
And almost burst the barriers in their heat,
Shouting, "Sir Galahad and Sir Percivale!"

'But when the next day brake from under ground—
O brother, had you known our Camelot,
Built by old kings, age after age, so old [340]
The King himself had fears that it would fall,
So strange, and rich, and dim; for where the roofs
Totter'd toward each other in the sky,
Met foreheads all along the street of those
Who watch'd us pass; and lower, and where the long
Rich galleries, lady-laden, weigh'd the necks
Of dragons clinging to the crazy walls,
Thicker than drops from thunder, showers of flowers

Fell as we past; and men and boys astride
On wyvern, lion, dragon, griffin, swan,°   [350]
At all the corners, named us each by name,
Calling "God speed!" but in the ways below
The knights and ladies wept, and rich and poor
Wept, and the King himself could hardly speak
For grief, and all in middle street the Queen,
Who rode by Lancelot, wail'd and shriek'd aloud,
"This madness has come on us for our sins."
So to the Gate of the three Queens we came,
Where Arthur's wars are render'd mystically,
And thence departed every one his way.   [360]

　　'And I was lifted up in heart, and thought
Of all my late-shown prowess in the lists,
How my strong lance had beaten down the knights,
So many and famous names; and never yet
Had heaven appear'd so blue, nor earth so green,
For all my blood danced in me, and I knew
That I should light upon the Holy Grail.

　　'Thereafter, the dark warning of our King,
That most of us would follow wandering fires,
Came like a driving gloom across my mind.   [370]
Then every evil word I had spoken once,
And every evil thought I had thought of old,
And every evil deed I ever did,
Awoke and cried, "This Quest is not for thee."
And lifting up mine eyes, I found myself
Alone, and in a land of sand and thorns,
And I was thirsty even unto death;
And I, too, cried, "This Quest is not for thee."

　　'And on I rode, and when I thought my thirst
Would slay me, saw deep lawns, and then a brook,   [380]
With one sharp rapid, where the crisping white
Play'd ever back upon the sloping wave,
And took both ear and eye; and o'er the brook
Were apple-trees, and apples by the brook
Fallen, and on the lawns. "I will rest here,"
I said, "I am not worthy of the Quest;"
But even while I drank the brook, and ate

The goodly apples, all these things at once
Fell into dust, and I was left alone,
And thirsting, in a land of sand and thorns.°   [390]

'And then behold a woman at a door
Spinning; and fair the house whereby she sat,
And kind the woman's eyes and innocent,
And all her bearing gracious; and she rose
Opening her arms to meet me, as who should say,
"Rest here;" but when I touch'd her, lo! she, too,
Fell into dust and nothing, and the house
Became no better than a broken shed,
And in it a dead babe; and also this
Fell into dust, and I was left alone.   [400]

'And on I rode, and greater was my thirst.
Then flash'd a yellow gleam across the world,
And where it smote the plowshare in the field,
The plowman left his plowing, and fell down
Before it; where it glitter'd on her pail,
The milkmaid left her milking, and fell down
Before it, and I knew not why, but thought
"The sun is rising," tho' the sun had risen.
Then was I ware of one that on me moved
In golden armour with a crown of gold   [410]
About a casque all jewels; and his horse
In golden armour jewell'd everywhere:
And on the splendour came, flashing me blind;
And seem'd to me the Lord of all the world,
Being so huge. But when I thought he meant
To crush me, moving on me, lo! he, too,
Open'd his arms to embrace me as he came,
And up I went and touch'd him, and he, too,
Fell into dust, and I was left alone
And wearying in a land of sand and thorns.   [420]

'And I rode on and found a mighty hill,
And on the top, a city wall'd: the spires
Prick'd with incredible pinnacles into heaven.
And by the gateway stirr'd a crowd; and these
Cried to me climbing, "Welcome, Percivale!
Thou mightiest and thou purest among men!"

And glad was I and clomb, but found at top
No man, nor any voice. And thence I past
Far thro' a ruinous city, and I saw
That man had once dwelt there; but there I found   [430]
Only one man of an exceeding age.
"Where is that goodly company," said I,
"That so cried out upon me?" and he had
Scarce any voice to answer, and yet gasp'd,
"Whence and what art thou?" and even as he spoke
Fell into dust, and disappear'd, and I
Was left alone once more, and cried in grief,
"Lo, if I find the Holy Grail itself
And touch it, it will crumble into dust."

    'And thence I dropt into a lowly vale,   [440]
Low as the hill was high, and where the vale
Was lowest, found a chapel, and thereby
A holy hermit in a hermitage,
To whom I told my phantoms, and he said:

    ' "O son, thou hast not true humility,
The highest virtue, mother of them all;
For when the Lord of all things made Himself
Naked of glory for His mortal change,
'Take thou my robe,' she said, 'for all is thine,'
And all her form shone forth with sudden light   [450]
So that the angels were amazed, and she
Follow'd Him down, and like a flying star
Led on the gray-hair'd wisdom of the east;°
But her thou hast not known: for what is this
Thou thoughtest of thy prowess and thy sins?
Thou hast not lost thyself to save thyself
As Galahad." When the hermit made an end,
In silver armour suddenly Galahad shone
Before us, and against the chapel door
Laid lance, and enter'd, and we knelt in prayer.   [460]
And there the hermit slaked my burning thirst,
And at the sacring of the mass I saw°
The holy elements alone; but he,
"Saw ye no more? I, Galahad, saw the Grail,
The Holy Grail, descend upon the shrine:
I saw the fiery face as of a child

That smote itself into the bread, and went;
And hither am I come; and never yet
Hath what thy sister taught me first to see,
This Holy Thing, fail'd from my side, nor come   [470]
Cover'd, but moving with me night and day,
Fainter by day, but always in the night
Blood-red, and sliding down the blacken'd marsh
Blood-red, and on the naked mountain top
Blood-red, and in the sleeping mere below
Blood-red. And in the strength of this I rode,
Shattering all evil customs everywhere,
And past thro' Pagan realms, and made them mine,
And clash'd with Pagan hordes, and bore them down,
And broke thro' all, and in the strength of this   [480]
Come victor. But my time is hard at hand,
And hence I go; and one will crown me king
Far in the spiritual city; and come thou, too,
For thou shalt see the vision when I go."

'While thus he spake, his eye, dwelling on mine,
Drew me, with power upon me, till I grew
One with him, to believe as he believed.
Then, when the day began to wane, we went.

'There rose a hill that none but man could climb,
Scarr'd with a hundred wintry water-courses—   [490]
Storm at the top, and when we gain'd it, storm
Round us and death; for every moment glanced
His silver arms and gloom'd: so quick and thick
The lightnings here and there to left and right
Struck, till the dry old trunks about us, dead,
Yea, rotten with a hundred years of death,
Sprang into fire: and at the base we found
On either hand, as far as eye could see,
A great black swamp and of an evil smell,
Part black, part whiten'd with the bones of men,   [500]
Not to be crost, save that some ancient king
Had built a way, where, link'd with many a bridge,
A thousand piers ran into the great Sea.
And Galahad fled along them bridge by bridge,
And every bridge as quickly as he crost
Sprang into fire and vanish'd, tho' I yearn'd

To follow; and thrice above him all the heavens
Open'd and blazed with thunder such as seem'd
Shoutings of all the sons of God: and first
At once I saw him far on the great Sea,   [510]
In silver-shining armour starry-clear;
And o'er his head the Holy Vessel hung
Clothed in white samite or a luminous cloud.
And with exceeding swiftness ran the boat,
If boat it were—I saw not whence it came.
And when the heavens open'd and blazed again
Roaring, I saw him like a silver star—
And had he set the sail, or had the boat
Become a living creature clad with wings?
And o'er his head the Holy Vessel hung   [520]
Redder than any rose, a joy to me,
For now I knew the veil had been withdrawn.
Then in a moment when they blazed again
Opening, I saw the least of little stars
Down on the waste, and straight beyond the star
I saw the spiritual city and all her spires
And gateways in a glory like one pearl—
No larger, tho' the goal of all the saints—
Strike from the sea; and from the star there shot
A rose-red sparkle to the city, and there   [530]
Dwelt, and I knew it was the Holy Grail,
Which never eyes on earth again shall see.
Then fell the floods of heaven drowning the deep.
And how my feet recrost the deathful ridge
No memory in me lives; but that I touch'd
The chapel-doors at dawn I know; and thence
Taking my war-horse from the holy man,
Glad that no phantom vext me more, return'd
To whence I came, the gate of Arthur's wars.'

'O brother,' ask'd Ambrosius,—'for in sooth   [540]
These ancient books—and they would win thee—teem,
Only I find not there this Holy Grail,
With miracles and marvels like to these,
Not all unlike; which oftentime I read,
Who read but on my breviary with ease,
Till my head swims; and then go forth and pass

Down to the little thorpe that lies so close,
And almost plaster'd like a martin's nest
To these old walls—and mingle with our folk;
And knowing every honest face of theirs [550]
As well as ever shepherd knew his sheep,
And every homely secret in their hearts,
Delight myself with gossip and old wives,
And ills and aches, and teethings, lyings-in,
And mirthful sayings, children of the place,
That have no meaning half a league away:
Or lulling random squabbles when they rise,
Chafferings and chatterings at the market-cross,
Rejoice, small man, in this small world of mine,
Yea, even in their hens and in their eggs— [560]
O brother, saving this Sir Galahad,
Came ye on none but phantoms in your quest,
No man, no woman?'
        Then Sir Percivale:
'All men, to one so bound by such a vow,
And women were as phantoms. O, my brother,
Why wilt thou shame me to confess to thee
How far I falter'd from my quest and vow?
For after I had lain so many nights,
A bedmate of the snail and eft and snake,°
In grass and burdock, I was changed to wan [570]
And meagre, and the vision had not come;
And then I chanced upon a goodly town
With one great dwelling in the middle of it;
Thither I made, and there was I disarm'd
By maidens each as fair as any flower:
But when they led me into hall, behold,
The Princess of that castle was the one,
Brother, and that one only, who had ever
Made my heart leap; for when I moved of old
A slender page about her father's hall, [580]
And she a slender maiden, all my heart
Went after her with longing: yet we twain
Had never kiss'd a kiss, or vow'd a vow.
And now I came upon her once again,
And one had wedded her, and he was dead,
And all his land and wealth and state were hers.

And while I tarried, every day she set
A banquet richer than the day before
By me; for all her longing and her will
Was toward me as of old; till one fair morn,   [590]
I walking to and fro beside a stream
That flash'd across her orchard underneath
Her castle-walls, she stole upon my walk,
And calling me the greatest of all knights,
Embraced me, and so kiss'd me the first time,
And gave herself and all her wealth to me.
Then I remember'd Arthur's warning word,
That most of us would follow wandering fires,
And the Quest faded in my heart. Anon,
The heads of all her people drew to me,   [600]
With supplication both of knees and tongue:
"We have heard of thee: thou art our greatest knight,—
Our Lady says it, and we well believe:
Wed thou our Lady, and rule over us,
And thou shalt be as Arthur in our land."
O me, my brother! but one night my vow
Burnt me within, so that I rose and fled,
But wail'd and wept, and hated mine own self,
And ev'n the Holy Quest, and all but her;
Then after I was join'd with Galahad   [610]
Cared not for her, nor anything upon earth.'

    Then said the monk, 'Poor men, when yule is cold,
Must be content to sit by little fires.
And this am I, so that ye care for me
Ever so little; yea, and blest be Heaven
That brought thee here to this poor house of ours
Where all the brethren are so hard, to warm
My cold heart with a friend: but O the pity
To find thine own first love once more—to hold,
Hold her a wealthy bride within thine arms,   [620]
Or all but hold, and then—cast her aside,
Foregoing all her sweetness, like a weed.
For we that want the warmth of double life,
We that are plagued with dreams of something sweet
Beyond all sweetness in a life so rich,—
Ah, blessèd Lord, I speak too earthlywise,

Seeing I never stray'd beyond the cell,
But live like an old badger in his earth,
With earth about him everywhere, despite
All fast and penance. Saw ye none beside,   [630]
None of your knights?'
              'Yea so,' said Percivale:
'One night my pathway swerving east, I saw
The pelican on the casque of our Sir Bors
All in the middle of the rising moon:
And toward him spurr'd, and hail'd him, and he me,
And each made joy of either; then he ask'd,
"Where is he? hast thou seen him—Lancelot?—Once,"
Said good Sir Bors, "he dash'd across me—mad,
And maddening what he rode: and when I cried,
'Ridest thou then so hotly on a quest   [640]
So holy,' Lancelot shouted, 'Stay me not!
I have been the sluggard, and I ride apace,
For now there is a lion in the way.'
So vanish'd."
            'Then Sir Bors had ridden on
Softly, and sorrowing for our Lancelot,
Because his former madness, once the talk
And scandal of our table, had return'd;
For Lancelot's kith and kin so worship him
That ill to him is ill to them; to Bors
Beyond the rest: he well had been content   [650]
Not to have seen, so Lancelot might have seen,
The Holy Cup of healing; and, indeed,
Being so clouded with his grief and love,
Small heart was his after the Holy Quest:
If God would send the vision, well: if not,
The Quest and he were in the hands of Heaven.

  'And then, with small adventure met, Sir Bors
Rode to the lonest tract of all the realm,
And found a people there among their crags,
Our race and blood, a remnant that were left   [660]
Paynim amid their circles, and the stones°
They pitch up straight to heaven: and their wise men
Were strong in that old magic which can trace
The wandering of the stars, and scoff'd at him

And this high Quest as at a simple thing:
Told him he follow'd—almost Arthur's words—
A mocking fire: "what other fire than he,°
Whereby the blood beats, and the blossom blows,
And the sea rolls, and all the world is warm'd?"
And when his answer chafed them, the rough crowd,   [670]
Hearing he had a difference with their priests,
Seized him, and bound and plunged him into a cell
Of great piled stones; and lying bounden there
In darkness thro' innumerable hours
He heard the hollow-ringing heaven sweep
Over him till by miracle—what else?—
Heavy as it was, a great stone slipt and fell,
Such as no wind could move: and thro' the gap
Glimmer'd the streaming scud: then came a night
Still as the day was loud; and thro' the gap   [680]
The seven clear stars of Arthur's Table Round—°
For, brother, so one night, because they roll
Thro' such a round in heaven, we named the stars,
Rejoicing in ourselves and in our King—
And these, like bright eyes of familiar friends,
In on him shone: "And then to me, to me,"
Said good Sir Bors, "beyond all hopes of mine,
Who scarce had pray'd or ask'd it for myself—
Across the seven clear stars—O grace to me—
In colour like the fingers of a hand   [690]
Before a burning taper, the sweet Grail
Glided and past, and close upon it peal'd
A sharp quick thunder." Afterwards, a maid,
Who kept our holy faith among her kin
In secret, entering, loosed and let him go.'

    To whom the monk: 'And I remember now
That pelican on the casque: Sir Bors it was
Who spake so low and sadly at our board;
And mighty reverent at our grace was he:
A square-set man and honest; and his eyes,   [700]
An out-door sign of all the warmth within,
Smiled with his lips—a smile beneath a cloud,
But heaven had meant it for a sunny one:
Ay, ay, Sir Bors, who else? But when ye reach'd

The city, found ye all your knights return'd,
Or was there sooth in Arthur's prophecy,
Tell me, and what said each, and what the King?'

Then answer'd Percivale: 'And that can I,
Brother, and truly; since the living words
Of so great men as Lancelot and our King   [710]
Pass not from door to door and out again,
But sit within the house. O, when we reach'd
The city, our horses stumbling as they trode
On heaps of ruin, hornless unicorns,
Crack'd basilisks, and splinter'd cockatrices,
And shatter'd talbots, which had left the stones°
Raw, that they fell from, brought us to the hall.

'And there sat Arthur on the daïs-throne,
And those that had gone out upon the Quest,
Wasted and worn, and but a tithe of them,   [720]
And those that had not, stood before the King,
Who, when he saw me, rose, and bad me hail,
Saying, "A welfare in thine eyes reproves
Our fear of some disastrous chance for thee
On hill, or plain, at sea, or flooding ford.
So fierce a gale made havoc here of late
Among the strange devices of our kings;
Yea, shook this newer, stronger hall of ours,
And from the statue Merlin moulded for us
Half-wrench'd a golden wing; but now—the Quest,   [730]
This vision—hast thou seen the Holy Cup,
That Joseph brought of old to Glastonbury?"

'So when I told him all thyself hast heard,
Ambrosius, and my fresh but fixt resolve
To pass away into the quiet life,
He answer'd not, but, sharply turning, ask'd
Of Gawain, "Gawain, was this Quest for thee?"

' "Nay, lord," said Gawain, "not for such as I.
Therefore I communed with a saintly man,
Who made me sure the Quest was not for me;   [740]
For I was much awearied of the Quest:
But found a silk pavilion in a field,

And merry maidens in it; and then this gale
Tore my pavilion from the tenting-pin,
And blew my merry maidens all about
With all discomfort; yea, and but for this,
My twelvemonth and a day were pleasant to me."

'He ceased; and Arthur turn'd to whom at first
He saw not, for Sir Bors, on entering, push'd
Athwart the throng to Lancelot, caught his hand,   [750]
Held it, and there, half-hidden by him, stood,
Until the King espied him, saying to him,
"Hail, Bors! if ever loyal man and true
Could see it, thou hast seen the Grail;" and Bors,
"Ask me not, for I may not speak of it:
I saw it;" and the tears were in his eyes.

'Then there remain'd but Lancelot, for the rest
Spake but of sundry perils in the storm;
Perhaps, like him of Cana in Holy Writ,°
Our Arthur kept his best until the last;   [760]
"Thou, too, my Lancelot," ask'd the King, "my friend,
Our mightiest, hath this Quest avail'd for thee?"

' "Our mightiest!" answer'd Lancelot, with a groan;
"O King!"—and when he paused, methought I spied
A dying fire of madness in his eyes—
"O King, my friend, if friend of thine I be,
Happier are those that welter in their sin,
Swine in the mud, that cannot see for slime,
Slime of the ditch: but in me lived a sin
So strange, of such a kind, that all of pure,   [770]
Noble, and knightly in me twined and clung
Round that one sin, until the wholesome flower
And poisonous grew together, each as each,
Not to be pluck'd asunder; and when thy knights
Sware, I sware with them only in the hope
That could I touch or see the Holy Grail
They might be pluck'd asunder. Then I spake
To one most holy saint, who wept and said,
That save they could be pluck'd asunder, all
My quest were but in vain; to whom I vow'd   [780]
That I would work according as he will'd.

And forth I went, and while I yearn'd and strove
To tear the twain asunder in my heart,
My madness came upon me as of old,
And whipt me into waste fields far away;
There was I beaten down by little men,
Mean knights, to whom the moving of my sword
And shadow of my spear had been enow
To scare them from me once; and then I came
All in my folly to the naked shore,   [790]
Wide flats, where nothing but coarse grasses grew:
But such a blast, my King, began to blow,
So loud a blast along the shore and sea,
Ye could not hear the waters for the blast,
Tho' heapt in mounds and ridges all the sea
Drove like a cataract, and all the sand
Swept like a river, and the clouded heavens
Were shaken with the motion and the sound.
And blackening in the sea-foam sway'd a boat,
Half-swallow'd in it, anchor'd with a chain;   [800]
And in my madness to myself I said,
'I will embark and I will lose myself,
And in the great sea wash away my sin.'
I burst the chain, I sprang into the boat.
Seven days I drove along the dreary deep,
And with me drove the moon and all the stars;
And the wind fell, and on the seventh night
I heard the shingle grinding in the surge,
And felt the boat shock earth, and looking up,
Behold, the enchanted towers of Carbonek,°   [810]
A castle like a rock upon a rock,
With chasm-like portals open to the sea,
And steps that met the breaker! there was none
Stood near it but a lion on each side
That kept the entry, and the moon was full.
Then from the boat I leapt, and up the stairs.
There drew my sword. With sudden-flaring manes
Those two great beasts rose upright like a man,
Each gript a shoulder, and I stood between;
And, when I would have smitten them, heard a voice,   [820]
'Doubt not, go forward; if thou doubt, the beasts
Will tear thee piecemeal.' Then with violence

The sword was dash'd from out my hand, and fell.
And up into the sounding hall I past;
But nothing in the sounding hall I saw,
No bench nor table, painting on the wall
Or shield of knight; only the rounded moon
Thro' the tall oriel on the rolling sea.°
But always in the quiet house I heard,
Clear as a lark, high o'er me as a lark,   [830]
A sweet voice singing in the topmost tower
To the eastward: up I climb'd a thousand steps
With pain: as in a dream I seem'd to climb
For ever: at the last I reach'd a door,
A light was in the crannies, and I heard,
'Glory and joy and honour to our Lord
And to the Holy Vessel of the Grail.'
Then in my madness I essay'd the door;
It gave; and thro' a stormy glare, a heat
As from a seventimes-heated furnace, I,   [840]
Blasted and burnt, and blinded as I was,
With such a fierceness that I swoon'd away—
O, yet methought I saw the Holy Grail,
All pall'd in crimson samite, and around
Great angels, awful shapes, and wings and eyes.
And but for all my madness and my sin,
And then my swooning, I had sworn I saw
That which I saw; but what I saw was veil'd
And cover'd; and this Quest was not for me."

  'So speaking, and here ceasing, Lancelot left   [850]
The hall long silent, till Sir Gawain—nay,
Brother, I need not tell thee foolish words,—
A reckless and irreverent knight was he,
Now bolden'd by the silence of his King,—
Well, I will tell thee: "O King, my liege," he said,
"Hath Gawain fail'd in any quest of thine?
When have I stinted stroke in foughten field?
But as for thine, my good friend Percivale,
Thy holy nun and thou have driven men mad,
Yea, made our mightiest madder than our least.   [860]
But by mine eyes and by mine ears I swear,
I will be deafer than the blue-eyed cat,

And thrice as blind as any noonday owl,
To holy virgins in their ecstasies,
Henceforward."

' "Deafer," said the blameless King,
"Gawain, and blinder unto holy things
Hope not to make thyself by idle vows,
Being too blind to have desire to see.
But if indeed there came a sign from heaven,
Blessèd are Bors, Lancelot and Percivale,   [870]
For these have seen according to their sight.
For every fiery prophet in old times,
And all the sacred madness of the bard,
When God made music thro' them, could but speak
His music by the framework and the chord;
And as ye saw it ye have spoken truth.

' "Nay—but thou errest, Lancelot: never yet
Could all of true and noble in knight and man
Twine round one sin, whatever it might be,
With such a closeness, but apart there grew,   [880]
Save that he were the swine thou spakest of,
Some root of knighthood and pure nobleness;
Whereto see thou, that it may bear its flower.

' "And spake I not too truly, O my knights?
Was I too dark a prophet when I said
To those who went upon the Holy Quest,
That most of them would follow wandering fires,
Lost in the quagmire?—lost to me and gone,
And left me gazing at a barren board,
And a lean Order—scarce return'd a tithe—   [890]
And out of those to whom the vision came
My greatest hardly will believe he saw;
Another hath beheld it afar off,
And leaving human wrongs to right themselves,
Cares but to pass into the silent life.
And one hath had the vision face to face,
And now his chair desires him here in vain,
However they may crown him otherwhere.

‘ "And some among you held, that if the King
Had seen the sight he would have sworn the vow: [900]
Not easily, seeing that the King must guard
That which he rules, and is but as the hind
To whom a space of land is given to plow.
Who may not wander from the allotted field
Before his work be done; but, being done,
Let visions of the night or of the day
Come, as they will; and many a time they come,
Until this earth he walks on seems not earth,
This light that strikes his eyeball is not light,
This air that smites his forehead is not air   [910]
But vision—yea, his very hand and foot—
In moments when he feels he cannot die,
And knows himself no vision to himself,
Nor the high God a vision, nor that One°
Who rose again: ye have seen what ye have seen."

‘So spake the King: I knew not all he meant.’

Rizpah

17—

I

Wailing, wailing, wailing, the wind over land and sea—
And Willy's voice in the wind, 'O mother, come out to me.'
Why should he call me to-night, when he knows that I cannot go?
For the downs are as bright as day, and the full moon stares at
    the snow.

II

We should be seen, my dear; they would spy us out of the town.
The loud black nights for us, and the storm rushing over the down,
When I cannot see my own hand, but am led by the creak of
    the chain,
And grovel and grope for my son till I find myself drenched with
    the rain.

III

Anything fallen again? nay—what was there left to fall?
I have taken them home, I have number'd the bones, I have
    hidden them all.   [10]
What am I saying? and what are *you*? do you come as a spy?
Falls? what falls? who knows? As the tree falls so must it lie.

IV

Who let her in? how long has she been? you—what have you
    heard?°
Why did you sit so quiet? you never have spoken a word.
O—to pray with me—yes—a lady—none of their spies—
But the night has crept into my heart, and begun to darken
    my eyes.

V

Ah—you, that have lived so soft, what should *you* know of
   the night,
The blast and the burning shame and the bitter frost and the
   fright?
I have done it, while you were asleep—you were only made for
   the day.
I have gather'd my baby together—and now you may go
   your way.   [20]

VI

Nay—for it's kind of you, Madam, to sit by an old dying wife.
But say nothing hard of my boy, I have only an hour of life.
I kiss'd my boy in the prison, before he went out to die.
'They dared me to do it,' he said, and he never has told me
   a lie.
I whipt him for robbing an orchard once when he was but
   a child—
'The farmer dared me to do it,' he said; he was always so wild—
And idle—and couldn't be idle—my Willy—he never could rest.
The King should have made him a soldier, he would have been
   one of his best.

VII

But he lived with a lot of wild mates, and they never would
   let him be good;
They swore that he dare not rob the mail, and he swore that
   he would;   [30]
And he took no life, but he took one purse, and when all was
   done
He flung it among his fellows—I'll none of it, said my son.

VIII

I came into court to the Judge and the lawyers. I told them
   my tale,
God's own truth—but they kill'd him, they kill'd him for
   robbing the mail.
They hang'd him in chains for a show—we had always
   borne a good name—

To be hang'd for a thief—and then put away—isn't that enough
   shame?
Dust to dust—low down—let us hide! but they set him so high
That all the ships of the world could stare at him, passing by.
God 'ill pardon the hell-black raven and horrible fowls of the air,
But not the black heart of the lawyer who kill'd him and
   hang'd him there. [40]

IX

And the jailer forced me away. I had bid him my last goodbye;
They had fasten'd the door of his cell. 'O mother!' I heard him
   cry.
I couldn't get back tho' I tried, he had something further to say,
And now I never shall know it. The jailer forced me away.

X

Then since I couldn't but hear that cry of my boy that was
   dead,
They seized me and shut me up: they fasten'd me down on
   my bed.
'Mother, O mother!'—he call'd in the dark to me year after year—
They beat me for that, they beat me—you know that I couldn't
   but hear;
And then at the last they found I had grown so stupid and still
They let me abroad again—but the creatures had worked
   their will. [50]

XI

Flesh of my flesh was gone, but bone of my bone was left—
I stole them all from the lawyers—and you, will you call it a
   theft?—
My baby, the bones that had suck'd me, the bones that had
   laughed and had cried—
Theirs? O no! they are mine—not theirs—they had moved in
   my side.

XII

Do you think I was scared by the bones? I kiss'd 'em, I buried
   'em all—

I can't dig deep, I am old—in the night by the churchyard wall.
My Willy 'ill rise up whole when the trumpet of judgment
    'ill sound,
But I charge you never to say that I laid him in holy ground.

XIII

They would scratch him up—they would hang him again on
    the cursed tree.
Sin? O yes—we are sinners, I know—let all that be,   [60]
And read me a Bible verse of the Lord's good will toward men—
'Full of compassion and mercy, the Lord'—let me hear it again;°
'Full of compassion and mercy—long-suffering.' Yes, O yes!
For the lawyer is born but to murder—the Saviour lives but to
    bless.
He'll never put on the black cap except for the worst of the worst,°
And the first may be last—I have heard it in church—and the
    last may be first.°
Suffering—O long-suffering—yes, as the Lord must know,
Year after year in the mist and the wind and the shower and
    the snow.

XIV

Heard, have you? what? they have told you he never repented
    his sin.
How do they know it? are *they* his mother? are *you* of his kin?   [70]
Heard! have you ever heard, when the storm on the downs began,
The wind that 'ill wail like a child and the sea that 'ill moan like
    a man?

XV

Election, Election and Reprobation—it's all very well.°
But I go to-night to my boy, and I shall not find him in Hell.
For I cared so much for my boy that the Lord has look'd into my
    care,
And He means me I'm sure to be happy with Willy, I know not
    where.

XVI

And if *he* be lost—but to save *my* soul, that is all your desire:
Do you think that I care for *my* soul if my boy be gone to the fire?

I have been with God in the dark—go, go, you may leave me
    alone—
You never have borne a child—you are just as hard as a stone.   [80]

XVII

Madam, I beg your pardon! I think that you mean to be kind,
But I cannot hear what you say for my Willy's voice in the wind—
The snow and the sky so bright—he used but to call in the dark,
And he calls to me now from the church and not from the
    gibbet—for hark!
Nay—you can hear it yourself—it is coming—shaking the walls—
Willy—the moon's in a cloud——Good-night. I am going.
    He calls.

The Revenge

A Ballad of the Fleet

I

At Flores in the Azores Sir Richard Grenville lay,
And a pinnace, like a flutter'd bird, came flying from far away:
'Spanish ships of war at sea! we have sighted fifty-three!'
Then sware Lord Thomas Howard: "Fore God I am no coward;
But I cannot meet them here, for my ships are out of gear,
And the half my men are sick. I must fly, but follow quick.
We are six ships of the line; can we fight with fifty-three?'

II

Then spake Sir Richard Grenville: 'I know you are no coward;
You fly them for a moment to fight with them again.
But I've ninety men and more that are lying sick ashore.   [10]
I should count myself the coward if I left them, my Lord Howard,
To these Inquisition dogs and the devildoms of Spain.'

III

So Lord Howard past away with five ships of war that day,
Till he melted like a cloud in the silent summer heaven;

But Sir Richard bore in hand all his sick men from the land
Very carefully and slow,
Men of Bideford in Devon,
And we laid them on the ballast down below;
For we brought them all aboard,
And they blest him in their pain, that they were not left to Spain,   [20]
To the thumbscrew and the stake, for the glory of the Lord.

IV

He had only a hundred seamen to work the ship and to fight,
And he sailed away from Flores till the Spaniard came in sight,
With his huge sea-castles heaving upon the weather bow.
'Shall we fight or shall we fly?
Good Sir Richard, tell us now,
For to fight is but to die!
There'll be little of us left by the time this sun be set.'
And Sir Richard said again: 'We be all good English men.
Let us bang these dogs of Seville, the children of the devil,   [30]
For I never turn'd my back upon Don or devil yet.'

V

Sir Richard spoke and he laugh'd, and we roar'd a hurrah, and so
The little Revenge ran on sheer into the heart of the foe,
With her hundred fighters on deck, and her ninety sick below;
For half of their fleet to the right and half to the left were seen,
And the little Revenge ran on thro' the long sea-lane between.

VI

Thousands of their soldiers look'd down from their decks and
    laugh'd,
Thousands of their seamen made mock at the mad little craft
Running on and on, till delay'd
By their mountain-like San Philip that, of fifteen hundred tons,   [40]
And up-shadowing high above us with her yawning tiers of guns,
Took the breath from our sails, and we stay'd.

VII

And while now the great San Philip hung above us like a cloud
Whence the thunderbolt will fall

Long and loud,
Four galleons drew away
From the Spanish fleet that day,
And two upon the larboard and two upon the starboard lay,
And the battle-thunder broke from them all.

VIII

But anon the great San Philip, she bethought herself and went [50]
Having that within her womb that had left her ill content;
And the rest they came aboard us, and they fought us hand to hand,
For a dozen times they came with their pikes and musketeers,
And a dozen times we shook 'em off as a dog that shakes his ears
When he leaps from the water to the land.

IX

And the sun went down, and the stars came out far over the summer
sea,
But never a moment ceased the fight of the one and the fifty-three.
Ship after ship, the whole night long, their high-built galleons came,
Ship after ship, the whole night long, with her battle-thunder and
flame;
Ship after ship, the whole night long, drew back with her dead
and her shame. [60]
For some were sunk and many were shatter'd, and so could fight
us no more—
God of battles, was ever a battle like this in the world before?

X

For he said 'Fight on! fight on!'
Tho' his vessel was all but a wreck;
And it chanced that, when half of the short summer night was gone,
With a grisly wound to be drest he had left the deck,
But a bullet struck him that was dressing it suddenly dead,
And himself he was wounded again in the side and the head,
And he said 'Fight on! fight on!'

XI

And the night went down, and the sun smiled out far over the
summer sea, [70]

And the Spanish fleet with broken sides lay round us all in a ring;
But they dared not touch us again, for they fear'd that we still
    could sting,
So they watch'd what the end would be.
And we had not fought them in vain,
But in perilous plight were we,
Seeing forty of our poor hundred were slain,
And half of the rest of us maim'd for life
In the crash of the cannonades and the desperate strife;
And the sick men down in the hold were most of them stark
    and cold,
And the pikes were all broken or bent, and the powder was all of
    it spent;   [80]
And the masts and the rigging were lying over the side;
But Sir Richard cried in his English pride,
'We have fought such a fight for a day and a night
As may never be fought again!
We have won great glory, my men!
And a day less or more
At sea or ashore,
We die—does it matter when?
Sink me the ship, Master Gunner—sink her, split her in twain!
Fall into the hands of God, not into the hands of Spain!'   [90]

XII

And the gunner said 'Ay, ay,' but the seamen made reply:
'We have children, we have wives,
And the Lord hath spared our lives.
We will make the Spaniard promise, if we yield, to let us go;
We shall live to fight again and to strike another blow.'
And the lion there lay dying, and they yielded to the foe.

XIII

And the stately Spanish men to their flagship bore him then,
Where they laid him by the mast, old Sir Richard caught at last,
And they praised him to his face with their courtly foreign
    grace;
But he rose upon their decks, and he cried: [100]
'I have fought for Queen and Faith like a valiant man and true;
I have only done my duty as a man is bound to do:

With a joyful spirit I Sir Richard Grenville die!'
And he fell upon their decks, and he died.

XIV

And they stared at the dead that had been so valiant and true,
And had holden the power and glory of Spain so cheap
That he dared her with one little ship and his English few;
Was he devil or man? He was devil for aught they knew,
But they sank his body with honour down into the deep,
And they mann'd the Revenge with a swarthier alien crew,   [110]
And away she sail'd with her loss and long'd for her own;
When a wind from the lands they had ruin'd awoke from sleep,
And the water began to heave and the weather to moan,
And or ever that evening ended a great gale blew,
And a wave like the wave that is raised by an earthquake grew,
Till it smote on their hulls and their sails and their masts and
    their flags,
And the whole sea plunged and fell on the shot-shatter'd navy
    of Spain,
And the little Revenge herself went down by the island crags
To be lost evermore in the main.

Battle of Brunanburh

Constantinus, King of the Scots, after having sworn allegiance to Athelstan,
allied himself with the Danes of Ireland under Anlaf, and invading England,
was defeated by Athelstan and his brother Edmund with great slaughter at
Brunanburh in the year 937.

I

Athelstan King,
Lord among Earls,
Bracelet-bestower and
Baron of Barons,
He with his brother,
Edmund Atheling,°
Gaining a lifelong

Glory in battle,
Slew with the sword-edge
There by Brunanburh,   [10]
Brake the shield-wall,
Hew'd the lindenwood,°
Hack'd the battleshield,
Sons of Edward with hammer'd brands.

II

Theirs was a greatness
Got from their Grandsires—
Theirs that so often in
Strife with their enemies
Struck for their hoards and their hearths and their homes.

III

Bow'd the spoiler,   [20]
Bent the Scotsman,
Fell the shipcrews
Doom'd to the death.
All the field with blood of the fighters
Flow'd, from when first the great
Sun-star of morningtide,
Lamp of the Lord God
Lord everlasting,
Glode over earth till the glorious creature°
Sank to his setting.   [30]

IV

There lay many a man
Marr'd by the javelin,
Men of the Northland
Shot over shield.
There was the Scotsman
Weary of war.

V

We the West-Saxons,
Long as the daylight

   Lasted, in companies
  Troubled the track of the host that we hated,   [40]
Grimly with swords that were sharp from the grindstone,
Fiercely we hack'd at the flyers before us.

        VI

  Mighty the Mercian,°
  Hard was his hand-play,
  Sparing not any of
  Those that with Anlaf,
  Warriors over the
  Weltering waters
  Borne in the bark's-bosom,
  Drew to this island: [50]
  Doom'd to the death.

        VII

Five young kings put asleep by the sword-stroke,
Seven strong Earls of the army of Anlaf
Fell on the war-field, numberless numbers,
Shipmen and Scotsmen.

        VIII

  Then the Norse leader,
  Dire was his need of it,
  Few were his following,
  Fled to his warship:
Fleeted his vessel to sea with the king in it,   [60]
Saving his life on the fallow flood.

        IX

  Also the crafty one,
  Constantinus,
  Crept to his North again,
  Hoar-headed hero!

        X

  Slender warrant had
  He to be proud of

The welcome of war-knives—
He that was reft of his
Folk and his friends that had   [70]
Fallen in conflict,
Leaving his son too
Lost in the carnage,
Mangled to morsels,
A youngster in war!

XI

Slender reason had
He to be glad of
The clash of the war glaive—°
Traitor and trickster
And spurner of treaties—   [80]
He nor had Anlaf
With armies so broken
A reason for bragging
That they had the better
In perils of battle
On places of slaughter—
The struggle of standards,
The rush of the javelins,
The crash of the charges,
The wielding of weapons—   [90]
The play that they play'd with
The children of Edward.

XII

Then with their nail'd prows
Parted the Norsemen, a
Blood-redden'd relic of
Javelins over
The jarring breaker, the deep-sea billow,
Shaping their way toward Dyflen again,°
Shamed in their souls.

XIII

Also the brethren,   [100]
King and Atheling,

Each in his glory,
Went to his own in his own West-Saxonland,
Glad of the war.

XIV

Many a carcase they left to be carrion,
Many a livid one, many a sallow-skin—
Left for the white-tail'd eagle to tear it, and
Left for the horny-nibb'd raven to rend it, and
Gave to the garbaging war-hawk to gorge it, and
That gray beast, the wolf of the weald.   [110]

XV

Never had huger
Slaughter of heroes
Slain by the sword-edge—
Such as old writers
Have writ of in histories—
Hapt in this isle, since
Up from the East hither
Saxon and Angle from
Over the broad billow
Broke into Britain with   [120]
Haughty war-workers who
Harried the Welshman, when
Earls that were lured by the
Hunger of glory gat
Hold of the land.

The Voyage of Maeldune

(Founded on an Irish legend A.D. 700)

I

I was the chief of the race—he had stricken my father dead—
But I gather'd my fellows together, I swore I would strike off his
head.

Each of them look'd like a king, and was noble in birth as in worth,
And each of them boasted he sprang from the oldest race upon
    earth.
Each was as brave in the fight as the bravest hero of song,
And each of them liefer had died than have done one another a
    wrong.
He lived on an isle in the ocean—we sail'd on a Friday morn—
He that had slain my father the day before I was born.

II

And we came to the isle in the ocean, and there on the shore was he.
But a sudden blast blew us out and away thro' a boundless sea.   [10]

III

And we came to the Silent Isle that we never had touch'd at before,
Where a silent ocean always broke on a silent shore,
And the brooks glitter'd on in the light without sound, and the
    long waterfalls
Pour'd in a thunderless plunge to the base of the mountain walls,
And the poplar and cypress unshaken by storm flourish'd up
    beyond sight,
And the pine shot aloft from the crag to an unbelievable height,
And high in the heaven above it there flicker'd a songless lark,
And the cock couldn't crow, and the bull couldn't low, and
    the dog couldn't bark.
And round it we went, and thro' it, but never a murmur, a breath—
It was all of it fair as life, it was all of it quiet as death,   [20]
And we hated the beautiful Isle, for whenever we strove to speak
Our voices were thinner and fainter than any flittermouse-shriek;°
And the men that were mighty of tongue and could raise such
    a battle-cry
That a hundred who heard it would rush on a thousand lances
    and die—
O they to be dumb'd by the charm!—so fluster'd with anger
    were they
They almost fell on each other; but after we sail'd away.

IV

And we came to the Isle of Shouting, we landed, a score of wild
    birds

Cried from the topmost summit with human voices and words;
Once in an hour they cried, and whenever their voices peal'd
The steer fell down at the plow and the harvest died from the
    field, [30]
And the men dropt dead in the valleys and half of the cattle went
    lame,
And the roof sank in on the hearth, and the dwelling broke into
    flame;
And the shouting of these wild birds ran into the hearts of my crew,
Till they shouted along with the shouting and seized one another
    and slew;
But I drew them the one from the other; I saw that we could not stay,
And we left the dead to the birds and we sail'd with our wounded
    away.

V

And we came to the Isle of Flowers: their breath met us out on
    the seas,
For the Spring and the middle Summer sat each on the lap of the
    breeze;
And the red passion-flower to the cliffs, and the dark-blue
    clematis, clung,
And starr'd with a myriad blossom the long convolvulus hung; [40]
And the topmost spire of the mountain was lilies in lieu of snow,
And the lilies like glaciers winded down, running out below
Thro' the fire of the tulip and poppy, the blaze of gorse, and the
    blush
Of millions of roses that sprang without leaf or a thorn from the
    bush;
And the whole isle-side flashing down from the peak without ever
    a tree
Swept like a torrent of gems from the sky to the blue of the sea;
And we roll'd upon capes of crocus and vaunted our kith and
    our kin,
And we wallow'd in beds of lilies, and chanted the triumph of
    Finn,°
Till each like a golden image was pollen'd from head to feet
And each was as dry as a cricket, with thirst in the middle-day
    heat. [50]
Blossom and blossom, and promise of blossom, but never a fruit!
And we hated the Flowering Isle, as we hated the isle that was mute,

And we tore up the flowers by the million and flung them in bight
 and bay,
And we left but a naked rock, and in anger we sail'd away.

VI

And we came to the Isle of Fruits: all round from the cliffs and the
 capes,
Purple or amber, dangled a hundred fathom of grapes,
And the warm melon lay like a little sun on the tawny sand,
And the fig ran up from the beach and rioted over the land,
And the mountain arose like a jewell'd throne thro' the fragrant air,
Glowing with all-colour'd plums and with golden masses of
 pear,   [60]
And the crimson and scarlet of berries that flamed upon bine
 and vine,
But in every berry and fruit was the poisonous pleasure of wine;
And the peak of the mountain was apples, the hugest that ever
 were seen,
And they prest, as they grew, on each other, with hardly
 a leaflet between,
And all of them redder than rosiest health or than utterest shame,
And setting, when Even descended, the very sunset aflame;
And we stay'd three days, and we gorged and we madden'd, till
 every one drew
His sword on his fellow to slay him, and ever they struck and
 they slew;
And myself, I had eaten but sparely, and fought till I sunder'd
 the fray,
Then I bad them remember my father's death, and we sail'd
 away.   [70]

VII

And we came to the Isle of Fire: we were lured by the light from
 afar,
For the peak sent up one league of fire to the Northern Star;
Lured by the glare and the blare, but scarcely could stand upright,
For the whole isle shudder'd and shook like a man in a mortal
 affright;
We were giddy besides with the fruits we had gorged, and so crazed
 that at last

There were some leap'd into the fire; and away we sail'd, and we past
Over that undersea isle, where the water is clearer than air:
Down we look'd: what a garden! O bliss, what a Paradise there!
Towers of a happier time, low down in a rainbow deep
Silent palaces, quiet fields of eternal sleep!   [80]
And three of the gentlest and best of my people, whate'er I could
    say,
Plunged head down in the sea, and the Paradise trembled away.

VIII

And we came to the Bounteous Isle, where the heavens lean low
    on the land,
And ever at dawn from the cloud glitter'd o'er us a sunbright hand,
Then it open'd and dropt at the side of each man, as he rose from
    his rest,
Bread enough for his need till the labourless day dipt under the
    West;
And we wander'd about it and thro' it. O never was time so good!
And we sang of the triumphs of Finn, and the boast of our
    ancient blood,
And we gazed at the wandering wave as we sat by the gurgle of
    springs,
And we chanted the songs of the Bards and the glories of fairy
    kings;   [90]
But at length we began to be weary, to sigh, and to stretch and
    yawn,
Till we hated the Bounteous Isle and the sunbright hand of the
    dawn,
For there was not an enemy near, but the whole green Isle was our
    own,
And we took to playing at ball, and we took to throwing the stone,
And we took to playing at battle, but that was a perilous play,
For the passion of battle was in us, we slew and we sail'd away.

IX

And we past to the Isle of Witches and heard their musical cry—
'Come to us, O come, come' in the stormy red of a sky
Dashing the fires and the shadows of dawn on the beautiful shapes,
For a wild witch naked as heaven stood on each of the loftiest
    capes,   [100]

And a hundred ranged on the rock like white seabirds in a row,
And a hundred gamboll'd and pranced on the wrecks in the sand
  below,
And a hundred splash'd from the ledges, and bosom'd the burst
  of the spray,
But I knew we should fall on each other, and hastily sail'd away.

X

And we came in an evil time to the Isle of the Double Towers,°
One was of smooth-cut stone, one carved all over with flowers,
But an earthquake always moved in the hollows under the dells,
And they shock'd on each other and butted each other with
  clashing of bells,
And the daws flew out of the Towers and jangled and wrangled
  in vain,
And the clash and boom of the bells rang into the heart and
  the brain,   [110]
Till the passion of battle was on us, and all took sides with the
  Towers,
There were some for the clean-cut stone, there were more for
  the carven flowers,
And the wrathful thunder of God peal'd over us all the day,
For the one half slew the other, and after we sail'd away.

XI

And we came to the Isle of a Saint who had sail'd with St
  Brendan of yore,°
He had lived ever since on the Isle and his winters were fifteen
  score,
And his voice was low as from other worlds, and his eyes were
  sweet,
And his white hair sank to his heels and his white beard fell to his
  feet,
And he spake to me, 'O Maeldune, let be this purpose of thine!
Remember the words of the Lord when he told us "Vengeance
  is mine!"   [120]
His fathers have slain thy fathers in war or in single strife,
Thy fathers have slain his fathers, each taken a life for a life,
Thy father had slain his father, how long shall the murder last?
Go back to the Isle of Finn and suffer the Past to be Past.'

And we kiss'd the fringe of his beard and we pray'd as we heard
    him pray,
And the Holy man he assoil'd us, and sadly we sail'd away.°

XII

And we came to the Isle we were blown from, and there on the
    shore was he,
The man that had slain my father. I saw him and let him be.
O weary was I of the travel, the trouble, the strife and the sin,
When I landed again, with a tithe of my men, on the Isle of
    Finn.°   [130]

De Profundis

The Two Greetings

I

Out of the deep, my child, out of the deep,
Where all that was to be, in all that was,
Whirl'd for a million æons thro' the vast
Waste dawn of multitudinous-eddying light—
Out of the deep, my child, out of the deep,
Thro' all this changing world of changeless law,
And every phase of ever-heightening life,
And nine long months of antenatal gloom,
With this last moon, this crescent—her dark orb
Touch'd with earth's light—thou comest, darling boy;   [10]
Our own; a babe in lineament and limb
Perfect, and prophet of the perfect man;
Whose face and form are hers and mine in one,
Indissolubly married like our love;
Live, and be happy in thyself, and serve
This mortal race thy kin so well, that men
May bless thee as we bless thee, O young life
Breaking with laughter from the dark; and may
The fated channel where thy motion lives
Be prosperously shaped, and sway thy course   [20]
Along the years of haste and random youth

Unshatter'd; then full-current thro' full man;
And last in kindly curves, with gentlest fall,
By quiet fields, a slowly-dying power,
To that last deep where we and thou are still.

II

I

Out of the deep, my child, out of the deep,
From that great deep, before our world begins,
Whereon the Spirit of God moves as he will—
Out of the deep, my child, out of the deep,
From that true world within the world we see, [30]
Whereof our world is but the bounding shore—
Out of the deep, Spirit, out of the deep,
With this ninth moon, that sends the hidden sun
Down yon dark sea, thou comest, darling boy.

II

For in the world, which is not ours, They said
'Let us make man' and that which should be man,
From that one light no man can look upon,
Drew to this shore lit by the suns and moons
And all the shadows. O dear Spirit half-lost
In thine own shadow and this fleshly sign [40]
That thou art thou—who wailest being born
And banish'd into mystery, and the pain
Of this divisible-indivisible world
Among the numerable-innumerable
Sun, sun, and sun, thro' finite-infinite space
In finite-infinite Time—our mortal veil
And shatter'd phantom of that infinite One,
Who made thee unconceivably Thyself
Out of His whole World-self and all in all—
Live thou! and of the grain and husk, the grape [50]
And ivyberry, choose; and still depart
From death to death thro' life and life, and find
Nearer and ever nearer Him, who wrought
Not Matter, nor the finite-infinite,
But this main-miracle, that thou art thou,
With power on thine own act and on the world.

'Frater Ave atque Vale'

Row us out from Desenzano, to your Sirmione row!°
So they row'd, and there we landed—'O venusta Sirmio!'°
There to me thro' all the groves of olive in the summer glow,
There beneath the Roman ruin where the purple flowers grow,
Came that 'Ave atque Vale' of the Poet's hopeless woe,
Tenderest of Roman poets nineteen-hundred years ago,
'Frater Ave atque Vale'—as we wander'd to and fro
Gazing at the Lydian laughter of the Garda Lake below°
Sweet Catullus's all-but-island, olive-silvery Sirmio!

To Virgil

Written at the Request of the Mantuans for the Nineteenth Centenary of Virgil's Death

I

Roman Virgil, thou that singest
    Ilion's lofty temples robed in fire,
Ilion falling, Rome arising,
    wars, and filial faith, and Dido's pyre;°

II

Landscape-lover, lord of language
    more than he that sang the Works and Days,°
All the chosen coin of fancy
    flashing out from many a golden phrase;

III

Thou that singest wheat and woodland,
    tilth and vineyard, hive and horse and herd;   [10]
All the charm of all the Muses
    often flowering in a lonely word;

IV

Poet of the happy Tityrus
    piping underneath his beechen bowers;
Poet of the poet-satyr°
    whom the laughing shepherd bound with flowers;

V

Chanter of the Pollio, glorying°
    in the blissful years again to be,
Summers of the snakeless meadow,
    unlaborious earth and oarless sea;   [20]

VI

Thou that seëst Universal
    Nature moved by Universal Mind;
Thou majestic in thy sadness
    at the doubtful doom of human kind;

VII

Light among the vanish'd ages;
    star that gildest yet this phantom shore;
Golden branch amid the shadows,
    kings and realms that pass to rise no more;

VIII

Now thy Forum roars no longer,
    fallen every purple Cæsar's dome—   [30]
Tho' thine ocean-roll of rhythm
    sound for ever of Imperial Rome—

IX

Now the Rome of slaves hath perish'd,
    and the Rome of freemen holds her place,°
I, from out the Northern Island
    sunder'd once from all the human race,

X

I salute thee, Mantovano,°
    I that loved thee since my day began,
Wielder of the stateliest measure
    ever moulded by the lips of man.   [40]

Vastness

I

Many a hearth upon our dark globe sighs after many a vanish'd
    face,
Many a planet by many a sun may roll with the dust of a vanish'd
    race.

II

Raving politics, never at rest—as this poor earth's pale history
    runs,—
What is it all but a trouble of ants in the gleam of a million
    million of suns?

III

Lies upon this side, lies upon that side, truthless violence
    mourn'd by the Wise,
Thousands of voices drowning his own in a popular torrent of
    lies upon lies;

IV

Stately purposes, valour in battle, glorious annals of army and fleet,
Death for the right cause, death for the wrong cause, trumpets
    of victory, groans of defeat;

V

Innocence seethed in her mother's milk, and Charity setting the
    martyr aflame;
Thraldom who walks with the banner of Freedom, and recks not
    to ruin a realm in her name.   [10]

VI

Faith at her zenith, or all but lost in the gloom of doubts that darken
the schools;
Craft with a bunch of all-heal in her hand, follow'd up by her
vassal legion of fools;°

VII

Trade flying over a thousand seas with her spice and her vintage,
her silk and her corn;
Desolate offing, sailorless harbours, famishing populace,
wharves forlorn;

VIII

Star of the morning, Hope in the sunrise; gloom of the evening,
Life at a close;
Pleasure who flaunts on her wide down-way with her flying robe
and her poison'd rose;

IX

Pain, that has crawl'd from the corpse of Pleasure, a worm
which writhes all day, and at night
Stirs up again in the heart of the sleeper, and stings him back to
the curse of the light;

X

Wealth with his wines and his wedded harlots; honest Poverty,
bare to the bone;
Opulent Avarice, lean as Poverty; Flattery gilding the rift in
a throne;   [20]

XI

Fame blowing out from her golden trumpet a jubilant challenge
to Time and to Fate;
Slander, her shadow, sowing the nettle on all the laurel'd graves
of the Great;

XII

Love for the maiden, crown'd with marriage, no regrets for aught
that has been,
Household happiness, gracious children, debtless competence,
golden mean;

XIII

National hatreds of whole generations, and pigmy spites of the
    village spire;
Vows that will last to the last death-ruckle, and vows that are
    snapt in a moment of fire;

XIV

He that has lived for the lust of the minute, and died in the doing it,
    flesh without mind;
He that has nail'd all flesh to the Cross, till Self died out in the love
    of his kind;

XV

Spring and Summer and Autumn and Winter, and all these old
    revolutions of earth;
All new-old revolutions of Empire—change of the tide—what
    is all of it worth?   [30]

XVI

What the philosophies, all the sciences, poesy, varying voices of
    prayer?
All that is noblest, all that is basest, all that is filthy with all that
    is fair?

XVII

What is it all, if we all of us end but in being our own corpse-
    coffins at last,
Swallow'd in Vastness, lost in Silence, drown'd in the deeps of
    a meaningless Past?

XVIII

What but a murmur of gnats in the gloom, or a moment's anger
    of bees in their hive?—

    .   .   .   .   .   .

Peace, let it be! for I loved him, and love him for ever: the dead
    are not dead but alive.°

Locksley Hall Sixty Years After

Late, my grandson! half the morning have I paced these sandy
   tracts,
Watch'd again the hollow ridges roaring into cataracts,

Wander'd back to living boyhood while I heard the curlews call,
I myself so close on death, and death itself in Locksley Hall.

So—your happy suit was blasted—she the faultless, the divine;
And you liken—boyish babble—this boy-love of yours with mine.

I myself have often babbled doubtless of a foolish past;
Babble, babble; our old England may go down in babble at last.

'Curse him!' curse your fellow-victim? call him dotard in your
   rage?
Eyes that lured a doting boyhood well might fool a dotard's age.   [10]

Jilted for a wealthier! wealthier? yet perhaps she was not wise;
I remember how you kiss'd the miniature with those sweet eyes.

In the hall there hangs a painting—Amy's arms about my neck—
Happy children in a sunbeam sitting on the ribs of wreck.

In my life there was a picture, she that clasp'd my neck had flown;
I was left within the shadow sitting on the wreck alone.

Yours has been a slighter ailment, will you sicken for her sake?
You, not you! your modern amourist is of easier, earthlier make.

Amy loved me, Amy fail'd me, Amy was a timid child;
But your Judith—but your worldling—*she* had never driven
   me wild.   [20]

She that holds the diamond necklace dearer than the golden ring,
She that finds a winter sunset fairer than a morn of Spring.°

She that in her heart is brooding on his briefer lease of life,
While she vows 'till death shall part us,' she the would-be-widow wife.

She the worldling born of worldlings—father, mother—be
   content,
Ev'n the homely farm can teach us there is something in descent.

Yonder in that chapel, slowly sinking now into the ground,
Lies the warrior, my forefather, with his feet upon the hound.

Cross'd! for once he sail'd the sea to crush the Moslem in his
    pride;°
Dead the warrior, dead his glory, dead the cause in which he
    died.   [30]

Yet how often I and Amy in the mouldering aisle have stood,
Gazing for one pensive moment on that founder of our blood.

There again I stood to-day, and where of old we knelt in prayer,
Close beneath the casement crimson with the shield of
    Locksley—there,

All in white Italian marble, looking still as if she smiled,
Lies my Amy dead in child-birth, dead the mother, dead the
    child.

Dead—and sixty years ago, and dead her aged husband now—
I this old white-headed dreamer stoopt and kiss'd her marble
    brow.

Gone the fires of youth, the follies, furies, curses, passionate
    tears,
Gone like fires and floods and earthquakes of the planet's
    dawning years.   [40]

Fires that shook me once, but now to silent ashes fall'n away.
Cold upon the dead volcano sleeps the gleam of dying day.

Gone the tyrant of my youth, and mute below the chancel
    stones,
All his virtues—I forgive them—black in white above his bones.°

Gone the comrades of my bivouac, some in fight against the foe,
Some thro' age and slow diseases, gone as all on earth will go.

Gone with whom for forty years my life in golden sequence ran,
She with all the charm of woman, she with all the breadth of man,

Strong in will and rich in wisdom, Edith, yet so lowly-sweet,
Woman to her inmost heart, and woman to her tender feet,   [50]

Very woman of very woman, nurse of ailing body and mind,
She that link'd again the broken chain that bound me to my kind.

Here to-day was Amy with me, while I wander'd down the coast,
Near us Edith's holy shadow, smiling at the slighter ghost.

Gone our sailor son thy father, Leonard early lost at sea;
Thou alone, my boy, of Amy's kin and mine art left to me.

Gone thy tender-natured mother, wearying to be left alone,
Pining for the stronger heart that once had beat beside her own.

Truth, for Truth is Truth, he worshipt, being true as he was
     brave;
Good, for Good is Good, he follow'd, yet he look'd beyond
     the grave,   [60]

Wiser there than you, that crowning barren Death as lord of all,
Deem this over-tragic drama's closing curtain is the pall!

Beautiful was death in him, who saw the death, but kept the deck,
Saving women and their babes, and sinking with the sinking wreck,

Gone for ever! Ever? no—for since our dying race began,
Ever, ever, and for ever was the leading light of man.

Those that in barbarian burials kill'd the slave, and slew the wife,
Felt within themselves the sacred passion of the second life.

Indian warriors dream of ampler hunting grounds beyond the
     night;
Ev'n the black Australian dying hopes he shall return, a white.   [70]

Truth for truth, and good for good! The Good, the True, the
     Pure, the Just—
Take the charm 'For ever' from them, and they crumble into
     dust.

Gone the cry of 'Forward, Forward,' lost within a growing
     gloom;
Lost, or only heard in silence from the silence of a tomb.

Half the marvels of my morning, triumphs over time and space,
Staled by frequence, shrunk by usage into commonest
     commonplace!

'Forward' rang the voices then, and of the many mine was one.
Let us hush this cry of 'Forward' till ten thousand years have gone.

Far among the vanish'd races, old Assyrian kings would flay
Captives whom they caught in battle—iron-hearted victors
     they.   [80]

Ages after, while in Asia, he that led the wild Moguls,
Timur built his ghastly tower of eighty thousand human skulls,°

Then, and here in Edward's time, an age of noblest English
names,°
Christian conquerors took and flung the conquer'd
Christian into flames.

Love your enemy, bless your haters, said the Greatest of the
great;
Christian love among the Churches look'd the twin of heathen
hate.

From the golden alms of Blessing man had coin'd himself a
curse:
Rome of Cæsar, Rome of Peter, which was crueller? which was
worse?°

France had shown a light to all men, preach'd a Gospel, all
men's good;
Celtic Demos rose a Demon, shriek'd and slaked the light
with blood.°   [90]

Hope was ever on her mountain, watching till the day begun—
Crown'd with sunlight—over darkness—from the still
unrisen sun.

Have we grown at last beyond the passions of the primal clan?
'Kill your enemy, for you hate him,' still, 'your enemy' was
a man.

Have we sunk below them? peasants maim the helpless horse,
and drive
Innocent cattle under thatch, and burn the kindlier brutes alive.

Brutes, the brutes are not your wrongers—burnt at midnight,
found at morn,
Twisted hard in mortal agony with their offspring, born-unborn,°

Clinging to the silent mother! Are we devils? are we men?
Sweet St Francis of Assisi, would that he were here again,°   [100]

He that in his Catholic wholeness used to call the very flowers
Sisters, brothers—and the beasts—whose pains are hardly
less than ours!

Chaos, Cosmos! Cosmos, Chaos! who can tell how all will end?
Read the wide world's annals, you, and take their wisdom
   for your friend.

Hope the best, but hold the Present fatal daughter of the Past,
Shape your heart to front the hour, but dream not that the
   hour will last.

Ay, if dynamite and revolver leave you courage to be wise:
When was age so cramm'd with menace? madness? written,
   spoken lies?

Envy wears the mask of Love, and, laughing sober fact to scorn,
Cries to Weakest as to Strongest, 'Ye are equals, equal-
   born.'   [110]

Equal-born? O yes, if yonder hill be level with the flat.
Charm us, Orator, till the Lion took no larger than the Cat,

Till the Cat thro' that mirage of overheated language loom
Larger than the Lion,—Demos end in working its own doom.

Russia bursts our Indian barrier, shall we fight her? shall we
   yield?°
Pause! before you sound the trumpet, hear the voices from the
   field.

Those three hundred millions under one Imperial sceptre now,
Shall we hold them? shall we loose them? take the suffrage of
   the plow.°

Nay, but these would feel and follow Truth if only you and you,
Rivals of realm-ruining party, when you speak were wholly
   true.   [120]

Plowmen, Shepherds, have I found, and more than once, and
   still could find,
Sons of God, and kings of men in utter nobleness of mind,

Truthful, trustful, looking upward to the practised hustings-
   liar;°
So the Higher wields the Lower, while the Lower is the Higher.

Here and there a cotter's babe is royal-born by right divine;
Here and there my lord is lower than his oxen or his swine.

Chaos, Cosmos! Cosmos, Chaos! once again the sickening
    game;
Freedom, free to slay herself, and dying while they shout her
    name.

Step by step we gain'd a freedom known to Europe, known to all;
Step by step we rose to greatness,—thro' the tonguesters
    we may fall.   [130]

You that woo the Voices—tell them 'old experience is a fool,'°
Teach your flatter'd kings that only those who cannot read can
    rule.

Pluck the mighty from their seat, but set no meek ones in their
    place;
Pillory Wisdom in your markets, pelt your offal at her face.

Tumble Nature heel o'er head, and, yelling with the yelling
    street,
Set the feet above the brain and swear the brain is in the feet.

Bring the old dark ages back without the faith, without the hope,
Break the State, the Church, the Throne, and roll their ruins
    down the slope.

Authors—essayist, atheist, novelist, realist, rhymester, play
    your part,
Paint the mortal shame of nature with the living hues of Art.   [140]

Rip your brothers' vices open, strip your own foul passions bare;
Down with Reticence, down with Reverence—forward—
    naked—let them stare.

Feed the budding rose of boyhood with the drainage of your
    sewer;
Send the drain into the fountain, lest the stream should issue
    pure.

Set the maiden fancies wallowing in the troughs of Zolaism,—°
Forward, forward, ay and backward, downward too into the
    abysm.

Do your best to charm the worst, to lower the rising race of
    men;
Have we risen from out the beast, then back into the beast again?

Only 'dust to dust' for me that sicken at your lawless din,
Dust in wholesome old-world dust before the newer world
    begin.   [150]

Heated am I? you—you wonder—well, it scarce becomes
    mine age—
Patience! let the dying actor mouth his last upon the stage.

Cries of unprogressive dotage ere the dotard fall asleep?
Noises of a current narrowing, not the music of a deep?

Ay, for doubtless I am old, and think gray thoughts, for I am gray:
After all the stormy changes shall we find a changeless May?

After madness, after massacre, Jacobinism and Jacquerie,°
Some diviner force to guide us thro' the days I shall not see?

When the schemes and all the systems, Kingdoms and
    Republics fall,
Something kindlier, higher, holier—all for each and each
    for all?   [160]

All the full-brain, half-brain races, led by Justice, Love, and Truth;
All the millions one at length with all the visions of my youth?

All diseases quench'd by Science, no man halt, or deaf or blind;
Stronger ever born of weaker, lustier body, larger mind?

Earth at last a warless world, a single race, a single tongue—
I have seen her far away—for is not Earth as yet so young?—

Every tiger madness muzzled, every serpent passion kill'd,
Every grim ravine a garden, every blazing desert till'd,

Robed in universal harvest up to either pole she smiles,
Universal ocean softly washing all her warless Isles.   [170]

Warless? when her tens are thousands, and her thousands
    millions, then—
All her harvest all too narrow—who can fancy warless men?

Warless? war will die out late then. Will it ever? late or soon?
Can it, till this outworn earth be dead as yon dead world
    the moon?

Dead the new astronomy calls her. . . . On this day and at this
    hour,

In this gap between the sandhills, whence you see the Locksley
    tower,

Here we met, our latest meeting—Amy—sixty years ago—
She and I—the moon was falling greenish thro' a rosy glow,

Just above the gateway tower, and even where you see her now—
Here we stood and claspt each other, swore the seeming-
    deathless vow. . . .   [180]

Dead, but how her living glory lights the hall, the dune, the
    grass!
Yet the moonlight is the sunlight, and the sun himself will pass.

Venus near her! smiling downward at this earthlier earth of ours,
Closer on the Sun, perhaps a world of never fading flowers.

Hesper, whom the poet call'd the Bringer home of all good
    things.°
All good things may move in Hesper, perfect peoples, perfect kings.

Hesper—Venus—were we native to that splendour or in Mars,
We should see the Globe we groan in, fairest of their evening stars.

Could we dream of wars and carnage, craft and madness, lust
    and spite,
Roaring London, raving Paris, in that point of peaceful light?   [190]

Might we not in glancing heavenward on a star so silver-fair,
Yearn, and clasp the hands and murmur, 'Would to God that
    we were there'?

Forward, backward, backward, forward, in the immeasurable sea,
Sway'd by vaster ebbs and flows than can be known to you or me.

All the suns—are these but symbols of innumerable man,
Man or Mind that sees a shadow of the planner or the plan?

Is there evil but on earth? or pain in every peopled sphere?
Well be grateful for the sounding watchword, 'Evolution' here,

Evolution ever climbing after some ideal good,
And Reversion ever dragging Evolution in the mud.   [200]

What are men that He should heed us? cried the king of sacred
    song;°
Insects of an hour, that hourly work their brother insect wrong,

While the silent Heavens roll, and Suns along their fiery way,
All their planets whirling round them, flash a million miles a day.

Many an Æon moulded earth before her highest, man, was born,
Many an Æon too may pass when earth is manless and forlorn,

Earth so huge, and yet so bounded—pools of salt, and plots
     of land—
Shallow skin of green and azure—chains of mountain, grains
     of sand!

Only That which made us, meant us to be mightier by and by,
Set the sphere of all the boundless Heavens within the human
     eye,   [210]

Sent the shadow of Himself, the boundless, thro' the human
     soul;
Boundless inward, in the atom, boundless outward, in the
     Whole.

     .   .   .   .

Here is Locksley Hall, my grandson, here the lion-guarded gate.
Not to-night in Locksley Hall—to-morrow—you, you come
     so late.

Wreck'd—your train—or all but wreck'd? a shatter'd wheel?
     a vicious boy!
Good, this forward, you that preach it, is it well to wish you joy?

Is it well that while we range with Science, glorying in the Time,
City children soak and blacken soul and sense in city slime?

There among the glooming alleys Progress halts on palsied feet,
Crime and hunger cast our maidens by the thousand on the
     street.   [220]

There the Master scrimps his haggard sempstress of her daily
     bread,
There a single sordid attic holds the living and the dead.

There the smouldering fire of fever creeps across the rotted floor,
And the crowded couch of incest in the warrens of the poor.

Nay, your pardon, cry your 'forward,' yours are hope and youth,
     but I—
Eighty winters leave the dog too lame to follow with the cry,

Lame and old, and past his time, and passing now into the night;
Yet I would the rising race were half as eager for the light.

Light the fading gleam of Even? light the glimmer of the dawn?
Aged eyes may take the growing glimmer for the gleam
    withdrawn.   [230]

Far away beyond her myriad coming changes earth will be
Something other than the wildest modern guess of you and me.

Earth may reach her earthly-worst, or if she gain her earthly-
    best,
Would she find her human offspring this ideal man at rest?

Forward then, but still remember how the course of Time will
    swerve,
Crook and turn upon itself in many a backward streaming curve.

Not the Hall to-night, my grandson! Death and Silence hold
    their own.
Leave the Master in the first dark hour of his last sleep alone.°

Worthier soul was he than I am, sound and honest, rustic
    Squire,
Kindly landlord, boon companion—youthful jealousy is a
    liar.   [240]

Cast the poison from your bosom, oust the madness from
    your brain.
Let the trampled serpent show you that you have not lived
    in vain.

Youthful! youth and age are scholars yet but in the lower school,
Nor is he the wisest man who never proved himself a fool.

Yonder lies our young sea-village—Art and Grace are less
    and less:
Science grows and Beauty dwindles—roofs of slated
    hideousness!

There is one old Hostel left us where they swing the Locksley
    shield,
Till the peasant cow shall butt the 'Lion passant' from his field.

Poor old Heraldry, poor old History, poor old Poetry, passing
    hence,

In the common deluge drowning old political common-sense!   [250]

Poor old voice of eighty crying after voices that have fled!
All I loved are vanish'd voices, all my steps are on the dead.

All the world is ghost to me, and as the phantom disappears,
Forward far and far from here is all the hope of eighty years.

.   .   .   .

In this Hostel—I remember—I repent it o'er his grave—
Like a clown—by chance he met me—I refused the hand he
    gave.

From that casement where the trailer mantles all the
    mouldering bricks—
I was then in early boyhood, Edith but a child of six—

While I shelter'd in this archway from a day of driving
    showers—
Peept the winsome face of Edith like a flower among the
    flowers.   [260]

Here to-night! the Hall to-morrow, when they toll the Chapel
    bell!
Shall I hear in one dark room a wailing, 'I have loved thee well.'

Then a peal that shakes the portal—one has come to claim his
    bride,
Her that shrank, and put me from her, shriek'd, and started
    from my side—

Silent echoes! You, my Leonard, use and not abuse your day,
Move among your people, know them, follow him who led
    the way,

Strove for sixty widow'd years to help his homelier brother men,
Served the poor, and built the cottage, raised the school, and
    drain'd the fen.

Hears he now the Voice that wrong'd him? who shall swear it
    cannot be?
Earth would never touch her worst, were one in fifty such
    as he.   [270]

Ere she gain her Heavenly-best, a God must mingle with
    the game:

Nay, there may be those about us whom we neither see nor
    name,

Felt within us as ourselves, the Powers of Good, the Powers of Ill,
Strowing balm, or shedding poison in the fountains of the Will.

Follow you the Star that lights a desert pathway, yours or mine.
Forward, till you see the highest Human Nature is divine.

Follow Light, and do the Right—for man can half-control his
    doom—
Till you find the deathless Angel seated in the vacant tomb.°

Forward, let the stormy moment fly and mingle with the Past.
I that loathed, have come to love him. Love will conquer at
    the last.   [280]

Gone at eighty, mine own age, and I and you will bear the pall;
Then I leave thee Lord and Master, latest Lord of Locksley Hall.

Far—Far—Away

(For Music)

What sight so lured him thro' the fields he knew
As where earth's green stole into heaven's own hue,
                Far—far—away?

What sound was dearest in his native dells?
The mellow lin-lan-lone of evening bells
                Far—far—away.

What vague world-whisper, mystic pain or joy,
Thro' those three words would haunt him when a boy,
                Far—far—away?

A whisper from his dawn of life? a breath   [10]
From some fair dawn beyond the doors of death
                Far—far—away?

Far, far, how far? from o'er the gates of Birth,
The faint horizons, all the bounds of earth,
                Far—far—away?

What charm in words, a charm no words could give?
O dying words, can Music make you live
                  Far—far—away?

Merlin and the Gleam

I

O young Mariner,
You from the haven
Under the sea-cliff,
You that are watching
The gray Magician
With eyes of wonder,
I am Merlin,
And *I* am dying,
I am Merlin
Who follow The Gleam.   [10]

II

Mighty the Wizard°
Who found me at sunrise
Sleeping, and woke me
And learn'd me Magic!
Great the Master,
And sweet the Magic,
When over the valley,
In early summers,
Over the mountain,
On human faces,   [20]
And all around me,
Moving to melody,
Floated The Gleam.

III

Once at the croak of a Raven who crost it,°
A barbarous people,

Blind to the magic,
And deaf to the melody,
Snarl'd at and cursed me.
A demon vext me,
The light retreated,   [30]
The landskip darken'd,
The melody deaden'd,
The Master whisper'd
'Follow The Gleam.'

IV

Then to the melody,
Over a wilderness
Gliding, and glancing at
Elf of the woodland,
Gnome of the cavern,
Griffin and Giant,   [40]
And dancing of Fairies
In desolate hollows,
And wraiths of the mountain,
And rolling of dragons
By warble of water,
Or cataract music
Of falling torrents,
Flitted The Gleam.

V

Down from the mountain
And over the level,
And streaming and shining on   [50]
Silent river,
Silvery willow,
Pasture and plowland,
Innocent maidens,
Garrulous children,
Homestead and harvest,
Reaper and gleaner,
And rough-ruddy faces
Of lowly labour,   [60]
Slided The Gleam—

VI

Then, with a melody
Stronger and statelier,
Led me at length
To the city and palace
Of Arthur the king;°
Touch'd at the golden
Cross of the churches,
Flash'd on the Tournament,
Flicker'd and bicker'd   [70]
From helmet to helmet,
And last on the forehead
Of Arthur the blameless
Rested The Gleam.

VII

Clouds and darkness
Closed upon Camelot;
Arthur had vanish'd°
I knew not whither,
The king who loved me,
And cannot die;   [80]
For out of the darkness
Silent and slowly
The Gleam, that had waned to a wintry glimmer
On icy fallow
And faded forest,
Drew to the valley
Named of the shadow,
And slowly brightening
Out of the glimmer,
And slowly moving again to a melody   [90]
Yearningly tender,
Fell on the shadow,
No longer a shadow,
But clothed with The Gleam.

VIII

And broader and brighter
The Gleam flying onward,

Wed to the melody,
Sang thro' the world;
And slower and fainter,
Old and weary, [100]
But eager to follow,
I saw, whenever
In passing it glanced upon
Hamlet or city,
That under the Crosses
The dead man's garden,
The mortal hillock,
Would break into blossom;
And so to the land's
Last limit I came— [110]
And can no longer,
But die rejoicing,
For thro' the Magic
Of Him the Mighty,
Who taught me in childhood,
There on the border
Of boundless Ocean,
And all but in Heaven
Hovers The Gleam.

IX

Not of the sunlight, [120]
Not of the moonlight,
Not of the starlight!
O young Mariner,
Down to the haven,
Call your companions,
Launch your vessel,
And crowd your canvas,
And, ere it vanishes
Over the margin,
After it, follow it, [130]
Follow The Gleam.

Crossing the Bar

Sunset and evening star,
    And one clear call for me!
And may there be no moaning of the bar,
    When I put out to sea,

But such a tide as moving seems asleep,
    Too full for sound and foam,
When that which drew from out the boundless deep
    Turns again home.

Twilight and evening bell,
    And after that the dark!   [10]
And may there be no sadness of farewell,
    When I embark;

For tho' from out our bourne of Time and Place
    The flood may bear me far,
I hope to see my Pilot face to face
    When I have crost the bar.

PROSE

LETTERS AND JOURNAL ENTRIES

1. *To* Mary Anne Fytche

My dear Aunt

When I was at Louth,° you used to tell me, that you should be obliged to me, if I would write to you, and give you my remarks on works and authors. I shall now fulfill this promise, which I made at that time. Going into the Library this morning, I picked up 'Sampson Agonistes,' on which (as I think it is a play you like) I shall send you my remarks. The first scene is the Lamentation of Sampson, which possesses much pathos and sublimity. This passage 'restless thoughts, that like a deadly swarm of hornets arm'd no sooner found alone, But rush upon me thronging, and present Times past, what once I was, and what am now,'° puts me in mind of that in Dante, which Lord Byron has prefixed to his Corsair. 'Nessun maggior dolore, Che recordarsi del tempo felice, nella miseria.'° His complaint of his blindness is particularly beautiful,

> 'Oh! loss of sight, of thee I most complain!
> 'Blind among enemies, O worse than chains,
> 'Dungeon, or beggary, or decrepit age!
> 'Light, the prime work of God, to me is extinct,
> 'And all her various objects of delight
> 'Annulled; which might in part my grief have eased,
> 'Inferior to the vilest now become
> 'Of man, or worm, the vilest here excel me,
> 'They weep, yet see; I dark in light exposed
> 'To daily fraud, contempt, abuse, and wrong—
> 'Scarce half I seem to live, dead more than half,
> 'O dark, dark, dark, amid the blaze of noon,
> 'Irrecoverably dark, total eclipse
> 'Without all hope of day.
> 'O first created beam, and thou great word
> 'Let there be light, and light was over all,
> 'Why was I thus bereaved thy prime decree?'

I think this is beautiful, particularly 'O dark, dark, dark, amid the blaze of Noon.' After a long lamentation of Sampson, the Chorus enters, saying these words: 'This, this is he, softly a while, Let us not break in upon him, O change beyond report, thought, or belief! See how he lies at random carelessly *diffused*.' If you look into Bishop Newton's° notes, you will find that he informs you that 'this beautiful application of the word "diffused," is borrowed from the Latin.' It has the same meaning as 'temere' in one of the Odes of Horace, Book the second.

> 'Sic temere, et rosâ
> 'Canos adorati capillos.'°

Of which this is a free Translation 'Why lie we not at random, under the shade of the plantain (sub platano) having our hoary head perfumed with rose-water.' To an English reader the metre of the Chorus may seem unusual, but the difficulty will vanish when I inform him, that it is taken from the Greek. In line 133d, there is this expression 'Chalybean tempered steel.' The Chalybes were a nation among the ancients very famous for the making of steel: hence the expression 'Chalybean' or 'peculiar to the Chalybes.' In line 147th 'the gates of Azza' this probably (as Bishop Newton observes) was to avoid too great an alliteration which the 'Gates of Gaza' would have caused, though (in my opinion) it would have rendered it more beautiful: and (though I do not affirm it as a fact), perhaps, Milton gave it that name for the sake of novelty, as all the world knows he was a great pedant. I have not, at present, time to write any more: perhaps I may continue my remarks in another letter to you: but (as I am very volatile and fickle) you must not depend on me for, I think, you do not know any one who is so fickle, as

> Your affectionate nephew
> A. Tennyson

Frederick informed me that Grandmamma was quite growing dissipated, going out to parties, every night. The Russells, and Grandmamma Tennyson are to be at Dalby on Tuesday the 23rd, and I also hope to be taken by Papa and Mama who are invited. Frederick made Mama promise to write him an account of the visit, but if I go, I shall take the trouble from Mamma.

2. *To* ELIZABETH RUSSELL

April 18, [1828]

My dear Aunt

I am sitting Owl-like and solitary in my rooms (nothing between me and the stars but a stratum of tiles) the hoof of the steed, the roll of the wheel, the shouts of drunken Gown and drunken Town come up from below with a sea-like murmur. I wish to Heaven I had Prince Houssain's° fairy carpet to transport me along the deeps of air to your Coterie—nay, I would even take up with his brother Aboul-something's glass for the mere pleasure of a peep. What a pity it is that the golden days of Faerie are over! What a misery not to be able to consolidate our gossamer dreams into reality! Be it so. I must take my cigar philosophically and evaporate them in smoke, twirl my thumbs rotatorily, cross one leg over the other and sink back in my chair. No—it won't do. The eternal riot of this place, the wear and tear of mind and body are a very insufficient balm to the wound of recollection. When my dearest Aunt may I hope to see you again? I know not how it is but I feel isolated here in the midst of society. The country is so disgustingly level, the revelry of the place so monotonous, the studies of the University so uninteresting, so much matter of fact—none but dryheaded calculating angular little gentlemen can take much delight in a $\sqrt{} + ba - b + c + d - e$ or $\sqrt[3]{a^2}$ etc., etc., 'Logarithms Involution and Evolution, properties of curvelines resuming Series, Indeterminate Analysis, Method of Increments' do not they look annihilatingly barbarous? 'There is no pleasure like proof' cries the Mathematician. I reverse it, 'There is no proof like pleasure.'

I have been seeking 'Falkland'° here for a long time without success. Those beautiful extracts of it which you shewed me at Tealby haunt me incessantly but wishes I think like Telescopes reversed seem to set their objects at a greater distance. I was at Dalby the other day and thought my Aunt looked remarkably well: she was then however labouring under the effects of a sprain in her leg which was painful but not of any consequence.

Whether Emma be or be not married give her my sincerest wishes for her happiness. You have had much previous uneasiness which was not perhaps utterly fruitless since what is more beautiful than sunshine succeeding storm and the hues of happiness like the colours of the rainbow may be brightest when pourtrayed on tears.

I fear you must accept this crude trash by way of Epistle from your

Ever affectionate Nephew

A. Tennyson

3. 'THE ACTS OF THE APOSTLES'

1829

Saturday, November 7th

On the question whether clergy of the established church should be allowed to sit in the House of Commons

Hallam votes *no* (Tennyson paid 5*s*. for non-attendance)

Saturday, November 14th

On the question whether the present law of libel calculated to allow freedom of discussion combined with the necessary protection of individuals.

Hallam votes *no*

Saturday, November 21st

On the question 'Whether the poems of Shelley have an immoral tendency'

Hallam and Tennyson vote *no*

Saturday, November 28th

On the question 'Whether there is any rule of moral action except general expediency'

Tennyson and Hallam vote 'aye'

Saturday, December 5th

Hallam read an essay on the question 'Whether the existence of an intelligent First Cause is deducible from the phenomena of the universe'

Tennyson and Hallam vote *no*

[1830]

February 6th

'Whether the monastic Institutions or the Saracenic invasions had the more beneficial effect on modern literature'

Hallam is neutral

February 13th

Tennyson is 'Moderator' (Essayist): but 'No essay was read to the Society this evening and Tennyson resigned his seat'

4. *To* ELIZABETH RUSSELL

March 18, [1832]

Dearest Azile°

I am grieved to hear nothing of or from thee, (for thy memory is more grateful to my spirit than the gale before a coming shower in the day of heat) and I know not in what solitary bower thou blossomest alone so that I cast my letter like a feather to the winds, hoping that some happy gale, attracted by thy fragrance, may blow it to thee; how is thine health, dearest Azile, since thou didst cease to enlighten with thy presence the muggy atmosphere that broods over the Chelt and the vicinity of the Boisragons? The first news I heard of thee since I saw thee last was from Smith, thy banker, who stated thy having paid £100 into his hands for me without giving me thy 'whereabout' that I might thank thee for it.

What thinkest thou of the state of affairs in Europe? Burking° and Cholera have ceased to create much alarm: they are our least evils, but reform and St Simonism are and will continue to be subjects of the highest interest: the future is so dark in the prospect that I am sometimes ready to cry out with the Poet

> 'The empty thrones call out for Kings
> But Kings are cheap as summer dust.
> The good old time hath taken wings
> And with it taken faith and trust
> And solid hope of better things.'°

Reform (not the measure, the passing of which is unavoidable)° but the instigating spirit of reform which is likely to subsist among the people long after the measure has past into a law, will bring on the confiscation of church property and maybe the downfall of the church altogether: but the existence of the Sect of the St Simonistes is at once a proof of the immense mass of evil that is existent in the 19th century and a focus which gathers all its rays. This sect is rapidly spreading in France, Germany and Italy and they have missionaries in London: but I hope and trust that there are hearts as true and pure as steel in old England that will never brook the sight of Baal in the sanctuary and St Simon in the Church of Christ.

I should delight in having a line from you or Emma and I wish I could *see* to write you a longer letter. My blindness increases daily. Believe me,

Ever yours most affectionately

A.T.

5. *To* WILLIAM HENRY BROOKFIELD

[mid-March 1832]

Hollo! Brooks, Brooks! for shame! what are you about—musing, and brooding and dreaming and opiumeating yourself out of this life into the next? Awake, arise or be for ever fallen. Shake yourself you Owl o' the turret you! come forth you cat-a-mountain°—you shall chew no more cud. I swear by Spedding's speech and Hallam's essay, by the right hand of Tennant and the eyes of Thompson, by the impetuous pomp of the taller—and the voluptuous quiverings of the eyeglass of the smaller—Scotchman, I swear by the mildness of Heath and the memory of Trench° that thou shalt chew no more cud. What! is St Anne dead? Is there not cakes and ale?° is there not toddies? is there not bacchies?° is there not pipes? smoke negrofoot an thou wilt but in the name of all that is near and dear unto thee I prythee take no opium—it were better that a millstone were hung about thy neck and that thou wert thrown into the Cam.° I have been and still continue to be very unwell, Brooks, and my eyes grow daily worse; otherwise, you should hear oftener from me, but you must not be sullen and fall out with me and abuse me in public and private because I am sometimes selfish enough to prefer a state of pur-blindness to one of utter amaurosis which would speedily succeed any continuous exertion of that sight which I am only anxious to preserve in order that I may look upon you once again—there now, the sentiment is pretty, though it be clumsily worded. I have told you the truth and I will hear no more growling.

You and Trench, I am told, grew very intimate with one another before he left Cambridge: it is impossible to look upon Trench and not to love him, though he be, as Fred° says, always strung to the highest pitch, and the earnestness which burns within him so flashes through all his words and actions, that when one is not in a mood of sympathetic ele-vation, it is difficult to prevent a sense of one's own inferiority and lack of all high, and holy feeling. Trench is a bold truehearted Idoloclast°— yet have I no faith in any one of his opinions. Hallam got a letter from Stradbally the other day. Trench writes that they keep armed watch and ward all night—a state of things, I should think, not very disagreeable to *him* who would have smitten off *both* ears (whose jest was that—the man who made it deserves to be cultivated?) The Spring is burgeoning fast about us and the crocus pierces through the dark moist moulds like a tongue of flame. You came to see us when there was an utter dearth of all beauty in holt and hill: perhaps we may see you sometime in the summer when the shining landskip is

> —crisp with woods
> and tufted knolls on wavy wolds.°

I think you mentioned a renewal of your acquaintance with the fisher-men, which may possibly occur if you will leave off the aforesaid drug, if you do not I can foresee nothing for you but stupefaction, aneurism, confusion, horror and death.

> Thine, dear Brooks, to the end of time,
> A.T.

P.S. Remembrances which vary through every shade of affectionate feeling according to the original constitution, and super-induced habits of the individual, from every member of the family.

6. *To* JAMES SPEDDING

[7 February 1833]

My dear James

I seize upon a dirty halfsheet (not of hotpress—but the blank half of a printed prospectus of a translation of 'Osman Sultaun's campaigns in the Western Asia from the reign of Bayezyd Ildirim to the death of Murad the fourth (1389–1640) from the German of Joseph Von Hammer—by Thomas Aquila Dale'—indeed mine ancient tutor and paidagogue in times of yore—which work commend everywhere for, I think, he is likely to do it well and the book will contain a map of the countries from Sinope to Tiflis and from Adana to Bagdad, which map will be three feet and a half by two and a half—and you will grant that our literature is marvellous deficient in works of Oriental history—and as I said before the man is mine ancient and trusty paidagogue,° and moreover a good man and one that is publishing at a loss and one that has *not* two cloaks°—wherefore it is reasonable that you should commend his book) in order to answer your last. This halfsheet has flown down on my escritoire, puffed with the balmy breath of Correspondence 'heav-enly maid' as Oxford has it.° For your letter I thank you heartily—my thanks have lost half their natural vigour and beauty because I was deliv-ered of them so long after conception—my confinement was very painful—the nurses said it was like to have proved a still birth—however you must recollect that half your epistle was to Hallam—indeed you confessed as much in your P.S.—are we not quits then or in the language of Mrs Jennings 'does not one shoulder of mutton drive out another.'°

You should not have written to me without telling me somewhat that was interesting to myself (always the first consideration) or that bore some reference to you and yours (always the second) or lastly without giving me some news of the great world; for know you not that I live so far apart from the bustle of life that news (even gossip) becomes interesting to me? Ironical sidehits at a person under the same roof with myself and filling more than a first half of the sheet—(i.e. not the person—but the sidehits—it looks as though I meant that the person in question slept with me and I assure you that we have a spare bed and that the bed is not so spare either, but a bed both plump and pulpy and fit for your dome-ship, whenever you can come and see us—I express myself very clum-sily but being overawed by the memory of your calm personal dignity and dome and melted likewise with the recollection of the many intel-lectual, spirituous, and spiritual evenings we have spent together in olden days—evenings, when spiritual things were spirituously dis-cerned, while we sat (O the Father!) looking smoky babies in each other's eyes (for you know, James, you were ever fond of a pipe) overawed (I repeat) with the crowd and cloud of my recollections (recollections of bacchies which alas! I never meet with in this Septentrional Province) I will yet endeavour to indite something not altogether unworthy of your thricefinèd tastes and liberal brows) ironical sidehits, I say, at my friend and guest, in a letter addressed to me,—moral kicks and punches through the medium of my epistle, and consequently to be delivered by me in a mellowed accent to the unhappy kickee (O fatal necessity and such as ought never to have been imposed!)—metaphysical flankers and crossbuttocks and wherein I was made the unhappy instrument of giv-ing pain to my dearest friend—Speak for me Aposiopesis, or rather do not—for thou art an unhappy figure, and born dumb, and of no earthly use but to cut the throat of a clause, though thou *cuttest* such a *dash*!

Write to me, now and then, lest I perish. Where is Tennant? I have not yet answered him, how shall I direct to him? You inquire after Charles°—we see little of him—I believe his spirits are pretty good, though he sometimes takes some drops of laudanum by way of stimulus. Is Brooks at Cambridge? to him I owe a letter and I mean to pay my debt.

Ever thine
A.T.

7. HENRY ELTON *to* ALFRED TENNYSON

October 1, 1833

My dear Sir

At the desire of a most afflicted family, I write to you, because they are unequal from the Abyss of grief into which they have fallen to do it themselves.

Your friend, Sir, and my much loved nephew, Arthur Hallam, is no more—it has pleased God, to remove him from this his first scene of Existence, to that better world, for which he was created.

He died at Vienna on his return from Buda, by Apoplexy, and I believe his Remains come by Sea from Trieste.

Mr Hallam arrived this morning in 3 Princes Buildings. May that Great Being, in whose hands are the Destinies of Man and who has promised to comfort all that Mourn, pour the Balm of Consolation on all the Families who are bowed down by this unexpected dispensation!

I have just seen Mr Hallam, who begs I will tell you, that he will write himself as soon as his Heart will let him. Poor Arthur had a slight attack of Ague—which he had often had—order'd his fire to be lighted and talked with as much cheerfulness as usual. He suddenly became insensible and his Spirit departed without Pain. The Physician endeavour'd to get any Blood from him—and on Examination it was the General Opinion, that he could not have lived long. This was also Dr Holland's opinion. The account I have endeavour'd to give you is merely what I have been able to gather, but the family of course are in too great distress to enter into details. I am, Dear Sir,

Your obedient Servant
Henry Elton

8. *To* RICHARD MONCKTON MILNES

[3 December 1833]

My dear Milnes

A letter from you was like a messenger from the land of shadows—it is so long since I have looked upon and conversed with you, that I will not deny but that you had withdrawn a little into the twilight—yet you do me wrong in supposing that I have forgotten you. I shall not easily forget you, for you have that about you which one remembers with pleasure.

I am rejoiced to hear that you intend to present us with your Grecian impressions.° Your gay and airy mind must have caught as many colours from the landskip you moved through, as a flying soapbubble—a comparison truly somewhat irreverent—yet I meant it not as such,—though I care not if you take it in an evil sense, for is it not owed to you, for your three-years silence to me whom you professt to love and to care for, and, in the second place, for your profane expression '*cleaning* one's mind of Greek thoughts and Greek feelings to make way for something better': it is a sad thing to have a dirty mind full of Greek thoughts and feelings— what an Augean [stable]° it must have been before the Greek thoughts got there.

To have done with this idle banter. I hope that in your book you have given us much glowing description and little mysticism. I know that you can describe richly and vividly—Give orders to Moxon and he will take care that the volume is conveyed to me. Believe me, dear Richard,

ever thine
A.T.

P.S. Charles and Frederick are neither of them here so that I am forced to coin their remembrances to you.

9. *To* SOFIA WALLS RAWNSLEY

[December 1833]

My dear Mrs Rawnsley

I am well aware how much I lose by not joining your party to day and it is only myself who have to regret that my state of health and spirits will not permit me that gratification. It would be of no use to come among you with an uncheerful mind—and old remembrances sometimes come most powerfully upon me in the midst of society. I have felt this so often to be the case that I am unwilling to go out when I feel any tendency to depression of spirits—at the same time believe me it is not without considerable uneasiness that I absent myself from a house where I visit with greater pleasure than at any other in the country if indeed I may be said to visit any other. Believe me therefore

Always yours
A.T.

10. *To* HENRY HALLAM

February 14, 1834

That you intend to print some of my friend's remains (though only for private circulation) has given me greater pleasure than anything I have experienced for a length of time. I attempted to draw up a memoir of his life and character, but I failed to do him justice. I failed even to please myself. I could scarcely have pleased you. I hope to be able at a future period to concentrate whatever powers I may possess on the construction of some tribute to those high speculative endowments and comprehensive sympathies which I ever loved to contemplate; but at present, though somewhat ashamed at my own weakness, I find the object yet is too near me to permit of any very accurate delineation. You, with your clear insight into human nature, may perhaps not wonder that in the dearest service I could have been employed in, I should be found most deficient. . . . I know not whether among the prose pieces you would include the one which he was accustomed to call his Theodicean Essay. I am inclined to think it does great honour to his originality of thought. Among the poems—if you print the one entitled *Timbuctoo*—I would request you, for my sake, to omit the initiatory note. The poem is everyway so much better than that wild and unmethodized performance of my own, that even his praise on such a subject would be painful.

11. *To* JAMES SPEDDING

[March 1835]

My dear James

I am sorry to disappoint myself (and perhaps in some slight measure you also) by postponing my visit. I am going to be from home for some time but not anywhere in your direction. The birds must sing and the furze bloom for you and Fitzgerald alone par nobile fratrum.° I sincerely hope you have not put off anyone else in the expectation of seeing me—though I did not state as much in my note it was only when I first proposed it that I could have come to you. Fortune will perhaps bring me whiter days.

I know not whether you are aware that Charles° has become an independent gentleman living in a big house among chalky wolds at Caistor. His and my great Uncle Samuel Turner to whom he was heir died some little time ago and left him property but he complains that it is at present unavailable, talks of debts to be paid etc. etc.

John Heath writes me word that Mill is going to review me in a new Magazine to be called the London Review—and favourably. But it is the last thing I wish for and I would that you or some other who may be friends of Mill would hint as much to him: I do not wish to be dragged forward again in any shape before the reading public at present, particularly on the score of my old poems most of which I have so corrected (particularly Oenone) as to make them much less imperfect which you who are a wise man would own if you had the corrections, which I may very possibly send you some time.

I am in much haste and obliged to conclude but absent or present believe me

Ever your true friend and admirer
A.T.

12. To RICHARD MONCKTON MILNES

[9 January 1837]

Why, what in the name of all the powers, my dear Richard, makes you run me down in this fashion? Now is my nose out of joint. Now is my tail not only not curled so tight as to lift me off my hindlegs, like Alfred Crowquill's° poodle, but fairly between them. Many sticks are broken about me. I am the ass in Homer.° I am blown. What has so jaundiced your good natured eyes as to make them mistake harmless banter for *insulting Irony*: harsh terms, applicable only to Lytton Bulwer,° who, big as he is, sits to all posterity astride upon the nipple of Literary Dandyism and 'takes her milk for gall.'° 'Insulting Irony,' and 'piscatory° vanity' as if you had been writing to St Anthony, who converted the soft souls of salmon—but may St Anthony's fire consume all misapprehension, the spleen-born mother of fivefold more evil on our turnip spheroid, than is Malice aforethought! Had I been writing to a nervous, morbidly-irritable man, down in the world, stark-spoiled with the staggers of a mismanaged imagination and equally opprest by Fortune and by the Reviews, it is possible that I might have halted to find expressions more suitable to his case—but that you, who seem, at least, to take the world as it comes, to doff it and let it pass—that you a man every way prosperous and talented, should have taken pet at my unhappy badinage made me—lay down my pipe and stare at the fire for ten minutes till the stranger fluttered up the chimney. You wish I had never written that passage. So do I, since it seems to have [given] such offence. Perhaps you likewise found a stumblingblock in the expression vapid books as the angry inversion of four commas seems to intimate. But are not annuals vapid?° Or coud I *possibly* mean that what you or Trench or Darley chose to write therein must be vapid? I thought you knew me better than even to insinuate these things. Had I spoken the same words to you, laughingly, in my chair, and with my own emphasis, you would have seen what they really meant, but coming to read them, peradventure, in a fit of indigestion or with a slight matutinal headache after your Apostolic symposium you subjected them to such misinterpretation as, if I had not sworn to be true friend to you, till my latest death-ruckle, would have gone far to make me indignant: but, least said, soonest mended! which comes with peculiar grace from me, after all this verbiage.

You judged me rightly in supposing that I would not be backward in doing a really charitable deed. I will either bring or send you something for your Annual. It is very problematical whether I shall be able to come and see you as I proposed; so do not return earlier from your tour on my account: and if I come, I should only be able to stop a few days, for as I and all my people are going to leave this place very shortly—never to return—I have much upon my hands—but whether I see you or not believe me

Always thine affectly*
A. Tennyson

* by the bye though I have adopted that mode of curtailing 'affectionately' from you, I don't like it. It looks like 'affectedly.' Moreover Mr D'Eyncourt always writes it so.

P.S. If I am not able to come and see you do not blame me for capricious change of purpose. I intended to have visited you immediately after Christmas, as I had a week or two to spare, but you were out, and if you had not been, the snowdrifts would have hindered me.

I have spoken with Charles who has promised to contribute to your Annual—Frederick will, I dare say, follow his example. See now whether I am not doing my best for you, and whether you had any occasion to threaten me with that black b—— Anacaona° and her cocoa-shadowed *coves* of niggers—I cannot have her strolling about the land in this way—it is neither good for her reputation nor mine. When is L[ord] N[orthampton]'s book to be publisht and how long may I wait before I send anything by way of contribution?

13. *To* LEIGH HUNT

[13 July 1837]

My dear Sir

I was obliged to leave town on the day after that when I was to have drunk tea with you, seen Carlyle, and tumbled your books. I did not like to put you to an expense of postage or I would have written to you from the country, though it had been merely to express my regret at not having seen you once more after that pleasant conversation. I only arrived here the other night and lit upon your parcel. It was very good of you to get all those poems written out for me and I can never be sufficiently grateful for the Paganini° full as it is of the most graceful and thickcoming fancies: of the others I like the cottage best but I return you (a poor exchange) all of what is most thankful in my nature for the whole flower garland.

With respect to Mr Hall°—I have to apologize for my seeming discourtesy. I did indeed write him an answer which however like a Sibylline leaf was flung somewhere to the winds: for when I parted from home I gave orders to the servant to send it to the post: but in the mean time an Auction took place in our house and our Penates made room for others and in the huddle and confusion consequent thereupon I suppose my letter was forgotten and I had hoped that Mr Hall had forgotten it likewise.

It goes somewhat against my grain to give any account of myself or mine to the public. You say he merely wants some 'family information.' Well then. I am the son of the Rev. George Clayton Tennyson LLD. I was born at Somersby, a small village in Lincolnshire, I was chiefly educated by my father, who was a man of considerable acquirements and when about 18 years of age I was entered at Trinity College, Cambridge. Will these dry dates serve, think you or does Mr Hall want more? I have no life to give—for mine has been one of feelings not of actions—can he not miss me out altogether? Addio,

Always yours
A. Tennyson

14. *To* EMILY SELLWOOD

[March or April] 1838

I saw from the high road through Hagworthingham the tops of the elms on the lawn at Somersby, beginning to kindle into green. I remember you sitting with me there on the iron garden chair one day when I had first come from London (and when Miss Bourn of Alford called). It was earlier in the year than now. The morning three years back seems fresh and pleasant; and you were in a silk pelisse, and I think I read some book with you.

15. *To* EMILY SELLWOOD

[October or November 1838]

I have dim mystic sympathies with tree and hill reaching far back into childhood. A known landskip is to me an old friend, that continually talks to me of my own youth and half-forgotten things, and does more for me than many an old friend that I know. An old park is my delight and I could tumble about it for ever.

Sculpture is particularly good for the mind: there is a height and divine stillness about it which preaches peace to our stormy passions. Methinks that in looking upon a great statue like the Theseus (maim'd and defaced as it is) one becomes as it were Godlike to feel things in the Idea.

There is the glory of being loved, for so have we 'laid great bases for Eternity.'

Through darkness and storm and weariness of mind and of body is there built a passage for His created ones to the gates of light.

That world of perfect chrysolite, a pure and noble heart.

16. *To* EMILY SELLWOOD

[January 1839]

I murmured (like a hen in the sunshine) lines and half lines of some poem to thee, I know not what: but I could not think of thee, thou white dove, brooding in thy lonely chamber without movements of the truest affection toward thee and an admiration of thee which no years can render less. God bless thee, sweetest, and God will bless thee for thou seemest to me such as pure eyes delight to dwell on.

17. *To* EMILY SELLWOOD

[November 1840]

[I dare not tell] thee how high I rate this faculty, which is generally most fruitful in the highest and most solemn human spirits. Dante is full of it. Shakespeare, Cervantes and almost all the greatest have been pregnant with this glorious power. Thou wilt find it even in the Gospel of Christ. How hast thou come to me. Thou didst make thyself wings of love and of faith and hast flown over the interval betwixt thee and me and hast settled in my bosom. But how thou should'st have found thyself there, without those wings, I know not.

If I have written aught of this from vanity may thy love leave me when I want it most. I scarce expect thee to agree with me in many things I have said—believe only that all is kindness to thee, to her, to Anne, to thy father and that I have but one wish with respect to them all, that they may be blest by the Father of all and that they may see the truth, not as I see it, (if not the truth) but the truth. Thine, dear, εἰς αἰῶνα[ς] τῶν αἰώνων (till the age of ages commonly translated ever and ever) A

18. *To* CHARLES STEARNS WHEELER

[August 26, 1841]

Dear Sir

Mr Brown called on me for about ten minutes this morning and stated that he was going to leave town tomorrow. This is the first time I

have met him since he has been in the old world and I am sorry that I have
seen so little of him as he seems a good genial sort of man, but he has
been in France and I in Holland, and we met at the eleventh hour and
settled nothing. He said he would see my publisher Moxon and arrange
with him, if he had time. However, I will take care that (when I publish)
he has the proofsheets in time to give him the start over other American
publishers.

I am glad to hear that I have friends in and about Boston. I met while
I was travelling two medical gentlemen from your side of the Atlantic,
who spoke very highly of Boston and its neighbourhood and so well of
yourself as to make me doubly desirous of knowing you personally, a
consummation which is I fear very far on in the future.

I am much obliged to you for the volume of Emerson's Essays.° I had
heard of him before and I know that Carlyle rates him highly. He has
great thoughts and imaginations, but he sometimes misleads himself
by his own facility of talking brilliantly. However, I have not perhaps
studied him sufficiently. I am, dear Sir,

Yours very truly
A. Tennyson

19. *To* EDMUND LUSHINGTON

[February 1842]

Dear Edmund

I was very glad to hear of the reconvalescence of your 'Geschwis-
ter'° for I had some fancy (as I told you) that all was not right. Your
lines I liked. Some doubt I had about 'πολυπίδακε' but Venables set
me right: not that I believed *you* could be out of your Greek, but the
'πολυπίδακος' Ἴδης'° ran in my head. 'Νασμῷ ἐν ἀμφιρύτῳ'° is a
wrong translation, the rest good. I have no news. I have not yet taken
my book to Moxon. Spedding's going to America has a little disheart-
ened me, for some fop will get the start of him in the *Edinburgh Review*
where he promised to put an article and I have had abuse enough.
Moreover Spedding was just the man to do it, both as knowing me, and
writing from clear conviction. However I intend to get it out shortly,
but I cannot say I have been what you professors call 'working' at it,
that indeed is not my way. I take my pipe and the muse descends in a
fume, not like your modern ladies who shriek at a pipe as if they saw a

'splacknuck':° do you know what a splacknuck is? I have been once into your grounds, the house looked very unhappy. Charles and I went together: he admired the place much, though everything was deep in snow.

Yours ever
A. Tennyson

20. *To* EDWARD FITZGERALD

[July 1842]

My dear Fitz

If you had known how much I have gone through since I saw you, you would pardon perhaps my ungracious silence in return for so many kind letters: if you had known—, but then I don't mean to tell you: you will very likely know soon enough: you have been a very good fellow to remember me in your correspondence; but then I know you like writing which I hate mortally: I have seen you scribble to Bernard Barton and others for the mere love of scribbling, and so perhaps I have not been so grateful for your notice as I might have been.

Don't abuse my book:° you can't hate it more than I do, but it does me no good to hear it abused; if it is bad, you and others are to blame who continually urged me to publish. Not for my sake but yours did I consent to submit my papers to the herd—d——m 'em! and all reproach comes too late.

I don't know whether the Dulwich days were 'good' days: something good no doubt about them, but I don't look back with *much* satisfaction on them: I have not had a good day, a perfect white day, for years; I think I require delicious scenery to make a perfect day as well as friends—I don't know.

Edwin the fair° I have not read: people say it is a weaker Philip.° You are unjust in calling the latter a solemn humbug: there is some very good stuff in it, though not of the highest class.

I do not know that I can make any expeditions this year: for I have neither money nor credit. Blenheim I should certainly like to see with you. O that glorious old chase! The great oaks are fresher in my recollection than the Raffaelle;° indeed I had not much time to study the latter: I was just getting into it when the old Duke sent a special blue-plush° to me to turn me out.

That is a fac-simile of the nib of my pen. The ink has
twice spurted right into the apple of my eye.—Therefore,
good bye, old Fitz,
Lest I lose my witz.
Never more my own than when

Yours
A.T.
Hoovery! Doovery! &c

21. THOMAS CARLYLE *to* RALPH WALDO EMERSON
(extract)

[August 5, 1844]

Today I get answer about Alfred Tennyson: all is right on that side.
Moxon informs us . . . that Tennyson is now in Town, and means to
come and see me. Of this latter result I shall be very glad: Alfred is one
of the few British or Foreign Figures (a not increasing Number, I think!)
who are and remain beautiful to me; a true human soul, or some authen-
tic approximation thereto, to whom your own soul can say, Brother!—
However, I doubt h[e] will not come; he often skips me, in these brief
visits to Town; skips [every]-body indeed; being a man solitary and sad,
as certain men are, dwelling in an element of gloom,—carrying a bit of
Chaos about him, in short, which he is manufacturing into Cosmos!

Alfred is the son of a Lincolnshire Gentleman Farmer, I think;
indeed you see in his verses that he is a native of 'moated granges,' and
green fat pastures, not of mountains and their torrents and storms. He
had his breeding at Cambridge, as if for the Law, or Church; being mas-
ter of a small annuity on his Father's decease, he preferred clubbing with
his Mother and some Sisters, to live unpromoted and write Poems. In
this way he lives still, now here now there; the family always within reach
of London, never in it; he himself making rare and brief visits, lodging
in some old comrade's rooms. I think he must be under forty, not much
under it. One of the finest looking men in the world. A great shock of
rough dusty-dark hair; bright-laughing hazel eyes; massive acquiline
face, most massive yet most delicate, of sallow brown complexion,
almost Indian-looking; clothes cynically loose, free-and-easy;—smokes
infinite tobacco. His voice is musical metallic,—fit for loud laughter and

piercing wail, and all that may lie between; speech and speculation free and plenteous: I do not meet, in these late decades, such company over a pipe!—We shall see what he will grow to. He is often unwell; very chaotic,—his way is thro' Chaos and the Bottomless and Pathless; not handy for making out many miles upon.

22. TENNYSON'S JOURNAL OF HIS TOUR OF SWITZERLAND, AUGUST 1846

1846. Went on a tour to the Isle of Wight and in August to Switzerland with Edward Moxon.

August 2nd. Up at 4 to go by 'Princess Maude.' Picturesque sunrise from the pier. Bruges. Englishman with moustache told us of festival at Bruges. I go down into fore-cabin and get the very worst breakfast I ever had in my life. Arrival at Ostend. Order from Belgian king that no passports need be shown. Inhuman conduct and superogatory fury of porters. We lose our presence of mind and run for it, but there is plenty of time. Arrive at Bruges, walk to Hôtel de Blé, recommended by moustached Englishman, missing the conveyance thitherward, which marked with gilt letters Fleur de Blé, rolls by us as we near our hotel. Great rejoicings of the people and hero-worship of Simon Stevin,° S on the banners, and names, busts and statues of all the Flanders great men, statesmen, sculptors, poets, etc. in an inner square within the great square. Horsemen riding in a circle for prize. High tower and clock in great square, picturesque groups in Cathedral, motioned from the seats we had taken opposite pulpit, depart to F. de Blé, dinner in salle— affected Englishwoman whom I took for Belge or German opposite, hot nervous night with me. Man 'hemmed' overhead° enough to shake the walls of Jericho.

August 3rd. Off to Grand Hôtel de Flandre, monkey, pleasant folk, commissionaire, pharmacien and opticien. J. Arteveld's house, townhall very fine, musée not good, go to Louvain, Hôtel de Suède, new town-hall, old café, row of poplars, nervous night.

August 4th. Off to Liège, two sons of Sir Robert Peel, Hôtel d'Angleterre good, money changed, too soon for rail which came very late, pretty scenery, Chaudefontaine, old man and little boy, railway bordered with young acacias. Cologne, Hôtel de Cologne, rooms overlooking moonlit Rhine, hotel full of light and festival, pillaring its lights in the quiet water, bridge of boats, three steamers lying quietly below windows, not quite four hours' sleep.

August 5th. Woke at 5 or earlier, clash and clang of steamboat departure under me, walk on the quay, Cathedral splendid but to my mind too narrow for its length.

> 'Gaspar and Melchior and Balthazar
> Came to Cologne on the broad-breasted Rhine,
> And founded there a temple which is yet
> A fragment, but the wonder of the world.'°

Embark, the bore of the Rhine, three Hyde Park drawling snobs, deck very hot, Nonnenwerth and Drachenfels, sad recollections; Coblentz, horrid row, king of Holland, shuffled off to the Rheinischerhof, stupid hotel. Coblentz as hateful as it was long years before, over the bridge to the Cheval Blanc, coffee there, back again, the bridge opening islanded us in the river.

August 6th. Off again by boat, three drawlers departed at Mainz, talk about language with Germans, sad old city of Worms among poplars, reach Mannheim, Hôtel de l'Europe, take a dark walk among shrubberies with M.

August 7th. Early next morning off by rail to Kehl, confusion about the two railways, douane, stop and see Cathedral, nave magnificent, rail to Basle, Three Kings, green swift Rhine roaring against the piers, Swiss fountain.

August 8th. Café in room, off by diligence° to Lucerne, vines, agreeable Swiss young lady to whom I quoted Goethe and she spouted *William Tell*, sorry to lose her, see Righi and Pilatus in the distance, walk before diligence but get in again, pass bridge over swift green stream, bureau, go to Schweizerhof, room at top of house, look out in the night and see the lake marbled with clouds, gabble of servants, bad night.

August 9th. Walk up the hill above the town, churchyard, innumerable gilt crosses, go to a villa, lie on the grass, return a different way from M., cross a part of the lake, walk back.

August 10th. Strolled about the painted bridges, M. met his friend, we bought Keller's map, off by 2 o'clock steamer to Weggis, hired a horse up the Righi, looked over and saw the little coves and wooded shores and villages under vast red ribs of rock, very fine, dismissed my horse at the Bains where we entered with an Englishman and found peasants waltzing, gave two francs to boy who had ordered beds, summit, crowd of people, very feeble sunset, tea, infernal chatter as of innumerable apes.

August 11th. Sunrise, strange look of clouds packed on the lake of Egeri, far off Jungfrau looking as if delicately pencilled. Rossberg, Küssnacht, breakfast, began to descend at 9, strange aspect of hill, cloud, and snow, as if the mountains were on fire, watch the clouds opening and shutting as we go down, and making framed pictures of the lake, etc., long hot descent, dined at Weggis, landlady takes me out to select live fish for dinner, I am too tender-hearted so we go without fish, boat touches, off to Fluelen, very sleepy, carriage road to Italy, Tell's chapel, go in to church, return to Sweizerhof.

August 12th. Lake, guide and boat to Alpnach, hire voiture up the vale of Sarnen, walk a little before, get in, nothing very remarkable, arrive at Lungern, pretty green Alpine 'thal' shut in with steep cliffs, one long waterfall, jolly old Radical who abused Dr Arnold, over the hills to Meyringen, home (after having seen Lauterbrunnen and the Bernese Alps, the best things in the tour).

23. CHARLES DICKENS *to* JOHN FORSTER

[August 24, 1846]

After dinner, at a little after seven o'clock, I was walking up and down under the little colonnade in the garden, racking my brain about *Dombey* and *Battle of Life*, when two travel-stained-looking men approached, of whom one, in a very limp and melancholy straw hat, ducked perpetually to me as he came up the walk. I couldn't make them out at all; and it wan't till I got close up to them that I recognised [Tennyson] and (in the straw hat) [Moxon]. They had come from Geneva by the steamer, and taken a scrambling dinner on board. I gave them some fine Rhine wine, and cigars innumerable. [Tennyson] enjoyed himself and was quite at home. [Moxon] (an odd companion for a man of genius) was snobbish, but pleased and good-natured. [Tennyson] had a five pound note in his pocket which he had worn down, by careless carrying about, to some two-thirds of its original size, and which was so ragged in its remains that when he took it out bits of it flew about the table. 'Oh Lor you know—now really—like Goldsmith you know—or any of those great men!' said [Moxon], with the very 'snatches in his voice and burst of speaking' that reminded Leigh Hunt of Cloten . . . The clouds were lying, as they do in such weather here, on the earth, and our friends saw no more of Lake Leman than of Battersea. Nor had they, it might appear, seen more of the Mer de Glace, on their way here; their talk about it bearing much resemblance to that of the man who had been to Niagara and said it was nothing but water.

24. *To* COVENTRY PATMORE

[February 28, 1849]

My dear Coventry

I went up to my room yesterday to get my book of elegies°—you know what I mean—a long butcher-ledger-like book. I was going to read one or two to an artist here. I could not find it. I have some obscure remembrance of having lent it to you. If so, all is well. If not will you go to my old chambers and institute a vigorous inquiry. I was coming up to-day on purpose to look after it, but the weather is so ferocious I have yielded to the wishes of my friends here to stop till tomorrow. I shall be, I expect in town tomorrow at 25 M.P. where I shall be glad to see you:—at 9.10 p.m. the train in which I come gets into London. I suppose I shall be in Mornington Place about 10 o'clock.

Perhaps you would in your walk Museum-ward call on Mrs Lloyd and tell her to prepare for me. With best remembrances to Mrs Patmore, believe me

Ever yours
A. Tennyson

25. *To* EMILY SELLWOOD TENNYSON

[July 13 1852]

I want to go to Redcliffe Scar which old Wordsworth once told me of, or perhaps to Bolton Abbey. If I go through Leeds, I should like to see James Marshall if he be there still. It is a pity you did not see Owen,° you called him Mr (do you mean the bone man, the professor?) and old Mr Jesse. Either of these would have told you about the bird. I suppose if the young ones have come out of the nest, they were going to fly and have all gone by this. You can send a sovereign if you like to the sapper and miner, but I think it is very hard that I am obliged to subscribe to all the bad poets, and I am indignant that I should be aidant in filling the world with more trash than there is at present. Besides this kind of demand (if it be found out that I respond to such claims) is likely to increase, and I do not believe that old Wordey paid any attention to such. He was far too canny. Tom Taylor I will answer, though I think it a great pity that your 'Sweet and low' hadn't the start of Mrs Taylor's and all these. I have had two very good days coasting, I mean walking along on and under the cliffs. Very singular they are with great bivalve shells sticking out of them. They are made of a great dark slate coloured shale (is it to be called) that comes showering down ever and anon from a great height; and on the hard flat rock which makes the beach on one side of the town (for on the other side are sands), you see beautiful little ammonites which you stoop to pick up but find them part of the solid rock. You know these are the snakes which St Hilda drove over the cliff and falling they lost their heads, and she changed them into stone. I found a strange fish on the shore with rainbows about its wild staring eyes, enclosed in a sort of sack with long tentacula beautifully coloured, quite dead, but when I took it up by the tail spotted all the sand underneath with great drops of ink, so I suppose a kind of cuttle fish. I found too a pale pink orchis on the sea bank and a pink vetch, a low sort of shrub with here and there a thorn. I am reading lots of novels. The worst is they do not last longer than the day. I am such a fierce reader I think I have had pretty well my quantum suff:° Venables' anecdotes are very interesting indeed one cannot help wishing that such a man as Gladstone may come to sit on the top branch of the tree.

26. *To* JOHN FORSTER

August 11, 1852

My dear John Forster
    I did not tell you of my marriage which you rather took in dudgeon. Now I will tell you of the birth of a little son this day. I have seen beautiful things in my life, but I never saw anything more beautiful than the mother's face as she lay by the young child an hour or two after, or heard anything sweeter than the little lamblike bleat of the young one. I had fancied that children after birth had been all shriek and roar; but he gave out a little note of satisfaction every now and then, as he lay by his

mother, which was the most pathetic sound in its helplessness I ever listened to. You see I talk almost like a bachelor, yet unused to these things: but you—I don't hear good reports of you. You should have been better by this. Get better quickly if you would have me be as I always am,

Yours most truly

A. Tennyson

27. *To* ROBERT JAMES MANN

[September 1855]

My dear Sir

I am glad that you like poor 'Maud', she has been beaten as black and blue by the penny-a-liners as the 'trampled wife' by the drunken ruffian in the opening poem.° I always calculated on a certain quantity of anonymous insolence but I have had more than my share this time and it goes on still. I one day got an anonymous letter, such a thing, signed pleasantly, 'Yours in aversion, a former admirer.' The best notices I have seen are first that in the *Examiner* (but then that I expected). My friend Forster would speak justly and honestly about it; the next are in two Edinburgh papers *The Daily Express* and another, I forget the name, and last comes your letter, so that poor 'Maud' begins to believe that if she can by any means get clear of the political *mob* and general calcitration she may yet have a chance for her life.

A.T.

28. *To* G. G. BRADLEY

August 25, 1855

Dear Mr Bradley

Many thanks for the Arnold:° nobody can deny that he is a poet. 'The Merman' was an old favourite of mine, and I like him as well as ever. 'The Scholar Gipsy' is quite new to me, and I have already an affection for him, which I think will increase. There are several others which seem very good, so that altogether I may say that you have conferred a great boon upon me. I have received a Scotch paper, in which it is stated that poor 'Maud' is to be slashed all to pieces by that mighty man, that pom-pholygous,° broad-blown Apollodorus, the gifted X.° Her best friends do not expect her to survive it! I am

Yours very truly
A. Tennyson

29. *To* GEORGE BRIMLEY

November 28, 1855

Sir

I wish to assure you that I quite close with your commentary on 'Maud'.° I may have agreed with portions of other critiques on the same poem, which have been sent to me; but when I saw your notice I laid my finger upon it and said, 'There, that is my meaning.' Poor little 'Maud,' after having run the gauntlet of so much brainless abuse and anonymous spite, has found a critic. Therefore believe her father (not the gray old wolf) to be

Yours not unthankfully
A. Tennyson

P.S. But there are two or three points in your comment to which I should take exception, e.g. 'The writer of the fragments, etc.,' surely the speaker or thinker rather than the writer; again, as to the character of the love, do any of the expressions 'rapturous,' 'painful' [*for* fanciful], 'childish,' however they may apply to some of the poems, fully characterize the 18th?° is it not something deeper? but perhaps some day I may discuss these things with you, and therefore I will say no more here, except that I shall be very glad to see you if ever you come to the Isle of Wight.

30. TENNYSON'S JOURNAL OF HIS TOUR OF PORTUGAL, AUGUST–SEPTEMBER 1859, WITH F. T. PALGRAVE AND F. C. GROVE

August 16th. Radley's Hotel, Southampton. Have been over the Vectis, the name of the vessel, not Tagus, Tagus being repaired, or running alternately with the Vectis. She is very prettily got up and painted, and apparently scrupulously clean. Brookfield° keeps up my spirits by wonderful tales, puns, etc. I find that neither Palgrave nor Grove wants to move except as I will and they are quite content to remain at Cintra.

August 17th. Have passed a night somewhat broken by railway whistles.

August 21st. Braganza Hotel, Lisbon. Just arrived at Lisbon and settled at the Braganza Hotel after a very prosperous voyage tho' with a good deal of rolling. We merely touched at Vigo which looked fruitful, rolled up in a hot mist, and saw Oporto from the sea, looking very white in a fat port-wine country. It is here just as hot as one would wish it to be but not at all too hot. There was a vast deal of mist and fog all along the coast as we came. Lisbon I have not yet seen except from the sea, and it does not equal expectation as far as seen. Palgrave and Grove have been helpful and pleasant companions, and so far all has gone well. We shall go to Cintra either to-morrow or next day. It is said to be Lisbon's Richmond and rather cockney tho' high and cool. The man who is landlord here is English and an Englishman keeps the hotel at Cintra. I hope with good hope that I shall not be pestered with the plagues of Egypt. I cannot say whether we shall stick at Cintra or go further on. Brookfield gave a good account of the cleanliness of Seville.

August 23rd. Cintra. We drove over Lisbon yesterday in a blazing heat and saw the Church of St Vincent, and the Botanical Gardens where palms and prickly pears and huge cactuses were growing, and enormous oleanders covered all over with the richest red blossom, and I thought of our poor one at Farringford that won't blossom. There were two strange barbaric statues at the gate of the garden, which were dug up on the top of a hill in Portugal: some call them Phœnician but no one knows much about them. I tried to see the grave of Fielding the novelist, who is buried in the Protestant cemetery, but could find no one to let me in; he lies among the cypresses. In the evening we came on here; the drive was a cold one, and the country dry, tawny, and wholly uninteresting. Cintra disappointed me at first sight, and perhaps will continue to disappoint, tho' to southern eyes from its ever green groves, in contrast to the parched barren look of the landscape, it must look very lovely. I climbed with Grove to the Peña, a Moorish-looking castle on the top of the hill, which is being repaired, and which has gateways fronted with tiles in pattern; these gates look like those in the illustrated *Arabian Nights* of Lane.

August 26th. It is, I think, now decided that we are to go on to Cadiz and Seville on the 2nd, and then to Gibraltar and possibly to Tangiers, possibly to Malaga and Granada. The King's Chamberlain has found me out by my name: his name is the Marquis of Figueros or some such sound; and yesterday even the Duke of Saldanha came into the *salle à manger*, described himself as 'having fought under the great Duke,° and having been in two and forty combats and successful in all, as having married two English wives, both perfect women,' etc., and ended with seizing my hand and crying out 'Who does not know England's Poet Laureate? I am the Duke of Saldanha.' I continue pretty well except for toothache; I like the place much better as I know it better. A visit to Santarem (the city of convents) was greatly enjoyed.

Sept. 2nd. Lisbon. The heat and the flies and the fleas and one thing or another have decided us to return by the boat to Southampton which starts from this place on the 7th. We propose on arriving at Southampton to pass on to Lyndhurst to spend two or three days in the Forest.

[Our visit, we gradually found, was not at the most favourable season: the fields browned and burnt by heat, the mosquitoes afflicting. Against the latter, Tennyson had provided himself with an elaborate tent (first contrived, I believe, by Sir C. Fellowes for use in Asia Minor, during the night-time): a sheet formed into a large bag, but ending in a muslin canopy, which was distended by a cane circle, and hung upwards, to accommodate head and shoulders, from a nail which I took the freedom to run into his bedroom wall. Into this shelter the occupant crept by a narrow sheet-funnel, which he closed by twisting; and once in, he was unable to light a match outside for fear lest the action should set the muslin on fire. Hence one night Tennyson, able to command the bell, summoned the waiter. I brought him in through my (contiguous) room with a light; and the man's terror at the spectacle of the great ghost, looking spectral within its white canopy, was delightful. He almost ran off. But I think that after this experience Tennyson abandoned the tent and took his chances: only pretending to wish that he had a little baby in bed with him, as a whiter and more tempting morsel to the insect world.

More serious than the mosquito was the sun. This so wrought upon and disturbed Tennyson, in a manner with which many English travellers to Italy during the heat will be unpleasantly familiar, that he now began gravely to talk about leaving his bones by the side of the great novelist Fielding, who died and was buried at Lisbon in 1754.]°

Sept. 13th. Southampton. Arrived, and going on to-morrow to Lyndhurst, where I shall stop two or three days, then I am going on to Cambridge with Palgrave from a longing desire that I have to be there once more.

31. *To* THE DUKE OF ARGYLL

[October 3, 1859]

My dear Duke

We are delighted to hear that your Duchess has added another scion to your race, and that Mother and child are both prospering. I had fancied that the event would have come off while I was in Portugal (for in Portugal I have been) and made enquiries 'thereanent' of Mr Henry Howard but he could tell me nothing.

If I came back with 'bullion'° in the Tagus, it was nowhere in my packages and the Captain and crew kept their treasure a profound secret. I went to see that Cintra which Byron and Beckford° have made so famous: but the orange trees were all dead of disease, and the crystal streams (with the exception of a few sprinkling springlets by the wayside) either dried up, or diverted through unseen tunnels into the great aqueduct of Lisbon. Moreover the place is cockney and when I was there, was crammed with Lisbon fashionables and Portuguese nobility; yet Cintra is not without its beauties, being a mountain of green pines rising out of an everywhere arid and tawny country, with a fantastic Moorish-looking castle on the peak, which commands a great sweep of the Atlantic and the mouth of the Tagus: here on the topmost tower sat the King (they say) day by day in the old times of Vasco da Gama watching for his return, till he saw him enter the river: there perhaps was a moment worth having been waited for. I made some pleasant acquaintances, but I could not escape autograph-hunters—a certain Don Pedro Something even telegraphed for one after I had returned to Lisbon.

As to Macaulay's suggestion of the Sangraal° I doubt whether such a subject could be handled in these days, without incurring a charge of irreverence. It would be too much like playing with sacred things. The old writers *believed* in the Sangraal. Many years ago I did write Lancelot's Quest of the Grail in as good verses as I ever wrote—no, I did not write—I made it in my head, and it has now altogether slipt out of memory. My wife, I am sorry to say, has been very unwell and is at this moment in bed with a severe cold—but desires her best remembrances.

Yours ever
A. Tennyson

32. *To* PRINCESS ALICE

[13 January 1862]

Madam

Having heard some time ago from Sir C. B. Phipps that your Royal Highness had expressed a strong desire that I should in some way 'idealize' our lamented Prince, and being at that time very unwell, I was unwilling to attempt the subject, because I feared that I might scarce be able to do it justice; nor did I well see how I should idealize a life which was in itself an ideal.

At last it seemed to me that I could do no better than dedicate to His memory a book which He Himself had told me was valued by him. I am the more emboldened to send these lines to your Royal Highness, because having asked the opinion of a lady who knew and truly loved and honoured Him, she gave me to understand by her reply that they were true and worthy of Him: whether they be so or not, I hardly know, but if they do not appear to be so to Your Royal Highness, forgive me as your Father would have forgiven me.

Though these lines conclude with an address to our beloved Queen I feel that I cannot do better than leave the occasion of presenting them to the discretion of your Royal Highness. Believe me, as altogether sympathizing with your sorrow,

Your Royal Highness' faithful and obedient servant
A. Tennyson

33. *To* FREDERICK LOCKER

[31 January 1863]

Dear Mr Locker

I am glad that your young lady approves of my little book. Why wouldn't you let me give it to her?

As to this canard of a Baronetcy, I remember the same foolish rumour arising some years ago, and with some little trouble I put it down, or it died down of itself. In this instance the notice had been out in the *Athenaeum* several days before I heard of it, but I answered the first letter which alluded to it by declaring that the rumour was *wholly* unfounded; so that as no Baronetcy has been offered, there is less reason for considering your friendly pros and cons as to acceptance or refusal;

if it had, I trust that I should have had grace and loyalty enough to think more of the Queen's feelings than my own in this matter. I mean whichever way I answered. Both myself and my wife have been somewhat vexed and annoyed by all this chatter.

Kind regards to Lady Charlotte. I shall be glad to see you here, whenever you like to come our way. Froude promised me he would come in January, but January is breathing his last to-day.

Yours very truly
Alfred Tennyson

34. *To* ALGERNON CHARLES SWINBURNE

[March 1865]

My dear Sir

Accept my congratulations on the success of your Greek play. I had some strong objections to parts but these I think have been modified by a reperusal and at any rate I dare say you would not care to hear them. Here however is one. Is it *fair* for a Greek chorus to abuse the Deity something in the style of the Hebrew prophets?

Altogether it is many a day since I have read anything so fine—for it is not only carefully written, but has both strength and splendour, and shows moreover that you have a fine metrical invention which I envy you.

Yours very truly
A. Tennyson

35. *To* RICHARD OWEN

[October, 1865]

My dear Owen

I suppose when you say 'quantity' like most English people you mean accent.° 'embryonic' would be the accent though the *syllable* is a short one, embryŏnic not embryōnic. As for 'embryonal' I never heard of such a word, but if there be such, it may be a moot point whether you laid the accent on the first syllable, or the one before the last: for there is a word 'embryonate' (being in the state of an embryo) which I find accented on the first: embryonal would be certainly wrong: but except you really want the two words for some scientific distinction, it would be better to stick to 'embryonic'.

I and my wife are grieved to hear that you have overtasked your muscular powers in your Highland holiday. Pray for your own and your friends' sake obey your doctors (you scarce have a better and kindlier than Paget) and cease to work for awhile that you may work better hereafter. We cannot afford to lose your brains. Not at least till all our lizards° are dug out, and this stretch of red cliff which I see from my attic windows no longer needs an interpreter. Believe me,

Ever truly yours
A. Tennyson

36. TENNYSON AND GLADSTONE IN CONVERSATION, 8 DECEMBER 1865

My father° came to us this afternoon. He is going to dine with Woolner, to meet Tennyson, Gladstone and Holman Hunt. I am to go in the evening at 9.30.

When I arrived at Woolner's, the maid said she supposed I was 'for the gentlemen.' On my replying 'Yes,' she showed me into the dining-room, where they were finishing dessert. Woolner sat of course at the bottom of the table, Tennyson on his left, my father on his right hand. Gladstone sat next Tennyson and Hunt next my father. I relapsed into an arm-chair between Woolner and my father.

The conversation continued. They were talking about the Jamaica business°—Gladstone bearing hard on Eyre, Tennyson excusing any cruelty in the case of putting down a savage mob. Gladstone had been reading official papers on the business all the morning and said, with an expression of intense gravity, just after I had entered, 'And that evidence wrung from a poor black boy with a revolver at his head!' He said this in an orator's tone, pity mingled with indignation, the pressure of the lips, the inclination of the head, the lifting of the eyes to heaven, all marking the man's moral earnestness. He has a face like a lion's; his head is small above it, though the forehead is broad and massive, something like Trajan's in its proportion to the features. Character, far more than intellect, strikes me in his physiognomy, and there is a remarkable duplicity of expression—iron, vice-like resolution combined with a subtle, mobile ingeniousness.

Tennyson did not argue. He kept asserting various prejudices and convictions. 'We are too tender to savages; we are more tender to a black than to ourselves.' 'Niggers are tigers; niggers are tigers,' in *obbligato*, *sotto voce*,° to Gladstone's declamation. 'But the Englishman is a cruel man—he is a strong man,' put in Gladstone. My father illustrated this by stories of the Indian Mutiny.° 'That's not like Oriental cruelty,' said Tennyson; 'but I could not kill a cat, not the tomcat who scratches and miawls over his disgusting amours, and keeps me awake,' thrown in with an indefinable impatience and rasping hatred. Gladstone looked glum and irate at this speech, thinking probably of Eyre. Then they turned to the insufficiency of evidence as yet in Eyre's case, and to other instances of his hasty butchery—the woman he hung, though [mercy] recommended by court-martial, because women had shown savageness in mutilating a corpse. 'Because *women*, not *the woman*—and that, too, after being recommended to mercy *by court-martial*, and he holding the Queen's commission!' said Gladstone with the same hostile emphasis. The question of his personal courage came up. That, said Gladstone, did not prove his capability of remaining cool under and dealing with such special circumstances. Anecdotes about sudden panics were related. Tennyson said to my father, 'As far as I know my own temperament, I could stand any sudden thing, but give me an hour to reflect, and I should go here and go there, and all would be confused. If the fiery gulf of Curtius° opened in the City, I would leap at once into it on horseback. But if I had to reflect on it, no—especially the thought of death—nothing can be weighed against that. It is the moral question, not the fear, which would perplex me. I have not got the English courage. I could not wait six hours in a square expecting a battery's fire.' Then stories of martial severity were told. My father repeated the anecdote of Bosquet in the Malakoff.° Gladstone said Cialdini° had shot a soldier for being without his regimental jacket. Tennyson put in, *sotto voce*, 'If they shot paupers, perhaps they wouldn't tear up their clothes,' and laughed very grimly.

Frank Palgrave here came in, a little man in morning dress, with short beard and moustache, well-cut features, and a slight cast in his eye, an impatient, unsatisfied look and some self-assertion in his manner. He directed the conversation to the subject of newspapers. Tennyson all the while kept drinking glasses of port and glowering round the room through his spectacles. His moustache hides the play of his mouth, but as far as I could see, that feature is as grim as the rest. He has cheek-bones carved out of iron. His head is domed, quite the reverse of Gladstone's—like an Elizabethan head, strong in the coronal, narrow in the frontal regions, but very finely moulded. It is like what Connington's head seems trying to be.

Something brought up the franchise. Tennyson said, 'That's what we're coming to when we get your Reform Bill, Mr Gladstone; not that I know anything about it.' 'No more does any man in England,' said Gladstone, taking him up quickly with a twinkling laugh, then adding, 'But I'm sorry to see you getting nervous.' 'Oh, I think a state in which every man would have a vote is the ideal. I always thought it might be realized in England, if anywhere, with our constitutional history. But how to do it?' This was the mere reflector. The man of practice said nothing. Soon after came coffee. Tennyson grew impatient, moved his great gaunt body about, and finally was left to smoke a pipe. It is hard to fix the difference between the two men, both with their strong provincial accent—Gladstone with his rich flexible voice, Tennyson with his deep drawl rising into an impatient falsetto when put out: Gladstone arguing, Tennyson putting in a prejudice; Gladstone asserting rashly, Tennyson denying with a bald negative; Gladstone full of facts, Tennyson relying on impressions; both of them humorous, but the one polished and delicate in repartee, the other broad and coarse and grotesque. Gladstone's hands are white and not remarkable. Tennyson's are huge, unwieldy, fit for moulding clay or dough. Gladstone is in some sort a man of the world: Tennyson a child, and treated by him like a child.

Woolner played the host well, with great simplicity. His manner was agreeably subdued. Palgrave rasped a little. Hunt was silent. My father made a good third to the two great people. I was like a man hearing a concerto; Gladstone first violin, my father second violin, Tennyson violoncello, Woolner bass viol, Palgrave viola, and, perhaps, Hunt a second but very subordinate viola.

When we left the dining-room we found Mrs Woolner and her sister, Miss Waugh (engaged to Holman Hunt), in the drawing-room. Both of these ladies are graceful. They affect the simplicity of pre-Raphaelite nature, and dress without crinoline very elegantly. Miss Waugh, though called 'the goddess,' is nowise unapproachable. She talked of Japanese fans like a common mortal. Mrs Woolner is a pretty little maidenly creature who seems to have walked out of a missal margin.

Woolner gave Gladstone a MS book, containing translations of the 'Iliad' by Tennyson, to read. Gladstone read it by himself till Tennyson appeared. Then Woolner went to him and said, 'You will read your translation, won't you? And Palgrave, 'Come you! A shout in the

trench!' 'No, I shan't,' said Tennyson, standing in the room, with a pet-
tish voice, and jerking his arms and body from the hips. 'No, I shan't read
it. It's only a little thing. Must be judged by comparison with the Greek.
Can only be appreciated by the difficulties overcome.' Then seeing the
MS in Gladstone's hand, 'This isn't fair; no, this isn't fair.' He took it
away, and nothing would pacify him. 'I meant to read it to Mr Gladstone
and Dr Symonds.' My father urged him to no purpose, told him he
would be φωνοῦντα συνετοῖσιν° but he cried, 'Yes, you and Glad-
stone, but the rest don't understand it.' 'Here's my son, an Oxford first-
class man.' 'Oh, I should be afraid of him.' Then my father talked
soothingly in an admirable low voice to him such as those who have to
deal with fractious people would do well to acquire. He talked to him of
his poems—'Mariana in the Moated Grange.' This took them to the
Lincolnshire flats—as impressive in their extent of plain as mountain
heights. My father tried to analyse the physical conditions of ideas of
size. But Tennyson preferred fixing his mind on the ideas themselves. 'I
do not know whether to think the universe great or little. When I think
about it, it seems now one and now the other. What makes its greatness?
Not one sun or one set of suns, or is it the whole together?' Then to illus-
trate his sense of size he pictured a journey through space like Jean Paul
Richter's,° leaving first one galaxy or spot of light behind him, then
another, and so on through infinity. Then about matter. Its incognisabil-
ity puzzled him. 'I cannot form the least notion of a brick. I don't know
what it is. It's no use talking about atoms, extension, colour, weight. I
cannot penetrate the brick. But I have far more distinct ideas of God, of
love and such emotions. I can sympathise with God in my poor way. The
human soul seems to me always in some way, how we do not know, iden-
tical with God. That's the value of prayer. Prayer is like opening a sluice
between the great ocean and our little channels.' Then of eternity and
creation: 'Huxley° says we may have come from monkeys. That makes
no difference to me. If it is God's way of creation, He sees the whole,
past, present, and future, as one' (entering on an elaborate statement of
eternity à la Sir Thomas Browne). Then of morality: 'I cannot but think
moral good is the crown of man. But what is it without immortality? Let
us eat and drink, for to-morrow we die. If I knew the world were coming
to an end in six hours, would I give my money to a starving beggar: No,
if I did not believe myself immortal. I have sometimes thought men of
sin might destroy their immortality. The eternity of punishment is quite
incredible. Christ's words were parables to suit the sense of the times.'
Further of morality: 'There are some young men who try to do away
with morality. They say "We won't be moral." Comte,° I believe, and

perhaps Mr Grote° too, deny that immortality has anything to do with being moral.' Then from material to moral difficulties: 'Why do mosquitoes exist? I believe that after God had made His world the devil began and added something.' (Cat and mouse—leopards. My father raised moral evil—morbid art.) The conversation turned on Swinburne for the moment, and then dropped.

In all this metaphysical vagueness about matter, morals, the existence of evil, and the evidences of God there was something almost childish. Such points pass with most men for settled as insoluble after a time. But Tennyson has a perfect simplicity about him which recognises the real greatness of such questions, and regards them as always worthy of consideration. He treats them with profound moral earnestness. His 'In Memoriam' and 'Two Voices' illustrate this habit. There is nothing original or startling—on the contrary, a general commonplaceness, about his metaphysics; yet, so far as they go, they express real agitating questions—express, in a poet's language, what most men feel and think about.

A move was made into the dining-room. Tennyson had consented to read his translations to Gladstone and my father. I followed them and sat unperceived behind them. He began by reading in a deep bass growl the passage of Achilles shouting in the trench. Gladstone continually interrupted him with small points about words. He has a combative, House of Commons mannerism, which gives him the appearance of thinking too much about himself. It was always to air some theory of his own that he broke Tennyson's recital; and he seemed listening only in order to catch something up. Tennyson invited criticism.

Tennyson was sorely puzzled about the variations in Homeric readings and interpretations. 'They change year after year. What we used to think right in my days I am told is all wrong. What is a poor translator to do?' But he piqued himself very much on his exact renderings. 'These lines are word for word. You could not have a closer translation: one poet could not express another better. There! those are good lines.' Gladstone would object, 'But you will say Jove and Greeks: can't we have Zeus and Achæans?' 'But the sound of Jove! Jove is much softer than Zeus—Zeus—Zeus.' 'Well, Mr Worsley gives us Achæans.' 'Mr Worsley has chosen a convenient long metre; he can give you Achæans, and a great deal else.' Much was said about the proper means of getting a certain pause, how to give equivalent suggestive sounds, and so on.

. . .

Could it [Homer] be got into hexameters? Tennyson repeated some quantitative hexameters, 'beastly bad,' which he had made. English people could not understand quantity. 'I showed 'em to a man, Allingham; he wanted to scan 'em; couldn't see they had quantity.' Gladstone observed that modern Greek readings of Homer must be all wrong. We have lost accent, which was not emphasis, but arsis and thesis of voice. At end of word, *e.g.*, the grave becomes the acute, and the voice is raised. There are three parts in pronunciation: time, emphasis, and pitch.

Palgrave suggested a translation of Homer into Biblical prose. He began it. Jowett° dissuaded him, saying he thought he had not enough command of English (How like Jowett!) 'Rather disparaging to you,' said Tennyson.

Tennyson said he had read out in Old English to his wife the 'Odyssey.' 'And it struck me I did it very well.'

Real difficulty of translation. No two languages hit each other off. Both have some words 'like shot silk' (Tennyson's metaphor, good). These cannot be rendered. We can never *quite* appreciate another nation's poetry on this account. Gave as an instance the end of 'Enoch Arden,' 'Calling of the sea,'° a phrase well known to sailors, for a clear night with a sea-sound on the shore in calm. A German translator rendered it 'Geschrei,' which suggested storm, etc., wrongly. He meant a big voice of the sea, but coming through the calm. (The Venetian sailors, however, say 'Chiama il mare.')

Gladstone, just before we parted, said he always slept well. He had only twice been kept awake by the exertion of a great speech in the House. On both occasions the recollection that he had made a misquotation haunted him.

At about one we broke up. Gladstone went off first. My father and I walked round the studio, then shook hands with Tennyson and got home.

37. *To* FRANCIS PALGRAVE

[December 24, 1868]

My dear Palgrave

You distress me when you tell me that, without leave given by me, you showed my poem° to Max Müller: not that I care about Max Müller's seeing it, but I do care for your not considering it a sacred deposit. Pray do so in future; otherwise I shall see some boy in some Magazine making a lame imitation of it, which a clever boy could do in twenty minutes—and, though his work would be worth nothing, it would take away the bloom and freshness from mine.

I can't conceive how the Grail M.M. mentions can well be treated by a poet of the 13th century from a similar point of view to mine, who write in the 19th, but, if so, I am rather sorry for it, as I rather piqued myself on my originality of treatment.

If Max Müller will give you or me the name of the book, which contains all the Mediaeval literature about the Grail, I will order it of the London Library; though, if it be in German prose, I fear I shan't have the patience to wade through a tenth of it.

The 'Grail' is not likely to be published for a year or two, and certainly not along with the other thing which you hate so much (too much it seems to me). I shall write three or four more of the 'Idylls,' and link them together as well as I may. Jowett comes on Saturday, and I will give him your message. The boys are both here and well, not at Farringford, which is getting scoured and cleaned, but at a house at Alum Bay (Headon Hall) where Nature in winter at least, seems always in a rage.

Please attend to my request about the 'Grail' and the 'Lover's Tale,' and show them to no one, or if you can't depend upon yourself, forward them to me.

Always yours
A. Tennyson

But of course you can depend upon yourself, even in [a] genial hour of pipe and grog. As for your advice, to make the whole thing larger, I will think of it but at present I do not see my way.

38. *To* WILLIAM COX BENNETT

[November 13, 1872]

My dear Mr Bennett

Thanks for your flattering poem. I could wish that I had something of what Master Swinburne calls 'the divine arrogance of Genius' that I might take it into my system and rejoice abundantly—but—as Marvell says—

> at my back I always hear
> Time's winged chariot hurrying near;
> And yonder all before us lie
> Deserts of vast eternity—°

where most of us will be lost and swallowed up. Nevertheless, true thanks.

Yours ever
A. Tennyson

39. *To* WILLIAM GLADSTONE

[March 30, 1873]

My dear Gladstone

I do not like to trouble you about my own personal matters in the midst of your absorbing public work; but not only on account of my feeling for yourself, but also for the sake of that memory which we share, I speak frankly to you, when I say, that I had rather we should remain plain Mr and Mrs, and that, if it were possible, the title should first be assumed by our son at any age it may be thought right to fix upon: but like enough this is against all precedent and could not be managed; and on no account would I have suggested it were there the least chance of the Queen's construing it into a slight of the proffered honour. I hope that I have too much of the old-world loyalty left in me not to wear my Lady's favour against all comers, should you think that it would be more agreeable to H.M. that I should do so.

In that case please to accept the accompanying letter (of the 28th) as the expression of my acceptance and believe me

Yours ever
A. Tennyson

40. *To* WILLIAM GLADSTONE

[April 16, 1873]

My dear Gladstone

Accept my thanks for having made clear my wish and my motives to the Queen. Now that I have H.M.'s sanction as well as your own I am not likely to change my mind on the subject.

Hallam to whom we have spoken regarding it since my last would not like to wear the honour during my lifetime. For the rest I leave myself in your hands being quite sure that you will do what is best and when best. You have much good work however to accomplish before the time of your retirement from office.

With kindest regards from my wife and myself I am

Yours ever
A. Tennyson

41. *To* BENJAMIN PAUL BLOOD

[May 7, 1874]

Sir

I have to thank you for your Essay and your Photograph. The face is that of one (it seems to me) born to grapple with difficulties metaphysical and other, and the Essay does not belie the face—a very notable sketch of Metaphysic—ending, apparently, yet once more in the strange history of human thought, with the placid Buddha, as verified by Nineteenth Century anaesthetics.

But what need you my praise, when you have secured the approval of him° who is by report our greatest, or one of our greatest Hegelians, whereas I, though I have a gleam of Kant have never turned a page of Hegel, all that I know of him having come to me obiter,° and obscurely through the talk of others; nor have I ever vigorously delivered myself to dialectics.

I have never had any revelations through anaesthetics: but 'a kind of waking trance' (this for lack of a better word) I have frequently had quite up from boyhood when I have been all alone. This has often come upon me through repeating my own name to myself silently, till all at once as it were out of the intensity of the consciousness of individuality the individuality itself seemed to dissolve and fade away into boundless being—and this not a confused state but the clearest of the clearest, the surest of the surest, utterly beyond words—where Death was an almost laughable impossibility—the loss of personality (if so it were) seeming no extinction but the only true life.

I am ashamed of my feeble description. Have I not said the state is utterly beyond words? But in a moment when I come back into my normal condition of 'sanity' I am ready to fight for 'Mein liebes Ich,'° and hold that it will last for Aeons of Aeons.

In Lucretius° 'What is Duty' was the first reading. It was altered because Lucretius nowhere I think makes any mention of Duty in that sense; but it now stands again as at first.

If ever you come to England I shall be glad to welcome you here. Believe me

Yours very truly
A. Tennyson

42. *To* MATTHEW FRASER

[May 7, 1880]

Dear Sir

I only consented to stand for your Lord Rectorship when informed by the letter of introduction which your agreeable deputation brought that my nomination was 'supported by a large majority if not a totality of the students of Glasgow.' It now seems necessary that I should by standing at your invitation appear what I had stedfastly refused to be—party candidate for the Conservative Club. The mere fact of a contest between the supporters of a nominee of a Liberal and that of a Conservative Club leads I suppose inevitably to this conclusion in the minds of the public. On this account I must beg to decline the honour of your candidature. You are probably aware that some years ago the Glasgow University Liberals asked me to be their candidate and that in like manner I declined. Yet I would gladly accept the honour of a nomination after what has occurred if at any time a club of students bearing no political party name should wish to nominate me or if both Liberals and Conservatives should ever happen to agree on foregoing the excitement of a political contest and to desire a Lord Rector who would not appear for installation and who would in fact be a 'roi-fainéant'° with nothing but the literary claims you are good enough to appreciate.

I thank you all for the trouble which you have taken, and I am with best wishes for the prosperity of your University

Yours faithfully
A. Tennyson

Matthew P. Fraser Esq.

I request that you will do me the favour to publish this letter.

43. *To* WILLIAM GLADSTONE

[early December 1883]

My dear Gladstone

Don't let Knowles° print A.H.H.'s letters—at least let them first be submitted to me. I think that I of all living men should be allowed a voice in this matter.

K. is a very clever man and a kindly, but he is—Knowles of the 19th Century. K would set the fame of his review above the fame of your old friend and mine. At least I fear so.

H.M.° must decide as to when I am to be Peered. The younger branch of my father's family, who succeeded to the fortune took the name of Tennyson-D'Eyncourt. Would that do?° They say they are descended from the old branch of the D'Eyncourts who came in with William and from the later creation of the same name in tempore° Charles II.—if they, then I. It is a small matter. I will let you know later on.

Many thanks for your congratulations on Hallam's engagement. I trust that Mrs Gladstone, to whom my best and kindest remembrances—is better.

Ever yours
A. Tennyson

P.S. I heard of an old lady the other day, to whom all the great men of her time had written. When Froude's Carlyle came out, she rushed up to her room and to an old chest there wherein she kept their letters, and she flung them into the fire. 'They were written to *me*,' she said, 'not to the public!' and she set her chimney on fire, and her children and grandchildren ran in—'The chimney's on fire.' 'Never mind,' she said, and went on burning. I should like to raise an altar to that old lady and burn incense upon it.

44. *To* FRANCISQUE MICHEL

[January 28, 1884]

I have such sheaves of letters, not only from here and there in Great Britain, but America, Australia, India, etc., that I am sometimes, as they say, 'at my wit's end,' how I am to answer them all; and my son generally answers them for me, for my eyes are failing, and I fear that I may be slowly growing blind; but I cannot resist responding to your kindly letter with my own hand.

I have not forgotten you, nor that pleasant day and night when you were with us, and enlivened us with hundreds of stories and anecdotes. You talked a whole volume. Very agreeable it was and very remember-able.

You will despise my ignorance. I am so little of an antiquarian that, though of course I have heard of John Gower, I don't think I have ever read more of him than a few lines in a chance quotation; and as for Chandos, I am ashamed to tell you that till I read your advertisement I knew not even his name; but I have no doubt that your forthcoming book supplies a want, and will be most interesting.

I thank you for your kind congratulations about the peerage; but being now in my 75th year, and having lost all my youthful contemporaries, I see myself, as it were, in an extra page of Holbein's 'Dance of Death,' and standing before the mouth of an open sepulchre while the Queen hands me a coronet, and the skeleton takes it away and points me downward into the darkness.

Pardon me, if this sound too tragic and believe me, my dear Translator

Yours very truly
Tennyson

45. *To* ELIZABETH CHAPMAN

[November 23, 1886]

Madam

I am grateful to you for your book which contains an analysis of 'In Memoriam.' I like this much better than Mr Gatty's, which perhaps you have seen, and which is too personal to please me. Yours is excellent in taste and judgement. I like too what you say about Comtism.° I really could almost fancy that p. 95° was written by myself. I have been saying the same thing for years in all but the same words. I think that you have not touched upon one argument against *their* subjective immortality, viz. that, according to astronomical and geological probabilities, this great goddess Humanity in a certain number of ages will breathe her last gasp, and leave the earth without even a Comtist.

I should say, as Napoleon is reported to have said. When someone was urging upon him how much more glorious was the immortality of a great artist, a painter for instance, than that of a great soldier, he asked

how long the best painted and best preserved picture would last. 'About
800 years.' 'Bah! quelle immortalité!'°

Yours very faithfully
Tennyson

46. *To* WALT WHITMAN

[November 15, 1887]

Dear Walt Whitman

I thank you for your kind thought of me. I value the photographs
much and I wish that I could see not only this sun-picture, excellent as I
am told it is, but also the living-original.

May he still live and flourish for many years to be! The coming year°
should give new life to every American who has breathed a breath of that
soul which inspired the great founders of your American Constitution
whose work you are to celebrate.

Truly the Mother Country, pondering on this, may feel that how
much soever the daughter owes to her she, the Mother, has nevertheless
something to learn from the daughter. Especially I would note the care
taken to guard a noble Constitution from rash and unwise innovators. I
am,

Always yours
Tennyson

47. *To* CHARLES ESMARCH

[April 18, 1888]

Sir

I thank you for the gift of your translation but I must object and
strongly to the statement in your preface that *I* am the hero in either
poem. I never had a cousin Amy. Locksley Hall is an entirely imaginative
edifice. My grandsons are little boys. I am not even white-haired, I never
had a gray hair in my head. The whole thing is a dramatic imperson-
ation, but I find in almost all modern criticism this absurd tendency to
personalities. Some of my thought *may* come out in the poem but am I

therefore the hero? *There is not one* touch of *autobiography in it from end to end.*

Thanking you again for your elegant volume, I am

Yours very faithfully
Tennyson

Charles Esmarch Esq.

EXCERPTS FROM HALLAM TENNYSON'S *MEMOIR*: TENNYSON IN HIS OWN WORDS

[*Tennyson's childhood in his own words*]

According to the best of my recollection, when I was about eight years old, I covered two sides of a slate with Thomsonian blank verse in praise of flowers for my brother Charles, who was a year older than I was, Thomson then being the only poet I knew. Before I could read, I was in the habit on a stormy day of spreading my arms to the wind, and crying out 'I hear a voice that's speaking in the wind,' and the words 'far, far away' had always a strange charm for me. About ten or eleven Pope's *Homer's Iliad* became a favourite of mine and I wrote hundreds and hundreds of lines in the regular Popeian metre, nay even could improvise them, so could my two elder brothers, for my father was a poet and could write regular metre very skilfully.

. . .

At about twelve and onward I wrote an epic of six thousand lines à la Walter Scott,—full of battles, dealing too with sea and mountain scenery,—with Scott's regularity of octo-syllables and his occasional varieties. Though the performance was very likely worth nothing I never felt myself more truly inspired. I wrote as much as seventy lines at one time, and used to go shouting them about the fields in the dark. All these early efforts have been destroyed, only my brother-in-law Edmund Lushington begged for a page or two of the Scott poem. Somewhat later (at fourteen) I wrote a Drama in blank verse, which I have still, and other things. It seems to me, I wrote them all in perfect metre.

[*Memoir*, i. 11–12]

[*Hallam recalls Tennyson's attitude to variant readings*]

From the volume of 1832 [my father] omitted several stanzas of 'The Palace of Art' because he thought that the poem was too full. 'The artist is known by his self-limitation' was a favourite adage of his. He allowed me however to print some of them in my notes, otherwise I should have hesitated to quote without his leave lines that he had excised. He 'gave the people of his best,' and he usually wished that his best should remain without variorum readings, 'the chips of the workshop,' as he called them. The love of bibliomaniacs for first editions filled him with horror, for the first editions are obviously in many cases the worst editions; and once he said to me:

'Why do they treasure the rubbish I shot from my full-finish'd cantos?
νήπιοι οὐδὲ ἴσασιν ὅσῳ πλέον ἥμισυ παντός.'

[nēpioi oude isasin hosōi pleon hēmisu pantos: 'children never realize how much more half is than all i.e. that less is more']

For himself many passages in Wordsworth and other poets had been entirely spoilt by the modern habit of giving every various reading along with the text. Besides, in his case, very often what is published as the latest edition has been the original version in his first manuscript, so that there is no possibility of really tracing the history of what may seem to be a new word or a new passage. 'For instance,' he said, 'in "Maud" a line in the first edition was "I will bury myself in *my books*, and the Devil may pipe to his own," which was afterwards altered to "I will bury myself *in myself*, etc.": this was highly commended by the critics as an improvement on the *original* reading—but it was actually in the first MS draft of the poem.'

[*Memoir*, i. 118]

[*Tennyson's work timetable, 1833*]

He lived for the most part at Somersby, and I give a list of his week's work; which he drew up.

Monday.	History, German.
Tuesday.	Chemistry, German.
Wednesday.	Botany, German.
Thursday.	Electricity, German.
Friday.	Animal Physiology, German.
Saturday.	Mechanics.
Sunday.	Theology.
Next Week.	Italian in the afternoon.
Third Week.	Greek. *Evenings.* Poetry.

[*Memoir*, i. 124]

[Tennyson's reading, 1835]

My father read them a great deal of Wordsworth, 'the dear old fellow,' as he called him. 'The Yews of Borrowdale,' 'The Simplon Pass,' the sonnet beginning 'Two Voices,' 'The Solitary Reaper,' 'Peele Castle,' the 'Ode on Intimations of Immortality,' 'The Fountain,' were among his favourites. Fitzgerald notes again:

I remember A.T. saying he remembered the time when he could see nothing in 'Michael' which he now read us in admiration; though he thought Wordsworth often clumsy and diffuse. There was no end of 'This Thorn' in the piece that bears the name: 'such hammering to set a scene for so small a drama.'

My father also read Keats and Milton: saying that 'Lycidas' was 'a test of any reader's poetic instinct,' and that 'Keats, with his high spiritual vision, would have been, if he had lived, the greatest of us all (tho' his blank verse was poor), and that there is something magic and of the innermost soul of poetry in almost everything which he wrote.' Then, perhaps in his weaker moments, he used to think Shakespeare greater in his sonnets than in his plays. 'But he soon returned to the thought which is indeed the thought of all the world. He would have seemed to me to be reverting for a moment to the great sorrow of his own mind; and in that peculiar phase of mind he found the sonnets a deeper expression of the never-to-be-forgotten love which he felt, more than any of the many moods of many minds which appear among Shakespeare's dramas.'

[Memoir, i. 151–2]

[Tennyson on politics, 1842]

The Chartist and Socialist agitations were then alarming the country. My father thought they should be met not by universal imprisonment and repression, but by a widespread National education, by more of a patriotic and less of a party spirit in the Press, by partial adoption of Free Trade principles, and by an increased energy and sympathy among those who belonged to the different forms of Christianity. He was sometimes described as advancing opposite opinions at different times. This was because from his firm sense of justice he had a dramatic way of representing an opinion adverse to his own in a favourable light, in order that he might give it the most generous interpretation possible.

[Memoir, i. 185]

[*Tennyson on* The Princess]

As for the various characters in the poem, they give all possible views of
Woman's higher education; and as for the heroine herself, the Princess
Ida, the poet who created her considered her as one of the noblest among
his women. The stronger the man or woman, the more of the lion or
lioness untamed, the greater the man or woman tamed. In the end we see
this lioness-like woman subduing the elements of her humanity to that
which is highest within her, and recognizing the relation in which she
stands towards the order of the world and toward God—

> A greater than all knowledge beat her down.
>
> [*Princess*, VII. 223]

His friends report my father to have said, that the two great social
questions impending in England were 'the housing and education of the
poor man before making him our master, and the higher education of
women'; and that the sooner woman finds out, before the great educa-
tional movement begins, that 'woman is not undevelopt man, but
diverse,' [*Princess*, VII. 259–60] the better it will be for the progress of
the world.

There have not been wanting those who have deemed the varied
characters and imagery of the poem wasted on something of a fairy tale
without the fairies. But, in this instance as in others involving the
supreme meaning and guidance of life, a parable is perhaps the teacher
that can most surely enter in at all doors.

It was no mere dramatic sentiment, but one of my father's strongest
convictions of the true relation between man and woman, which
impelled him to write:

> Let this proud watchword rest
> Of equal; seeing either sex alone
> Is half itself, and in true marriage lies
> Nor equal, nor unequal: each fulfils
> Defect in each, and always thought in thought,
> Purpose in purpose, will in will, they grow,
> The single pure and perfect animal,
> The two-cell'd heart beating, with one full stroke,
> Life.
>
> [*Princess*, VII. 282–90]

And if woman in her appointed place 'stays all the fair young planet
in her hands,' she may be well content. She has space enough to

Burgeon out of all
Within her—let her make herself her own
To give or keep, to live and learn and be
All that not harms distinctive womanhood.

[*Princess*, VII. 255–8]

She must train herself to do the large work that lies before her, even though she may not be destined to be wife or mother, cultivating her understanding not her memory only, her imagination in its highest phases, her inborn spirituality and her sympathy with all that is pure, noble and beautiful, rather than mere social accomplishments; then and then only will she further the progress of humanity, then and then only men will continue to hold her in reverence.

On the other hand one of the poet's main tests of manhood is 'the chivalrous reverence' for womanhood.

To love one maiden only, cleave to her,
And worship her by years of noble deeds,
Until they win her; for indeed I know
Of no more subtle master under heaven
Than is the maiden passion for a maid,
Not only to keep down the base in man,
But teach high thought and amiable words,
And courtliness and the desire of fame,
And love of truth, and all that makes a man.

[*The Idylls of the King*, 'Guinevere', 472–80]

He would say, 'I would pluck my hand from a man even if he were my greatest hero, or dearest friend, if he wronged a woman or told her a lie.'

After 1847 'The Princess' underwent considerable alterations. The second edition was published in 1848 with a few amendments, and dedicated to Henry Lushington, but in 1850 a third edition appeared with omissions and many additions, and notably six songs were introduced, which help to express more clearly the meaning of 'the medley.'

These songs

The women sang
Between the rougher voices of the men,
Like linnets in the pauses of the wind.

[*Princess*, 'Prologue', 236–8]

In 1851 the 'weird seizures' of the Prince were inserted. His too emotional temperament was intended from an artistic point of view to emphasize his comparative want of power. 'Moreover,' my father writes, 'the words "dream-shadow," "were and were not" doubtless refer to the anachronisms and improbabilities of the story: compare the prologue,

> Seven and yet one, like shadows in a dream,
>
> [Prologue, 222]

and v. 466,

> And like a flash the weird affection came,
>
> .   .   .   .   .   .
>
> I seem'd to move in old memorial tilts,
> And doing battle with forgotten ghosts,
> To dream myself the shadow of a dream.

'It may be remarked that there is scarcely anything in the story which is not prophetically glanced at in the prologue.'

[*Memoir*, i. 248–51]

[*Tennyson in 1846*]

One acquaintance would keep on assuring my father that it was the greatest honour of his life to have met him. My father's answer to such praise was, 'Don't talk d——d nonsense.'

. . .

A year or two before, my father had lived some weeks in a Hydro-pathic Establishment at the very primitive village of Prestbury, and the village boys were in the habit of following him and the other inmates whenever they showed themselves on the roads and shouting, 'Shiver and shake.' This made him very nervous at the time, and the thought even of passing through Prestbury revived the feeling.

[*Memoir*, i. 264–5]

[*A friend recalls Tennyson, and Tennyson's mother*]

Two wishes I used to hear him express; one was to see the West Indies, the other to see the earth from a balloon.

Few things delighted me more than to see the mother and son together. You cannot remember your grandmother, I think. She was a perfect picture, a beautiful specimen of the English gentlewoman, lov-ing and loveable, 'no angel but a dearer being,' and so sensitive that touch her feelings ever so lightly and the tears rushed to her eyes. Then it was we used to hear your father say, 'Dam your eyes, mother, dam your eyes!' and then she smiled and applied the white pocket-handkerchief and shook her head at her son. He often jested with her about Dr Cumming and his 'bottles,' the bottles being the seven vials of St John's Revelation! You have heard, I dare say, that your grandmother confined her reading at that time to two books, the *Bible* and Dr Cumming's work on *Prophecy.* He used to jest with his mother about her monkey, a clever little black thing that was generally seen in the garden perched on the top of a pole. Your father naturally christened it St Simeon Stylites. I once ventured to ask him whether his mother had not sat for the picture of the Prince's mother in 'The Princess,' and he allowed that no one else had.

[*Memoir*, i. 265]

[*Tennyson and Carlyle, 1840s*]

During the 'forties' he was in the habit of walking with Carlyle at night, and Carlyle would rail against the 'governments of Jackasserie which cared more for commerce than for the greatness of our empire'; or would rave against the stuccoed houses in London as 'acrid putrescence,' or against the suburbs as a 'black jumble of black cottages where there used to be pleasant fields'; and they would both agree that it was growing into 'a strange chaos of odds and ends, this London.' They were not in the least afraid of one another although many were afraid of them, and they had long and free discussions on every conceivable subject, and once only almost quarrelled, when Carlyle asserted that my father talked of poetry as 'high art,' which he flatly contradicted, 'I never in my whole life spoke of "high art." '

They had—both of them—lost MSS of their works; Carlyle his *French Revolution*, my father *Poems, chiefly Lyrical*. When my father asked Carlyle how he felt after the disappearance of his MS, he answered, 'Well, I just felt like a man swimming without water.'

My uncle Frederick writes:

I am sure I could not perform such a feat as I know Alfred to have done, any more than raise the dead. The earliest MS of the *Poems, chiefly Lyrical* he lost out of his great-coat pocket one night while returning from a neighbouring market town. This was enough to reduce an ordinary man to despair, but the invisible ink was made to reappear, all the thoughts and fancies in their orderly series and with their entire drapery of words arose and lived again. I wonder what under such circumstances would become of the 'mob of gentlemen who write with ease.' Of course it would not much matter as they could easily indite something new.

My father's poems were generally based on some single phrase like 'Someone had blundered': and were rolled about, so to speak, in his head, before he wrote them down: and hence they did not easily slip from his memory.

[*Memoir*, i. 267–8]

[*Tennyson on* In Memoriam]

'It must be remembered,' writes my father, 'that this is a poem, *not* an actual biography. It is founded on our friendship, on the engagement of Arthur Hallam to my sister, on his sudden death at Vienna, just before the time fixed for their marriage, and on his burial at Clevedon Church. The poem concludes with the marriage of my youngest sister Cecilia. It was meant to be a kind of *Divina Commedia*, ending with happiness. The sections were written at many different places, and as the phases of our intercourse came to my memory and suggested them. I did not write them with any view of weaving them into a whole, or for publication, until I found that I had written so many. The different moods of sorrow as in a drama are dramatically given, and my conviction that fear, doubts, and suffering will find answer and relief only through Faith in a God of Love. "I" is not always the author speaking of himself, but the voice of the human race speaking thro' him. After the Death of A.H.H., the divisions of the poem are made by First Xmas Eve (Section XXVIII.), Second Xmas (LXXVIII.), Third Xmas Eve (CIV. and CV. etc.). I myself did not see Clevedon till years after the burial of A.H.H. Jan. 3rd, 1834, and then in later editions of "In Memoriam" I altered the word "chancel," which was the word used by Mr Hallam in his Memoir, to "dark church." As to the localities in which the poems were written, some were written in Lincolnshire, some in London, Essex, Gloucestershire, Wales, anywhere where I happened to be.'

'And as for the metre of "In Memoriam" I had no notion till 1880 that Lord Herbert of Cherbury had written his occasional verses in the same metre. I believed myself the originator of the metre, until after "In Memoriam" came out, when some one told me that Ben Jonson and Sir Philip Sidney had used it. The following poems were omitted from "In Memoriam" when I published, because I thought them redundant.

The Grave (originally No. LVII.) (*Unpublished*)

I keep no more a lone distress,
    The crowd have come to see thy grave,
    Small thanks or credit shall I have,
But these shall see it none the less.

The happy maiden's tears are free
    And she will weep and give them way;
    Yet one unschool'd in want will say
'The dead are dead and let them be.'

Another whispers sick with loss:
    'O let the simple slab remain!
    The "Mercy Jesu" in the rain!
The "Miserere" in the moss!'

'I love the daisy weeping dew,
    I hate the trim-set plots of art!'
    My friend, thou speakest from the heart,
But look, for these are nature too.

To A.H.H. (originally No. CVIII.) (*Unpublished*)

Young is the grief I entertain,
    And ever new the tale she tells,
    And ever young the face that dwells
With reason cloister'd in the brain:

Yet grief deserves a nobler name:
    She spurs an imitative will;
    'Tis shame to fail so far, and still
My failing shall be less my shame:

Considering what mine eyes have seen,
    And all the sweetness which thou wast
    In thy beginnings in the past,
And all the strength thou wouldst have been:

A master mind with master minds,
    An orb repulsive of all hate,
    A will concentric with all fate,
A life four-square to all the winds.

The Victor Hours (originally No. CXXVII.) (*Unpublished*)

Are those the far-famed Victor Hours
    That ride to death the griefs of men?
    I fear not; if I fear'd them, then
Is this blind flight the winged Powers.

Behold, ye cannot bring but good,
    And see, ye dare not touch the truth,

> Nor Sorrow beauteous in her youth,
> Nor Love that holds a constant mood.
>
> Ye must be wiser than your looks,
>   Or wise yourselves, or wisdom-led,
>   Else this wild whisper round my head
> Were idler than a flight of rooks.
>
> Go forward! crumble down a throne,
>   Dissolve a world, condense a star,
>   Unsocket all the joints of war,
> And fuse the peoples into one.

That my father was a student of the Bible, those who have read 'In Memoriam' know. He also eagerly read all notable works within his reach relating to the Bible, and traced with deep interest such fundamental truths as underlie the great religions of the world. He hoped that the Bible would be more and more studied by all ranks of people, and expounded simply by their teachers; for he maintained that the religion of a people could never be founded on mere moral philosophy: and that it could only come home to them in the simple, noble thoughts and facts of a Scripture like ours.

Soon after his marriage he took to reading different systems of philosophy [including Spinoza, Kant, and Hegel], yet none particularly influenced him. The result I think is shown in a more ordered arrangement of religious, metaphysical and scientific thought throughout the 'Idylls' and his later works. 'In Poems like "De Profundis" and the "Ancient Sage," ' Jowett said, 'he often brings up metaphysical truths from the deepest depths.' But as a rule he knew that poetry must touch on metaphysical topics rather by allusion than systematically. In the following pages I shall not give any of his subtler arguments; but only attempt to illustrate from 'In Memoriam,' with some of the other poems, and from his conversation, the *general* everyday attitude of his mind toward the highest problems that confront us. In dealing with these none was readier in the discovery of fallacies, none was more resolute in proclaiming what seemed to him realities.

His creed, he always said, he would not formulate, for people would not understand him if he did; but he considered that his poems expressed the principles at the foundation of his faith.

He thought, with Arthur Hallam, that 'the essential feelings of religion subsist in the utmost diversity of forms,' that 'different language does not always imply different opinions, nor different opinions any difference in *real* faith.' 'It is impossible,' he said, 'to imagine that the

Almighty will ask you, when you come before Him in the next life what your particular form of creed was: but the question will rather be, "Have you been true to yourself, and given in My Name a cup of cold water to one of these little ones?" '

'This is a terrible age of unfaith,' he would say. 'I hate utter unfaith, I cannot endure that men should sacrifice everything at the cold altar of what with their imperfect knowledge they choose to call truth and reason. One can easily lose all belief, through giving up the continual thought and care for spiritual things.'

And again, 'In this vale of Time the hills of Time often shut out the mountains of Eternity.'

[*Memoir*, i. 304–9]

[*Tennyson on evolution*]

Of Evolution he said: 'That makes no difference to me, even if the Darwinians did not, as they do, exaggerate Darwinism. To God all is present. He sees present, past, and future as one.'

. . .

To Tyndall he once said, 'No evolutionist is able to explain the mind of Man or how any possible physiological change of tissue can produce conscious thought.' Yet he was inclined to think that the theory of Evolution caused the world to regard more clearly the 'Life of Nature as a lower stage in the manifestation of a principle which is more fully manifested in the spiritual life of man, with the idea that in this process of Evolution the lower is to be regarded as a means to the higher.'

[*Memoir*, i. 322–3]

[*Tennyson on being translated*]

Translations into French of 'Ring out, wild bells,' and 'Mariana in the Moated Grange,' were sent him from France.

He pointed out 'what a poor language French is for translating English poetry, although it is the best language for delicate *nuances* of meaning. How absurd "Ring out, wild bells" sounds in the translation "Sonnez, Cloches, Sonnez," and what a ridiculous rendering of "He cometh not, she said" is "Tom ne vient pas"!'

[*Memoir*, i. 385]

[Tennyson judges]

A most pathetic incident . . . my father told me, happened to him at Twickenham, when a Waterloo soldier brought twelve large cantos on the battle of Waterloo. The veteran had actually taught himself in his old age to read and write that he might thus commemorate Wellington's great victory. The epic lay for some time under the sofa in my father's study, and was a source of much anxiety to him. How could he go through such a vast poem? One day he mustered up courage and took a portion out. It opened on the heading of a canto: 'The Angels encamped above the field of Waterloo.' On that day, at least, he 'read no more.' He gave the author, when he called for his manuscript, this criticism: 'Though great images loom here and there, your poem could not be published as a whole.' The old man answered nothing, wrapt up each of the twelve cantos carefully, placed them in a strong oak case and carried them off. He was asked to come again but he never came.

[Memoir, i. 392]

[Tennyson's Lincolnshire dialect poems (Northern Farmer, New Style)]

My father was fond of telling stories . . . in Lincolnshire dialect. The three following are examples:

A housemaid, who was born in the fen country, and accustomed to drink the strong fen water, went to Caistor on the Wolds, famous for its splendid springs. However, she soon gave warning for this reason—'She liked Caistor, but could not abear the watter, for that taästed o' nowt [nothing].' Another story was of a Lincolnshire farmer coming home on Sunday after a sermon about the endless fires of hell and talking to his wife—'Noä, Sally, it woän't do, noä constitootion cud stan' it.' A third was of a Lincolnshire minister praying for rain: 'O God, send us rain, and especially on John Stubbs' field in the middle marsh, and if Thou doest not know it, it has a big thorn-tree in the middle of it.'

The Lincolnshire dialect poems are so true in dialect and feeling, that when they were first read in that county a farmer's daughter exclaimed: 'That's Lincoln labourers' talk, and I thought Mr Tennyson was a gentleman.'

[Memoir, ii. 10]

[*Tennyson on metre and prosody*]

Among the experiments in classical quantity, the Alcaic 'Ode to Milton' was annotated thus: 'My Alcaics are not intended for Horatian Alcaics, nor are Horace's Alcaics the Greek Alcaics, nor are his Sapphics, which are vastly inferior to Sappho's, the Greek Sapphics. The Horatian Alcaic is perhaps the stateliest metre in the world except the Virgilian hexameter at its best; but the Greek Alcaic, if we may judge from the two or three specimens left, had a much freer and lighter movement: and I have no doubt that an old Greek if he knew our language would admit my Alcaics as legitimate, only Milton must not be pronounced Mil*ton*.'

His hexameters directed against the translation of Homer into accentual English hexameters are well known. German hexameters he disliked even more than English. He once said—' "Was die Neugier nicht thut": What a beginning of an hexameter!' and 'What a line "Hab' ich den Markt und die Strassen, doch nie so einsam gesehen!" ' '

Indeed he thought that even quantitative English hexameters were as a rule only fit for comic subjects, 'tho' of course you might go on with perfect hexameters of the following kind, but they would grow monotonous:

> High woods roaring above me, dark leaves falling about me.

I remember a comic end of an Alcaic in quantity, which he made at this time:

> Thine early rising well repaid thee,
> Munificently rewarded artist.

. . .

I have heard him say, 'Englishmen *will* spoil English verses by scanning when they are reading, and they confound accent and quantity.'

. . .

I need not dwell on my father's love of the perfection of classical literary art, on his sympathy with the temper of the old world, on his love of the old metres, and on his views as to how the classical subject ought to be treated in English poetry.

He purposely chose those classical subjects from mythology and legend, which had been before but imperfectly treated, or of which the stories were slight, so that he might have free scope for his imagination. 'The Lotos-Eaters,' 'Ulysses,' 'Tithonus,' 'Œnone,' 'The Death of Œnone,' 'Tiresias,' 'Demeter and Persephone,' 'Lucretius.' A modern feeling was to some extent introduced into the themes, but they were dealt with according to the canons of antique art. The blank verse was often intentionally restrained.

About his blank verse he said something of this kind to me: 'The English public think that blank verse is the easiest thing in the world to write, mere prose cut up into five-foot lines; whereas it is one of the most difficult. In a blank verse you can have from three up to eight beats; but, if you vary the beats unusually, your ordinary newspaper critic sets up a howl. The varying of the beats, of the construction of the feet, of the emphasis, of the extra-metrical syllables and of the pauses, helps to make the greatness of blank verse. There are many other things besides, for instance a fine ear for vowel-sounds, and the kicking of the geese out of the boat (i.e. doing away with sibilations); but few educated men really understand the structure of blank verse. I never put two "ss" together in any verse of mine. My line is not, as often quoted,

> And freedom broadens slowly down—

but

> And freedom slowly broadens down.
> ['You ask me why, tho' ill at ease', 11]

People sometimes say how "studiedly alliterative" Tennyson's verse is. Why, when I spout my lines first, they come out so alliteratively that I have sometimes no end of trouble to get rid of the alliteration.'

The note by my father, that originally headed his blank verse translation from the *Iliad* beginning

> He ceased, and sea-like roar'd the Trojan host,

ran: 'Some, and among these one at least of our best and greatest, have endeavoured to give us the *Iliad* in English hexameters, and by what appears to me their failure have gone far to prove the impossibility of the task. I have long held by our blank verse in this matter, and now after having spoken so disrespectfully here of these hexameters, I venture or rather feel bound to subjoin a specimen (however brief and with whatever demerits) of a blank verse translation.'

> [*Memoir*, ii. 11–15]

[*Notes made by Tennyson in Switzerland, 1869*]

'The last cloud clinging to the peak when all the mists have risen.' 'Snow and rock thro' cloud unbelievably high.' 'The top of the Jungfrau rich saffron colour at dawn, the faded moon beside it.' 'The vision over the valley of Schwarenbach.' 'Splendour of sunlit clouds passing over the shadowed peak of the Eiger.'

[*Memoir*, ii. 65]

[*Tennyson on Byron, 1869*]

He spoke with great regard of X—, then he added: 'I think that I believe more of revealed religion than X— does. He believes in a God, but knows nothing more.' I said: 'I wonder if he is happy.' He replied: 'So good a man must be happy.' Then he added: 'I am not blasé, I see the nothingness of life, I know its emptiness, but I believe in Love, and Virtue, and Duty. Perhaps, thanks to Byron, I was more blasé at fourteen than I am now.'

We talked of Byron and Wordsworth. 'Of course,' said Tennyson, 'Byron's merits are on the surface. This is not the case with Wordsworth. You must love Wordsworth ere he will seem worthy of your love. As a boy I was an enormous admirer of Byron, so much so that I got a surfeit of him, and now I cannot read him as I should like to do. I was fourteen when I heard of his death. It seemed an awful calamity; I remember I rushed out of doors, sat down by myself, shouted aloud, and wrote on the sandstone: "*Byron is dead!*" '

[*Memoir*, ii. 69]

[*Tennyson on the immensity of the Universe, and on Jane Austen*]

January 25th, 1870. The Ritchies and Annie Thackeray dined with us.

My father said to them: 'I don't find it difficult to believe in the Infinity of Worlds.' Then, after trying to make us all realize the rate at which the earth whirls through space, and that every two days the solar system has rushed one million miles towards a certain point in the constellation of Hercules, and that light takes millions of years to travel from some of the stars, the light of which has not yet reached us, and other astronomical sublimities—he observed, 'From the starry spheres to think of the airs given themselves by county families in ball-rooms! One lady I remember early in the century in Lincolnshire, drawing herself up on hearing that the daughters of a neighbouring family were taking lessons in drawing and singing, and saying, "My daughters don't learn drawing." ' He continued: 'Miss Austen understood the smallness of life to perfection. She was a great artist, equal in her small sphere to Shakespeare. I think *Persuasion* and *Mansfield Park* are my favourites. There is a saying that if God made the country, and man the town, the devil made the little country town. There is nothing equal to the smallness of a small town.'

[*Memoir*, ii. 96]

[*Tennyson's prose sketches for an Arthurian epic*]

The earliest fragment of an epic that I can find among my father's MSS in my possession was probably written about 1833, and is a sketch in prose. I give it as it stands.

King Arthur

On the latest limit of the West in the land of Lyonnesse, where, save the rocky Isles of Scilly, all is now wild sea, rose the sacred Mount of Camelot. It rose from the deeps with gardens and bowers and palaces, and at the top of the Mount was King Arthur's hall, and the holy Minster with the Cross of gold. Here dwelt the King in glory apart, while the Saxons whom he had overthrown in twelve battles ravaged the land, and ever came nearer and nearer.

The Mount was the most beautiful in the world, sometimes green and fresh in the beam of morning, sometimes all one splendour, folded in the golden mists of the West. But all underneath it was hollow, and the mountain trembled, when the seas rushed bellowing through the porphyry caves; and there ran a prophecy that the mountain and the city on some wild morning would topple into the abyss and be no more.

It was night. The King sat in his Hall. Beside him sat the sumptuous Guinevere and about him were all his lords and knights of the Table Round. There they feasted, and when the feast was over the Bards sang to the King's glory.

The following memorandum was presented by my father to Mr Knowles at Aldworth on October 1, 1869, who told him that it was between thirty and forty years old. It was probably written at the same time as the fragment which I have just quoted. However the allegorical drift here marked out was fundamentally changed in the later scheme of the 'Idylls.'

K. A. Religious Faith.

King Arthur's three Guineveres.

The Lady of the Lake.

Two Guineveres. ye first prim. Christianity. 2^d Roman Catholicism. ye first is put away and dwells apart. 2^d Guinevere flies. Arthur takes to the first again but finds her changed by lapse of Time.

Modred, the sceptical understanding. He pulls Guinevere, Arthur's latest wife, from the throne.

Merlin Emrys, the enchanter. Science. Marries his daughter to Modred. Excalibur, war.

The sea, the people. ⎱ the S. are a sea-people and it is
The Saxons, the people. ⎰ theirs and a type of them.

The Round Table: liberal institutions.

Battle of Camlan.

2^d Guinevere with the enchanted book and cup.

Before 1840 it is evident that my father wavered between casting the Arthurian legends into the form of an epic or into that of a musical masque; for in one of his 1833–1840 MS books there is the following first rough draft of a scenario, into which the Lancelot and Elaine scenes were afterwards introduced.

First Act

Sir Mordred and his party. Mordred inveighs against the King and the Round Table. The knights, and the quest. Mordred scoffs at the Ladies of the Lake, doubts whether they are supernatural beings, etc. Mordred's cringing interview with Guinevere. Mordred and the Lady of the Lake. Arthur lands in Albyn.

Second Act

Lancelot's embassy and Guinevere. The Lady of the Lake meets Arthur and endeavours to persuade him not to fight with Sir Mordred. Arthur will not be moved from his purpose. Lamentation of the Lady of the Lake. Elaine. Marriage of Arthur.

Third Act

Oak tomb of Merlin. The song of Nimue. Sir Mordred comes to consult Merlin. Coming away meets Arthur. Their fierce dialogue. Arthur consults Sir L. and Sir Bedivere. Arthur weeps over Merlin and is reproved by Nimue, who inveighs against Merlin. Arthur asks Merlin the issue of the battle. Merlin will not enlighten him. Nimue requests Arthur to question Merlin again. Merlin tells him he shall bear rule again, but that the Ladies of the Lake can return no more. Guinevere throws away the diamonds into the river. The Court and the dead Elaine.

Fourth Act

Discovery by Mordred and Nimue of Lancelot and Guinevere. Arthur and Guinevere's meeting and parting.

Fifth Act

The battle. Chorus of the Ladies of the Lake. The throwing away of Excalibur and departure of Arthur.

After this my father began to study the epical King Arthur in earnest. He had travelled in Wales, and meditated a tour in Cornwall. He thought, read, talked about King Arthur. He made a poem on Lancelot's quest of the San Graal; 'in as good verse,' he said, 'as I ever wrote—no, I did not write, I made it in my head, and it has altogether slipt out of memory.' What he called 'the greatest of all poetical subjects' perpetually haunted him. But it was not till 1855 that he determined upon the final shape of the poem, and not until 1859 that he published the first instalment, 'Enid,' 'Vivien,' 'Elaine,' 'Guinevere.' In spite of the public applause he did not rush headlong into the other 'Idylls of the King,' although he had carried a more or less perfected scheme of them in his head over thirty years. For one thing, he did not consider that the time was ripe. In addition to this, he did not find himself in the proper mood to write them, and he never could work except at what his heart impelled him to do.—Then, however, he devoted himself with all his energies and with infinite enthusiasm to that work alone.

He also gave some other reasons for pausing in the production of the 'Idylls.' 'One,' he wrote, 'is because I could hardly light upon a finer close than that ghost-like passing away of the King' (in 'Guinevere'), although the 'Morte d'Arthur' was the natural close. The second was that he was not sure he could keep up to the same high level throughout the remaining 'Idylls.' 'I have thought about it,' he writes in 1862, 'and arranged all the intervening "Idylls," but I dare not set to work for fear of a failure and time lost.' The third was, to give it in his own words, 'I doubt whether such a subject as the San Graal could be handled in these days without incurring a charge of irreverence. It would be too much like playing with sacred things.' 'The Holy Grail' however later on seemed to come suddenly, as if by a breath of inspiration; and that volume was given to the world in 1869, containing . . . 'The Coming of Arthur,' 'The Holy Grail,' 'Pelleas and Ettarre,' and 'The Passing of Arthur.'

In 1871 'The Last Tournament' was privately printed, and then published in the *Contemporary Review*: republished with 'Gareth and Lynette' in 1872. These with 'Balin and Balan' (published in 1885) make up the 'twelve books,'—the number mentioned in the Introduction to the 'Morte d'Arthur.'

[*Memoir*, ii. 122–6]

[*Tennyson and George Eliot*]

Two or three times we [Tennyson and his son] met George Eliot in town, and she expressed herself much pleased that the poet who, she said, had 'so much human blood in his poems and plays,' should have told her that her 'flight of Hetty in *Adam Bede* and Thackeray's gradual breaking down of Colonel Newcome were the two most pathetic things in modern prose fiction.' He had the highest admiration for her insight into character, but did not think her quite so true to nature as Shakespeare and Miss Austen.

I read somewhere an account of a quarrel between her and my father, carried on in loud tones, with red faces and clenched fists, the subject being her want of belief in an after-life. I showed this to him, and he wrote down what actually happened. 'I and she never had one moment of discussion, much less of quarrel. She called, and when she went away I pressed her hand kindly and sweetly, and said, "I wish you well with your molecules." She replied as gently, "I get on very well with my molecules." '

I have also the record of a later conversation between them which took place at Aldworth. They agreed as to 'the namby-pambyism of the age, which hates a story to end in tragedy, as if the greatest moral lessons were not taught by tragedies.' My father added, 'What the public do not understand is that the great tragedy is all balance throughout.' She then objected to the many English writers who set up French literature against our own, for 'Is not ours,' she said, 'one of the greatest in the world?'

She wanted my father to make a poem of this story, which she narrated as true, and as having occurred in one of the midland counties. A drunkard boasted that he would 'fight any bull ever born.' He went out into the starlight and walked up to a well-known ferocious bull, dealing him a blow on the forehead which felled both man and bull. By that shock the man became 'undrunk' and never drank again, so great was the terror which seized on him while lying there: the bull 'nozzling' him; those big eyes, head and horns between him and the sky. George Eliot thought that my father would make a fine analysis of what passed in the man's mind as he lay there under the starry heavens.

[*Memoir*, ii. 225–6]

[*Tennyson on quantity*]

My father . . . confessed that he believed he knew the quantity of every word in the English language except perhaps 'scissors.' We asked him to make a Sapphic stanza in quantity, with the Greek cadence. He gave us this:

Sapphics

Faded ev'ry violet, all the roses;
Gone the glorious promise; and the victim,
Broken in this anger of Aphrodite,
      Yields to the victor.

[*Memoir*, ii. 231]

[*Tennyson and Carlyle in conversation, 1879*]

I subjoin some talks which my father had with Carlyle, jotted down in my note-book.

A.T. People say you are writing your autobiography.

Carlyle. Do they? Do they want me to make away with myself that they talk like that?

A.T. Why don't you try your hand at a great novel? you have seen life enough.

Carlyle. No, no. I write a novel! I know nothing of human character.

After going with my father to the British Museum and looking at the Greek and Roman statues, Carlyle said, 'Neither man nor god can get on without a decent jaw-bone, and not one of them has a decent jaw-bone.' Carlyle became in later years reconciled to my father's writing poetry. He admired 'Harold,' saying that it was 'full of wild pathos,' and founded on the Bayeux tapestry, which he called 'a very blessed work indeed.'

My father read him 'The Revenge.'

Carlyle. Eh! Alfred, you have got the grip of it.

A.T. There's a man for you. The Spaniards declared he would 'carouse' three or four glasses of wine and take the glasses between his teeth and crush them to pieces and swallow them down.

Carlyle. (Half to himself.) I knew that Alfred would treat that episode in a masterful manner, and he'd not allude to Elizabeth's starving the poor sailors.

And then he spoke of 'The May Queen.' 'Oh! but that's tender and true; my niece says it sometimes to me!'

Through 'The First Quarrel' he gave little cries of sympathy.

Carlyle. Ah, but that's a dreary tragic tale.

A.T. That's a true tale. My doctor in the Isle of Wight told it me.

Carlyle, going on about the poem: Ech! poor fellow, he was just an honest plain man, and she was a curious production of the century, and I'm very sorry for that poor girl too.

One day Carlyle was full of Holman Hunt's 'Shadow of the Cross.'

Carlyle. I think, poor fellow, he painted that picture in a distraction.

A.T. The Christ I call Christ-like is Sebastian del Piombo's in the National Gallery.

Then they talked of Goldsmith and Goethe.

Carlyle. Goldie was just an Irish blackguard, with a fine brain and sun-like eyes, and a great fund of goosery.

A.T. And of tender-heartedness: I love Goldie.

He made Carlyle laugh by giving a humorous imitation of Dr Johnson and Goldsmith talking together.

Carlyle. Goldsmith was much read in Germany in Goethe's time.

A.T. You know we visited Goethe's house at Weimar. The 'Salve' on the door-mat, and the legion of Goethe's old boots there looked to me terribly pathetic.

Then my father told how we had found a book 'From T. Carlyle' on his table, which pleased the old man mightily.

They made merry over the statues of Goethe and Schiller in the market-place, 'for all the world like drunken sailors quarrelling over a wreath.'

Carlyle. Ay, ay. Art is at a low ebb; and among the nations England, unless she takes great heed, will go down to the devil.

A.T. Come! we are not so bad as in Charles II.'s reign.

Carlyle. O yes, there were more Andrew Marvells then. True, the Parliament was so coxcombed at having cut a king's head off that there was no doing anything with them. Those days indeed were very like the days now, no real strong ruler, all just a confusion of jackassery.

He called Gladstone 'The man with the immeasurable power of vocables.'

A.T. I love the man, but no Prime Minister ought to be an orator.

They touched on Macaulay.

A.T. Macaulay, Guizot, Hallam and I went over the Houses of Parliament and Westminster Hall together; Macaulay said to me on going away, 'I am delighted to have met you, Mr Tennyson'; but I never saw him afterwards.

Carlyle. Eh (looking at him grimly), Alfred, Macaulay was afraid of you, you are such a black man (with a tremendous guffaw).

The last time we saw Carlyle he was in his dressing-gown, reading Masson's *Milton.*

A.T. Milton is a grand old fellow.

Carlyle. Yes, yes, and this man Masson is the first man who has properly sorted the Mosaic cosmogony, and I can now tell which way Satan went; but Masson has hung on his Milton peg *all* the politics, which Milton, poor fellow, had never much to do with except to print a pamphlet or two.

They then talked about death.

A.T. In my old age I should like to get away from all this tumult and turmoil of civilization and live on the top of a tropical mountain! I should at least like to see the splendours of the Brazilian forests before I die.

Carlyle. I would also like to quit it all.

A.T. If I were a young man, I would head a colony out somewhere or other.

Carlyle. O, ay, so would I, to India or somewhere: but the scraggiest bit of heath in Scotland is more to me than all the forests of Brazil. I am just twinkling away, and I wish I had had my Dimittis long ago.

Carlyle gave my father his tobacco box as a pledge of eternal brotherhood.

[*Memoir*, ii. 234–7]

[*Tennyson on Poets*]

It may not be out of place if I give here some of my father's criticisms on poets,—'who,' as he said, 'enrich the blood of the world,'—in addition to those already quoted. I put down a few random notes of his sayings at this time and at other times on the subject.

Chaucer was to him a kindred spirit, as a lover of nature and as a word-painter of character: and he enjoyed reading him aloud more than any poet except Shakespeare and Milton.

When he talked of the 'grand style' of poetic diction he would emphasize his opinion that he considered that of Milton even finer than that of Virgil, 'the lord of language.' 'Verse should be *beau comme la prose*.'

'Browning,' he said, 'never greatly cares about the glory of words or beauty of form: he has told me that the world must take him as it finds him. As for his obscurity in his great imaginative analyses, I believe it is a mistake to explain poetry too much, people have really a pleasure in discovering their own interpretations. He has a mighty intellect, but sometimes I cannot read him. He seldom attempts the marriage of sense with sound, although he shows a spontaneous felicity in the adaptation of words to ideas and feelings. I wish I had written his two lines:

> "The little more and how much it is,
> The little less and what worlds away."

['By the Fireside', 191–2]

He has plenty of music in him, but he cannot get it out.'

He would cite 'Rabbi Ben Ezra,' 'Death in the Desert,' 'Caliban upon Setebos,' 'The Englishman in Italy,' and 'A Grammarian's Funeral,' as poems of fine thought, and 'Mr Sludge, the Medium' as an example of exceeding ingenuity of mind. The last, however, he said to Browning, is 'two-thirds too long.'

Among modern sonnets he liked some of Rossetti's, Mrs Browning's 'Sonnets from the Portuguese,' and Charles Turner's. For Christina Rossetti, as a true artist, he expressed profound respect.

Of Shelley he said: 'He is often too much in the clouds for me. I admire his "Alastor," "Adonais," "Prometheus Unbound," and "Epipsychidion," and some of his short lyrics are exquisite. As for "The Lover's Tale," that was written before I had ever seen a Shelley, though it is called Shelleyan.'

Of Swinburne: 'He is a reed through which all things blow into music.'

He was not a great reader of William Morris; but he liked *The Life and Death of Jason*.

Keats he placed on a lofty pinnacle. 'He would have been among the very greatest of us if he had lived. There is something of the innermost soul of poetry in almost everything he ever wrote.' He gave the unfinished 'Eve of St Mark,' and the following lines from the 'Ode to a Nightingale' in illustration:

> 'Perhaps the self-same song that found a path
> Through the sad heart of Ruth, when, sick for home,
> She stood in tears amid the alien corn;
> The same that oft-times hath
> Charm'd magic casements, opening on the foam
> Of perilous seas, in faery lands forlorn.'

'If the beginning of "Hyperion," as now published, were shorter,' he said, 'it would be a deal finer: that is, if from "Not so much" to "feathered grass" were omitted.'

He felt what Cowper calls the 'musical finesse' of Pope, and admired single lines and couplets very much; but he found the 'regular da da, da da' of his heroic metre monotonous. He quoted

> 'What dire offence from amorous causes springs.'

[*The Rape of the Lock*, 1]

' "Amrus causiz springs," horrible! I would sooner die than write such a line!! Archbishop Trench (not then archbishop) was the only critic who said of my first volume, "What a singular absence of the 's'!" '

[*Memoir*, ii. 284–6]

[*Tennyson on Shakespeare*]

Of Shakespeare's sonnets he would say, 'Henry Hallam made a great mistake about them: they are noble. Look how beautiful such lines as these are:

> "The summer flower is to the summer sweet,
> Though to itself it only live and die,"

and

> "And peace proclaims olives of endless age." '

Of Shakespeare's blank verse he said, 'Almost any prose can be cut up into blank verse, but blank verse becomes the finest vehicle of thought in the language of Shakespeare and Milton. As far as I am aware, no one has noticed what great Æschylean lines there are in Shakespeare, particularly in *King John*: for instance,

> "The burning crest
> Of the old, feeble, and day-wearied sun,"

or again,

> "The sepulchre
> Hath oped his ponderous and marble jaws." '

He would say, 'There are three repartees in Shakespeare which always bring tears to my eyes from their simplicity.

One is in *King Lear* when Lear says to Cordelia, "So young and so untender," and Cordelia lovingly answers, "So young, my lord, and true." And in *The Winter's Tale*, when Florizel takes Perdita's hand to lead her to the dance, and says, "So turtles pair that never mean to part," and the little Perdita answers, giving her hand to Florizel, "I'll swear for 'em." And in *Cymbeline*, when Imogen in tender rebuke says to her husband,

> "Why did you throw your wedded lady from you?
> Think that you are upon a rock; and now
> Throw me again!"

and Posthumus does not ask forgiveness, but answers, kissing her,

> "Hang there like fruit, my soul,
> Till the tree die." '

After reading *Pericles*, Act V. aloud:

'That is glorious Shakespeare: most of the rest of the play is poor, and not by Shakespeare, but in that act the conception of Marina's character is exquisite.'

Of *Henry VI.* he said, 'I am certain that *Henry VI.* is in the main not Shakespeare's, though here and there he may have put in a touch, as he undoubtedly did in *The Two Noble Kinsmen*. There is a great deal of fine Shakespeare in that. Spedding insisted that Shakespeare, among the many plays that he edited for the stage, had corrected a play on Sir Thomas More in the British Museum. It is a poor play, but Spedding believed that the corrections were possibly in Shakespeare's actual handwriting.'

'I have no doubt that much of *Henry VIII.* also is not Shakespeare. It is largely written by Fletcher, with passages unmistakeably by Shakespeare, notably the two first scenes in the first Act, which are sane and compact in thought, expression and simile. I could swear to Shakespeare in the *Field of the Cloth of Gold*:

> "To-day the French
> All clinquant, all in gold like heathen gods,
> Shone down the English; and to-morrow they
> *Made Britain India; every man that stood*
> *Show'd like a mine.*"

'*Hamlet* is the greatest creation in literature that I know of: though there may be elsewhere finer scenes and passages of poetry. Ugolino and Paolo and Francesca in Dante equal anything anywhere. It is said that Shakespeare was such a poor actor that he never got beyond his ghost in this play, but then the ghost is the most real ghost that ever was. The Queen did not think that Ophelia committed suicide, neither do I.'

'Is there a more delightful love-poem than *Romeo and Juliet*? yet it is full of conceits.

'One of the most passionate things in Shakespeare is Romeo's speech:

> "Amen, amen! but come what sorrow can,
> It cannot countervail the exchange of joy
> That one short minute gives me in her sight," etc.

More passionate than anything in Shelley. No one has drawn the true passion of love like Shakespeare.'

For inimitably natural talk between husband and wife he would quote the scene between Hotspur and Lady Percy (*King Henry IV.*, Pt. I.), and would exclaim: 'How deliciously playful is that—

"In faith, I'll break thy little finger, Harry,
An if thou wilt not tell me all things true"!'

'Macbeth is not, as is too often represented, a noisy swash-buckler; he is a full-furnished, ambitious man. In the scene with Duncan, the excess of courtesy adds a touch to the tragedy. It is like Clytemnestra's profusion to Agamemnon; who, by the way, always strikes me as uncommonly cold and haughty to his wife whom he had not seen for years.'

'*King Lear* cannot possibly be acted, it is too titanic. At the beginning of the play Lear, in his old age, has grown half mad, choleric and despotic, and therefore cannot brook Cordelia's silence. This play shows a state of society where men's passions are savage and uncurbed. No play like this anywhere—not even the *Agamemnon*—is so terrifically human.'

'Actors do not comprehend that Shakespeare's greatest villains, Iago among them, have always a touch of conscience. You see the conscience working—therein lies one of Shakespeare's pre-eminences. Iago ought to be acted as the "honest Iago," not the stage villain; he is the essentially jealous man, not Othello.'

Parts of *The Two Noble Kinsmen* he considered were by Shakespeare. 'For instance such lines as these bear his impress:

"That makes the stream seem flowers,"

and

"Who dost pluck
With hand armipotent from forth blue clouds
The mason'd turrets: that both mak'st and break'st
The stony girths of cities." '

[*Memoir*, ii. 289–92]

[*Tennyson on race and Ireland, 1887*]

Speaking of Ireland and England, he said: 'The Celtic race does not easily amalgamate with other races, as those of Scandinavian origin do, as for instance Saxon and Norman, which have fused perfectly. The Teuton has no poetry in his nature like the Celt, and this makes the Celt much more dangerous in politics, for he yields more to his imagination than his common-sense. Yet his imagination does not allow of his realizing the sufferings of poor dumb beasts. The Irish are difficult for us to deal with. For one thing the English do not understand their innate love of fighting, words and blows. If on either side of an Irishman's road to Paradise shillelahs grew, which automatically hit him on the head, yet he would not be satisfied. Suppose that we allowed Ireland to separate from us: owing to its factions she would soon fall a prey to some foreign power. She has absolute freedom now, and a more than full share in the government of one of the mightiest empires in the world. Whatever she may say, she is not only feudal, but oriental, and loves those in authority over her to have the iron hand in the silken glove.'

[*Memoir*, ii. 338]

[*Tennyson on society*]

He acknowledged that there is a greater feeling of the Unity of Society than there was in his young days. But he would say: 'The whole of Society at present is too like a jelly; when it is touched, it shakes from base to summit. As yet the Unity is of weakness rather than of strength. The difference of individualities must always exist, and since we are members of one body, different gifts are needed to supply the wants of that body. Our aim therefore ought to be not to merge the individual in the community, but to strengthen the social life of the community, and foster the individuality.'

Speaking of the ultra-Radicals' passion for change, he said: 'Stagnation is more dangerous than Revolution. But *sudden* change means a house on sand. Action and Reaction is the miserable see-saw of our child-world. If these extreme men had their way, the end of the century would be plunged in blood, a universal French Revolution. What we have to bear in mind is that, even in a Republic, there must be a guiding hand. Men of education, experience, weight, and wisdom, must continue to come forward. They who will not be ruled by the rudder will in the end be ruled by the rock.

[*Memoir*, ii. 339]

['*Crossing the Bar*']

'Crossing the Bar' was written in my father's eighty-first year, on a day in October when we came from Aldworth to Farringford. Before reaching Farringford he had the Moaning of the Bar in his mind, and after dinner he showed me this poem written out.

I said, 'That is the crown of your life's work.' He answered, 'It came in a moment.' He explained the 'Pilot' as 'That Divine and Unseen Who is always guiding us.'

A few days before my father's death he said to me: 'Mind you put "Crossing the Bar" at the end of all editions of my poems.'

[*Memoir*, ii. 366–7]

[*Tennyson on novels*]

'Scott is the most chivalrous literary figure of this century, and the author with the widest range since Shakespeare. I think *Old Mortality* is his greatest novel. The realism and life-likeness of Miss Austen's Dramatis Personæ come nearest to those of Shakespeare. Shakespeare however is a sun to which Jane Austen, tho' a bright and true little world, is but an asteroid.'

Of *Clarissa Harlowe* [by Samuel Richardson] he would say: 'I like those great *still* books,' and 'I wish there were a great novel in hundreds of volumes that I might go on and on; I hate some of your modern novels with numberless characters thrust into the first chapter and nothing but modern society talk; and also those morbid, and introspective tales, with their oceans of sham philosophy. To read these last is like wading through glue.'

[*Memoir*, ii. 372]

[*Tennyson's unfulfilled plans for poems*]

My father would have liked to make a poem of one of those great Egyptian legends, which describe how despair and death came upon him who was mad enough to try and probe the secret of the Universe; and he thought of weaving into a great stage drama the legend of 'Tristram of Lyonnesse,' as he had been obliged to cut it down to suit his treatment of the 'Idylls of the King.'

This narrative from the *Spectator*, given him by the Bishop of Ripon (Boyd Carpenter), he felt was a noble theme, and he laid it aside for future use:

In December last, the American ship '*Cleopatra*' was descried by Captain Hughes of the Liverpool steamer '*Lord Gough*,' near the St George's Shoal, with her colours at half-mast and evidently sinking. The gale and the sea were so terrible that it seemed madness to help her; but volunteers came forward, and a boat was manned, when suddenly, the colours were hauled down. Captain Hughes however persevered, the desperate adventure succeeded, and the crew of the '*Cleopatra*' was saved.

The United States Government forwarded thanks and rewards to Captain Hughes and his men; but noble as their conduct was, Captain Pendleton of the '*Cleopatra*' had done a nobler thing. He was asked why his colours were hauled down, and replied, 'Because we had no boats, and thought it wrong to imperil other lives in a hopeless attempt.' The '*Cleopatra*' was then water-logged, and Captain Pendleton and his men faced the certainty of death by drowning rather than tempt others, strangers, into danger.

Honour to the name of the brave! That deed on the '*Cleopatra*' is equal to the conduct of the soldiers on the '*Birkenhead*,' and should live like it in song.

[*Memoir*, ii. 372–3]

NOTES

Tennyson's own annotations (recorded by Hallam Tennyson in the 'Eversley' edition of the poems) are recorded in these notes with the attribution '(T)'. All annotators of Tennyson owe a debt of gratitude to the work of Christopher Ricks, whose edition of the complete poems remains definitive; I acknowledge the more egregious of these debts to Ricks in the notes below. All translations unless otherwise specified are my own. Abbreviations in these notes refer to the following:

Letters   C. Y. Lang and E. F. Shannon (eds.), *The Letters of Alfred Lord Tennyson* (3 vols.; Oxford: Clarendon Press, 1982–90)

Memoir   Hallam Tennyson, *Alfred Lord Tennyson, a Memoir, by his Son* (2 vols., 1897)

Ricks   Christopher Ricks (ed.), *The Poems of Tennyson* (2nd edn., 3 vols.; London: Longman, 1987)

1830   *Poems, Chiefly Lyrical* (1830)

1832   *Poems* (1832)

1842   *Poems* (2 vols., 1842; the first volume includes a selection of earlier poems).

POEMS

3 *Timbuctoo*. Encouraged by his grandfather to compete for the Chancellor's Medal in Poetry at Cambridge, Tennyson took an earlier work called *Armageddon* and adapted it to the theme required by the Prize Committee. He was awarded the prize on 6 June 1829, but declined the usual public recitation of the poem in the Senate House (his friend Charles Merivale stood in for him). Always diffident about this work, he wrote to a printer called Metcalf who wanted to bring out a volume of various Cambridge Prize Poems that 'prize poems . . . are not properly speaking "Poems" at all, and ought to be forgotten as soon as recited. I could have wished that poor "Timbuctoo" might have been suffered to slide quietly off, with all its errors, into forgetfulness' (*Memoir*, i. 45). The poem was published in the *Cambridge Chronicle and Journal* in 1829, and in the same year in a volume called *Prolusiones Academicae*. Tennyson did not include it in any edition of his own poetry during his lifetime.

l. 1. *Mountain*. The narrator is at the Straits of Gibraltar.

l. 11. *Giant of old Time*. Hercules, who is reputed to have erected 'the Pillars of Hercules' at the Straits.

l. 15. *yeasty*. Frothy, foaming. 'Yeasty wave' is from *Macbeth*, IV. i. 73–4 ('Though the yeasty wave | Confound and swallow navigation up').

4 l. 33. *Genius*. In the Greek sense of the spirit or god of the temple.

l. 66. *orbs*. Eyes.

5 l. 71. *zone*. Belt (from the Greek *zonē*, 'girdle').

l. 109. *wan sapphire*. Dark blue (Tennyson's colour for outer space).

6 l. 142. *shallop*. Boat.

l. 147. *house*. Live.

7 l. 176. *valve*. Double door.

8 l. 196. *glory' of Heaven*. Tennyson puts in the apostrophe to indicate that the words should be elided for the rhythm of the line ('glory'f Heaven').

l. 218. *Fable*. Tennyson's view that myth and story, no matter how fanciful, could be proper media for imaginative truth was timely. Wordsworth's *Excursion*, iv. 630–940 makes similar points.

ll. 227–8. *imaging | The soft inversion*. Mirroring.

9 ll. 230–1. *pagods*. Idol temples or Pagodas.   *chrysolite*. A precious green-coloured stone.

l. 233. *gulphs*. Swallows.

l. 247. *Calpe*. The mountain at the Straits of Gibraltar (from line 1).

'*The Idealist*'. Written in 1829, but not published during Tennyson's lifetime. An 'idealist' in philosophy is somebody who believes that the external world is not concrete or 'real', but is in some sense a collection of 'ideas'. Religious idealists (like the English philosopher Berkeley) believe the world to be an Idea in the mind of God; transcendental idealists (following the great German philosopher Kant, whose works were popularized in Britain by Coleridge) believe that the world may indeed be 'real', but can only be known to us via our mental ideas.

l. 13. *Tadmor*. Ancient Syrian city, also known as Palmyra, now famous chiefly (as with 'Rome' and 'Cairo') for its ruins.

11 *Mariana*. First published in *1830*, Tennyson later classified this work as 'juvenilia'. The epigraph is adapted from Shakespeare's *Measure for Measure*, III. i. 277, where the Duke announces: 'I will presently to St Luke's: there, at the moated grange, resides this dejected Mariana'. A 'moated grange' is a farmhouse or cottage with a moat around it. In the play Mariana is betrothed to Angelo, who acts as deputy for the Duke of Vienna in the latter's absence. The Duke returns in disguise to see how badly Angelo is doing, and explains Mariana's situation to another character.

> DUKE. Her brother Frederick was wracked at sea, having in that perished vessel the dowry of his sister. But mark how heavily this befell to the poor gentlewoman: there she lost a noble and renowned brother, in his love toward her ever most kind and natural; with him, the portion and sinew of her fortune, her marriage-dowry; with both, her combinate husband, this well-seeming Angelo.
> ISABELLA. Can this be so? Did Angelo leave her?

DUKE. Left her in tears, and dried not one of them with his comfort. Swallowed his vows whole, pretending in her discoveries of dishonour: in few, bestowed her on her own lamentation, which she yet wears for his sake; and he, a marble to her tears, is washed with them, but relents not. (*Measure for Measure*, III. i)

Tennyson seems to have written, or planned, a prologue to this poem (to be called 'Prologue to the Marianas'), but this has not survived. His sequel, 'Mariana in the South', is printed on pp. 26–8.

12 l. 38. *sluice*. A place where the stream had been dammed to make a small pool.

l. 40. *marish-mosses*. 'The little marsh-moss lumps that float on the surface of water' (T). 'Marish' is an old form of the word 'marsh'.

l. 63. *blue fly*. The bluebottle fly.

l. 64. *wainscot*. Wood panelling lining the walls.

13 *Supposed Confessions of a Second-Rate Sensitive Mind*. Written in Cambridge 1829 and first published in *1830*, where it was titled 'Supposed Confessions of a Second-Rate Sensitive Mind Not in Unity With Itself'. The title may make reference to Goethe's *Wilhelm Meister's Travels* (which had been translated by Carlyle in 1827), whose seventh chapter is called 'The Confessions of some mind not yet in unity with itself'. There may also be an allusion to James Hogg's popular pseudo-Gothic novel, *The Private Memoirs and Confessions of a Justified Sinner* (1824).

l. 11. *rive*. Cleave, split, break asunder.

15 l. 56. *salient*. Leaping or jumping up.

l. 83. *scathe*. Harm.

16 l. 97. *reboant*. Re-echoing loudly (literally 're-bellowing').

l. 126. *slope*. i.e. 'sloping'.

ll. 128–9. *broad-imbased*. Uncertain. This may mean simply 'broad-based'; or it might mean 'broad and low', particularly with overtones of a lowering in dignity or status.   *tarn*. Small lake.

l. 131. *mere*. Small lake or pond.

17 l. 158. *fere*. Companion.

18 l. 181. *Shadow*. Protect.

Song ('I' the glooming light'). First published in *1830*, but not reprinted by Tennyson during his life.

19 *Song ('A spirit haunts the year's last hours')*. The first stanza was written 1828, the second probably in 1830. First published in *1830*, and later reprinted by Tennyson as 'juvenilia'.

l. 19. *box*. A variety of evergreen shrub.

20 *The Kraken*. Printed in *1830*, and later reprinted by Tennyson as 'juvenilia'. 'Kraken' is the Norwegian name of a mythical sea-monster; it was

introduced to English via a 1755 translation of a work called *The Natural History of Norway*. 'See the account which Erik Pontoppidan, the Norwegian bishop, born 1698, gives of the fabulous sea-monster—the Kraken (*Biographie Universelle*)' (T).

l. 12. *Battening*. Feeding, growing fat.

l. 13. *latter fire*. The fire that attends the end of the world. Tennyson is alluding to the biblical *Revelation*, chapter 8.

21 *The Lady of Shalott*. Tennyson was working on this poem in Oct. 1831, and then finished it in May 1832. It was published in *1832*, but revised fairly extensively for *1842* (the later version is printed here). The subject of this Arthurian poem is Elaine, who loved Lancelot; she was known as 'the lily maid of Astolat', which is Tennyson's 'Shalott'. He later claimed not to have read Malory before writing this poem, but to have found the story in a 14th-century Italian romance called 'La Donna di Scalotta' (the actual title is *Qui conta come la Damigella di Scalot morì per amore di Lancialotto de Lac*). He changed 'Scalotta' because 'Shalott was a softer sound than Scalott'. In 1868 Tennyson told F. J. Furnivell that 'I met the story first in some Italian *nouvelle*: but the web, mirror, island, etc., were my own. Indeed, I doubt whether I should ever have put it in that shape if I had been then aware of the Maid of Astolat in *Mort Arthur*' (quoted in Ricks, i. 387).

l. 10. *Willows whiten*. Willow leaves have pale undersides, and these are being rippled upwards by the wind.

l. 22. *shallop*. Small boat.

22 l. 56. *pad*. Non-thoroughbred horse.

23 l. 71. *'I am half sick of shadows'*. 'Shadows' means 'reflected images'. Hallam's *Memoir* says that 'the key to this tale of magic "symbolism" is of deep human significance, and is to be found in the lines [69–72]'. He then quotes Tennyson's own interpretation: 'the new-born love for something, for some one in the wide world from which she has been so long secluded, takes her out of the region of shadows into that of realities' (*Memoir*, i. 116–17).

l. 76. *greaves*. Armour for the shins.

l. 78. *red-cross knight*. Tennyson is thinking primarily of 'the Red-Crosse Knight' from book 1 of Spenser's *Faerie Queene* (there are a number of Spenserian allusions in the poem); but as the Red Cross was the emblem of St George, the patron saint of England, this shield-blazon also has the effect of Anglicizing the (French) Sir Lancelot.

l. 87. *baldric*. A shoulder strap from which the shield could be hung. 'Blazon'd' means ornamented with heraldic devices.

24 l. 107. *Tirra lirra*. As critics have pointed out, Lancelot's song is the same as Shakespeare's Autolycus (from *The Winter's Tale*), who sings a song with this refrain whose subject is 'tumbling in the hay' with women. The point is to underline the Lady's sexual frustration.

25 ll. 163–71. *Who is this? . . . 'The Lady of Shalott'*. The last stanza of the poem was different in the original publication:

> They crossed themselves, their stars they blest
> Knight, minstrel, abbot, squire and guest.
> There lay a parchment at her breast,
> That puzzled more than all the rest,
>   The wellfed wits at Camelot.
> *'The web was woven curiously*
> *The charm is broken utterly,*
> *Draw near and fear not—this is I,*
>   *The Lady of Shalott.'*

Tennyson, in his decision to rewrite the stanza, may have been influenced by John Stuart Mill's reference to the original as 'a lame and impotent conclusion' in a review from 1835.

26 *Mariana in the South*. Written 1830–1, first published in *1832*, and revised fairly extensively for *1842* (the later version is printed here). The scenery described is southern France, after a journey Tennyson and Arthur Hallam had undertaken through that country 'between Narbonne and Perpignan' (*Memoir*, i. 117) in 1830. A letter from Arthur Hallam to W. B. Donne talks about the poem in these terms: 'it is intended, you will perceive, as a kind of pendant to his former poem of "Mariana", the idea of both being the expression of desolate loneliness . . . When we were journeying together this summer through the South of France we came upon a range of country just corresponding to his preconceived thought of a barrenness' (*Memoir*, i. 500).

28 l. 85. *cicala*. Cicada.

Œnone. Written 1830–2, and published in *1832*, but revised fairly extensively for *1842* (the later version is printed here). Tennyson wrote to his friend Spedding (Mar. 1835) with news of 'my old poems, most of which I have so corrected (particularly "Œnone") as to make them much less imperfect', *Memoir*, i. 145). The pastoral aspects of this poem recall Theocritus, whose 'idylls' were to be a continuing influence on Tennyson. He wrote a sequel to it 'The Death of Œnone', at the end of his career (written 1889–90 and published 1892).

l. 1. *Ida*. A mountain south of the ancient city of Troy, in Asia Minor.

l. 2. *Ionian*. The 'Ionians' were Greeks who settled widely in Greece, Sicily, and in Asia Minor, a portion of which was called 'Ionia' in their honour.

l. 10. *Gargarus*. 'The highest part of Mount Ida' (T). The name means 'big heap' in Greek.

l. 16. *Paris*. A prince of ancient Troy, who has abandoned Œnone for Helen. Helen's husband, Menelaus, sailed to Troy with an army to get his wife back, and the Trojan War began.

29 l. 37. *River-God*. The river Simois, one of two rivers on the plain of Troy (see line 51).

30 l. 60. *foam-bow*. 'The rainbow in the cataract' (T).

l. 65. *Hesperian*. The evening star, Hesperus, had four daughters—the Hesperides—who were given the job of guarding certain golden apples by Herè, queen of the gods. The apples were magic, with healing powers, and symbolized happiness. See 'The Hesperides' on p. 43.

l. 72. *Oread*. A type of mountain-nymph.

l. 79. *Peleus*. Peleus was king of Thessaly, married to the immortal Thetis, and father of the great Greek warrior Achilles. At the wedding between Peleus and Thetis, the goddess Eris ('Strife') brought a golden apple to be given to 'the fairest'. Three goddesses, Herè the queen of the gods, Pallas Athene the goddess of wisdom, and Aphrodite the goddess of love, all claimed this prize. The apple was given to the mortal man Paris, for him to judge who most deserved it (this is the Judgement of Paris).

31 l. 105. *her*. Herè, wife of Zeus and queen of the gods. She offers Paris 'royal power' in return for the apple.

32 l. 151. *Sequel of guerdon*. 'Addition of reward' (T).

33 ll. 170–1. *Idalian . . . Paphian*. Both Idalium and Paphos were cities in Cyprus, the island most sacred to Aphrodite. The goddess is 'fresh as the foam' because her name is derived from *aphros*, the Greek for 'foam'.

l. 195. *pard*. Panther or leopard.

34 l. 220. *The Abominable*. Eris, Goddess Strife, whose gift of the apple had started all the trouble (see ll. 179 f. above).

35 l. 259. *Cassandra*. A beautiful Trojan princess, given the gift of prophecy by the god Apollo when wooing her. She rejected Apollo's suit, and he then overturned his gift by making sure nobody would believe her prophecies. Cassandra foresaw the doom of Troy, but was not heeded.

The Palace of Art. Written 1831–2 and first published *1832*. It was revised many times between 1832 and 1835, mostly by dropping or adding whole stanzas. Tennyson later claimed the poem originated in a discussion with R. C. Trench at Cambridge: 'Trench said to me, when we were at Trinity together, "Tennyson, we cannot live in art" '. His own gloss on the poem (' "The Palace of Art" is the embodiment of my own belief that the God-like life is with man and for man') has seemed reductive to many critics (*Memoir*, i. 118–19).

l. 1. Echo of Coleridge's 'Kubla Khan'; 'In Xanadu did Kubla Khan | A stately pleasure-dome decree' [1–2].

ll. 15–16. *Saturn . . . luminous ring*. This sort of precise astronomical imagery, drawn from the latest scientific discourses, is characteristic of Tennyson. Saturn, a gas giant much larger than Earth, none the less revolves much more rapidly than does our world, with a ten-and-a-half-hour cycle. Despite this, the shadow the planet throws across its own ring-system appears motionless.

36 l. 41. *she*. The soul, for whom the palace has been built, is traditionally female (*anima*).

37 l. 61. *arras*. Hanging tapestries that cover the walls, woven with various designs.

l. 80. *hoary to the wind*. A similar observation to 'Lady of Shalott', l. 10 (see above, p. 559). Tennyson himself glossed: 'the underside of the olive leaf is white'.

38 l. 95. *sardonyx*. A variety of stone with reddish layers. 'The Parisian jewellers apply graduated degrees of heat to the sardonyx, by which the original colour is changed to various colours. They imitate thus, among other things, bunches of grapes with green tendrils' (T).

l. 99. *St Cecily*. More usually Saint Cecilia, the patron-saint of music.

l. 102. *Houris*. Beautiful women who will attend the Muslim (or 'Islamite', l. 103) faithful when they enter Paradise.

ll. 105–7. *Uther's deeply-wounded son . . . Avalon*. Arthur, son of Uther Pendragon, was badly injured in the Last Battle. He was carried away to the mystic island of Avalon to heal his hurt.

l. 111. *Ausonian king*. The story was that Numa Pompilius, an early king of Rome, was given the laws that formed the basis of the Roman legal canon by a wood-nymph called Egeria. 'Ausonian' is a poetic name for middle and lower Italy.

l. 113. *engrail'd*. Indented, or marked at the edge with notches.

l. 115. *Indian Cama*. 'The Hindu God of young love, son of Brahma' (T).

l. 117. *Europa*. Europa was the beautiful daughter of the king of Tyre. Zeus fell in love with her, and transformed himself into the shape of a great white bull with golden horns to carry her away.

l. 121. *Ganymede*. Another mortal beloved of Zeus, this time a beautiful young boy. Zeus sent down his eagle to carry him up to the home of the gods, where he became a cup-bearer.

39 l. 137. *Ionian father*. Homer.

l. 159. *Oriels*. Large recesses with a window.

40 l. 163. *Verulam*. The English scientist and philosopher Francis Bacon, who had been created Lord Verulam, Viscount St Albans by James I.

l. 171. *Memnon*. A mythical statue at Thebes in Egypt, which the Ancient Greeks believed to be of the fabled Ethiopian King Memnon. It was reputed to give out beautiful music when the dawning sun's rays touched it.

41 ll. 203–4. *brainless devil . . . deep*. The reference is to Matt. 8: 28–34, where Jesus meets two people possessed by devils and casts the demons into a nearby herd of swine, 'and behold, the whole herd of swine ran violently down a steep place into the sea, and perished in the waters'.

l. 219. *Herod*. 'And upon a set day Herod, arrayed in royal apparel, sat upon his throne, and made an oration unto them. And the people gave a shout, saying, It is the voice of a god, and not of a man. And immediately the angel of the Lord smote him, because he gave not God the glory: and he was eaten of worms, and gave up the ghost' (Acts 12: 21–3).

l. 227. *Mene, mene.* This is part of 'the writing on the wall' that scares Balshazzar at his feast (Dan. 5: 23–7). Daniel, called in to interpret the mystic words, announces 'This is the interpretation of the thing: MENE; God hath numbered thy kingdom, and finished it. TEKEL; Thou art weighed in the balances, and art found wanting. PERES; Thy kingdom is divided.'

43   *The Hesperides.* Published in *1832*, Tennyson withdrew the poem after it was severely criticized by reviewers. Later Tennyson said 'he regretted that he had done away with it from among his Juvenilia' (*Memoir*, i. 61). Hesperus, the evening star, lived in the far west (sometimes identified with Western Africa) with his three (or four) daughters, the Hesperides. Together with a dragon called Ladon, they guarded the tree that bore the magical golden apples, which had been a wedding gift from earth (Gaea) to Hera on her marriage to Zeus, King of the Gods. One of the twelve labours of Hercules was to steal these apples, which he did by killing the dragon; or, alternatively, by persuading Atlas to steal them whilst he took over Atlas's job of supporting the world. The accents on words in this poem are Tennyson's own.

Epigraph. From Milton's masque, *Comus*, 982–3.

ll. 2–4. *Zidonian Hanno . . . Soloë . . . Thymiaterion.* Hanno was a celebrated sailor and navigator from Phoenicia (Zidon or Sidon is a Phoenician city). He explored the western coast of Africa many hundred years BC, his voyages being recorded in a Greek text called the *Periplus of Hanno*. Soloë and Thymiaterion are places on the Moroccan coast, as found in the *Periplus*.

44   l. 7. *Lotus-flute.* The lotus flower, eating which produced a state of dreamy happiness. Tennyson returns to this land with 'The Lotos-Eaters', on p. 47.

l. 28. *Five and three.* There are many discussions of this sort of sacred numerology in Tennysonian criticism. 5 + 3 is eight, known to Gnostic mystics as 'the ogdoad' and a specially holy number (there were eight divine beings in some Gnostic traditions). In Christian traditions, there were five wounds suffered by Christ on the cross and three elements to the Divine Trinity. Strictly in terms of the poem, there are five guarding the apples (Hesper, his three daughters and the dragon) plus the 'threefold music' of the three daughters' singing.

45   l. 42. *one.* Hercules.

46   l. 74. *Himala . . . Caucasus.* The Himalayas in Tibet, and the more westerly Caucasus mountains.

l. 82. *Phosphor.* The morning star.

47   *The Lotos-Eaters.* Written 1830–2 and first published in *1832*, it was revised by having various sections added for *1842*. The Lotos is a mythical plant, eating which produced a state of dreamy happiness. In Homer's *Odyssey*, Odysseus and his crew are returning from the battle of Troy by sea.

Odyssey, ix. 82 ff. describes how they put in at the land of the Lotus-eaters 'who eat a flowery food'.

47 l. 1. *he.* Odysseus.

l. 11. *lawn.* Fine cloth, used in theatres to imitate falling water. When a critic suggested that Tennyson should draw his images from nature, not theatrical props, he indignantly replied that he had indeed come up with the image in nature, whilst sitting beside a waterfall in the Pyrenees.

l. 23. *galingale.* An aromatic herb.

51 l. 133. *amaranth.* A mythic plant, reputed never to decay ('amaranth' means 'never fading').   *moly.* A magical plant with white flower and black root (perhaps the mandrake), given to Odysseus by Hermes as a charm against the magic of Circe (*Odyssey*, x).

l. 142. *acanthus.* Prickly leafy plant, known as 'Bears-breech'.

l. 156. *bolts.* Thunderbolts.

52 l. 170. *asphodel.* A yellow lily-like flower. Its name sounds soft, but actually its petals are rigid and rather spiky, not unlike daffodils, so it would make an uncomfortable sort of bed.

A Dream of Fair Women. Written 1831–2, published in *1832*, and later revised. As the *Memoir* tells us, 'The "Dream of Fair Women" begins in the first edition of 1832 with some stanzas about a man sailing in a balloon, but my father did not like the "balloon stanzas" so they were cut out' (*Memoir*, i. 121). Tennyson alludes in his title and opening lines to Chaucer's poem *The Legend of Good Women* (written between 1372 and 1386), in which the god of love scolds Chaucer for having only written negative things about women. Chaucer, by way of reparation, composes a poem in praise of those women who have been faithful in love: Cleopatra, Thisbe, Dido, Hypsipyle and Medea, Lucrece, Ariadne, Philomela, Phyllis, and Hypermnestra.

l. 5. *Dan Chaucer.* 'Dan' means 'Lord', short for 'Dominus'; Tennyson is being respectful (the phrase is from Spenser's *Faerie Queene*, IV. ii. 32, 'Dan Chaucer, well of English undefyled').

53 l. 27. *tortoise.* Roman military formation (the 'testudo'), where a troop of soldiers link their shields over their heads to provide defence against attack from above (for instance, as when attacking the base of a defended wall).

l. 36. *seraglios.* Harems.

l. 54. *an old wood.* Tennyson's own gloss was that 'the wood is the Past'.

54 l. 85. *lady.* The first 'fair woman' is Helen of Troy.

55 l. 100. *one.* The next is Iphigenia, beautiful daughter of Agamemnon, who, needing fair winds for his war-fleet to sail to Troy, sacrificed her at Aulis on the Greek coast to appease the gods.

l. 126. *One.* Next is Cleopatra, Queen of Egypt, who loved first Julius Caesar, then Mark Antony, but could not win over Octavius Caesar (Augustus) (l. 139).

l. 127. *swarthy cheeks*. Tennyson's later comments on this passage betray a certain racial anxiety: 'I was thinking of Shakespeare's Cleopatra: "Think of me | That am with Phoebus' amorous pinches black" [this is from *Antony and Cleopatra*, 1. v. 28] . . . I know perfectly well she was a Greek. "Swarthy" merely means sunburnt. I should not have spoken of her breast as "polished silver" if I had not known her as a white woman. Read "sunburnt" if you like it better' (in Ricks, i. 486). The slightly hysterical tone here, the over-insistence that this 'fair woman' was not Black, is representative of the ambient racism of the time.

56 l. 146. *Canopus*. Bright star visible in the southern sky.

57 l. 178. *one*. The next 'fair woman' is Jephthah's daughter, whose name is not recorded. Jephthah the Gileadite went to war with the children of Ammon, promising God that if he were victorious then 'whatsoever cometh forth of the doors of my house to meet me, when I return in peace . . . shall surely be the LORD's, and I will offer it up for a burnt offering'. After defeating the children of Ammon, 'Jephthah came to Mizpeh unto his house, and, behold, his daughter came out to meet him with timbrels and with dances: and she was his only child' (Judges 11: 31–4). Jephthah goes on to sacrifice her.

59 ll. 238–9. *Hew'd Ammon . . . Minneth*. 'And he [Jephthah] smote them [the children of Ammon] from Aroer, even till thou come to Minnith, even twenty cities' (Judges 11: 33).

l. 243. *Thridding the sombre boskage*. Threading her way between the trees in the dark thicket.

l. 249. *a low voice*. Belonging to Rosamond de Clifford, known as 'Fair Rosamond', mistress of Henry II, to whom she bore two sons. The story goes that she was poisoned by Henry's Queen, Eleanor. Henry erected a cross to her memory at Charing in central London (the place has been called Charing Cross ever since).

l. 258. *Egyptian*. Cleopatra speaks again; reminded by Rosamond's story of her own problems with Mark Antony's wife, Fulvia.

l. 263. *The captain*. 'Venus, the star of the morning' (T).

l. 266. *her*. Margaret Roper, daughter of Sir (or Saint) Thomas More. After her father's decapitation, she retrieved the head from a spike on London Bridge. Her coffin was later opened, and she was discovered still holding the leaden box that contained the head.

l. 269. *her*. 'Eleanor, wife of Edward I, went with him to the Holy Land (1269), where he was stabbed at Acre with a poisoned dagger. She sucked the poison from the wound' (T).

61 *The Two Voices*. Written 1833 (according to Tennyson, it was 'begun under the cloud of [my] overwhelming sorrow after the death of Arthur Hallam'; although portions of it had been written before Tennyson heard of Hallam's death). First published in *1842*. Originally titled 'Thoughts of a Suicide', Tennyson told his son 'when I wrote "The Two Voices" I was so

utterly miserable, a burden to myself and to my family, that I said, "Is life worth anything?" ' (*Memoir*, i. 193).

61   l. 7. *dragon-fly*. The 'still small voice' negates the narrator's assertion that he is valuable because 'wonderfully made' by instancing a lower animal even more marvellously constructed.

ll. 17–18. *five cycles . . . man*. Based on the biblical account of the Creation in Genesis, where God creates the world in five days, man on the sixth day, resting on the seventh. Some scientists tried to reconcile this account with natural history by replacing God with Nature, and the 'days' with certain ages, lasting thousands or millions of years.

64   l. 127. *Pæan*. Hymn of praise.

66   l. 186. *cope*. Top.

l. 195. *Ixion-like*. Ixion, a mortal king, was favoured by Zeus and invited to the home of the gods. But he repaid this hospitality by trying to seduce Zeus's wife, Hera. Zeus fooled Ixion with a mock-Hera made out of cloud, and later punished him by binding him to a wheel of fire in Hades.

67   l. 219. *Stephen*. The Apostle Stephen was martyred by stoning, 'but he, being full of the Holy Ghost, looked up stedfastly into heaven, and saw the glory of God' (Acts 7: 55).

68   l. 271. *him*. Death. This is a reference to Tennyson's early melancholia.

70   l. 325. *ducts*. In Tennyson's day 'duct' was a general medical term referring to any vessel or tube in the body—here, those in his mother's body that delivered the material ('lime' is a form of calcium) to build him; or else his own boyish 'ducts' that supplied his bones with the nutrients to grow.

l. 350. *Lethe*. The river of forgetfulness in the classical underworld; newly dead spirits were reputed to drink from this river to forget their mortal existence before entering Hades.

73   l. 436. *Æolian harp*. A device usually hung in a window, so that breezes could make spontaneous music upon it (not unlike 'wind chimes'). The Aeolian harp is a common symbol for Romantic writers of the Nature-inspired poet.

74   *St Simeon Stylites*. Written before 1833 (a manuscript of the poem circulated amongst Tennyson's university friends); published in *1842*. Simeon (AD 388–460) was a saint of the early Church, an ascetic who decided to sit on top of a pillar (*stulos* in Greek, whence 'Stylites') in 423. This pillar was gradually increased in height (from six cubits to forty, i.e. from 9 ft. to nearly 60 ft.) but Simeon never came down, spending the last thirty-seven years of his life in this fashion. He had a basket on a rope, which he would lower for people to put in food and water; and is said to have passed the time working miracles and prophesying for the large crowds that came to see him. Tennyson's satire on this extreme form of the ascetic impulse represents one of his earliest historical dramatic monologues. He seems to have been particularly fond of its grotesqueness: Edward Fitzgerald remembered that 'this is one of the poems A.T. would read with grotesque grimness, especially such

passages as "coughs, aches, stitches," [l. 13] etc., laughing aloud at times' (*Memoir*, i. 193).

76 l. 94. *dial.* Sundial.

78 l. 153. *chrysalis.* The cocoon from which an insect emerges. A traditional image for the separation of Soul from the body.

ll. 165–6. *Pontius . . . seraphs.* Pontius Pilate, who 'washed his hands' of Christ's fate, and Judas Iscariot, who betrayed Christ, would appear as 'seraphs' (angels) next to Simeon.

l. 169. *Abaddon and Asmodeus.* Devils. 'The [fallen] angel of the bottomless pit, whose name in the Hebrew tongue is Abaddon' (Rev. 9: 11); 'Asmodeus the evil spirit' (Tobit 3: 8).

79 l. 205. *the crown.* Christ promises a crown to the faithful in Rev. 2: 10 ('To him that overcometh . . . I will give thee a crown of life').

80 *Ulysses.* Written 20 Oct. 1833, after hearing the news of Arthur Hallam's death; published in *1842*. 'Ulysses . . . was written soon after Arthur Hallam's death, and gave my feeling about the need of going forward, and braving the struggle of life perhaps more simply than anything in "In Memoriam" ' (*Memoir*, i. 196). The poem is often linked to another mythological treatment of the bereavement, 'Tithonus' (p. 348), which Tennyson claimed was a 'pendant' to 'Ulysses'.

Details of what became of Odysseus (Ulysses is the Latin version of his name) after the adventures related in Homer's *Odyssey* are hinted at in *Odyssey*, xi. 100–37, where Tiresias utters a prophecy: 'But when you have slain the suitors for your wife's hand in your halls [which Odysseus does at the end of the poem] . . . then you will go travelling again, taking a well-shaped oar, until you come to men that know nothing of ships . . . And death will find you far from the sea, a mild death that will lay you down when you have been overcome by sleek old age, and your people shall grow prosperous around you'. Dante puts Ulysses in Hell, after a rather different story (*Inferno*, xxvi. 90 ff.): 'Forth I sail'd | Into the deep illimitable main, | With but one bark, and the small faithful band | That yet cleav'd to me' (trans. by H. F. Carey, 1805). Dante's Ulysses sails to the southern ocean, sees the mountain of Purgatory and is consumed by the sea.

l. 3. *mete and dole.* Assess and give out.

l. 10. *Hyades.* A group of stars near the constellation Taurus. The rising of the Hyades was associated with the rainy season (Tennyson quotes from Virgil's *Aeneid*, i. 744, 'pluviasque Hyades' [rainy Hyades]).

81 l. 64. *Achilles.* Odysseus' companion-in-arms, the greatest of all warriors, had died at the battle of Troy. In Greek thought, most mortals died and descended to an extremely attenuated existence in the underworld; only a few heroes and semi-divine figures were allowed to go to the 'Isles of the Blest' in the western ocean, where the afterlife was more agreeable. In fact, Odysseus has already met Achilles, much-reduced and miserable, as a shade in Hades in *Odyssey* xi; whether Tennyson has forgotten this, or

intends us to assume that Odysseus is blocking the memory from his mind, is unclear.

81 *Tithon*. Tennyson's first version of this poem was completed in 1833, shortly after Arthur Hallam's death; he considered it a 'pendant' to 'Ulysses' (above). The poem was not published in this form, but, much revised, appeared as 'Tithonus' in 1860 (see p. 348). According to the legend, Tithonus was a beautiful young man, with whom the goddess Aurora (the Dawn) fell in love. He was allowed to live with her, and asked for eternal life to keep her company through eternity—but he should have asked for eternal *youth*, because he aged and grew more infirm and shrunken, but could not die. Eventually he was transformed into the grasshopper.

82 l. 22. *ordinance*. The allotted span of mortal life.

83 l. 53. *Ilion*. Troy, which was built to the sound of Apollo playing his lyre.

The Epic / Morte d'Arthur. The 'Morte d'Arthur' itself was written 1833–4, soon after hearing of Arthur Hallam's death. Tennyson later composed the frame pieces of 'The Epic', probably in 1837–8, in order 'to anticipate or excuse the "faint Homeric echoes" . . . and to give a reason for telling an old-world tale' (this is Edward Fitzgerald's opinion, *Memoir*, i. 194). The poem and its frame were published together in *1842*. Tennyson had had youthful ambitions to write an Arthurian epic, but had more or less abandoned them by this stage. He later took them up again, and eventually put together the *Idylls of the King* (see p. 605). 'Morte d'Arthur' was later incorporated wholesale in the last book of the *Idylls* ('The Passing of Arthur'), although it is stylistically a very different sort of poem, much more markedly archaic in vocabulary and syntax.

The Epic

l. 3. *sacred bush*. Mistletoe.

l. 10. *cutting eights*. skating figures-of-eight.

84 l. 16. *Geology and schism*. Recent geological science (as represented by Charles Lyell's *Principles of Geology*, 1830–3, which Tennyson had been reading) had cast doubt on traditional religious belief that the world was only a few thousand years old.

l. 36. *Mastodon*. Extinct mammoth.

85 *Morte d'Arthur*

l. 4. *Lyonnesse*. 'The country of legend that lay between Cornwall and the Scilly Islands' (T).

l. 38. *lightly*. Quickly.

86 l. 56. *haft*. Hilt of the sword.

l. 57. *jacinth*. Reddish gem-stone.

87 l. 80. *lief*. Beloved.

88 l. 139. *streamer of the northern morn*. The Northern Lights.

l. 140. *moving isles*. Presumably icebergs.

90 l. 198. *Three Queens*. Malory (Tennyson's source) identifies these queens: 'that one was King Arthur's sister Morgan le Fay; the other was the Queen of Northgalis; and the third was the Queen of the Waste Lands' (Malory, *Morte D'Arthur*, iii. 169). Tennyson himself commented, 'some say that the three Queens are Faith, Hope, and Charity ... They are three of the noblest of women. They are also those three Graces, but they are much more' (in Ricks, ii. 15).

l. 209. *casque*. Helmet.

ll. 215–16. *greaves and cuisses*. Shin guard armour and armour for the front of the thighs. 'Cuisse' is pronounced 'kwish'.   *drops | Of onset*. Blood from the King's wounds. 'Onset' is used in its archaic sense of 'battle' or 'attack'.

91 l. 259. *Avilion*. More usually Avalon, the mythical Isle of the Blessed where Arthur remains to this day. The spelling 'Avilion' is that found in Malory.

92 *'You ask me, why, thou' ill at ease'*. Written 1833, expressing Tennyson's concern at the political unrest that followed the House of Lords' rejection of the 1832 Reform Act. Published in *1842*.

93 l. 17. *banded unions*. Tennyson's animus is directed against the early manifestations of workers' co-operative organizations, many of which fed into Chartism (a nation-wide movement for democratic rights, that began with the publication of The Worker's Charter in May 1838). Trade unions as we understand the term did not really come about until later in the century.

Audley Court. Written autumn 1838 and published in *1842* as one of Tennyson's 'English Idylls'. As with all his Idylls, including the Arthurian *Idylls of the King*, Tennyson owes much in this form to the pastoral poems of the Greek poet Theocritus.

94 ll. 22–3. *pasty*. Pie.   *leveret*. Young hare.

l. 34. *corn-laws*. The Corn Laws were passed in 1815 forbidding the import of wheat at anything less than 80 shillings a bushel. The idea was to help domestic farmers by preventing cheap imports, but there was much popular agitation against these laws on the grounds that they kept the price of bread artificially high. The Corn Laws were repealed in 1846.

l. 37. *pippin*. Apple tree.

95 l. 86. *Sole star of phosphorescence in the calm*. 'The little buoy appearing and disappearing in the dark sea' (T).

96 *'Break, break, break'*. Written sometime after the death of Hallam, to which it makes oblique reference. Published in *1842*.

Sir Galahad. Written 1834, published in *1842*.

l. 1. *casques*. Helmets.

97 l. 25. *crescent*. i.e. when the moon sets.

l. 42. *Grail*. The cup or platter used by Christ at the last supper. Joseph of

Arimathea caught drops of blood in it from Christ on the cross, and later brought it to England. The quest for the holy grail has a central place in Arthurian legend; in some versions, only Galahad is able to achieve the grail, because 'his heart is pure'.

98   l. 82. *pale.* Fence.

99   *'A Farewell'.* Written 1837, addressed to the stream that ran past the Tennyson house at Somersby on the occasion of the family moving away. Published in *1842.*

     'Oh! that 'twere possible'. The germ of this poem (more or less the first eleven stanzas) was written in 1833, after the death of Arthur Hallam, to which it refers. Later Tennyson revised the poem somewhat and added the final four stanzas, before publishing it under the title 'Stanzas' in *The Tribute* (Sept. 1837). The poem was reused as Part II, Section IV of *Maud* (see pp. 339–42).

102   *Locksley Hall.* Probably written 1838, published *1842.* Tennyson commented: ' "Locksley Hall" is an imaginary place (tho' the coast is Lincolnshire) and the hero is imaginary. The whole poem represents young life, its good side, its deficiencies, and its yearnings. Mr Hallam [Arthur Hallam's father] said to me that the English people liked verse in Trochaics, so I wrote the poem in this metre' (*Memoir*, i. 195). Critics have made much play with the autobiographical provenance of this avowedly fictional dramatic monologue; the narrator's relationship with Amy has some parallels with Tennyson's own thwarted love-affair with a young woman called Rosa Baring between 1834 and 1836; their relationship, never hopeful given Tennyson's then-precarious financial prospects, was finally ended by her parents. Baring married somebody else in 1838, which may have reopened the wound for Tennyson and played its part in the mood of the poem.

     l. 1. *Comrades.* It is not stated explicitly in the poem, but the implication seems to be that the speaker has joined the army, and has come to take his leave of Locksley Hall. These 'comrades', then, would be his fellow soldiers.

     l. 9. *Pleiads.* The constellation more usually known as the Pleiades.

104   l. 41. *fathoms.* Comprehends.

     l. 47. *clown.* A rustic lout.

     l. 62. *straiten'd forehead.* Narrow head (sign of stupidity).

105   l. 75. *the poet.* Dante. Tennyson is thinking of a passage from *Inferno*, v. 121–3.

     l. 82. *widow'd.* In the sense that she should have married the speaker, but now that chance is gone forever.

106   l. 100. *gold.* i.e. money.

     l. 118. *earnest.* Future pledge.

     l. 121. *argosies of magic sails.* An 'argosy' is a merchant ship of the largest size, a sort of sailing supertanker. Tennyson here anticipates air-freight, and (in the next couplet) aerial warfare.

108 l. 149. *wroth*. Angry.

ll. 154–5. *Orient . . . Mahratta-battle*. The narrator tells us he was born in India, and that his father died in the war between the British and the Mahratta (more usually Maratha), Indian soldiers from Bombay, in 1818.

l. 162. *trailer*. Jungle creeper or vine.

109 l. 180. *Joshua*. 'Then Joshua spoke to the LORD . . . and he said in the sight of Israel, Sun, stand thou still upon Gibeon; and thou, Moon, in the valley of Ajalon. And the sun stood still, and the moon stayed' (Josh. 10: 12–13).

l. 182. *ringing grooves*. Tennyson remembered: 'when I went by the first train from Liverpool to Manchester (1830), I thought that the wheels ran in a groove. It was a black night and there was such a vast crowd round the train at the station that we could not see the wheels. Then I made this line' (*Memoir*, i. 195).

l. 184. *Cathay*. China.

The Vision of Sin. Written in the later 1830s and published in *1842*. A dream-allegory, like 'The Palace of Art' (pp. 35–43) with which it may be connected, this was always one of Tennyson's favourites amongst his poems. He described the poem as concerning 'the soul of a youth who has given himself up to pleasure and Epicurianism. He at length is worn out and wrapt in the mists of satiety. Afterwards he grows into a cynical old man afflicted with the "curse of nature", and joining in the Feast of Death. Then we see the landscape which symbolises God, Law and the future life' (quoted in Ricks, ii. 156).

l. 3. *horse with wings*. The protagonist (poet) rides Pegasus, the winged horse from Greek myth, because it was associated with the Muses and hence with poetry.

110 l. 41. *Furies*. Supernatural and fearsome females who punished criminals by remorselessly chasing them down.   *Graces*. Three goddesses who symbolized beauty.

111 l. 63. *ostler*. Servant employed by this inn (called the 'Dragon', l. 72) to attend to travellers' horses.

112 l. 91. *saved by works*. The debate as to whether Christians needed to do good in the world (i.e. works), or merely to be holy (i.e. grace) in order to find salvation was much debated in the 18th- and 19th-centuries.

l. 93. *forks*. Legs.

113 l. 136. *Freedom*. Tennyson presumably has in mind the 'liberté' of the French Revolution, or more particularly the Terror that followed it.

114 l. 179. *Vivat Rex*. Latin for 'Long Live the King!'

115 l. 189. *Buss*. Kiss.

115 l. 211. *shards and scurf.* Scales and flakes.

116 *The Eagle.* Written on 2 May 1846, but not published (as a 'Fragment')
until 1851. The original version was more obviously fragmentary, begin-
ning with an extra line and a half: '—to sit apart | And triumph in the
eagle's heart; | | Who clasps the crag . . .'.

117 *The Princess.* Tennyson was planning this poem as early as 1839, but he did
not start writing it properly until 1845. It was published on Christmas Day
1847. For the third edition Tennyson revised fairly extensively, in particu-
lar interspersing a number of short lyrics between the sections of the
poem. These songs (not the blank verse lyrics within the body of the poem,
such as 'Tears, Idle Tears', which were always part of the work) have been
much anthologized separately. For the fourth edition of 1851 Tennyson
added some more material, relating to the 'weird seizures' of the Prince
(see Part I, l.14 and note). This later text is the one printed here.
     Tennyson's own opinions on women's rights were less than radical.
Hallam reported: 'his friends report my father to have said, that the two
great social questions impending in England were "the housing and educa-
tion of the poor man before making him our master [i.e. to avoid 'mob
rule'], and the higher education of women"; and that the sooner woman
finds out, before the great educational movement begins, that "woman is
not undevelopt man, but diverse," [*Princess*, vii. 259–60] the better it will
be for the progress of the world' (*Memoir*, i. 249).

Prologue

l. 5. *Institute.* An organization dedicated to the advancement of working
men, such as the Mechanics' Institute. Tennyson based the frame poem on
a day organized by this society. 'The Prologue was written about a feast of
the Mechanics' Institute held in the Lushingtons' grounds at Park House,
near Maidstone, 6th July 1842' (T).

l. 15. *Ammonites.* Fossils of the segmented shells of an extinct variety of
large sea-snails.

ll. 17–18. *celts.* Ancient stone or metal axes.   *calumets.* Native Amer-
ican peace-pipe.   *Claymore.* Broadsword of the old Scottish High-
landers.

l. 19. *sandal.* Sandalwood.

l. 21. *cursed Malayan crease.* The 'kris', a dagger with a blade shaped in a
wavy form. It is 'cursed' because it was thought to be an instrument used in
particularly brutal ways.

ll. 25–6. *Agincourt.* Battle (1415) where a small English force led by Henry
V and armed chiefly with bows defeated a much larger French army.
Ascalon. Battle in the Crusades (1192), where Richard I ('the Lionheart')
defeated the Saracens. Both these engagements have, for the English, con-
notations of heroism and glory.

118 l. 32. *a lady.* This was Ida, Countess of Mountfort, who led troops out of
the besieged city of Hanybount riding a horse and dressed in armour, and

drove away the attackers. The story is found in Froissart's *Chronicle* (see l. 49), a French contemporary history of the Hundred Years War (which was a war fought between France and England in the 14th and 15th centuries over English territorial claims on the continent).

ll. 59–79. Tennyson's descriptions of the various mechanical and electrical devices displayed by the 'Institute' is bang up to date for the 1840s: a fountain of water controlled by a pump, a cannon fired electrically rather than by hand, telescopes, a battery giving people the relatively new sensation of mild electric shocks, a model steamer run on clockwork and model trains, a hot-air balloon that drops packets with miniature parachutes attached, and a telegraph wire run from one side of the garden to the other.

119 l. 82. *stump'd the wicket*. From the game of cricket. A bowler throws balls from one wicket (three sticks in the ground) at another, attempting to strike it; a batsman uses his bat to knock the ball away, and score runs by running between the wickets. If the wicket is 'stumped' (i.e. struck so that the loose bails balanced on top fall off) the batsman is dismissed. Strictly speaking, Tennyson is wrong here: he seems to be describing not a batsman who has been 'stumped', but one who has been 'bowled'.

l. 85. *Soldier-laddie*. A folk tune.

120 l. 113. *breathed the Proctor's dogs*. 'Made the proctor's attendants out of breath' (T). The Proctor is an officer at an Oxford or Cambridge College, amongst whose duties is the enforcement of the College curfew. His 'attendants' are 'dogs' only in a slang sense.

l. 116. *in grain*. Thoroughly, to the core; i.e. 'a deep-dyed rogue'.

121 l. 148. *sward*. Grass.

l. 178. *Muses of the cube and square*. i.e. mathematics.

l. 184. *wassail*. Sociable drinking (an archaic term).

122 l. 199. *Chimeras, crotchets*. Illusions, whimsical fancies.

l. 204. *a winter's tale*. Playing with the title of Shakespeare's *The Winter's Tale*, in which is said 'a sad tale's best for winter' (II. i. 25).

Part I

123 l. 14. *weird seizures*. Tennyson added many passages that relate to the epilepsy of the Prince in the fourth edition of 1851, changes that have divided critics. P. M. Wallace edited an edition of the poem in 1891, and Tennyson read the proofs of this, endorsing Wallace's view on the seizures: 'It must be clearly shown that it was not the glamour of [The Prince's] physical or moral brilliance that won his lady from her isolation. His too emotional temperament and susceptibility to cataleptic seizures, added for the first time in the fourth Edition of the Poem, was no doubt [T. changed this to 'probably'] intended to emphasise this point' (quoted in Ricks, ii. 186).

124 l. 19. *court-Galen*. i.e. Court Physician. Galen was Claudius Galenus, a highly renowned doctor from Pergamus in Asia Minor in the 2nd century AD, who wrote extensively on medical and physiological matters.

124   l. 33. *proxy-wedded with a bootless calf.* 'Proxy wedding' was a ceremony whereby a long-distance betrothal was formalized by somebody (the proxy) standing in on behalf of the affianced party; this would involve a sort of ritualized getting into bed with the bride-to-be, whereby the proxy would place his bare leg (his 'bootless calf') under the sheets with the woman.

l. 36. *puissance.* Strength, power.

125   l. 65. *cook'd his spleen.* Matured or developed his anger.

126   l. 100. *silver sickle.* The Moon.

ll. 109–10. *tilth.* Tilled fields.   *grange.* Farmhouses.   *blowing bosks.* 'Blossoming thickets' (T).

128   l. 198. *holp.* Archaic form of 'helped'.

l. 201. *guerdon.* Reward (archaic).

129   l. 219. *Pallas.* Pallas Athene, the Greek Goddess of wisdom. She was, suitably, a virgin.

l. 223. *Ostleress.* Cod female form of 'ostler', the stableman at an inn.

l. 239. *Uranian Venus.* Venus (the Greek Aphrodite) was the goddess of sexual love; but the epithet 'Uranian' refers to a higher, purer form of love, postulated in Plato's *Symposium* (the word derives from the Greek for 'the heavens', and can mean 'heavenly or spiritual love'). It acquired common currency as a synonym for 'homosexual love' only later in the century, and it is unlikely that Tennyson was aware of this usage.

Part II

130   l. 4. *zoned.* Girdled.

131   l. 63. *Odalisques.* Female Harem-slaves.

132   l. 65. *the Sabine.* A people from central Italy whose women fought the Romans. The Princess itemizes a number of famous strong women. *she.* Semiramis, fabled Babylonian Queen proverbial for her beauty and cruelty.

ll. 67–8. *Carian Artemisia.* 'She who fought so bravely for Xerxes at Salamis that he said his women had become men and his men women' (T). Xerxes, the Persian monarch, was trying to invade Greece, but was stopped at the battle of Salamis in 480 BC.   *Rhodope.* 'A celebrated Greek courtesan of Thracian origin, who was said to have built a pyramid near Memphis' (T).

ll. 69–71. *Clelia.* Roman woman 'who swam the Tiber in escaping from Porsenna's camp' (T).   *Cornelia.* 'Mother of the Gracchi' (T). The Gracchi were brothers who, as Tribunes in early Rome, battled against aristocratic power and became popular heroes; their mother (born 189 BC) was renowned as a model of virtue and learning, and was so beloved of the people of Rome that they erected a statue to her inscribed 'Cornelia, Mother of the Gracchi'.   *Palmyrene.* 'Zenobia, Queen of Palmyra'

(T). She battled against the Roman Emperor Marcus Aurelius Antoninus in the 2nd century AD. *Agrippina.* 'Grand-daughter of Augustus, married to Germanicus'. She accompanied her husband on military expeditions, and on one occasion used her sagacity and heroism to suppress a rebellion in the camp.

l. 94. *headed like a star.* 'With bright golden hair' (T).

l. 97. *the dame.* The fabled Greek King Midas possessed the hairy ears of an ass, a deformity concerning which he confided only to his wife on condition she tell nobody else. Unable to keep the secret, she whispered to the grass ('sedge') that 'Midas has asses' ears', and the wind spread the rumour around Midas' kingdom.

133 l. 105. *woaded.* Ancient Britons were reputed to paint themselves with a blue daub called 'woad'.

l. 110. *Amazon.* Mighty female warriors of Greek myth.

ll. 112–13. *Lycian.* 'Herodotus says that the Lycians took their names from their mothers instead of their fathers' (T). *Lar and Lucumo.* Roman for 'nobleman' (more properly, a household deity) and Etruscan for 'prince of the priestly caste' (the sense of the line is 'a society in which women were allowed to hob-nob with the male aristocracy'; Roman custom was to eat and drink lying down).

ll. 117–18. *Salique.* French laws that forbad inheritance by women; Henry V used them as a pretext to invade France, claiming that the French king of the time traced his lineage through a female line and so was not legitimate. *little-footed.* The old Chinese custom of binding women's feet to keep them small (and, supposedly but erroneously, more beautiful). *Mahomet.* 'Had she heard that, according to Mohammedan doctrine, hell was chiefly occupied by women?' (T).

l. 142. *Kaffir.* Disparaging term applied to Black Africans. *Hottentot.* A people indigenous to South-West Africa; Tennyson is again using the term disparagingly.

l. 143. *horn-handed breakers of the glebe.* Peasants. 'Horn-handed' because their hands are callused with wielding their spades to dig up the ground ('glebe').

134 l. 144. *Verulam.* Sir Francis Bacon, the noted Renaissance philosopher and scientist, was Lord Verulam.

ll. 146–8. *Elizabeth.* Queen Elizabeth I, renowned 16th-century English monarch. *peasant Joan.* Joan of Arc. *Sappho.* Highly regarded lyric poet from the island of Lesbos, 6th century BC.

l. 169. *Tacks.* 'Tacking' is the technique of sailing into the wind by following a zigzag path.

l. 180. *softer Adams.* Like Adam, in being the first, but female ('softer').

l. 181. *Sirens.* In the *Odyssey*, creatures with bird-bodies but beautiful female faces and entrancing voices, that lured mariners to their death.

135   l. 209. *clapper*. Device for scaring away birds.   *garth*. Enclosed ground.

137   ll. 263–4. *Spartan Mother*. 'Who condemned her sons to death for conspiracy against the city (Livy, ii. 5)' (T).   *Lucius Junius Brutus*. One of the first consuls of Rome, Brutus discovered a conspiracy against the city involving his own two sons; putting civic duty first, he had them both put to death.

l. 269. *secular*. Long-lasting.

138   l. 306. *agates*. A banded semi-precious stone.

l. 319. *Danaïd*. The daughters of Danaus murdered their husbands, and were punished in Hades by being given the task of carrying water in a leaky sieve.

l. 323. *Aspasia*. One of the most famous women of 5th-century BC Athens, the mistress of Pericles and hostess of philosophical parties.

l. 325. *Sheba*. 'And when the queen of Sheba heard of the fame of Solomon concerning the name of the LORD, she came to prove him with hard questions' (1 Kings 10: 1). Solomon received her in his famous house, made of 'cedar trees out of Lebanon' (1 Kings 5: 6).

140   l. 382. *bigger boy*. Cupid, the son of Venus, who also fell in love with a woman called Psyche.

141   l. 420. *Astræan*. 'Astræ, daughter of Zeus and Themis, is to come back first of the celestials on the return of the Golden Age' (T).

l. 433. *oar'd a shallop*. Rowed a boat.

Part III

143   ll. 55–6. *Ganymedes . . . Vulcans*. 'They mounted like Ganymede (a beautiful mortal who was snatched up to heaven) only to tumble like Vulcan (or Hephaestus, who fell from Olympus and injured himself)'.

144   l. 73. *inosculated*. Intertwined.

l. 97. *Hebes*. Hebe was a goddess of youth who was originally a cupbearer to the gods (who would eat 'ambrosia', the delicious food of the gods, and drink 'nectar'). A 'Hebe' became a poeticism for a waitress or barmaid.

145   l. 99. *Samian Herè*. 'The Greek Herè [or Hera, queen of the gods], whose favourite abode was Samos' (T).

l. 100. *Memnon*. 'The statue in Egypt which gave forth a musical note when "smitten with the morning sun" ' (T).

l. 104. *champaign*. Field (archaic).

l. 126. *limed*. Trapped (twigs smeared with sticky lime were set to trap birds).

146   l. 154. *dip of certain strata*. She intends to go to examine some exposed rock layers.

l. 159. *platans*. Tropical fruit trees, similar to the banana.

147   l. 199. *Quoit*. 'Quoits' is a game where players attempt to throw a hoop or ring over a target.   *tennis*. So-called 'real tennis' played in an enclosed court.

l. 212. *Vashti*. 'Ahasuerus sat on the throne of his kingdom, which was Sushan . . . On the seventh day, when the heart of the king was merry with wine, he commanded [his chamberlains] . . . to bring Vashti the queen before the king with the crown royal, to shew the people and the princes her beauty: for she was fair to look on. But the queen Vashti refused to come at the king's commandment by his chamberlains: therefore was the king very wroth' (Esther 1: 2–12). Ahasuerus goes on to issue a commandment 'that every man should bear rule in his own house'.

l. 215. *breathes full East*. Meaning both 'like an Eastern Queen' and 'like the East wind' (which was notoriously chill).

148   l. 246. *POU STO*. Greek for 'a place to stand'; after Archimedes, who experimented with levers and was impressed. 'Give me a place to stand,' he said, 'and I could move the world.'

149   l. 262. *gynæceum*. 'Women's quarters in a Greek house' (T).

l. 285. *Diotima*. 'Said to have been an instructress of Socrates. She was a priestess of Mantinea. (Cf. Plato's *Symposium*)' (T). Socrates went on to drink hemlock willingly and die, although it had been given to him in order to carry out his public execution for corrupting the morals of the Athenian young.

l. 290. *anatomic*. Anatomist, student of anatomy. The Princess replies that she didn't want her women to study anatomy after hearing stories of male vivisection of live animals ('carve the living hound') or of anatomy students who fed human body parts to their dogs (a detail Tennyson took from one of Hogarth's engravings in the series 'Stages of Cruelty').

150   l. 324. *Elysian lawns*. The 'Elysian Fields' were the realm of the gods and the happy dead in Greek mythology.

l. 331. *Corinna*. 'She is the Boeotian poetess who is said to have triumphed over Pindar in poetical competition (Pausanias, ix. 22). The Princess probably exaggerates' (T).

151   ll. 344–5. *shale . . . trachyte*. Ricks (ii. 230) usefully quotes from the glossary to Lyell's *Principles of Geology* (1830–3), which Tennyson certainly read, by way of explaining these terms as follows: *shale*. 'Indurated slaty clay'.   *hornblende*. 'A simple mineral of a dark green or black colour'.   *trap*. 'Volcanic rocks'.   *tuff*. 'A variety of volcanic rock of an earthy texture'.   *Amygdaloid*. 'One of the forms of the trap-rocks'.   *trachyte*. 'A variety of lava'.   *rag* is a hard, rough stone.

Part IV

l. 2. *hypothesis of theirs*. The 'hypothesis' that the sun was 'nebulous' (i.e. composed of gases) was first promulgated by the French cosmologist Pierre Laplace (1749–1827). It is, as it happens, largely true.

152 l. 13. *satin dome*. The Princess's tent.

153 l. 59. *Babels*. The tower that human hubris wanted to build 'whose top may reach unto heaven' (Gen. 11: 4); this ambition was broken by God. *kex*. The name for the stem of a number of herbacious plants.

154 l. 100. *Ithacensian*. Odysseus took ten years to sail back from the Siege of Troy; and during that time a large number of suitors from his home island of Ithaca pressed their various suits on his wife, Penelope. Odysseus finally returned home in disguise and killed the suitors.

l. 101. *alien lips*. A quotation from Homer, *Odyssey*, xx. 347: 'And now they (the suitors) laughed with alien lips' (not realizing who Odysseus was; they are killed soon after).

l. 104. *Bulbul . . . Gulistan*. Persian words, meaning 'nightingale' and 'rose garden' respectively.

l. 106. *meadow-crake*. Corn-crake, a bird like the pheasant that hides amongst the grass, from where its harsh call may be heard.

l. 110. *made bricks in Egypt*. i.e. 'when we were slaves' (like the Hebrews, who were forced to make bricks for the Egyptian Pharaoh).

l. 117. *canzonets*. Love songs.

155 l. 121. *Valkyrian*. In Norse mythology, the Valkyrie were twelve statuesque war-maidens who conducted the souls of slain warriors to Valhalla.

156 l. 126. *Mock-Hymen*. Mock-marriage.

l. 138. *master'd*. Cyril is drunk.

l. 183. *Caryatids*. 'Female figures used as bearing shafts . . . e.g. the maidens supporting the light entablature of the portico of the Erechtheum at Athens' (T).

l. 184. *valves*. Gates. These ones carry designs of Actaeon the hunter, who accidentally caught sight of Artemis (Diana) naked and as punishment was turned into a stag and devoured by his own hounds.

l. 194. *the Bear*. The constellation Ursa Minor.

157 l. 207. *a Judith*. Picture of the biblical heroine, who decapitated the General Holofernes (in the Apocryphal book of Judith) and thus prevented him destroying the peoples of Israel.

158 l. 243. *boles*. Trunks of the trees.

l. 255. *fire*. St Elmo's fire, a freak electrical phenomenon that can gather about the masts of ships in a storm.

l. 260. *blowzed*. Ruddy.

l. 261. *Druid rock*. Ancient British standing stone, such as are found at Stonehenge; thought once to have been erected by the cast of pagan priests, the Druids.

l. 275. *Castalies*. Castaly was a fountain sacred to the Muses; so: 'I lead you to all the arts connected with the Muses'.

159   l. 292. *Jonah's gourd*. A 'gourd' is a fleshy vegetable, or the tree that produces this fruit. Jonah was sitting in the sun, and God 'prepared a gourd, and made it to come up over Jonah, that it might be a shadow over his head. So Jonah was exceeding glad of the gourd.' But the next day God 'smote the gourd that it withered . . . and the sun beat upon the head of Jonah, that he fainted, and wished himself to die' (Jonah 4: 6–8).

l. 306. *lidless*. With wide-open eyes.

l. 314. *touchwood*. Wood decayed by a certain fungus into a crumbly, flammable material.

160   l. 352. *Niobëan daughter*. 'Niobe was proud of her twelve children, and in consequence boasted herself as superior to Leto, mother of Apollo and Artemis, who in revenge shot them all dead' (T).

162   ll. 418–19. *Cassiopëia*. In Greek myth, a Queen of Ethiopia who was memorialized in the sky as a constellation. *Persephonè*. Wife of the King of the Underworld (Hades), who spends half the year down there and half the year above ground. The Prince means he would have come after Ida no matter how out of reach she seemed to be.

l. 427. *the dwarfs of presage*. i.e. not living up to expectations.

164   l. 484. *protomartyr*. The first martyr (with the implication that many would copy her martyrdom).

Part V

167   l. 25. *mawkin*. Kitchen-wench.

l. 36. *ferule*. Walking stick.

l. 37. *transient*. Passing.

170   l. 121. *year*. A year's growth, crop.

l. 142. *mammoth bulk'd in ice*. 'Bulky mammoth buried in ice' (T).

172   l. 213. *bussed*. Kissed.

173   l. 250. *airy Giant's zone*. 'The stars in the belt of Orion' (T).

l. 254. *morions*. Steel helmets.

l. 266. '*sdeath!* Shakespearean swear-word (shortened form of 'God's Death').

174   l. 284. *Her*. 'St Catherine of Alexandria, niece of Constantine the Great' (T). The Emperor Maximan, who was trying to suppress Christianity, sent fifty of his wisest men to try and convert her away from the faith; he failed, and had her executed in AD 307.

176   l. 355. *Tomyris*. 'Queen of the Massagetæ, who cut off the head of Cyrus the Great after defeating him, and dipped it in a skin which she had filled with blood and bade him, as he was insatiate of blood, to drink his fill, gorge himself with blood' (T). Cyrus, who had unified the Medes and Persians into the Persian Empire with many battles, died in 529 BC.

l. 369. *fire*. 'Suttee in India' (T). 'Suttee' was the practice of burning the widow on her husband's funeral pyre.

176   l. 372. *running flood*. 'Ganges' (T).

l. 376. *leaven*. The allusion is to 1 Cor. 5: 6–7: 'know ye not that a little leaven leaveneth the whole lump. Purge out therefore the old leaven'.

l. 382. *institutes*. Laws.

177   l. 417. *Egypt-plague*. Like the plagues Moses visited upon Egypt (Exodus, chs. 7–12).

178   ll. 448–9. *bantling scald*. Allow their small children (bantlings) to get burnt at home.   *potherbs*. Herbs used in cooking.

179   l. 500. *cymbal'd Miriam*. 'And Miriam the prophetess, the sister of Aaron, took a timbrel in her hand; and all the women went out after her with timbrels and dances' (Exod. 15: 20).   *Jael*. In Judges, God sells the Children of Israel into the hands of the king of Canaan, the captain of whose army was called Sisera—'then Jael, Heber's wife, took a nail of the tent, and took a hammer in her hand, and went softly unto him, and smote the nail into his temples . . . So he died' (Judges 4: 21).

Part VI

181   l. 16. *dame of Lapidoth*. Deborah, who was married to Lapidoth, was an Old Testament prophetess, who rejoiced at Jael's killing of Sisera (above). 'Then sang Deborah and Barak the son of Abinoam on that day, saying, Praise ye the Lord for the avenging of Israel' (Judges 5: 1–2).

182   l. 59. *valves*. Doors (as at IV, l. 184 above).

184   l. 118. *brede*. Embroidery.

185   l. 166. *port*. Haven.

l. 186. *dead prime*. 'Earliest dawn' (T).

186   l. 224. *Lot's wife*. Who was turned to a pillar of salt.

187   l. 239. *sine . . . azimuth*. All trigonometric terms. An *arc* is a curved line; a *sine of arc* is a line from one end of an arc parallel to the tangent at the other end; *spheroid* means spherical and *azimuth* is defined by Hallam Tennyson in the following terms: 'the azimuth of any point on a horizontal plane is the angle between a line drawn to that point, and a fixed line in the horizontal plane, usually chosen to be a line drawn due North' (quoted in Ricks, ii. 275).

188   l. 283. *adit*. Access.

189   l. 319. *Pharos*. The lighthouse outside the harbour of classical Alexandria, named after the rocky island on which it was set.

Part VII

191   l. 19. *void was her use*. 'She felt she was of no use'.

l. 31. *gyres*. A twisting or turning motion.

192   l. 56. *obtain'd*. 'Prevailed' (T).

193   l. 109. *Oppian law*. 'When Hannibal was nearing Rome a law was carried by C. Oppius, Trib. Pleb. [Tribune of the people], B.C. 125 [215], forbidding

women to wear more than half an ounce of gold, or brilliant dresses, and no woman was to come within a mile of Rome or of any town save on account of public sacrifices in a conveyance drawn by horses' (T). There was a great deal of public pressure to repeal this law, pressure which was opposed by Cato, the Roman Statesman and soldier. None the less, the law was repealed in 95 BC.

l. 112. *Hortensia*. After Julius Caesar was assassinated in 44 BC, the Triumvirate (l. 116) of Mark Antony, Octavius Caesar (afterwards Augustus), and Lepidus proposed to raise a tax on Roman matrons in order to help finance the war against the assassins, Brutus and Cassius. Hortensia was one such matron who spoke eloquently against the tax.

194 l. 159. *Poets of her land*. The lyric that follows is Tennyson's own, but is based on a Persian form called a 'ghazal', a sort of love poetry, that may suggest that Ida's land is a fictional version of Persia.

195 l. 167. *Danaë*. 'Zeus came down to Danaë when shut up in the tower in a shower of gold stars' (T). The stars are Tennyson's addition; more conventionally Zeus is said to have descended just in 'a shower of gold'.

l. 176. *Idyl*. The 'idyll' is a Greek form of descriptive poetry, mostly on rural topics, practised by Theocritus. Tennyson was happy to accept that he had been influenced by Theocritus in much of his writing, but denied it for the lyric 'Come down, O maid' ('said [by some] to be taken from Theocritus, but there is no real likeness except perhaps in the Greek Idyllic feeling' (T)). Tennyson considered this lyric one of his most successful pieces.

197 l. 255. *burgeon*. Grow.

Conclusion

202 l. 87. *pine*. Pineapple.

l. 89. *guano*. Seabird excrement, valuable as a fertilizer.

203 *In Memoriam A.H.H.* Written over many years, from 1833 when Arthur Hallam died into the late 1840s. It was published, anonymously, in 1850. Hallam had been Tennyson's closest friend since their days together in Cambridge in 1829. The two had travelled together in Europe in 1830, and Hallam had fallen in love with and become engaged to Tennyson's sister Emily in the same year. He also enthusiastically supported Tennyson's poetic vocation, reading his work carefully and positively, providing encouragement and advice. He wrote a review of Tennyson's 1830 *Poems, Chiefly Lyrical* in *Englishman's Magazine* called 'On Some of the Characteristics of Modern Poetry and on the Lyrical Poetry of Alfred Tennyson', the first serious, positive assessment of Tennyson's genius. Indeed, Hallam was generally regarded as the most promising individual of his generation, with a wide circle of friends (including future Prime Minister William Gladstone, who always said that had he not died Hallam would certainly have been Prime Minister himself).

Hallam died suddenly in Vienna, 15 Sept. 1833, apparently of a brain haemorrhage. Tennyson received the news on 1 October in a letter from Hallam's uncle. 'Your friend, and my much-beloved nephew, Arthur Hallam, is no more ... He died at Vienna, on his return from Buda, by apoplexy, and I believe his remains come by sea from Trieste' (*Memoir*, i. 105). The body was brought back to Britain, and he was buried in Clevedon, Somerset, 3 Jan. 1834.

The force of this bereavement focused Tennyson's already sometimes melancholic poetic talent in a single direction. It seems clear that the shock of this death was indeed the most significant emotional event of his life. Tennyson's brother Charles was of the opinion that 'to both Alfred and Emily the blow was overwhelming ... For Alfred a sudden and brutal stroke had annihilated in a moment a love "passing the love of women". The prop, round which his own growth had twined itself for four fruitful years, was suddenly removed. A lifelong prospect, founded on his own friendship and Emily's hoped-for union with his friend, was blotted out instantly and forever' (*Memoir*, i. 145). That biblical quotation referring to a love 'passing the love of women' (2 Sam. 1: 26, about the love of David for Jonathan) is apropos. The intensity of love expressed as loss in this poem is so great as to verge often on the erotic. At least one reviewer of the first edition mistook the gender of the author ('these touching lines evidently come from the full heart of the widow of a military man', *Memoir*, i. 298).

Tennyson's comments on the poem try to bring out a latent structure in what remains a loosely accumulated congregation of lyrics. To James Knowles, he said: 'It is rather the cry of the whole human race than mine. In the poem altogether private grief swells out into thought of, and hope for, the whole world. It begins with a funeral and ends with a marriage—begins with death and ends in promise of new life—a sort of Divine Comedy, cheerful at the close. It is a very impersonal poem, as well as personal' (quoted in Ricks, ii. 312). Tennyson was fond of the comparison with Dante:

> It must be remembered that this is a poem, not an actual biography. It is founded on our friendship, on the engagement of Arthur Hallam to my sister, on his sudden death in Vienna, just before the time fixed for their marriage, and on his burial at Clevedon Church. The poem concludes with the marriage of my youngest sister Cecilia. It was meant to be a kind of *Divina Commedia*, ending with happiness. The sections were written at many different places, and as the phases of our intercourse came to my memory and suggested them, I did not write them with any view to weaving them into a whole, or with any view of publication, until I found that I had written so many. The different moods of sorrow as in a drama are dramatically given, and my conviction that fear, doubts, and suffering will find answer and relief comes from Faith in a God of Love. 'I' is not always the author speaking of himself, but the voice of the human race speaking through him. After the death of A.H.H., the divisions are made by First Xmas Eve (section xxviii), Second Xmas (lxxviii), Third Xmas Eve (civ and cv etc.) (*Memoir*, i. 304-5).

Critics still disagree on this question of structure. To Knowles, Tennyson suggested a different nine-part 'structure' for the poem, that doesn't quite map onto the tripartite model of the 'three Christmases', although it does draw out the Dantean parallels (see Ricks, ii. 313).

1.	First Part ('Inferno')	(i)	I–VIII
		(ii)	IX–XX ('all connected—all about the Ship')
		(iii)	XXI–XXVII
2.	Second Part ('Purgatorio')	(iv)	XXVIII–XLIX
		(v)	L–LVIII
		(vi)	LIX–LXXI
3.	Third Part ('Paradiso')	(vii)	LXXII–XCVIII
		(viii)	XCIX–CIII
		(ix)	CIV–CXXXI

Critics today are more likely to stress the freer form of the piece, on the analogy of (for instance) Shakespeare's *Sonnets*, which is also a manifest influence on Tennyson's elegy. As he also said to Knowles, 'the general way of its being written was so queer that if there were a blank space I would put in a poem.'

[Prologue], l. 5. *orbs*. 'Sun and moon' (T).

l. 28. *as before*. 'As in the ages of faith' (T).

204 *I.* l. 1. *him*. Asked in later life to identify 'him', Tennyson wrote: 'I believe I alluded to Goethe. Among his last words were these: "Von Aenderungen zu höheren Aenderungen", "from changes to higher changes" ' (*Memoir*, ii. 391). Nobody has found anything in Goethe that corresponds to this.

l. 13. *Hours*. In Greek mythology, the 'Horai' (Hours) were goddesses who personified time and presided over the changing seasons.

205 *II.* l. 7. *clock*. The clock in the church-tower overlooking the graveyard.

l. 14. *Sick for*. Sick with envy for.

III. l. 14. *her*. i.e. Sorrow.

206 *IV.* l. 6. *fail*. Fall away from.

V. l. 9. *weeds*. Clothes. This archaic term survives now chiefly in the phrase 'widow's weeds' (or the black clothes worn to indicate mourning), and Tennyson's use of it has that connotation.

207 *VI.* l. 25. *dove*. Term of affection for a woman. 'Ranging' in the next line means 'arranging'.

208 *VII.* l. 1. *Dark house*. Hallam's house at 67 Wimpole Street, London.

209 *IX.* l. 1. *Fair ship*. Sections IX–XX all concern the ship bringing Hallam's remains back to Britain (it arrived 31 Dec. 1833). Tennyson later said that this lyric was 'the first written' (Ricks, ii. 327).

209 l. 10. *Phosphor*. Venus, the morning star.

210 *X*. ll. 15–16. *drains | The chalice*. Takes communion in church.

l. 20. *tangle*. Seaweed.

XI. l. 5. *wold*. An old English word for uncultivated uplands. Here the scene is the Lincolnshire flats of Tennyson's childhood.

212 *XIII*. l. 13. *many years*. i.e. 'for many years'.

XIV. l. 2. *thou*. This whole lyric is addressed to the ship.

215 *XIX*. l. 1. *Danube to the Severn*. The route Tennyson imagines Hallam's body to have taken; Vienna, where he died, is on the Danube; the ship carrying his remains would travel up the Bristol Channel into the Severn, and eventually the Wye (l. 7), near where Hallam is buried.

216 *XXI*. l. 4. *pipes*. The syrinx, or pan-pipes, a standard prop of classical Pastoral. Sections XXI–XXV see Tennyson drawing more self-consciously on the conventions of pastoral elegy; according to Robert Hill they form 'an interlude . . . his recourse to the pastoral convention allows him to think of his verses in terms of a larger, more durable context' (Hill (ed.), *Tennyson's Poetry* (2nd edn., New York: Norton, 1999), 218).

l. 16. *power?* Alluding to popular radical movements such as Chartism, as well as to Tennyson's continuing bugbear the French Revolution.

217 *XXII*. l. 3. *four sweet years*. Tennyson knew Hallam from 1829 to 1833.

l. 12. *Shadow*. Death. 'Shadow of Death' is a common biblical locution (for instance, Job 10: 22, Psalms 23: 4).

218 *XXIII*. l. 5. *keys*. The Shadow (Death) keeps the keys of all faiths; a grim parallel to the traditional image of St Peter keeping the keys to the (Christian) Heaven.

l. 12. *Pan*. The half-human, half-goat Greek god Pan (whose name means 'everything') is a stock figure in Pastoral poetry.

l. 22. *Argive*. Homeric term for 'Greek'.

l. 24. *Arcady*. The hilly area of central Greece, the scene of a great many classical Pastoral poems.

XXIV. l. 3. *fount of Day*. The Sun; the 'wandering isles of night' are sunspots.

219 l. 15. *orb into the perfect star*. The sense is that, with enough distance, even a spotted disc like the Sun would be seen only as a pure point of light (a star); which is to say, with the distance of time the 'spots' in Tennyson and Hallam's relationship would become invisible.

XXV. l. 11. *lading*. Piling on.

220 *XXVI*. l. 16. *proper*. Personal (i.e. his scorn of himself).

XXVII. l. 12. *want-begotten*. Ill-deserved.

ll. 15–16. *'Tis better . . . loved at all*. This famous couplet modifies Section I, lines 15–16. It is repeated in LXXXV, lines 3–4.

XXVIII. l. 1. *The time*. The first Christmas after Hallam's death ushers in the second part of the poem. Sequences XXVIII–XLIX are largely concerned with questions of Hallam's supposed immortality. The scene is set at Somersby, Tennyson's home of 1833.

l. 9. *changes*. Bell-ringing term. Each of the four churches within earshot of Somersby are ringing out their (different) chimes.

221 *XXIX*. l. 11. *Wont*. Custom, habit.

l. 13. *Old sisters*. i.e. Use and Wont.

XXX. l. 8. *Shadow*. Now Hallam-in-Death.

222 l. 18. *meet*. Proper, fitting.

l. 27. *seraphic*. Angelic.

XXXI. l. 1. *Lazarus*. 'Then when Jesus came, he found that he [Lazarus] had lain in the grave four days already . . . he cried with a loud voice, Lazarus, come forth. And he that was dead came forth' (John 11: 17–44). The Bible records that Lazarus was the brother of Mary, but contains no such meeting envisaged here by Tennyson.

223 l. 12. *Olivet*. The Mount of Olives, near Jerusalem.

l. 15. *He*. Lazarus.

l. 16. *Evangelist*. John, whose gospel is the only one to contain the story of Lazarus.

XXXII. l. 1. *Her*. Mary, sister of Lazarus. This section continues on from the one before.

l. 8. *Life*. Jesus (who tells Mary, as she mourns for the dead Lazarus, 'I am the resurrection and the Life', John 11: 25).

l. 12. *spikenard*. A costly oil. Mary had earlier bathed Christ's feet in this oil and wiped them clean with her hair.

XXXIII. l. 1. *thou*. It is not clear who is addressed. The section as a whole concerns a brother (the 'thou') whose religious faith does not need to be attached to any particular thing, and a sister whose faith is simpler and fixed on a 'form', but whose beliefs are just as valid (and whom the narrator exhorts the brother not to disturb). Following on from the earlier lyrics this could be Lazarus and Mary, or perhaps Tennyson and his sister Emily (who had both been bereaved).

224 *XXXIV*. l. 5. *round of green, this orb of flame*. i.e. the Earth and the Sun.

225 *XXXV*. l. 11. *Æonian hills*. Hills that are aeons old.

l. 14. *that forgetful shore*. The banks of Lethe ('Forgetfulness'), the river which all the dead must cross.

ll. 18–19. *If Death . . . had not been*. If death really were death—that is, complete extinction—then love would not be possible ('Love had not been' means 'Love could not have been').

l. 22. *Satyr-shape*. Man at his most bestial, like a satyr. 'Batten'd' in l. 24 means 'stuffed himself with food'.

225   *XXXVI*. l. 7. *truth embodied in a tale*. The 'tale' of the gospels.

l. 9. *the Word*. Tennyson commented: ' "The Word" as used by St. John, the Revelation of the Eternal Thought of the Universe' (*Memoir*, i. 312). The reference is to the beginning of John's gospel: 'In the beginning was the Word, and the Word was with God, and the Word was God' (John 1: 1).

l. 15. *wild eyes*. 'The Pacific Islanders' (T). They were being Christianized in the mid-19th century.

226   *XXXVII*. l. 1. *Urania*. One of the Muses; originally connected with astronomy, Milton made her the 'Muse of Heavenly Poetry' in *Paradise Lost* (Milton's invocation to Urania at the beginning of book vii is behind Tennyson's use here).

l. 6. *Parnassus*. Mountain in Greece where the Muses were reputed to live.

l. 9. *Melpomene*. Muse of Tragedy, and hence of elegy (following Hallam's 'tragic' death).

227   *XXXIX*. l. 1. *Old warder*. The yew growing in the cemetery where Hallam is buried (see Section II). It is now 'fruitful' because the poem has moved on to spring. Tennyson observed: 'the yew, when flowering, in a wind or if struck, sends up its pollen like smoke' (quoted in Ricks, ii. 356).

ll. 11–12. *Thy gloom . . . gloom again*. The sense isn't clear here. The yew has traditionally been regarded as symbolic of sadness (Shakespeare talks, for instance, of 'the dismal yew', *Titus Andronicus* II. iii. 107) which is perhaps what 'gloom' means; the sense could be 'you represented gloom once before—for instance, in Section II—and although now you represent spring and new growth (you are 'kindled' at your 'tips' with pollen) it is inevitable, as Sorrow says, that you will pass back into your wintry state of gloom again'.

228   *XL*. l. 17. *thee*. Hallam.

l. 32. *undiscover'd lands*. Allusion to Hamlet's 'to be or not to be' soliloquy, where death is 'the undiscovered country, from whose bourn | No traveller returns' (*Hamlet* III. i. 79–80).

XLI. l. 16. *The howlings*. The reference is to Dante's grim vision of Hell; 'The eternal miseries of the Inferno' (T).

229   l. 24. *behind*. The speaker is worried that when he dies and goes to Heaven, Hallam will already have progressed through the stages of the afterlife such that Tennyson could not hope to catch up with him 'tho' following with an upward mind'.

XLIII. l. 3. *interval*. Existing between two lives or stages of existence.

230   *XLIV*. l. 4. *shut the doorways of his head*. When a baby is born, the plates in its skull are not joined, but soon become so. Believers in reincarnation used to believe that before this happened, the baby could remember its past life (although, being a baby, it could not talk about it), and that the 'closing' of the skull destroyed this memory. Tennyson seems to have something like this in mind here—that perhaps God effects a similar change after death,

and that accordingly perhaps Hallam will not be able to remember his previous existence.

231   *XLVI*. l. 5. *there*. In the afterlife.

l. 7. *marge to marge*. From edge to edge; i.e. from birth to death.

XLVII. l. 4. *the general Soul*. After the philosophy of the 12th-century thinker Averrhoès, a school of thought grew up that denied individual immortality, suggesting that after death the soul was blended back into the Universal Oversoul whence it came. Tennyson was uncomfortable with this Averroism: 'if the absorption into the divine in the after-life be the creed of some,' he said, 'let them at all events allow us many existences of individuality before this absorption; since this short lived individuality seems to be too short a preparation for so mighty a union' (*Memoir*, i. 319).

232   *XLVIII*. l. 5. *Her*. Sorrow's.

XLIX. l. 8. *crisp*. Curl or become wavy.

233   *L*. From this section to section LVIII constitutes another element in the pattern identified by Tennyson (see above, p. 583).

234   *LII*. l. 11. *sinless years*. The life of Christ. 'Syria' (l. 12) is used generally, as the land east of the Mediterranean, where Christ lived his life.

LIII. l. 5. *give*. 'Give in', surrender.

235   *LV*. l. 7. *type*. Species. The sense is that whilst Nature may preserve an entire species—say mankind—she has no care for or interest in any particular individual. Tennyson once told his son that 'the lavish profusion' of the natural world 'appals me, from the growths of the tropical forest to the capacity of man to multiply, the torrent of babies . . . If we look at Nature alone, full of perfection and imperfection, she tells us that God is disease, murder and rapine' (*Memoir*, i. 314).

236   *LVI*. One of the most famous sections of *In Memoriam*, not least because it seems to anticipate Darwin so presciently. Tennyson's interest in fossils dates from before 1844, when he obtained a copy of Robert Chambers's *Vestiges of Creation* in which the fossil record is discussed (of this influential volume, Tennyson said 'it seems to contain many speculations with which I have been familiar for years, and on which I have written more than one poem', *Memoir*, i. 222–3). He was also familiar with Lyell's geological study *Principles of Geology* (1830–3), which similarly discusses fossil finds.

l. 2. *scarped*. Cut open.

l. 3. *She*. Nature (referring back to Section LV).

l. 12. *fanes*. Temples.

ll. 19–20. *Be blown . . . hills?* The syntax picks up and concludes the clause that began with the 'Shall he . . .?' of l. 8. 'Seal'd within the iron hills' means 'turned into fossils'.

237   l. 22. *Dragons*. Dinosaurs. 'Tare' in the next line is a variant of 'tore' (i.e. injured one another in fighting).

237 l. 26. *thy*. Hallam's.

LVII. l. 15. *Ave*. Latin for 'hail!' Famous lines by the Roman poet Catullus bid farewell to the poet's dead brother with the words 'atque in perpetuum frater ave atque vale', 'and forever brother, hail and farewell'. Tennyson thought there was 'no modern elegy' that could 'equal in pathos the desolation of that everlasting farewell' of Catullus (*Memoir*, ii. 239).

238 *LIX*. This up to Section LXXI supposedly constitutes the sixth section of the poem, and the conclusion to the second third of the whole.

239 *LXI*. l. 12. *Shakspeare*. The usual spelling of 'Shakespeare' in the 19th century.

LXII. l. 2. *blench*. Quail, flinch.

l. 5. *declined*. Lowered himself.

242 *LXVII*. l. 2. *place of rest*. Hallam is buried at Clevedon, beside the Severn.

243 *LXIX*. l. 14. *found*. Had a vision of.

LXX. l. 7. *palled*. Covered in a pall; veiled.

244 *LXXI*. l. 4. *France*. The reference is to a happy holiday Tennyson and Hallam took together through France in 1830.

LXXII. l. 1. *dim dawn*. The occasion is the first anniversary of Hallam's death: 15 Sept. 1834. Tennyson himself suggested that this lyric stood at the beginning of the third 'part' of the loosely structured *In Memoriam* (see above, p. 583).

l. 5. *crown'd estate*. When he first began wearing the 'crown of thorns' of sorrow at Hallam's death (as in LXIX, ll. 7–8, 'I took the thorns to bind my brows, | I wore them like a civic crown').

245 l. 25. *up thy vault*. Fill the sky.

l. 27. *goal*. Seeing the sunset as the 'goal' of the day certainly seems gloomy and death-oriented enough.

LXXIII. l. 3. *thee*. Hallam.

247 *LXXVI*. l. 9. *matin songs*. 'Matins' is a morning prayer; here the sense is of the 'morning' of the human race. Tennyson glosses: 'the great early poets'.

l. 12. *oak*. Tree with particularly English associations; oaks can live many hundreds of years. Tennyson is contrasting the oak with the (similarly long-lived) yew of l. 8.

LXXVII. l. 7. *curl a maiden's locks*. Heated metal tongs were used to impress fashionable curls in hair, waste paper (such as the speaker imagines his poems becoming) being placed between the tong and the hair to stop the latter singeing.

248 *LXXVIII*. l. 1. *Christmas*. This is Christmas 1834, the second after Hallam's death. See Section XXX with its equivalent l. 4: 'And sadly fell our Christmas-eve'.

l. 5. *yule-clog*. Northern dialect variant of 'yule log', the log that was placed on the fire to burn throughout Christmas.

ll. 11–12. *mimic picture's*. *Tableaux vivants*, a parlour game in which people acted out still poses of famous scenes and players had to guess which.   *hoodman-blind*. Blind man's buff.

LXXIX. l. 2. *thee*. Tennyson's brother, Charles Tennyson Turner. The first line is quoted from Section IX, l. 20.

249 *LXXX*. l. 8. *stay'd*. Acted as a stay, propped up.

LXXXI. l. 4. *ear*. Of grain. The section elaborates this winter-wheat metaphor, although there is also a pun here on the organ of hearing (see the next section, ll. 13–16).

250 *LXXXIII*. ll. 9–12. *orchis . . . laburnums*. All the flowers mentioned here bloom in late spring, early summer.

251 *LXXXIV*. l. 11. *link thy life with one*. Hallam had been engaged to Emily, Tennyson's sister.

l. 15. *cypress*. Symbolic of sadness and mourning.   *orange flower*. Symbolic of weddings and (therefore) happiness.

253 *LXXXV*. l. 21. *Intelligences*. Angels.

255 l. 100. *my friend*. This section is addressed to Edmund Lushington, who went on to marry Tennyson's sister Cecilia in 1842—which marriage functions as the epilogue to *In Memoriam*. Tennyson was friendly with Lushington, but (as this section makes clear) the friendship could not substitute for Hallam's.

256 *LXXXVI*. ll. 4–5. *breathing bare | The round of space*. i.e. the wind clears the sky of clouds. This section was written at Barmouth in 1839.

LXXXVII. l. 1. *reverend walls*. Trinity College Cambridge, where Tennyson had been a student.

l. 5. *fanes*. Chapels.

270 l. 21. *a band*. The reference is to 'The Apostles', the undergraduate debating society that had included both Tennyson and Hallam.

l. 31. *him*. Hallam, the 'master-bowman' of debate.

l. 40. *The bar of Michael Angelo*. The celebrated Renaissance artist had a prominent forehead ridge of bone over his eyes, as did Hallam. It was thought indicative of an astute and contemplative cast of mind. Hallam had once said to Tennyson: 'Alfred, look over my eyes; surely I have the bar of Michael Angelo' (*Memoir*, i. 38).

LXXXVIII. l. 1. *Wild bird*. 'To the Nightingale' (T).

l. 2. *budded quicks*. Blossoming hedgerows.

258 *LXXXIX*. l. 1. *counterchange*. A heraldic term for 'chequer'.

l. 12. *purlieus*. Outskirts. Hallam had left university to become a lawyer.

l. 24. *Tuscan poets*. Dante and Petrarch.

259 l. 36. *Socratic*. In the dialectical investigative manner of the Greek philosopher Socrates. Tennyson originally wrote 'Platonic', which is to say in the like manner of Plato, Socrates' student; but he may have changed it because 'Platonic' was sometimes used as a euphemism for 'homosexual'.

ll. 47–8. *crimson-circled . . . grave*. 'Before Venus, the evening star, had dipt into the sunset. The planets, according to Laplace, were evolved from the sun' (T).

XC. l. 6. *wail*. Lament.

260 l. 21. *dear*. Tennyson told Knowles in 1870: 'if any body thinks I ever called him "dearest" in his life they are much mistaken, for I never even called him "dear" (quoted in Ricks, ii. 441–2). See also Section CXXII.

XCI. l. 2. *rarely*. With rare beauty.

l. 4. *sea-blue bird*. Kingfisher.

261 *XCII*. l. 14. *spiritual presentiments*. The sense is that even if a 'vision' of Hallam appeared and spoke prophecies about the future that turned out to be true, the speaker might not believe; because the prophecies might be nothing but his own 'presentiments', the reflection ('refraction') of events in his own mind.

XCIII. l. 9. *sightless range*. Invisible land.

262 *XCIV*. l. 16. *jar*. Make unpleasant noise.

XCV. l. 2. *herb*. Grass. The scene is on the lawn at Somersby, where a family party is going on into the evening. Tennyson told friends of 'one singularly still starlit evening' when 'he and his friends had once sat out far into the night having tea at a table on the lawn beneath the stars, and that the candles had burned with steady upright flame, disturbed from time to time by the inrush of a moth or cockchafer, as tho' in a closed room' (*Memoir*, i. 205).

l. 8. *fluttering urn*. The urn contains tea; it is 'fluttering' because there is a flame underneath it, keeping the tea hot.

l. 15. *kine*. Cattle.

263 l. 22. *that glad year*. When Hallam was still alive. Perhaps Tennyson is reading letters to him from Hallam.

l. 38. *empyreal*. Of highest heaven.

l. 41. *Æonian music*. Eons-old music; the music of the spheres.

264 *XCVI*. l. 1. *You*. Probably addressed to Emily Sellwood, whom Tennyson was to marry in 1850; one of the reasons their engagement was so prolonged had to do with Emily's doubts about his religious faith.

l. 5. *one*. Hallam.

265 ll. 22–4. *Sinai's peaks . . . trumpets blew so loud*. Whilst Moses went up Mount Sinai to receive the Ten Commandments, the Israelites set up a golden calf as an object of worship, thus displeasing both Moses and God: 'And it came to pass on the third day in the morning, that there were

thunders and lightnings, and a thick cloud upon the mount, and the voice of the trumpet exceeding loud; so that all the people that was in the camp trembled . . . And when the voice of the trumpet sounded long, and waxed louder and louder, Moses spake, and God answered him by a voice' (Exod. 19: 16–19).

XCVII. l. 5. *partners of a married life.* No actual married couple was intended here; a fictional pair where the woman looks up to her husband, even though he (he seems to be a man of science 'rapt in matters dark and deep') neglects her because of his work.

l. 15. *earnest.* A pledge.

266　*XCVIII.* l. 1. *You.* This section is addressed to Tennyson's brother, Charles, who married in 1836 and went on honeymoon to central Europe, visiting many of the places that Tennyson associates with Hallam (the Rhine where Hallam and Tennyson holidayed, and Vienna, on the Danube, where Hallam died).

l. 11. *I will not see.* Indeed, Tennyson never visited Vienna.

l. 17. *Gnarr.* 'Snarl' (T).

l. 21. *mother town.* The word 'metropolis' is derived from the Greek for 'mother town'.

267　*XCIX.* l. 1. *dim dawn.* The second anniversary of Hallam's death. From here to CIII constitutes a separate subsection of the larger tripartite 'structure' of the whole, according to Tennyson's scheme (see above, p. 583).

l. 18. *Betwixt the slumber of the poles.* Between the poles, which is to say anywhere on Earth. The poles are said to be 'slumbering' either because they do not move as they rotate, or else because they are covered with ice.

268　*CI.* l. 1. *Unwatch'd.* The scenes described will be 'unloved' and 'unwatched' because the Tennysons are moving from Somersby, with its memories of Hallam, to a new home at High Beech, north of London. Compare the lyric 'A Farewell' (p. 99), also concerned with this move.

l. 11. *lesser wain.* The constellation of Ursa Minor, the Little Bear, which contains the pole star.

l. 14. *hern and crake.* Heron and corncrake.

269　*CII.* l. 7. *two spirits.* 'Referring to the double loss of his father and of his friend' (*Memoir*, i. 72).

l. 10. *matin song.* Songs of praise sung in the morning; figuratively, Tennyson's earliest poetry.

270　*CIII.* l. 6. *maidens.* 'They are the Muses, poetry, arts—all that made life beautiful here, which we hope will pass with us beyond the grave' (T).

l. 7. *summits.* 'The divine' (T).

l. 8. *river.* 'Life' (T).

l. 16. *sea.* 'Eternity' (T).

270 ll. 25–8. *And still . . . than before.* 'The progress of the age' (T).

ll. 31–2. *Anakim.* Sons of Anak. 'And there we saw giants, the sons of Anak, which come of the giants: and we were in our own sight as grasshoppers, and so we were in their sight' (Num. 13: 33). *Titans.* Race of giants from Greek mythology, overthrown and superseded by the Olympian gods.

ll. 33–6. *As one would . . . of a star.* 'The great hopes of humanity and science' (T).

271 *CIV.* l. 1. *The time.* It is the third Christmas after Hallam's death. From this section until the end of the poem constitutes the final subsection identified by Tennyson as part of the 'structure' of *In Memoriam.*

272 *CV.* l. 4. Compare line 4 of Sections XXX and LXXVIII.

l. 5. *father's dust.* Tennyson's father had died in 1831.

l. 18. *wassail mantle warm.* Christmas punch bubble over the heat.

CVI. l. 4. *him.* The Old Year, but with suggestive implication for the passing of Tennyson's grief.

273 *CVII.* l. 1. *the day when he was born.* Coming so soon after the Christmas sections this is also suggestive; but Hallam's date of birth was 1 Feb. 1811.

274 l. 11. *grides.* Rubs, grates.

275 *CIX.* The descriptions in this section all apply to Hallam.

CX. l. 1. *Thy.* The poet continues with his descriptions of Hallam.

l. 2. *rathe.* Young.

276 *CXI.* l. 3. *golden ball.* Symbolic prop of monarchy.

277 l. 18. *villain.* Low-born; i.e. not a gentleman.

CXII. l. 3. *glorious insufficiencies.* 'Unaccomplished greatness such as Arthur Hallam's' (T). The sense of this stanza seems to be that Tennyson 'sets only light store' on the fully accomplished achievements of narrower men, preferring the 'unaccomplished greatness' of a figure such as Hallam.

l. 5. *thou.* Hallam.

278 *CXIV.* l. 4. *pillars.* 'Wisdom hath builded her house, she hath hewn out her seven pillars' (Prov. 9: 1).

l. 12. *Pallas.* Pallas Athene, the Greek goddess of wisdom. The myth was that she was not born in the conventional manner, but leapt out already fully armed from the forehead of Zeus.

l. 17. *A higher hand.* i.e. God. 'The fear of the Lord is the beginning of wisdom' (Prov. 9: 10).

279 *CXV.* l. 2. *quick.* Life. The 'maze of quick' is presumably vegetation.

l. 3. *flowering squares.* Fields full of flowers.

l. 8. *sightless.* Invisible.

l. 14. *greening gleam.* i.e. the sea.

280 *CXVII*. ll. 10–11. *span of shade*. 'The sun-dial' (T). *toothed wheels*. Clockwork wheels of a clock.

CXVIII. l. 7. *They*. Scientists such as Laplace, who first theorized that the Earth had accumulated out of gas.

281 l. 16. *type*. Used as a verb, to mean 'prefigure'.

CXIX. l. 1. *Doors*. The speaker is once again (after Section VII) at Hallam's house in Wimpole Street, London.

CXX. l. 4. *Like Paul*. St Paul said: 'If after the manner of men I have fought with beasts at Ephesus, what advantageth it me, if the dead rise not? Let us eat and drink, for to morrow we die' (1 Cor. 15: 32).

ll. 9–11. *Let him . . . greater ape*. The later publication (1859) of Darwin's *Origin of Species* was greeted with interest by Tennyson, and he considered he had prefigured many Darwinian points. Of these three lines he later said: 'spoken ironically against mere materialism, not against evolution' (quoted in Ricks, ii. 440).

CXXI. l. 1. *Hesper*. The evening star. 'Phosphor' (l. 9) is the morning star. In fact they are both the same star, or rather the same planet (Venus).

l. 5. *wain*. Wagon.

283 *CXXII*. l. 2. *doom*. Fate.

l. 16. *slip*. Let slip, i.e. let go.

l. 18. *bow*. Rainbow.

l. 19. *wizard lightnings*. The Northern Lights.

285 *CXXVII*. l. 2. *the night of fear*. The French Revolution (where the river of Paris, the Seine, was reddened with blood, l. 7); one of Tennyson's perennial bugbears.

l. 10. *lazar*. Leper, here the lowest of the low; but also suggesting 'Lazarus', who was touched by Christ and came back from the dead (so, the highest).

286 l. 16. *Æon*. Age.

288 *CXXXI*. l. 1. *living will*. 'That which we know as Free-will, the higher and enduring part of man' (*Memoir*, i. 319).

[Epilogue]. This is an epithalamium, a poem or song celebrating a marriage. The marriage in question was between Edmund Lushington, Tennyson's friend (addressed in Section LXXXV) and Cecilia, Tennyson's sister, in 1842. As Tennyson said, 'the poem concludes with the marriage of my youngest sister Cecilia. It was meant to be a kind of *Divina Commedia*, ending with happiness' (*Memoir*, i. 304).

l. 6. *he*. Hallam, who, like Lushington, was in love with one of Tennyson's sisters.

l. 10. *thrice three years*. Since Hallam's death; the poem is being composed in 1842.

289 l. 40. *learning*. Lushington was a Professor of Greek at Glasgow University.

289 l. 51. *tablets*. Gravestones. The wedding party is now in the graveyard of the church ('her feet . . . on the dead').

290 l. 57. *sign your names*. An English church wedding is not complete until both parties have signed the parish register. They usually retire to a special room to do this, whilst the organist amuses the congregation with organ pieces.

l. 86. *guest*. Hallam.

291 l. 104. *three-times-three*. The toast ('three-times-three cheers for the bride and groom!').

293 *To the Queen*. Written 1 Mar. 1851, this was Tennyson's first work as Poet Laureate. It was published as the dedication to the seventh edition of 1851's *Poems*. It uses the *In Memoriam* stanza: according to his son, Tennyson 'was appointed Poet Laureate, owing chiefly to Prince Albert's admiration for *In Memoriam*' (*Memoir*, i. 334). After Albert's death in 1861, Victoria grew even fonder of the volume, keeping it on her bedside table.

l. 14. *throstle*. Song thrush.

294 *Ode on the Death of the Duke of Wellington*. Published by itself on 16 Nov. 1852, in time for Wellington's funeral on the 18th (he had died on the 14th). Tennyson's first separate publication as laureate attracted much attention though little praise, although more recent critics have seen this elegiac ode as one of the great pieces of occasional verse in English, connecting it particularly with *In Memoriam* and *Morte d'Arthur*. Wellington had been born Arthur Wellesley in 1769 and had joined the army in 1787. He fought with distinction in Flanders and India, before commanding the British forces in the Napoleonic Wars. After defeating the French and invading France, Wellesley was created 1st Duke of Wellington. Following Napoleon's escape from imprisonment and the 'hundred days', Wellington commanded the Anglo-Dutch forces at Waterloo. Victory there assured him hero status in British popular consciousness, and he subsequently went into politics. During his first term as Prime Minister he passed a bill freeing Catholics from the legal restraints placed upon them (Catholic Emancipation became law in 1829); but despite this piece of liberal legislation in general his two terms of office were characterized by extreme conservatism. His later career divided public opinion, and 'the Great Duke' was as like to have his house stoned by an angry mob as he was to be greeted by cheering crowds. He was buried in St Paul's Cathedral, London.

295 l. 42. *World-victor's victor*. The 'World-victor' is Napoleon, who conquered most of Europe and a large piece of Russia. Wellington, however, was victorious over the 'world victor'.

l. 49. *cross of gold*. St Paul's is topped with a large golden cross.

296 l. 84. *Seaman*. Nelson, another British hero of the Napoleonic wars (who is supposed to have spoken the preceding three lines), was already interred in St Paul's, having been killed at the battle of Trafalgar in 1805.

297 l. 99. *Assaye*. A battle fought in Hindustan, 1803; superior firepower enabled Wellington to defeat a much larger force of Indians.

l. 103. *Lisbon*. In Portugal. Wellington fought a number of engagements with the French in the Peninsular War, 1808–14, eventually heavily defeating them in 1813. He was then able to invade France through the Pyrenees.

l. 119. *eagle*. Napoleon's symbol.

l. 123. *sabbath*. Sunday, 18 June 1815; the day on which the battle of Waterloo was fought.

l. 127. *Prussian*. The Prussian arrival, to aid Wellington's Anglo–Dutch force, tipped the balance.

298 l. 137. *Baltic and the Nile*. Nelson had defeated the French navy at the battle of the Nile in 1798; he defeated the Danish fleet in the Baltic in 1801.

299 l. 188. *Alfred*. The English King Alfred the Great (849–901), known as (amongst other things) the 'truth-teller'.

302 *The Charge of the Light Brigade*. Britain (allied with France and the Ottoman empire) was at war with Russia in the Crimea, 1853–6. At one engagement in this war, the battle of Balaclava 25 Oct. 1854, the Light Brigade, a troop of 700 horse, was ordered to retrieve some abandoned Russian cannons. Misinterpreting the order, the Brigade charged at the main concentration of Russian artillery, losing over 500 men. Tennyson wrote the poem on 2 Dec. 1854, 'in a few minutes, after reading the description in the *Times* in which occurred the phrase "someone had blundered", and this was the origin of the metre of the poem' (*Memoir*, i. 381). He changed the 700 to 600 because 'six is much better than seven hundred (as I think) metrically' (*Letters*, ii. 101).

304 *Maud; A Monodrama*. The first part of this poem to be written was the lyric 'Oh that 'twere possible' (above, p. 99), which Tennyson apparently wrote after Hallam's death in 1833 (it is *Maud*, II. 141–238). Aubrey de Vere says of the composition: 'Its origin and composition were, as he described them, singular. He had accidentally lighted upon a poem of his own which begins, "O that 'twere possible", and which had long before been published in a selected volume got up by Lord Northampton for the aid of a sick clergyman. It had struck him, in consequence, I think, of a suggestion made by Sir John Simeon, that, to render the poem fully intelligible, a preceding one was necessary. He wrote it; the second poem too required a predecessor; and thus the whole work was written, as it were, *backwards*' (*Memoir*, i. 379). Most of this 'backwards' writing took place in 1854.

A 'Monodrama' is a dramatic performance for one speaker, usually on the stage or in opera. To his son, Tennyson claimed that his psychological dramatic monologue (the more usual modern term) was 'a little *Hamlet*', and not a work like *In Memoriam* rooted in autobiography: 'the history of a morbid poetic soul, under the blighting influence of a recklessly speculative age. He is the heir to madness, an egoist with the makings of a cynic, raised to sanity by a pure and holy love which elevates his whole nature, passing from the height of triumph to the lowest depth of misery into madness by the loss of her whom he has loved, and, when he has at length passed through the fiery furnace, and has recovered his reason, giving himself up to work for the good of mankind. . . . "The peculiarity of this poem," my father added, "is that different phases of passion in one person take the place of different characters' (*Memoir*, i. 396). The *Memoir* also includes Tennyson's headings and notes, which help elaborate the narrative. Since Tennyson's lyric technique in this work tends to obscure the narrative line, it is worth reproducing these here; the following is all Tennyson's:

Part I	I.	Before the arrival of Maud.
	II.	First sight of Maud.
	III.	Visions of the night. The broad-flung shipwrecking roar. In the Isle of Wight the roar can be heard nine miles away from the beach. (Many of the descriptions of Nature are taken from observations of natural phenomena at Farringford, although the localities in the poem are all imaginary.)
	IV.	Mood of bitterness after fancied disdain.
	V.	He fights against his growing passion.
	VI.	First interview [i.e. conversation] with Maud.
	VII.	He remembers his own and her father talking just before the birth of Maud.
	VIII.	That she did not return his love.
	IX.	First sight of the young lord.
	X.	Hero fulminates against peace-at-all-price men.
	XI.	
	XII.	Interview with Maud.
	XIII.	Mainly prophetic. He sees Maud's brother who will not recognize him.
	XIV.	
	XV.	
	XVI.	He will declare his love.
	XVII.	Accepted.
	XVIII.	Happy. The sigh in the cedar branches seems to chime in with his own yearning.
	XXI.	Before the Ball.
	XXII.	In the Hall-Garden.
Part II	I.	The Phantom (after the duel with Maud's brother).

    II. In Brittany. The shell undestroyed amid the storm perhaps symbolizes to him his own first and highest nature preserved amid the storms of passion.

    III. He felt himself going mad.

    IV. Haunted after Maud's death.

    V. In the mad-house. The second corpse is Maud's brother, the lover's father being the first corpse, whom the lover thinks that Maud's father has murdered.

Part III   VI. Sane but shattered. Written when the cannon was heard booming from the battle-ships in the Solent before the Crimean War.

In other words, the narrator loves Maud, with whom he has been betrothed since a child. But Maud's imperious brother opposes the match, insisting that Maud marry a 'young Lord'. The narrator and the brother fight a duel, the brother dying. The narrator runs away to France, where he hears that Maud, grief-stricken, has also died. He goes mad, but returns to a form of sanity at the end of the poem with the decision to enlist and go to seek a purging glory as a soldier in the Crimean War. This ending, which is certainly ambiguous (pro-war or anti-?), has provoked the greatest proportion of critical discussion.

Part I

304 l. 2. *blood-red heath*. Hallam Tennyson said: 'my father would say that in calling heath "blood"-red the hero showed his extravagant fancy, which is already on the road to madness' (quoted in Ricks, ii. 519).

    l. 9. *speculation*. i.e. financial speculation. We never learn precisely how the narrator's father was ruined; a great many people lost money in Railway shares in the 1840s and early 1850s.

305 l. 37. *vitriol*. Virulent, acrimonious.

    l. 41. *centre-bits*. Metalwork tools, here used by burglars breaking into houses.

306 l. 45. *Mammonite*. Follower of Mammon, the biblical personification of money (for instance, the 'mammon of unrighteousness' of Luke 16: 9). A 'burial fee' was money paid by instalments into a society, to be used if necessary to pay for a decent burial. Carlyle's attack on contemporary evils *Past and Present* contains the story: 'a Mother and a Father' in 1841 'arraigned and found guilty of poisoning three of their children to defraud a "burial-society" of some £3. 8s. [£3. 40 in decimal currency] due on the death of each child' (quoted in Ricks, ii. 522–3).

    l. 46. *Timour-Mammon*. 'Timour' is Tamerlane or Tamburlaine the Great, Mongol conqueror of much of Asia (1335–1405), who is credited with many atrocities. At Sebsewar in Khorasan he is reputed to have built the people of the town (including children) into a pyramid, cementing their bodies together with mortar as if they were stones and leaving them to die.

Tennyson's point is that the atrocities of a notional modern-day Timour are inseparably connected with money ('Mammon').

306   l. 52. *yardwand*. Measuring stick (such as might be used by a shop worker).

307   l. 78. *neither savour nor salt*. 'But if the salt have lost his savour, wherewith shall it be salted?' (Matt. 5: 13).

308   l. 101. *Orion*. The constellation, visible from Britain low in the sky.

l. 110. *lies as a Czar*. Reflecting the climate of anti-Russian feeling in the run-up to the Crimean War (which began in 1853).

309   l. 132. *eft*. Lizard. The word 'dinosaur', which had been coined in 1841, is from the Greek for 'terrible lizard'.

l. 144. *Isis*. 'The great Goddess of the Egyptians' (T).

l. 147. *Poland*. In 1846 Russia and Austria had occupied and partitioned Poland, an act that contributed to the opinion that Russia was following a policy of active aggrandizement of its empire and needed to be stopped (hence, in part, the Crimean War).   *Hungary*. Hungary was part of the Austrian Habsburg Empire; in 1848 a revolution led by Kossuth failed to gain freedom from Emperor Franz Joseph.

l. 148. *knout*. Russian flogging scourge, notoriously brutal. The sense of the line is a question as to whether the West (the rod) or Russia (the knout) should be in the ascendancy in post-Napoleonic Europe.

312   l. 233. *Assyrian Bull*. 'With hair curled like that of the bulls on Assyrian sculpture' (T). The narrator consistently describes both his rival for Maud's affections and Maud's brother with orientalizing terms, that feed into the 'eastern' theatre of war of the Crimea.

l. 243. *hustings*. Platforms from which candidates for parliamentary seats make their speeches to the crowd. They are 'rotten' either because the speaker despises democracy (very likely), or else because the 1832 reforms to the largely corrupt system had left many loopholes and problems that were not rectified until the two subsequent Reform Acts of 1867 and 1884.

314   l. 289. *Men*. Maud's father and the father of the narrator, speaking whilst the latter is only a child; they are discussing the future union of their respective children.

l. 295. *Viziers*. High-ranking advisers to the Sultan in many *Arabian Nights* stories.

316   l. 347. *gewgaw*. Showily ornamented.

l. 359. *bought commission*. Officers in the British Army are said to have 'the King's (or Queen's) Commission'. This may be awarded on appointment, or achieved through promotion; alternatively, in the 19th century, if one were wealthy enough one could simply buy a commission. The narrator is contemptuous of Maud's admirer for having done this, but 'purchasing your commission' remained standard practice in the Army until late in the century.

l. 366. *one.* A Quaker preacher, in a distinctive wide-brimmed black hat (l. 370). Quakers were and are implacably opposed to war. The narrator disagrees with this position, arguing that the preacher is playing into the hands of the Czar and men like him ('play[ing] the game of the despot kings').

319 l. 435. *rosy.* 'Because if you tread on the daisy, it turns up a rosy underside' (T).

l. 441. *King Charley.* King Charles Spaniel, a small yappy dog.

320 l. 464. *Gorgonised me.* Turned me to stone.

322 l. 537. *lump of earth.* Maud's brother, who has gone to London.

l. 544. *Oread.* Maud. An 'Oread' is a beautiful mountain-nymph from Greek mythology.

323 l. 560. *fasten'd.* Married.

324 l. 613. *thou.* The Lebanon Cedar of l. 616.

325 l. 634. *sad astrology.* 'The "sad astrology" is modern astronomy, for of old astrology was thought to sympathise with and rule man's fate' (T).

326 l. 666. *false death.* Sleep.

l. 674. *ye.* The 'happy stars' of l. 679.

330 l. 790. *The Sultan.* Another orientalized nickname for Maud's brother.

331 l. 819. *Tory.* Local landowners are likely to be members of the right-wing Tory party, not the centre-left Liberals.

332 l. 850. *Come into the garden, Maud.* This was set to music during Tennyson's lifetime, and remains one of the most distinctive and famous Victorian parlour songs, although it is very bad. Tennyson always said he 'hated the valse [waltz] to which "Come into the Garden Maud", was made to dance. Nothing fit for it but the human voice' (quoted in Ricks, ii. 562).

Part II

335 l. 29. *he.* Maud's brother, dying after his duel with the narrator.

l. 32. *Wraith.* Maud, ghostlike in her grief.

337 l. 96. *Lamech.* 'And Lamech said to his wives, Adah and Zillah, Hear my voice; ye wives of Lamech, hearken unto my speech: for I have slain a man to my wounding, and a young man to my hurt. If Cain shall be avenged sevenfold [for killing his brother Abel], truly Lamech seventy and sevenfold' (Gen. 4: 23–4).

338 l. 135. *left for ever alone.* Maud has now died.

342 *V.* Tennyson is reputed to have written the whole of this scene (ll. 239–342) in twenty minutes. 'He called out to his wife "now I am going to begin the mad scene", & in 20 minutes it was done' (quoted in Ricks, ii. 576). He was proud of it: 'about the mad-scene one of the best-known doctors for the insane wrote that it was "the most faithful representation of madness since Shakespeare" ' (*Memoir*, i. 398).

343   l. 280. *prophecy*. Christ's prophecy: 'Therefore whatsoever ye have spoken
      in darkness shall be heard in the light; and that which ye have spoken in the
      ear in closets shall be proclaimed upon the housetops. And I say unto you
      my friends, Be not afraid of them that kill the body, and after that have no
      more that they can do. But I will forewarn him you whom ye shall fear: Fear
      him, which after he hath killed hath power to cast into hell; yea, I say unto
      you, Fear him' (Luke 12: 3–5).

      l. 290. him. Maud's dead brother.

      l. 291. *wolf*. Maud's father.

      l. 296. *rat*. The common brown or grey rat (Rattus Norvegicus) was
      introduced to Britain in the 18th century and proceeded to force out the
      native black rat (of Great Plague fame), which is now almost extinct.
      One story, put about by Jacobites (Catholic opponents of the Protestant
      royal family imported onto the British throne in 1714) was that the
      'Norwegian Rat' came over from Hanover with the first Hanoverian
      monarch.

344   l. 317. *keeper*. Maud's brother.

      l. 318. *dead man*. The narrator considers himself dead.   *spectral bride*.
      Maud.

      Part III

345   l. 4. *time of year*. The passing daffodils (l. 6) tell us it is now late spring.

      ll. 6–7. *Charioteer | And starry Gemini*. Constellations in the British sky, to
      the north and west respectively.

      l. 10. *She*. Maud.

      l. 14. *Lion's breast*. In the constellation of Leo. The Lion is the symbolic
      animal of Britain.

346   l. 34. *giant deck*. The deck of a giant troop ship, preparing to sail to the
      Crimea.

      l. 36. *dreary phantom*. 'Of Maud' (T). The narrator has two different
      visions of Maud, as an accusing Phantom (for instance at II. 32, 82) and as
      a spirit in 'a band of the blest' (III. 10). His resolve banishes the grimmer of
      these two apparitions.

      l. 45. *a giant liar*. The Russian Czar, Nicholas I.

      l. 50. *peace, that I deem'd no peace*. In the first edition Tennyson had put 'the
      long, long canker of peace', and was attacked by the critics. *Tait's Edin-
      burgh Magazine* (Sept. 1855), for instance, said: 'if any man comes forward
      to say that the slaughter of 30,000 Englishmen in the Crimea tends to pre-
      vent women poisoning their babies, for the sake of the burial fees, in Birm-
      ingham, he is bound to show cause, and not bewilder our notions of morals
      and lexicography by calling thirty years of intermitted war (absolute peace
      we have *not* had during the interval) a "long, long *canker* of peace" '
      (quoted in Ricks, ii. 584). The issue of Tennyson's identification with a
      pro-war philosophy, or alternatively his criticism of such a philosophy by

putting these words into the mouth of a madman who had recently killed a man, has been much debated by critics.

346 l. 51. *Black*. i.e. the Black Sea.

348 *Tithonus (Final version)*. For the earlier version of this poem, written soon after Hallam's death, see above, p. 81. Tennyson's friend Thackeray (the novelist) was editor of the *Cornhill Magazine*, and asked the poet for copy in 1859. 'I ferreted among my old books and found this *Tithonus*, written upwards of a quarter of a century ago' (*Memoir*, i. 459). He revised it, adding lengthy passages, and it was published in the *Cornhill*, Feb. 1860. According to the legend, Tithonus was a beautiful young man, with whom the goddess Aurora (the Dawn) fell in love. He was allowed to live with her, and asked for eternal life to keep her company through eternity—but he should have asked for eternal *youth*, because he aged and grew more infirm and shrunken, but unable to die. Eventually he was transformed into the grasshopper.

l. 30. *ordinance*. The allotted span of mortal life.

349 ll. 62–3. *Apollo . . . towers*. Troy (Ilion) was built to the sound of Apollo playing his lyre.

351 *Enoch Arden*. Written from Nov. 1861 to Apr. 1862, and published in *Enoch Arden and Other Poems* (1864). Tennyson conceded that the poem was 'founded on a theme given me by the sculptor Woolner. I believe that this particular story came out of Suffolk, but something like the same story is told in Brittany' (*Memoir*, ii. 7). Critics today tend to be sneeringly dismissive of the alleged sentimentality of this tale, and its last three lines (ll. 909–11) are sometimes put forward as amongst the most bathetic, worst poetry of the 19th century. Yet *Enoch Arden* was enormously successful in the poet's own day, and there are reasons for that: it remains a powerfully compressed example of the poetry of affect.

l. 7. *Danish barrows*. There are many burial-mounds and barrows in England associated with the Danish invasions of the 9th century.

353 l. 100. *Friday fare*. Fish were traditionally eaten on Fridays.

354 l. 131. *isles a light*. The sun makes 'islands of light on the sea' (T). The 'offing' is the sea far enough away from land that a ship needs no pilot to navigate it.

357 l. 239. *glass*. Telescope.

359 l. 326. *garth*. Kitchen garden.

363 l. 494. *'Under the palm-tree'*. The method of seeking guidance by consulting the Bible at random has a long pedigree. Annie has lighted on Judges 4: 5: 'And she dwelt under the palm tree of Deborah between Ramah and Beth-el in Mount Ephraim: and the children of Israel came up to her for judgment.'

364 l. 527. *the summer of the world*. 'The equator' (T).

367 l. 657. *ghostly wall*. The chalk cliffs of much of the southern English coastline are strikingly white.

373 l. 866. *bairns*. Dialect for 'children'.

375 *Milton: Alcaics*. One of a number of 'experiments in classical quantity' (*Memoir*, ii. 11) undertaken by Tennyson (another is 'Hendecasyllabics', below). It was written 16 Nov. 1863 and published in the *Cornhill* in December. Unlike English verse, which is metrical (based, that is, on the patterning of stressed and unstressed syllables) Greek and Latin verse was quantitative (based *not* on stress, but on the patterning of long and short vowels—so, for instance, 'pain' includes a long vowel and 'pan' a short one). Alcaics were a form of verse invented by the Greek poet Alcaeus (from around 600 BC) with a distinctive prosody and a stanza form, both imitated accurately by Tennyson here.

l. 5. *Gabriel, Abdiel*. Two great angels who, in *Paradise Lost* are given important, powerfully written speeches.

Hendecasyllabics. For the details of publication see 'Alcaics' (above) with which this was printed. Written autumn 1863. 'Hendecasyllabics' are verses in which the lines have eleven syllables; it was used by (amongst others) Sappho and Catullus, and is particularly associated with the latter.

376 *Helen's Tower*. Written, Sept. to Oct. 1861, at the request of Tennyson's friend Frederick Temple-Blackwood, 4th Baron Dufferin, who built a tower on the Ulster coast and named it after his mother.

l. 4. *Mother's love in letter'd gold*. Dufferin placed a golden tablet inside the tower on which were inscribed some verses written by his mother on the occasion of his coming-of-age.

Northern Farmer, New Style. Tennyson wrote this and another experiment in Lincolnshire dialect verse ('Northern Farmer: Old Style') in 1864–5. He said of the poem that it was 'founded on a single sentence, "When I canters my 'earse along the ramper (highway) I 'ears proputty, proputty, proputty". I had been told that a rich farmer in our neighbourhood was in the habit of saying this. I never saw the man and know no more of him. It was also reported of the wife of this worthy that, when she entered the *salle à manger* [dining room] of a sea bathing-place, she slapt her pockets and said, "When I married I brought him £5000 on each shoulder" ' (*Memoir*, ii. 9).

l. 2. *proputty*. 'Property'.

377 l. 5. *theer's a craw to pluck wi' tha*. There's a crow to pluck [i.e. dispute to settle] with you.

l. 7. *to weeäk*. This week.

l. 14. *scoors o' gells*. Scores of girls.

l. 17. *stunt*. Stubborn.

l. 24. *'ant nowt?* Has nothing.

l. 26. *addle*. Earn.

l. 27. *nobbut*. Nothing but.

l. 28. *ligs*. Lies.   *shere*. Shire.

378 l. 29. *Varsity*. University.

l. 30. *shut on*. Shot of.

l. 31. *grip*. Ditch.

l. 32. *far-welter'd yowe*. Fow-weltered ewe (one lying on its back).

l. 38. *burn*. Born.

l. 39. *mays nowt*. Makes nothing.

l. 40. *the bees is as fell as owt*. The flies are as fierce as anything.

l. 41. *esh*. Ash (an ash-branch would be attached to an ass's head to keep the flies away).

l. 52. *tued an' moil'd 'issén deäd*. Toiled and struggled himself dead.

379 l. 53. *beck*. Stream.

l. 55. *brig*. Bridge.

'*Flower in the crannied wall*'. Published in 1869.

The Higher Pantheism. Written Dec. 1867; it was read aloud at the first meeting of the Metaphysical Society (2 June 1869) and published in the same year. 'Pantheism' is a belief that sees God in everything; either by asserting that the entire Universe is God, or else by stressing (as did Wordsworth) that the natural world of things is entirely suffused with the being of God. A 'lower pantheism' would be close to the animism of pagan religions, where various natural objects (trees, stones, and rivers say) were worshipped as gods; Tennyson's 'higher pantheism' sees instead an immanent spirit in all aspects of the universe. The poem prompted the atheist Swinburne to write one of the finest parodies of the 19th century, which begins and ends:

> One, who is not, we see: but one, whom we see not, is;
> Surely this is not that: but that is assuredly this.

> . . . .

> God, who we see not, is: and God who is not, we see;
> Fiddle we know is diddle: and diddle, we take it, is dee.

380 *Lucretius*. Written between Oct. 1865 and Jan. 1868, this dramatic monologue was first published in *Macmillan's Magazine*, May 1868. Titus Carus Lucretius was a Roman philosopher (99–55 BC), most famous for his *De Rerum Natura* (*On the Nature of Things*), a six-book philosophical epic poem on the subject of, as its title suggests, everything. There were two versions of his death; one that he killed himself after a fit of melancholy, the other that he died as a result of a love-potion (this is the version Tennyson found in St Jerome's *Chronicle* and followed—Jerome as an early Christian was, of course, highly critical of the Epicurean philosophy of Lucretius, which denies the immortality of the soul and advises us to maximize pleasure for ourselves whilst we are still alive). The poem's treatment of the erotic life was considered daring by some contemporaries, although Tennyson was proud of the restraint with which he detailed it.

380 l. 11. *Hexameter*. The (epic) metre of the *De Rerum Natura*.

l. 13. *the Teacher*. Epicurus, the founder of the Epicurean school of philosophy which Lucretius followed.

381 l. 38. *atom-streams*. The *De Rerum Natura* defines the universe in these terms—an enormous collection of atoms, falling eternally through space.

l. 47. *Sylla*. The 'mulberry-faced Dictator' of l. 54; Sulla seized power in Rome in 82 BC and reigned ruthlessly for three years.

l. 50. *Cadmean teeth*. The myth has to do with the founding of the Greek city of Thebes. Cadmus had killed a dragon, and on the instruction of the goddess Athena he sowed its teeth like seeds in the earth; from them sprang up a race of fierce warriors.

l. 52. *Hetairai*. Prostitutes (a Greek word).

l. 61. *Helen*. Helen of Troy, the most beautiful woman in the world, whose abduction led to the siege and destruction of Troy (the Ilion of l. 65).

382 l. 70. *proœmion*. Proem, prelude to a poem. The proem to the *De Rerum Natura* invokes Venus as the symbol of natural fertility.

l. 82. *Mavors*. Mars the god of war, with whom Venus (though married to Vulcan) had a passionate affair.

ll. 88–91. *Trojan . . . wounded hunter . . . beardless apple-arbiter*. Three mortal men loved by Venus. The 'Trojan' is Anchises, who fathered Aeneas on Venus; the hunter is the beautiful youth Adonis, with whom Venus fell in love but who was killed by a bull; the 'apple-arbiter', Paris, who had to award a golden apple to the fairest goddess, and chose Venus.

ll. 93–4. *Sicilian*. Empedocles.   *Calliope*. Muse of epic poetry, to whom Empedocles wrote a dedicatory poem.

l. 95. *Kypris*. Cyprian (Venus was born in Cyprus).

383 l. 119. *Memmius*. Lucretius dedicated the *De Rerum Natura* to Caius Memmius Gemellus.

384 l. 147. *Plato*. The Greek philosopher opposes suicide in these terms: 'We men are as it were on guard, and a man ought not to free himself from it, nor to run away' (*Phaedo* 6).

385 l. 181. *he*. Numa, legendary king of Rome. He 'snared' the 'rustic gods' Picus and Faunus in an attempt to find out from them the secrets of the universe.

l. 188. *Oread*. Mountain nymph.

l. 193. *proved impossible*. The *De Rerum* denies the existence of satyrs, the lustful half-human half-goat deities of the countryside.

386 l. 224. *Heliconian*. Helicon was the mountain in Greece dedicated to the Muses.

l. 235. *her*. Lucretia (the female form of the name Lucretius) was a Roman matron raped by Tarquin, one of the early Roman kings. She subsequently committed suicide by stabbing herself; and outrage at this event led to the overthrow of the Tarquin line and the establishment of the Roman Republic (the 'Commonwealth' of l. 241).

386   l. 238. *Collatine*. Tarquin.

l. 254. *fanes*. Temples.

l. 260. *Ixionian*. Ixion was punished by the gods by being tied to a fiery, spinning wheel.

l. 261. *Fury's ringlet-snake*. The Furies were mythological goddesses, with snakes twined in their hair, who pursued wrongdoers and criminals.

387   l. 275. *She*. Lucilia, Lucretius' wife.

388   *The Idylls of the King*. Tennyson first formed the ambition to write an Arthurian epic young. His 'Morte d'Arthur' (see above, p. 85) was written in the aftermath of Arthur Hallam's death, but the framing poem 'The Epic' suggests the reasons why he abandoned these youthful ambitions. By the time he resurrected plans for an epic on what he called 'the greatest of all poetical subjects' (*Memoir*, ii. 125) it was the mid-1850s, and instead of writing a poeticized version of Malory, full of archaic idiom and static *tableaux* like the 'Morte d'Arthur', he found himself writing a series of poems designed to contrast false love and true love. 'Merlin and Vivien' (under the title 'Nimuë') was being written 1855–6, 'Geraint and Enid' (originally titled 'Enid') in 1856, 'Guinevere' from 1857 to 1858, and 'Lancelot and Elaine' (originally titled 'Elaine', and first published under that title) in 1858–9. These four 'idylls' (Tennyson always pronounced this word as 'eidylls', remembering that the derivation was from the Greek *eidullion*, which means a short descriptive poem, usually on pastoral subjects) were published together in 1859. Mostly positive critical response reinforced in him the idea that he should write an epic, complete in twelve books. He worked on four more *Idylls* towards the end of the 1860s: 'The Holy Grail' in 1868; the first of the idylls 'The Coming of Arthur' in 1868–9; 'Pelleas and Ettarre' later in 1869; and the final idyll 'The Passing of Arthur' (incorporating the earlier 'Morte d'Arthur' whole—rather jarringly, in that the earlier poem is written in a much more starkly archaic idiom) in 1869. They were published together as *The Holy Grail and Other Poems* in 1869. This gave him eight 'books' for his intended epic, even though each book was effectively a separate poem. Tennyson pressed on: 'The Last Tournament' was written 1871; 'Gareth and Lynette', which he had begun in 1869, was completed in 1872; they were published together as *Gareth and Lynette and other poems* in 1872. 'Balin and Balan' was mostly composed in 1872, although it was not published until 1885. Finally he broke 'Enid' into two separate idylls—'The Marriage of Geraint' and 'Geraint and Enid'—in 1888. The whole was completed, and eventually published as *The Idylls of the King* in the following order:

1. 'The Coming of Arthur'
2. 'Gareth and Lynette'
3. 'The Marriage of Geraint'

4. 'Geraint and Enid'
5. 'Balin and Balan'
6. 'Merlin and Vivien'
7. 'Lancelot and Elaine'
8. 'The Holy Grail'
9. 'Pelleas and Ettarre'
10. 'The Last Tournament'
11. 'Guinevere'
12. 'The Passing of Arthur'.

Clearly it was always going to be hard to bring coherence and aesthetic unity to an epic composed so piecemeal, over such a long time (55 years), and the truth of the matter is that Tennyson does not quite manage to do so. In a poem such as *In Memoriam*, a certain looseness and a sense of a poetic drift does not harm the aesthetic achievement of the piece, because it is not primarily concerned with narrative. *The Idylls of the King* do set out to tell a story—the coming of Arthur and the establishment of his kingdom, the adventures of his knights, the decay that adulterous love introduces with the passion of Lancelot and Guinevere, the quest for the Holy Grail, the decline of the kingdom and the last battle and passing of Arthur—but the discontinuous mode of this work vitiates the narrative drive. Tennyson did not help his case by the blatantly allegorical cast of several of the *Idylls*, particularly 'Gareth and Lynette' and 'The Holy Grail'. His own notes on the poem point up the narrowly allegorical reading, and he himself glossed the poem as concerning the battle of soul and flesh in the ideal man: 'the whole is the dream of man coming into practical life and ruined by one sin. Birth is a mystery and death is a mystery, and in the midst lies the table-land of life, of its struggles and performances. It is not the history of one man or of one generation but of a whole cycle of generations' (*Memoir*, ii. 127). On the other hand, he also rebelled against too literally allegorical readings by critics, saying 'they have taken my hobby and ridden it too hard, and have explained some things too allegorically, although there is an allegorical or perhaps rather a parabolic drift in the poem' (*Memoir*, ii. 126–7).

Too long to include whole in this edition, the *Idylls* suffer least of all Tennyson's longer works by selective representation. Included here are 'Merlin and Vivien' and 'The Holy Grail'.

Merlin and Vivien. For composition and publication details, see above. In terms of Tennyson's allegorical scheme Merlin represents wisdom, intellect, and knowledge, which proves unable to resist the attractions of sex (Vivien): 'Some even among the highest intellects become the slaves of the evil which is at first half disdained' (T).

l. 2. *Broceliande.* Forest in Brittany ('Little Britain'), Northern France.

l. 10. *Tintagil.* Tintagel in Cornwall, where Arthur sometimes held court. Tennyson pronounced the word with a hard 'g' and the emphasis on the first syllable.

388 l. 12. *Lancelot worshipt no unmarried girl*. In the broader scheme of the poem, the illicit love between Lancelot, Arthur's greatest knight and friend, and Guinevere, Arthur's Queen, has begun poisoning the utopia of Arthur's kingdom.

389 l. 52. *Holy Writ*. 'Who can say, I have made my heart clean, I am pure from my sin?' (Prov. 20: 9).

l. 62. *Camelot*. Arthur's capital, the site of his great palace.

391 l. 107. *gray cricket*. The Minstrel (ll. 9–29).

l. 122. *seeling . . . lure*. All terms to do with the training of falcons and other birds of prey. 'Seeling' is closing the bird's eyes up by sewing the lids together; 'jesses' are leather straps that hold the leg, the 'leash' is connected to the jesses and held by the falconer to prevent the bird from escaping, and the 'lure' is the piece of meat used in training.

ll. 123–4. *pies*. Magpies. The bird is too noble to hunt magpies. *rake*. To hunt indiscriminately.

l. 128. *tower'd*. Flew high.

ll. 144–5. *left | Death in the living waters*. Poisoned the water source.

400 ll. 472–3. *Azure . . . dexter chief*. This is the specialized language of heraldry. It describes an image with a blue background, a golden eagle rising and the sun in the top right-hand corner.

401 l. 505. *misty star*. Tennyson's own rather clinical note reads: 'θ Orionis— the nebula in which is embedded the great multiple star. When this was written some astronomers fancied that this nebula in Orion was the vastest object in the Universe—a firmament of suns too far away to be resolved into stars by the telescope, and yet so huge as to be seen by the naked eye' (T).

402 l. 552. *king*. Tennyson invented this king and the legend associated with him.

406 l. 706. *reckling*. Puny infant.

407 l. 750. *Hic Jacets*. 'Hic iacet' is Latin for 'Here Lies . . .', the first words on many tombstones.

l. 762. *holy king*. The biblical King David, author of the Psalms.

408 l. 791. *leal*. Loyal, honest.

410 l. 866. *Seethed . . . mother's milk*. Alluding to the biblical interdiction: 'Thou shalt not seeth a kid in his mother's milk' (Exod. 35: 26).

411 l. 936. *white-listed*. 'Striped with white' (T).

413 *The Holy Grail*. For composition and publication details, see the headnote above. The Holy Grail was the platter or cup used by Christ at the Last Supper; alternatively (or additionally) it was the vessel in which Joseph of Arimathea caught some drops of Christ's blood at the crucifixion, and which he subsequently brought to England. As a religious symbol it also incorporates aspects of pagan symbolic vessels, such as the Cauldron of

Bran. In 1859 Tennyson wrote to the Duke of Argyll: 'as to Macaulay's suggestion of the Sangreal [i.e. Holy Grail], I doubt whether such a subject could be handled in these days, without incurring the charge of irreverence. It would be too much like playing with sacred things. The old writers *believed* in the Sangreal' (*Memoir*, i. 456–7). Tennyson's strong religious commitment to the poem weighted the allegory of the piece towards a Protestant restraint as opposed to the spiritual excesses of what he considered to be the Catholic religious imagination (of Percivale's surreal journey); or, as he put it 'Faith declines, religion in many turns from practical goodness [i.e. Tennyson's Protestantism] to the quest after supernatural and marvellous and selfish religious excitement [i.e. Continental Catholicism]. Few are those for whom the quest is a source of spiritual strength ... *The Holy Grail* is one of the most imaginative of my poems. I have expressed there my strong feelings as to the Reality of the Unseen. The end, where the King speaks of his work and of his visions, is intended to be the summing up of all in the highest note by the highest of men' (T).

413   l. 18. *smoke*. 'The pollen in Spring which, blown abroad by the wind, looks like smoke' (T).

414   l. 48. *Aromat*. More odorous poetic variation of Arimathea.

l. 50. *Moriah*. Mountain near Jerusalem.

l. 52. *Glastonbury*. In the West Country. Joseph of Arimathea was reputed to have come to England with the Grail, and to have established the first Christian church at Glastonbury. There is a thorn-bush there even today supposed to have been planted by him.

l. 61. *Arviragus*. King of the Britons at the time of Joseph's arrival.

417   l. 172. *Siege perilous*. 'Siege' is an archaic word for seat or throne; and the Siege Perilous was the vacant seat at Arthur's Round Table, which only the knight destined to achieve the Holy Grail could occupy without peril. 'The perilous seat which stands for the spiritual imagination' (T).

418   l. 227. *Camelot*. Merlin constructed Arthur's great city by magical means. Tennyson claimed 'it is everywhere symbolic of the gradual growth of human beliefs and institutions, and of the spiritual development of man' (*Memoir*, ii. 127).

419   l. 232. *four great zones*. Hallam Tennyson glossed: 'the four zones represent human progress: the savage state of society; the state where man lords it over the beast; the full development of man; the progress toward spiritual ideas' (quoted in Ricks, iii. 471).

420   l. 300. *Taliessin*. Or Taliesin, famous Welsh bard.

421   l. 312. *White Horse*. Emblem of the Saxons (there is a famous large white horse carved into the Berkshire Downs near Wantage, in southern England).

422   l. 350. *wyvern*. A sort of dragon with two feet like an eagle and a serpent's tail.   *griffin*. Fantastic beast whose lower half is that of a lion and upper half an eagle.

423 l. 390. *a land of sand and thorns*. Symbolic of spiritual discontent. Tennyson comments on this episode and the ones that follow: 'the gratification of sensual appetite brings Percivale no content. Nor does wifely love and the love of the family; nor does wealth, which is worshipt by labour; nor does glory; nor does Fame' (T).

424 l. 453. *wisdom of the east*. 'The Magi' (T).

l. 462. *sacring*. Making sacred (i.e. the consecration of the host).

427 l. 569. *eft*. Newt.

429 l. 661. *Paynim*. Pagan.   *circles*. Stone circles, like Stonehenge.

430 l. 667. *he*. The Sun.

l. 681. *seven clear stars*. 'The Great Bear' (T).

431 ll. 715–16. *basilisks*. Fabulous reptile, hatched by a serpent from a cock's egg, whose mere look was lethal.   *cockatrices*. Winged serpents. *talbots*. Large white hunting dogs.

432 l. 759. *Cana*. The marriage feast where Jesus turned the water into wine; the host praised the bridegroom, saying 'every man doth set forth good wine; and when men have well drunk, then that which is worse: but thou hast kept the good wine until now' (John 2: 10).

433 l. 810. *Carbonek*. Reputed to be the home of the Grail.

434 l. 828. *oriel*. Tall bay window.

436 ll. 912–14. Tennyson said that 'these three lines in Arthur's speech are the (spiritually) central lines of the Idylls' (*Memoir*, i. 90).

437 *Rizpah*. Written 1878, first published in 1880. It is based on the true story of a man executed in 1793 in Brighton, southern England, which Tennyson read in a magazine called *Leisure Hour*. The story concerns two men, Rooke and Howell, who were arrested and convicted of robbing the mail-coach. To quote from the *Leisure Hour* account: 'they were gibbeted on the spot where the robbery was committed, and there is an affecting story connected with the body of Rooke. When the elements had caused the clothes and flesh to decay, his aged mother, night after night, in all weathers, and the more tempestuous the weather the more frequent the visits, made a special pilgrimage to the lonely spot on the Downs, and it was noticed that on her return she always brought something away with her in her apron. Upon being watched it was discovered that the bones of the hanging man were the objects of her search, and as the wind and rain scattered them on the ground she conveyed them to her home. There she kept them, and, when the gibbet was stripped of its horrid burden, in the dead silence of the night she interred them in the hallowed enclosure of Old Shoreham Churchyard. What a sad story of a Brighton Rizpah!' (*Memoir*, ii. 250–1). The woman had to resort to these tactics because the body of her son, as an executed criminal, would not legally have been entitled to burial in consecrated ground.

The biblical story of Rizpah concerns a mother whose two sons are hanged by a king in the days of harvest: 'And Rizpah the daughter of Aiah took sackcloth, and spread it for her upon the rock, from the beginning of harvest until water dropped upon them [i.e. the bones] out of heaven, and suffered neither the birds of the air to rest on them by day, nor the beasts of the field by night' (2 Sam. 21: 10).

437 l. 13. *her*. A female visitor, who has come to be with the old woman on her deathbed and encourage her to make her peace with God.

440 l. 62. *Full of compassion and mercy, the Lord*. 'But thou, O Lord, art a God full of compassion, and gracious, long-suffering, and plenteous in mercy and truth' (Psalm 86: 15).

l. 65. *black cap*. A British judge when passing the sentence of death used to wear a special black cap.

l. 66. *first may be last . . . last may be first*. 'But many that are first shall be last; and the last shall be first' (Matt. 20: 30).

l. 73. *Election and Reprobation*. Terminology from Calvinist doctrine of predestination, whereby some individuals are fated to go to heaven regardless of how well or ill they act during their life (they are 'elect'), and some doomed to hell no matter how much good they do ('reprobation').

441 *The Revenge: A Ballad of the Fleet*. Begun in 1873, and taken up again and completed in 1877. First published in *Nineteenth Century*, Mar. 1878. Following the defeat of the Spanish Armada (an invasion fleet sent by Spain against Britain in 1588) by Sir Walter Ralegh, relations between Britain and Spain were hostile for years. In 1591 Lord Howard was sent to the Azores with a fleet of sixteen ships, including the *Revenge* captained by Sir Richard Grenville: his business was to capture Spanish treasure ships that were on route from the West Indies to Spain and take their cargo. The Spanish, understandably anxious not to lose their ships and treasure, sent out a fleet of 53 warships. Many British ships were lost, and Howard got away with only five remaining; but Grenville refused to go, and engaged the entire Spanish fleet single-handed at close quarters for fifteen hours, before surrendering because he himself was mortally wounded and only twenty of his ship's complement were left alive. The Victorian historian Froude, whom Tennyson read, was of the opinion that 'this story of "The Revenge" struck a deeper terror, though it was but the action of a single ship, into the hearts of the Spanish people, and it dealt a more deadly blow upon their fame and moral strength than the Armada itself' (*Memoir*, ii. 251). Tennyson's intensely patriotic poem was extremely popular in Britain, or more particularly in England, throughout the 19th and early 20th centuries, as long as patriotism remained in vogue. It is less regarded today.

445 *Battle of Brunanburh*. Hallam Tennyson translated this Old English poem into prose for the *Contemporary Review* (Nov. 1876), and Tennyson drew on this when producing his own poetic translation for the first number of his friend Knowles's new journal *The Nineteenth Century* in 1877. Athelstan (895–941) was the son of Edward the Elder and grandson of Alfred the Great, and is the king most credited with unifying by conquest the various

nations and tribes of England into one kingdom. In 937 Constantine of Scotland and Anlaf, an exiled Northumbrian prince, formed a league against him; but Athelstan totally defeated them at the battle of Brunanburh. The 10th-century poem, whose author is unknown, celebrates this victory.

l. 6. *Atheling*. Member of royal family.

446   l. 12. *lindenwood*. 'Shields of lindenwood' (T).

l. 29. *Glode*. Glided.

447   l. 43. *Mercian*. Athelstan. Mercia was a kingdom in what is now central England.

448   l. 78. *glaive*. Sword.

l. 98. *Dyflen*. Dublin.

449   *The Voyage of Maeldune*. Written 1879–80, published in 1880. This Celtic Odyssey is founded on an old Irish story: 'the oldest form of Maeldune is in *The Book of the Dun Cow* (1160 A.D.). I read the legend in Joyce's *Celtic Legends*'—P. W. Joyce's *Old Celtic Romances*, published in 1879—'but most of the details are mine' (*Memoir*, ii. 255).

450   l. 22. *flittermouse-shriek*. Bat's cry.

451   l. 48. *Finn*. Legendary Irish hero.

454   l. 105. *Double Towers*. According to Hallam Tennyson, this stanza is 'symbolical of the contest between Roman Catholics and Protestants' (quoted in Ricks, iii. 66).

l. 115. *St Brendan*. Famed Irish navigator of the 6th century, reputed to have sailed all the way to America.

455   l. 126. *assoil'd*. Absolved.

l. 130. *tithe*. Tenth.

De Profundis. Tennyson began writing this poem in 1852, at the birth of his son Hallam; but it was not completed until 1880. The title is from the Vulgate (Latin Bible) and means 'out of the depths' ('Out of the depths I have cried unto thee, O LORD' Psalm 130: 1).

457   *Frater Ave atque Vale*. Written on a visit to the peninsula of Sirmio or Sirmione in Lake Garda, Italy, June 1880; first published in the *Nineteenth Century*, 1883. The title ('Brother, Hail and Farewell') is from Catullus' elegy to his dead brother. Tennyson's own brother Charles had died in 1879.

l. 1. *Desenzano*. Town on the shores of Lake Garda.

l. 2. *O venusta Sirmio*. 'O lovely Sirmione' (Italian).

l. 8. *Lydian*. The inhabitants of this part of Italy are supposed to be descended from the inhabitants of ancient Lydia.

To Virgil. The great Roman poet Publius Vergilius Maro (Vergil or Virgil in English) was born in Mantua in 70 BC and died 19 BC. Tennyson received a letter from the Vergilian Academy of Mantua, 23 June 1882: 'one verse of yours, one writing however small, that could be published in the Vergilian album will be agreeable, not only to us . . .' (quoted in Ricks, iii. 99–100). The poem was given to the Mantuans, and also published in *Nineteenth Century*, Sept. 1882.

457   ll. 2–4. *Ilion's . . . Dido's pyre*. All events detailed in Vergil's *Aeneid*.

l. 6. *he*. Hesiod, the much earlier Greek poet (8th century BC) whose *Works and Days* was an influence on Vergil's *Georgics*.

458   ll. 13–15. *Tityrus*. Shepherd from *Eclogues* i.   *poet-satyr*. Silenus, in *Eclogues* vi.

l. 17. *Pollio*. One of Vergil's patrons.

l. 34. *freemen*. Rome had been occupied by Austrian troops since 1849, but in 1870 Italian troops had recaptured the city and made it part of the new Italian state.

459   l. 37. *Mantovano*. You from Mantua (Vergil's birthplace).

Vastness. First published in *Macmillan's Magazine*, Nov. 1885, and presumably written shortly before this date. Tennyson commented on the thought behind the poem: 'Hast Thou made all this for naught! Is all this trouble of life worth undergoing if we only end in our own corpse-coffins at last? If you allow God, and God allows this strong instinct and universal yearning for another life, surely that is in a measure a presumption of its truth. We cannot give up the mighty hopes that make us men' (*Memoir*, i. 321).

460   l. 12. *all-heal*. A herb with many medicinal uses.

461   l. 36. *him*. Critics are divided as to whether the reference is to Arthur Hallam, or to Tennyson's brother Charles who had died in 1879. Manuscript drafts make reference to a brother in the original version of this final couplet so it could be Charles, but then again Hallam is called 'brother' several times in *In Memoriam*.

462   *Locksley Hall Sixty Years After*. Written in 1886 and published the same year, forty-four years after the original *Locksley Hall* (see above, p. 102). Hallam Tennyson recorded that 'my father said that the old man in the second *Locksley Hall* had a stronger faith in God and in human goodness than he had had in his youth; but he had also endeavoured to give the moods of despondency which are caused by the decreased energy of life'. Tennyson himself asserted several times that 'there is not one touch of biography in it from beginning to end' (*Memoir*, ii. 329–31).

l. 22. *winter sunset*. Presumably Judith prefers a much older man to the narrator's grandson.

463   l. 29. *Cross'd*. The statue's legs are crossed—an indication that he had fought as a crusader in the Holy Land.

l. 44. *above his bones*. i.e. inscribed over his tomb (black letters on a white background).

465   l. 82. *Timur*. Also called Tamerlane (1336–1405), the Mongol conqueror who was infamous for his barbarities.

l. 83. *Edward's time*. The reign of Edward VI (1547–53), when many Catholics were burnt at the stake.

l. 88. *Rome of Cæsar, Rome of Peter*. The Roman Empire and the Roman Catholic Church.

l. 90. *Demos*. Greek for 'People', here personified as the 'Demon' of the French Revolution and subsequent Terror.

ll. 95–8. *peasants maim . . . born-unborn*. 'The modern Irish cruelties' (T). Irish agitation for Home Rule (self-determination and secession from the United Kingdom) prompted a variety of violent acts, including attacking livestock as listed here.

l. 100. *St Francis of Assisi*. Famous for his kindness to animals.

466 l. 115. *Russia bursts our Indian barrier*. It was a perennial concern of Britain that Russia was poised to invade British India. On 30 Mar. 1885 Russian troops attacked Pehjdeh in Afghanistan in an attempt to move through, and for a while war loomed.

l. 118. *suffrage of the plow*. The Third Reform Act of 1884 had significantly broadened the franchise, including all adult males (even farm labourers) who owned or rented property and were not in receipt of Poor Relief. It is this electorate which is now to decide issues such as whether India remain part of the British Empire.

l. 123. *hustings-liar*. One who tells lies on the hustings (the platform from which Parliamentary candidates addressed the electorate).

467 l. 131. *Voices*. Votes.

l. 145. *Zolaism*. Émile Zola (1840–1902), the French novelist, who was a leading figure in the French school of 'realist' or 'naturalistic' fiction. His insistence on rendering life as it actually was meant that his novels often deal with unsavoury themes—low life, prostitution, and ignoble living. Tennyson was not alone in Britain in deploring this aesthetic.

468 l. 157. *Jacobinism*. French Revolutionary doctrine, particularly associated with the atrocities of the Terror.   *Jacquerie*. 'Originally a revolt in 1358 against Picardy nobles; and afterwards applied to insurrections of the mob' (T).

469 l. 185. *the poet*. Sappho, one of whose fragments addresses Hesperus: 'Evening star, you bring back everything that Dawn scattered, you bring the sheep, you bring the goat, you bring the child home to the mother'.

l. 201. *the king*. David. 'O Lord our Lord, how excellent is thy name in all the earth! . . . What is man, that thou art mindful of him? and the son of man that thou visitest him?' (Psalm 8: 1–4).

471 l. 238. *the Master*. Of Locksley Hall. It was this man who married the speaker's love, Amy, and against whom the speaker vented his spleen in the first 'Locksley Hall'.

473 l. 278. *vacant tomb*. Of Christ. Mary Magdalene and the other Mary come

to see Christ's tomb but find it empty and an angel sitting inside, who says 'he is not here: for he is risen' (Matt. 28: 6).

473   *Far—Far—Away.* Written late 1888. Tennyson recalled his childhood, and declared that 'the words "far, far away" always had a strange charm for me' (quoted in Ricks, iii. 197).

474   *Merlin and the Gleam.* Written Aug. 1889. This poem constitutes a poetic autobiography, a looking back over Tennyson's life with the figure of Merlin as himself, the poet. 'In the story of "Merlin and Nimue",' he said, 'I have read that [the name] Nimue means the Gleam,—which signifies in my poem the higher poetic imagination. Verse IV is the early imagination, Verse V alludes to the Pastorals [i.e. Tennyson's 'English Idylls']' (*Memoir*, ii. 366). Various critics have made various attempts to identify all the allegorical episodes as relating to Tennyson's life, with varying success: it is not straightforward.

l. 11. *the Wizard.* Anybody's guess. It could be Wordsworth, Scott, Byron, Milton, Shakespeare, any of the profound literary influences on Tennyson's youth; it might, alternatively, mean Arthur Hallam.

l. 24. *a Raven.* Generally taken as representative of the 'harsh' reviewers who panned Tennyson's early work.

476   l. 66. *Arthur the King.* Presumably Tennyson's *Idylls of the King*, which he was composing off and on between 1833 and the 1880s.

l. 77. *Arthur had vanish'd.* Presumably the death of Arthur Hallam.

478   *Crossing the Bar.* Written Oct. 1889, whilst crossing the Solent. Hallam Tennyson recalled that: ' "Crossing the Bar" was written in my father's eighty-first year, on a day in October when we came from Aldworth to Farringford. Before reaching Farringford he had the Moaning of the Bar in his mind, and after dinner he showed me this poem written out. I said "that is the crown of your life's work." He answered, "it came in a moment." He explained the "Pilot" as "That Divine and Unseen Who is always guiding us." A few days before my father's death he said to me: "Mind you put 'Crossing the Bar' at the end of all editions of my poems' (*Memoir*, ii. 366–7). In deference to his wishes, editors almost always place this poem at the end of any editions of his work. The 'bar' is the sandbar across the harbour mouth that helps keep the harbour waters calm; a pilot is necessary to help guide ships past the bar, and then is 'dropped' or sent back to the land. Tennyson reverses this, hoping to see his 'pilot' *after* the bar is crossed, a fact which has annoyed some critics.

LETTERS

481   *1. To Mary Anne Fytche [Oct. 1821].* Fytche was Tennyson's maternal aunt.

Louth. Tennyson's school.

restless thoughts ... am now. Tennyson quotes from Milton's *Samson Agonistes*, 19–22; the other quotations from Milton in this letter are from 64–76, 79–85, 115–18.

Nessun... miseria. Dante's *Inferno*, v. 121–3. This passage is referred to in 'Locksley Hall', 76.

482   *Bishop Newton.* Thomas Newton, whose edition of Milton Tennyson possessed.

Sic... capillos. Horace, *Odes* II. xi. 13–15.

483   2. *To Elizabeth Russell 18 Apr. [1828]*

Prince Houssain. A character from *The Arabian Nights*.

Falkland. The first novel of Edward Bulwer-Lytton, which had been published in 1827.

484   3. *'The Acts of the Apostles'.* 'The Apostles' was a Cambridge debating group which Tennyson and Arthur Hallam joined. These 'Acts' are some of the topics debated in 1829 and 1830.

485   4. *To Elizabeth Russell 18 Mar. [1832]*

Azile. Tennyson's nickname for his aunt is 'Eliza' spelt backwards.

Burking. Digging up buried corpses and selling them to medical schools for dissection, after William Burke, who was famously hanged for this grisly crime in 1829.

The empty... better things. Unidentified poetry; possibly Tennyson's own.

Reform... unavoidable. The First Reform Act was indeed passed in June 1832.

486   5. *William Henry Brookfield [mid-Mar. 1832].* Brookfield was a friend of Tennyson's at Cambridge. He later became a Curate.

cat-a-mountain. Shakespeare, *Merry Wives of Windsor*, II. ii. 27.

Trench. Another Cambridge undergraduate friend; he had not died (despite Tennyson's jocular intimations here), but he had left the university.

cakes and ale? Shakespeare, *Twelfth Night*, II. iii. 123.

bacchies. Tobacco: 'negrofoot' is a variety of strong tobacco.

Cam. The river that runs through Cambridge. Tennyson is playing with a passage from Luke 17: 2.

Fred. Tennyson's brother, Frederick.

Idoloclast. 'Breaker of idols' (a form of iconoclast).

487   *Crisp... wavy wolds.* Tennyson is the author here.

6. *To James Spedding [7 Feb. 1833]*

paidogogue. Greek for 'teacher'.

two cloaks. Luke 3: 11.

Oxford. 'Balmy breath' is from Shakespeare, *Othello*, V. ii. 16, so 'Oxford' may have been a rival Cambridge student nickname for Shakespeare (because of the proximity of Stratford-upon-Avon to Oxford); or else because the Earl of Oxford was sometimes thought to have been the real author of Shakespeare's plays.

487 *Does not ... drive out another*. Quoted from Jane Austen, *Sense and Sensibility*, II. 8.

488 *Charles*. Tennyson's brother.

489 *7. Henry Elton to Alfred Tennyson 1 Oct. 1833*. Elton was Hallam's uncle.

  8. To Richard Monkton Milnes [3 Dec. 1833]

490 *Grecian impressions*. Milnes had travelled in Greece, and published *Memoirs of a Tour in Some Parts of Greece, Chiefly Poetical* in 1834.

  Augean stable. One of the labours of Heracles was to clean the enormously filthy stables of King Augeus, which he did by diverting a river through them.

  9. To Sofia Walls Rawnsley [Dec. 1833]. Rawnsley was an elderly friend of the family.

491 *10. To Henry Hallam 14 Feb. 1834*. Henry Hallam was Hallam's father.

  11. To James Spedding [Mar. 1835]

  par nobile fratrum. A well-known pair of brothers.

  Charles. Tennyson's brother. He later changed his name to Charles Tennyson-Turner, on account of his inheritance from Samuel Turner (mentioned here), who was great-uncle to the Tennyson brothers.

492 *12. To Richard Monckton Milnes [9 Jan. 1837]*

  Alfred Crowquill. A popular comic writer (actually the pseudonym under which two writers worked).

  the ass in Homer. The 'lazy ass' of *Iliad* xi. 558–61, 'upon whose ribs many sticks are broken'.

  Lytton Bulwer. Bulwer Lytton, novelist and playwright (1803–73) was obviously the butt of Tennyson's circle of friends, presumably because his 'silver fork' novels of the aristocracy gave him an air of 'literary dandyism'.

  takes her milk for gall. Shakespeare's *Macbeth*, I. iv. 48.

  piscatory. Fishy (with a play on the fact that the Pope wears a signet ring called the 'piscatory ring', hence the later humour about converting salmon).

493 *are not annuals vapid?* Milnes was editing an 'annual', a collection of literary bits and pieces, and clearly had been a little upset by Tennyson's mockery of the form. Tennyson (later in this letter) agrees to send one of his poems for Milnes's project (he sent him 'O! that 'twere possible').

  Anacaona. Unpublished poem by Tennyson about a 'dark Indian maid'.

494 *13. To Leigh Hunt [13 July 1837]*. Leigh Hunt, the poet and man of letters, was by this stage of his life a grand old man of the London literary scene.

  Paganini. A poem by Leigh Hunt, which was later printed in *Leigh Hunt's London Journal*.

  Mr Hall. Samuel Hall was assembling an edition of various short poems and poetic excerpts called *Poetic Gems*; he eventually included six poems by Tennyson.

495 *14. To Emily Sellwood [Mar./Apr.] 1838*. Tennyson was courting Emily Sellwood at this time, but it was not until 1850 that she finally married him, her family being unsatisfied with his prospects and her finding his religious doubts disconcerting. This and the following three letters are excerpted from his courtship correspondence (we do not have the full texts of the letters).

496 *18. To Charles Stearns Wheeler [26 Aug. 1841]*. Wheeler was an American from Cambridge, Massachusetts, who had a wide range of literary and publishing friends. This letter concerns Tennyson's contact with James Brown, who had recently set up the American publishing house of Little, Brown & Co, about an American edition of Tennyson's poems.

497 *Emerson's Essays*. Emerson's *Essays* had been published in 1841; Wheeler was a friend of Emerson.

19. To Edmund Lushington [Feb. 1842]. Lushington had translated Tennyson's 'Œnone' into Greek.

'Geschwister'. Siblings.

πολυπίδακε (*polupidake*). 'many-fountained'. See 'Œnone', line 22.

πολυπίδακος Ἴδης (*polupidakos Idēs*). 'Many-fountained Ida'. 'Œnone', line 22. This is a quotation from Homer, which is why Tennyson prefers this version.

Νασμῷ ἐν ἀμφιρύτῳ (*Nasmōi en amphirutōi*). '. . . the stream that flowed around . . .'. This could be a mistranslation of 'Œnone', line 3, or 8, or 67.

498 *splacknuck*. The word comes from Swift's *Gulliver's Travels* (1726), where it refers to a strange animal from the land of giants, Brobdingnag.

20. To Edward Fitzgerald [July 1842]

my book. Tennyson's *Poems* (1842) had been published on 14 May.

Edwin the fair. A drama in verse by Henry Taylor.

Philip. *Philip van Artevelde* (1834), Taylor's more highly regarded verse-play.

Raffaelle. Raphael, the Renaissance artist. Tennyson is thinking of 'The Ansidei Madonna'.

blue-plush. Servant in livery.

499 *21. Carlyle to Ralph Waldo Emerson [5 Aug. 1844]*. Emerson, the celebrated American man of letters, was visiting Britain.

500 *22. Tennyson's Journal of his Tour of Switzerland, Aug. 1846*

Simon Stevin. Sixteenth-century mathematician and engineer from Bruges.

Man 'hemmed' overhead. The man in the room above kept clearing his throat.

501 *'Gaspar . . . of the world'*. Tennyson's own verses.

diligence. Continental stage-coach.

502　23. *Charles Dickens to John Forster [24 Aug. 1846]*. Dickens was in Switzerland writing *Dombey and Son* and preparing another of his successful Christmas books.

503　24. *To Coventry Patmore [28 Feb. 1849]*. Patmore was a poet, whose *Angel in the House* began to appear in 1854. By this stage he had published only a few things.

my book of elegies. The manuscript of *In Memoriam*, which Tennyson is fearful he has lost.

25. *To Emily Sellwood Tennyson [13 July 1852]*

Owen. Richard Owen (1804–82), the celebrated scientist. He specialized in anatomy and natural history. Tennyson had visited him earlier in the year but Emily, feeling poorly, had stayed in the carriage outside.

504　*quantum suff.* 'Quantum sufficet' [Latin], sufficient amount.

505　27. *To Robert James Mann [Sept. 1855]*

in the opening poem. *Maud*, I. 37–8.

28. *To G. G. Bradley 25 Aug. 1855*

Arnold. Matthew Arnold's *Poems* (1855).

506　*pompholygous*. Greek for 'bubbling up' or 'puffed-up'.

Apollodorus. Apollodorus of Cassandria (not the more famous mythographer) was a demagogue of the 3rd century BC. 'X' is probably Archer Thompson Gurney, who attacked *Maud* in a satirical poem called *A Satire for the Age: The Transcendentalists* (2nd edn., 1855).

29. *To George Brimley 28 Nov. 1855*

Maud. Brimley had written favourably on *Maud* for *Cambridge Essays* (1855).

18th. Part I, Lyric 18.

30. *Tennyson's Journal of his Tour of Portugal, Aug.–Sept. 1859*

507　*Brookfield*. Tennyson's friend W. H. Brookfield, who had come to see them off at Southampton.

508　*the great Duke*. The Duke of Wellington, who fought the Peninsular War against Napoleon in Portugal and Spain 1808–14.

Our visit . . . 1754. This passage is added by Tennyson's travelling companion, F. T. Palgrave.

509　31. *To the Duke of Argyll [3 Oct. 1859]*

bullion. Argyll, surprised because he had not known Tennyson had gone abroad, had written telling of a newspaper report that announced that 'a Lisbon steamer had brought a lot of Bullion *and* the Poet Laureate' back from Portugal.

Byron and Beckford. Byron wrote about Cintra in *Childe Harold's Pilgrimage* (i. 236–314); William Beckford, author of *Vathek*, lived there 1794–5.

509 *Sangraal*. The Quest for the Holy Grail, which Macaulay had suggested to Tennyson as a possible subject for poetry. *The Holy Grail* appeared 1869.

510 *32. To Princess Alice [13 Jan. 1862]*. Alice was Victoria and Albert's second daughter. She married Prince Louis, Grand Duke of Hesse, later in the year. Albert had died in Dec. 1861. Tennyson added a 'Dedication' to the *Idylls of the King* in Albert's honour, on the grounds that the Prince had particularly liked the volume.

33. To Frederick Locker [31 Jan. 1863]. Locker was a poet, author of *London Lyrics* (1857) and a friend of Tennyson; his daughter (the 'your young lady' of the first line of this letter) married Tennyson's brother in 1878.

511 *34. To Algernon Charles Swinburne [Mar. 1865]*. Swinburne's first significant publication, his Greek-style drama *Atalanta in Calydon* was published in 1865. It includes a number of atheist pronouncements in the Choruses, including an attack on 'the supreme evil God'.

35. To Richard Owen [Oct. 1865]

quantity . . . accent. Tennyson was more aware than most of the distinction between metrical (accentual) and quantitative (length of vowel) verse. See, for instance, his 'experiments at versification' above, p. 375 and note.

512 *lizards*. Dinosaur fossils. Owen was particularly interested in these.

36. Tennyson and Gladstone in Conversation, 8 Dec. 1865

My father. The text is from the *Letters and Papers of John Addington Symonds* (London, 1923), 1–10. Symonds's father, also a John, was a celebrated physician who knew Tennyson. Woolner, whose dinner-party this extract describes, was an old friend of Tennyson's, and Gladstone had known both Tennyson and Hallam at Cambridge in the 1830s. The other person at the party was William Holman Hunt, the Pre-Raphaelite painter.

the Jamaica business. Plantation workers in Jamaica rebelled against English rule in October 1865; Edward Eyre, the Governor of the island, put this insurrection down with extreme force and barbarity. The atrocities committed by Eyre divided public opinion in Britain sharply.

513 *obbligato*. Musical term, here meaning 'additional to the conversation' (i.e. Tennyson is just repeating the phrase without reference to what Gladstone is saying).   *sotto voce*. In a low voice.

Indian Mutiny. 1857–8. A rebellion against British rule in India began in the Hindu and Muslim regiments of the British army, but soon spread across the subcontinent. There were atrocities committed on both sides, and the mutiny was squashed within months.

Curtius. A chasm opened in ancient Rome, and oracles said that it would only close after it had consumed 'that on which Rome was based'. Curtius put on full armour to represent 'the Roman soldier' and rode his horse into the gulf, after which it closed.

Malakoff. A battle in the Crimean War, where the French general Bosquet was severely wounded. It was Bosquet who is reputed to have said, after seeing the charge of the Light Brigade, 'c'est magnifique, mais ce n'est pas la guerre'.

513 *Cialdini*. Italian general, who fought against Garibaldi.

514 φωνοῦντα συνετοῖσιν (*fōnounta sunetoisin*). Talking to those in the know.

Richter. Friedrich 'Jean-Paul' Richter (1763–1825), novelist and humourist. Tennyson refers to his *Quintus Fixlein* (1796).

Huxley. Thomas Huxley (1825–95); scientist and close friend of Darwin's, whose *Descent of Man* was to appear in 1871.

Comte. French philosopher (1798–1857).

516 *Grote*. George Grote (1794–1871), philosopher and author of an influential *History of Greece*.

517 *Jowett*. Benjamin Jowett (1817–93), professor of Greek at Oxford and Tennyson's friend.

Calling . . . sea. Enoch Arden, 904.

37. To Francis Palgrave [24 Dec. 1868]

my poem. 'The Holy Grail' (see above, p. 413).

518 *38. To William Cox Bennett [13 Nov. 1872]*. Bennett had sent Tennyson a flattering poem, now lost.

Marvell. . . . eternity. Tennyson quotes 'To His Coy Mistress', 21–4.

519 *39. To Gladstone [30 Mar. 1873]*. Tennyson was once again being offered a baronetcy. Here he attempts to decline for himself, but accept on behalf of his son. After a certain negotiation, the offer was refused.

520 *41. To Benjamin Paul Blood [7 May 1874]*. Blood (1832–1919) was an American philosopher and mystic; he had sent Tennyson a copy of *The Anaesthetic Revelation and the Gist of Philosophy* (1874), in which he argued that the then relatively new science of anaesthesia opened the mind to an important mystic trance state.

him. Benjamin Jowett.

obiter. By the way (Latin).

Mein liebes Ich. 'My love's I' (German).

Lucretius. The phrase altered is in the last line of 'Lucretius' (above, p. 387).

521 *42. To Matthew Fraser [7 May 1880]*. Fraser, a student at the university of Glasgow, had written to offer Tennyson the Rectorship of the University; he wrote later explaining that Tennyson would be the candidate of the Conservative students, against John Bright who was the Liberal candidate.

roi-fainéant. Imitation king.

522 *43. To Gladstone [early Dec. 1883]*. Gladstone had written again offering a peerage (a Barony, which ranks higher than the baronetcy which he had been offering previously), which Tennyson here finally accepts.

522 *Knowles.* Also in Gladstone's letter was the news that James Knowles, Tennyson's friend and editor of the journal *The Nineteenth Century*, was thinking of publishing some letters by Arthur Hallam.

H.M. Her Majesty (Queen Victoria).

Would that do? A Lord must be a Lord *of* somewhere. Tennyson's first suggestion, that he be Lord Tennyson d'Eyncourt, met with difficulties on discovering that there already was a Baron d'Eyncourt. He eventually settled on 'Lord Tennyson of Aldworth' (in Sussex).

in tempore. 'In the time of' (Latin).

44. To Francisque Michel [28 Jan. 1884]. Michel had written to Tennyson about the 14th-century poets Gower and Chandos.

523 *45. To Elizabeth Chapman [23 Nov. 1886].* Chapman (1831–1904) was a poet and writer. She had published 'An Analysis of *In Memoriam*' in a collection of essays in 1886, and later published *A Companion to In Memoriam* as a separate volume in 1888.

Comtism. The school of the French positivist philosopher Comte.

p. 95. Tennyson is referring to a passage declaring that life would be meaningless without the hope of the immortality of the soul.

524 *Bah! . . . immortalité!* 'Bah! Such immortality!'

46. To Walt Whitman [15 Nov. 1887]

The coming year. 1888 was the hundreth anniversary of the ratification of the US Constitution.

47. To Charles Esmarch [18 Apr. 1888]. Esmarch was professor of Law at Prague University. He sent Tennyson a copy of *Locksley Hall sechzig Jahre später*, his translation of 'Locksley Hall Sixty Years After' (above, p. 462), along with speculations on the original's autobiographical provenance, which produced this acerbic reply.

FURTHER READING

Modern Collected Editions

Cecil Y. Lang and Edgar F. Shannon (eds.), *The Letters of Alfred Lord Tennyson* (3 vols., Oxford: Clarendon Press, 1982–90).

Christopher Ricks (ed.), *The Poems of Tennyson* (2nd edn. in 3 vols., London: Longman, 1987).

Susan Shatto and Marion Shaw (eds.), *In Memoriam* (Oxford: Clarendon Press, 1982).

Secondary Criticism

Isobel Armstrong, *Victorian Poetry: Poetry, Poetics and Politics* (London: Routledge, 1993).

Chris R. Vanden Bossche, 'Realism Versus Romance: the War of Cultural Codes in Tennyson's *Maud*', *Victorian Poetry* 24 (1986), 69–82.

Jerome H. Buckley, *Tennyson: the Growth of a Poet* (Cambridge MA: Harvard University Press, 1960).

Philip Collins (ed.), *Tennyson: Seven Essays* (New York: St Martin's Press, 1992).

Richard Cronin, *Romantic Victorians: English Literature 1824–1840* (New York: Palgrave, 2002).

A. Dwight Culler, *The Poetry of Tennyson* (New Haven: Yale University Press, 1977).

Aidan Day, *Tennyson's Scepticism* (London: Palgrave Macmillan, 2005).

T. S. Eliot, '*In Memoriam*', *Selected Essays* (London: Faber and Faber, 1932), 286–95.

Eric Griffiths, *The Printed Voice of Victorian Poetry* (Oxford: Clarendon Press, 1989).

Donald S. Hair, *Tennyson's Language* (Toronto: University of Toronto Press, 1991).

Elaine Jordan, *Alfred Tennyson* (Cambridge: Cambridge University Press, 1988).

Gerhard Joseph, *Tennyson and the Text: The Weaver's Shuttle* (Cambridge University Press, 1992).

John D. Jump (ed.), *Tennyson: the Critical Heritage* (London: Routledge, 1967).

Jerome J. McGann, 'Tennyson and the Histories of Criticism', in *The Beauty of Inflections: Literary Investigations in Historical Method and Theory* (Oxford: Clarendon Press, 1988), 173–203.

Darrel Mansell, 'Displacing Hallam's Tomb in Tennyson's *In Memoriam*', *Victorian Poetry* 36 (1998), 97–111.

Robert Bernard Martin, *Tennyson: the Unquiet Heart* (Oxford: Oxford University Press, 1980; London: Faber and Faber, 1983).

Laurence W. Mazzeno, *Alfred Tennyson: The Critical Legacy* (Boydell & Brewer, 2004).

J. Hillis Miller, 'Temporal Topographies: Tennyson's Tears', *Topographies* (Stanford: Stanford University Press, 1995), 134–49.

Jeff Nunakawa, '*In Memoriam* and the Extinction of the Homosexual', *ELH* 58 (1991), 427–38.

Leonée Ormond, *Alfred Tennyson: A Literary Life* (London: Macmillan, 1993).

Norman Page (ed.), *Tennyson: Interviews and Recollections* (London: Macmillan, 1983).

Cornelia D. J. Pearsall, *Tennyson's Rapture: Transformation in the Victorian Dramatic Monologue* (Oxford University Press, 2008).

Seamus Perry, *Alfred Tennyson* (Northcote House, 2005).

Matthew Reynolds, 'Tennyson's Britain', *The Realms of Verse: English Poetry in a Time of Nation-Building* (Oxford University Press, 2001), 203–72.

Christopher Ricks, *Tennyson* (London: Macmillan, 1972; 2nd edn. Macmillan, 1989).

Edgar F. Shannon Jr., *Tennyson and the Reviewers* (Cambridge MA: Harvard University Press, 1952).

Marion Shaw, '*In Memoriam* and Popular Religious Poetry', *Victorian Poetry*, 15 (1977), 1–8.

——'Tennyson's Dark Continent', *Victorian Poetry*, 32 (1994), 157–69.

W. David Shaw, *Tennyson's Style* (Cornell University Press, 1976).

——*The Lucid Veil: Poetic Truth in the Victorian Age* (London: Athlone, 1987).

Alan Sinfield, *Alfred Tennyson* ('Rereading Literature Series', Oxford: Blackwell, 1986).

E. Warwick Slinn, 'Absence and Desire in *Maud*', *The Discourse of the Self in Victorian Poetry* (London: Macmillan, 1991).

Rebecca Stott (ed.), *Tennyson* (Longman Critical Readers; London: Longman, 1996).

Ann Thwaite, *Emily Tennyson: the Poet's Wife* (London: Faber and Faber, 1997).

Paul Turner, *Tennyson* (London: Routledge, 1976).

INDEX OF TITLES

INDEX OF FIRST LINES

American Literature

British and Irish Literature

Children's Literature

Classics and Ancient Literature

Colonial Literature

Eastern Literature

European Literature

Gothic Literature

History

Medieval Literature

Oxford English Drama

Poetry

Philosophy

Politics

Religion

The Oxford Shakespeare

A complete list of Oxford World's Classics, including Authors in Context, Oxford English Drama, and the Oxford Shakespeare, is available in the UK from the Marketing Services Department, Oxford University Press, Great Clarendon Street, Oxford OX2 6DP, or visit the website at www.oup.com/uk/worldsclassics.

In the USA, visit www.oup.com/us/owc for a complete title list.

Oxford World's Classics are available from all good bookshops. In case of difficulty, customers in the UK should contact Oxford University Press Bookshop, 116 High Street, Oxford OX1 4BR.